California Real Estate Practice

Seventh Edition

Kathryn Haupt
Megan Dorsey

Rockwell Publishing Company

Copyright © 2015
By Rockwell Publishing, Inc.
13218 N.E. 20th
Bellevue, WA 98005
(425)747-7272 / 1-800-221-9347

Seventh edition

ISBN: 978-1-939259-69-1

PRINTED IN THE UNITED STATES OF AMERICA

Table of Contents

1

Real Estate Agency Relationships

Agency and Agency Law

- Agency relationships
- Agent's duties to the principal
- Agent's duties to third parties
- Other legal effects of agency relationships

How an Agency is Created and Terminated

Agency Disclosure

- Disclosure requirements
- Acting in accordance with the disclosures
- Licensee acting as a principal

Types of Real Estate Agency Relationships

- Seller agency
- Buyer agency
- Dual agency
- Finder or middleman

Introduction

You have just closed a sale. The seller was pleased with the sales price; the buyers are happy to be moving into their dream house. Your broker is smiling. Her office will now reach this month's sales goal, thanks to your sale. And you can't wait to take your commission check to the bank.

But wait! Now the buyers are talking to their attorney about breach of agency duties and threatening to cancel the contract because of undisclosed material facts. The Bureau of Real Estate has notified you that it has received a complaint against you: the seller is claiming that you failed to disclose your agency status. Plus, the seller is refusing to pay the commission. Your broker is worried about a lawsuit, and she thinks that it's all your fault. What a disaster!

What went wrong? In this hypothetical situation, as sometimes happens in real life, there was confusion about agency relationships and what they meant for the real estate licensee. In today's increasingly complicated legal environment, it is crucial to understand the practical aspects of agency relationships. In this chapter, we will discuss real estate agency law, the ways in which agency relationships can be established, agency disclosure requirements, and the different types of agency relationships.

Agency and Agency Law

Agency law is the body of statutes and court decisions that govern agency relationships in a wide variety of contexts. For example, agency law applies to the relationship between lawyer and client, or between trustee and beneficiary. It is also the legal basis for a real estate agent's relationship with her clients.

Agency Relationships

An **agent** is a person who has been authorized by a **principal** to represent the principal in dealings with **third parties**. A real estate agent's principal may be a real estate seller, buyer, landlord, or tenant. A real estate agent's principal may also be called his **client**. When a real estate agent negotiates with buyers or tenants on a client's behalf, those third parties are sometimes called **customers**.

Example: Sullivan asks Broker Harris to find a buyer for her house. Harris shows the house to Brown, who makes an offer on it. Sullivan is Harris's client, or principal; Harris is Sullivan's agent; and Brown is a customer or third party.

The term "real estate agent" is commonly used to refer to either a licensed real estate broker or a licensed real estate salesperson. Technically, however, only a broker can be the agent of a member of the public (a seller, buyer, landlord, or tenant). When a real estate salesperson works with a seller, for example, the salesperson does so as an agent of her broker, not as the agent of the seller. The broker is legally responsible for the actions of the salesperson. So even though the salesperson as well as the broker may be referred to as the seller's agent, strictly speaking only the broker is the seller's agent in the eyes of the law. Although this technical distinction doesn't necessarily make much difference in the day-to-day work of a salesperson, it should be kept in mind.

Another point to be aware of: a real estate broker isn't necessarily an individual; it may be a real estate firm with a corporate license, headed by an individually licensed broker. In that case, strictly speaking, the client's agent is the firm (McNally Real Estate, Inc.) rather than an individual licensee. Most licensees work for brokerages structured in this way.

In many residential sales transactions, one real estate licensee (the listing agent) acts as the **seller's agent** and another licensee (the selling agent) acts as the **buyer's agent**. A licensee may also act as a **dual agent**, representing both the seller and the buyer in the same transaction. (Note that a listing agent may act as a dual agent, but may not represent *only* the buyer; the listing agent always represents the seller.) In some cases a licensee may prefer not to act as the agent of either party, choosing instead to act merely as a middleman or **finder**. We'll discuss each of these roles in more detail later in this chapter.

Why does it matter which party in a transaction a real estate licensee is representing? Because an agency relationship has a number of very important legal implications. For a third party, dealing with the agent can be the legal equivalent of dealing with the principal. For instance, if an agent is authorized to do so, she can enter into a contract that will be legally binding on the principal. And if the agent makes a mistake or commits fraud, the principal could be held liable to a third party who was injured by the agent's action. Perhaps most importantly, an agent owes legal duties to her principal beyond those she owes to third parties. We'll cover each of these issues in more detail. Let's start with the agent's legal duties.

Agent's Duties to the Principal

The duties that agents owe to their principals are called fiduciary duties. A **fiduciary** is a person who occupies a position of special trust in relation to another person. An agent owes the principal these five basic fiduciary duties:

- utmost care,
- obedience and good faith,
- accounting,
- loyalty, and
- disclosure of material facts.

A real estate agent owes his client(s) these duties regardless of whether he is representing the seller, the buyer, or both parties.

Utmost Care. An agent owes her principal the duty of utmost care in carrying out the agency. A real estate agent is required to act with the level of care and skill generally expected of a competent real estate agent. If her performance fails to meet that standard, she may be found liable for any harm to the principal that results from her negligence.

Obedience and Good Faith. An agent must obey the principal's instructions and carry them out in good faith, with honesty and integrity. The agent's actions must conform to the purpose and intent of the instructions. If a real estate agent fails to obey the client's instructions, the agent (or the agent's broker) may be held liable for any loss to the client that results.

Accounting. Agents must be able to account to their clients for all funds (or other valuables) entrusted to their care. These are referred to as **trust funds**. California's Real Estate Law requires brokers to report to their clients on the status of all trust funds on a regular basis. They must also avoid mixing, or **commingling**, trust funds with their own funds.

Loyalty. The duty of loyalty means that agents must put the interests of their clients above their own interests and above the interests of any other party. An agent must not make any **secret profits** from the agency. For example, it is a breach of agency duty for a broker to list a property for less than it is worth, secretly buy it from the principal through an intermediary, and then sell it for a profit.

One of the most important aspects of the duty of loyalty is the requirement of **confidentiality**. An agent may not disclose any confidential information about the principal, even after the agency relationship terminates. Information is generally considered confidential if it was:

1. given to the agent by the principal in confidence, and/or
2. acquired by the agent during the course of or on account of the fiduciary relationship.

Confidential information cannot be disclosed to other parties or otherwise used in a manner that is detrimental to the principal.

Example: A buyer privately tells her agent that she is independently wealthy and can easily afford the listing price, but would like to offer $5,000 less than the listing price as an opening offer. The buyer's agent must keep this information confidential, since it was told to the agent in confidence, and revealing the information to the seller would not be in the buyer's best interest.

Of course, information is not confidential if it is already available to the general public. Also, information is not confidential if the law requires the principal to disclose it. For example, as we'll discuss later in this chapter and in Chapter 2, the seller in a real estate transaction must make a number of disclosures to the buyer. One kind of information that must be disclosed is the presence of latent defects in the property. A **latent defect** is a problem that would not be discovered by ordinary inspection.

Information about latent defects must never be concealed on the grounds that the information is confidential. Because the principal would be legally obligated to disclose a latent defect to buyers, by definition it is not confidential information.

Example: A seller tells Parker, his agent, that the roof of his house leaks during heavy rain, and asks her not to mention this information to prospective buyers. Although this was told to Parker in confidence, she must disclose it to buyers.

Confidential information about a principal can't be disclosed even after the transaction has ended. This is particularly important if a person who once was an agent's principal is now represented by another agent.

Example: Agent Vance helped Torino purchase an expensive house. While Vance was representing him, Torino told Vance a considerable amount of confidential information about his extensive financial holdings.

Over a year later, Vance is representing Cortez in the sale of an investment property. Torino, who is now represented by another agent, is interested in buying Cortez's property. Vance knows that Torino is extremely wealthy and can easily afford to pay the property's full listing price. But because this knowledge is based on confidential information he learned while he was acting as Torino's agent, Vance cannot disclose this to his current client, Cortez. This is true even though Vance's agency relationship with Torino ended a long time ago.

Disclosure of Material Facts. While an agent must not disclose the principal's confidential information to third parties, she must disclose all material facts that she knows about to her principal (and also to the other party, as we'll discuss shortly). For a real estate agent, a **material fact** is any information that affects the value or desirability of the property, or that could affect the principal's decision as to whether or not to enter into a transaction. Material facts that must be disclosed to the principal include:

- all offers to purchase the property,
- the true value of the property, and
- any relationship between the agent and another party.

A seller's agent must present all offers to the principal in a timely manner. It's the seller, not the agent, who decides whether an offer is acceptable. The duty to present all offers continues even after the property is subject to an existing contract.

Example: Seller Sanders has just accepted an offer from Buyer Barton. Garcia, the listing agent, receives another written offer for the same property from Buyer Bell. Garcia has a duty to present Bell's offer to Sanders, even though Sanders has already accepted Barton's offer.

A seller's agent must also inform his principal of the property's true value. Since sellers usually rely on their agent's advice in setting a listing price, an agent could arrange to collect a secret profit by telling the seller that the property is worth less than it actually is, and then arranging to purchase it at an unfairly low price. This would breach the agent's fiduciary duties.

Any **conflicts of interest** must also be disclosed to the principal. For instance, the seller's agent must inform the seller if there is any relationship between the agent and a prospective buyer. If the other party is a friend, relative, or business associate of the agent, or a company in which the agent has an interest, there is a conflict of interest. The principal has the right to this information before she decides whether to make or accept an offer.

An agent isn't merely expected to disclose material facts to the principal, but also to discuss the ramifications of the information in order to help the principal make sound decisions. However, a real estate agent's advice should not exceed the agent's expertise. For example, a real estate agent must never offer legal advice; when appropriate, she should recommend that the principal consult with a real estate attorney.

Agent's Duties to Third Parties

A real estate agent also owes certain legal duties to parties that the agent is not representing. These duties are:

- reasonable care and skill,
- good faith and fair dealing, and
- disclosure of material facts.

Reasonable Care and Skill. As mentioned earlier, an agent must use the degree of care and skill expected of a reasonably competent real estate agent. If an agent harms a third party because of carelessness or incompetence, he may be liable to the third party for any loss caused by his negligence.

Good Faith and Fair Dealing. The duty of good faith and fair dealing requires a real estate agent to treat third parties honestly. Making inaccurate statements or misrepresentations to customers would breach this duty. Even an unintentional misrepresentation may constitute fraud. The party to whom the misrepresentation was made could rescind the transaction and/or sue for damages.

It's not only the real estate agent who has a duty of good faith and fair dealing: the parties do as well. If a seller or a buyer makes misrepresentations to the other party, the other party can rescind the transaction and/or sue for damages.

Disclosure of Material Facts. Sellers and their agents are required to disclose material facts to prospective buyers. They must disclose any information that materially affects the value, desirability, or intended use of the property, unless the information should already be apparent to buyers. Of course, this includes latent defects: problems with the property that wouldn't be obvious to a buyer during a casual inspection. The seller and the seller's agent cannot conceal latent defects; they must disclose them even if the buyer doesn't ask about them.

In most residential transactions, the seller must give the buyer a transfer disclosure statement. This requirement applies to all sales of one- to four-unit residential properties, although there are exemptions for new homes in subdivisions being sold for the first time, and certain other types of transfers. We discuss the transfer disclosure statement in more detail in Chapter 2.

You can usually be held liable for failure to disclose a material fact only if you knew about it and the fact was not readily apparent or ascertainable by the other party. Also, you don't have to explain the ramifications of a material fact to a third party; you're only required to disclose the fact itself.

If it's unclear whether an observed condition is a latent defect, it is best to err on the side of disclosure. Even small problems should be disclosed, because they might indicate a much bigger problem when considered together.

Example: The seller's agent notices that the house is built on a hillside that consists mostly of fill dirt, which can be unstable. There is netting further down the hill that was probably used to shore up slumping soil. Also, the surface of the garage floor is somewhat uneven.

The agent should consider these facts to be latent defects and disclose them. Although they don't conclusively show that the property is at risk for landslides, taken together they are red flags that suggest a possible geologic hazard.

The disclosure of latent defects cannot be waived by the buyer or the buyer's agent. Even if there is an "as is" clause in the purchase agreement, the seller and the seller's agent must still reveal all known latent defects.

Investigation or inspection. An agent generally isn't required to search for and discover material facts that she doesn't already know. For instance, an agent does not need to investigate a party's financial position, or to verify statements that come from a reliable source, such as a title insurance company.

California law does, however, require real estate agents to perform a reasonably competent and diligent visual inspection of the property being sold, if it is a residential property with one to four units. Any latent defects or other material facts discovered during the inspection must be reported to a prospective buyer.

Exceptions to disclosure requirement. The fact that someone has died on a property can stigmatize that property, even though the death has no actual effect on the property's condition or title. California law offers some protection in this situation from the duty to disclose. Sellers and agents don't need to disclose to buyers that someone died on the property more than three years ago, regardless of the cause of death. However, if there has been a death on the property within the last three years, and the death could affect the desirability of the property, you should disclose it. In addition, if the buyer asks you about the subject directly, you must answer truthfully.

Example: Agent Kipling is showing Buyer Green a house. Green has three children and wants a safe family home to live in. Kipling knows that the property he's showing Green was the site of a brutal murder-suicide ten years ago. This information does not have to be disclosed to Green, because the deaths occurred more than three years ago.

Note, however, that if Green asks Kipling whether any crimes have occurred on the property, Kipling will have to answer honestly.

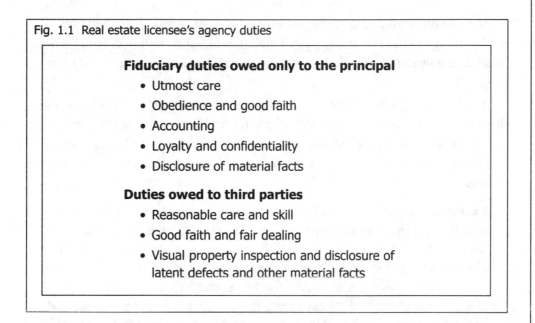

Fig. 1.1 Real estate licensee's agency duties

Fiduciary duties owed only to the principal
- Utmost care
- Obedience and good faith
- Accounting
- Loyalty and confidentiality
- Disclosure of material facts

Duties owed to third parties
- Reasonable care and skill
- Good faith and fair dealing
- Visual property inspection and disclosure of latent defects and other material facts

Also, California civil rights laws prohibit agents and sellers from disclosing certain information. For example, sellers and agents can't tell prospective buyers that the property was occupied by someone who had AIDS or was HIV-positive. If a buyer asks whether anyone with AIDS lives or lived in the seller's house, you should explain that answering that question could violate fair housing laws. The same response is appropriate for questions about race, religion, or other protected classes (see Chapter 3).

Other Legal Effects of Agency Relationships

An agency relationship has other significant legal implications beyond the issue of an agent's duties. As we mentioned earlier, for a third party, dealing with an agent can be the legal equivalent of dealing with the principal. When an authorized agent signs a document or makes a promise, it's as if the principal signed or promised. The principal is bound by the agent's actions if they are within the actual or apparent scope of the agency. Third parties are expected to inquire into the actual scope of the agent's authority, however. If they fail to do so, the principal will usually not be liable for actions that exceeded the agent's authority.

In addition, communication to an agent is the legal equivalent of communication to the principal. If a third party gives the agent information about a certain problem or requirement, the principal is deemed to have been informed of it—even if the agent never actually passed the information on to the principal. This is called the **imputed knowledge** rule; the agent's knowledge is imputed to the principal.

Furthermore, under certain circumstances, if an agent does something wrong, the principal may be held liable to third parties for harm resulting from the agent's actions. This is called **vicarious liability**. Vicarious liability may apply whether or not the principal approved or knew of the agent's acts, either before or after the fact.

> **Example:** Broker Burroughs is representing Sawyer in the sale of her property. While inspecting the property, Burroughs notices indications of previous flooding. Sawyer doesn't know about the flooding, and Burroughs doesn't tell either Sawyer or prospective buyers about the problem.
>
> Hassan purchases Sawyer's property, and soon afterward it floods again. Hassan must pay a repair bill of $15,000. Hassan can sue both Burroughs and Sawyer. Sawyer may be held vicariously liable for her agent's failure to disclose a material fact to the buyer.

If the third party prevails in a lawsuit based on vicarious liability, the agent and principal are usually jointly liable for the damages. In other words, either of them can be required to pay the full amount if the other does not pay his or her share. This is called **joint and several liability**. However, if the principal did nothing wrong, the principal may turn around and sue the agent for the amount the principal had to pay to the injured party.

> **Example:** Continuing with the previous example, the court awards Hassan $15,000 in damages. To prevent a judgment lien from attaching to the property she currently owns, Sawyer (the seller) pays the full $15,000 to Hassan. But since Sawyer actually did nothing wrong herself and wasn't aware that Burroughs was withholding information, she may now sue Burroughs (her agent) for the $15,000 that she had to pay to Hassan.

Joint and several liability creates an incentive for the agent and the principal to watch each other's conduct, instead of purposefully remaining ignorant of the other's behavior (perhaps in hope of benefiting from it). Joint and several liability also makes it more likely that an injured party will be able to collect the full amount of a judgment, even if one of the judgment debtors is insolvent.

Note that when it's a real estate salesperson rather than a broker whose action harms a third party, both the salesperson's broker and the client (the seller or buyer) could be held liable. The broker would be vicariously liable as the salesperson's principal, and the client would be vicariously liable as the broker's principal.

How an Agency is Created and Terminated

Agency duties arise when an agency relationship begins and last until it ends (although the duty of confidentiality continues even after termination). Let's discuss how agency relationships are created and terminated.

Creating an Agency

The key requirement for the creation of an agency relationship is very simple: the consent of both parties. There are four ways to establish an agency:

1. **express agreement** (the principal appoints someone to act as an agent, and the agent accepts the appointment);
2. **ratification** (the principal gives approval after the fact to acts performed by a person who was without authority to act for the principal);
3. **estoppel** (when it would be unfair to a third party to deny an agent's authority, because the principal allowed the third party to believe there was an agency relationship); or
4. **implication** (when one person behaves toward another in a way that implies that she is acting as that person's agent).

The vast majority of real estate agency relationships are created by express agreement, either with a listing agreement, a buyer representation agreement (discussed later in this chapter), or a property management agreement (see Chapter 12). A power of attorney is another way of creating an agency by express agreement; real estate agents do not ordinarily have power of attorney for their clients, however.

If a seller's agent creates an agency by implication with a buyer, this results in an **inadvertent dual agency**.

Example: Agent Phillips has been working with the Glenn family for a few weeks, showing them a number of houses that they might want to buy and providing them with a lot of information and advice. Phillips doesn't have a signed buyer representation agreement with the Glenns, and in fact he is acting as a seller's agent in connection with all of these properties. But he doesn't explain that to the Glenns, and they develop the impression that Phillips is acting as their agent.

Under these circumstances, Phillips could be considered the Glenns' agent by implication. In that case, Phillips is acting as an inadvertent dual agent in regard to the houses that the Glenns are considering, since he was already representing the sellers.

When the Glenns decide to make an offer on one of those houses, they tell Phillips that they're willing to pay the full listing price but would like to begin by offering $15,000 less. This puts Phillips in a very awkward position. He would be breaching his fiduciary duties to the sellers if he didn't tell them what the Glenns said about the price. However, the Glenns disclosed that information to him because they believed he was their agent and would keep it confidential. So if Phillips does repeat the Glenns' remarks to the sellers, a court could rule that he has breached his fiduciary duties to the Glenns.

Inadvertent dual agency was once a common problem. But as we'll discuss shortly, agency disclosure laws have done much to prevent it.

Terminating an Agency

An agency relationship may be terminated either by the actions of the parties or through the operation of law. Once an agency has been terminated, the agent is no longer authorized to represent the principal.

Termination by the Parties. Since agency requires the consent of both the principal and the agent, they can end the agency relationship at any time. This may occur by mutual agreement, revocation, or renunciation.

Mutual agreement. In some cases, the principal and the agent simply agree to end the agency. If the agency was originally established with a written document, it's advisable to formally terminate it in writing, too.

Revocation. A principal may revoke an agent's authority at any time. Under some circumstances, however, the revocation may be a breach of contract. In that case, the principal may be liable to the agent for damages resulting from the breach of contract.

Example: Davidson decides she distrusts and dislikes the broker she listed her house with, but their exclusive listing won't expire for another two months. Even though Davidson could terminate the listing unilaterally, revoking the broker's authority to represent her, it would be much better if she could get the broker to agree to the termination instead. A unilateral revocation would be a breach of the listing agreement, and the broker could sue Davidson for his commission.

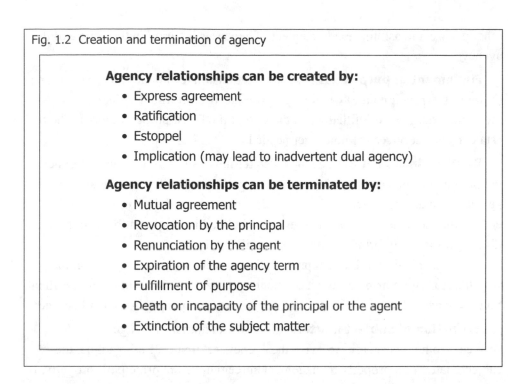

Fig. 1.2 Creation and termination of agency

Agency relationships can be created by:
- Express agreement
- Ratification
- Estoppel
- Implication (may lead to inadvertent dual agency)

Agency relationships can be terminated by:
- Mutual agreement
- Revocation by the principal
- Renunciation by the agent
- Expiration of the agency term
- Fulfillment of purpose
- Death or incapacity of the principal or the agent
- Extinction of the subject matter

Renunciation. An agent also has the right to terminate the agency relationship unilaterally, without the principal's consent. This is called renouncing the agency. Like revocation, renunciation may be a breach of contract, and the agent could end up owing the principal damages for the breach. But damages are usually not an issue when a real estate broker renounces an agency.

Termination by Operation of Law. An agency relationship can also terminate by operation of law, without any action on the part of the principal or agent. This can happen as a result of the expiration of the agency, fulfillment of purpose, death or incapacity, or the extinction of the subject matter.

Expiration. If an agency agreement has a termination date, the agent's authority to represent the principal terminates automatically when the expiration date arrives. If there is no termination date, the agency will be deemed to expire within a reasonable time. How long a period is considered reasonable will depend on the circumstances and may be decided by a court.

If an agency agreement lacks a termination date—a relatively rare occurrence, because California law requires exclusive agreements to have one—the agreement can usually be ended by either party without liability for damages; unilateral termination does not represent a breach of the agreement. In some situations, the other party could ask for reimbursement of expenses incurred in the course of the agency.

Fulfillment of purpose. An agency relationship terminates automatically (before its expiration date) when its purpose has been fulfilled. A listing agreement, for example, is fulfilled when the sale of the listed property closes. The real estate agent's services are no longer needed.

Death or incapacity. An agency also terminates before it expires if either the principal or the agent dies or becomes legally incapacitated (mentally incompetent). As a general rule, the agent's authority to act on behalf of the principal ends at the moment the principal dies or is declared incompetent by a court, even if the agent is not informed of the event until later on.

Note that a listing or buyer representation agreement is typically a contract with the real estate firm, not the individual licensee who's working with the client. So the agency relationship continues even if something happens to that licensee.

Extinction of subject matter. If the subject matter of an agency is destroyed or otherwise ceases to exist, the agency terminates. For example, the subject matter of a property management agreement is the principal's property. If the principal sells the property, the agent's authority terminates.

Agency Disclosure

As we've said, confusion about which party an agent represents can lead to loss of the commission, a lawsuit (perhaps even more than one), and disciplinary action. The best way to prevent confusion is with proper agency disclosure. Agency disclosure is required by state law and should make clear to all parties who is representing whom.

Agency Disclosure Requirements

California's agency disclosure law, adopted in 1988, applies to transactions involving residential property with one to four dwelling units. It requires the real estate agents involved in a transaction to disclose their agency status to the parties and give each of them two different written disclosures: an agency disclosure form and an agency confirmation statement.

Agency Disclosure Form. The agency disclosure form is essentially a general consumer information form for real estate sellers and buyers. It explains the legal duties of a seller's agent, a buyer's agent, and a dual agent. The back of the form sets forth the statutory provisions that govern agency relationships in real estate transactions. An example of this form is shown in Figure 1.3.

A listing agent must provide a copy of this disclosure form to a seller before the seller signs a listing agreement. A selling agent must give the form to a buyer as soon as it is practical to do so, and before the buyer signs an offer to purchase. The selling agent must also give the form to the seller as soon as it's practical to do so, and before presenting the buyer's offer to the seller. (If the selling agent isn't dealing directly with the seller, the selling agent can deliver the form to the seller through the listing agent or by certified mail.) Each disclosure form must be signed by the party who receives it, to acknowledge receipt. The agent who furnished the form must also sign it and keep a copy for her transaction records.

Notice that the agency disclosure form does not state which party the agent represents in this transaction. That disclosure is made in the agency confirmation statement.

Agency Confirmation Statement. As soon as it's practical to do so, a real estate agent must disclose to each party in the transaction which party or parties he represents. The initial disclosure may be spoken rather than written, but each party must sign a written agency confirmation statement before signing a purchase agreement form.

This confirmation statement may be (and usually is) included in the purchase agreement form, as long as it's clearly presented in a separate agency disclosure paragraph. Alternatively, the confirmation statement may be a separate document. The parties accept the described agency relationships when they sign the purchase agreement or the separate agency confirmation document.

Figure 1.4 shows an example of an agency confirmation form. This would be used if the purchase agreement form didn't have an agency confirmation provision. Each agent checks off which party he or she represents and signs the document. Both the seller and the buyer also sign it to acknowledge receipt of a copy.

Acting in Accordance with the Disclosures

The disclosures mandated by state law are fairly straightforward. However, once the disclosures have been made, a real estate agent also must act in accordance with them. This can be more difficult than it sounds.

Fig. 1.3 Agency disclosure form

DISCLOSURE REGARDING REAL ESTATE AGENCY RELATIONSHIP
(As required by the Civil Code)
(C.A.R. Form AD, Revised 12/14)

CALIFORNIA ASSOCIATION OF REALTORS ®

❑ (If checked) This form is being provided in connection with a transaction for a leasehold interest exceeding one year as per Civil Code section 2079.13(k), (l), and (m).

When you enter into a discussion with a real estate agent regarding a real estate transaction, you should from the outset understand what type of agency relationship or representation you wish to have with the agent in the transaction.

SELLER'S AGENT

A Seller's agent under a listing agreement with the Seller acts as the agent for the Seller only. A Seller's agent or a subagent of that agent has the following affirmative obligations:
To the Seller: A Fiduciary duty of utmost care, integrity, honesty and loyalty in dealings with the Seller.
To the Buyer and the Seller:
(a) Diligent exercise of reasonable skill and care in performance of the agent's duties.
(b) A duty of honest and fair dealing and good faith.
(c) A duty to disclose all facts known to the agent materially affecting the value or desirability of the property that are not known to, or within the diligent attention and observation of, the parties. An agent is not obligated to reveal to either party any confidential information obtained from the other party that does not involve the affirmative duties set forth above.

BUYER'S AGENT

A selling agent can, with a Buyer's consent, agree to act as agent for the Buyer only. In these situations, the agent is not the Seller's agent, even if by agreement the agent may receive compensation for services rendered, either in full or in part from the Seller. An agent acting only for a Buyer has the following affirmative obligations:
To the Buyer: A fiduciary duty of utmost care, integrity, honesty and loyalty in dealings with the Buyer.
To the Buyer and the Seller:
(a) Diligent exercise of reasonable skill and care in performance of the agent's duties.
(b) A duty of honest and fair dealing and good faith.
(c) A duty to disclose all facts known to the agent materially affecting the value or desirability of the property that are not known to, or within the diligent attention and observation of, the parties.
An agent is not obligated to reveal to either party any confidential information obtained from the other party that does not involve the affirmative duties set forth above.

AGENT REPRESENTING BOTH SELLER AND BUYER

A real estate agent, either acting directly or through one or more associate licensees, can legally be the agent of both the Seller and the Buyer in a transaction, but only with the knowledge and consent of both the Seller and the Buyer.
In a dual agency situation, the agent has the following affirmative obligations to both the Seller and the Buyer:
(a) A fiduciary duty of utmost care, integrity, honesty and loyalty in the dealings with either the Seller or the Buyer.
(b) Other duties to the Seller and the Buyer as stated above in their respective sections.
In representing both Seller and Buyer, the agent may not, without the express permission of the respective party, disclose to the other party that the
Seller will accept a price less than the listing price or that the Buyer will pay a price greater than the price offered.
The above duties of the agent in a real estate transaction do not relieve a Seller or Buyer from the responsibility to protect his or her own interests. You should carefully read all agreements to assure that they adequately express your understanding of the transaction. A real estate agent is a person qualified to advise about real estate. If legal or tax advice is desired, consult a competent professional.
Throughout your real property transaction you may receive more than one disclosure form, depending upon the number of agents assisting in the transaction. The law requires each agent with whom you have more than a casual relationship to present you with this disclosure form. You should read its contents each time it is presented to you, considering the relationship between you and the real estate agent in your specific transaction. **This disclosure form includes the provisions of Sections 2079.13 to 2079.24, inclusive, of the Civil Code set forth on page 2. Read it carefully. I/WE ACKNOWLEDGE RECEIPT OF A COPY OF THIS DISCLOSURE AND THE PORTIONS OF THE CIVIL CODE PRINTED ON THE BACK (OR A SEPARATE PAGE).**

Buyer/Seller/Landlord/Tenant _____ Date _____
Buyer/Seller/Landlord/Tenant _____ Date _____
Agent _____ DRE Lic. # _____
Real Estate Broker (Firm)
By _____ DRE Lic. # _____ Date _____
(Salesperson or Broker-Associate)

Agency Disclosure Compliance (Civil Code §2079.14):
• When the listing brokerage company also represents Buyer/Tenant: The Listing Agent shall have one AD form signed by Seller/Landlord and a different AD form signed by Buyer/Tenant.
• When Seller/Landlord and Buyer/Tenant are represented by different brokerage companies: (i) the Listing Agent shall have one AD form signed by Seller/Landlord and (ii) the Buyer's/Tenant's Agent shall have one AD form signed by Buyer/Tenant and either that same or a different AD form presented to Seller/Landlord for signature prior to presentation of the offer. If the same form is used, Seller may sign here:

Seller/Landlord _____ Date _____   Seller/Landlord _____ Date _____

The copyright laws of the United States (Title 17 U.S. Code) forbid the unauthorized reproduction of this form, or any portion thereof, by photocopy machine or any other means, including facsimile or computerized formats. Copyright © 1991-2010, CALIFORNIA ASSOCIATION OF REALTORS®, INC. ALL RIGHTS RESERVED.
AD REVISED 12/14 (PAGE 1 OF 2) Print Date

Reviewed by _____ Date _____

DISCLOSURE REGARDING REAL ESTATE AGENCY RELATIONSHIP (AD PAGE 1 OF 2)

Reprinted with permission, California Association of Realtors®. Endorsement not implied.

2079.13 As used in Sections 2079.14 to 2079.24, inclusive, the following terms have the following meanings: **(a)** "Agent" means a person acting under provisions of Title 9 (commencing with Section 2295) in a real property transaction, and includes a person who is licensed as a real estate broker under Chapter 3 (commencing with Section 10130) of Part 1 of Division 4 of the Business and Professions Code, and under whose license a listing is executed or an offer to purchase is obtained. **(b)** "Associate licensee" means a person who is licensed as a real estate broker or salesperson under Chapter 3 (commencing with Section 10130) of Part 1 of Division 4 of the Business and Professions Code and who is either licensed under a broker or has entered into a written contract with a broker to act as the broker's agent in connection with acts requiring a real estate license and to function under the broker's supervision in the capacity of an associate licensee. The agent in the real property transaction bears responsibility for his or her associate licensees who perform as agents of the agent. When an associate licensee owes a duty to any principal, or to any buyer or seller who is not a principal, in a real property transaction, that duty is equivalent to the duty owed to that party by the broker for whom the associate licensee functions. **(c)** "Buyer" means a transferee in a real property transaction, and includes a person who executes an offer to purchase real property from a seller through an agent, or who seeks the services of an agent in more than a casual, transitory, or preliminary manner, with the object of entering into a real property transaction. "Buyer" includes vendee or lessee. **(d)** "Commercial real property" means all real property in the state, except single-family residential real property, dwelling units made subject to Chapter 2 (commencing with Section 1940) of Title 5, mobilehomes, as defined in Section 798.3, or recreational vehicles, as defined in Section 799.29. **(e)** "Dual agent" means an agent acting, either directly or through an associate licensee, as agent for both the seller and the buyer in a real property transaction. **(f)** "Listing agreement" means a contract between an owner of real property and an agent, by which the agent has been authorized to sell the real property or to find or obtain a buyer. **(g)** "Listing agent" means a person who has obtained a listing of real property to act as an agent for compensation. **(h)** "Listing price" is the amount expressed in dollars specified in the listing for which the seller is willing to sell the real property through the listing agent. **(i)** "Offering price" is the amount expressed in dollars specified in an offer to purchase for which the buyer is willing to buy the real property. **(j)** "Offer to purchase" means a written contract executed by a buyer acting through a selling agent that becomes the contract for the sale of the real property upon acceptance by the seller. **(k)** "Real property" means any estate specified by subdivision (1) or (2) of Section 761 in property that constitutes or is improved with one to four dwelling units, any commercial real property, any leasehold in these types of property exceeding one year's duration, and mobilehomes, when offered for sale or sold through an agent pursuant to the authority contained in Section 10131.6 of the Business and Professions Code. **(l)** "Real property transaction" means a transaction for the sale of real property in which an agent is employed by one or more of the principals to act in that transaction, and includes a listing or an offer to purchase. **(m)** "Sell," "sale," or "sold" refers to a transaction for the transfer of real property from the seller to the buyer, and includes exchanges of real property between the seller and buyer, transactions for the creation of a real property sales contract within the meaning of Section 2985, and transactions for the creation of a leasehold exceeding one year's duration. **(n)** "Seller" means the transferor in a real property transaction, and includes an owner who lists real property with an agent, whether or not a transfer results, or who receives an offer to purchase real property of which he or she is the owner from an agent on behalf of another. "Seller" includes both a vendor and a lessor. **(o)** "Selling agent" means a listing agent who acts alone, or an agent who acts in cooperation with a listing agent, and who sells or finds and obtains a buyer for the real property, or an agent who locates property for a buyer or who finds a buyer for a property for which no listing exists and presents an offer to purchase to the seller. **(p)** "Subagent" means a person to whom an agent delegates agency powers as provided in Article 5 (commencing with Section 2349) of Chapter 1 of Title 9. However, "subagent" does not include an associate licensee who is acting under the supervision of an agent in a real property transaction.

2079.14 Listing agents and selling agents shall provide the seller and buyer in a real property transaction with a copy of the disclosure form specified in Section 2079.16, and, except as provided in subdivision (c), shall obtain a signed acknowledgement of receipt from that seller or buyer, except as provided in this section or Section 2079.15, as follows: **(a)** The listing agent, if any, shall provide the disclosure form to the seller prior to entering into the listing agreement. **(b)** The selling agent shall provide the disclosure form to the seller as soon as practicable prior to presenting the seller with an offer to purchase, unless the selling agent previously provided the seller with a copy of the disclosure form pursuant to subdivision (a). **(c)** Where the selling agent does not deal on a face-to-face basis with the seller, the disclosure form prepared by the selling agent may be furnished to the seller (and acknowledgement of receipt obtained for the selling agent from the seller) by the listing agent, or the selling agent may deliver the disclosure form by certified mail addressed to the seller at his or her last known address, in which case no signed acknowledgement of receipt is required. **(d)** The selling agent shall provide the disclosure form to the buyer as soon as practicable prior to execution of the buyer's offer to purchase, except that if the offer to purchase is not prepared by the selling agent, the selling agent shall present the disclosure form to the buyer not later than the next business day after the selling agent receives the offer to purchase from the buyer.

2079.15 In any circumstance in which the seller or buyer refuses to sign an acknowledgement of receipt pursuant to Section 2079.14, the agent, or an associate licensee acting for an agent, shall set forth, sign, and date a written declaration of the facts of the refusal.

2079.16 Reproduced on Page 1 of this AD form.

2079.17(a) As soon as practicable, the selling agent shall disclose to the buyer and seller whether the selling agent is acting in the real property transaction exclusively as the buyer's agent, exclusively as the seller's agent, or as a dual agent representing both the buyer and the seller. This relationship shall be confirmed in the contract to purchase and sell real property or in a separate writing executed or acknowledged by the seller, the buyer, and the selling agent prior to or coincident with execution of that contract by the buyer and the seller, respectively. **(b)** As soon as practicable, the listing agent shall disclose to the seller whether the listing agent is acting in the real property transaction exclusively as the seller's agent, or as a dual agent representing both the buyer and seller. This relationship shall be confirmed in the contract to purchase and sell real property or in a separate writing executed or acknowledged by the seller and the listing agent prior to or coincident with the execution of that contract by the seller.

(c) The confirmation required by subdivisions (a) and (b) shall be in the following form.

_____(DO NOT COMPLETE. SAMPLE ONLY)_____ is the agent of (check one): ❑ the seller exclusively; or ❑ both the buyer and seller.
(Name of Listing Agent)

_____(DO NOT COMPLETE. SAMPLE ONLY)_____ is the agent of (check one): ❑ the buyer exclusively; or ❑ the seller exclusively; or
(Name of Selling Agent if not the same as the Listing Agent)   ❑ both the buyer and seller.

(d) The disclosures and confirmation required by this section shall be in addition to the disclosure required by Section 2079.14.

2079.18 No selling agent in a real property transaction may act as an agent for the buyer only, when the selling agent is also acting as the listing agent in the transaction.

2079.19 The payment of compensation or the obligation to pay compensation to an agent by the seller or buyer is not necessarily determinative of a particular agency relationship between an agent and the seller or buyer. A listing agent and a selling agent may agree to share any compensation or commission paid, or any right to any compensation or commission for which an obligation arises as the result of a real estate transaction, and the terms of any such agreement shall not necessarily be determinative of a particular relationship.

2079.20 Nothing in this article prevents an agent from selecting, as a condition of the agent's employment, a specific form of agency relationship not specifically prohibited by this article if the requirements of Section 2079.14 and Section 2079.17 are complied with.

2079.21 A dual agent shall not disclose to the buyer that the seller is willing to sell the property at a price less than the listing price, without the express written consent of the seller. A dual agent shall not disclose to the seller that the buyer is willing to pay a price greater than the offering price, without the express written consent of the buyer. This section does not alter in any way the duty or responsibility of a dual agent to any principal with respect to confidential information other than price.

2079.22 Nothing in this article precludes a listing agent from also being a selling agent, and the combination of these functions in one agent does not, of itself, make that agent a dual agent.

2079.23 A contract between the principal and agent may be modified or altered to change the agency relationship at any time before the performance of the act which is the object of the agency with the written consent of the parties to the agency relationship.

2079.24 Nothing in this article shall be construed to either diminish the duty of disclosure owed buyers and sellers by agents and their associate licensees, subagents, and employees or to relieve agents and their associate licensees, subagents, and employees from liability for their conduct in connection with acts governed by this article or for any breach of a fiduciary duty or a duty of disclosure.

Published and Distributed by:
REAL ESTATE BUSINESS SERVICES, INC.
a subsidiary of the California Association of REALTORS®
525 South Virgil Avenue, Los Angeles, California 90020

Reviewed by _____ Date _____

AD REVISED 12/14 (PAGE 2 OF 2)

DISCLOSURE REGARDING REAL ESTATE AGENCY RELATIONSHIP (AD PAGE 2 OF 2)

Fig. 1.4 Agency confirmation statement

CALIFORNIA ASSOCIATION OF REALTORS ®

CONFIRMATION OF REAL ESTATE AGENCY RELATIONSHIPS
(As required by the Civil Code)
(C.A.R. Form AC, Revised 04/08)

Subject Property Address _____

The following agency relationship(s) is/are hereby confirmed for this transaction:

LISTING AGENT: _____
(Print Firm Name)

is the agent of (check one):

❏ the Seller/ Landlord exclusively; or

❏ both the Buyer/Tenant and Seller/Landlord

SELLING AGENT: _____
(Print Firm Name)
(if not the same as Listing Agent)

is the agent of (check one):

❏ the Buyer/Tenant exclusively; or

❏ the Seller/Landlord exclusively; or

❏ both the Buyer/Tenant and Seller/Landlord

I/WE ACKNOWLEDGE RECEIPT OF A COPY OF THIS CONFIRMATION.

Seller/Landlord _____ Date _____

Seller/Landlord _____ Date _____

Buyer/Tenant _____ Date _____

Buyer/Tenant _____ Date _____

Real Estate Broker (Selling Firm) _____

By _____ Date _____

Real Estate Broker (Listing Firm) _____

By _____ Date _____

A REAL ESTATE BROKER IS QUALIFIED TO ADVISE ON REAL ESTATE. IF YOU DESIRE LEGAL ADVICE, CONSULT YOUR ATTORNEY.

This form is available for use by the entire real estate industry. It is not intended to identify the user as a REALTOR®. REALTOR® is a registered collective membership mark which may be used only by members of the NATIONAL ASSOCIATION OF REALTORS® who subscribe to its Code of Ethics.

The copyright laws of the United States (17 U.S. Code) forbid the unauthorized reproduction of this form by any means, including facsimile or computerized formats. Copyright © 1987-2008, CALIFORNIA ASSOCIATION OF REALTORS®

Published and Distributed by:
REAL ESTATE BUSINESS SERVICES, INC.
a subsidiary of the California Association of REALTORS®
525 South Virgil Avenue, Los Angeles, California 90020

Reviewed by _____ Date _____

EQUAL HOUSING OPPORTUNITY

CONFIRMATION REAL ESTATE AGENCY RELATIONSHIPS (AC PAGE 1 OF 1)

Reprinted with permission, California Association of Realtors®. Endorsement not implied.

Example: Carville is the listing agent for Sharp's house; he represents only the seller. Carville discloses this fact, in writing, to Blaine, a potential buyer.

But Carville and Blaine get along well, and over the course of a few days he acts more and more like Blaine's agent. He gives Blaine a lot of advice about making an offer and negotiating the best terms. Blaine begins to rely on Carville's advice, and by the time Blaine is ready to make an offer on Sharp's house, he feels confident that Carville is working in his (Blaine's) best interests.

In this case, even though Carville properly disclosed his status as the seller's agent, his actions may have implied an agency relationship with Blaine and created an inadvertent dual agency. If Blaine or Sharp later became dissatisfied with the transaction, either of them could accuse Carville of breaching his agency duties.

As this example shows, the agency disclosure law has not completely eliminated the problem of inadvertent dual agency.

If a real estate agent's conduct is not consistent with his agency disclosure, he may be subject to disciplinary action by the Bureau of Real Estate, and the following sanctions may be imposed:

- suspension or revocation of his real estate license, and/or
- a fine of up to $10,000.

Licensee Acting as a Principal

When a real estate agent is selling or buying property for herself, there's a greater potential for misunderstandings. In this situation you should disclose that you are a licensed real estate agent and that you are selling or buying the property for your own benefit and not acting as anyone's agent. Make the disclosure in writing. If the other party is unrepresented, it's also a good idea to recommend that he seek representation with another agent.

Don't try to act as the other party's agent yourself. Disclose your licensed status, but avoid using your business cards, brokerage stationery, or other items that may create the impression that you're acting in your capacity as a real estate licensee.

In certain situations, you might change your role from agent to principal. For example, this would happen if you decided to buy one of your own listings. Then it's especially important to explain your conflict of interest to the seller and strongly advise her to find another agent or consult a lawyer about the transaction. If you are planning to resell the property at a profit, disclose the amount of profit you expect to make and obtain the seller's consent. Again, do all of this in writing.

Your broker may have office policies about agents buying or selling their own properties. If so, you should become familiar with these rules and follow them. Ask your broker to review any contracts involved before you make or accept an offer.

Types of Real Estate Agency Relationships

Now let's examine more closely the three basic types of real estate agency relationships: seller agency, buyer agency, and dual agency. We'll also discuss how a real estate licensee can act as a finder instead of as an agent.

Seller Agency

Seller agency, which is ordinarily established with a listing agreement, is the traditional type of real estate agency. At one time all of the agents involved in a typical residential transaction—the listing agent, the selling agent, and any other cooperating agents—were representing the seller. It was relatively uncommon for residential buyers to be represented by an agent. Now most buyers have their own agents.

Seller's Agent's Duties to Seller. As we discussed earlier, a real estate agent owes agency duties to his principal that go above and beyond the duties that he owes to any party. In general, a seller's agent must use his best efforts to promote the interests of the seller.

Services to Buyers. A seller's agent must treat a prospective buyer fairly and act in good faith. But the agent must not act as if she is representing the buyer. Although the seller's agent is required to fully disclose all material facts and answer the buyer's questions honestly, the agent should not give the buyer advice. For example, it would obviously be inappropriate for the seller's agent to suggest to the buyer how much to offer for the listed property.

Even so, there are many services that a seller's agent can provide to a buyer without violating his fiduciary duties to the seller. In fact, these services actually promote the interests of the seller, because they increase the chances of a sale and then enable the sales transaction to close smoothly. The services a seller's agent can offer a buyer include:

- discussing the buyer's housing needs;
- showing the property to the buyer;

- answering questions about the property and the neighborhood;
- discussing financing alternatives;
- furnishing copies of documents that affect the property (such as CC&Rs and easements);
- filling out the purchase agreement form;
- explaining the process of presenting the offer, negotiation, and closing the transaction; and
- referring the buyer to other professionals, if necessary.

Pre-existing Relationships. A seller's agent can provide all of these services without creating an agency relationship with the buyer. However, sometimes the seller's agent has had a previous relationship with the buyer. In this situation, it may be difficult for the agent to represent the seller's interests without feeling some loyalty to the buyer as well.

Example: Agent Jensen helped Sterling sell her home. Sterling was so pleased with Jensen's work, she wants him to help her find her next home. Jensen selects a suitable property that he has listed and shows it to Sterling.

Under the circumstances, it would be easy for Sterling to assume that Jensen is acting as her agent. But unless otherwise agreed, Jensen is only the seller's agent, and he should emphasize this fact to Sterling. Jensen should disclose his agency relationship with the seller to Sterling, remind Sterling that he is obligated to tell the seller any material information Sterling reveals to him, and emphasize to Sterling that he will be representing the seller in all negotiations.

Remember, however, that an agent must keep information learned from a prior client confidential even after the agency relationship has terminated. So even though Jensen currently represents the seller, he cannot disclose confidential information that he learned when Sterling was his principal, even if that information would benefit Jensen's current seller.

Buyer Agency

Most home buyers in California are represented by their own agent. A buyer's agent can go beyond the limited list of services that a seller's agent can provide to a buyer. And buyers with their own agent can freely discuss their housing needs and financial condition, knowing that their agent must keep this information confidential.

Benefits of Buyer Agency. The benefits of a buyer agency relationship can be broken down into four categories:

- agency duties,
- objective advice,
- help with negotiations, and
- access to more properties.

Agency duties. A buyer's agent owes fiduciary duties to the buyer rather than to the seller. For many buyers, the loyalty their agent owes them is the most important benefit of a buyer agency relationship. A buyer's agent must put the buyer's interests ahead of anyone else's, and any private information the buyer discloses to the agent must be kept confidential.

Example: Ashworth is a first-time home buyer. Broker Donnelly is helping him find a home. Donnelly shows him a home he's very interested in. Its listing price is $359,000 and Ashworth could easily afford a home that costs $30,000 more. Donnelly must put Ashworth's interests before her own, so she encourages him to make an offer on the home, even though she would receive a larger commission if he purchased a more expensive property.

Ashworth is eager to buy the home and suggests making a full price offer. Donnelly is pretty sure Ashworth can get the property for less than the listing price, so she advises him to start by offering $354,000. Even though Donnelly knows Ashworth is willing to pay the full listing price, she is obligated to keep that information confidential. If she had been the seller's agent, she would have been required to disclose this information to the seller.

Objective advice. Seller's agents develop expert sales techniques that are designed to convince the buyer to sign on the dotted line. Buyer's agents, on the other hand, are free to advise the buyer on the pros and cons of purchasing any given home.

Example: The Whittiers looked very seriously at two homes before they purchased a third one. Their agent, Smith, gave them invaluable advice throughout the house-hunting process.

The Whittiers responded emotionally to the beautiful landscaping and lovely interior of the first home, and they were immediately ready to make a full price offer. Then Smith helped them look into the property taxes, heating costs, and upkeep, and the Whittiers realized that the house would cost too much to maintain.

The second home they were interested in was much more affordable, but Smith made sure they got all the pertinent information about the structural condition of the house. Once they realized how much it would cost to replace the roof and what three previous termite infestations meant, they quickly decided against the purchase.

The third home seemed ideal, even after Smith helped them evaluate all the information about it. Because Smith was familiar with the housing market, he advised the Whittiers to offer $8,000 less than the listing price. Their offer was accepted and the transaction closed without a hitch. If it weren't for Smith's objective advice, they might have ended up with a property that wasn't right for them.

Help with negotiations. While some buyers are happiest when they're dickering over a sales price, many buyers are decidedly uncomfortable negotiating for a home they want. They are afraid to offer full price, because they don't want to pay too much for the home. On the other hand, they are afraid to make an offer that's too low, for fear of offending the seller and ruining any chance of reaching an agreement. A buyer's agent is extremely useful during the negotiation phase. The agent can use her knowledge of the real estate market to help the buyer get the property on the best possible terms.

Example: The Browns are first-time buyers. They have decided to make an offer on a starter home, but they are unsure about how much to offer. Their agent, Cohen, knows the going price for similar homes and suggests an amount for a strategic opening offer. She also discusses other important terms of the offer, such as the amount of the good faith deposit, the closing date, and how the parties will divide the closing costs. With her help, the Browns are able to purchase the home on very favorable terms.

Access to more properties. A buyer's agent who enters into a written representation agreement with the buyer (see below) will usually be compensated if the buyer purchases any home, even one that isn't listed with a broker. So a buyer's agent may pursue less traditional means of searching for properties, considering properties that are for sale by owner, properties with open listings, and properties in foreclosure or probate proceedings.

Example: McHugh has very specific housing requirements. Among other things, he wants lake frontage, a boat ramp, an outbuilding to use as a shop, and fruit trees. A property with these features in McHugh's price range simply can't be found through the multiple listing service.

McHugh enters into a buyer representation agreement with Morris and agrees to pay a commission if Morris finds him a property that is not listed with the MLS. Morris scours legal notices for foreclosure, bankruptcy, and estate sales. He also carefully reviews "for sale by owner" (FSBO) ads in the local and regional papers. Finally, after driving through several lakeshore neighborhoods, he spots a FSBO that meets most of McHugh's requirements.

McHugh makes an offer on the house and the parties successfully close the transaction.

Buyer Representation Agreements. If a buyer and a broker choose to create a buyer agency relationship, they should enter into a written **representation agreement** that establishes the rights and duties of both parties. The agreement will set forth the agent's duty to use his professional expertise to locate a property for the buyer and negotiate the terms of the sale, and also the circumstances in which the buyer will be required to compensate the agent. Most buyer representation agreements contain other important provisions as well. These may include:

- the term of the agreement;
- the general characteristics of the property the buyer wants;
- a price range for the property;
- any warranties or representations made by the agent; and
- how the buyer agency relationship will affect the agent's relationship with other property buyers and sellers.

An example of a buyer representation agreement is shown in Figure 1.5. This form authorizes the broker to locate properties and show them to the buyer, present offers on the buyer's behalf, assist in the negotiation process, and assist the buyer in obtaining financing, inspections, and escrow services.

Unless the buyer checks a "Single Agency Only" provision, this agreement provides that the broker may act as a dual agent if necessary or appropriate. If the broker shows the buyer a property that he listed, the broker will be a dual agent in respect to that property. (See the section on in-house transactions in the discussion of dual agency later in this chapter.) The dual agency must immediately be disclosed to the buyer, and the broker cannot reveal either party's negotiating position to the other party. In this agreement, the buyer also acknowledges that salespersons affiliated with the broker may represent different buyers in competing transactions involving the same property.

Warranties are another issue that's often addressed in a buyer representation agreement. In most cases, the buyer's agent does not make any warranties or representations regarding the value of any property or its suitability for the buyer's purposes. Investigating the physical condition and legal status of a property is the buyer's responsibility.

Buyer's Agent's Compensation. Naturally, real estate agents are concerned about how they will be compensated for their time and effort. The way a seller's agent is compensated is well established: the seller agrees to pay the listing broker a percentage of the sales price when the property is sold. If another brokerage is involved in bringing the sale about, the listing broker and the selling broker will split the commission.

The arrangements for paying a buyer's agent's fee are not so clear-cut. There are three common methods of compensating a buyer's agent:

- a seller-paid fee,
- a buyer-paid fee, and
- a retainer.

The buyer and the buyer's agent may agree to one of these methods, or a combination of two or more methods.

Seller-paid fee. Under the terms of most listing agreements, the buyer's agent will be paid by the seller, as a result of a commission split. The seller pays the commission to the listing agent, and the listing agent then splits the commission with the buyer's agent. This arrangement is based on a provision found in most listing agreements that entitles any cooperating agent who procures a buyer to receive the selling broker's portion of the commission, regardless of which party that cooperating agent represents. (The source of the commission does not determine the identity of the agent's principal.)

Example: Seller Forbes lists his property with Broker Winston. He agrees to pay Winston a commission of 6% of the sales price. The listing agreement includes a clause that entitles any cooperating broker who procures a buyer to be paid the selling broker's portion of the commission.

Broker Lopez is representing Buyer Brown. Brown offers $600,000 for Forbes's house and Forbes accepts the offer. When the transaction closes, the $36,000 commission paid by Forbes is split between Winston and Lopez. Accepting a share of the commission paid by the seller does not affect Lopez's agency relationship with the buyer.

Fig. 1.5 Buyer representation agreement

BUYER REPRESENTATION AGREEMENT - EXCLUSIVE

CALIFORNIA ASSOCIATION OF REALTORS®

(C.A.R. Form BRE, Revised 4/13)

1. **EXCLUSIVE RIGHT TO REPRESENT:** _____ ("Buyer")
grants _____ ("Broker")
beginning on (date) _____ and ending at: **(i)** 11:59 P.M. on (date) _____, or **(ii)** completion of
a resulting transaction, whichever occurs first ("Representation Period"), the exclusive and irrevocable right, on the terms specified
in this Agreement, to represent Buyer in acquiring real property or a manufactured home as follows:
   A. **PROPERTY TO BE ACQUIRED:**
      (1) Any purchase, lease or other acquisition of any real property or manufactured home described as
      Location:_____
      Other:_____
      Price range: $ _____ to $ _____
OR ☐ **(2)** The following specified properties only:_____
OR ☐ **(3)** Only the properties identified on the attached list.
   B. Broker agrees to exercise due diligence and reasonable efforts to fulfill the following authorizations and obligations.
   C. Broker will perform its obligations under this Agreement through the individual signing for Broker below or another real estate
      licensee assigned by Broker, who is either Broker individually or an associate-licensee (an individual licensed as a real estate
      salesperson or Broker who works under Broker's real estate license). Buyer agrees that Broker's duties are limited by the terms of
      this Agreement, including those limitations set forth in paragraphs 5 and 6.
2. **AGENCY RELATIONSHIPS:**
   A. **DISCLOSURE:** If the property described in paragraph 4 includes residential property with one to four dwelling units, Buyer
      acknowledges receipt of the "Disclosure Regarding Real Estate Agency Relationships" (C.A.R. Form AD) prior to entering into
      this Agreement.
   B. **BUYER REPRESENTATION:** Broker will represent, as described in this Agreement, Buyer in any resulting transaction.
   C. **(1) POSSIBLE DUAL AGENCY WITH SELLER:** (C(1) APPLIES UNLESS C(2)(i) or (ii) is checked below.)
      Depending on the circumstances, it may be necessary or appropriate for Broker to act as an agent for both Buyer and a seller,
      exchange party, or one or more additional parties ("Seller"). Broker shall, as soon as practicable, disclose to Buyer any election
      to act as a dual agent representing both Buyer and Seller. If Buyer is shown property listed with Broker, Buyer consents to
      Broker becoming a dual agent representing both Buyer and Seller with respect to those properties. In event of dual agency,
      Buyer agrees that: **(a)** Broker, without the prior written consent of Buyer, will not disclose to Seller that the Buyer is willing to pay
      a price greater than the price offered; **(b)** Broker, without the prior written consent of Seller, will not disclose to Buyer that Seller
      is willing to sell Property at a price less than the listing price; and **(c)** other than as set forth in (a) and (b) above, a dual agent
      is obligated to disclose known facts materially affecting the value or desirability of the property to both parties.
   OR (2) SINGLE AGENCY ONLY: (APPLIES ONLY IF (i) or (ii) is checked below.)
      ☐ **(i) Broker's firm lists properties for sale:** Buyer understands that this election will prevent Broker from showing Buyer
      those properties that are listed with Broker's firm or from representing Buyer in connection with those properties. Buyer's
      acquisition of a property listed with Broker's firm shall not affect Broker's right to be compensated under paragraph 3. In any
      resulting transaction in which Seller's property is not listed with Broker's firm, Broker will be the exclusive agent of Buyer and not
      a dual agent also representing Seller.
   OR ☐ **(ii) Broker's firm DOES NOT list property:** Entire brokerage firm only represents buyers and does not list property. In any
      resulting transaction, Broker will be the exclusive agent of Buyer and not a dual agent also representing Seller.
   D. **OTHER POTENTIAL BUYERS:** Buyer understands that other potential buyers may, through Broker, consider, make offers on
      or acquire the same or similar properties as those Buyer is seeking to acquire. Buyer consents to Broker's representation of such
      other potential buyers before, during and after the Representation Period, or any extension thereof.
   E. **NON CONFIDENTIALITY OF OFFERS:** Buyer is advised that Seller or Listing Agent may disclose the existence, terms, or
      conditions of Buyer's offer unless all parties and their agent have signed a written confidentiality agreement. Whether any such
      information is actually disclosed depends on many factors, such as current market conditions, the prevailing practice in the real
      estate community, the Listing Agent's marketing strategy and the instructions of the Seller.
   F. **CONFIRMATION:** If the Property (as defined below) includes residential property with one to four dwelling units, Broker shall
      confirm the agency relationship described above, or as modified, in writing, prior to or coincident with Buyer's execution of a
      Property Contract (as defined below).
3. **COMPENSATION TO BROKER:**
   **NOTICE: The amount or rate of real estate commissions is not fixed by law. They are set by each Broker
   individually and may be negotiable between Buyer and Broker (real estate commissions include all
   compensation and fees to Broker).**
   Buyer agrees to pay to Broker, irrespective of agency relationship(s), as follows:
   A. **AMOUNT OF COMPENSATION: (Check (1), (2) or (3). Check only one.)**
      ☐ **(1)** _____ percent of the acquisition price AND (if checked ☐) $ _____,
   OR ☐ **(2)** $_____,
   OR ☐ **(3)** Pursuant to the compensation schedule attached as an addendum _____.

Buyer's Initials (_____)(_____)

BRE REVISED 4/13 (PAGE 1 OF 4) Print Date

Reviewed by _____ Date _____

EQUAL HOUSING OPPORTUNITY

BUYER REPRESENTATION AGREEMENT – EXCLUSIVE (BRE PAGE 1 OF 4)

Buyer: _____ Date: _____

B. COMPENSATION PAYMENTS AND CREDITS: Buyer is responsible for payment of compensation provided for in this Agreement. **However, if anyone other than Buyer compensates Broker for services covered by this Agreement, that amount shall be credited toward Buyer's obligation to pay compensation.** If the amount of compensation Broker receives from anyone other than Buyer exceeds Buyer's obligation, the excess amount shall be disclosed to Buyer and if allowed by law paid to Broker, or (if checked) ☐ credited to Buyer, or ☐ other _____.

C. BROKER RIGHT TO COMPENSATION: Broker shall be entitled to the compensation provided for in paragraph 3A:

(1) If during the Representation Period, or any extension thereof, Buyer enters into an agreement to acquire property described in paragraph **1A**, on terms acceptable to Buyer provided Seller completes the transaction or is prevented from doing so by Buyer. (Broker shall be entitled to compensation whether any escrow resulting from such agreement closes during or after the expiration of the Representation Period.)

(2) If, within ___ **calendar days** after expiration of the Representation Period or any extension thereof, Buyer enters into an agreement to acquire property described in paragraph 1, which property Broker introduced to Buyer, or for which Broker acted on Buyer's behalf. The obligation to pay compensation pursuant to this paragraph shall arise only if, prior to or within **3 (or ☐ _____) calendar days** after expiration of this Agreement or any extension thereof, Broker gives Buyer a written notice of those properties which Broker introduced to Buyer, or for which Broker acted on Buyer's behalf.

D. TIMING OF COMPENSATION: Compensation is payable:

(1) Upon completion of any resulting transaction, and if an escrow is used, through escrow.

(2) If acquisition is prevented by default of Buyer, upon Buyer's default.

(3) If acquisition is prevented by a party to the transaction other than Buyer, when Buyer collects damages by suit, settlement or otherwise. Compensation shall equal one-half of the damages recovered, not to exceed the compensation provided for in paragraph 3A, after first deducting the unreimbursed payments, credits and expenses of collection, if any.

E. Buyer hereby irrevocably assigns to Broker the compensation provided for in paragraph 3A from Buyer's funds and proceeds in escrow. Buyer agrees to submit to escrow any funds needed to compensate Broker under this Agreement. Broker may submit this Agreement, as instructions to compensate Broker, to any escrow regarding property involving Buyer and a seller or other transferor.

F. "BUYER" includes any person or entity, other than Broker, related to Buyer or who in any manner acts on Buyer's behalf to acquire property described in paragraph 1A.

G. (1) Buyer has not previously entered into a representation agreement with another broker regarding property described in paragraph **1A**, unless specified as follows (name other broker here): _____
_____

(2) Buyer warrants that Buyer has no obligation to pay compensation to any other broker regarding property described in paragraph **1A**, unless Buyer acquires the following property(ies): _____

(3) If Buyer acquires a property specified in G(2) above during the time Buyer is obligated to compensate another broker, Broker is neither: **(i)** entitled to compensation under this Agreement, nor **(ii)** obligated to represent Buyer in such transaction.

4. INTERNET ADVERTISING; INTERNET BLOGS; SOCIAL MEDIA: Buyer acknowledges and agrees that: **(i)** properties presented to them may have been marketed through a "virtual tour" on the Internet, permitting potential buyers to view properties over the Internet, or that the properties may have been the subject of comments or opinions of value by others on Internet blogs or other social media sites; **(ii)** neither the service provider(s) nor Broker has control over who will obtain access to such services or what action such persons might take; and **(iii)** Broker has no control over how long the information concerning the properties will be available on the Internet or social media sites.

5. BROKER AUTHORIZATIONS AND OBLIGATIONS:

A. Buyer authorizes Broker to: **(i)** locate and present selected properties to Buyer, present offers authorized by Buyer, and assist Buyer in negotiating for acceptance of such offers; **(ii)** assist Buyer with the financing process, including obtaining loan pre-qualification; **(iii)** upon request, provide Buyer with a list of professionals or vendors who perform the services described in the attached Buyer's Inspection Advisory; **(iv)** order reports, and schedule and attend meetings and appointments with professionals chosen by Buyer; **(v)** provide guidance to help Buyer with the acquisition of property; and **(vi)** obtain a credit report on Buyer.

B. For property transactions of which Broker is aware and not precluded from participating in by Buyer, Broker shall provide and review forms to create a property contract ("Property Contract") for the acquisition of a specific property ("Property"). With respect to such Property, Broker shall: **(i)** if the Property contains residential property with one to four dwelling units, conduct a reasonably competent and diligent on-site visual inspection of the accessible areas of the Property (excluding any common areas), and disclose to Buyer all facts materially affecting the value or desirability of such Property that are revealed by this inspection; **(ii)** deliver or communicate to Buyer any disclosures, materials or information received by, in the personal possession of or personally known to the individual signing for Broker below during the Representation Period; and **(iii)** facilitate the escrow process, including assisting Buyer in negotiating with Seller. Unless otherwise specified in writing, any information provided through Broker in the course of representing Buyer has not been and will not be verified by Broker. Broker's services are

Buyer's Initials (_____)(_____)

Reviewed by _____ Date _____

BUYER REPRESENTATION AGREEMENT – EXCLUSIVE (BRE PAGE 2 OF 4)

Buyer: _____ Date: _____

performed in compliance with federal, state and local anti-discrimination laws.

6. SCOPE OF BROKER DUTY:

    A. While Broker will perform the duties described in paragraph 6B, Broker recommends that Buyer select other professionals, as described in the attached Buyer's Inspection Advisory, to investigate the Property through inspections, investigations, tests, surveys, reports, studies and other available information ("Inspections") during the transaction. Buyer agrees that these Inspections, to the extent they exceed the obligations described in paragraph 6B, are not within the scope of Broker's agency duties. Broker informs Buyer that it is in Buyer's best interest to obtain such Inspections.

    B. Buyer acknowledges and agrees that Broker: **(i)** does not decide what price Buyer should pay or Seller should accept; **(ii)** does not guarantee the condition of the Property; **(iii)** does not guarantee the performance, adequacy or completeness of inspections, services, products or repairs provided or made by Seller or others; **(iv)** does not have an obligation to conduct an inspection of common areas or offsite areas of the Property; **(v)** shall not be responsible for identifying defects on the Property, in common areas or offsite areas unless such defects are visually observable by an inspection of reasonably accessible areas of the Property or are known to Broker; **(vi)** shall not be responsible for inspecting public records or permits concerning the title or use of the Property; **(vii)** shall not be responsible for identifying the location of boundary lines or other items affecting title; **(viii)** shall not be responsible for verifying square footage, representations of others or information contained in Investigation reports, Multiple Listing Service, advertisements, flyers or other promotional material; **(ix)** shall not be responsible for providing legal or tax advice regarding any aspect of a transaction entered into by Buyer or Seller; and **(x)** shall not be responsible for providing other advice or information that exceeds the knowledge, education and experience required to perform real estate licensed activity. Buyer agrees to seek legal, tax, insurance, title and other desired assistance from appropriate professionals.

    C. Broker owes no duty to inspect for common environmental hazards, earthquake weaknesses, or geologic and seismic hazards. If Buyer receives the booklets titled "Environmental Hazards: A Guide for Homeowners, Buyers, Landlords and Tenants," "The Homeowner's Guide to Earthquake Safety," or "The Commercial Property Owner's Guide to Earthquake Safety," the booklets are deemed adequate to inform Buyer regarding the information contained in the booklets and, other than as specified in 6B above, Broker is not required to provide Buyer with additional information about the matters described in the booklets.

7. BUYER OBLIGATIONS:

    A. Buyer agrees to timely view and consider properties selected by Broker and to negotiate in good faith to acquire a property. Buyer further agrees to act in good faith toward the completion of any Property Contract entered into in furtherance of this Agreement. Within **5 (or ☐ _____) calendar days** from the execution of this Agreement, Buyer shall provide relevant personal and financial information to Broker to assure Buyer's ability to acquire property described in paragraph 4. If Buyer fails to provide such information, or if Buyer does not qualify financially to acquire property described in paragraph 4, then Broker may cancel this Agreement in writing. Buyer has an affirmative duty to take steps to protect him/herself, including discovery of the legal, practical and technical implications of discovered or disclosed facts, and investigation of information and facts which are known to Buyer or are within the diligent attention and observation of Buyer. Buyer is obligated, and agrees, to read all documents provided to Buyer. Buyer agrees to seek desired assistance from appropriate professionals, selected by Buyer, such as those referenced in the attached Buyer's Inspection Advisory.

    B. Buyer shall notify Broker in writing (C.A.R. Form BMI) of any material issue to Buyer, such as, but not limited to, Buyer requests for information on, or concerns regarding, any particular area of interest or importance to Buyer ("Material Issues").

    C. Buyer agrees to: **(i)** indemnify, defend and hold Broker harmless from all claims, disputes, litigation, judgments, costs and attorney fees arising from any incorrect information supplied by Buyer, or from any Material Issues that Buyer fails to disclose in writing to Broker; and **(ii)** pay for reports, Inspections and meetings arranged by Broker on Buyer's behalf.

    D. Buyer is advised to read the attached Buyer's Inspection Advisory for a list of items and other concerns that typically warrant Inspections or investigation by Buyer or other professionals.

8. OTHER TERMS AND CONDITIONS: The following disclosures or addenda are attached:

    A. ☑ Buyer's Inspection Advisory (C.A.R. Form BIA-B) _____

    B. ☐ Statewide Buyer and Seller Advisory (C.A.R. Form SBSA) _____

    C. ☐ _____

    D. ☐ _____

9. ATTORNEY FEES: In any action, proceeding or arbitration between Buyer and Broker regarding the obligation to pay compensation under this Agreement, the prevailing Buyer or Broker shall be entitled to reasonable attorney fees and costs, except as provided in paragraph 11A.

10. ENTIRE AGREEMENT: All understandings between the parties are incorporated in this Agreement. Its terms are intended by the parties as a final, complete and exclusive expression of their agreement with respect to its subject matter, and may not be contradicted by evidence of any prior agreement or contemporaneous oral agreement. This Agreement may not be extended, amended, modified, altered or changed, except in writing signed by Buyer and Broker. In the event that any provision of this Agreement is held to be ineffective or invalid, the remaining provisions will nevertheless be given full force and effect. This Agreement and any supplement, addendum or modification, including any copy, whether by copier, facsimile, NCR or electronic, may

Buyer's Initials (_____)(_____)

BRE REVISED 4/13 (PAGE 3 OF 4)

Reviewed by _____ Date _____

BUYER REPRESENTATION AGREEMENT – EXCLUSIVE (BRE PAGE 3 OF 4)

Buyer: _____ Date: _____

be signed in two or more counterparts, all of which shall constitute one and the same writing.

11. DISPUTE RESOLUTION:

A. MEDIATION: Buyer and Broker agree to mediate any dispute or claim arising between them out of this Agreement, or any resulting transaction, before resorting to arbitration or court action, subject to paragraph 11B(2) below. Paragraph 11B(2) below applies whether or not the arbitration provision is initialed. Mediation fees, if any, shall be divided equally among the parties involved. If, for any dispute or claim to which this paragraph applies, any party commences an action without first attempting to resolve the matter through mediation, or refuses to mediate after a request has been made, then that party shall not be entitled to recover attorney's fees, even if they would otherwise be available to that party in any such action. THIS MEDIATION PROVISION APPLIES WHETHER OR NOT THE ARBITRATION PROVISION IS INITIALED.

B. ARBITRATION OF DISPUTES: (1) Buyer and Broker agree that any dispute or claim in Law or equity arising between them regarding the obligation to pay compensation under this Agreement, which is not settled through mediation, shall be decided by neutral, binding arbitration, including and subject to paragraph 11B(2) below. The arbitrator shall be a retired judge or justice, or an attorney with at least five years of residential real estate law experience, unless the parties mutually agree to a different arbitrator, who shall render an award in accordance with substantive California law. The parties shall have the right to discovery in accordance with California Code of Civil Procedure §1283.05. In all other respects, the arbitration shall be conducted in accordance with Title 9 of Part III, of the California Code of Civil Procedure. Judgment upon the award of the arbitrator(s) may be entered in any court having jurisdiction. Interpretation of this Agreement to arbitrate shall be governed by the Federal Arbitration Act.

(2) EXCLUSIONS FROM MEDIATION AND ARBITRATION: The following matters are excluded from mediation and arbitration: (i) a judicial or non-judicial foreclosure or other action or proceeding to enforce a deed of trust, mortgage or installment land sale contract as defined in California Civil Code §2985; (ii) an unlawful detainer action; (iii) the filing or enforcement of a mechanic's lien; and (iv) any matter that is within the jurisdiction of a probate, small claims or bankruptcy court. The filing of a court action to enable the recording of a notice of pending action, for order of attachment, receivership, injunction, or other provisional remedies, shall not constitute a waiver of the mediation and arbitration provisions.

"NOTICE: BY INITIALING IN THE SPACE BELOW YOU ARE AGREEING TO HAVE ANY DISPUTE ARISING OUT OF THE MATTERS INCLUDED IN THE 'ARBITRATION OF DISPUTES' PROVISION DECIDED BY NEUTRAL ARBITRATION AS PROVIDED BY CALIFORNIA LAW. YOU ARE GIVING UP ANY RIGHTS YOU MIGHT POSSESS TO HAVE THE DISPUTE LITIGATED IN A COURT OR JURY TRIAL. BY INITIALING IN THE SPACE BELOW YOU ARE GIVING UP YOUR JUDICIAL RIGHTS TO DISCOVERY AND APPEAL, UNLESS THOSE RIGHTS ARE SPECIFICALLY INCLUDED IN THE 'ARBITRATION OF DISPUTES' PROVISION. IF YOU REFUSE TO SUBMIT TO ARBITRATION AFTER AGREEING TO THIS PROVISION, YOU MAY BE COMPELLED TO ARBITRATE UNDER THE AUTHORITY OF THE CALIFORNIA CODE OF CIVIL PROCEDURE. YOUR AGREEMENT TO THIS ARBITRATION PROVISION IS VOLUNTARY."

"WE HAVE READ AND UNDERSTAND THE FOREGOING AND AGREE TO SUBMIT DISPUTES ARISING OUT OF THE MATTERS INCLUDED IN THE 'ARBITRATION OF DISPUTES' PROVISION TO NEUTRAL ARBITRATION."

Buyer's Initials _____/_____ Broker's Initials _____/_____

Buyer acknowledges that Buyer has read, understands, received a copy of and agrees to the terms of this Agreement.

Buyer _____ Date _____
Address _____ City _____ State _____ Zip _____
Telephone _____ Fax _____ E-mail _____

Buyer _____ Date _____
Address _____ City _____ State _____ Zip _____
Telephone _____ Fax _____ E-mail _____

Real Estate Broker (Firm) _____ DRE License # _____
By (Agent) _____ DRE License # _____ Date _____
Address _____ City _____ State _____ Zip _____
Telephone _____ Fax _____ E-mail _____

BRE REVISED 4/13 (PAGE 4 OF 4)   Reviewed by _____ Date _____

BUYER REPRESENTATION AGREEMENT – EXCLUSIVE (BRE PAGE 4 OF 4)

Since the commission split arrangement does not change the amount of the commission the seller is obligated to pay, sellers rarely object to paying the buyer's agent's fee in this way. Most buyer representation agreements provide that the buyer's agent will be paid by a commission split if the buyer purchases a home that is listed through a multiple listing service.

Buyer-paid fee. Buyer representation agreements may also provide for a buyer-paid fee. The fee may be based on an hourly rate, an arrangement that turns the agent into a consultant. Alternatively, a buyer's agent may charge a percentage fee, requiring the buyer to pay the agent a percentage of the purchase price of the property as a commission. A third possibility is a flat fee—a specified sum that is payable if the buyer purchases a property found by the broker.

Many buyer representation agreements provide that the buyer's agent will accept a commission split if one is available, but that the buyer will pay the fee if the purchased property was unlisted (for example, if the property was for sale by owner). In some situations, a buyer promises to pay a flat fee to a broker but then purchases a property that is subject to a commission split. If the commission split only covers a part of that fee, the buyer will need to pay the broker the difference.

Retainer. Some agents insist on a retainer—a fee paid up front—before agreeing to a buyer agency relationship. The retainer is usually nonrefundable, but will be credited against any fee or commission that the buyer's agent becomes entitled to.

Dual Agency

A dual agency relationship exists when an agent represents both the seller and the buyer in the same transaction. A dual agent owes fiduciary duties to both principals. However, because the interests of the buyer and the seller nearly always conflict, it is difficult to represent them both without being disloyal to one or the other.

Example: Woodman represents both the buyer and the seller in a real estate transaction. The seller informs Woodman that she is in a big hurry to sell and will accept any reasonable offer. The buyer tells Woodman that he is very interested in the house and is willing to pay the full listing price. Should Woodman tell the buyer about the seller's eagerness to sell? Should Woodman tell the seller about the buyer's willingness to pay full price?

In fact, it is really impossible for a dual agent to fully represent both parties. Thus, a dual agent should explain to both of her principals that neither of them will receive full representation. Certain facts must necessarily be withheld from each party; the dual agent cannot divulge confidential information about one party to the other. California law provides that a dual agent cannot tell the buyer that the seller is willing to sell for less than the listing price unless the seller consents to the disclosure in writing. Nor can the dual agent tell the seller that the buyer is willing to pay more than the offered price without the buyer's written consent.

In-house Transactions. Dual agency most commonly arises in in-house transactions. A sale is an **in-house transaction** when the listing agent and the selling agent both work for the same broker. The listing agent represents the seller, so if the selling agent is representing the buyer, then their broker becomes a dual agent.

> **Example:** Salesperson Werner, who works for Starboard Realty, is acting as Buyer Miller's agent. They've looked at many houses. Finally, Miller decides to make an offer on a house listed by Salesperson Nagano, who also works for Starboard. Since the salesperson representing the seller (the listing agent, Nagano) and the salesperson representing the buyer (the selling agent, Werner) both work for the same firm, Starboard Realty is a dual agent in this transaction. As a result, both Nagano and Werner are now considered dual agents too. Although Nagano may continue to work exclusively with the seller and Werner may continue to work exclusively with the buyer, both agents owe fiduciary duties to both parties.

Informed Consent to Dual Agency. Before acting as a dual agent, a broker must have the informed written consent of both parties to the transaction. Acting as a dual agent without full disclosure and written consent is a violation of California's Real Estate Law, and may lead to disciplinary action.

Real estate licensees should be especially careful about their agency disclosures in this context. Buyers and sellers, eager to get on with the business of buying and selling a home, may agree to a dual agency without really understanding what it means. They may accept the agent's explanation at face value and sign an agency confirmation statement without question. Later, one party may feel that his or her interests were neglected and that agency duties were breached. This kind of disappointment often leads to legal action.

Fig. 1.6 Types of real estate agency

Seller's Agent
- Owes fiduciary duties only to the seller

Buyer's Agent
- Owes fiduciary duties only to the buyer

Dual Agent
- Owes fiduciary duties to both seller and buyer
- Must not disclose confidential information to either party

Finder or Middleman
- Introduces buyer to seller
- Owes fiduciary duties to neither party

Finder or Middleman

It's possible for a real estate licensee to be involved in a transaction without forming an agency relationship with either party. This happens when a licensee acts as a **finder** or middleman. In order to be considered a finder rather than an agent, the licensee can have no involvement in the transaction beyond arranging an introduction between the seller and a prospective buyer.

A licensee acting as a finder does not owe fiduciary duties to either party. Any activity aside from a mere introduction, such as participating in the negotiations, will create an agency relationship. Forming an agency relationship without the proper disclosure can lead to disciplinary action and the loss of the finder's fee.

Note that it is not necessary to be a real estate licensee to act as a finder and collect a finder's fee. Again, however, the finder must do nothing more than introduce the parties. If an unlicensed person did anything beyond that, she would be acting as a real estate licensee without a license and could face penalties from the Real Estate Commissioner.

Chapter Summary

1. When a real estate licensee enters into an agency relationship, he owes fiduciary duties to his principal. These duties include the duty of utmost care, obedience and good faith, accounting, loyalty and confidentiality, and disclosure of material facts.

2. A real estate licensee owes third parties the duties of reasonable care and skill, good faith and fair dealing, and disclosure of material facts. Agents representing sellers and the sellers themselves are legally required to disclose latent defects and other material facts about the property to prospective buyers.

3. California law requires real estate agents to perform a reasonably competent and diligent visual inspection of the property and disclose any problems they discover to the buyer.

4. In California, real estate agents must disclose to the parties in a transaction which party they are representing. The parties must be given an agency disclosure form, and they must also sign an agency confirmation form or provision in the purchase agreement.

5. A seller agency relationship is ordinarily created with a listing agreement. A buyer agency relationship should also be created by written agreement. A licensee may act as a dual agent with the written consent of both parties, but must be careful not to create a dual agency inadvertently.

6. A real estate licensee (or an unlicensed person) may collect a finder's fee for introducing a seller and a buyer. A finder is not considered to be an agent and does not owe fiduciary duties to either party.

Key Terms

Agent: A person authorized to represent another (the principal) in dealings with third parties.

Principal: A person who grants another person (an agent) authority to represent her in dealings with third parties.

Third party: A person seeking to deal with a principal through an agent. Also referred to as a customer.

Client: A person who employs a real estate agent. A real estate broker's client can be the seller, the buyer, or both.

Dual agent: An agent who represents both parties to a transaction, as when a broker represents both the buyer and the seller.

Finder: Someone who introduces a real estate buyer and seller, but does not help them negotiate their contract. A finder is not the agent of either party and does not have to be licensed. Also called a middleman.

Fiduciary relationship: A relationship of trust and confidence, where one party owes the other (or both parties owe each other) loyalty and a higher standard of good faith than is owed to third parties. For example, an agent is a fiduciary in relation to the principal; husband and wife are fiduciaries in relation to one another.

Trust funds: Money or things of value received by an agent, not belonging to the agent but being held for the benefit of others.

Commingling: Illegally mixing trust funds held on behalf of a client with personal funds.

Secret profit: A financial benefit that an agent takes from a transaction without informing the principal.

Latent defects: Defects that are not visible or apparent (as opposed to patent defects).

Material fact: An important fact; one that is likely to influence a decision.

Imputed knowledge: A legal doctrine stating that a principal is considered to have notice of information that the agent has, even if the agent never told the principal.

Vicarious liability: A legal doctrine holding that a principal can be held liable for harm to third parties resulting from an agent's actions.

Joint and several liability: A form of liability in which two or more persons are responsible for a debt both individually and as a group.

In-house transaction: A sale in which the buyer and the seller are brought together by salespersons working for the same broker.

Chapter Quiz

1. The listing agent knows that a suicide took place in the house four years ago. A buyer asks the agent if he knows about any deaths that have occurred on the property. The agent says he's not aware of any. What duty has the agent breached?
   a. The duty to disclose material facts
   b. The duty of reasonable care and skill
   c. The duty of good faith and fair dealing
   d. None; the agent acted properly

2. Under California law, which of the following must not be disclosed?
   a. The agent found indications of flooding in the basement during a visual inspection
   b. A person diagnosed with AIDS lived on the property until last year
   c. The property was the site of an illegal drug lab, and chemical residues may linger
   d. The roof of the house leaks during heavy rains

3. The duty of accounting does not include which of the following responsibilities?
   a. To disclose the terms of the listing salesperson's share of the commission
   b. To be able to account for all funds or valuables entrusted to the broker
   c. To avoid commingling trust funds with the broker's own funds
   d. To report to clients on the status of all trust funds regularly

4. A buyer's agent is most commonly compensated with a/an:
   a. hourly rate
   b. seller-paid commission split
   c. retainer
   d. flat fee

5. Which of the following situations clearly does not involve dual agency?
   a. A listing agent gives advice to prospective buyers about how much to offer for the property
   b. A licensee introduces a seller to a prospective buyer without providing further representation
   c. A buyer and a seller consent in writing to be represented by the same broker
   d. A broker employs both the selling agent, who is representing the buyer in this transaction, and the listing agent, who represents the seller

6. Because of the fiduciary duty of loyalty, an agent must:
   a. keep secret profits out of the client's trust account
   b. put the interests of third parties above his own interests
   c. keep confidential information from third parties
   d. refuse net listings

7. Whether or not you have an agency relationship with a particular party in a transaction does not affect:
   a. whether that party may be held liable for your actions
   b. the extent of the duties you owe to that party
   c. whether your actions will be binding on that party
   d. whether you are required to answer that party's questions in good faith

8. Proper agency confirmation may be made:
   a. anywhere in the purchase agreement
   b. in a separate document
   c. in a separate paragraph in the purchase agreement
   d. Both b and c

9. Which of the following is not one of the basic types of real estate agency relationships in California?
   a. Net agency
   b. Seller agency
   c. Dual agency
   d. Buyer agency

10. Which of the following situations involves a change from one type of agency relationship to another?
    a. A finder explains to the seller and the buyer that she is acting only as a facilitator in the transaction
    b. The buyer's agent receives the selling broker's share of the commission, even though the commission was paid by the seller
    c. A real estate agent representing a buyer helps the buyer make an offer on one of the agent's own listings
    d. A buyer representation agreement provides that the buyer's agent will accept a commission split if available, but otherwise the buyer will pay the agent's fee

Answer Key

1. c. The agent was not required to disclose the suicide as a material fact, because it took place more than three years ago. But by responding untruthfully to a specific question, the agent breached the duty of good faith and fair dealing that he owes to potential buyers.

2. b. An agent may not disclose that a property was occupied by a person who had AIDS or was HIV-positive. Other problems that may affect the value or desirability of the property are material facts and must be disclosed as latent defects.

3. a. The duty of accounting requires a broker to account for all trust funds she holds. The broker must keep the client updated as to the status of the funds. She must also avoid commingling them with her personal or general business funds. (The listing salesperson's share of the brokerage commission does not have to be disclosed to the client.)

4. b. Unless the property was unlisted, a buyer's agent is ordinarily compensated with a portion of the commission paid by the seller to the listing agent.

5. b. A finder can avoid creating an agency relationship with either party by providing no services beyond introducing them to one another. A dual agency can be created through express agreement or inadvertently. In an in-house transaction, the broker becomes a dual agent (but the listing agent continues to represent only the seller and the selling agent continues to represent only the buyer).

6. c. The duty of loyalty is owed only to the principal. Among other things, it requires the agent to keep the principal's confidential information confidential.

7. d. An agency relationship with one of the parties in a transaction does not allow you to give false or misleading information to third parties, even on your principal's orders.

8. d. The agency confirmation statement may be included in the purchase agreement or provided in a separate document. If it is incorporated into the purchase agreement, it must be in a separate paragraph.

9. a. The basic types of real estate agency relationships in California are seller agency, buyer agency, and dual agency.

10. c. A listing agent always represents the seller. So when a buyer's agent shows the buyer one of her own listings and the buyer makes an offer on it, a dual agency is created. The agent must disclose this to both parties and obtain their written consent.

2

Listing Agreements and Property Disclosures

Types of Listing Agreements

- Open listings
- Exclusive agency listings
- Exclusive right to sell listings

Elements of a Listing Agreement

- Basic legal requirements
- Provisions of a typical listing agreement form
- Modifying a listing agreement

Mandatory Disclosures Concerning the Property

- Transfer disclosure statement
- Environmental hazards booklet
- Natural hazard disclosure statement
- Residential earthquake hazards report
- Lead-based paint disclosure
- Supplemental statutory disclosure form
- Mello-Roos lien disclosure

Introduction

When you begin your real estate career, your broker will encourage you to start looking for listings. Listings generate a lot of business activity for you and your brokerage.

- When you submit a listing agreement to the multiple listing service, all of the agents at your office (as well as other agents who belong to the MLS) can start trying to find a buyer.
- When a new "For Sale" sign shows up in a neighborhood, "drive-by" buyers will call your office for more information. Even if ultimately they aren't interested in that particular property, they could wind up buying another listed property.
- When you hold an open house for the listed property, you attract potential buyers and sellers that you may be able to do business with in the future.
- And when the listed property sells, you get a portion of the commission, no matter who finds the buyer. Plus, a "Sold!" banner across your "For Sale" sign is good advertising for you and your broker.

Obtaining a listing is a positive and financially rewarding experience. There are a variety of techniques you can learn to help you get listings; these methods are thoroughly explained in courses and books on sales techniques. However, using a listing agreement properly and fulfilling the legal obligations it imposes are just as important as finding an interested seller to list with you. If you aren't thoroughly familiar with the terms of your listing agreement form and able to use it correctly, your career may get off to a very rocky start.

This chapter describes the different types of listing agreements, the elements of a valid listing agreement, and the standard provisions that are found in most listing agreement forms. It also discusses the transfer disclosure statement form that you will give to sellers to fill out when they list their property with you. The chapter also covers a variety of other disclosures that California law requires sellers to make to prospective buyers.

Types of Listing Agreements

A **listing agreement** is a written employment contract between a property owner and a real estate broker. The owner hires the broker to find a buyer (or a tenant) who is **ready, willing, and able** to buy (or lease) the property on the owner's terms.

There are three different types of listing agreements:

- the open listing,
- the exclusive agency listing, and
- the exclusive right to sell listing.

Open Listing Agreements

Open listings are rarely used in residential transactions (and some multiple listing services don't allow them), but you still need to understand how they work. Under an open listing, the seller must pay your broker a commission only if you are the **procuring cause** of the sale. The procuring cause is the person primarily responsible for bringing about an agreement between the seller and a ready, willing, and able buyer. To be the procuring cause, you usually must have personally negotiated the offer the seller accepts, or an offer that meets the seller's stated terms.

An open listing is rarely in the best interests of either the real estate agent or the seller. Here are some of the disadvantages of open listings:

- A seller may enter into open listings with as many brokers as he wants. Only the broker whose salesperson makes the sale is entitled to a commission; the other brokers and their sales agents are not compensated for their time and effort. And if the seller himself makes the sale, he does not have to pay any of the brokers.
- Since a listing agent has little assurance of earning a commission from an open listing, she might not put as much effort into marketing the property.
- If agents working for two competing brokers negotiate with the person who ends up buying the property, there may be a dispute over which agent was the procuring cause.

Because of these problems, open listings are generally used only when a seller is unwilling to execute an exclusive agency or exclusive right to sell listing.

Exclusive Agency Listing Agreements

In an exclusive agency listing, the seller agrees to list with only one broker, but retains the right to sell the property herself without being obligated to pay the broker a commission. The broker is entitled to a commission if anyone other than the seller finds a buyer for the property, but not if the seller finds the buyer without the help of an agent.

Exclusive agency listings are uncommon in residential transactions because they present the chance of a commission dispute between the seller and the broker as to who was the procuring cause of the sale.

Fig. 2.1 Types of listing agreements

Open Listing
- Seller may give open listings to several brokers
- Only the broker whose agent was the procuring cause
  is compensated

Exclusive Agency Listing
- Seller gives listing to only one broker
- No compensation if seller finds a buyer without help
- Listing broker compensated if anyone other than seller finds a buyer

Exclusive Right to Sell Listing
- Seller gives listing to only one broker
- Listing broker compensated if anyone finds a buyer

Exclusive Right to Sell Listing Agreements

In an exclusive right to sell listing, the seller agrees to list with only one broker, and that broker is entitled to a commission if the property sells during the listing term, regardless of who finds the buyer. Even if the seller makes the sale directly, without the help of an agent, the broker is still entitled to the commission.

Not surprisingly, the exclusive right to sell listing is the type preferred by most brokers. It provides the most protection for the listing broker, and the potential for conflict with the seller over who was the procuring cause is limited. The brokers involved in the transaction might disagree about who's entitled to the selling broker's share of the commission, but the seller will have to pay the listing broker in any event.

Because of these advantages, the great majority of residential listing agreements are exclusive right to sell listings.

Elements of a Listing Agreement

When you go to a listing appointment, you take along the listing agreement form used by your office. It is probably a form provided by your local multiple listing service or Association of REALTORS®. Brokers rarely use their own individual listing forms, and you aren't allowed to come up with one yourself. (If you did, you would be guilty of the unauthorized practice of law.) Even so, you should understand the basic legal requirements for a valid listing agreement. Later in the chapter we will look at the standard provisions found in a typical listing agreement form.

Basic Legal Requirements

Of course, a listing agreement must have all of the elements that are required for any valid contract: competent parties, offer and acceptance, consideration, and a legal purpose. In addition, a listing agreement should:

- identify the property to be sold,
- include the terms of sale,
- establish the broker's authority,
- establish the broker's compensation,
- specify the listing's termination date, and
- be in writing and signed by the seller.

Identify the Property. The listing agreement must clearly identify the property. The best practice is to use a legal description. A street address is useful and should be included, but it's not adequate by itself. You can get the property's legal description from a title insurance company or from the seller's deed. If you don't have access to the legal description when you fill out the form, you may write "Legal description to be provided by agent" in the blank for the property description, and have the seller sign the agreement. (Be sure, though, to follow through and add the description later.)

If the legal description is lengthy, put it on a separate sheet of paper or an addendum form and attach it to the agreement, writing "See attached" or "See addendum" in the space provided for a description on the listing agreement form. Remember that the parties must sign or initial any attachments or addenda to a contract.

Terms of Sale. A listing agreement should indicate what kind of offer the seller wants from prospective buyers. Most importantly, the agreement should state the listing price—that is, the cash price that the seller would like for the property. It should also state any other terms of sale the seller requires (for example, a closing date after January 1) or is willing to provide (for example, secondary financing, or assumption of an existing loan).

The seller ought to specify any unusual terms that would affect whether he would accept an offer. Otherwise he could become liable for the brokerage commission if he refuses an offer that meets all the stated terms of sale but is nonetheless undesirable.

The listing agreement should also list any items of personal property the seller intends to leave behind for the buyer, and any fixtures the seller intends to remove.

Broker's Authority. Since the listing agreement is an employment contract, it should specify the listing agent's duties and the scope of her authority. Typically, the seller gives the broker the authority to list the property with a multiple listing service, advertise the property, cooperate with buyers' agents, and receive offers and good faith deposits.

Promise of Compensation. Of course, the seller's promise to compensate the broker is a key provision in a listing agreement. The conditions of payment should be clearly stated. For example, the seller could promise to pay the broker when the broker has found a ready, willing, and able buyer, or not until a contract is signed, or not unless a sale actually closes. A **ready, willing, and able buyer** is one who:

1. makes an offer to purchase that meets the seller's terms, and
2. is financially able to complete the transaction.

In addition to the conditions of payment, the listing agreement should state the amount or rate of the listing broker's compensation. The compensation—the brokerage commission—is usually stated as a percentage of the sales price, but it may be a specified dollar amount instead.

In listing agreements for one- to four-unit residential properties, state law requires a provision in boldface type stating that the amount or rate of the commission is not fixed by law, and is negotiable between the seller and broker.

In a **net listing**, the seller stipulates a certain net amount that she wants from the sale of the property. If the sales price exceeds that net figure, the listing agent is entitled to keep the excess as his compensation. In California, net listings are allowed only if the listing agent discloses the amount of his commission to the seller before the seller becomes committed to the transaction.

Example: Warshaw wants you to sell her home. She wants to get $235,000 from the sale, and she says you can have anything over that. In other words, if you can sell the property for $245,000, you get a $10,000 commission. If you sell the property for $250,000, you get a $15,000 commission.

It is legal to take Warshaw's listing on this basis only if you inform her how much your commission will amount to before she accepts an offer to purchase.

Net listings are generally disfavored because they give unscrupulous brokers an opportunity to take advantage of clients who don't know the true value of their property. They are illegal in some states.

Termination Date. California law requires an exclusive agency or exclusive right to sell listing agreement to have a definite termination date. There is no minimum or maximum listing period; the parties may agree to whatever listing period suits their needs. But the listing period's termination date must be included in the listing agreement.

In Writing. California's statute of frauds requires all listing agreements to be in writing and signed by the seller. Without a written, signed listing agreement, the broker can't sue for the commission. Note, however, that the writing requirement doesn't mean that you must have a formal listing agreement. Some notes jotted on a piece of paper could be sufficient.

> **Example:** George runs into his old friend Brad. Brad wants to put his house up for sale, and he's delighted to discover that George is now a real estate broker. He wants to list his property with George right away.
>
> George doesn't have a listing agreement form with him, so he jots down the following on a piece of paper: "I will pay George Hanson 6% of the selling price when he finds a ready, willing, and able buyer for the only piece of property I own—Hillshire Orchards—in Fresno County." Brad signs the paper. This would probably be enforceable in California, as long as Brad is legally competent and the description is sufficient to identify the property.

Provisions of a Typical Listing Agreement Form

Of course, printed listing agreement forms contain much more information than the handwritten note in the example above. Let's take a look at the many provisions found in a typical listing form.

In California (as in most states), there is no single standard listing agreement form. Various forms are available from multiple listing services, brokers' associations, and general publishers of legal forms. Although these forms have many elements in common, there may also be significant differences between them. You must be sure to learn the provisions of the specific form used by your broker.

The following is a general discussion of provisions that are likely to be encountered in a typical form, but any given form might omit some of these provisions and include others not discussed here. As an example, an exclusive right to sell listing form published by the California Association of REALTORS® is shown in Figure 2.2.

Broker's Authority and Listing Period. The first section in a listing agreement form usually identifies the parties, establishes the broker's agency authority, and specifies the date on which the listing period will expire.

Broker's name. Although a listing agreement form is frequently filled out and signed by a salesperson, the listing agreement is actually a contract between the seller and the broker. Remember, only a broker may directly contract with members of the public for brokerage services (see Chapter 1).

Agency authority. Even though the most commonly used type of listing agreement is called an "exclusive right to sell" listing, it does not literally give the broker authority to sell the property (to do that, the seller would have to give the broker a power of attorney). It is up to the seller to accept an offer and transfer the property to the buyer.

> **Example:** You take a listing on Sorenson's house. Wilson is very interested in purchasing the house, and he makes an offer that meets all of Sorenson's terms. You do not have the authority to accept this offer; you only have the authority to present the offer to Sorenson. Sorenson will choose whether or not to accept the offer.

Listing period. As mentioned, a listing agreement should include a termination date. This is required for exclusive listing agreements, because an exclusive listing effectively prevents the seller from hiring a different agent until it expires. (If the seller hired another agent, she might end up owing a commission to both the first agent and the new one.)

Of course, a listing agreement may terminate before its termination date even without a sale of the property. This can happen in a number of ways, generally corresponding to the ways in which any agency relationship can terminate (see Chapter 1):

- termination by mutual agreement of the seller and the broker;
- revocation by the seller;
- renunciation by the broker;
- death or mental incompetence of the seller or broker; or
- the loss of the broker's license.

Fig. 2.2 Exclusive right to sell listing agreement form

CALIFORNIA ASSOCIATION OF REALTORS®

RESIDENTIAL LISTING AGREEMENT
(Exclusive Authorization and Right to Sell)
(C.A.R. Form RLA, Revised 11/13)

1. **EXCLUSIVE RIGHT TO SELL:** _____ ("Seller")
hereby employs and grants _____ ("Broker")
beginning (date) _____ and ending at 11:59 P.M. on (date) _____ ("Listing Period")
the exclusive and irrevocable right to sell or exchange the real property in the City of _____,
County of_____, Assessor's Parcel No. _____
California, described as: _____ ("Property").

2. **ITEMS EXCLUDED AND INCLUDED:** Unless otherwise specified in a real estate purchase agreement, all fixtures and fittings that are attached to the Property are included, and personal property items are excluded, from the purchase price.
ADDITIONAL ITEMS EXCLUDED: _____.
ADDITIONAL ITEMS INCLUDED: _____.
Seller intends that the above items be excluded or included In offering the Property for sale, but understands that: (i) the purchase agreement supersedes any intention expressed above and will ultimately determine which items are excluded and included in the sale; and (ii) Broker is not responsible for and does not guarantee that the above exclusions and/or inclusions will be in the purchase agreement.

3. **LISTING PRICE AND TERMS:**
   A. The listing price shall be: _____
   _____ Dollars ($ _____).
   B. Additional Terms _____
   _____

4. **COMPENSATION TO BROKER:**
   Notice: The amount or rate of real estate commissions is not fixed by law. They are set by each Broker individually and may be negotiable between Seller and Broker (real estate commissions include all compensation and fees to Broker).
   A. Seller agrees to pay to Broker as compensation for services irrespective of agency relationship(s), either ☐ _____ percent of the listing price (or if a purchase agreement is entered into, of the purchase price), or ☐ $ _____
   AND _____, as follows:
      (1) If during the Listing Period, or any extension, Broker, cooperating broker, Seller or any other person procures a ready, willing, and able buyer(s) whose offer to purchase the Property on any price and terms is accepted by Seller, provided the Buyer completes the transaction or is prevented from doing so by Seller. (Broker is entitled to compensation whether any escrow resulting from such offer closes during or after the expiration of the Listing Period, or any extension.)
   OR (2) If within _____ calendar days (a) after the end of the Listing Period or any extension; or (b) after any cancellation of this Agreement, unless otherwise agreed, Seller enters into a contract to sell, convey, lease or otherwise transfer the Property to anyone ("Prospective Buyer") or that person's related entity: (i) who physically entered and was shown the Property during the Listing Period or any extension by Broker or a cooperating broker; or (ii) for whom Broker or any cooperating broker submitted to Seller a signed, written offer to acquire, lease, exchange or obtain an option on the Property. Seller, however, shall have no obligation to Broker under paragraph 4A(2) unless, not later than 3 calendar days after the end of the Listing Period or any extension or cancellation, Broker has given Seller a written notice of the names of such Prospective Buyers.
   OR (3) If, without Broker's prior written consent, the Property is withdrawn from sale, conveyed, leased, rented, otherwise transferred, or made unmarketable by a voluntary act of Seller during the Listing Period, or any extension.
   B. If completion of the sale is prevented by a party to the transaction other than Seller, then compensation due under paragraph 4A shall be payable only if and when Seller collects damages by suit, arbitration, settlement or otherwise, and then in an amount equal to the lesser of one-half of the damages recovered or the above compensation, after first deducting title and escrow expenses and the expenses of collection, if any.
   C. In addition, Seller agrees to pay Broker: _____
   D. Seller has been advised of Broker's policy regarding cooperation with, and the amount of compensation offered to, other brokers.
      (1) Broker is authorized to cooperate with and compensate brokers participating through the multiple listing service(s) ("MLS") by offering to MLS brokers out of Broker's compensation specified in 4A, either ☐ _____ percent of the purchase price, or ☐ $ _____
      (2) Broker is authorized to cooperate with and compensate brokers operating outside the MLS as per Broker's policy.
   E. Seller hereby irrevocably assigns to Broker the above compensation from Seller's funds and proceeds in escrow. Broker may submit this Agreement, as instructions to compensate Broker pursuant to paragraph 4A, to any escrow regarding the Property involving Seller and a buyer, Prospective Buyer or other transferee.
   F. **(1)** Seller represents that Seller has not previously entered into a listing agreement with another broker regarding the Property, unless specified as follows: _____
      (2) Seller warrants that Seller has no obligation to pay compensation to any other broker regarding the Property unless the Property is transferred to any of the following individuals or entities: _____
      (3) If the Property is sold to anyone listed above during the time Seller is obligated to compensate another broker: (i) Broker is

© 2013, California Association of REALTORS®, Inc.

RLA REVISED 11/13 (PAGE 1 OF 5)   Print Date

Seller's Initials (_____)(_____)

Reviewed by _____ Date _____

EQUAL HOUSING OPPORTUNITY

RESIDENTIAL LISTING AGREEMENT - EXCLUSIVE (RLA PAGE 1 OF 5)

Reprinted with permission, California Association of Realtors®. Endorsement not implied.

Property Address:_____ Date:_____

not entitled to compensation under this Agreement; and (ii) Broker is not obligated to represent Seller in such transaction.

5. MULTIPLE LISTING SERVICE:

A. Broker is a participant/subscriber to _____ Multiple Listing Service (MLS) and possibly others. Unless otherwise instructed in writing the Property will be listed with the MLS(s) specified above. That MLS is (or if checked ☐ is not) the primary MLS for the geographic area of the Property. All terms of the transaction, including sales price and financing, if applicable, (i) will be provided to the MLS in which the property is listed for publication, dissemination and use by persons and entities on terms approved by the MLS and (ii) may be provided to the MLS even if the Property is not listed with the MLS.

BENEFITS OF USING THE MLS; IMPACT OF OPTING OUT OF THE MLS; PRESENTING ALL OFFERS

WHAT IS AN MLS? The MLS is a database of properties for sale that is available and disseminated to and accessible by all other real estate agents who are participants or subscribers to the MLS. Property information submitted to the MLS describes the price, terms and conditions under which the Seller's property is offered for sale (including but not limited to the listing broker's offer of compensation to other brokers). It is likely that a significant number of real estate practitioners in any given area are participants or subscribers to the MLS. The MLS may also be part of a reciprocal agreement to which other multiple listing services belong. Real estate agents belonging to other multiple listing services that have reciprocal agreements with the MLS also have access to the information submitted to the MLS. The MLS may further transmit the MLS database to Internet sites that post property listings online.

EXPOSURE TO BUYERS THROUGH MLS: Listing property with an MLS exposes a seller's property to all real estate agents and brokers (and their potential buyer clients) who are participants or subscribers to the MLS or a reciprocating MLS.

CLOSED/PRIVATE LISTING CLUBS OR GROUPS: Closed or private listing clubs or groups are not the same as the MLS. The MLS referred to above is accessible to all eligible real estate licensees and provides broad exposure for a listed property. Private or closed listing clubs or groups of licensees may have been formed outside the MLS. Private or closed listing clubs or groups are accessible to a more limited number of licensees and generally offer less exposure for listed property. Whether listing property through a closed, private network - and excluding it from the MLS - is advantageous or disadvantageous to a seller, and why, should be discussed with the agent taking the Seller's listing.

NOT LISTING PROPERTY IN A LOCAL MLS: If the Property is listed in an MLS which does not cover the geographic area where the Property is located then real estate agents and brokers working that territory, and Buyers they represent looking for property in the neighborhood, may not be aware the Property is for sale.

OPTING OUT OF MLS: If Seller elects to exclude the Property from the MLS, Seller understands and acknowledges that: (a) real estate agents and brokers from other real estate offices, and their buyer clients, who have access to that MLS may not be aware that Seller's Property is offered for sale; (b) Information about Seller's Property will not be transmitted to various real estate Internet sites that are used by the public to search for property listings; (c) real estate agents, brokers and members of the public may be unaware of the terms and conditions under which Seller is marketing the Property.

REDUCTION IN EXPOSURE: Any reduction in exposure of the Property may lower the number of offers and negatively impact the sales price.

PRESENTING ALL OFFERS: Seller understands that Broker must present all offers received for Seller's Property unless Seller gives Broker written instructions to the contrary.

Seller's Initials (_____)(_____)	Broker's Initials (_____)(_____)

B. MLS rules generally provide that residential real property and vacant lot listings be submitted to the MLS within 2 days or some other period of time after all necessary signatures have been obtained on the listing agreement. Broker will not have to submit this listing to the MLS if, within that time, Broker submits to the MLS a form signed by Seller (C.A.R. Form SELM or the local equivalent form).

C. MLS rules allow MLS data to be made available by the MLS to additional Internet sites unless Broker gives the MLS instructions to the contrary. Seller acknowledges that for any of the below opt-out instructions to be effective, Seller must make them on a separate instruction to Broker signed by Seller (C.A.R. Form SELI or the local equivalent form). Specific information that can be excluded from the Internet as permitted by (or in accordance with) the MLS is as follows:
(1) Property Availability: Seller can instruct Broker to have the MLS not display the Property on the Internet.
(2) Property Address: Seller can instruct Broker to have the MLS not display the Property address on the Internet.
Seller understands that the above opt-outs would mean consumers searching for listings on the Internet may not see the Property or Property's address in response to their search.
(3) Feature Opt-Outs: Seller can instruct Broker to advise the MLS that Seller does not want visitors to MLS Participant or Subscriber Websites or Electronic Displays that display the Property listing to have the features below. Seller understands (i) that these opt-outs apply only to Websites or Electronic Displays of MLS Participants and Subscribers who are real estate broker and agent members of the MLS; (ii) that other Internet sites may or may not have the features set forth herein; and (iii) that neither Broker nor the MLS may have the ability to control or block such features on other Internet sites.
(a) Comments And Reviews: The ability to write comments or reviews about the Property on those sites; or the ability to link to another site containing such comments or reviews if the link is in immediate conjunction with the Property.

RLA REVISED 11/13 (PAGE 2 OF 5)

Seller's Initials (_____)(_____)
Reviewed by _____ Date _____

RESIDENTIAL LISTING AGREEMENT - EXCLUSIVE (RLA PAGE 2 OF 5)

Property Address:_____ Date:_____

(b) Automated Estimate Of Value: The ability to create an automated estimate of value or to link to another site containing such an estimate of value if the link is in immediate conjunction with the Property.

6. **SELLER REPRESENTATIONS:** Seller represents that, unless otherwise specified in writing, Seller is unaware of: (i) any Notice of Default recorded against the Property; (ii) any delinquent amounts due under any loan secured by, or other obligation affecting, the Property; (iii) any bankruptcy, insolvency or similar proceeding affecting the Property; (iv) any litigation, arbitration, administrative action, government investigation or other pending or threatened action that affects or may affect the Property or Seller's ability to transfer it; and (v) any current, pending or proposed special assessments affecting the Property. Seller shall promptly notify Broker in writing if Seller becomes aware of any of these items during the Listing Period or any extension thereof.

7. **BROKER'S AND SELLER'S DUTIES:** (a) Broker agrees to exercise reasonable effort and due diligence to achieve the purposes of this Agreement. Unless Seller gives Broker written instructions to the contrary, Broker is authorized to (i) order reports and disclosures as necessary, (ii) advertise and market the Property by any method and in any medium selected by Broker, including MLS and the Internet, and, to the extent permitted by these media, control the dissemination of the information submitted to any medium; and (iii) disclose to any real estate licensee making an inquiry the receipt of any offers on the Property and the offering price of such offers. (b) Seller agrees to consider offers presented by Broker, and to act in good faith to accomplish the sale of the Property by, among other things, making the Property available for showing at reasonable times and, subject to paragraph 4F, referring to Broker all inquiries of any party interested in the Property. Seller is responsible for determining at what price to list and sell the Property. Seller further agrees to indemnify, defend and hold Broker harmless from all claims, disputes, litigation, judgments attorney fees and costs arising from any incorrect information supplied by Seller, or from any material facts that Seller knows but fails to disclose.

8. **DEPOSIT:** Broker is authorized to accept and hold on Seller's behalf any deposits to be applied toward the purchase price.

9. **AGENCY RELATIONSHIPS:**
   A. Disclosure: If the Property includes residential property with one-to-four dwelling units, Seller shall receive a "Disclosure Regarding Agency Relationships" (C.A.R. Form AD) prior to entering into this Agreement.
   B. Seller Representation: Broker shall represent Seller in any resulting transaction, except as specified in paragraph 4F.
   C. Possible Dual Agency With Buyer: Depending upon the circumstances, it may be necessary or appropriate for Broker to act as an agent for both Seller and buyer, exchange party, or one or more additional parties ("Buyer"). Broker shall, as soon as practicable, disclose to Seller any election to act as a dual agent representing both Seller and Buyer. If a Buyer is procured directly by Broker or an associate-licensee in Broker's firm, Seller hereby consents to Broker acting as a dual agent for Seller and Buyer. In the event of an exchange, Seller hereby consents to Broker collecting compensation from additional parties for services rendered, provided there is disclosure to all parties of such agency and compensation. Seller understands and agrees that: (i) Broker, without the prior written consent of Seller, will not disclose to Buyer that Seller is willing to sell the Property at a price less than the listing price; (ii) Broker, without the prior written consent of Buyer, will not disclose to Seller that Buyer is willing to pay a price greater than the offered price; and (iii) except for (i) and (ii) above, a dual agent is obligated to disclose known facts materially affecting the value or desirability of the Property to both parties.
   D. Other Sellers: Seller understands that Broker may have or obtain listings on other properties, and that potential buyers may consider, make offers on, or purchase through Broker, property the same as or similar to Seller's Property. Seller consents to Broker's representation of sellers and buyers of other properties before, during and after the end of this Agreement.
   E. Confirmation: If the Property includes residential property with one-to-four dwelling units, Broker shall confirm the agency relationship described above, or as modified, in writing, prior to or concurrent with Seller's execution of a purchase agreement.

10. **SECURITY AND INSURANCE:** Broker is not responsible for loss of or damage to personal or real property, or person, whether attributable to use of a keysafe/lockbox, a showing of the Property, or otherwise. Third parties, including, but not limited to, appraisers, inspectors, brokers and prospective buyers, may have access to, and take videos and photographs of, the interior of the Property. Seller agrees: (i) to take reasonable precautions to safeguard and protect valuables that might be accessible during showings of the Property; and (ii) to obtain insurance to protect against these risks. Broker does not maintain insurance to protect Seller.

11. **PHOTOGRAPHS AND INTERNET ADVERTISING:**
    A. In order to effectively market the Property for sale it is often necessary to provide photographs, virtual tours and other media to buyers. Seller agrees (or ☐ if checked, does not agree) that Broker may photograph or otherwise electronically capture images of the exterior and interior of the Property ("Images") for static and/or virtual tours of the Property by buyers and others on Broker's website, the MLS, and other marketing sites. Seller acknowledges that once Images are placed on the Internet neither Broker nor Seller has control over who can view such Images and what use viewers may make of the Images, or how long such Images may remain available on the Internet. Seller further agrees that such Images are the property of Broker and that Broker may use such Images for advertisement of Broker's business in the future.
    B. Seller acknowledges that prospective buyers and/or other persons coming onto the property may take photographs, videos or other images of the property. Seller understands that Broker does not have the ability to control or block the taking and use of Images by any such persons. (If checked) ☐ Seller instructs Broker to publish in the MLS that taking of Images is limited to those persons preparing Appraisal or Inspection reports. Seller acknowledges that unauthorized persons may take images who do not have access to or have not read any limiting instruction in the MLS or who take images regardless of any limiting instruction in the MLS. Once Images are taken and/or put into electronic display on the Internet or otherwise, neither Broker nor Seller has control over who views such Images nor what use viewers may make of the Images.

12. **KEYSAFE/LOCKBOX:** A keysafe/lockbox is designed to hold a key to the Property to permit access to the Property by Broker, cooperating brokers, MLS participants, their authorized licensees and representatives, authorized inspectors, and accompanied prospective buyers. Broker, cooperating brokers, MLS and Associations/Boards of REALTORS® are not insurers against injury, theft, loss, vandalism or damage attributed to the use of a keysafe/lockbox. Seller does (or if checked ☐ does not) authorize Broker to install a keysafe/lockbox. If Seller does not occupy the Property, Seller shall be responsible for obtaining occupant(s)' written permission for use of a keysafe/lockbox (C.A.R. Form KLA).

RLA REVISED 11/13 (PAGE 3 OF 5)

Seller's Initials (_____)(_____)

Reviewed by _____ Date _____

RESIDENTIAL LISTING AGREEMENT - EXCLUSIVE (RLA PAGE 3 OF 5)

Property Address: _____ Date: _____

13. **SIGN:** Seller does (or if checked ☐ does not) authorize Broker to install a FOR SALE/SOLD sign on the Property.

14. **EQUAL HOUSING OPPORTUNITY:** The Property is offered in compliance with federal, state and local anti-discrimination laws.

15. **ATTORNEY FEES:** In any action, proceeding or arbitration between Seller and Broker regarding the obligation to pay compensation under this Agreement, the prevailing Seller or Broker shall be entitled to reasonable attorney fees and costs from the non-prevailing Seller or Broker, except as provided in paragraph 19A.

16. **ADDITIONAL TERMS:** ☐ REO Advisory Listing (C.A.R. Form REOL) ☐ Short Sale Information and Advisory (C.A.R. Form SSIA)

_____

_____

_____

_____

_____

_____

17. **MANAGEMENT APPROVAL:** If an associate-licensee in Broker's office (salesperson or broker-associate) enters into this Agreement on Broker's behalf, and Broker or Manager does not approve of its terms, Broker or Manager has the right to cancel this Agreement, in writing, within **5 Days** After its execution.

18. **SUCCESSORS AND ASSIGNS:** This Agreement shall be binding upon Seller and Seller's successors and assigns.

19. **DISPUTE RESOLUTION:**

   A. MEDIATION: Seller and Broker agree to mediate any dispute or claim arising between them regarding the obligation to pay compensation under this Agreement, before resorting to arbitration or court action. Mediation fees, if any, shall be divided equally among the parties involved. If, for any dispute or claim to which this paragraph applies, any party (i) commences an action without first attempting to resolve the matter through mediation, or (ii) before commencement of an action, refuses to mediate after a request has been made, then that party shall not be entitled to recover attorney fees, even if they would otherwise be available to that party in any such action. THIS MEDIATION PROVISION APPLIES WHETHER OR NOT THE ARBITRATION PROVISION IS INITIALED. **Exclusions from this mediation agreement are specified in paragraph 19C.**

   B. ARBITRATION OF DISPUTES:
   Seller and Broker agree that any dispute or claim in Law or equity arising between them regarding the obligation to pay compensation under this Agreement, which is not settled through mediation, shall be decided by neutral, binding arbitration. The arbitrator shall be a retired judge or justice, or an attorney with at least 5 years of residential real estate Law experience, unless the parties mutually agree to a different arbitrator. The parties shall have the right to discovery in accordance with Code of Civil Procedure §1283.05. In all other respects, the arbitration shall be conducted in accordance with Title 9 of Part 3 of the Code of Civil Procedure. Judgment upon the award of the arbitrator(s) may be entered into any court having jurisdiction. Enforcement of this agreement to arbitrate shall be governed by the Federal Arbitration Act. Exclusions from this arbitration agreement are specified in paragraph 19C.
   "NOTICE: BY INITIALING IN THE SPACE BELOW YOU ARE AGREEING TO HAVE ANY DISPUTE ARISING OUT OF THE MATTERS INCLUDED IN THE 'ARBITRATION OF DISPUTES' PROVISION DECIDED BY NEUTRAL ARBITRATION AS PROVIDED BY CALIFORNIA LAW AND YOU ARE GIVING UP ANY RIGHTS YOU MIGHT POSSESS TO HAVE THE DISPUTE LITIGATED IN A COURT OR JURY TRIAL. BY INITIALING IN THE SPACE BELOW YOU ARE GIVING UP YOUR JUDICIAL RIGHTS TO DISCOVERY AND APPEAL, UNLESS THOSE RIGHTS ARE SPECIFICALLY INCLUDED IN THE 'ARBITRATION OF DISPUTES' PROVISION. IF YOU REFUSE TO SUBMIT TO ARBITRATION AFTER AGREEING TO THIS PROVISION, YOU MAY BE COMPELLED TO ARBITRATE UNDER THE AUTHORITY OF THE CALIFORNIA CODE OF CIVIL PROCEDURE. YOUR AGREEMENT TO THIS ARBITRATION PROVISION IS VOLUNTARY."
   "WE HAVE READ AND UNDERSTAND THE FOREGOING AND AGREE TO SUBMIT DISPUTES ARISING OUT OF THE MATTERS INCLUDED IN THE 'ARBITRATION OF DISPUTES' PROVISION TO NEUTRAL ARBITRATION."

Seller's Initials	/	Broker's Initials	/

   C. ADDITIONAL MEDIATION AND ARBITRATION TERMS: The following matters shall be excluded from mediation and arbitration: (i) a judicial or non-judicial foreclosure or other action or proceeding to enforce a deed of trust, mortgage or installment land sale contract as defined in Civil Code §2985; (ii) an unlawful detainer action; (iii) the filing or enforcement of a mechanic's lien; and (iv) any matter that is within the jurisdiction of a probate, small claims or bankruptcy court. The filing of a court action to enable the recording of a notice of pending action, for order of attachment, receivership, injunction, or other provisional remedies, shall not constitute a waiver or violation of the mediation and arbitration provisions.

RLA REVISED 11/13 (PAGE 4 OF 5)

Seller's Initials (_____)(_____)

Reviewed by _____ Date _____

RESIDENTIAL LISTING AGREEMENT - EXCLUSIVE (RLA PAGE 4 OF 5)

Property Address:_____ Date:_____

20. **ENTIRE AGREEMENT:** All prior discussions, negotiations and agreements between the parties concerning the subject matter of this Agreement are superseded by this Agreement, which constitutes the entire contract and a complete and exclusive expression of their agreement, and may not be contradicted by evidence of any prior agreement or contemporaneous oral agreement. If any provision of this Agreement is held to be ineffective or invalid, the remaining provisions will nevertheless be given full force and effect. This Agreement and any supplement, addendum or modification, including any photocopy or facsimile, may be executed in counterparts.

21. **OWNERSHIP, TITLE AND AUTHORITY:** Seller warrants that: (i) Seller is the owner of the Property; (ii) no other persons or entities have title to the Property; and (iii) Seller has the authority to both execute this Agreement and sell the Property. Exceptions to ownership, title and authority are as follows: _____
_____.

By signing below, Seller acknowledges that Seller has read, understands, received a copy of and agrees to the terms of this Agreement.

Seller_____ Date _____
Address _____ City _____ State _____ Zip _____
Telephone _____ Fax _____ Email _____

Seller _____ Date _____
Address _____ City _____ State _____ Zip _____
Telephone _____ Fax _____ Email _____

Real Estate Broker (Firm) _____ Cal BRE Lic.# _____
By (Agent) _____ Cal BRE Lic.# _____ Date _____
Address _____ City _____ State _____ Zip _____
Telephone _____ Fax _____ Email _____

Published and Distributed by:
REAL ESTATE BUSINESS SERVICES, INC.
a subsidiary of the California Association of
REALTORS®

Reviewed by _____ Date _____

RLA REVISED 11/13 (PAGE 5 OF 5)

RESIDENTIAL LISTING AGREEMENT - EXCLUSIVE (RLA PAGE 5 OF 5)

The seller and the listing broker may terminate the listing by mutual agreement at any time. Alternatively, the seller may revoke the listing agreement by firing the broker whenever he wishes. As we discussed in Chapter 1, revocation of an agency agreement may be a breach of contract. In the case of a listing agreement, this could mean that the seller will be required to pay the broker's commission.

On the other hand, the listing broker can renounce the listing agreement. Like revocation, renunciation would constitute a breach of contract, in which case the broker could be liable for the seller's resulting damages (if any).

Commission. A listing agreement form includes a blank in which to fill in the percentage or amount of the broker's commission. It also explains how and when the broker earns the commission. An exclusive right to sell listing might provide that the broker will earn a commission if any of these events occur:

1. during the listing period, the listing agent—or anyone else—secures a buyer who is willing to buy on the exact terms specified by the seller in the listing agreement or on other terms acceptable to the seller (in other words, a ready, willing, and able buyer);
2. during the listing period, the seller sells, exchanges, or enters into a contract to sell or exchange the property; or
3. within a certain period (for example, six months) after the listing expires, the seller sells the property to anyone who first became aware of the property through any advertising or other marketing activities of the listing agent or other agents in the MLS.

The agreement usually also provides that MLS members are considered "cooperating brokers" and may act as the agent of the buyer, as the agent of the seller, or in some other capacity as agreed to by the parties. The selling office is entitled to its share of the commission no matter which party the selling agent represents.

Most purchase agreements state that if the buyer breaches the contract, the seller can keep the good faith deposit as liquidated damages (see Chapter 6). Listing agreements commonly provide that under those circumstances the deposit will first be applied to cover any costs incurred (title and escrow expenses, for example); then the seller and the broker will split the remainder of the deposit, with half going to the broker as compensation for the broker's services.

Under the terms of many listing agreement forms, the seller agrees not to interfere with the broker's right to market the property. For example, if the seller leases the property, grants an option on the property, or enters into any other agreement that might interfere with selling the property, she owes the full commission.

Safety clause. Number three on the list shown above is an example of a safety clause (sometimes called a "protection period clause," "protection clause," or "extender clause"). Occasionally, behind the listing agent's back, a buyer and a seller agree to postpone entering into a contract until after the listing expires, to save the cost of the broker's commission. A safety clause prevents this strategy from working (unless the buyer and seller are willing to wait a long time).

Safety clauses differ from one listing agreement form to another. Sometimes the obligation to pay a commission after the listing has expired is triggered only when the property is sold to a buyer that the agent actually negotiated with during the listing period.

Example: You have listed Baker's property. The safety clause in your listing agreement applies only to buyers you've negotiated with.

One buyer, Abrams, is very interested in Baker's property. You present her offer to Baker and spend a few days trying to negotiate the terms of the sale. Finally, Abrams decides that she isn't willing to raise her final offer by the extra $1,000 that Baker wants, and she walks away from the property. Another buyer, Thornwood, sees your "For Sale" sign posted on the property and calls you on the phone to ask some questions about the property. You have no further contact with Thornwood, who doesn't seem very interested in the property after all.

Suppose Abrams buys the property after your listing agreement with Baker expires. Since you actually negotiated with Abrams, your safety clause applies and Baker owes you a commission. On the other hand, if Thornwood were to purchase the property, Baker would not owe you a commission. Under the terms of the listing agreement, since you never actually negotiated with Thornwood, the safety clause does not apply.

Some safety clauses are broader and require the seller to pay a commission if the property is sold within a specified period of time to anyone who learned about it in any way that can be traced to the listing agent or another MLS agent.

Example: Returning to the previous example, now suppose that the safety clause in the listing requires the seller to pay the commission if the property is sold to anyone who learned of it from you or another MLS agent. With this type of safety clause, if Thornwood were to buy Baker's property during the period of time covered by the safety clause, Baker would still owe you a commission. Even though you never actually negotiated with Thornwood, he learned the property was for sale because of your "For Sale" sign and then contacted you to find out more about the property.

Some safety clauses provide safeguards for the seller. For example, you may be required to give the seller a list of all the potential buyers you had contact with during the listing period. Or the safety clause might state that a commission will not be due if the property is listed with another real estate broker during the extension period. This protects the seller from becoming liable for two commissions.

Example: Your listing agreement with Baker expires and Baker immediately lists the property with a new agent. Shortly afterward, Abrams (a buyer you negotiated with before your listing expired) purchases the property. Under some safety clauses, Baker could be held liable for two commissions—one to you (because of your safety clause) and one to the new agent (under the terms of the new agent's listing agreement). But your safety clause excluded this kind of situation, so Baker only owes a commission to the new listing agent.

Some safety clauses state that, in these circumstances, if the commission owed to the second listing agent is less than the commission that would have been owed to the first listing agent, then the first listing agent is entitled to the excess amount.

Seller's Warranties. A listing agreement form often includes some warranties or representations by the seller, such as:

- the seller has the right to sell the property on the terms stated in the listing agreement;
- the information about the property included in the listing is accurate; and
- there are no undisclosed encumbrances against the property, such as loan delinquencies, special assessments, or pending legal actions.

There is usually also a "hold harmless" clause to protect the broker. This clause states that the seller takes responsibility for the information given and will indemnify the broker against any losses caused by the seller's errors or omissions.

Example: You have listed Carr's property. You are unaware of the fact that the roof leaks, and the seller doesn't include this information in the listing agreement. The Bolts purchase the property, and when they discover the leaky roof, they sue both Carr and you. Since you relied on the information in the listing agreement and had no reason to doubt it, Carr will be obligated to reimburse you for any damages you are required to pay the buyers because of his omission.

Multiple Listing Service Provision. Most listing agreements provide that unless the seller instructs otherwise, you will submit the listing to your local multiple listing service. The MLS provision also reminds the seller that (unless the seller instructs otherwise) the information in the listing is not confidential; it will be shared with the members of the MLS, and most of it will also be accessible to the public online. The seller may need to use a form separate from the listing agreement itself to opt out of MLS participation.

The multiple listing service is not a party to the listing agreement. Its only function is to provide information about the property to other MLS members. The MLS will not be responsible for verifying any information provided by the seller or the listing agent.

Deposit. The listing agreement usually authorizes the broker to receive and hold the buyer's good faith deposit on the seller's behalf. Without this authorization, the listing broker may still hold the deposit, but will be considered the buyer's agent as far as the deposit is concerned. This complicates the agency relationships in a transaction, so it is always best to use a listing agreement that specifically authorizes the broker to hold the buyer's deposit.

Agency Relationships. The "Agency Relationships" paragraph in the listing agreement form in Figure 2.2 states that the broker will represent the seller. The form then goes on to describe the circumstances in which a dual agency will arise: if the property is sold to a buyer who's represented by the same broker as the seller. (That's true even if the agent working with the buyer isn't the listing agent, but another agent affiliated with the same broker.) The seller gives her consent to this dual agency. The seller also acknowledges that a dual agent is not permitted to disclose either party's negotiating position to the other party without written consent. (We discussed dual agency in Chapter 1.)

Photographs and Internet Advertising. Unless the seller checks a box forbidding it, the listing agreement usually gives the broker permission to take pictures of the property for use on the broker's website, the MLS website, and other Internet marketing sites. In the form in Figure 2.2, the seller acknowledges that once these photos are online, the broker has no control over who will see them, how they may be used, or how long they will remain online. The seller also agrees that these images belong to the broker and can be used in the future to advertise the broker's real estate business.

Access and Keyboxes. A listing agreement form typically gives you the right to enter the property at reasonable times so you can show it to prospective buyers. And since other MLS members will be acting as cooperating agents—helping to find a buyer—they need a way to gain access to the property as well. Keyboxes are the standard method of facilitating access to listed properties when the owners aren't home. Thus, MLS listing forms usually include a provision authorizing the installation of a keybox on the property and permitting MLS agents to enter and show the home. It's common to include a disclaimer of liability for any loss of or damage to the seller's property that may occur because of misuse of a keybox.

In many listing agreement forms, the seller agrees to take precautions to secure valuables within the house during showings, and to obtain insurance needed to protect the contents of the house. Most sellers already have homeowner's insurance, but they should notify the insurer that the property is for sale and that open houses will be held during the selling process.

Attorney's Fees. Most listing agreement forms provide that if either the broker or the seller has to resort to a lawsuit to enforce the contract, the losing party must pay the winning party's attorney's fees.

Dispute Resolution. Many listing forms include a provision that, if initialed, requires the parties to attempt to settle any dispute using alternative methods such as mediation or arbitration rather than a lawsuit. Either party may refuse to initial such a clause, though, and retain the right to pursue legal action in a court of law instead.

Mediation and arbitration are frequently confused. In mediation, a neutral party helps the parties find a mutually satisfactory solution; the mediator does not impose a solution on the parties. By contrast, arbitration is overseen by a third party (usually a retired judge) who hears evidence and then issues a decision that is binding on both parties. Generally, arbitration can resolve a case much more quickly and cheaply than a lawsuit.

Listing Information. Most listing agreement forms used by multiple listing services are accompanied by a **listing input sheet**. The purpose of a listing input sheet is to generate detailed information about the property and the listing that will be distributed in the MLS publications. Much of the information is coded to make computer input easier.

All of the following basic information is typically required on a listing input sheet for residential property:

- property address,
- location on a coded map,
- architectural style of the home,
- listing price,
- identification of the listing agent,
- expiration date of the listing,
- age of the home,
- number of bedrooms,
- number of bathrooms,
- county tax identification number,
- commission split,
- name of the present occupant, and
- name, address, and phone number of the owner.

The rest of the input sheet usually has spaces to fill in or boxes to check off to describe a wide variety of property features and amenities. There is also a place for information about any existing encumbrances and the annual property taxes.

Signatures. A listing agreement should be signed by both parties: the listing broker and the seller. When you prepare a listing agreement form, you will sign on behalf of your broker. Write your broker's name (as licensed) on the line labeled "Agent" and sign your own name on the "By" line underneath. (The agent isn't legally required to sign the listing agreement, however. As long as it's signed by the seller, it's an enforceable contract, even without the signature of the agent or the agent's representative.)

If more than one person owns the property, make sure that all of the owners sign the form.

Example: You prepare a listing agreement for property owned by the Mastersons, a married couple. Unless both spouses sign the listing agreement form, the contract might turn out to be unenforceable.

In some cases, the sellers are unsure of the names of all the owners. For example, this might happen if the property was inherited by several people, or if it is owned by a partnership. If the sellers seem at all uncertain, or if you simply want to double-check the ownership, you could:

1. get a copy of the deed from the seller;
2. check with a title company; or
3. check the county's property records.

Receipt of Copy. You must give the parties, at the time of signature, a copy of any legal document you prepare. So a listing agreement form often includes the seller's acknowledgment of receipt of a copy of the agreement.

Modifying a Listing Agreement

Once a listing agreement (or any contract) has been signed, it can be modified only with the written consent of all of the parties.

Example: You and the Mastersons sign a 90-day listing agreement, but two days later you realize that a 120-day listing would be more appropriate in the current market, which is quite slow. The Mastersons agree to the longer listing period. So you cross out the old expiration date on the form and write in a new expiration date. To make this change legally effective, you must write your initials and the date beside the change, and both of the Mastersons must do the same.

It's acceptable to modify the terms of a listing agreement by crossing out what you originally filled in and replacing it with new information (as long as all parties initial and date the change, as in the example above). However, if your multiple listing service has an amendment form specifically designed for changing the terms of a listing agreement, it's a better practice to use that. Of course, all parties must sign and date the amendment form.

Mandatory Disclosures Concerning the Property

When real property is sold, California law requires certain information about the property to be disclosed to potential buyers. The disclosures necessary for a particular transaction may include:

- a transfer disclosure statement,
- an environmental hazards booklet,
- a natural hazard disclosure statement,
- a residential earthquake hazards report,
- a lead-based paint disclosure,

- a supplemental statutory disclosure form, and
- disclosure of Mello-Roos liens.

Transfer Disclosure Statement

California requires sellers of residential property to give their buyers a comprehensive disclosure form called a **real estate transfer disclosure statement**. The disclosure law applies to single-family homes, multi-family properties with up to four units, homes for sale by owner, mobile homes, and condominiums and cooperatives. A transfer disclosure statement isn't required for the sale of new construction in a subdivision where a public report has been delivered, or for a sale pursuant to court order, such as a probate sale. Also exempt from this requirement are transfers between spouses or co-owners, transfers between divorcing spouses, transfers to lineal descendants, and foreclosure sales.

In the transfer disclosure statement, the seller must disclose her knowledge about the condition of the buildings and utilities, the existence of easements or other encumbrances, and other information about the property's physical condition and title. Buyers should understand that the statement is merely a disclosure of information; it isn't a warranty by the seller or the seller's agents.

An example of a transfer disclosure statement form is shown in Figure 2.3. The content of the form is prescribed by statute, so neither a seller nor an agent should ever change the form's wording. Some cities and counties require additional disclosures; in that case, the standard local disclosure form should be used in addition to the state form.

Filling Out the Form. The "Seller's Information" section takes up the majority of the transfer disclosure statement form. You should explain the purpose of the disclosure statement to the sellers you represent, but you shouldn't fill out any part of the Seller's Information section for them. If you did, you could be held liable for any inaccuracies.

The first part of the Seller's Information section is a checklist of features that are present on the property. The next part asks if the seller knows of any problems with the basic structural or functional components of the property, such as the frame, the foundation, and the plumbing and electrical systems.

Next, the seller must check "Yes" or "No" to answer 16 questions concerning other potential problems, such as environmental concerns, drainage problems, zoning issues, private restrictions, and lawsuits that may affect the property. If the seller answers "Yes" to any of these questions, she must provide more information (attaching additional sheets of paper if necessary).

Fig. 2.3   Transfer disclosure statement

CALIFORNIA ASSOCIATION OF REALTORS®

REAL ESTATE TRANSFER DISCLOSURE STATEMENT
(CALIFORNIA CIVIL CODE §1102, ET SEQ.)
(C.A.R. Form TDS, Revised 4/14)

THIS DISCLOSURE STATEMENT CONCERNS THE REAL PROPERTY SITUATED IN THE CITY OF _____
_____, COUNTY OF _____, STATE OF CALIFORNIA,
DESCRIBED AS _____.
THIS STATEMENT IS A DISCLOSURE OF THE CONDITION OF THE ABOVE DESCRIBED PROPERTY IN COMPLIANCE
WITH SECTION 1102 OF THE CIVIL CODE AS OF (date) _____. IT IS NOT A WARRANTY OF ANY
KIND BY THE SELLER(S) OR ANY AGENT(S) REPRESENTING ANY PRINCIPAL(S) IN THIS TRANSACTION, AND IS
NOT A SUBSTITUTE FOR ANY INSPECTIONS OR WARRANTIES THE PRINCIPAL(S) MAY WISH TO OBTAIN.

I. COORDINATION WITH OTHER DISCLOSURE FORMS

This Real Estate Transfer Disclosure Statement is made pursuant to Section 1102 of the Civil Code. Other statutes require disclosures, depending upon the details of the particular real estate transaction (for example: special study zone and purchase-money liens on residential property).

Substituted Disclosures: The following disclosures and other disclosures required by law, including the Natural Hazard Disclosure Report/Statement that may include airport annoyances, earthquake, fire, flood, or special assessment information, have or will be made in connection with this real estate transfer, and are intended to satisfy the disclosure obligations on this form, where the subject matter is the same:

☐   Inspection reports completed pursuant to the contract of sale or receipt for deposit.
☐   Additional inspection reports or disclosures: _____

II. SELLER'S INFORMATION

The Seller discloses the following information with the knowledge that even though this is not a warranty, prospective Buyers may rely on this information in deciding whether and on what terms to purchase the subject property. Seller hereby authorizes any agent(s) representing any principal(s) in this transaction to provide a copy of this statement to any person or entity in connection with any actual or anticipated sale of the property.

THE FOLLOWING ARE REPRESENTATIONS MADE BY THE SELLER(S) AND ARE NOT THE REPRESENTATIONS OF THE AGENT(S), IF ANY. THIS INFORMATION IS A DISCLOSURE AND IS NOT INTENDED TO BE PART OF ANY CONTRACT BETWEEN THE BUYER AND SELLER.

Seller ☐ is ☐ is not occupying the property.

A. The subject property has the items checked below:*

☐ Range	☐ Wall/Window Air Conditioning	☐ Pool:
☐ Oven	☐ Sprinklers	☐ Child Resistant Barrier
☐ Microwave	☐ Public Sewer System	☐ Pool/Spa Heater:
☐ Dishwasher	☐ Septic Tank	☐ Gas ☐ Solar ☐ Electric
☐ Trash Compactor	☐ Sump Pump	☐ Water Heater:
☐ Garbage Disposal	☐ Water Softener	☐ Gas ☐ Solar ☐ Electric
☐ Washer/Dryer Hookups	☐ Patio/Decking	☐ Water Supply:
☐ Rain Gutters	☐ Built-in Barbecue	☐ City ☐ Well
☐ Burglar Alarms	☐ Gazebo	☐ Private Utility or
☐ Carbon Monoxide Device(s)	☐ Security Gate(s)	Other_____
☐ Smoke Detector(s)	☐ Garage:	☐ Gas Supply:
☐ Fire Alarm	☐ Attached ☐ Not Attached	☐ Utility ☐ Bottled (Tank)
☐ TV Antenna	☐ Carport	☐ Window Screens
☐ Satellite Dish	☐ Automatic Garage Door Opener(s)	☐ Window Security Bars
☐ Intercom	☐ Number Remote Controls	☐ Quick Release Mechanism on
☐ Central Heating	☐ Sauna	Bedroom Windows
☐ Central Air Conditioning	☐ Hot Tub/Spa:	☐ Water-Conserving Plumbing Fixtures
☐ Evaporator Cooler(s)	☐ Locking Safety Cover	

Exhaust Fan(s) in _____ 220 Volt Wiring in _____ Fireplace(s) in _____
☐ Gas Starter _____ ☐ Roof(s): Type: _____ Age: _____ (approx.)
☐ Other: _____
Are there, to the best of your (Seller's) knowledge, any of the above that are not in operating condition? ☐ Yes ☐ No. If yes, then describe. (Attach additional sheets if necessary):_____

(*see note on page 2)

Buyer's Initials (_____)(_____)

Seller's Initials (_____)(_____)

TDS REVISED 4/14 (PAGE 1 OF 3) Print Date

Reviewed by _____ Date _____

REAL ESTATE TRANSFER DISCLOSURE STATEMENT (TDS PAGE 1 OF 3)

Property Address: _____ Date:_____

B. Are you (Seller) aware of any significant defects/malfunctions in any of the following? ☐ Yes ☐ No. If yes, check appropriate space(s) below.

☐ Interior Walls ☐ Ceilings ☐ Floors ☐ Exterior Walls ☐ Insulation ☐ Roof(s) ☐ Windows ☐ Doors ☐ Foundation ☐ Slab(s) ☐ Driveways ☐ Sidewalks ☐ Walls/Fences ☐ Electrical Systems ☐ Plumbing/Sewers/Septics ☐ Other Structural Components

(Describe: _____
_____)

If any of the above is checked, explain. (Attach additional sheets if necessary.): _____
_____
_____

*Installation of a listed appliance, device, or amenity is not a precondition of sale or transfer of the dwelling. The carbon monoxide device, garage door opener, or child-resistant pool barrier may not be in compliance with the safety standards relating to, respectively, carbon monoxide device standards of Chapter 8 (commencing with Section 13260) of Part 2 of Division 12 of, automatic reversing device standards of Chapter 12.5 (commencing with Section 19890) of Part 3 of Division 13 of, or the pool safety standards of Article 2.5 (commencing with Section 115920) of Chapter 5 of Part 10 of Division 104 of, the Health and Safety Code. Window security bars may not have quick-release mechanisms in compliance with the 1995 edition of the California Building Standards Code. Section 1101.4 of the Civil Code requires all single-family residences built on or before January 1, 1994, to be equipped with water-conserving plumbing fixtures after January 1, 2017. Additionally, on and after January 1, 2014, a single-family residence built on or before January 1, 1994, that is altered or improved is required to be equipped with water-conserving plumbing fixtures as a condition of final approval. Fixtures in this dwelling may not comply with section 1101.4 of the Civil Code.

C. Are you (Seller) aware of any of the following:

1. Substances, materials, or products which may be an environmental hazard such as, but not limited to, asbestos, formaldehyde, radon gas, lead-based paint, mold, fuel or chemical storage tanks, and contaminated soil or water on the subject property .... ☐ Yes ☐ No
2. Features of the property shared in common with adjoining landowners, such as walls, fences, and driveways, whose use or responsibility for maintenance may have an effect on the subject property .... ☐ Yes ☐ No
3. Any encroachments, easements or similar matters that may affect your interest in the subject property .... ☐ Yes ☐ No
4. Room additions, structural modifications, or other alterations or repairs made without necessary permits .... ☐ Yes ☐ No
5. Room additions, structural modifications, or other alterations or repairs not in compliance with building codes .... ☐ Yes ☐ No
6. Fill (compacted or otherwise) on the property or any portion thereof... ☐ Yes ☐ No
7. Any settling from any cause, or slippage, sliding, or other soil problems... ☐ Yes ☐ No
8. Flooding, drainage or grading problems .... ☐ Yes ☐ No
9. Major damage to the property or any of the structures from fire, earthquake, floods, or landslides .... ☐ Yes ☐ No
10. Any zoning violations, nonconforming uses, violations of "setback" requirements .... ☐ Yes ☐ No
11. Neighborhood noise problems or other nuisances .... ☐ Yes ☐ No
12. CC&R's or other deed restrictions or obligations .... ☐ Yes ☐ No
13. Homeowners' Association which has any authority over the subject property.. ☐ Yes ☐ No
14. Any "common area" (facilities such as pools, tennis courts, walkways, or other areas co-owned in undivided interest with others).. ☐ Yes ☐ No
15. Any notices of abatement or citations against the property .... ☐ Yes ☐ No
16. Any lawsuits by or against the Seller threatening to or affecting this real property, claims for damages by the Seller pursuant to Section 910 or 914 threatening to or affecting this real property, claims for breach of warranty pursuant to Section 900 threatening to or affecting this real property, or claims for breach of an enhanced protection agreement pursuant to Section 903 threatening to or affecting this real property, including any lawsuits or claims for damages pursuant to Section 910 or 914 alleging a defect or deficiency in this real property or "common areas" (facilities such as pools, tennis courts, walkways, or other areas co-owned in undivided interest with others) .... ☐ Yes ☐ No

If the answer to any of these is yes, explain. (Attach additional sheets if necessary.): _____
_____
_____
_____
_____

D. 1. The Seller certifies that the property, as of the close of escrow, will be in compliance with Section 13113.8 of the Health and Safety Code by having operable smoke detector(s) which are approved, listed, and installed in accordance with the State Fire Marshal's regulations and applicable local standards.

2. The Seller certifies that the property, as of the close of escrow, will be in compliance with Section 19211 of the Health and Safety Code by having the water heater tank(s) braced, anchored, or strapped in place in accordance with applicable law.

Buyer's Initials (_____)(_____)   Seller's Initials (_____)(_____)

TDS REVISED 4/14 (PAGE 2 OF 3) | Reviewed by _____ Date _____ |

REAL ESTATE TRANSFER DISCLOSURE STATEMENT (TDS PAGE 2 OF 3)

Property Address: _____ Date: _____

Seller certifies that the information herein is true and correct to the best of the Seller's knowledge as of the date signed by the Seller.

Seller_____ Date _____

Seller_____ Date _____

III. AGENT'S INSPECTION DISCLOSURE

(To be completed only if the Seller is represented by an agent in this transaction.)

THE UNDERSIGNED, BASED ON THE ABOVE INQUIRY OF THE SELLER(S) AS TO THE CONDITION OF THE PROPERTY AND BASED ON A REASONABLY COMPETENT AND DILIGENT VISUAL INSPECTION OF THE ACCESSIBLE AREAS OF THE PROPERTY IN CONJUNCTION WITH THAT INQUIRY, STATES THE FOLLOWING:

☐ See attached Agent Visual Inspection Disclosure (AVID Form)

☐ Agent notes no items for disclosure.

☐ Agent notes the following items: _____

_____

_____

_____

Agent (Broker Representing Seller) _____ By _____ Date_____
 (Please Print) (Associate Licensee or Broker Signature)

IV. AGENT'S INSPECTION DISCLOSURE

(To be completed only if the agent who has obtained the offer is other than the agent above.)

THE UNDERSIGNED, BASED ON A REASONABLY COMPETENT AND DILIGENT VISUAL INSPECTION OF THE ACCESSIBLE AREAS OF THE PROPERTY, STATES THE FOLLOWING:

☐ See attached Agent Visual Inspection Disclosure (AVID Form)

☐ Agent notes no items for disclosure.

☐ Agent notes the following items: _____

_____

_____

_____

Agent (Broker Obtaining the Offer) _____ By _____ Date_____
 (Please Print) (Associate Licensee or Broker Signature)

V. BUYER(S) AND SELLER(S) MAY WISH TO OBTAIN PROFESSIONAL ADVICE AND/OR INSPECTIONS OF THE PROPERTY AND TO PROVIDE FOR APPROPRIATE PROVISIONS IN A CONTRACT BETWEEN BUYER AND SELLER(S) WITH RESPECT TO ANY ADVICE/INSPECTIONS/DEFECTS.

I/WE ACKNOWLEDGE RECEIPT OF A COPY OF THIS STATEMENT.

Seller _____ Date _____ Buyer _____ Date_____

Seller _____ Date _____ Buyer _____ Date_____

Agent (Broker Representing Seller) _____ By _____ Date_____
 (Please Print) (Associate Licensee or Broker Signature)

Agent (Broker Obtaining the Offer) _____ By _____ Date_____
 (Please Print) (Associate Licensee or Broker Signature)

SECTION 1102.3 OF THE CIVIL CODE PROVIDES A BUYER WITH THE RIGHT TO RESCIND A PURCHASE CONTRACT FOR AT LEAST THREE DAYS AFTER THE DELIVERY OF THIS DISCLOSURE IF DELIVERY OCCURS AFTER THE SIGNING OF AN OFFER TO PURCHASE. IF YOU WISH TO RESCIND THE CONTRACT, YOU MUST ACT WITHIN THE PRESCRIBED PERIOD.

A REAL ESTATE BROKER IS QUALIFIED TO ADVISE ON REAL ESTATE. IF YOU DESIRE LEGAL ADVICE, CONSULT YOUR ATTORNEY.

Published and Distributed by:
REAL ESTATE BUSINESS SERVICES, INC.
a subsidiary of the California Association of REALTORS®
525 South Virgil Avenue, Los Angeles, California 90020

TDS REVISED 4/14 (PAGE 3 OF 3)

Reviewed by _____ Date _____

REAL ESTATE TRANSFER DISCLOSURE STATEMENT (TDS PAGE 3 OF 3)

California law requires single-family homes to have an operable smoke detector. In addition, water heaters are required to be braced, anchored, or strapped to prevent damage in an earthquake. The transfer disclosure statement must include a statement from the seller verifying that the house being sold complies with these state laws.

The last page of the transfer disclosure statement has sections to be completed by the listing agent and the selling agent (the agent who obtained the offer), if there are agents involved in the transaction. Each agent must perform a visual inspection of the property and list any problems he or she observes that require disclosure (see Chapter 1). Alternatively, the agent may use an agent visual inspection disclosure form (see Figure 2.4), which provides space for the agent to note what was observed in each room and area of the home. Using this type of form allows the agent to include more information about his or her findings, creating a more detailed record of the inspection. The agent inspection form is also useful in transactions that do not require a transfer disclosure statement (such as court-ordered sales); remember that the agents in these transactions are still required by law to perform visual inspections and document their findings.

The final part of the transfer disclosure statement encourages the buyer and seller to have professional inspections of the property performed, and to include appropriate provisions regarding the inspections (such as a contingency clause) in the purchase contract.

Timing and Effect of Disclosure. The buyer must ordinarily be given the disclosure statement as soon as practicable after the purchase agreement is signed and before transfer of title. (Note that the disclosure statement does not become part of the purchase contract between the parties.) The buyer may not waive the right to receive a completed statement, even if the property is being sold subject to an "as is" clause. If there's more than one agent involved in the transaction, it's the selling agent's responsibility to deliver the statement to the buyer, unless the seller instructs otherwise.

Within three business days after personal delivery of a completed disclosure statement, or five days after the completed statement is deposited in the mail, the buyer can either accept the disclosure or rescind the purchase agreement. The choice between acceptance and rescission is completely up to the buyer. If he does not like the information in the disclosure for any reason, however trivial, he can rescind the agreement.

Fig. 2.4 Agent visual inspection disclosure form

CALIFORNIA ASSOCIATION OF REALTORS®

AGENT VISUAL INSPECTION DISCLOSURE
(CALIFORNIA CIVIL CODE § 2079 ET SEQ.)
For use by an agent when a transfer disclosure statement is
required or when a seller is exempt from completing a TDS
(C.A.R. Form AVID, Revised 11/13)

This inspection disclosure concerns the residential property situated in the City of_____,
County of _____, State of California, described as _____
_____ ("Property").

☐ This Property is a duplex, triplex, or fourplex. This AVID form is for unit # _____. Additional AVID forms required
for other units.

Inspection Performed By (Real Estate Broker Firm Name) _____

California law requires, with limited exceptions, that a real estate broker or salesperson (collectively, "Agent") conduct a reasonably competent and diligent **visual** inspection of reasonably and normally accessible areas of certain properties offered for sale and then disclose to the prospective purchaser material facts affecting the value or desirability of that property that the inspection reveals. The duty applies regardless of whom that Agent represents. The duty applies to residential real properties containing one-to-four dwelling units, and manufactured homes (mobilehomes). The duty applies to a stand-alone detached dwelling (whether or not located in a subdivision or a planned development) or to an attached dwelling such as a condominium. The duty also applies to a lease with an option to purchase, a ground lease or a real property sales contract of one of those properties.

California law does not require the Agent to inspect the following:
• Areas that are not reasonably and normally accessible
• Areas off site of the property
• Public records or permits
• Common areas of planned developments, condominiums, stock cooperatives and the like.

Agent Inspection Limitations: Because the Agent's duty is limited to conducting a reasonably competent and diligent visual inspection of reasonably and normally accessible areas of only the Property being offered for sale, there are several things that the Agent will not do. What follows is a non-exclusive list of examples of limitations on the scope of the Agent's duty.

Roof and Attic: Agent will not climb onto a roof or into an attic.

Interior: Agent will not move or look under or behind furniture, pictures, wall hangings or floor coverings. Agent will not look up chimneys or into cabinets, or open locked doors.

Exterior: Agent will not inspect beneath a house or other structure on the Property, climb up or down a hillside, move or look behind plants, bushes, shrubbery and other vegetation or fences, walls or other barriers.

Appliances and Systems: Agent will not operate appliances or systems (such as, but not limited to, electrical, plumbing, pool or spa, heating, cooling, septic, sprinkler, communication, entertainment, well or water) to determine their functionality.

Size of Property or Improvements: Agent will not measure square footage of lot or improvements, or identify or locate boundary lines, easements or encroachments.

Environmental Hazards: Agent will not determine if the Property has mold, asbestos, lead or lead-based paint, radon, formaldehyde or any other hazardous substance or analyze soil or geologic condition.

Off-Property Conditions: By statute, Agent is not obligated to pull permits or inspect public records. Agent will not guarantee views or zoning, identify proposed construction or development or changes or proximity to transportation, schools, or law enforcement.

Analysis of Agent Disclosures: For any items disclosed as a result of Agent's visual inspection, or by others, Agent will not provide an analysis of or determine the cause or source of the disclosed matter, nor determine the cost of any possible repair.

What this means to you: An Agent's inspection is not intended to take the place of any other type of inspection, nor is it a substitute for a full and complete disclosure by a seller. Regardless of what the Agent's inspection reveals, or what disclosures are made by sellers, California Law specifies that a buyer has a duty to exercise reasonable care to protect himself or herself. This duty encompasses facts which are known to or within the diligent attention and observation of the buyer. Therefore, in order to determine for themselves whether or not the Property meets their needs and intended uses, as well as the cost to remedy any disclosed or discovered defect, **BUYER SHOULD: (1) REVIEW ANY DISCLOSURES OBTAINED FROM SELLER; (2) OBTAIN ADVICE ABOUT, AND INSPECTIONS OF, THE PROPERTY FROM OTHER APPROPRIATE PROFESSIONALS; AND (3) REVIEW ANY FINDINGS OF THOSE PROFESSIONALS WITH THE PERSONS WHO PREPARED THEM. IF BUYER FAILS TO DO SO, BUYER IS ACTING AGAINST THE ADVICE OF BROKER.**

Buyer's Initials (_____)(_____)   Seller's Initials (_____)(_____)

AVID REVISED 11/13 (PAGE 1 OF 3)   Print Date

Reviewed by _____ Date _____

EQUAL HOUSING OPPORTUNITY

AGENT VISUAL INSPECTION DISCLOSURE (AVID PAGE 1 OF 3)

Reprinted with permission, California Association of Realtors®. Endorsement not implied.

Property Address: _____ Date: _____

If this Property is a duplex, triplex, or fourplex, this AVID is for unit # _____.

Inspection Performed By (Real Estate Broker Firm Name) _____

Inspection Date/Time:_____ Weather conditions: _____

Other persons present: _____

THE UNDERSIGNED, BASED ON A REASONABLY COMPETENT AND DILIGENT VISUAL INSPECTION OF THE REASONABLY AND NORMALLY ACCESSIBLE AREAS OF THE PROPERTY, STATES THE FOLLOWING:

Entry (excluding common areas): _____

Living Room: _____

Dining Room: _____

Kitchen: _____

Other Room: _____

Hall/Stairs (excluding common areas): _____

Bedroom # __: _____

Bedroom # __: _____

Bedroom # __: _____

Bath # ___: _____

Bath # ___: _____

Bath # ___: _____

Other Room: _____

Buyer's Initials (_____)(_____)   Seller's Initials (_____)(_____)

AVID REVISED 11/13 (PAGE 2 OF 3)   Reviewed by _____ Date _____

AGENT VISUAL INSPECTION DISCLOSURE (AVID PAGE 2 OF 3)

Property Address: _____ Date: _____

If this Property is a duplex, triplex, or fourplex, this AVID is for unit # _____.

Other Room: _____
_____
_____

Other: _____
_____
_____

Other: _____
_____
_____

Other: _____
_____

Garage/Parking (excluding common areas): _____
_____
_____

Exterior Building and Yard - Front/Sides/Back: _____
_____
_____

Other Observed or Known Conditions Not Specified Above: _____
_____
_____

This disclosure is based on a reasonably competent and diligent visual inspection of reasonably and normally accessible areas of the Property on the date specified above.

Real Estate Broker (Firm who performed the Inspection)_____
By _____ Date _____
       (Signature of Associate Licensee or Broker)

Reminder: Not all defects are observable by a real estate licensee conducting an inspection. The inspection does not include testing of any system or component. Real Estate Licensees are not home inspectors or contractors. **BUYER SHOULD OBTAIN ADVICE ABOUT AND INSPECTIONS OF THE PROPERTY FROM OTHER APPROPRIATE PROFESSIONALS. IF BUYER FAILS TO DO SO, BUYER IS ACTING AGAINST THE ADVICE OF BROKER.**

I/we acknowledge that I/we have read, understand and received a copy of this disclosure.
SELLER _____ Date _____
SELLER _____ Date _____
BUYER _____ Date _____
BUYER _____ Date _____
Real Estate Broker(FirmRepresentingSeller) _____
By _____ Date _____
       (Associate Licensee or Broker Signature)

Real Estate Broker (Firm Representing Buyer) _____
By _____ Date _____

Published and Distributed by:
REAL ESTATE BUSINESS SERVICES, INC.
a subsidiary of the California Association of REALTORS®
525 South Virgil Avenue, Los Angeles, California 90020

Reviewed by _____ Date _____

AVID REVISED 11/13 (PAGE 3 OF 3)

AGENT VISUAL INSPECTION DISCLOSURE (AVID PAGE 3 OF 3)

If the buyer decides to rescind the agreement, he must notify the seller or the seller's real estate agent in writing. The buyer will then be entitled to a full refund of the good faith deposit.

If the buyer is not given a disclosure statement, the transaction is still valid, but the person who failed to comply with the disclosure law (either the seller or one of the agents) is liable for any damages the buyer suffers as a result.

When Circumstances Change. After the buyer accepts the transfer disclosure statement, information may come to light that makes the statement inaccurate.

> **Example:** Stein and O'Neil signed a purchase agreement. Stein filled out the transfer disclosure statement and gave it to O'Neil. O'Neil examined the statement, was satisfied with it, and decided to go ahead with the purchase. Two weeks later, Stein discovers that the roof has started leaking. Since this wasn't disclosed in the transfer disclosure statement she gave O'Neil, the disclosure statement is no longer accurate.

When this happens, the seller may either give the buyer an amended disclosure statement, or else fix the problem so that the disclosure statement is made accurate once again. If the seller amends the disclosure statement, the buyer again has three or five days (depending on the delivery method) to either accept the amended disclosure statement or rescind the purchase agreement.

> **Example:** Stein gives O'Neil an amended disclosure statement, this time listing the true condition of the roof. O'Neil, who has had second thoughts about buying the property anyway, decides to rescind the purchase agreement.

Once the sale has closed, the buyer can no longer rescind, even if new information is discovered.

Disclosure of Latent Defects. Even if there's no question on the disclosure statement form that prompts disclosure of a particular problem, the seller and the agent must disclose the problem if they are aware of it. The transfer disclosure statement does not limit the responsibility of the seller and the real estate agent to disclose latent defects and other material facts to the buyer.

Environmental Hazards Booklet

As we've discussed, the disclosures that must be made in the transfer disclosure statement include any specific environmental problems on the property that the seller or the agents are aware of. In addition, the seller or the seller's agent should also make sure the buyer receives a copy of a pamphlet prepared by the Bureau of Real Estate entitled "Environmental Hazards: A Guide for Homeowners, Buyers, Landlords, and Tenants." If the buyer is given this general information pamphlet, the seller and the seller's agent do not need to provide further information regarding environmental hazards, beyond the disclosure of known problems on the property.

Natural Hazard Disclosure Statement

Additional disclosures are required for properties that are at higher risk for natural disasters, such as earthquakes or landslides. These hazards should be disclosed separately on the natural hazard disclosure statement, rather than on the transfer disclosure statement.

An example of a natural hazard disclosure statement form is shown in Figure 2.5. If a property is in an earthquake fault zone, a seismic hazard zone (an area subject to landslides or liquefaction), an area designated a flood hazard area or subject to potential flooding in the event of a dam failure, or an area with high forest fire risks, the seller should check "Yes" for that particular hazard.

Although sellers and agents can rely on their own knowledge when they fill out the transfer disclosure statement, they can't do that for the natural hazard disclosure statement. To determine whether or not the property is in a hazard area, they may consult maps issued by the state or federal government (and generally available online). Or they may base their disclosures on a relatively inexpensive report generated by a consulting company.

Buyers have the same rescission rights in connection with the natural hazard disclosure statement that they have in connection with the transfer disclosure statement. In other words, they can rescind the purchase agreement within three days after receiving the natural hazard disclosure statement in person, or within five days after the statement is mailed to them.

Residential Earthquake Hazards Report

For one- to four-unit residences built before 1960, the listing agent must give the buyer a copy of a pamphlet published by the California Seismic Safety Commission entitled "The Homeowner's Guide to Earthquake Safety." The guide contains a disclosure form called the Residential Earthquake Hazards Report, which the seller should complete and give to the buyer. The disclosure form asks the seller whether seismic retrofitting has been performed on the house, and also whether the property is in an earthquake fault zone or seismic hazard zone.

Fig. 2.5 Natural hazard disclosure statement

CALIFORNIA
ASSOCIATION
OF REALTORS®

NATURAL HAZARD DISCLOSURE STATEMENT
(C.A.R. Form NHD, Revised 10/04)

This statement applies to the following property: _____

The transferor and his or her agent(s) or a third-party consultant disclose the following information with the knowledge that even though this is not a warranty, prospective transferees may rely on this information in deciding whether and on what terms to purchase the subject property. Transferor hereby authorizes any agent(s) representing any principal(s) in this action to provide a copy of this statement to any person or entity in connection with any actual or anticipated sale of the property.

The following are representations made by the transferor and his or her agent(s) based on their knowledge and maps drawn by the state and federal governments. This information is a disclosure and is not intended to be part of any contract between the transferee and transferor.

THIS REAL PROPERTY LIES WITHIN THE FOLLOWING HAZARDOUS AREA(S):

A SPECIAL FLOOD HAZARD AREA (Any type Zone "A" or "V") designated by the Federal Emergency Management Agency.
Yes _____ No _____ Do not know and information not available from local jurisdiction _____

AN AREA OF POTENTIAL FLOODING shown on a dam failure inundation map pursuant to Section 8589.5 of the Government Code.
Yes _____ No _____ Do not know and information not available from local jurisdiction _____

A VERY HIGH FIRE HAZARD SEVERITY ZONE pursuant to Section 51178 or 51179 of the Government Code. The owner of this property is subject to the maintenance requirements of Section 51182 of the Government Code.
Yes _____ No _____

A WILDLAND AREA THAT MAY CONTAIN SUBSTANTIAL FOREST FIRE RISKS AND HAZARDS pursuant to Section 4125 of the Public Resources Code. The owner of this property is subject to the maintenance requirements of Section 4291 of the Public Resources Code. Additionally, it is not the state's responsibility to provide fire protection services to any building or structure located within the wildlands unless the Department of Forestry and Fire Protection has entered into a cooperative agreement with a local agency for those purposes pursuant to Section 4142 of the Public Resources Code.
Yes _____ No _____

AN EARTHQUAKE FAULT ZONE pursuant to Section 2622 of the Public Resources Code.
Yes _____ No _____

A SEISMIC HAZARD ZONE pursuant to Section 2696 of the Public Resources Code.
Yes (Landslide Zone) _____   Yes (Liquefaction Zone) _____
No _____   Map not yet released by state ____

NHD REVISED 10/04 (PAGE 1 OF 2)

Buyer's Initials (_____) (_____)
Seller's Initials (_____) (_____)

Reviewed by _____ Date _____

EQUAL HOUSING OPPORTUNITY

NATURAL HAZARD DISCLOSURE STATEMENT (NHD PAGE 1 OF 2)

Property Address: _____ Date: _____

THESE HAZARDS MAY LIMIT YOUR ABILITY TO DEVELOP THE REAL PROPERTY, TO OBTAIN INSURANCE, OR TO RECEIVE ASSISTANCE AFTER A DISASTER.

THE MAPS ON WHICH THESE DISCLOSURES ARE BASED ESTIMATE WHERE NATURAL HAZARDS EXIST. THEY ARE NOT DEFINITIVE INDICATORS OF WHETHER OR NOT A PROPERTY WILL BE AFFECTED BY A NATURAL DISASTER. TRANSFEREE(S) AND TRANSFEROR(S) MAY WISH TO OBTAIN PROFESSIONAL ADVICE REGARDING THOSE HAZARDS AND OTHER HAZARDS THAT MAY AFFECT THE PROPERTY

Signature of Transferor(s) _____ Date _____

Signature of Transferor(s) _____ Date _____

Agent(s) _____ Date _____

Agent(s) _____ Date _____

Check only one of the following:

☐ Transferor(s) and their agent(s) represent that the information herein is true and correct to the best of their knowledge as of the date signed by the transferor(s) and agent(s).

☐ Transferor(s) and their agent(s) acknowledge that they have exercised good faith in the selection of a third-party report provider as required in Civil Code Section 1103.7, and that the representations made in this Natural Hazard Disclosure Statement are based upon information provided by the independent third-party disclosure provider as a substituted disclosure pursuant to Civil Code Section 1103.4. Neither transferor(s) nor their agent(s) (1) has independently verified the information contained in this statement and report or (2) is personally aware of any errors or inaccuracies in the information contained on the statement. This statement was prepared by the provider below:

Third-Party Disclosure Provider(s) _____ Date _____

Transferee represents that he or she has read and understands this document. Pursuant to Civil Code Section 1103.8, the representations made in this Natural Hazard Disclosure Statement do not constitute all of the transferor's or agent's disclosure obligations in this transaction.

Signature of Transferee(s) _____ Date _____

Signature of Transferee(s) _____ Date _____

SURE TRAC
The System for Success

Published and Distributed by:
REAL ESTATE BUSINESS SERVICES, INC.
a subsidiary of the California Association of REALTORS®
525 South Virgil Avenue, Los Angeles, California 90020

Reviewed by _____ Date _____

EQUAL HOUSING OPPORTUNITY

NHD REVISED 10/04 (PAGE 2 OF 2)

NATURAL HAZARD DISCLOSURE STATEMENT (NHD PAGE 2 OF 2)

Lead-Based Paint Disclosure

In sale or lease transactions that involve housing built before 1978, federal law requires the seller or landlord to disclose information about lead-based paint on the property to potential buyers or tenants. Many homes built before 1978 contain some lead-based paint. The paint is usually not dangerous if properly maintained, but if it deteriorates and is ingested, it may cause brain damage and organ damage in young children.

The federal law requires the seller of a dwelling built before 1978 to do all of the following:

- disclose the location of any lead-based paint in the home that he is aware of;
- provide a copy of any report concerning lead-based paint in the home, if the home has been inspected;
- give buyers a copy of a pamphlet on lead-based paint prepared by the U.S. Environmental Protection Agency, and
- allow buyers at least a ten-day period in which to have the home tested for lead-based paint.

A disclosure form such as the one shown in Figure 2.6 can be used to comply with this law. It must be signed by the parties and the agents, and it becomes part of the purchase agreement.

Agent's Responsibilities. A real estate agent is required to ensure that the seller knows her obligations under the lead-based paint disclosure law and fulfills those obligations. An agent is also responsible for making sure that the purchase agreement contains a lead warning statement and all of the disclosures and signatures that the law requires.

Penalties. Sellers and real estate agents who fail to fulfill their obligations under the lead-based paint disclosure law may be ordered to pay the buyer treble damages (three times the amount of any actual damages suffered by the buyer). Civil and criminal penalties may also be imposed.

Fig. 2.6   Lead-based paint disclosure

Reprinted with permission, California Association of Realtors®. Endorsement not implied.

Property Address: _____ Date _____

2. LISTING AGENT'S ACKNOWLEDGMENT

Agent has informed Seller or Landlord of Seller's or Landlord's obligations under §42 U.S.C. 4852d and is aware of Agent's responsibility to ensure compliance.

I have reviewed the information above and certify, to the best of my knowledge, that the information provided is true and correct.

_____ By _____
(Please Print) Agent (Broker representing Seller or Landlord)   Associate-Licensee or Broker Signature   Date

3. BUYER'S OR TENANT'S ACKNOWLEDGMENT

I (we) have received copies of all information listed, if any, in 1 above and the pamphlet "*Protect Your Family From Lead In Your Home*" or an equivalent pamphlet approved for use in the State such as "*The Homeowner's Guide to Environmental Hazards and Earthquake Safety.*" **If delivery of any of the disclosures or pamphlet referenced in paragraph 1 above occurs after Acceptance of an offer to purchase, Buyer has a right to cancel pursuant to the purchase contract. If you wish to cancel, you must act within the prescribed period.**

For Sales Transactions Only. Buyer acknowledges the right for 10 days, unless otherwise agreed in the real estate purchase contract, to conduct a risk assessment or inspection for the presence of lead-based paint and/or lead-based paint hazards; OR, (if checked) ☐ Buyer waives the right to conduct a risk assessment or inspection for the presence of lead-based paint and/or lead-based paint hazards.

I (we) have reviewed the information above and certify, to the best of my (our) knowledge, that the information provided is true and correct.

_____ _____ _____ _____
Buyer or Tenant   Date   Buyer or Tenant   Date

4. COOPERATING AGENT'S ACKNOWLEDGMENT

Agent has informed Seller or Landlord, through the Listing Agent if the property is listed, of Seller's or Landlord's obligations under §42 U.S.C. 4852d and is aware of Agent's responsibility to ensure compliance.

I have reviewed the information above and certify, to the best of my knowledge, that the information provided is true and correct.

_____ By _____
Agent (Broker obtaining the Offer)   Associate-Licensee or Broker Signature   Date

Published and Distributed by:
REAL ESTATE BUSINESS SERVICES, INC.
a subsidiary of the California Association of REALTORS®
525 South Virgil Avenue, Los Angeles, California 90020
FLD REVISED 11/10 (PAGE 2 OF 2)

Reviewed by _____ Date _____

LEAD-BASED PAINT AND LEAD-BASED PAINT HAZARDS DISCLOSURE (FLD PAGE 2 OF 2)

Supplemental Statutory Disclosure Form

California state law requires a number of other disclosures that don't have their own disclosure forms. It may be necessary to disclose that:

- the property is located in a commercial or industrial zone,
- the property is affected by a nearby airport,
- the property is near a former military site that may have live munitions on it,
- illegal controlled substances were released on the property, or
- a death occurred on the property within the last three years.

Many organizations publish a supplemental disclosure form that can be used to make any of these disclosures.

Mello-Roos Lien Disclosure

The Mello-Roos Community Facilities Act is a state law that allows communities to form special taxing districts and make special assessments to provide public services and facilities such as police protection and parks. When property that is subject to a Mello-Roos assessment lien is sold, the lien must be disclosed to the buyer.

Ordinarily, the seller complies with this requirement by obtaining a copy of the tax notice from the local agency that levied the special assessment. If the seller or listing agent delivers a copy of this notice to the buyer, no further disclosure is required. Even so, it's generally a good idea to disclose the lien on the transfer disclosure statement as well.

Chapter Summary

1. The listing agreement is an employment contract between the seller and the real estate broker. The seller agrees to pay the broker a stated commission if a ready, willing, and able buyer is found during the listing period.

2. The three basic types of listing agreements are the open listing, the exclusive agency listing, and the exclusive right to sell listing. The type of listing determines the circumstances under which the broker is entitled to be paid a commission.

3. A listing agreement must be in writing. It should identify the property to be sold, specify the listing price and other terms of sale, state the broker's authority, include a promise to compensate the broker, set a termination date, and be signed by the seller.

4. The listing agreement should also state the items included and excluded, the conditions under which the commission will be paid, and the seller's warranties and representations regarding the accuracy of the information provided about the property.

5. A safety clause provides that the seller will be liable for the broker's commission if the property is sold during a certain period after the listing expires to a buyer the broker dealt with during the listing period.

6. When residential property is sold, the seller is required to give the buyer a transfer disclosure statement, disclosing any problems concerning the title or condition of the property. On the basis of the information in the disclosure statement, the buyer may choose to rescind the purchase agreement.

7. Other disclosures concerning the property that may be required in a transaction include a natural hazard disclosure statement, a residential earthquake hazards report, a lead-based paint disclosure, and a Mello-Roos lien disclosure. A supplemental form may be used for disclosures that do not call for their own separate form.

Key Terms

Ready, willing, and able: A buyer is ready, willing, and able if he makes an offer that meets the seller's stated terms, and has the contractual capacity and financial resources to complete the transaction.

Procuring cause: The real estate agent who is primarily responsible for bringing about a sale; for example, by negotiating the agreement between the buyer and seller.

Open listing: A nonexclusive listing, given by a seller to as many brokers as she chooses. If the property is sold, a broker is entitled to a commission only if he was the procuring cause of the sale.

Exclusive agency listing: A listing agreement that entitles the broker to a commission if anyone other than the seller finds a buyer for the property during the listing term.

Exclusive right to sell listing: A listing agreement that entitles the broker to a commission if anyone—including the seller—finds a buyer for the property during the listing term.

Safety clause: A clause in a listing agreement providing that for a specified period after the listing expires, the broker will still be entitled to a commission if the property is sold to someone the broker dealt with during the listing term. Also called an extender clause or protection clause.

Real estate transfer disclosure statement: A statement containing information about the property that a seller of residential property is required to give to the buyer.

Mello-Roos lien: A lien based on a type of special assessment allowed under the Mello-Roos Community Facilities Act, which allows communities to create special districts to finance certain kinds of improvements or services.

Chapter Quiz

1. One disadvantage of an open listing agreement is that it:

   a. does not state the broker's compensation as a fixed amount

   b. requires the agent to put more effort into marketing the property

   c. may lead to a dispute over which agent was the procuring cause, if the seller gives the listing to more than one broker

   d. prevents sellers from listing their property with as many brokers as they want

2. Which of the following types of listings offers the listing agent the greatest protection?

   a. Open listing

   b. Exclusive agency listing

   c. Exclusive right to sell listing

   d. Non-exclusive listing

3. A typical listing agreement form does not authorize the broker to:

   a. act as the agent of the seller

   b. accept good faith deposits from prospective buyers on behalf of the seller

   c. accept an offer to purchase the property

   d. submit offers to purchase to the seller

4. A hold harmless clause:

   a. protects the broker in that the seller takes responsibility for information given in the listing

   b. relieves the agent from liability for any theft or damage during an open house

   c. states that the seller will pay the agent's attorney's fees if the seller loses a legal dispute with the agent regarding payment of a commission

   d. contains a warranty that there are no undisclosed encumbrances against the property

5. A transfer disclosure statement:

   a. is considered part of the listing agreement

   b. is considered part of the purchase contract between the seller and the buyer

   c. provides warranty protection to a buyer who acts in reliance on the statement

   d. reflects the seller's knowledge of the condition of the property and the title

6. A safety clause might provide that:
   a. the seller must pay a commission if the property is sold within the extension period to a buyer you negotiated with during the listing period
   b. the seller will not owe you a commission if the property is listed with another broker during the extension period
   c. the provision will not be enforceable unless you give the seller a list of all potential buyers you negotiated with during the listing period
   d. All of the above

7. Which of the following disclosures does not require a separate disclosure form?
   a. Disclosure that the property is in a flood hazard zone
   b. Disclosure of a Mello-Roos lien
   c. Disclosure of presence of lead-based paint
   d. Disclosure that the house has not been seismically retrofitted

8. The purpose of a listing input sheet is to:
   a. explain the agency relationships of MLS members to the seller
   b. allow the MLS to verify the accuracy of information about the listing
   c. gather information about the property for distribution in MLS publications
   d. disclose information the seller is required to give to the buyer

9. With respect to the transfer disclosure statement, all of the following statements concerning the buyer's rights are true, except:
   a. if the buyer rescinds the purchase agreement based on the disclosure statement, she gives up her good faith deposit
   b. the buyer can rescind the purchase agreement if she does not like something in the disclosure statement, no matter how trivial
   c. the buyer has three days after personal delivery of the disclosure statement to accept it or rescind the purchase agreement
   d. if the seller fails to provide a disclosure statement, the transaction is still valid but the seller may be liable for any damages suffered by the buyer as a result

10. If new information comes to light that makes the transfer disclosure statement inaccurate, the:
    a. seller is required to take action to fix the problem so that the disclosure statement is accurate again
    b. seller does not have to give the buyer an amended disclosure statement if he can correct the problem so that the original statement is accurate again
    c. buyer must accept the amended disclosure statement if she accepted the original disclosure statement
    d. buyer has the right to rescind the purchase agreement after the sale closes

Answer Key

1. c. Because a seller can give open listings to more than one broker, they can lead to disputes over which agent was the procuring cause of a sale.

2. c. An exclusive right to sell listing pays a commission to the listing broker regardless of whether the property is sold by one of his own agents, an agent working for another broker, or the seller herself. This provides the most protection to the listing agent.

3. c. Under the terms of nearly any listing agreement, the broker may submit offers to the seller, but only the seller can accept an offer. A broker cannot ordinarily accept an offer and create a contract that will be binding on the seller.

4. a. In a hold harmless clause, the seller takes responsibility for the information given to the listing agent in the listing agreement.

5. d. In filling out a transfer disclosure statement, a seller relies on her own knowledge of the property's condition and title. The disclosure statement is not part of the listing agreement or the purchase agreement, and it does not establish any warranties.

6. d. In addition to protecting the broker's commission for a specified period after the listing expires, a safety clause may also contain protections for the seller, such as the ones described in options b and c.

7. b. Disclosure of a Mello-Roos lien can be made simply by providing the buyer with a copy of the tax notice from the taxing authority that levied the assessment. Special forms should be used for each of the other disclosures.

8. c. The listing input sheet is filled in with information for the MLS to distribute to its members and use in listing the property. The MLS does not verify the information or take legal responsibility for it.

9. a. Within three days after receiving the transfer disclosure statement or five days after the statement is deposited in the mail, the buyer may rescind the purchase agreement for any reason without penalty. If a disclosure statement is not provided, the buyer can rescind the agreement at any time until closing, but not after closing.

10. b. The seller has two choices. He can either give the buyer an amended disclosure statement, or else he can correct the problem to make the original disclosure statement accurate again.

3

Listing Regulations

The Real Estate Law

- Commissions
- Ownership of a listing

Mortgage Foreclosure Consultant Law

Antidiscrimination Laws

- Federal Fair Housing Act
- California state antidiscrimination laws
- Complying with fair housing laws
- Americans with Disabilities Act

Antitrust Laws and Listing Practices

- Price fixing
- Group boycotts
- Tie-in arrangements
- Market allocation

Environmental Issues

- Environmental laws
- Environmental hazards
- Real estate agent's responsibilities

Introduction

The previous chapter covered two of the main legal issues you face when you take a listing: the validity of the listing agreement, and the disclosures concerning the property that the seller is required to make to buyers. But those are by no means the only legal issues you may confront as a listing agent. What would happen if the seller refused to pay your commission? Could you sue her? What should you do if the seller indicates that she doesn't want you to show the property to non-white buyers? What if you suspect there's an environmental problem with the property?

A wide variety of laws affect real estate listing and marketing practices, and you'll need to be familiar with them if you're going to avoid some of the pitfalls of selling real estate. These laws include the Real Estate Law, antidiscrimination laws, antitrust laws, and environmental laws. In this chapter, we'll discuss the provisions of these laws that pertain to listing and marketing properties and to brokerage commissions.

The Real Estate Law

California's Real Estate Law includes rules concerning payment of brokers' commissions and control of listings.

Commissions

As you know, a seller ordinarily pays the brokerage commission to the listing broker. In most cases, if two different brokerages are involved, the listing broker then pays a share of the commission to his own agent (the listing agent) and another share to the selling broker. The selling broker, in turn, pays a share of what she received to her own agent (the selling agent).

These steps are necessary because the Real Estate Law allows a broker to share a commission only with another licensed broker or with one of his own affiliated sales agents. A broker may not pay any compensation directly to a sales agent who is affiliated with another broker. Payment must be made to that agent's broker, who then pays the agent.

> **Example:** You work for Broker Winston. You found a buyer for a property that was listed by an agent working for Broker Andreas. When the sale closes, the seller pays Andreas a $10,000 commission.

Of that $10,000, Andreas gets to keep $2,500 for herself. She will pay her own agent (the one who listed the property) another $2,500. She pays the other $5,000 to your broker, Winston, because Winston is the selling broker. Winston pays you $2,500, because you found the buyer. It would be unlawful for Andreas to pay your $2,500 directly to you. Your compensation must come from your own broker.

Note that a real estate salesperson is not allowed to share her compensation with another salesperson, whether they work for different brokers or the same broker. If two sales agents are going to split a commission, the split must be handled by their broker or brokers.

A valid written agency agreement (either a listing agreement or a buyer representation agreement) is required before a broker can sue for a commission. Only the broker can sue the seller (or buyer, if appropriate) for the commission. A salesperson can't sue a principal for a commission. However, if the broker fails to pay the salesperson's share of the commission, the salesperson can sue the broker for it.

Ownership of a Listing

Under the Real Estate Law, only a broker can directly represent a member of the public (see Chapter 1). As a result, even though a listing agreement is usually prepared and signed by a salesperson, the listing is in the name of the broker and belongs to the broker.

Example: You work for Broker Yamaguchi. You are making a listing presentation to Piper. He decides to list his property with you, and you and he both sign the listing agreement form. However, the listing agreement is actually a contract between Yamaguchi and Piper. When you sign the form, you are signing it as an agent of Yamaguchi.

Because the listing agreement is between the broker and the seller, if the salesperson who took the listing goes to work for another broker, the listing stays with the original broker.

Example: You don't want to work for Yamaguchi anymore, so you start working for Broker Wilder instead. Piper's listing agreement was with Yamaguchi, not with you, so Yamaguchi keeps the listing.

Mortgage Foreclosure Consultant Law

California's Mortgage Foreclosure Consultant Law helps protect homeowners in financial distress from exploitative foreclosure rescue scams. This type of scam occurs, for example, when a consultant offers to help a homeowner fight foreclosure by "temporarily" transferring title to the property to the consultant; after the owner transfers title, the consultant sells the property to someone else or simply refuses to return title to the (former) owner.

Although this consumer protection law exempts real estate agents from most of its provisions, licensees need a general understanding of its requirements. It applies to dwellings with up to four units, if one of the units is the property owner's principal residence.

Definition of Foreclosure Consultant

Generally, the law imposes special duties on foreclosure consultants. A **foreclosure consultant** is anyone who offers (in exchange for compensation) to perform any service to:

- stop or postpone a foreclosure sale;
- obtain a forbearance from the lender;
- assist the homeowner in exercising a right of reinstatement (or extending the period during which reinstatement may occur);
- obtain a waiver of an acceleration clause;
- assist the owner in obtaining a loan or advance of funds;
- avoid or ameliorate the impairment of the owner's credit;
- save the home from foreclosure; or
- assist the owner in obtaining any surplus proceeds after the foreclosure sale.

Exemptions

The act contains certain exemptions; most significantly, it exempts real estate licensees who provide brokerage services in connection with the listing of a residence in foreclosure, as long as they don't accept any compensation until after the services have been provided. However, if a licensee provides any foreclosure services without a listing agreement, the exemption doesn't apply. It also doesn't apply if a licensee loans money to or accepts an advance fee from the homeowner. A real estate licensee who did any of those things would meet the definition of a foreclosure consultant and would therefore be required to comply with all of the law's requirements.

Requirements

Foreclosure consultants are required to register with the California Department of Justice and provide a surety bond. A consultant must enter into a formal written contract with the homeowner, known as a foreclosure consultant service agreement. The contract must be written in the same language used by the foreclosure consultant and the owner.

The foreclosure consultant service agreement must fully disclose the services that will be provided and the terms of the consultant's compensation, including the total amount of compensation she will receive. The agreement must contain a number of other disclosures as well, including a notice that the homeowner may cancel the agreement within three business days.

The foreclosure consultant may not receive compensation from the homeowner until she has performed every service promised in the agreement. Perhaps most importantly, the consultant may not acquire any interest in the property from the owner; in other words, the consultant cannot purchase the property or any rights to it.

Penalties

The penalties for violating the Mortgage Foreclosure Consultant Law are severe. A wronged homeowner can sue the consultant for any violation of the act and may receive actual damages and attorney's fees. In extreme cases, punitive damages (of up to three times the actual damages) may be awarded. Moreover, any violations of the law are considered crimes, with each violation punishable by a fine of up to $10,000, up to a year in prison, or both.

Antidiscrimination Laws

Fair housing laws and other antidiscrimination laws affect both how you obtain listings and how you market properties once they are listed. Before we discuss the impact of these laws on listing and marketing practices, we'll review the basic provisions of the main federal and state antidiscrimination laws that apply in real estate transactions.

Federal Fair Housing Act

The federal Fair Housing Act, part of the Civil Rights Act of 1968, makes it illegal to discriminate on the basis of **race, color, religion, sex, national origin,**

disability, or **familial status** in the sale or lease of residential property, or in the sale or lease of vacant land for the construction of residential buildings. The law also prohibits discrimination in advertising, lending, real estate brokerage, and other services in connection with residential real estate transactions.

Prohibited Acts. The Fair Housing Act prohibits any of the following actions if based on discrimination against the protected classes listed above, or against members of those protected classes.

- Refusing to rent or sell residential property after receiving a bona fide offer.
- Refusing to negotiate for the sale or rental of residential property, or otherwise making it unavailable.
- Changing the terms of sale or lease for different potential buyers or tenants.
- Using advertising that indicates a preference or intent to discriminate.
- Representing that property is not available for inspection, sale, or rent when it is in fact available.
- Discrimination by an institutional lender in making a housing loan.
- Limiting participation in a multiple listing service or similar service.
- Coercing, intimidating, threatening, or interfering with anyone on account of his or her enjoyment, attempt to enjoy, or encouragement or assistance to others in enjoying the rights granted by the Fair Housing Act.

The discriminatory practices known as blockbusting, steering, and redlining are also prohibited.

1. **Blockbusting:** This occurs when someone tries to induce homeowners to list or sell their properties by predicting that people of another race (or disabled people, people of a particular ethnic background, etc.) will be moving into the neighborhood, and that this will have undesirable consequences, such as a higher crime rate or lower property values. The blockbuster then profits by purchasing the homes at reduced prices, or (in the case of a real estate agent) by collecting commissions on the induced sales. Blockbusting is also known as panic selling.
2. **Steering:** This refers to channeling prospective buyers or tenants toward or away from specific neighborhoods based on their race (or religion, national origin, etc.) in order to maintain or change the character of those neighborhoods.
3. **Redlining:** This is a refusal to make a loan because of the racial or ethnic composition of the neighborhood in which the proposed security

property is located. Rejection of a loan application must be based on objective financial considerations concerning the buyer or the property.

Exemptions. There are some exemptions from the Fair Housing Act. However, these exemptions are very limited and apply only rarely. The most important thing to remember about the exemptions is that they *never* apply when a real estate agent is involved in a transaction.

Enforcement. The Fair Housing Act is enforced by the Department of Housing and Urban Development (HUD), through its Office of Fair Housing and Equal Opportunity. In California, HUD may also refer complaints to the California Department of Fair Employment and Housing.

When someone is held to have violated the Fair Housing Act, a court may issue an injunction ordering the violator to stop the discriminatory conduct. The violator may also be ordered to pay compensatory damages and attorney's fees to the injured party. In addition, the violator may be required to pay punitive damages to the injured party or a significant civil penalty to the government.

California State Antidiscrimination Laws

Real estate agents must also comply with the state laws that prohibit discrimination. These include the Unruh Civil Rights Act, the Fair Employment and Housing Act, and the Housing Financial Discrimination Act. In addition, California's Real Estate Law and the Commissioner's regulations prohibit discrimination by real estate licensees.

Unruh Civil Rights Act. One major state antidiscrimination law affecting real estate agents in California is the Unruh Civil Rights Act, which applies to business establishments. A brokerage is a business establishment, so the professional activities of real estate agents are subject to this law.

The Unruh Act prohibits any discrimination based on **sex**, **race**, **color**, **religion**, **ancestry**, **national origin**, **disability**, **medical condition**, **genetic information**, **marital status**, or **sexual orientation**. (The Unruh Act states that "sex" includes gender, gender identity, and gender expression, mirroring the state's Fair Employment and Housing Act, discussed below.) In transactions related to housing, business establishments are also not allowed to discriminate based on **age**. (Although the law specifically mentions only the classes of persons listed above, California courts have long interpreted the law more expansively.

For example, although familial status isn't specifically mentioned in the Unruh Act, families with children are nevertheless a protected class under the law.)

Apartment and condominium complexes are also considered business establishments, so they must comply with the law. There is an exemption, however, for developments that qualify as housing for senior citizens. Developments that meet the requirements of the senior housing exemption may discriminate on the basis of age and familial status to exclude families with children (but they cannot discriminate against other protected groups).

Penalties. Someone who violates the Unruh Act is liable for the injured party's actual damages and attorney's fees. In some cases an additional penalty may be imposed.

Fair Employment and Housing Act. The Fair Employment and Housing Act, also known as the **Rumford Act**, makes it unlawful to discriminate in the selling or leasing of housing. It applies not only to real estate agents and housing developments, but also to individual property owners.

The Fair Employment and Housing Act specifically prohibits a seller or landlord from asking about the **race, color, religion, sex, gender, gender identity, gender expression, sexual orientation, marital status, national origin, ancestry, familial status, source of income, disability, or genetic information** of any prospective buyer or tenant. You should refuse to answer such a question from a seller or landlord.

The law also specifically prohibits anyone from advertising housing for sale or rent in discriminatory terms. This includes advertising that suggests a preference for a particular group.

Example: A landlord places an advertisement listing an apartment for rent. The ad states: "Married couples only, please." The landlord has violated the Fair Employment and Housing Act.

Exemptions. There are a few exemptions from the Fair Employment and Housing Act. It doesn't apply to accommodations operated by nonprofit religious, fraternal, or charitable organizations, so long as their membership isn't restricted by race, color, or national origin. It also doesn't apply when part of a single-family, owner-occupied home is rented to a single boarder.

Example: Judy is a 75-year-old widow who owns a house and lives alone. She has extra space and needs some additional income, so she decides to rent out a room in her house. Judy believes she will only feel comfortable with another single, older woman as a tenant. She places an advertisement specifically looking for such a tenant. This is permissible under the Fair Employment and Housing Act.

In addition, if a rental involves shared living space, the advertising may specify only male or only female tenants. And the law's familial status protections do not apply to housing for senior citizens.

Penalties. Housing discrimination complaints are investigated by the Department of Fair Employment and Housing (DFEH). If DFEH determines that a complaint should be pursued, it will require the parties to participate in mediation (at no cost). If mediation is ineffective, DFEH will file a lawsuit with the California Superior Court. A violator who is found guilty may be ordered to sell or lease the property or a similar property to the injured party, and/or to pay damages to the injured party. In especially serious cases, the violator may also be required to pay the state a substantial civil penalty.

Fig. 3.1 Comparison of antidiscrimination laws

Federal Fair Housing Act
- Applies to residential real estate transactions
- Protected classes: race, color, religion, sex, national origin, disability, and familial status
- No exemptions for transactions involving real estate agents

Unruh Civil Rights Act
- Applies to business establishments, including real estate brokerages
- Protected classes: sex, race, color, religion, ancestry, national origin, disability, medical condition, genetic information, marital status, sexual orientation, age, and familial status
- Exemption for housing for senior citizens

Fair Employment and Housing Act (Rumford Act)
- Applies to the sale or lease of housing
- Protected classes: race, color, religion, sex, gender, gender identity, gender expression, sexual orientation, marital status, national origin, ancestry, familial status, source of income, disability, and genetic information

Housing Financial Discrimination Act. Another state law you should be aware of is the Housing Financial Discrimination Act, also known as the **Holden Act**. This law requires a lender to make a lending decision based on the merits of the borrower and the security property, rather than on the property's neighborhood or location.

The Holden Act prohibits lenders from considering the racial, ethnic, religious, or national origin composition of the neighborhood. Like the federal Fair Housing Act, the Holden Act makes the practice of redlining illegal. The Holden Act also bars lenders from discriminating based on race, color, religion, sex, marital status, national origin, or ancestry.

California Real Estate Law. In addition to the federal and state laws already discussed, real estate licensees must comply with antidiscrimination provisions in the Real Estate Law and the Commissioner's regulations.

A licensee who engages in discriminatory activity in violation of these provisions is subject to disciplinary action by the Bureau of Real Estate. His license could be suspended or revoked, and he could face a fine of up to $10,000.

The Real Estate Commissioner's regulations contain a list of prohibited discriminatory conduct. If it's based on race, color, sex, religion, ancestry, physical handicap, marital status, or national origin, it is against the law for a real estate licensee to:

- refuse to negotiate for the sale, rental, or financing of the purchase of real estate, or otherwise make it unavailable;
- refuse or fail to show, rent, sell, or finance the purchase of real estate;
- refuse or fail to provide information to any person about a property;
- discriminate in the sale, purchase, or negotiation of real estate;
- discriminate in the terms and conditions of a real estate transaction;
- discriminate in providing services or facilities in connection with a real estate transaction;
- represent that property is not available for inspection, sale, or rental when it is in fact available;
- act to delay, hinder, or avoid a real estate transaction;
- make any effort to encourage discrimination in a real estate transaction;
- refuse or fail to cooperate with another real estate licensee in a transaction;
- ask any question or make any statement that expresses or implies an intent to discriminate;

- make any effort to interfere with any person in the exercise of their rights;
- solicit sales, rentals, or listings in a discriminatory manner;
- discriminate in informing persons of waiting lists or other procedures with respect to the future availability of real estate;
- make any effort to discourage or prevent a real estate transaction;
- provide information or advice concerning real estate in a discriminatory manner;
- refuse to accept a listing or application for financing;
- enter into an agreement or carry out instructions with the understanding that a person may be discriminated against;
- advertise property in a way that indicates a discriminatory preference or limitation;
- selectively advertise property in a manner that causes discrimination;
- quote or charge a different price, rental, or deposit amount;
- discriminate in making any determination of financial ability or in processing a loan application;
- advise a person of the value of a property based on neighborhood characteristics related to a protected class;
- discriminate against owners or tenants in providing property management services;
- make any effort to instruct or encourage other licensees to engage in discriminatory acts;
- establish discriminatory rules through a multiple listing service or other real estate service; or
- assist any person in a real estate transaction where there are reasonable grounds to believe that the person intends to discriminate.

The Commissioner's regulations cover just about every activity a real estate agent might engage in. Note that the discriminatory conduct in this list normally violates other antidiscrimination laws as well.

Complying with Fair Housing Laws

As you can see, these antidiscrimination laws cover a lot of territory. You must become familiar with their provisions and know what activities are prohibited. And you must remember that violating an antidiscrimination law does not require intent; if you do something that is considered discriminatory, you may be found guilty of violating the law even if you had only the best intentions.

Example: You're giving a listing presentation at the seller's home. The sellers are from Central America and speak only limited English. You do not speak Spanish. During the listing presentation, you feel increasingly uncomfortable because of the communication barrier. When you finish your presentation, the sellers tell you they want to list their property with you right away. Somewhat awkwardly, you suggest that they may want to list their property with an agent who speaks Spanish. You explain tactfully that you have a very difficult time understanding them and believe that they would be happier with a Spanish-speaking agent. They insist that they want to list with you. You tell them, in all honesty, that you think another agent would be able to give them better service. Your well-intentioned refusal to list their property could be regarded as discrimination on the basis of national origin, and you could be found guilty of violating federal or state antidiscrimination laws.

To help you avoid unintentional discrimination, we'll discuss some basic guidelines to follow when you list property and when you advertise the properties you list.

Compliance When Listing Property. When you're taking a listing, you should remember the following general rules.

Never say or imply that the presence of persons of a particular protected class (race, national origin, etc.) in a neighborhood could or will result in:

- lower property values,
- a change in the composition of the neighborhood,
- a more dangerous neighborhood, or
- a decline in the quality of the schools in the neighborhood.

Example: Chadwick is making a listing presentation to Thompson, a home-owner who is considering selling her property but isn't sure this is the right time. During the presentation, Chadwick says to Thompson, "I hear your neighbor, Bowen, has an offer on his house from a minority couple. You know, it might be a good idea to get your house listed and an offer nailed down be-fore any minority families move into the neighborhood. That way, you can get the best price for your house. If you wait until Bowen's house is sold—well, you just might not get as much for your house." This is an example of block-busting. Chadwick has violated the antidiscrimination laws.

Remember that you can't refuse to list property in a market area served by your office because of the presence or absence of particular protected groups. Nor can you state or imply that a home will be more difficult (or easier) to sell based on the presence or absence of a particular group of people.

Example: Norquist is discussing the listing price with the sellers. She tells them with enthusiasm, "Your house is in a great neighborhood! There aren't very many safe, white, middle-class neighborhoods left these days. Your home's really going to sell fast!" Norquist has just violated antidiscrimination laws.

Most agents would not act in an overtly discriminatory way; for example, they wouldn't turn away a prospective buyer because of the buyer's race. Yet some of those same agents might tell racial or ethnic jokes or make derogatory remarks about a particular group of people. Although these jokes or remarks don't necessarily indicate a willingness to actually discriminate in a transaction, a listener might assume that they do. Avoid participating in or going along with slurs against protected classes, no matter what the source.

When taking a listing, if the seller makes remarks that suggest that he might act in a discriminatory manner, you should discuss the fair housing laws and explain that you will strictly abide by them. Ask the seller to commit to complying with fair housing laws. If she refuses, you should not take the listing.

Example: You're making a listing presentation to the Boyds, a white couple who live in a predominantly white neighborhood. While you are discussing the listing terms, Mr. Boyd says, "You know, we certainly want the best price for our house. But we want you to be pretty careful who you show it to. We spent a lot of time fixing up this house, and we raised our kids here. We don't really want to change the neighborhood. Our neighbors are good, traditional, hard-working folks. We don't want a buyer who would lower everybody else's property values. You know what we mean."

Even though the Boyds don't come out and say so, they could easily be implying that they would not accept an offer from a buyer with a different racial or ethnic background. Mr. Boyd's comments are red flags. You should discuss fair housing principles with the couple, emphasizing that equal opportunity is the law. If the Boyds seem uncomfortable with what you are saying, you should refuse to take the listing.

If you refuse a listing because you think the sellers would discriminate against potential buyers, you should immediately report that to your broker.

In your relationships with potential sellers, be sure to provide equal service without regard to the seller's race, creed, color, religion, national origin, or membership in any other protected class. You should always follow the same listing procedures no matter who your client is.

Compliance When Advertising Properties. After you list a property, your next step is usually to advertise it. Keep in mind that you need to avoid discrimination in the way you market the property.

Sometimes statements or actions that seem innocent to you may be interpreted as discriminatory. Suppose that you're preparing and mailing out a flyer about your listing. You could be accused of discrimination if:

- you send flyers only to neighborhoods where the residents are all predominantly of the same race or ethnic background as the seller;
- you send flyers to all the neighboring properties except those owned by people of a particular race or ethnic background; or
- the wording of the flyer suggests that the recipient can control the type of person who will buy the property.

    Example: Your flyer says that a neighbor can, by referring potential buyers, "uphold the standards of the community." But you fail to specify what community standards you're referring to. Unless you clearly describe these standards in nondiscriminatory language, a reader might infer that he can control the race or ethnic background of the buyer. A court could rule that your flyer violates antidiscrimination laws.

As a real estate agent, you're likely to place many ads online and in print. Here are some things to watch out for when you're deciding on an advertising strategy after you take a listing.

- Where you choose to advertise, for example, could be seen as a form of racial steering.

    Example: You've listed a home in a predominantly minority neighborhood. Your sellers are members of the predominant minority group. You decide to advertise the property in the neighborhood weekly newspaper rather than the city newspaper or any other neighborhood weeklies. You feel this is the best choice, because you think other minority residents from the same neighborhood would be more interested in the home than residents of other neighborhoods. This is discriminatory.

- The choice of models you use in display advertising could also lead to charges of discrimination.

    Example: A broker is the listing agent for a large, exclusive housing development. She advertises the homes in the development by putting display ads in the local paper. In every ad she places, the buyers and sellers are depicted only by white models, even though 38% of the city's population is non-white. The use of only white models could be grounds for a discrimination suit.

    When pictures of people are used in advertising, you should take all reasonable steps to make sure that the pictures give the impression that the housing is open to everyone.

- All your residential advertising should contain the Equal Housing Opportunity logo or slogan. Your brochures, circulars, business cards, direct mail advertising, and all other forms of advertising should also include the logo or slogan. In addition, you must display a fair housing poster that includes the logo at any place of business involving the sale, rental, or financing of residential property.

Fig. 3.2 Fair housing logo

Actions That Do Not Violate Fair Housing Laws. Certain actions may initially appear to violate antidiscrimination laws, but in fact are not considered to be violations. Here are some examples.

- You may provide information required by a federal, state, or local agency for data collection or civil rights enforcement purposes.
- You may ask questions and provide information on forms in regard to marital status, in an effort to comply with the state's community property laws concerning the purchase, sale, or financing of real estate.
- You may ask questions or make statements as necessary to best serve the needs of a disabled person. This may include calling the attention of disabled clients or customers to particular buildings built or modified to meet their needs.
- You may use an affirmative marketing plan that tries to attract members of a particular group to an area or property that they might not otherwise be aware of. A brokerage or real estate board may also take affirmative steps to recruit minority employees or members.

Example: The developer of a large, moderately priced subdivision located on the fringes of the metropolitan area contacts you to assist in the sale of properties in the subdivision. The developer encourages you to target your marketing efforts toward recent immigrants who might be looking for affordable entry-level housing. In your area, most of the recent immigrants are non-white and live in a few older urban neighborhoods. You could devote extra effort to advertising in immigrant community newspapers or leafleting these neighborhoods, as long as you also advertise in other neighborhoods or in newspapers of wider circulation.

- You may truthfully answer questions about the racial composition of neighborhoods, even if this results in unintentional racial steering. If a buyer expresses a desire not to be shown homes in a particular neighborhood, even if the buyer makes that decision because of the race or other characteristics of the residents, you are not obligated to show them homes in that neighborhood.

Example: You are representing the Duvalls, who have only a limited amount of money to spend on their first home. You suggest a variety of neighborhoods where there are listings that fit their price range and other preferences, including the Greengate neighborhood. When Mr. Duvall asks about the people who live in Greengate, you truthfully respond that most of the residents belong to a particular immigrant group. Mr. Duvall says, "I'm not sure we'd feel comfortable there; we'd rather look in other areas." So long as you do not discourage the Duvalls from looking at properties in this neighborhood, you aren't required to show them houses in this area against their wishes.

Americans with Disabilities Act

To avoid discrimination and promote equal treatment, real estate licensees need to be familiar not only with the fair housing laws but also with the Americans with Disabilities Act. This federal law helps guarantee people with disabilities equal access to employment, goods, and services.

As we discussed, housing discrimination on the basis of disability is prohibited under the federal Fair Housing Act. The ADA has a different application. Under this law, no one may be discriminated against on the basis of disability in places of public accommodation or other commercial facilities.

The ADA defines a **disability** as any physical or mental impairment that substantially limits one or more major life activities. (This is the same definition of disability that's used in the Fair Housing Act.) The definition of **public accommodation** in the ADA covers any nonresidential place that is owned, operated, or leased by a private entity and that is open to the public, if operation of the facility affects commerce.

The ADA requires places of public accommodation and other commercial facilities to be accessible to the disabled. Physical barriers to access may have to be removed, wheelchair ramps added, and restrooms and other facilities modified.

Places of Public Accommodation and Commercial Facilities. A wide variety of facilities open to the public meet the ADA's definition of public accommodation. Hotels, restaurants, retail stores, schools, theaters, and the offices of service professionals are all covered. For instance, the office of a real estate brokerage is open to the public and therefore must be accessible to people with disabilities. Even commercial offices that aren't regularly visited by members of the public may fall within the broader category of commercial facilities and need to be made accessible.

ADA Requirements. If you frequently deal with commercial or retail properties, it's particularly important to be familiar with the ADA's requirements. The person who owns, leases, or operates a place of public accommodation is legally responsible for the removal of barriers to accessibility, so you may have to advise clients about modifications that may be necessary for the properties that they're considering purchasing or leasing.

Changes that the owner or tenant of a commercial property might need to make so that the building complies with the ADA include:

- creating an accessible entrance by installing ramps, adding parking spaces, or widening doorways;
- providing access to goods and services within a building by installing elevators, widening aisles, or adding Braille or raised-lettering signage;
- improving restrooms by adding larger stalls, grab bars, or more easily operated faucets and door handles; or
- relocating other features such as drinking fountains or pay phones so they are more easily reached.

Note that barrier removal is required only in public areas, and is not required where it is not "readily achievable." For example, the owner of a small, independently owned two-story retail business would not necessarily be required to install an elevator to the second story. However, the business would be required to make other accommodations to serve a disabled customer, such as having a salesperson bring items down to the customer on the first floor.

New construction. If you are representing someone who plans to build a new building, you should be aware that all new construction of places of public accommodation or other commercial facilities must comply with ADA requirements.

Model homes are not ordinarily required to meet ADA requirements. However, if a model home is also serving as a sales office for a subdivision or complex, then the area used as a sales office would be considered a place of public accommodation.

Antitrust Laws and Listing Practices

As you go about the business of obtaining listings and negotiating listing terms, you need to be aware of the restrictions imposed by federal antitrust laws. The purpose of antitrust laws is to foster fair business practices among competitors. These laws are based on the belief that free enterprise and healthy competition are good both for individual consumers and for the economy as a whole.

The most important federal antitrust law is the **Sherman Antitrust Act**, which was passed in 1890. The Sherman Act prohibits any agreement that has the effect of restraining trade. This includes a **conspiracy**, which is defined in the law as two or more business entities participating in a common scheme, the effect of which is the unreasonable restraint of trade.

The Sherman Act doesn't apply only to monolithic computer companies and oil companies. Since 1950, antitrust laws have also applied to the real estate industry. In a landmark case, the United States Supreme Court held that mandatory fee schedules established and enforced by a real estate board violated the Sherman Act (*United States v. National Association of Real Estate Boards*).

The penalties for violating antitrust laws are severe:

- If an individual is found guilty of violating the Sherman Act, he can be fined up to one million dollars and/or sentenced to ten years' imprisonment.
- If a corporation is found guilty of violating the Sherman Act, it can be fined up to one hundred million dollars.

To avoid violations, you need to be aware of four types of prohibited activities. These are:

- price fixing,
- group boycotts,
- tie-in arrangements, and
- market allocation.

Price Fixing

Price fixing is defined as the cooperative setting of prices or price ranges by competing firms. Real estate brokers can run afoul of the law against price fixing by setting, or appearing to set, uniform commission rates.

Example: Members of a local organization of real estate brokers decide that they should all insist on 7% commissions. They arrange for 7% to be pre-printed in all their listing forms. When potential sellers question the commission rate, the real estate agents say, "It's the same rate everybody charges." This would be considered a blatant case of illegal price fixing.

One of the best ways to avoid the appearance of price fixing is to scrupulously avoid discussing commission rates with competing agents. (Note that it's a discussion between *competing* agents that is dangerous—it's all right for a broker to discuss commission rates with her own sales agents.) The only exception to this general rule is that two competing brokers may discuss a commission split in a cooperative sale. In other words, a listing broker and a selling broker may discuss what percentage of the sales commission each of them will receive.

Even casually mentioning that you're changing your commission rate could lead to antitrust problems.

Example: A prominent broker attends a meeting of the local real estate brokers' organization. He's asked to give a brief speech about his firm's sales goals. In the middle of his comments, he mentions that he's going to raise his firm's commission rate, even if nobody else raises theirs. The profitability of his firm depends on it.

The broker's statements could be interpreted as an invitation to conspire to fix prices. If any other members of the brokers' organization follow his lead and raise their rates, they might be accused of accepting his invitation to fix prices.

As this example illustrates, a broker doesn't have to actually consult with other brokers to be accused of conspiring to fix commission rates. Merely mentioning, among competing brokers, an intent to increase rates could be enough to lead to an antitrust lawsuit.

When you're taking a listing, it's important to emphasize to the seller that the commission rate is freely negotiable. You should never imply that commission rates are set by law or by your local MLS or Board of REALTORS®. Don't mention the rates of competing agents, either.

Example: Harris is making a listing presentation to Bell. When Bell asks Harris about the commission, Harris casually says, "Oh, the commission rate is 7%." When Bell asks if she has to pay a 7% commission, Harris replies, "All the agents around here charge a 7% commission. In fact, if you and I agreed to a lower commission rate, I'm not even sure that the MLS would accept the listing." Harris has violated the antitrust laws.

Remember that in California, a listing agreement for a residential property with up to four units must have a provision in boldface type stating that the amount or rate of the commission is negotiable between the seller and broker, not fixed by law. (See Chapter 2.)

Group Boycotts

Antitrust laws also prohibit group boycotts. A **group boycott** is an agreement between business competitors to exclude another competitor from fair participation in business activities. For example, an agreement between two or more real estate brokers to exclude another broker from fair participation in real estate activities would be a group boycott. The purpose of a group boycott is to hurt or destroy a competitor, and this is automatically unlawful under the antitrust laws.

A group boycott doesn't have to be based on a formal arrangement or carried out by a large group of people.

> **Example:** Barker and Jaffrey, two real estate brokers, meet to discuss an offer on a house. After discussing the offer, they begin talking about the business practices of a third broker, Hutton. Barker, angry with Hutton because of a past business transaction, claims that Hutton is dishonest. Barker says, "That sleazy jerk! I'll never do business with him again!" Jaffrey laughs. Barker then says, "You know, I've stopped returning Hutton's calls when he's asking about my listings. You should do the same thing. With any luck, the guy will be out of business in a few months." Jaffrey, who also disapproves of Hutton, agrees to go along with what Barker has suggested. Barker and Jaffrey could be found guilty of a conspiracy to boycott Hutton.

It's one thing to think another broker is dishonest or unethical and to choose to avoid him. It's another matter entirely to encourage other brokers to do the same. You should never tell clients or other agents not to work with a competing agent because (for example) you have doubts about that agent's competence or integrity.

It would also be considered a group boycott if a multiple listing service refused to allow a broker to become a member because he had a different kind of fee schedule. For example, an MLS can't refuse membership to a brokerage firm just because it charges a small flat fee for a listing, rather than a percentage of the sales price.

Tie-in Arrangements

Another type of business practice that antitrust laws prohibit is a tie-in arrangement. A **tie-in arrangement** is defined as an agreement to sell one product only on the condition that the buyer also purchases a different (or "tied") product.

Example: Fisher is a subdivision developer. Tyler, a builder, wants to buy a lot. Fisher tells Tyler that he will sell him a lot only if Tyler agrees that after Tyler builds a house on the lot, he will list the improved property with Fisher.

The type of agreement described in this example is called a **list-back agreement**. List-back agreements are not unlawful. But requiring a lot buyer to enter into a list-back agreement as a condition of the sale is a tie-in arrangement and violates the antitrust laws.

Another danger area for real estate agents is agreeing to manage property only if the owner agrees to list that property with you.

Example: Dahl, a broker, is negotiating a property management agreement with Heinz, a property owner. Dahl wants to include a clause in the agreement that provides that if Heinz ever decides to sell the managed property, he will list the property with Dahl. If Dahl tells Heinz that she'll enter into a management agreement only if it includes this listing clause, Dahl is violating the antitrust laws.

Market Allocation

Market allocation occurs when competing brokers agree not to sell: 1) certain products or services in certain specified areas; 2) in specified areas; or 3) to certain customers in specified areas. Market allocation between competing brokers is illegal, as it limits competition.

As with group boycotts, it's the collective action that makes market allocation illegal. An individual broker is free to determine the market areas in which she wants her brokerage to specialize; similarly, she can allocate territory to particular salespersons within her brokerage. It's allocation of territory between competing firms that is considered group action and therefore a violation of antitrust law.

Example: Broker Nguyen of ABC Realty assigns Salesperson Brentano to handle all incoming customers in the luxury home market, and assigns Salesperson Paxton to all incoming customers in the vacant land market. This practice does not violate antitrust law.

However, if Broker Nguyen of ABC Realty and Broker Carson of XYZ Realty agree to allocate customers so that ABC Realty will handle all luxury homes and XYZ Realty will handle all vacant land, that would be an antitrust violation.

Environmental Issues

As you saw in Chapter 2, the transfer disclosure statement calls for the disclosure of environmental hazards. Because of the growing concern about environmental hazards related to real estate—even residential real estate—it's important to discuss some of those hazards and the laws related to them. While you aren't expected to be an environmental expert, you should have a basic understanding of the environmental problems facing property owners and buyers today.

Environmental Laws

A number of federal and state environmental laws affect real estate agents and property sellers and buyers. We will just highlight some of the most important laws.

National Environmental Policy Act. The National Environmental Policy Act (NEPA) requires federal agencies to provide an **environmental impact statement** (EIS) for any action that may have a significant effect on the environment. NEPA applies to all types of federal development, such as construction projects, the building of highways, and waste control. NEPA also applies to private uses or developments that require the approval of a federal agency in the form of a license, a permit, or even a federal loan guaranty. In these cases, federal agencies may require submission of an EIS before approving the use or development.

An EIS should disclose the impact of the development on energy consumption, sewage systems, school population, drainage, water facilities, and other environmental, economic, and social factors.

California Environmental Quality Act. California has its own version of NEPA, the California Environmental Quality Act (CEQA). This law applies to public or private projects that receive any form of state or local approval or permit if they may have a significant effect on the environment.

To meet CEQA requirements, the public agency overseeing the project must prepare an environmental impact report (EIR), which is similar to the EIS required under NEPA. An EIR is not required when the public agency overseeing the project rules that it will not have significant adverse effects on the environment.

California Coastal Act. The California Coastal Act regulates development along the state's coastline. This law established the California Coastal Commission, which researches ways to protect the California coastline and controls development along the coast.

The Coastal Commission has several regional divisions that oversee coastal programs at the local level. No development is allowed in the coastal zone without a coastal development permit from the appropriate agency.

CERCLA. One of the most important environmental laws is the federal Comprehensive Environmental Response, Compensation, and Liability Act (CERCLA). CERCLA concerns liability for environmental cleanup costs and has dramatically changed the way property buyers view potential environmental liability.

CERCLA is best known for its creation of a multibillion-dollar fund called the **Superfund**. The purpose of the Superfund is to clean up hazardous waste dumps and respond to spills of hazardous materials. CERCLA also created a process for identifying the parties who are responsible for cleanup costs. Cleanup costs may include both the cost of cleaning up a particular property and the cost of cleaning up any neighboring property that may have been contaminated by the hazardous substances.

The parties responsible for the cleanup may include both present and previous landowners. In some cases, the current owners of contaminated property may be required to pay for the cleanup even if they did not cause the contamination. A buyer who is considering purchasing property that may have been contaminated should consult an environmental engineer and/or an attorney specializing in environmental law.

Clean Water Act. Of particular concern to land developers is the federal law protecting **wetlands**—swamps, marshes, ponds, and similar areas where the soil is saturated for part of the year. Section 404 of the Clean Water Act makes it illegal for a private landowner to fill or drain wetlands on his property without obtaining a permit from the U.S. Army Corps of Engineers. Violations may be punished with an order to restore the wetlands, civil penalties, and even criminal sanctions.

The presence of a wetland is not necessarily a complete barrier to the development of a property, though. A landowner may fill a wetland for development if she creates or restores new wetlands elsewhere, so that there is no net loss of wetland area. Alternatively, the landowner may purchase the right to develop in wetland areas by paying into a government fund that is used to develop new wetlands elsewhere.

Endangered Species Act. Both the federal government and the state of California have passed an Endangered Species Act. The purpose of these laws is to conserve habitats that shelter endangered or threatened species.

The federal and state governments each maintain their own lists of endangered species. A species may be included in either the federal list or the state list, or both. In California, there are dozens of listed species, many of which make their habitat primarily on private lands.

As with wetlands, however, the presence of an endangered species on a property does not completely bar development; private landowners may develop land supporting listed species if they agree to a Habitat Conservation Plan and undertake conservation measures. Landowners who agree to a plan and carry it out won't be required to take additional steps later on, even if the environmental circumstances change.

As a real estate agent, you should be familiar with the basics of all of these environmental laws. And you shouldn't hesitate to refer prospective buyers of developable land to the U.S. Environmental Protection Agency, the U.S. Fish and Wildlife Service, or the California Department of Fish and Game if they have any questions as to whether these laws may limit how they can use the land.

Environmental Hazards

Now let's take a look at some of the more common environmental hazards that real estate agents need to know about.

Asbestos. Asbestos was used for many years in insulation on plumbing pipes and heat ducts, and as general insulation material. It can also be found in floor tile and roofing material. In its original condition, asbestos is considered relatively harmless; but when asbestos dust filters into the air, it can cause lung cancer. Asbestos becomes a hazard in two ways: when it gets old and starts to disintegrate into a fine dust, and when it is damaged or removed during remodeling projects.

There are three methods of dealing with the presence of asbestos:

1. enclosure (this involves placing an airtight barrier between the asbestos and the rest of the space);
2. encapsulation (this involves covering the asbestos with an adhesive that will permanently seal in the asbestos fibers); or
3. removal.

Each of these three methods should only be undertaken by an experienced professional.

Urea Formaldehyde. Urea formaldehyde may be found in the adhesives used in pressed wood building materials, which are widely used in furniture, kitchen cabinets, and some types of paneling.

Urea formaldehyde may cause cancer, skin rashes, and breathing problems. However, it emits significant amounts of dangerous gas only in the first few years. Older urea formaldehyde materials are not considered dangerous.

Radon. Radon, a colorless, odorless gas, is actually present almost everywhere. It is found wherever uranium is deposited in the earth's crust. As uranium decays, radon gas is formed and seeps from the earth, usually into the atmosphere. However, radon sometimes collects in buildings. For example, radon may enter a house through cracks in the foundation or through floor drains. Exposure to dangerous levels of radon gas may cause lung cancer.

There are three ways to lower radon levels in a home:

1. sealing the holes and cracks that allow the gas to enter the home;
2. increasing ventilation to dilute the gas, especially in the areas where radon enters, such as the basement or crawl space; and
3. pressurizing the home to keep the gas out.

Lead-based Paint. Lead, though useful for many things, is extremely toxic to human beings. Children are especially susceptible to lead poisoning because they absorb it more quickly and have a more adverse reaction to its toxicity. Lead damages the brain, the kidneys, and the central nervous system.

The most common source of lead in the home is lead-based paint. Lead is now banned in consumer paint, but lead-based paint is still found in many homes built before 1978. As lead-based paint deteriorates, or if it is sanded or scraped, it forms a lead dust that accumulates inside and outside the home. This dust can be breathed in or ingested, increasing the risk of toxic lead exposure.

If there is lead-based paint in a home, it can be either eliminated or covered with non-lead-based paint. This requires special equipment and training; homeowners shouldn't try to handle the problem on their own.

In some cases, a seller or landlord is required by law to make disclosures concerning lead-based paint to prospective buyers or tenants. This disclosure law is discussed in Chapter 2.

Underground Storage Tanks. Underground storage tanks are found not only on commercial and industrial properties, but also on residential properties. A storage tank is considered underground if at least 10% of its volume (including piping) is below the earth's surface. Probably the most common commercial use of underground storage tanks is for gas stations. Chemical plants, paint manufacturers, and other industries use underground storage tanks to store toxic liquids. In the residential setting, older homes used underground storage tanks to store fuel oil.

The principal danger from underground storage tanks is that when they grow old they begin to rust, leaking toxic products into the soil or, even more dangerously, into the groundwater.

Removing underground storage tanks and cleaning up the contaminated soil can be time-consuming and expensive. Both federal and state laws regulate the removal of storage tanks and the necessary cleanup.

Water Contamination. Water can be contaminated by a variety of agents, including bacteria, viruses, nitrates, metals such as lead or mercury, fertilizers and pesticides, and radon. These contaminants may come from underground storage tanks, industrial discharge, urban area runoff, malfunctioning septic systems, and runoff from agricultural areas. Drinking contaminated water can cause physical symptoms that range from mild stomachaches to kidney and liver damage, cancer, and death.

If a homeowner uses a well as a water source, it should be tested by health authorities or private laboratories at least once a year. If well water becomes contaminated, the property owner may have to dig a new well.

Illegal Drug Manufacturing. If a property has been the site of illegal drug manufacturing, there may be substantial health risks for the occupants. The chemicals used to manufacture certain illegal drugs are highly toxic, and the effects of the contamination can linger for a long time.

If property is currently being used to manufacture illegal drugs, it can be seized by the government. This can occur even if the owner has no knowledge of the illegal drug activity.

> **Example:** Meyers owns a single-family home that has been used as a rental property for several years. Unknown to Meyers, the current tenants are

manufacturing illegal drugs in the basement of the home. The property could be seized by the government, even though Meyers knows nothing about the drug activity.

Of course, a property should not be listed or sold until any conditions that could subject the property to seizure have been eliminated.

Mold. Mold is a commonplace problem, especially in damp parts of houses such as basements and bathrooms. For most people, the presence of mold does not cause any adverse effects. However, for people who are allergic to mold or who have respiratory problems, the presence of mold may render a house unlivable. You may hear references to "toxic mold," which is something of a misnomer; certain varieties of black mold can be particularly problematic for those who are sensitive to mold, but generally do not pose any more of a health hazard for most people than other types of mold.

Mold can never be completely eliminated, but it can be controlled by cutting off sources of moisture. Mold that is already growing can be removed by scrubbing with a water and bleach solution. Carpet or tile that is affected by mold may need to be removed and thrown out.

Mold problems that you're aware of should be treated as a latent defect and disclosed to prospective buyers. You should also disclose any knowledge of previous incidents of flooding or water damage, since that can start the growth of mold. Bear in mind that mold may grow out of sight, inside walls or heating ducts, and will not necessarily be discovered in an inspection, so your disclosure is particularly important.

"Mold contingencies" are sometimes written into purchase agreements. A mold contingency allows the buyer to back out of the sale if mold is found during the inspection process.

Geologic Hazards. Geologic hazards are a significant concern for many property owners in California. Major potential geologic problems include landslides, flooding, subsidence, and earthquakes.

As with other environmental hazards, you should disclose any geologic hazards affecting a property as latent defects. In addition, information about designated hazard areas for flooding and earthquakes must be included in the natural hazards disclosure statement, which is discussed in Chapter 2.

Fig. 3.3 Environmental hazards

Environmental Hazards that May Affect Homes

- Asbestos
- Urea formaldehyde
- Radon gas
- Lead-based paint
- Underground storage tanks
- Water contamination
- Illegal drug manufacturing
- Mold
- Geologic hazards: landslides, flooding, subsidence, earthquakes

Landslides. Probably the most costly geologic problem affecting homeowners is landslides. It's quite common for a house to be built close to the top of a cliff overlooking a body of water, in order to take advantage of the view. However, the weight of the house on unstable soil, particularly after heavy rainfall, can cause ground movement downhill, damaging the foundation or even tearing the house apart.

When you're dealing with a property located on or near a steep slope, you should always look for signs of ground movement. Tilting trees, active soil erosion, and cracking, dipping, or slumping ground are all indicators of slide activity. A property owner may take corrective steps, such as building retaining walls or rockeries, but they are expensive and unlikely to completely solve the problem.

If you see any evidence of landslide activity, it may be wise to consult with a geologist, in order to assess the magnitude of the problem. In addition, if you have listed a property where there is any evidence of ground movement, that should be considered a latent defect and disclosed to potential buyers.

Flooding. Flooding can also be a serious problem for property owners. Whenever property is located in a flood plain—in the low-lying, flat areas immediately adjacent to a river—there is cause for concern. A prudent agent will check for signs of previous flood damage to structures, particularly in basements and foundations, and disclose any problems. An agent listing a flood-prone property should disclose frequent flooding as a latent defect.

Subsidence. Another potential geologic problem is subsidence, the collapse of ground into underground cavities. This can occur naturally, but only in areas of particularly porous bedrock. In most cases, subsidence is caused by man-made cavities. It may happen when forgotten underground storage tanks collapse, or when underground tanks have been removed but the soil has not been properly replaced. It is most common where mining has occurred. Over 50,000 abandoned mines exist throughout California, so before engaging in new construction in areas where mining once occurred, it may be advisable to obtain maps from government agencies that depict old mines.

Earthquakes. Earthquakes are the least predictable and least controllable of geologic problems. They are also potentially the most destructive.

However, steps can be taken to protect buildings against earthquakes. In fact, seismic retrofitting can make a property more desirable and increase its value. The most important step in this process involves bolting elements of a home's wood frame to the underlying foundation. Many contractors are able to perform this type of work, and information about seismic retrofitting is widely available from state and local government agencies.

Real Estate Agent's Responsibilities

As you make your listing presentation and later prepare offers to purchase, keep environmental issues in mind. Learn to recognize signs of environmental hazards. If you suspect that the property has environmental issues, recommend that your client consult an environmental attorney or other environmental expert.

If you are representing a seller whose property has environmental problems, it's best to have an attorney draft the appropriate disclosures. And if you represent buyers who are interested in purchasing a property with environmental problems, it's crucial to make sure that they understand the potential risks of such a purchase. These risks should be explained to them by their attorney.

Naturally, contaminated property should only change hands after the cleanup has been completed. But even then, under federal environmental laws, the buyers may be assuming more potential liability than they are aware of. As the new owners of the property, the buyers may be held responsible for any additional cleanup costs, even though they had nothing to do with the contamination.

Chapter Summary

1. California's Real Estate Law imposes certain restrictions on your listing activities. As a salesperson, you can be paid your commission only by your own broker. You can't be paid by other brokers or sales agents, or by the principal. And you may not sue the principal for a commission; only the broker may sue the principal.

2. A listing agreement belongs to the listing broker. It is a contract between the property seller and the broker; you sign the listing agreement only as an agent of your broker. Should you stop working for the listing broker, the listing remains with the broker. You can't take it with you to your new broker.

3. The federal Fair Housing Act prohibits discrimination based on race, color, religion, sex, national origin, disability, or familial status. In transactions related to housing, California antidiscrimination laws prohibit discrimination based on race, color, religion, ancestry, national origin, sex, gender, gender expression, gender identity, disability, medical condition, age, sexual orientation, marital status, familial status, genetic information, or source of income. Any discriminatory conduct by a real estate licensee is unlawful without exception.

4. While dealing with potential clients and taking listings, you need to scrupulously follow all fair housing laws. Never imply that the presence of a particular group of residents will change property values or other characteristics of a neighborhood. Never refuse to list a property because of the seller's race, national origin, or another protected characteristic. Avoid any kind of discriminatory slur, including telling racial or ethnic jokes or passively listening to them. You should also discuss fair housing laws with the seller before taking a listing. If you think the seller may discriminate against potential purchasers, refuse to take the listing.

5. When you advertise listed properties, make sure that all your advertising complies with fair housing laws. Never send flyers or choose advertising media based on discriminatory ideas, and make sure any models included in ads do not present discriminatory implications. Remember to include the fair housing logo or slogan in your ads.

6. Antitrust laws prohibit price fixing, group boycotts, tie-in arrangements, and market allocation. To avoid charges of price fixing, you should never discuss your commission rates with competing agents, and you must be sure to explain to sellers that the commission rate is fully negotiable. Never use a listing agreement form that has a commission amount or rate already set.

7. Environmental laws that may affect a real estate transaction include the National Environmental Policy Act (NEPA), the California Environmental Quality Act (CEQA), the California Coastal Act, and the Comprehensive Environmental Response, Compensation, and Liability Act (CERCLA). CERCLA is particularly important, because it may impose liability on present owners for the cost of cleaning up hazardous substances, regardless of fault.

8. Environmental hazards you need to be aware of include asbestos, urea formaldehyde, radon, lead-based paint, underground storage tanks, water contamination, the effects of illegal drug manufacturing, mold, and geologic problems. If you recognize potential environmental hazards in a listed property, advise the seller to consult an environmental professional.

Key Terms

Blockbusting: Attempting to induce owners to list or sell their homes by predicting that members of another race or ethnic group, or people with a disability, will be moving into the neighborhood.

Steering: Channeling prospective buyers or tenants to or away from particular neighborhoods based on their race, religion, national origin, or membership in any other protected class.

Redlining: The refusal by a lender to make loans secured by property in a certain neighborhood because of the racial or ethnic composition of the neighborhood.

Place of public accommodation: A nonresidential facility operated by a private entity and open to the public, if operation of the facility affects commerce.

Conspiracy: An agreement or plan between two or more persons to perform an unlawful act.

Price fixing: The cooperative setting of prices by competing firms. Price fixing is an automatic violation of antitrust laws.

Group boycott: In the real estate profession, an agreement between two or more real estate brokers to exclude other brokers from equal participation in real estate activities.

Tie-in arrangement: An agreement to sell one product, only on the condition that the buyer also purchases a different product. A tie-in arrangement is an automatic violation of antitrust laws.

Market allocation: When competing brokers agree not to sell: 1) certain products or services in certain specified areas; 2) in specified areas; or 3) to certain customers in specified areas.

Environmental hazards: Dangerous elements or conditions present on the property that real estate agents should be aware of, and warn clients about, including asbestos, urea formaldehyde, radon, lead-based paint, underground storage tanks, water contamination, illegal drug manufacturing, mold, and geologic hazards.

Chapter Quiz

1. Salesperson Jackson and Salesperson Robinson work for the same broker, Stellar Properties. They've both worked closely with a particular buyer. When that buyer finally purchases a house, Stellar Properties receives the selling broker's share of the commission and pays Jackson half of it. Jackson then gives half of her share of the commission to Robinson. This is:
   a. legal, because once a commission share has been paid to a salesperson, she is entitled to do whatever she wants with it
   b. legal, because agents are allowed to share compensation if they work for the same broker
   c. illegal, because a broker can share a commission only with another licensed broker
   d. illegal, because a commission split must be handled by the broker or brokers involved

2. Violations of the Rumford Act are investigated by the:
   a. Bureau of Real Estate
   b. Department of Fair Employment and Housing
   c. Department of Housing and Urban Development
   d. California Coastal Commission

3. Which of the following is not an example of illegal steering?
   a. An agent working with a buyer who has a disability calls his attention to a property with modifications that meet his needs
   b. An agent avoids showing an unmarried buyer houses in neighborhoods where most residents are married couples with children
   c. An agent working with a white couple doesn't tell them about homes in predominantly minority neighborhoods
   d. An agent working with a minority couple doesn't tell them about homes in predominantly white neighborhoods

4. Your advertising for residential properties should always include:
   a. models from the same ethnic group as the residents of the neighborhood you are advertising in
   b. models of a different ethnic background from the residents of the neighborhood you are advertising in
   c. the Equal Housing Opportunity logo or slogan
   d. a specific explanation of the standards of the community

5. Which of the following actions is most likely to be considered discriminatory?
    a. When a white buyer asks about the racial composition of a neighborhood, an agent truthfully answers that it is predominantly minority
    b. The listing agent for a home in a predominantly minority neighborhood decides to advertise only in the neighborhood newspaper because he thinks other minorities are most likely to be interested in the home
    c. A brokerage uses a marketing plan to let minority buyers know about properties in predominantly white neighborhoods that they might not otherwise be aware of
    d. A white couple expresses a desire not to be shown homes in a minority neighborhood, and their agent complies with their request

6. Which of the following is an example of price fixing?
    a. A listing broker and a selling broker discuss a commission split in a cooperative sale
    b. An agent making a listing presentation tells the seller that she is asking for a 7% commission, but emphasizes that the commission is negotiable
    c. A broker holds a staff meeting with her sales agents to discuss commission rates for the office
    d. A broker is having lunch with two other brokers and mentions that he is raising his commission rate, but there is no further discussion of the matter

7. Which law requires an environmental impact report (EIR) for projects that may have a significant effect on the environment?
    a. California Environmental Quality Act
    b. California Coastal Act
    c. Clean Water Act
    d. CERCLA

8. Which environmental law requires developers to obtain a permit from the U.S. Army Corps of Engineers?
    a. Clean Water Act
    b. Endangered Species Act
    c. National Environmental Policy Act
    d. California Coastal Act

9. Urea formaldehyde is found:
    a. in some floor tiles and roofing material
    b. wherever uranium is deposited in the earth's crust
    c. in the adhesives used in some pressed wood building materials
    d. in underground storage tanks

10. As a real estate agent, what is your responsibility with respect to environmental issues?

    a. Recommending that your clients obtain expert advice if you see signs of environmental hazards

    b. Making sure that an environmental impact statement is provided to the buyer

    c. Deciding what corrective action needs to be taken to solve the problem

    d. All of the above

Answer Key

1. d. Two salespersons working for the same broker may split a commission, but the commission split must be handled by their broker. A salesperson can only receive a commission through her broker.

2. b. Under the Rumford Act, also known as the Fair Employment and Housing Act, housing discrimination complaints are investigated by the Department of Fair Employment and Housing.

3. a. An agent can legitimately bring properties that are especially suited to the needs of a disabled buyer to the buyer's attention.

4. c. Regardless of what type of advertising you use to market a home, it should always include the Equal Housing Opportunity logo or slogan.

5. b. Advertising can be considered discriminatory if it appears only in a publication directed toward the minority neighborhood where the property is located. The advertising should also appear where it will be seen by a broader spectrum of the population.

6. d. Any communication between competing brokers about prices could be considered an invitation to engage in price fixing, even if the brokers don't explicitly decide to cooperate in fixing prices.

7. a. The California Environmental Quality Act (CEQA) requires an EIR for projects that may have a significant effect on the environment.

8. a. The Clean Water Act makes it illegal for a private landowner to fill or drain wetlands without a permit from the U.S. Army Corps of Engineers.

9. c. Urea formaldehyde is found in the adhesives used in some pressed wood building materials.

10. a. If there are environmental issues concerning a property, you should always recommend that your clients seek expert advice from an environmental engineer or attorney.

4

Evaluating and Pricing Property

The Agent's Role in Pricing Property

Value

- Types of value
- Value vs. price or cost

Competitive Market Analysis

- Analyzing the seller's property
- Choosing comparable properties
- Making adjustments to the comparables
- Estimating market value
- Completing a CMA
- CMA form

The Problem of a Low Appraisal

Introduction

Under normal conditions, a property that is listed at a competitive price will sell within a reasonable time frame. So, just what is involved in determining a competitive listing price? And what happens if your seller insists on listing her home at a ridiculously inflated price? What then? Should you simply take the listing and hope for the best?

In this chapter, we will discuss the listing agent's role in evaluating and pricing a seller's home, the dangers of setting a listing price too high, the concept of value, and how to complete a competitive market analysis.

The Agent's Role in Pricing Property

It is your seller's responsibility—not yours—to decide on a listing price for his home. But the average seller does not have the expertise to arrive at a realistic price. Your seller depends on you for information and advice about this important decision. Without your expertise, the seller could easily underprice or overprice his property. Either of these mistakes could have serious consequences for your client, and for you.

Example: Jeffries is listing his home with you. He asks you for advice on setting a listing price, but you tell him that the price is up to him.

Jeffries has checked some real estate websites and learned about a few nearby houses that have been for sale for many months. He believes the houses haven't sold because they're overpriced. He thinks his house is comparable to these other houses, but he wants a quick sale. So Jeffries sets his listing price by deducting $10,000 from the listing price of the other houses. He ends up listing his house for $620,000.

Jeffries's house is actually very appealing and sells quickly at that price. When his house is appraised, he discovers to his dismay that it was actually worth about $650,000. He's very angry—he just lost $30,000, and he considers it entirely your fault. If he decided to sue, your broker could lose the commission and might even have to pay additional damages as well.

On the other hand, suppose that when Jeffries sets his listing price, he thinks his house is worth much more than it really is. He sets the listing price at $690,000, and his house languishes on the market for several months. Finally, your listing agreement expires and Jeffries decides to list the property with another firm. Because of an inflated listing price, Jeffries waited in vain for a sale, you wasted a good deal of effort trying to sell an overpriced house, and your reputation in the neighborhood suffered as your "For Sale" sign faded and was then removed without a "Sold!" banner.

Your ability to suggest a competitive listing price is one of the most important services you can provide a seller. Your advice on a listing price will generally take the form of a **competitive market analysis** (CMA). A CMA compares your seller's house to other similar houses that are on the market or have recently sold. The listing or sales prices of those other houses help the seller set a realistic listing price for her own house.

A CMA is similar to an appraisal, but it is not an appraisal. As the listing agent, your role is very different from that of an appraiser. Your job is to provide the seller with information about the sales prices of similar homes. This is the information that is contained in your CMA. The seller uses this information to decide how much to ask for her property.

An appraiser, on the other hand, uses his professional experience to estimate the property's market value as of a specific date. The appraiser usually does this for a lender, to help the lender set a maximum loan amount for the loan applicant who wants to buy the property. The appraiser bases this estimate on a wide variety of data, including general social and economic data. An appraisal is much more complex than a competitive market analysis and is based on more information.

Value

The value of a home has many consequences for the owner. The value largely determines not only how much it costs to purchase the home, but also the financing, the property tax assessment, the insurance coverage, the potential rental rate, the eventual selling price, and the income tax consequences of its sale.

To estimate the value of a home, you need a general understanding of the concept of value. First of all, keep in mind that value is created by people. It is not so much the intrinsic qualities of an item that make it valuable, but rather our attitudes toward it. For example, if it were to begin raining gold instead of water, gold would become a nuisance and its value would disappear. Yet its intrinsic qualities would be the same whether it was a rare and precious metal or a too-common nuisance.

Types of Value

Appraisers distinguish between several different types of value. A property's value can vary depending on which type of value is in question in a given situation. For example, **value in use** is the subjective value placed on a property by someone who owns or uses it. By contrast, **value in exchange** (commonly referred to as **market value**) is the objective value of a property in the eyes of the average person. The difference between these two types of value is one reason the seller needs your help in setting a listing price.

Example: Darnell owns a large old house that has been in her family for generations. Because of the history of the house, it is very valuable to Darnell. In other words, its value in use is very high. Yet if an objective third party were considering buying the house, he would not be willing to pay very much for it. The plumbing is poor and the design is very outdated. The property's value in exchange is not nearly as high as its value in use.

Real estate agents are concerned with value in exchange, or market value. Here is the most widely accepted definition of market value, the one used by financial institution regulatory agencies:

The most probable price which a property should bring in a competitive and open market under all conditions requisite to a fair sale, the buyer and seller each acting prudently and knowledgeably, and assuming the price is not affected by undue stimulus.

Value vs. Price or Cost

When you're estimating the value of property, always remember that there's an important distinction between market value and market price. **Market price** is the price actually paid for a property, regardless of whether the parties to the transaction were informed and acting free of unusual pressure. Market value, as you've seen, is what should be paid if a property is purchased and sold under all the conditions requisite to a fair sale.

Another related concept is that of cost. **Cost** is the amount of money that was paid to acquire the property and build the structures on it. A property's cost, value, and price may all be different.

Example: A developer paid $75,000 for a parcel of vacant land and then spent $240,000 to build a house on the land. After the house was completed, the property was worth $350,000. But the developer needed some fast cash, so he sold the property at the "fire sale" price of $330,000. The cost of the house was $315,000, the value of the house was $350,000, and the price of the house was $330,000.

The basis for a good listing price for a home is its market value, not its original cost or purchase price. And the real estate agent's best tool for estimating market value is competitive market analysis.

Competitive Market Analysis

Although competitive market analysis isn't the only way to arrive at a listing price, it's often the best option. For instance, it has two key advantages over the "eyeball" approach to setting a listing price: It's reliable, and it's easy to explain.

With the eyeball approach, the real estate agent simply walks through the seller's house, observes its features, and then mentally compares them to features he's observed in other houses. The agent then decides on what he feels is a competitive price. A price reached in this way can be far from the true market value. And the agent won't have any data to support his conclusion if the seller questions him about it.

An estimate of value based on your gut feelings is especially problematic when the seller is expecting to get more for her property than it's worth. Unless you can back up your "low" estimate with facts and figures that are easy to understand, you will lose credibility as well as the seller's good will. So it's important to have a simple method of valuing property that is easy to apply and to explain.

In a formal appraisal, the appraiser may estimate the property's value by applying these three methods:

1. **Cost approach to value.** Estimating how much it would cost to build a similar structure, and then subtracting the depreciation that has accrued.
2. **Income approach to value.** Estimating value based on the income the property could potentially generate.
3. **Sales comparison approach to value.** Estimating value by comparing the property to similar properties that have recently sold.

The first two methods can be complicated, time-consuming, and difficult for many sellers to understand. The third method, the sales comparison approach, is much simpler to use and easier for the seller to understand. It's also considered the most reliable method for appraising residential property. As a result, real estate agents have borrowed the sales comparison approach to value and modified it for their own use. This modified sales comparison approach is called competitive market analysis, or CMA.

With a CMA, you estimate the value of your seller's property by comparing it to similar nearby properties that have sold recently or are for sale. (These are referred to as comparable properties or **comparables**.) CMAs are effective because an informed buyer acting free of pressure will not pay more for a particular property than she would have to pay for an equally desirable substitute property. Thus, if the seller is objective, he will base the listing price on the prices recently paid for similar properties in the same area.

The steps involved in completing a CMA include:

1. collecting and analyzing information about the seller's property;
2. choosing the comparable properties;
3. comparing the seller's property to the comparables and adjusting the value of the comparables accordingly; and
4. estimating a realistic listing price for the seller's property.

There are a variety of computer programs available to help you prepare a CMA. (Your broker's office or the MLS may provide one for your use.) However, even though these programs simplify the task considerably, you still need to understand the principles underlying the process.

Analyzing the Seller's Property

The first step in creating a CMA is to gather and study information about the seller's property. Naturally, you should pay the most attention to the elements that have the greatest impact on value. These elements fall into three categories:

1. the property's neighborhood,
2. the property (or site) itself, and
3. the improvements on the property.

As you collect information about the seller's property (sometimes called the **subject property**), keep in mind that you will need to gather the same information about the properties you choose as comparables.

Neighborhood Analysis. Few factors have as much impact on a property's value as its location, or neighborhood. A neighborhood is an area that contains similar types of properties; it may be residential, commercial, industrial, or agricultural. Its boundaries may be determined by physical obstacles (such as highways and bodies of water), land use patterns, the ages and values of homes or other buildings, and/or the economic status of the residents.

Neighborhood characteristics set the upper and lower limits of a property's value. A high-quality property cannot overcome the adverse influence of a poor neighborhood. And the value of a relatively weak property is enhanced by a desirable neighborhood.

Here are some specific factors to look at when gathering data about a residential neighborhood:

1. **Percentage of homeownership.** Is there a high degree of owner-occupancy, or do rental properties predominate? Owner-occupied homes are generally better maintained and less susceptible to deterioration.

2. **Vacant homes and lots.** An unusual number of vacant homes or lots suggests a low level of interest in the area, which has a negative effect on property values. On the other hand, significant construction activity indicates strong interest in the area.

3. **Conformity.** The homes in a neighborhood should be reasonably similar in style, age, size, and quality. Strictly enforced zoning and private restrictions promote conformity and protect property values.

4. **Changing land use.** Is the neighborhood in the middle of a transition from residential use to some other type of use? If so, the properties may be losing their value.

5. **Contour of the land.** Mildly rolling topography is preferable to terrain that is either monotonously flat or excessively hilly.

6. **Streets.** Wide, gently curving streets are more appealing than narrow or straight streets. Streets should be hard-surfaced and well maintained.

7. **Utilities.** Does the neighborhood have electricity, gas, water, sewers, and telephones? What about cable television and Internet access?

8. **Nuisances.** Not surprisingly, nuisances (odors, eyesores, industrial noises or pollutants, or exposure to unusual winds, smog, or fog) in or near a neighborhood hurt property values.

9. **Reputation.** Is the neighborhood considered prestigious, in comparison to others in the community? If so, that will increase property values.

10. **Proximity.** How far is it to traffic arterials and to important points such as downtown, employment centers, and shopping centers?

Fig. 4.1 Neighborhood data form

NEIGHBORHOOD DATA

Property adjacent to:

NORTH _____ Plum Boulevard, garden apartments _____
SOUTH _____ Cherry Street, single-family homes _____
EAST _____ 14th Avenue, single-family homes _____
WEST _____ 12th Avenue, single-family homes _____

Population: __ increasing   __ decreasing   x stable

Life cycle stage: __ integration x equilibrium __disintegration __rebirth

Tax rate: __ higher __ lower x same as competing areas

Services: x police x fire x garbage __ other: _____

Average family size: __3.5_____

Occupational status: __White collar; skilled trades_____

Distance from:

Commercial areas __3 miles_____
Elementary school __6 blocks_____
Secondary school __1 mile_____
Recreational areas__2 miles_____
Cultural centers __3 miles_____
Places of worship __Methodist, Catholic, Baptist_____
Transportation __Bus stop 1 block; frequent service to downtown
Freeway/highway __10 blocks_____

Typical Properties	Age	Price Range	Owner-occupancy
Vacant lots: 0%			
Single-family homes: 80%	20 yrs	$275,000-$340,000	93%
Apartments, 2- to 4-unit: 15%	10 yrs		
Apartments, over 4 units: 5%	5 yrs		
Non-residential: 0%			

Nuisances (odors, noise, etc.) __None_____
Environmental hazards (chemical storage, etc.) __None_____

11. **Schools.** What schools serve the neighborhood? Are they highly regarded? Are they within walking distance? The quality of a school or school district can make a major difference in property values in a residential neighborhood.

12. **Public services.** How well is the neighborhood served by public transportation, police, and fire units?

13. **Zoning.** Does zoning in and around the neighborhood promote residential use and insulate the property owner from nuisances?

14. **Neighborhood life cycle.** Neighborhoods progress through four phases as they age. The terminology varies, but a recently built neighborhood is in the **integration** or development phase. A stable, mature neighborhood is in **equilibrium**. An older neighborhood where properties are starting to fall into disrepair is in the **disintegration** or decline phase. Some neighborhoods progress to a point where old buildings are torn down or renovated and the properties become more valuable again; this phase is known as **rebirth** or rejuvenation. Which phase of its life cycle is this neighborhood in?

You can use a form (on paper or on a computer) such as the one shown in Figure 4.1 to record your neighborhood information. (Some CMA software may gather neighborhood information from your local MLS or other sources.) Of course, as you gain more experience, you'll become familiar with all of the neighborhoods in your area and their distinguishing characteristics. Before long, you'll be able to gauge the effect of the neighborhood on a property's value as soon as you hear where the property is located.

Site Analysis. Studying the site of the subject property means collecting information about the following factors:

1. **Width.** This refers to the lot's measurements from one side boundary to the other. Width can vary from front to back, as in the case of a pie-shaped lot on a cul-de-sac.

2. **Frontage.** Frontage is the length of the front boundary of the lot, the boundary that abuts a street or a body of water. The amount of frontage can be an important consideration if it measures the property's access or exposure to something desirable.

3. **Depth.** Depth is the distance between the site's front boundary and its rear boundary. Greater depth (more than the norm) can mean greater

Fig. 4.2 Site data form

```
┌─────────────────────────────────────────────────────────────┐
│                         SITE DATA                             │
│                                                               │
│   Address    10157 - 13th Avenue                              │
│   Legal description  Lot 6, Block 4, Caldwell's Addition, vol. 72, pg. 25 │
│   Dimensions  50' x 200'          Shape  Rectangular          │
│   Square feet  10,000             Street paving  Asphalt      │
│   Landscaping  Adequate           Topsoil  Good               │
│   Drainage  Good                  Frontage  (Street)          │
│   Easements  Utility S 15'        Corner lot __  Inside lot x   View __ │
│   Encroachments  Fence on west property line?                 │
│   Improvements:  x Driveway   x Sidewalks    x Curbs    __ Alley │
│   Utilities:  x Electricity   __ Gas   x Water   x Sewers   x Storm drains │
│               x Telephone   x Cable TV   x High-speed Internet │
└─────────────────────────────────────────────────────────────┘
```

value, but it doesn't always. For example, suppose Lot 1 and Lot 2 are the same, except that Lot 2 is deeper; Lot 2 is not necessarily more valuable than Lot 1. Each situation must be analyzed individually to determine whether more depth translates into greater value.

4. **Area.** Area is the total size of the site, usually measured in square feet or acres. Comparisons between lots often focus on the features of frontage and area.

Commercial land is usually valued in terms of frontage; that is, it is worth a certain number of dollars per front foot. Industrial land, on the other hand, tends to be valued in terms of square feet or acreage. Residential lots are measured both ways: by square feet or by acreage in most instances, but by front foot when the property abuts a lake or river, or some other desirable feature.

Under certain circumstances, combining two or more adjoining lots to achieve greater width, depth, or area will make the larger parcel more valuable than the sum of the values of its component parcels. The increment of value that results when two or more lots are combined to produce greater value is called **plottage**. The process of assembling lots to increase their value is most frequently part of industrial or commercial land development.

5. **Shape.** Lots with uniform width and depth (such as rectangular lots) are almost always more useful than irregularly shaped lots; a standard shape is more versatile for building purposes. This is true for any kind of lot—residential, commercial, or industrial.

6. **Topography.** A site is generally more valuable if it is aesthetically appealing. Rolling terrain is preferable to flat, monotonous land. On the other hand, if the site would be costly to develop because it sits well above or below the street or is excessively hilly, that lessens its value.

7. **Position and orientation.** How a lot is situated relative to the surrounding area influences its value. Consider whether the site has a view, and how much sunshine it gets during the day. And is it sheltered, or exposed to the elements and/or to traffic noise?

8. **Title.** Of course, any title problems will have an adverse effect on the value of the property. When you examine the site, look for signs of easements or encroachments. If a utility company has an easement across the rear portion of the property, for example, this would reduce the value of the property in comparison to a similar property with no easement.

You may want to use a form such as the one shown in Figure 4.2 to record the information you gather about the site.

Building Analysis. After examining the neighborhood and the site of the seller's property, the next step is to examine the improvements built on the property. For the typical residential property, this means a house and garage, and perhaps a garden shed or workshop. Here are some of the primary factors to analyze:

1. **Construction quality.** Is the quality of the materials and workmanship good, average, or poor?

2. **Age/condition.** How old is the home? Is its overall condition good, average, or poor? Depending on the condition, the effective age of the home may be more or less than its actual age.

3. **Size of house (square footage).** This includes the improved living area, excluding the garage, basement, and porches. (Note that an appraisal may exclude the square footage of any addition that was built without a valid permit.)

4. **Basement.** A functional basement, especially a finished basement, contributes to value. However, the amount a finished basement contributes to value is almost never enough to recover the cost of the finish work.

5. **Number of rooms.** Add up the total number of rooms in the house, excluding bathrooms and basement rooms.

6. **Number of bedrooms.** The number of bedrooms has a major impact on value. For instance, if all else is equal, a two-bedroom home is worth considerably less than a three-bedroom home.

7. **Number of bathrooms.** A full bath is a wash basin, toilet, shower, and bathtub; a three-quarter bath is a wash basin, toilet, and either a shower or tub. A half bath is a wash basin and toilet only. The number of bathrooms can have a noticeable effect on value.

8. **Air conditioning.** The presence of an air conditioning system and the system's condition are important in many areas of California.

9. **Energy efficiency.** A home that is energy-efficient is more valuable than a comparable one that is not. Energy-efficient features such as double-paned windows, good insulation, and weather stripping increase value.

10. **Garage or carport.** An enclosed garage is generally better than a carport. How many cars can it accommodate? Is there work or storage space in addition to space for parking? Is it possible to enter the home directly from the garage or carport, protected from the weather?

11. **Design and layout.** Is the floor plan functional and convenient? Are the design and layout attractive and efficient, or are there obvious design deficiencies that will decrease the value of the home? (We'll discuss design and layout in more detail in the next section of the chapter.)

You might want to use a form such as the one shown in Figure 4.3 to record the information you gather about the quality and condition of the improvements.

Design and Layout. A well-designed house is one that is the right size, shape, and configuration to produce the maximum value. Here are some questions to ask yourself as you examine the design of a house:

1. **General design.** The number of bedrooms in a house usually determines which buyers will consider purchasing it. Keep in mind the family size of potential buyers as you evaluate the house.

   In relation to the number of bedrooms, is the house large enough overall? Are there enough bathrooms, and an adequate number of closets? Is there a separate family room, children's playroom, or other recreational space? Is there sufficient work space in the kitchen and laundry room, and is there storage space for cleaning and gardening tools?

Fig. 4.3 Building data form

BUILDING DATA

Address ___10157 - 13th Avenue___

Age ___7 years___   Square feet ___1,350___

Number of rooms ___6___   Construction quality ___very good___

Style ___ranch___   General condition ___very good___

Feature	Good	Fair	Bad
Exterior: brick, frame, veneer, stucco, alum	x		
Foundation: slab, bsmt., crawl sp.	x		
Garage: attached, 1-car, 2-car, 3-car	x		
Patio, deck, porch, shed, other		x	
Interior (general condition)	x		
Walls: drywall, wood, plaster	x		
Ceilings	x		
Floors: wood, tile, lino, concrete, carpet		x	
Electrical wiring	x		
Heating: electric, gas, oil, other	x		
Air conditioning		x	
Fireplace(s) None			
Kitchen	x		
Bathroom(s) 2 full	x		
Bedroom(s) 1 large, 2 medium	x		

Additional amenities ___Large windows in living areas___

Design advantages ___Convenient, sunny kitchen___

Design flaws ___Inadequate closets in the two smaller bedrooms___

Energy efficiency ___Insulation, weather-stripping___

Location	Living Rm	Dining Rm	Kitchen	Bedrms	Baths	Family Rm
Basement						
First floor	x	x	x	3	2	None
Second floor						
Attic						

Depreciation:

  Deferred maintenance ___Normal wear, except for deck railings___

  Functional obsolescence ___No family room___

  External obsolescence ___None___

Are there enough windows and natural light, especially in the kitchen and other work or recreational spaces?

2. **Living room and family room.** How large are the living room and the family or recreation room (if any)? Will the shape of each room and the available wall space accommodate the furniture that will probably be placed in it?

3. **Dining room or dining area.** Is the dining area convenient to the kitchen and large enough for the number of people who will be eating there?

4. **Kitchen.** Is the kitchen convenient to an outside entrance and to the garage or carport? Is there adequate counter and cabinet space?

5. **Bedrooms.** How large are the bedrooms? Is there a master bedroom that's significantly larger than the other bedrooms? Are the bedroom closets big enough? Where are the bedrooms located in the house? It's better for the bedrooms to be located apart from the living room, family room, kitchen, and other work or recreational spaces.

6. **Bathrooms.** There should be at least two bathrooms if the house has more than two bedrooms. In many areas, particularly in newer houses, a private bathroom off the master bedroom is standard. Are there windows or ceiling fans in the bathrooms to provide adequate ventilation?

Design Deficiencies. Here is a brief list of some of the most common design deficiencies to watch out for:

- There's no front hall closet.
- The back door is difficult to reach from the kitchen, or from the driveway or garage.
- There's no comfortable area in or near the kitchen where the family can eat informally.
- The dining room is not easily accessible from the kitchen.
- The stairway leading to the second story is off of a room rather than in a hallway or foyer.
- A bathroom or some of the bedrooms are visible from the living room or foyer.
- The family room or recreation room is not visible from the kitchen.
- There is no direct access to the basement from outside the house.
- The bedrooms are not separated by a bathroom or closet wall (for sound-proofing).

- It's necessary to pass through one of the bedrooms to reach another bedroom.
- Outdoor living areas (such as a patio or deck) are not accessible from the kitchen.

Choosing Comparable Properties

Once you've gathered information about the seller's property, the next step in your CMA is choosing comparable properties that have recently sold, are now for sale, or were listed recently but failed to sell before the listing expired. (Expired listings show what buyers won't pay for a comparable property, so those set an upper limit on what you might suggest as a listing price.) By evaluating the sales prices or listing prices of these comparable properties, you will be able to estimate a reasonable listing price for the seller's property.

Before you can choose your comparables, you'll need to obtain comprehensive market data, including the listing and sales prices of properties in the seller's neighborhood, the financing terms of the sales transactions, and the physical characteristics of the properties. The most reliable source of this information is your multiple listing service. An MLS usually requires active members to assemble and share complete records of transactions, showing not only listing prices but also other useful data such as consummated sales, financing terms, and length of time on the market. Other sources of information include:

- real estate search websites, such as Zillow;
- real estate advertisements (both online and in local newspapers);
- other brokers and salespersons, loan officers, escrow officers, or anyone else actively involved with the local real estate market; and
- practical, everyday experience gained from previewing properties in a neighborhood over time.

Comparable properties must be truly comparable to the subject property in the areas of greatest importance, which are listed below. In choosing your comparables, these are the areas you should focus on. If a potential comparable is a listed property or a recently expired listing, you will be concerned with two key factors:

1. **Location of comparable.** We already mentioned how important location is to the value of a home. Ideally, a comparable property should be in the same neighborhood as the seller's property. If you can't find enough

comparables in the seller's neighborhood, you can choose comparables from similar neighborhoods nearby.

Even if your comparable is located in the same neighborhood as the seller's home, you may have to take into account differences in value due to location *within* a neighborhood.

> **Example:** Two basically identical properties located one block apart in the same neighborhood may have very different values if one of the properties borders a lake and the other does not. The values of the properties could also differ if one is located on a busy main avenue, while the other is on a quiet side street.

If a comparable is in an inferior neighborhood, it is probably less valuable than the subject property, even if it's structurally identical. The opposite is true of a comparable from a superior neighborhood.

2. **Physical characteristics.** To qualify as a comparable, a property should have physical characteristics that are similar to the subject property, including size, style, layout and design, construction materials, and condition of the building.

If the comparable has recently sold, you will also be concerned with the following factors, in addition to location and physical characteristics.

3. **Date of comparable sale.** The sale should be recent. The comparison is more reliable if the sale occurred within the last six months. Sales more than six months old should be used only if no alternatives are available. Older sales aren't reliable enough because market conditions (such as sales prices, interest rates, and construction costs) change over time. If the comparable you're considering sold more than six months ago (or even more recently in a rapidly changing market), you will probably have to make adjustments for the time factor, allowing for inflationary or deflationary trends or other changes in the market since the sale of the comparable.

4. **Terms of sale.** Was the sale financed? That is, did the buyer borrow money to complete the sale? (In most cases, the answer is yes.) If the price paid for the property was not affected by the financing terms, then the financing is referred to as **cash equivalent**. For example, if the buyer used a standard institutional loan to finance the sale of the home, the financing would be considered cash equivalent. But if the financing terms were unusual, they may have affected the sales price of the comparable.

Nonstandard financing can take a variety of forms, from seller financing to an interest rate buydown. (See Chapter 10.) In some cases, the effect of a special financing arrangement may be fairly obvious.

Example: The buyer's lender is charging $3,000 in discount points. The seller is going to pay the points to help the buyer qualify for the loan. The purchase price the buyer has agreed to pay is about $3,000 more than he would otherwise have paid, to compensate the seller for paying the points. In this case, the effect on the sales price equals the amount paid by the seller.

Other cases are not so clear-cut. In a sale that involves seller financing, for instance, the buyer may benefit in any of several ways. A below-market interest rate, a small downpayment, reduced (or zero) loan fees, and easier loan qualification are some of the possible benefits of seller financing.

Calculating the effect of nonstandard financing on price is rarely a simple task. If you don't feel comfortable making those calculations, it may be best to find another comparable with cash equivalent financing terms.

5. **Conditions of sale.** This factor concerns the motivations of the buyer and seller in a particular transaction. A sale can be used as a comparable only if it took place under normal market conditions: it was an **arm's length transaction** (between unrelated parties), neither party was acting under unusual pressure, both parties acted prudently and knowledgeably and in their own best interests, and the property was exposed on the open market for a reasonable length of time.

If a sale did not take place under normal conditions, the price paid is not a reliable indicator of market value, because the buyer and seller were acting under the influence of forces that do not affect the market in general.

Example: Morgan has been transferred to another city, and she's due to begin her new job in four weeks. She owns her home, and will need to sell before she moves. Her employer is paying for her moving expenses and has also offered to make up the difference between the market value of her house and any reasonable offer that is made in the first three weeks. Morgan can accept a low offer just to make a quick sale, since she won't personally lose any money on the transaction. This seller is not typically motivated, so this transaction should not be used as a comparable.

Making Adjustments to the Comparables

Now that you have chosen your comparable properties, you must compare each one to the seller's property. The comparison is made on the basis of the same elements you used to choose the comparables in the first place: 1) location, 2) physical characteristics, 3) date of sale, and 4) terms of sale. (The conditions of sale have already been taken into account, because a sale that did not take place under normal conditions would not be used as a comparable.) Before, you used these elements to weed out noncomparable properties. Now you'll use them to make minor adjustments in the sales prices or listing prices of the comparables.

Of course, the more similar the comparable, the easier the comparison. A comparable that was identical in design, neighborhood, site characteristics, and condition that sold under typical financing terms the previous month would give you an excellent indication of the market value of the subject property with no adjustments necessary. However, except in some new housing developments, you're not likely to find comparables that similar to the seller's property. Instead, there will nearly always be at least a few significant differences between the comparables and the seller's property. So you'll have to make the proper adjustments to the values of the comparables.

> **Example:** You've found a comparable that's very similar to the subject property, except that it has three bedrooms and the subject property has only two. The comparable recently sold for $735,000. If you know that a third bedroom is worth approximately $49,000, you'll subtract $49,000 from the sales price of the comparable. This adjusted price reflects the difference in the number of bedrooms.

One of the greatest challenges of completing a CMA is determining the value of the differences between the comparables and the subject property. How do you know how much an extra bedroom or bathroom, or proximity to a good elementary school, is really worth?

Sometimes you can find reliable data on the value of certain home features in your area online, or as part of a CMA computer program. In other cases, placing a value on individual features is a matter of careful research and comparison.

> **Example:** You know of two recently sold properties, A and B. They are virtually identical except that A has two bathrooms and B has three. Property A

Fig. 4.4 Finding the adjustment value for individual features

Sales Price Adjustment Chart								
Features	**Comparables**							
	A	B	C	D	E	F	G	H
Sales price	$332,500	$326,000	$332,500	$342,500	$341,000	$332,500	$324,500	$322,500
Location	Riverbend	Riverbend	Riverbend	Riverbend	Riverbend	Riverbend	Riverbend	Wood Hill
Age	8 yrs	7 yrs	8 yrs	6 yrs	8 yrs	7 yrs	6 yrs	7 yrs
Lot size	75 x 200	80 x 200	75 x 200	75 x 200	100 x 200	75 x 200	75 x 200	80 x 200
Construction	frame	frame	frame	frame	frame	frame	frame	frame
Style	ranch	ranch	ranch	ranch	ranch	ranch	ranch	ranch
No. of rooms	7	7	7	8	7	7	6	7
No. of bedrooms	3	3	3	4	3	3	2	3
No. of baths	2	1	2	2	2	2	2	2
Square feet	1,300	1,300	1,300	1,425	1,300	1,300	1,250	1,300
Exterior	good	good	good	good	good	good	good	good
Interior	good	good	good	good	good	good	good	good
Garage	2-car, att.	2-car, att.	2-car, att.	2-car, att.	2-car, att.	2-car, att.	2-car, att.	2-car, att.
Other	basement	basement	basement	basement	basement	basement	basement	basement
Financing	80% S/L	80% S/L	90% S/L	90% S/L	80% S/L	90% S/L	90% S/L	90% S/L
Date of sale	8 wk.	7 wk.	6 wk.	8 wk.	5 wk.	7 wk.	6 wk.	9 wk.
Typical house value	$332,500	$332,500	$332,500	$332,500	$332,500	$332,500	$332,500	$332,500
Variable feature		1 bath		4 bdrm.	larger lot		2 bdrm	poor loc.
Adjustment value for variable		$6,500		$10,000	$8,500		$8,000	$10,000

sold for $347,000 and B sold for $353,500. Since the number of bathrooms is the only real difference between the two properties, the value of the third bathroom is about $6,500.

By comparing many different properties in this way, you will be able to place a particular value on several different features. Of course, in the real world you may not find properties with only one distinguishing feature, like the one in our example. But with time and experience, you'll able to place a value on each of the many features that differ from one property to another.

The chart in Figure 4.4 illustrates how you can estimate the value of individual features. As you examine the chart, note that a few of the properties had no variables, so they were used as the standard against which the value of each distinguishing feature was measured.

Remember that you adjust the sales or listing price of the comparable to indicate the probable market value of the subject property. Never try to make the adjustments to the value of the subject property. If a comparable lacks a feature that the subject property has, *add* the value of the missing feature to the comparable's price. If a comparable has a feature that the subject property lacks, *subtract* the value of the feature from the comparable's price. The completed comparison chart shown in Figure 4.5 illustrates this process.

Estimating Market Value

After making all the required adjustments for varying features, you will have an adjusted market value figure for each comparable. You'll use these figures to estimate the market value of the seller's property, a process called **reconciliation**. To do this, you have to evaluate the reliability of each comparable. The comparables that are most like the subject property (and consequently have the fewest adjustments) offer the most reliable indication of market value.

Example: You have found three comparables with the values shown in Figure 4.6. Obviously, Comparable C has a significant number of variables (differences between the comparable and the subject property), which makes it less reliable as a comparable. Comparables A and B are much more similar to the subject property, with A being most like it. Therefore, the market value of A should be given the most weight and C the least. In this situation, you might estimate the market value of the seller's property to be about $339,000.

Fig. 4.5 Comparable sales comparison chart

		Comparables			
Features	**Subject Property**	**1**	**2**	**3**	**4**
Sales price		$341,750	$346,500	$332,000	$336,500
Location	quiet street				
Age	7 yrs.				
Lot size	80 x 200				
Construction	frame			+ $7,000	
Style	ranch				
Number of rooms	7		– $7,500		
Number of bedrooms	3			+ $8,500	+ $8,500
Number of baths	2	+ 6,500			
Square feet	1,400				
Exterior	good				
Interior	good				
Garage	2-car att.				
Other improvements		– $3,000			
Financing					
Date of sale			+ $3,000		
Net adjustments		+ $3,500	– $4,500	+ $15,500	+ $8,500
Adjusted value		$345,250	$342,000	$347,500	$345,000

Table title: Comparable Sales Comparison Chart

Fig. 4.6 Comparables requiring fewer adjustments are more reliable

	Comparables		
	A	B	C
Selling price	$346,500	$353,150	$370,050
Extra bedroom	-$8,000	-$8,000	-$8,000
Two-car garage			-$6,300
Large lot			-$8,750
Aluminum siding		-$4,750	
Final value	$338,500	$340,400	$347,000

Of course, when you're estimating market value to help the seller set a realistic listing price, you don't need to provide an exact figure. You can give the seller a range of figures, such as "between $338,000 and $341,000." It's then up to the seller to choose the listing price he wants.

Completing a CMA

Let's walk through the process of doing a competitive market analysis for a hypothetical property. Although the steps we will follow are the same ones you'll use when preparing CMAs in real life, the data we'll be using is simplified. (The actual CMAs you'll prepare will usually involve more complex data and a greater number of variables.)

Suppose some prospective sellers have asked you for advice on how much their house could sell for on the current market. They'll give you the listing if they're happy with the suggested price.

Your first step is to gather information about the sellers' house, the subject property. You walk through the house with the sellers, taking notes. You observe the property's amenities and defects; you also discuss the sellers' motivation for selling and their time parameters. When you leave, you drive through the neighborhood, noting the benefits and drawbacks of the area. You look for other properties that are on the market or that have recently sold.

After viewing the property, talking with the sellers, and studying the neighborhood, you have the following information: The house is located in Cedar Hills, which is a small, stable, middle-income neighborhood three miles north of the business district of Jeffersville. The house has three bedrooms, two full bathrooms, a dining room, and a large, well-landscaped back yard. It's a two-story house with a double garage. The house is four years old and in excellent condition.

The next step is to select comparable properties and gather information about them. You browse the MLS database and check some real estate search websites. You find several potential comparable properties, walk through the ones that are currently for sale, and drive by the properties that have sold or that have expired listings. After analyzing them as to date of sale, location, physical characteristics, and terms and conditions of sale, you choose the comparables listed in Figure 4.7. Like the sellers' property, all of them are located in the Cedar Hills neighborhood, have two stories, and are in excellent condition.

In preparing a CMA, remember that sales prices are better indications of value than listing prices. Sales prices represent what buyers were actually willing to pay in this marketplace. Listing prices are more likely to represent the ceiling of values in the area, since buyers rarely pay more for a property than the asking price, unless the market is exceptionally competitive.

Fig. 4.7 Comparables for Cedar Hills CMA

- **Comparable A:** 3 bedrooms, 2 baths, dining room, 3-car garage, large back yard, 3½ yrs old. Sold 5 months ago for $445,500.

- **Comparable B:** 4 bedrooms, 2 baths, dining room, 2-car garage, large side yard, 4 yrs old. Sold 2 months ago for $447,700.

- **Comparable C:** 3 bedrooms, 3 baths, large back yard, 3-car garage, 3½ yrs old, no dining room. Sold 7 months ago for $441,000.

- **Comparable D:** 3 bedrooms, 3 baths, 2-car garage, large back yard, 5 yrs old, no dining room. Currently listed for $449,500.

- **Comparable E:** 4 bedrooms, 2 baths, dining room, 3-car garage, large back yard, 4 yrs old. Listing expired 2 weeks ago; price was $473,500.

Next, you compare the comparables you've chosen to your sellers' property. Of course, there are differences between the subject property and the comparables that will require some adjustments, including:

1. a double garage versus a three-car garage,
2. three bedrooms versus four bedrooms,
3. two bathrooms versus three bathrooms, and
4. the presence or absence of a dining room.

Before you can make the appropriate adjustments for these differences, you must determine the adjustment value of each distinguishing feature. By referring to your online sources, you find four pairs of properties that provide the information you need.

1. Two houses are nearly identical to one another, except that one has a double garage and the other has a three-car garage. One sold for $478,700 and the other for $485,500. From this you conclude that a three-car garage is worth approximately $6,800 more than a double garage.
2. Two other houses are nearly identical except that one has three bedrooms and the other has four. The first sold for $453,000 and the other for $464,500. So you conclude that a fourth bedroom is worth about $11,500.
3. Two more houses are nearly identical except that one has three bathrooms and the other has only two. The first sold for $474,750 and the other sold for $461,550. The third bathroom is apparently worth about $13,200.
4. Finally, two other houses are nearly identical except that one has a dining room and the other does not. The one with the dining room sold for $427,000 and the other for $420,800. Thus, the dining room is worth about $6,200.

Based on these other sales, you have a general idea of how each of the variables in question should be valued. Now you make the adjustments for each of these features, as shown in Figure 4.8.

You now have the adjusted market values for the five comparables and can formulate an opinion of the subject property's market value. First you consider the reliability of each comparable. Comparable C has the most distinguishing features and thus the most adjustments, so it is the least reliable. Comparables A

Fig. 4.8 Adjusted values for comparables

	Comparables				
	A	B	C	D	E
Market value	$445,500	$447,700	$441,000	$449,500	$473,500
Three-car garage	-$6,800		-$6,800		-$6,800
Fourth bedroom		-$11,500			-$11,500
Third bathroom			-$13,200	-$13,200	
Dining room			+$6,200	+$6,200	
Total adjustments	-$6,800	-$11,500	-$13,800	-$7,000	-$18,300
Total adjusted value	$438,700	$436,200	$427,200	$442,500	$455,200

and B each have only one adjustment, but the variable between Comparable A and the subject property (the three-car garage) is less important to the property's overall value. Comparable A is probably the most reliable; but note how close the market values of A and B are anyway. Comparable D has not yet sold, so its listing price can be considered the ceiling of value. The listing on Comparable E expired, so its price was evidently unreasonable in current market conditions. Overall, you decide that a reasonable estimate of market value for the subject property is $438,000.

You present your estimate of value and give the sellers a range of reasonable listing prices—from $436,000 to $439,000. You explain the supporting data to them, discussing each comparable and how it affected your estimated price range. Impressed with your professional competence, the sellers give you their listing. They decide on a listing price of $438,500, a price you all feel comfortable with.

CMA Form

When you prepare a CMA and present it to the seller, you will probably be using a form such as the one shown in Figure 4.9. (Again, your CMA software will either fill out such a form for you, based on data entered into the program, or allow you to easily fill out the form yourself.)

Fig. 4.9 Competitive market analysis form

Competitive Market Analysis

Subject Property Address: 458 Maple

Address	Price	Age	Lot Size	Style	Exterior	No. of Rooms	Sq. Ft.	No. of Bedrms	Baths	Garage	Condition	Other Impr.	Terms	$ per sq. ft.	List Date	Date Sold
Subject	$332,500	7 yrs	80 x 150	ranch	wood	7	1,350	3	2	1-car, att.	excellent	—	cash	$239		
Current Listings																
291 Maple	$320,000	8 yrs	70 x 140	ranch	wood	6	1,250	3	1	1-car, att.	excellent	basement	cash	$256	July	
175 Main	$318,700	12 yrs	70 x 140	ranch	brick	7	1,350	3	2	1-car, att.	good		cash	$236	Aug.	
389 - 5th	$323,000	10 yrs	80 x 150	ranch	brick	7	1,420	3	2	2-car, att.	good	basement	cash	$227	Aug.	
995 Merrit	$314,500	5 yrs	80 x 150	ranch	wood	6	1,415	2	2	1-car, att.	good		cash	$222	June	
Recently Sold																
256 Oak	$315,400	10 yrs	80 x 140	ranch	wood	7	1,270	3	2	2-car, att.	good		cash	$248	March	May
1156 Larch	$312,000	6 yrs	80 x 150	ranch	brick	6	1,400	3	1	1-car, att.	excellent		cash	$223	Feb.	April
1052 - 8th	$305,250	7 yrs	80 x 140	ranch	brick	7	1,300	3	2	1-car, att.	good		cash	$235	April	June
Expired Listings																
2782 Cherry	$333,600	6 yrs	80 x 150	ranch	wood	6	1,150	2	2	1-car, att.	good		cash	$290	Jan.	
10012 - 7th	$338,800	4 yrs	80 x 140	ranch	brick	7	1,300	3	2	2-car, att.	excellent		cash	$261	March	

Location: centrally located, convenient to business center and public transportation	General Comments:
Assets: excellent condition, professionally landscaped yard	
Drawbacks: no basement	
Market Conditions: market is very competitive, sales price within 2% of market value	Company: Smith Realty
Financing Terms: cash	Agent: Susan James
Probable Market Value: $322,500	Phone: 555-8811

This form is easy to use and to explain. A major advantage is that it shows the seller what buyers can pay, will pay, and will not pay for a home in her neighborhood. It also helps you plan your presentation in a logical sequence.

You can include a dozen or more comparables on the form. The more similar they are to the seller's property, the more likely the seller is to accept your estimate of value.

The first section of the form calls for homes that are for sale now. Their prices represent what a buyer could pay for a similar home today on the open market. Select the currently listed homes that are the most like the seller's property. For each one, list the address, age, style, number of rooms, number of bedrooms and baths, condition, financing terms, date listed, and other characteristics.

The next section is for homes that have sold in the past 12 months. These show what buyers have actually paid for comparable homes. Choose the most recent sales transactions with the homes most similar to the seller's property, and fill in the pertinent information. Of course, the most important information is how much the comparable sold for and the terms on which it sold.

The next section deals with listings that have expired in the past 12 months. These represent what buyers would not pay for a similar home in this market. List all of the information called for on the form.

Other items to be filled in include the subject property's location, strong points, and drawbacks; market conditions; financing terms; and general comments.

All the information you have gathered and analyzed concerning both the seller's property and the comparable properties should be presented to the seller during your listing presentation. You should also explain how this information indicates market value. If carefully prepared and presented, your CMA can correct any misconceptions the seller has regarding the current market conditions in his neighborhood. It should help the seller take a realistic approach to pricing.

The Problem of a Low Appraisal

In spite of your best efforts to help sellers choose a listing price based on the market value of their home, you're likely to run into the problem of a low appraisal from time to time.

A low appraisal is an appraiser's estimate of value that is significantly lower than the price a seller and a buyer have agreed on. They've entered into a contract at a sales price that both of them are pleased with. But when the property is formally appraised for the buyer's lender, the appraiser concludes that the property is not worth as much as the buyer has agreed to pay.

A low appraisal puts a heavily financed sale in jeopardy. If the transaction is contingent on financing, the contingency often states that the buyer doesn't have to complete the sale if the appraised value turns out to be less than the agreed price. Even when a buyer would like to go ahead with the purchase in spite of the low appraisal, she may not be able to afford to do so. The purchase loan is based on the sales price or the appraised value, whichever is less, so in many cases a low appraisal means a smaller loan—and a bigger downpayment.

Example:

1. Buyer is prepared to make a 10% downpayment and obtain a 90% loan.
2. Sales price is $310,000.
3. Appraisal is issued at $300,000.
4. Maximum loan amount is 90% of $300,000.

$$\$300,000 \text{ Appraised value} \times 90\% \text{ Loan-to-value ratio} =$$
$$\$270,000 \text{ Maximum loan amount}$$

Because of the low appraisal ($10,000 less than the sales price), the loan amount is limited to $270,000. The buyer expected to make a $31,000 downpayment ($310,000 sales price × 90% = $279,000 loan). But the buyer would now have to make a $40,000 downpayment ($310,000 – $270,000 loan = $40,000) to pay the $310,000 price.

The easy solution to the problem of a low appraisal is for the seller to lower the sales price to the appraised value. But the seller may not be willing to do this; once a seller has become accustomed to a certain sales price, he'll be very reluctant to give it up.

Sometimes the buyer and seller will agree to a compromise price between the appraised value and the original sales price. More often, this solution runs up against both the seller's reluctance to lower the price and the buyer's reluctance (or inability) to pay any more than the appraised value.

Because of these problems, when there's a significant gap between the sales price and the appraised value and financing makes up the bulk of the purchase price, the most likely result is termination of the sale. It's the real estate agent's job to help the parties avoid this outcome whenever possible.

In some cases, the agent should ask the lender to reconsider the appraised value, in the hope that it will be increased to a figure more acceptable to the buyer and seller. This is called a request for reconsideration of value.

Request for Reconsideration of Value

Although appraisers try to be objective, subjective considerations are a part of every appraisal. In the end, the appraiser's conclusions are only an opinion of value. When you get a low appraisal and you genuinely believe the appraiser is mistaken, you can appeal the appraisal by submitting a request for reconsideration of value to the lender. With the proper documentation, you may be able to get the appraised value increased, possibly to the figure the buyer and seller originally agreed on.

Evaluating a Low Appraisal. The sooner you find out about a low appraisal, the better. After the appraiser has inspected the seller's property, ask a representative of the lender (for example, the loan officer) to call you with the results of the appraisal as soon as they are received. Don't try to get the results directly from the appraiser; she has a fiduciary relationship with the lender and is not allowed to divulge information about the appraisal to others without the lender's permission.

If the appraisal comes in low, ask the loan officer for the following information:

1. the final value estimate,
2. the value indicated by the sales comparison method, and
3. the addresses of the three comparables the appraiser used.

This is the essential information, because the sales comparison analysis is the heart of a residential appraisal, the part that the lender really relies on in deciding whether to approve a loan.

Evaluate the appraiser's comparables and update your competitive market analysis. Then decide if a request for reconsideration of value is a realistic option. You will have to support your request with at least three comparable sales (not listings) that indicate a higher value estimate is in order. If you're going to persuade the lender to accept your comparables over the appraiser's, yours must be at least as similar to the subject property as the appraiser's are.

If you believe the lender is likely to grant a request for reconsideration, your next step is to prepare the request and a cover letter.

Preparing a Reconsideration Request. Some lenders have their own form for requests for reconsideration of value. If so, you should use their form (in fact, you may even be required to do so). Otherwise, you can prepare your own. You may want to present your information in the same format as the Sales Comparison section of the Uniform Residential Appraisal Report form. Make four columns for the properties, with the subject property in the first column and the three comparables to the right.

Write a cover letter making your request and attach your competitive market analysis to it. The cover letter should be simple and very polite; do not criticize the appraiser.

Sometimes appraisers don't use the best information available, and when they don't, their findings can be successfully challenged. If your request for reconsideration of value contains well-researched, properly documented information and is presented in a professional manner, your chances of success are good.

Keep in mind that federal law prohibits anyone with an interest in a real estate transaction from inappropriately influencing the appraiser. Similarly, California law prohibits improperly influencing the development, reporting, result, or review of an appraisal. The law prohibits a licensee from (among other things) providing an appraiser with an anticipated value, conditioning the payment of the appraiser's fee on the appraisal result, or otherwise encouraging a specific outcome. Violation of this law is grounds for disciplinary action. However, the law specifically permits asking an appraiser to:

1. consider additional information about the property,
2. provide further detail or explanation for the appraiser's conclusion, or
3. correct any factual errors in the appraisal report.

So as long as your request for reconsideration of value is presented properly, you are in no danger of violating the law.

Chapter Summary

1. It is the seller's responsibility to establish a listing price. However, your sellers will rely on you for advice about the listing price. Your advice should usually take the form of a competitive market analysis, which presents information about similar properties that are currently for sale or that have sold recently in the seller's neighborhood.

2. While there are many different types of value, you will be most concerned with market value, which should be the basis for the seller's listing price. Market value is defined as the most probable price that a property should bring in under normal market conditions. (Remember to distinguish value from price and cost. Price is what a buyer actually paid for a property; cost is what was paid to purchase a property and build an improvement on it.)

3. When you estimate the value of a seller's property, your first step is to collect and study information about the property. Your information will come from a neighborhood analysis, a site analysis, and a building analysis. As you study the house itself, you should pay particular attention to its design and layout. Once you have a clear picture of all the features, amenities, and drawbacks of the seller's property, you can choose your comparables.

4. Comparables are properties in the seller's neighborhood (or a similar neighborhood) that are similar to the seller's property and that are currently for sale or have sold recently. Once you've picked your comparables, you'll note the differences between the comparables and the seller's property and adjust the value of the comparables accordingly. Features that a comparable property lacks are taken into account by adding the value of the missing feature to the comparable's price. Features that a comparable property has that the seller's property lacks are taken into account by deducting the value of the feature from the comparable's price. You'll then use the adjusted prices of the comparables as the basis for a reasonable price range for the seller's property.

5. Present the results of your competitive market analysis to the seller on a CMA form that sets out all the key information. The form will help him understand how you arrived at the listing price range you're recommending for his property.

6. A low appraisal is one that concludes the property is worth less than the buyer has agreed to pay for it. Many sales contingent on financing require the property to appraise at or above the sales price; if it doesn't, the buyer won't be required to complete the transaction. In some cases, you can appeal a low appraisal by submitting a request for reconsideration of value to the lender.

Key Terms

Competitive market analysis: A comparison of homes that are similar in location, style, and amenities to the subject property, in order to set a realistic listing price. Similar to the sales comparison approach to value.

Value in use: The value of a property to its owner or to a user. Also called use value.

Value in exchange (market value): The most probable price which a property should bring in a competitive and open market under all conditions requisite to a fair sale, the buyer and seller each acting prudently and knowledgeably, and assuming the price is not affected by undue stimulus.

Market price: The price actually paid for a property.

Comparable: In appraisal, a property that is similar to the subject property and that has recently been sold. The sales prices of comparables provide data for estimating the value of the subject property using the sales comparison approach. Also called a comp or a comparable sale.

Cash equivalent: When a property's financing terms do not affect the market value of the property, the financing is said to be cash equivalent.

Arm's length transaction: A transaction in which there is no pre-existing family or business relationship between the parties.

Request for reconsideration of value: A request to a lender to reconsider the appraised value of a property, when the appraisal comes in lower than expected. The request is supported by data on comparable sales that would support a higher market value for the subject property.

Chapter Quiz

1. The value of an item comes primarily from the:
    a. average of its cost and its market price
    b. intrinsic qualities of the item
    c. perceptions and attitudes people have about the item
    d. rarity of the item

2. A competitive market analysis (CMA) is an effective way to estimate value because:
    a. an informed buyer acting free of pressure will not pay more for a property than she could pay for another property that is equally desirable
    b. a buyer will never pay more than market value for a property
    c. it takes more neighborhoods into account in evaluating the property
    d. the income method of appraisal is the most reliable way to value residential property

3. Which of the following is true about neighborhood characteristics?
    a. The boundaries are defined by the county planning board
    b. Neighborhood characteristics set the upper limit of value for the properties located there
    c. Neighborhood characteristics do not affect the value of vacant lots located there
    d. A neighborhood's effect on property values is determined by the most expensive properties located there

4. What kind of topography is considered most desirable for a residential neighborhood?
    a. Level
    b. Sloping
    c. Gently subsiding
    d. Mildly rolling

5. A bathroom with a wash basin and toilet, but no shower or bathtub, is a:
    a. half bath
    b. three-quarter bath
    c. full bath
    d. design deficiency

6. Which of the following is a common design deficiency?
    a. More bathrooms than bedrooms
    b. Bedrooms not separated by bathroom or closets
    c. Bedrooms not visible from living room
    d. Kitchen too close to garage

7. Which of the following is an example of "normal market conditions"?

   a. The seller of the property is the buyer's uncle, but both the buyer and the seller are being advised by attorneys

   b. The seller of the property is the buyer's aunt, but the buyer and the seller are represented by different brokers

   c. The seller is relocating to take a new job, so she lets her employer take care of selling the house for her

   d. The seller finds a buyer after the property has been on the market for two months and the buyer has been looking in this area for some time

8. In a CMA, which of the following elements may make it necessary to adjust the prices of the comparables?

   a. Date of sale

   b. Value in use

   c. Cost

   d. Conditions of sale

9. To prepare a CMA for your seller's property, you choose three properties as comparables. You make all the necessary adjustments to reflect how the comparables differ from the subject property. Comparable A has an adjusted value of $311,000. Comparable B has an adjusted value of $327,500. Comparable C has an adjusted value of $314,000. How do you arrive at an estimate of the value of the subject property?

   a. Take the average of the adjusted values of the comparables

   b. Let the seller choose between the three values to set a listing price

   c. Evaluate the reliability of each comparable and use that as a basis for deciding on a suggested price

   d. Choose the value of the comparable property with the fewest adjustments

10. To have the best chance of succeeding with a request for reconsideration of value, you should use:

    a. exactly the same comparables as the appraiser

    b. the income approach to value method of appraisal

    c. only currently listed properties as comparables

    d. comparable sales that are at least as similar to the subject property as the appraiser's comparables

Answer Key

1. c. Value is created by people. Our perceptions and attitudes do more to determine the value of an item than the characteristics of the item itself.

2. a. Competitive market analysis is a modified form of the sales comparison method of appraisal. It is based on the assumption that a buyer will not want to pay more for a property than she could pay for a similar comparable property.

3. b. Neighborhood characteristics set both the upper and lower limits of a property's value.

4. d. Mildly rolling terrain is usually considered preferable, both as a neighborhood characteristic and for the property site itself.

5. a. A bathroom with only a wash basin and a toilet is considered a half bath.

6. b. It's considered a design deficiency when two bedrooms share a wall without a bathroom or closets between them to provide soundproofing.

7. d. A sale under normal market conditions is one in which the parties were unrelated, neither party was acting under unusual pressure, both parties acted prudently and knowledgeably and in their own best interests, and the property was exposed on the open market for a reasonable length of time.

8. a. If a comparable did not sell recently, it may be necessary to make an adjustment to take into account changes in the market since the date of sale.

9. c. You have to evaluate the reliability of each comparable to estimate the market value of the subject property. The comparables that are most like the subject property offer the most reliable indication of market value.

10. d. To persuade the lender to accept your estimate of value over the appraiser's, you need to select comparable sales that are at least as similar to the subject property as the appraiser's comparables.

5

Sales Techniques and Practices

Listing Practices

- Listing sources
  - Farming
  - Cold calls
  - Expired listings
  - For sale by owners
  - Referrals
- Listing presentations
- Servicing the listing

Selling Practices

- Types of buyers
- Finding a buyer
- Showing properties
- Making an offer

Safety Issues

Real Estate Assistants

Introduction

To be successful, a real estate agent must list properties, find buyers for properties, or both. Finding a seller or finding a buyer is the main way to earn a commission. Therefore, listing and selling practices are the lifeblood of a real estate career. This chapter reviews the basic steps of listing a property, and the basic steps of finding a buyer for a property. It also covers the ways in which an assistant, licensed or unlicensed, can help an agent with listing and selling practices.

Listing Practices

A listing agent's job involves more than just filling out a listing agreement form and waiting for a buyer to come along. First, you must work to locate listing prospects. Then you might need to convince prospective sellers to list their property for sale with you. Once you have entered into a listing agreement with the seller, you'll need to continue to service the listing. This includes researching the property and neighborhood, marketing the property, staging open houses, and communicating with the sellers about the work you're doing and the progress you're making.

Listing Sources

Agents should be familiar with a number of listing sources and activities that can generate listings. These include:

- farming,
- cold calls,
- expired listings,
- for sale by owners, and
- referrals.

If you use advertising materials to generate listings, keep in mind that California law requires real estate licensees to include their license number on all solicitation materials, including business cards, stationery, and flyers.

Farming. Farming is a technique that involves choosing a neighborhood where you wish to concentrate your activities, and then becoming a well-known name in that neighborhood.

Example: Marty Thompson is a new real estate agent. He needs to generate some listings, so he decides to "farm" an area. He decides that the area he knows best is his own neighborhood—a development containing about 150 homes. He starts out by sending an introductory letter to every home, introducing himself and describing the services he can offer. He follows up the letter with a personal visit, leaving a refrigerator magnet with his name and contact information at each home. Twice a year he sends newsletters to every home in the neighborhood; these contain neighborhood news, such as who's graduating from high school or who offers babysitting services, as well as information on local property values and market trends. He also looks for opportunities to sponsor local events, such as the annual summer barbecue. He visits each home during the winter holidays, dropping off a calendar pre-printed with his name and contact information. Soon, whenever neighborhood residents think about listing their homes, they immediately think of their neighbor, Marty Thompson.

By farming an area effectively and consistently, an agent can reasonably expect a constant supply of listings.

Many agents choose their "farm" based on three factors. The first factor is **diversity**—diversity of floor plans, square footage, exteriors, amenities, and values. Diversity guarantees that a variety of buyers will be attracted to the area. The second factor is **affinity**. An agent will be more successful if she chooses an area that feels comfortable. She should be enthusiastic about her "farm." The third factor is **turnover**. A neighborhood that is too stable will not offer many opportunities for listings. On the other hand, an area with a lot of recent turnover may be ready for a dry spell. An area with a steady stream of new listings is ideal.

Many licensees are enthusiastic proponents of farming, and it can be very successful. Other agents are not comfortable farming and prefer to use other methods of generating listings. Also, farming is a long-term strategy that may take years to pay dividends, so a new agent struggling to round up business may need to use additional methods that produce quicker results.

Cold Calls. The **cold call** technique is also popular with agents. This method involves calling homeowners on the telephone and asking whether they are interested in selling their homes or if they know someone who is. The homeowners who are called may be chosen randomly, or may be part of a systematic plan (such as calling all of the homeowners in a particular area).

Cold calling works only if the agent is willing to make many calls. Cold calling is often described as a "numbers game." One hundred calls may generate one listing appointment. As with farming, many agents feel that cold calls are a waste of precious time, or they feel uncomfortable with the process. Other agents, however, are very successful generating listings through cold calls.

An agent making cold calls probably doesn't think of himself as a telemarketer, but he is bound by some of the same laws as other telemarketers. An agent may not call those who have registered with the Do Not Call Registry maintained by the Federal Trade Commission. It is the agent's responsibility to consult the online registry before making cold calls. Even when contacting persons not on the registry, an agent must always honor requests not to be called again, may not block Caller ID, and may not call outside permissible calling hours.

Expired Listings. Real estate agents often keep an eye on listings that are about to expire. Expired listings can be opportunities in disguise. There are many reasons why a listing might not have sold: it was not marketed properly, minor repairs should have been made that were not, or the price was not reduced when it should have been. If so, a fresh approach may generate both the listing and a quick sale. (If the listing did not sell because the owners were not motivated, there is probably little that another agent can do to move the property.)

After a listing has expired, the new agent can approach the homeowners and see if they are interested in relisting their property. Note that these sellers may be wary of signing another listing agreement because they've just had a negative experience with a real estate agent.

Agents must never try to convince sellers to terminate an existing listing so that the seller can switch to another agent. Agents should also exercise extreme caution when discussing a previous agent's actions. Criticizing another agent's selling efforts is unprofessional. Instead, agents should focus on what they can do for their clients.

For Sale by Owners. Another way to obtain listings is to call sellers who are trying to sell their homes on their own. Calling "for sale by owners" (FSBOs) can be very effective, as these homeowners have already decided to sell their homes. All the agent needs to do is convince the FSBO that the agent can do a better job selling the home, in a shorter period of time, and for a higher sales price with a greater net return.

Agents keep track of FSBOs by noticing "For Sale" signs and reading classified ads in the newspaper or online. Some agents will contact any FSBO, while others have a more systematic approach, such as only contacting those in a certain price range.

Fig. 5.1 Listing information form

Listing Information	
Property:	
Seller name:	
Seller address:	
Seller phone: (H) (W)	
Date listed: Date expires:	
List price: Estimated market value:	
Seller wants to move by:	
First Loan	**Second Loan**
Lender:	Lender:
Phone:	Phone:
Loan type: [ ] conventional [ ] FHA [ ] VA [ ] seller	Loan type: [ ] conventional [ ] FHA [ ] VA [ ] seller
Balance: $ [ ] verified	Balance: $ [ ] verified
Monthly payment: $	Monthly payment: $
Interest rate: [ ] fixed [ ] adjustable	Interest rate: [ ] fixed [ ] adjustable
Assumable:	Assumable:
Assumption fee:	Assumption fee:
Seller's terms:	Seller's terms:
30-Day Marketing Strategy	
[ ] Submit to MLS	[ ] Meet with seller
[ ] Install lock box	[ ] Collect all agent business cards
[ ] Install for sale sign	[ ] Discuss agents' comments
[ ] Key at office	[ ] Review market value estimate
[ ] Office tour date	[ ] Other:
[ ] MLS tour date	[ ] Other:
[ ] Submit ad	[ ] Other:
Suggestions for Showing Property Better	

Agents approach FSBOs in a number of different ways. One approach includes sending several letters to the homeowner. These letters include helpful advice on selling a home. Another approach is to deliver free "service packages" to FSBOs. These packages include forms, helpful hints and articles on selling a home, and sample settlement instructions. Some agents may simply phone for an appointment or knock on the door. The key to any approach is to convince the homeowner that selling real estate is a complicated business that an agent can do better and faster.

Even agents who shy away from FSBOs will contact one if they have a particular buyer in mind. Under those circumstances, an agent can call the FSBO and ask for a one-party listing. A **one-party listing** is a listing agreement that is valid only in regard to one particular buyer. FSBOs may be initially skeptical of agents who request one-party listings. They may not believe the agent actually has a particular buyer in mind. However, they will often agree to a one-party listing if they are convinced that there is a legitimate prospect.

Referrals. Perhaps the most effective way to get listings is through referrals. Referrals may come from other real estate or finance professionals, such as attorneys, accountants, mortgage brokers, or escrow officers; these people are often happy to recommend prospects to a real estate agent, with the expectation that the agent might return the favor by referring clients who might need their services. Referrals may also come from satisfied clients or customers, in the form of repeat business or word-of-mouth.

Seeking referrals is really no different from the sort of **networking** any job-seeker uses. The first step is for an agent to contact friends, family, professionals whose services he uses, and other people in the community, and inform them of the services the agent provides. The goal is to create an **endless chain** of recommendations: if an agent receives two referral prospects from a friend, the agent should contact those two referral prospects and try to garner another two referrals from each of those prospects. If an agent tries out every link in the chain, the potential for hundreds of listings exists.

It may be particularly helpful for an agent to cultivate the friendship of influential persons in his neighborhood or community. These **centers of influence** can be a fruitful source of referrals, since they tend to have many acquaintances, some of whom might need an agent's services. When thinking of centers of influence, people often think of professionals such as attorneys, doctors, or public officials, but they can just as easily be store owners, bartenders, bank tellers, or anyone who interacts with a wide variety of people.

A key source for meeting centers of influence and other useful contacts is local community service groups. Many of the most successful agents build their referral networks through membership in groups such as churches, the PTA, the Chamber of Commerce, political organizations, or fraternal groups. An agent should focus on deeper involvement in only one or two organizations, rather than superficial involvement in a wide number of groups. An agent's main focus should be on the group's mission rather than aggressively seeking referrals; the referrals will come naturally as one becomes more deeply involved in the community.

An agent should always maintain a referral file, preferably using a contact management database. These programs will allow an agent to generate either mass or personalized mailings, and can even remind an agent when it is time to write or call in order to maintain steady contact.

Listing Presentations

Once a prospective seller has been located, a **listing presentation** may be necessary to convince the seller to list the property with the agent. Many sellers "shop around" for a real estate agent by asking two or three agents to make a listing presentation. That way, sellers can judge the strengths and weaknesses of different agents before making a final choice. Thus, it is important for the agent to come across as professional and well-prepared at the listing presentation; otherwise, the listing may go to someone else.

Even if an owner needs no convincing and is ready to list, the agent may want to use a listing presentation as an opportunity to discuss pricing. It's important to ensure that the owner is willing to put the property on the market at a competitive price.

Before the Presentation. As soon as an agent has an appointment to make a listing presentation, he should begin preparing for it. A variety of tasks should be completed prior to the listing appointment, including:

- researching the property,
- visiting the property,
- completing a competitive market analysis, and
- preparing a marketing plan.

Research the property. The agent should begin by gathering basic information about the property, including the legal description, a plat map, tax information, and ownership information. This information often can be obtained from a local title company at no charge.

Visit the property. The agent should ask the owner if she can stop by to inspect the property prior to the listing appointment. During this visit, the agent counts and measures rooms, notes any special features (such as a gourmet kitchen or a dazzling view), and gets a general impression of the soundness of the construction. The agent also drives through the neighborhood to get a general feel for the area. Are neighboring homes well-kept? Are there nearby parks? How close are the schools?

Complete a competitive market analysis. Once the agent has become familiar with the home and the neighborhood, it's time to complete a competitive market analysis. As you will recall from Chapter 4, a CMA is a comparison of the prices of homes that are similar in location, style, and amenities to the subject property. The purpose of a CMA is to help the seller set a realistic listing price—it is only by comparing the prices of similar homes that a seller can establish a reasonable price for his own home.

Three types of properties are used to prepare a CMA:

1. homes that are for sale now,
2. homes that have recently sold, and
3. homes whose listings have expired.

The prices of homes that are currently for sale tell the seller what a buyer could pay now for a similar home on the open market. The prices of homes that recently sold tell the seller what a buyer did pay for a similar home. And expired listings tell the seller what a buyer would not pay for a similar home. Note that the prices paid for properties are better indications of value than list prices, because sales prices represent what buyers were actually willing to pay in a competitive market situation. List prices represent the ceiling of values in the area—generally, buyers will balk at paying more than the list price.

There are forms, software, and online tools to help agents prepare CMAs. A sample CMA form is shown in Chapter 4 (Figure 4.9).

Prepare a marketing plan. The agent should be prepared to discuss all the different ways she plans to promote the seller's property to prospective buyers. Most marketing plans will include a combination of traditional marketing prac-

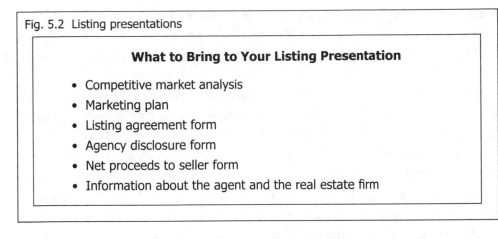

Fig. 5.2 Listing presentations

What to Bring to Your Listing Presentation

- Competitive market analysis
- Marketing plan
- Listing agreement form
- Agency disclosure form
- Net proceeds to seller form
- Information about the agent and the real estate firm

tices (such as MLS listings and "For Sale" signs) and newer marketing practices (such as online advertising and virtual tours of the home).

Listing Appointment. The agent should arrive at the seller's home armed with the CMA, a marketing plan, a listing agreement form, an agency disclosure form, a net proceeds to seller form (discussed later in this chapter), and information about the agent and the agent's firm. These items will help the agent explain the listing process to the seller and help the seller set a listing price. But the listing presentation is more than just an exchange of information; it is also the best opportunity the agent has to gain the seller's confidence and build rapport.

CMA. A major benefit of a real estate agent's services is her ability to help establish a realistic listing price. The seller is probably more interested in hearing the agent's opinion of the value of the home than any other piece of information.

All the information that was gathered and analyzed for the CMA should be presented to the seller, along with an explanation of how that information helps determine market value. A CMA form helps the agent present the information in an orderly way that's easy to understand. Plus, a CMA form makes it clear that the agent's estimate of value is based on facts, not personal opinion.

When the agent discusses value, it is best to focus on objective criteria: size, number of rooms, age, location, and terms of sale. This way, the seller (and the agent) won't get sidetracked with subjective issues, such as the fact that it took three years to complete the fancy deck, or cost hundreds of dollars to purchase just the right plants for the rock garden.

Agents often present three figures to the seller. The first figure is the general price range. The second figure is a suggested listing price, which is typically higher than the estimated selling price, to leave room for negotiation. The third figure is what the agent believes the property will actually sell for—the estimated selling price. The estimated selling price should be close to the property's market value.

During the discussion of listing prices, the agent should emphasize that it is the seller, not the agent, who will ultimately decide on the listing price. The agent can offer opinions and advice, but it is the seller who must set the price.

Many owners expect to receive more for their property than it is worth, because of market misinformation, inflated expectations, or the owner's personal attachment to the property. The information presented in the CMA can correct any misconceptions the seller has regarding current market conditions in her neighborhood, and force a more realistic approach to pricing.

Marketing plan. The agent should present the marketing plan to the seller, explaining each step in the marketing process so the seller will know what to expect. For instance, the agent might explain that open houses rarely produce a buyer for the property, but do provide valuable feedback concerning the listing price and the presentation of the home. It's also a good idea to bring samples of flyers and other advertising, showing the seller what type of marketing materials the agent would provide.

Background information. The seller will want to know something about the agent making the presentation and the real estate firm that the agent works for. The agent should be prepared to discuss the success rate of the firm, its membership in the local MLS, and how the MLS operates. Information about the agent's career is also important, such as how many of years of real estate experience the agent has, awards or achievements, and relevant education.

Listing agreement. The agent should review the listing agreement with the seller. This includes showing the seller the form, going over its most important provisions, and answering any questions the seller may have. It's a good idea to leave a copy of the form with the seller for a closer reading. (Of course, if the seller signs the agreement, the Real Estate Law requires the agent to give the seller a copy. Listing agreements are covered in Chapter 2.)

Agency disclosure. When a listing agreement is signed, it creates an agency relationship between the seller and the listing agent. So if the seller decides to list the property with the agent's firm, the agent must provide the seller with a copy of the agency disclosure form (see Chapter 1).

Net proceeds to seller. Along with the listing price, sellers are very interested in their net proceeds. They want to know how much cash they will walk away with after the sale has closed and all the expenses have been paid. Agents often use a "net proceeds to seller" form to arrive at the seller's bottom line. Of course, at this point the expenses can only be estimated, but it is possible to arrive at a fairly accurate figure. The steps for determining the net proceeds are discussed in Chapter 11, and a net proceeds to seller form is shown in Figure 11.5.

Servicing the Listing

Once the listing has been taken, the work of servicing the listing begins. This includes helping prepare the property for showing, marketing the property, and maintaining ongoing communication with the seller. In some cases, servicing the listing also includes modifying the original listing agreement.

Preparing the Property. It's a rare house that's in prime condition and ready to go on the market. Most homes need at least some work, and many need a lot of work. At a minimum, the house must be cleaned thoroughly before it's shown to prospective buyers. Some minor repairs are also likely to be necessary.

Both the interior and exterior should be cleaned and tidied up. Curb appeal—how the property looks from the street—is extremely important, since first impressions are often lasting impressions. It's preferable for the interior of the home to be decorated in neutral colors. Closets should be cleaned and organized; bulging closets give the impression that the house lacks storage space. All fixtures should work properly. Leaky faucets, squeaking doors, creaking floors, broken fences, and torn window screens should all be repaired.

Renovations to make a home more marketable are worthwhile if they increase the selling price by more than they cost. For example, sellers can often recoup more than 100% of what they spend on minor kitchen renovations. Fresh paint inside and/or outside can also pay for itself in some cases.

The following are some tasks that should be completed before a home is shown. Some of these items need to be done on a regular basis to keep the property in top condition during the listing period:

- mow and water lawns;
- weed flower beds;
- plant extra flowers or shrubs (after removing all dead or damaged plantings);
- prune trees and shrubs;
- rake up all old leaves and other debris;

- cover bare ground with bark chips or gravel;
- pressure wash the roof and replace any missing shingles;
- mend broken fences or railings;
- clean up porches and decks;
- repaint when necessary (especially trim);
- remove children's toys and bikes from walkways and driveways;
- straighten up the garage and shed;
- fix broken door and window screens;
- replace or fix the mailbox;
- remove any old vehicles;
- clean and remove clutter from rooms;
- reorganize the closets, basement, attic, and other storage spaces;
- repaint any brightly colored walls in a neutral shade;
- replace any old or outdated carpeting and wallpaper;
- repair any cracks in the walls;
- fix leaky faucets;
- put new hardware on drawers and cabinets; and
- oil squeaky doors.

Security. The seller should remove any small items of value, such as jewelry or coins, and keep them in a safety deposit box for the duration of the listing period. It may also be a good idea to rearrange or otherwise secure any delicate pieces of furniture or artwork.

Keys and keyboxes. The seller needs to provide the agent with keys to the property, which are generally stored in a lockbox attached to the front door.

Marketing the Property. Real estate agents market listed properties in many ways. One of the first and most important marketing activities occurs when the agent submits the listing to the MLS. Typically, this is done right after the listing agreement is signed. All the other MLS members become aware that the property is for sale and that they can begin showing it to their prospective buyers.

"For Sale" signs are also an extremely effective form of advertising. Many prospective buyers drive around the neighborhoods they're interested in, looking for signs. If they see a listed property that they want to find out more about, they follow up with a phone call to the listing agent or their own agent.

Flyers with information about the property should be prepared and left in an obvious spot in the house (such as a kitchen counter, or a table in the entryway).

That way, whenever any agent shows the home to a prospect, all the pertinent information is close at hand. Copies can also be placed in an information box attached to the "For Sale" sign in front of the home. A flyer should include the price, the terms of sale, the number of bedrooms and bathrooms, and other key features, along with one or more photographs of the property.

The Internet is an essential tool in real estate marketing. Brokerages and businesses such as Zillow maintain **websites** with photos, video clips, and detailed information about properties, and many individual agents have web pages for their listings. Prospective buyers can search these sites, then contact the agent if they find a property that interests them.

Real estate websites have reduced the importance of standard **advertisements**, but those can still be worthwhile. Agents place ads online and in print publications such as newspapers and local magazines.

Often properties are advertised more to make the real estate office's phone ring than to sell the homes featured in the ad. It's a rare buyer who sees a home in an ad and ends up deciding to purchase that particular property. Buyers are more likely to call about a home, find out it isn't right for them, and talk to the agent about other possibilities. Agents use advertising that features especially appealing properties as a way to bring in potential buyers for all of their listings.

Regardless of the marketing tools you use, you should always be sure that the money you spend on marketing activities is cost-effective. The key factor in any marketing strategy is to measure the dollars spent against the outcome achieved. Many agents find it helpful to keep a log of their marketing efforts. For example, an agent who spends $100 sending an email flyer about a new listing to 5,000 licensees will want to keep track of how many of those flyers result in showings, calls, offers, and/or sales. In her local market, she may find that the same $100 is better spent on an ad in the community newspaper. Tracking results will help you determine which marketing strategies work best for a particular type of property in your area.

Real estate agents must be aware of many restrictions on real estate advertising, both state and federal. Some restrictions involve the truthfulness of the ad; others involve making full disclosure. The laws apply both to print ads and to online advertising.

License law restrictions. Advertisements published or distributed by a real estate licensee (when acting as an agent) must include a licensee designation, such as "agent" or "REALTOR®." An advertisement that doesn't fulfill this requirement is called a "blind ad" and violates the license law. The advertisement must also state the agent's license number.

Truth in Lending Act. The federal Truth in Lending Act (TILA) is another law with provisions that apply to advertising. Generally, anyone who places a consumer credit advertisement must comply with the act. This includes real estate agents who include financing information when advertising homes for sale.

Before this law was passed, advertisers often disclosed only the most attractive aspects of their credit terms, distorting the true cost of the financing. For example, an ad might have touted low monthly payments ("Only $450 a month!") without mentioning the large downpayment necessary to qualify for that payment level. The Truth in Lending Act prohibits that kind of deception.

If an advertisement covered by TILA includes specific information about certain financing terms, then certain other information about the credit being offered must also be disclosed in the ad. These financing terms are referred to as "trigger terms," because they trigger the disclosure requirement. In other words, if the advertiser includes a trigger term in the ad, the Truth in Lending Act disclosures must be made; if no trigger terms are mentioned, then no disclosures are required. Trigger terms for real estate advertisements include:

- the amount of the downpayment ("20% down");
- the amount of any payment ("Pay less than $1,700 per month");
- the number of payments ("260 monthly payments");
- the period of repayment ("30-year financing available"); and
- the amount of any finance charge ("1% origination fee").

Example: Broker Simms places a classified ad that reads "Fantastic buy! Three-bedroom, two-bath house in the Wildwood neighborhood. Buyer can assume seller's VA loan. Payments are only $1,525 a month!"

This ad contains a trigger term, the amount of the monthly payment, so certain disclosures must also be included in the ad.

If any trigger terms are used in an advertisement, all of the following must be disclosed in the ad:

- the amount of the downpayment;
- the terms of repayment; and
- the annual percentage rate, using that term spelled out in full.

The **annual percentage rate** (APR) expresses the relationship of the total finance charge to the total amount financed as an annualized percentage. It takes into account the interest rate, loan fees, and other charges. (See Chapter 9.)

Here are some examples of phrases that would not trigger TILA's disclosure requirement:

- "No downpayment!"
- "5% Annual Percentage Rate loan available."
- "Easy monthly payments!"
- "Adjustable-rate financing available."
- "VA and FHA financing available."
- "Terms to fit your budget."

Example: Returning to the previous example, Broker Simms decides that he does not want to clutter up the ad with a lot of disclosures, so he rewrites the ad to read: "Fantastic buy! Three-bedroom, two-bath house in the Wildwood neighborhood. Buyer can assume seller's VA loan and take advantage of low monthly payments." This ad complies with the requirements of the Truth in Lending Act; since no trigger terms are used, no additional disclosures are required.

Advertising must also comply with fair housing laws. See Chapter 3 for a discussion of that topic.

Holding Open Houses. Most open houses do not directly result in the sale of the home, and some real estate agents consider them a questionable use of time (at least in an active market). However, most sellers expect their agent to hold an open house. From the agent's perspective, the main benefit of an open house is finding prospective buyers who might also be interested in other listed homes, or prospective sellers who are ready to list their own homes.

The basic steps involved in holding an open house include arranging a day and time with the sellers when they can be out of the home, advertising the open house, preparing informational packets about the property, making sure the home is ready for showing, setting up open house directional signs, putting out a guest log, staying at the property during the scheduled open house hours, and following up with thank-you notes to those visitors who signed the guest log.

Setting the day and time. Sellers should never remain in the house during an open house, so it is important for the agent to choose a day and time when it is convenient for the sellers to be away from their home. If a seller questions the need to be absent during an open house, the agent must tactfully explain that most buyers do not feel comfortable looking at a home when the owner is present.

Advertising. After the date is set, the open house can be advertised in the newspaper and on the Internet. The ad for the open house should target a specific audience. For example, an ad for a small two-bedroom home might be written to appeal to young couples or retirees.

Flyers are often sent to neighbors. Neighbors may know of someone in the market for a home, or may be interested in listing their own home (potential sellers like to know which agents are active in their neighborhood).

Flyer packets can be given to interested prospects who tour the home. These packages generally include a flyer about the home, the agent's business card, flyers on other listings in the area, and information about the agent.

Preparing the home. For an open house to accomplish anything, the listed property must be in top condition. The home should be sparkling clean, the rooms brightly lit and fresh smelling. All clutter should be put away. The grounds should be mowed, trimmed, and tidied. Some sellers need an extra nudge to get their homes in shape for an open house. But for that all-important first impression, order and cleanliness are a must.

Directional signs. "Open House" signs with arrows that point prospects in the right direction should be placed at strategic locations. Never count on a prospect's ability to find an address. Show the prospects how to get there, or they may not show up at all.

Guest logs. Guest logs are used to keep track of who views the property. A guest log can be a source of new leads as well as a security measure. Of course, not every prospect will want to sign the log; it is usually a mistake to try to push everyone to sign in.

Presence during open house hours. An agent should never leave an open house early, even if business is slow. Sellers are not very happy to come home to an empty house when they are expecting a positive report from an enthusiastic agent. Prospects that arrive at the property after the agent has left are sure to be disappointed and wary of dealing with that agent in the future. If an emergency arises and the agent must leave early, she should call another agent for backup. If business is slow, an agent can work on other aspects of the business during open house hours, such as calling FSBOs. (Agents should never use the seller's phone without the seller's permission.)

Of course, when the open house is over, it is imperative to lock up the home properly if the sellers have not yet returned.

Follow-up. Agents generally follow up on the leads who signed the guest log, in the form of a thank-you card or a personal note. It is especially important to keep any promises that were made. For instance, if an agent promised to go to a prospect's home and perform a CMA, it is vital that she do so.

Showing the Property. Open houses occur only occasionally—usually when a property is first listed—and rarely generate sales. The way most properties are sold is by showing them to individual prospects. Showing homes will be discussed in more detail later in the chapter.

Listing Modifications and Extensions. Sometimes a property is listed at a price that both the real estate agent and seller believe to be reasonable, yet weeks pass without significant interest from buyers. This may be due to a slow real estate market, or it may reflect a changing market. For example, if comparable homes have subsequently been put on the market at lower prices, this may decrease the interest in the listing. Of course, it's also possible that the listing simply was overpriced in the first place.

When a listing isn't attracting interested buyers, the agent should meet with the seller to discuss the situation and reevaluate the listing price. The seller may be resistant to the idea of lowering the price, so the agent should be prepared with data on new listings or comparable sales. Documentation of the agent's marketing efforts, such as flyers or printouts of online advertising, may also help convince the seller that the price (not the agent) is the problem.

Modifications to a listing agreement such as a change in listing price should be made using an appropriate form, and all of the parties to the original agreement must sign the form. (Listing agreement modifications are discussed in Chapter 2.) The new price should be submitted to the multiple listing service promptly.

If a listing's expiration date is approaching and no sale is scheduled to close, the agent will want to obtain a listing extension. Like a listing price modification, an extension involves meeting with the seller to discuss the efforts the agent has made and the possible reasons why the property hasn't sold yet. If the seller agrees to extend the listing, a separate modification form should be used to set a new expiration date.

Communicating with the Seller. An important aspect of servicing the listing is communication with the seller. Even though the agent's efforts will be focused on marketing the property, it's important to remain in contact with the seller. Informing the seller of what to expect and providing regular progress reports reassures the seller that the agent is working hard, and reduces the chance of any misunderstandings.

The agent should also provide the seller with regular updates summarizing the number of inquiries about and/or showings of the property, and any advertising used. The reports may also include copies of advertisements for the property, and any comments from other agents or prospective buyers.

Selling Practices

Real estate agents work to obtain listings, and they also work to find buyers. An agent working with a prospective buyer must determine the buyer's needs, choose suitable properties, and show the homes.

Types of Buyers

Buyers can be categorized in roughly four ways:

- first-time buyers,
- trade-up buyers,
- empty-nesters, and
- retirees.

First-time buyers are the novices—typically they know little about buying a home, have limited funds, and are looking for smaller homes. They have lots of questions about buying a home and often rely on a parent or older friend for advice. Sometimes a parent will be helping to finance the home, by giving the son or daughter some money towards a downpayment or by co-signing the loan.

Trade-up buyers are selling one house in order to purchase a newer and/or larger house. They are more experienced at buying a home, have a better idea of what they want, and rely less (if at all) on the advice of parents or friends. Because they are selling their present home, they may be able to make a fairly large downpayment on their new home.

Empty-nesters are couples whose children have left home. These buyers no longer need all the space available in a large family home. They typically look for smaller homes that require less upkeep. Often, these buyers can afford a hefty downpayment, using the equity they have in their present home.

Retirees are also looking for smaller, easily maintained homes. Monthly payments may be a concern, because retirees have a fixed income. They may be interested in condominium units or other attached housing.

Finding a Buyer

All types of buyers are found using the techniques previously discussed, such as advertising and open houses. Many buyers call real estate agents after seeing a "For Sale" sign posted on an attractive property, which is why most agents post

Fig. 5.3 Worksheet for tracking leads

Seller Prospect	
Name:	
Address:	
Phone: (H)	(W)
Reason for Selling:	
Must Sell By:	
Property Data	
Location:	
Age:	Family Room:
Lot size:	Square Footage:
Style:	Garage:
Bedroom:	Fireplace:
Bathroom:	Heating:
Dining Room:	Condition:
Asking Price:	Estimated Value:
Existing Financing:	
Minimum Net to Seller:	
Buyer Prospect	
Name:	
Address:	
Phone: (H)	(W)
Must Take Possession By:	
Property Desired	
Location:	Family Room:
Style:	Square Footage:
Bedroom:	Garage:
Bathroom:	Fireplace:
Dining Room:	Other:
Price Range: Maximum Downpayment:	Maximum Mortgage Payment:
Comments:	

their personal "name rider" on signs. Other buyers find properties by browsing websites. And others simply call or visit a real estate office because they want an agent to show them some properties. These "call-ins" or "walk-ins" are helped by the agent who is "working the floor" at the time.

Floor duty is the practice of assigning one agent to handle telephone calls and office visits for a specific period of time. If those calling or visiting do not ask to speak with a particular agent, the agent on floor duty can help them and, hopefully, retain them as customers. Some agents find it helpful to use a prospect form (such as the one shown in Figure 5.3) while they are on floor duty. With a prospect form, an agent can quickly jot down the pertinent information about callers or walk-in customers, be they potential buyers or potential sellers.

Using social media such as blogging or tweeting can be a great way to find potential buyers (and sellers). Of course, to be successful you have to pick a form of social media that appeals to you. The Internet is a rich source of information on how to use social media to build a clientele.

Regional or national companies often transfer workers from office to office. Transferees need agents to help them with both sides of the move: selling their present home and helping them to buy a home in a new community. Many real estate offices specialize in relocation or have relocation programs. These programs can be a lucrative source of business.

Determining Needs. Once an agent has found a prospective buyer, he must determine the buyer's housing needs. Determining a buyer's needs is a two-step process. First the agent helps the buyer determine how much she can afford, and then the agent helps the buyer define specific housing requirements (such as number of bedrooms and bathrooms).

Most real estate agents advise buyers to get **preapproved** by a lender. When a buyer is preapproved, the lender agrees in advance to loan her up to a specified amount of money, as long as the home she eventually chooses meets the lender's standards.

The preapproval process is discussed in more detail in Chapter 9; for now, though, it is enough to know that showing buyers homes they cannot afford is extremely counterproductive. It wastes the time of both the buyer and the agent, and it needlessly disappoints the buyer. There is probably nothing so discouraging to a buyer as getting excited about a dream home, only to discover that it is completely out of his price range. Suddenly other, more affordable housing loses its appeal, and the buyer may despair of ever finding the right home for the right price.

Buyers usually know what kind of home they want. The difficult part is prioritizing their needs.

Example: Stan and Nancy Cooke meet with Agent Sandin to discuss their housing needs. Stan and Nancy have two children and a lot of out-of-town guests. They tell Agent Sandin that they need a four-bedroom, two-bathroom house. They need a large kitchen, a family room, at least one fireplace, a three-car garage, a large yard, and room for a kennel for their three dogs. "And a laundry room," says Stan. "And a tool shed," Nancy adds.

Agent Sandin knows there's no way he is going to find a house with all of these attributes in the price range the Cookes can afford. After asking a lot of questions and listening carefully to the Cookes' answers, Agent Sandin says, "It sounds like four bedrooms, two bathrooms, and a large kitchen are the three most important criteria. The fourth item is room for your dogs, and the fifth is a large family room. Is that right?" After a moment's thought, the Cookes readily agree. Now Agent Sandin can begin looking for a house that fits their needs.

Sometimes creative problem-solving can help meet a housing need.

Example: Agent Sandin has found what he thinks is the perfect home for the Cookes, but it has only three bedrooms instead of four. However, the den could easily double as a guest room, especially since there is a third bathroom right off the den. The Cookes are more than willing to compromise on the guest bedroom and are delighted with a third bathroom.

An agent should never try to manipulate a buyer into considering a home just because that agent listed the home. If buyers feel they are being pressured to view homes that don't meet their needs, they will quickly find another agent who is more willing to accommodate them. If buyers sense a conflict of interest, they might even pursue disciplinary measures.

Showing Properties

The ability to show property effectively is vital to a successful real estate career. An agent should always take the time to research and plan her efforts in order to make showings as efficient and useful as possible. Thorough preparation includes developing sales speeches and keeping current with the local market and general real estate trends.

Selecting Listings. When choosing properties to show a prospective buyer, only pick homes the buyer can afford. An agent can lose a sale by showing a buyer homes that are priced too high. As noted above, buyers should be preapproved to determine their affordable price range. However, sometimes buyers choose to buy a less expensive house than they could afford. An agent must respect the buyer's wishes—it is up to the buyer to decide how much to spend on a home.

Don't show too many houses on one trip. After five or six houses, most buyers begin to tire and may forget or confuse impressions and details. It does no good to show a home to a buyer who is not going to remember it.

Previewing the Properties. Before taking buyers on a showing, the agent should always preview the listed homes and research the area. Knowing a home's best and worst attributes in advance allows the agent to choose what to highlight and what to downplay during the showing. It also helps the agent prepare to handle any objections that might be raised by the buyers.

Learning the local streets and planning a route will help avoid the embarrassment of getting lost. It's also a good idea to become familiar with school district boundaries and to know the location of neighborhood shopping and recreational facilities.

Inside the Homes. It's important to read the buyer's signals. The buyer will let the agent know, either verbally or by body language, how she feels about the house. It's important for the agent to listen to what the buyer says and pick up any nonverbal cues. Is this the kind of house the buyer loves? Hates? The buyer's reaction to one house will help the agent choose what to show her next.

The agent should give the buyers a chance to picture themselves in the home. Most buyers need to picture themselves in a house before they will make an offer on it. In order to do this, they need some time to themselves. Agents don't have to talk nonstop during a showing. A little silence can be an effective sales tool.

Making an Offer

Once a buyer has found a house that she would like to buy, the selling agent's next step is to prepare an offer. To purchase real estate, an offer must be made in writing. Once the offer has been signed by the seller, it forms a binding purchase agreement. (We will discuss offers and the purchase agreement in greater detail in the next two chapters.)

Offers and Counteroffers. Agents are required to submit any offer to the seller, even if that offer seems unreasonable. It is the seller who decides whether to accept an offer, not the real estate agent.

When a buyer's agent prepares a written offer, it should be passed on to the listing agent, who then presents it to the seller. Often, the selling agent will be present when the listing agent presents the offer, so if the seller has any questions about the buyer (regarding financial stability, for example), the questions can be answered by the selling agent.

Typically, once an offer is presented to the seller, a period of negotiation begins. This is perhaps one of the most valuable services an agent can provide:

shepherding the parties through the process of making offers and counteroffers, and helping the buyer and seller reach an agreement that satisfies them both.

Negotiation. When presenting the offer, agents often present the most positive aspects first, and then the more negative aspects. This prevents the seller from immediately rejecting the offer before the seller has had a chance to listen to and carefully consider all the terms. Even if the seller is unwilling to accept a negative term (such as a low sales price or a quick closing date), the seller is more likely to counter with another offer than to reject the buyer outright.

During the negotiation process, agents should remember to maintain their professionalism and avoid hostility between the parties. They must also give the parties copies of any documents they sign when they sign them. This means that the buyer must get a copy of any offer as soon as it is signed, the seller must get a copy of any counteroffer as soon as it is signed, and both parties must get a copy of the final purchase agreement as soon as it is signed.

Multiple Offers. In an active real estate market, it is likely that more than one offer will be submitted to a seller. In such a situation, the listing agent should present all available offers to the seller at the same time, without presenting them in a prejudicial fashion. The seller has the option of rejecting all offers, accepting one offer, making a counteroffer to one offer, or accepting one offer and making a contingent backup counteroffer to another offer.

When a seller has multiple offers to choose from, his decision hinges mainly on the prices offered; but there are ways to help a buyer's offer stand out from the crowd. Because a home sale is an emotional as well as a financial decision, in a tight market some selling agents have prospective buyers write a brief statement about themselves and why the seller's house appeals to them. Sellers are sometimes reluctant to sell, and they may feel better about selling to someone who has articulated her enthusiasm for the property.

Example: A prospective buyer might write a statement such as this: "We are a young married couple looking to purchase our first house, as we are planning to start a family and will need more room as our family grows. My husband is an accountant with an investment firm, and I am a veterinarian. You might say we're both animal lovers; we have several dogs, as well as some smaller pets, and love that your house has a large yard for the dogs to play in, along with ample kennel space in the utility room. We were also won over by the lush landscaping and the terrific school district."

Also bear in mind that most buyers are interested in other properties as well, and it can be helpful to let a seller know about other properties that the buyer was interested in. Not only does this remind the sellers that their house is competing against other properties, it also helps reassure the sellers that their house will be appreciated.

Example: A selling agent might inform the sellers: "The buyers were undecided between your home and a nearby property on Willow Way. While that property had a fourth bedroom and was about the same price, they opted for your property because they thought your home was in better condition, requiring less touching-up before they move in, and because they loved the big yard and the well-maintained landscaping."

Again, it's best for all buyers to be preapproved for a loan before making an offer, and this is even more important in a competitive market. Preapproval shows the buyer is serious about making a purchase; it also eases the concerns the seller might have about the buyer's ability to obtain the necessary financing. If a seller has to choose between two otherwise equal offers and only one buyer is preapproved, the seller will almost certainly choose the offer from the preapproved buyer.

Agency Disclosure. As you'll recall from Chapter 1, California law requires a selling agent (the agent working with the buyer) to give the agency disclosure form to each party as soon as it's practical to do so. The buyer must receive it before signing the offer to purchase, and the seller must receive it before the offer is presented. This is also the point at which the selling agent and the listing agent are required to provide an agency confirmation statement, indicating which party or parties they're representing in this transaction. The agency confirmation statement is usually included in the purchase agreement form.

Safety Issues

Throughout the listing and selling process, real estate agents must be conscious of safety and security issues.

Real estate agents must take care to protect the safety of clients and customers. For example, agents should never show buyers homes that are in the middle of construction. Instead, agents should arrange to have the contractor show the buyer the home. Construction sites are dangerous places, and can present grave hazards. This is particularly true if the buyer is accompanied by young children.

Real estate agents should also take precautions to secure a seller's possessions during open houses or when showing the property. Sellers should be warned to remove valuable items from the home prior to showing. Agents should never leave prospects unattended in a home and should encourage all visitors to sign a log. Agents should be especially wary when a couple attends an open house and one partner keeps the agent occupied while the other partner disappears into another part of the house—this behavior is a signal that trouble may be brewing. And, naturally, agents must be sure to leave the property securely locked.

Keys and keyboxes pose special hazards. Agents must make every effort to keep house keys in a safe place, and to make sure that keyboxes are as secure as possible. For example, when a salesperson terminates affiliation with a broker, that broker must notify the MLS immediately and make sure the salesperson's keybox code is deactivated.

Real estate agents must also be conscious of their own safety. Because real estate agents often work alone with virtual strangers, they should take extra precautions. While physical violence is rare, instances do occur.

If at all possible, agents should work in pairs when showing properties or holding open houses. If that is not possible, agents should ask their customers to meet them at their offices. This avoids the dangers of meeting a stranger at an empty house. And when meeting with customers for the first time, it is wise to ask for photo I.D.

Customers who call up and insist on meeting the agent at the property because they are pressed for time, or who "simply cannot" leave a number where they can be reached are poor risks. Legitimate customers are generally willing to reschedule appointments and are also happy to comply with personal safety rules. Remember, if the agent and the customer meet for the first time at the property rather than the office, the customer is also at risk. The customer is also meeting a stranger (the real estate agent) at a deserted property. If the agent explains that it is in everyone's best interest to meet first at the office, most customers will readily agree.

When agents are showing properties, they should leave word with their office as to where they are going and when they will return. They can also arrange to check in with someone on a regular basis. Keeping a cell phone handy is a necessary safety measure.

In areas where crime is a problem and agents are worried about their personal safety, most local police departments are happy to provide training and give advice on ways to foster personal safety.

Real Estate Assistants

Depending on the amount of business a real estate agent handles, he may decide to hire a real estate assistant. Many administrative and other tasks can be delegated to an assistant, freeing up more time for the agent to spend working face-to-face with clients. An assistant may work on a part-time or full-time basis, and is typically paid on a salary or salary-plus-commission basis.

Under the license law, many of the day-to-day activities performed by a real estate agent require a real estate license. Generally, it is unlawful for an unlicensed person (when acting on behalf of another, for compensation or in the expectation of compensation) to engage in any of the following acts:

1. selling, buying, or exchanging real property or a business opportunity;
2. leasing or collecting rents from real property or a business opportunity, or buying, selling, or exchanging leases on real property or a business opportunity;
3. soliciting prospective sellers, buyers, or tenants, or listing real property or a business opportunity for sale or lease;
4. locating or filing an application for the purchase or lease of lands owned by the state or federal government;
5. charging or collecting an advance fee to promote the sale or lease of real property or a business opportunity (by advertising or listing it, by obtaining financing, or in some other way);
6. soliciting borrowers or lenders for or negotiating loans secured by liens on real property or business opportunities, or collecting payments or performing other services in connection with such loans; and/or
7. selling, buying, or exchanging real property securities, land contracts, or promissory notes secured by liens on real property or business opportunities, and performing services for the holders of contracts or notes.

Because of these restrictions, an agent who's looking for a real estate assistant may want to consider hiring another real estate licensee.

A licensee might decide to work as a real estate assistant instead of as an agent for a variety of reasons. For example, a new licensee might want more experience before taking on full-scale agent responsibilities. Working as an assistant gives the licensee a chance to become more familiar with the business and to benefit from the knowledge and guidance of a mentor. A licensee might choose to work as an assistant because he can't afford to work full-time on a commission basis until he is more established and has a dependable stream of income. And some licensees simply find that they are not comfortable performing the marketing and sales duties associated with being an agent. Working as a real estate assistant allows them to limit their negotiation and sales responsibilities while remaining in the business.

If the agent decides to hire an assistant who is not a real estate licensee, both the agent and assistant must take care to ensure that none of the assistant's activities require a license. The Bureau of Real Estate has issued guidelines (currently available on the Bureau's website) explaining what unlicensed real estate assistants are allowed to do. Both agent and assistant should carefully review these guidelines.

Typical Duties of a Real Estate Assistant

A real estate agent may delegate any of a variety of tasks and responsibilities to a real estate assistant, depending on how much experience the assistant has, and whether she is a real estate licensee. Office procedures and business practices will vary from broker to broker, but the following is a discussion of some of the duties a real estate assistant might be expected to fulfill.

Office Administration. Whether licensed or not, most real estate assistants will be expected to help with basic office administration tasks. Real estate transactions generate a significant amount of paperwork; for example, the license law requires brokers to keep transaction records for a minimum of three years after closing (some records must be kept at least four years). A transaction folder might include a listing agreement, purchase agreement, modifications or addenda to those agreements, and a settlement statement. By the time the transaction is completed, the folder might also hold photographs, disclosure forms, offers to purchase, an appraisal, escrow papers, and closing documents. An assistant will likely be responsible for organizing and filing these documents accordingly. If any documents must be duplicated and distributed to different parties, this task might also fall to an assistant.

In addition to handling paperwork, an assistant may answer and direct phone calls, and greet current or prospective clients visiting the office. When handling inquiries, an assistant can provide general information about the broker's services, but should refer questions about a specific listing to the agent.

Updating Information. When a real estate agent takes a listing, the information should be given to the MLS as soon as possible. In addition, listing status changes must be updated with the MLS. If the listing information is not kept current, another agent may end up wasting time considering or showing a home that is no longer available. Failing to report a pending or closed sale is not only unprofessional, but may also subject the listing broker to a penalty. For example, some multiple listing services or professional organizations may impose fines for failing to report listing status changes within a certain period of time. An assistant can be invaluable in helping an agent to submit listing information to the MLS. However, depending on the requirements of the particular MLS, this task may require a real estate license.

If the agent maintains a website with current listing information, it must also be updated regularly. Advertising homes that are no longer available (or failing to advertise homes that have come on the market) is at best useless; at worst, it is counterproductive. If a prospective buyer is interested in a listing advertised on the agent's website, she will not be impressed to learn that it actually sold two months ago.

Client Communication. Keeping in contact with clients is essential to a successful real estate business, but can be extremely time-consuming. A busy agent might be able to handle exchanges with current clients, such as answering questions or providing updates. But the agent may not have time to stay in touch with former and prospective clients, even though this type of contact is an important component of marketing.

An agent may choose to delegate this work to an assistant, who may or may not be licensed. For example, an unlicensed assistant might be responsible for preparing and sending mass mailings of newsletters, seasonal cards, or other promotional materials.

Appointments and Open Houses. Even the most organized agent may need help managing a busy schedule. An unlicensed assistant can coordinate the agent's appointments and remind the agent of upcoming meetings and showings.

High volume listing agents often hire "showing assistants," to help hold open houses. However, an unlicensed assistant's contact with prospective buyers must be somewhat limited. For example, the assistant may distribute property flyers and provide information from those flyers, but cannot otherwise discuss the property's price or condition or answer questions regarding financing. In other words, an unlicensed assistant cannot truly "show" the property.

A licensed assistant can take on more responsibility. For instance, a licensed assistant could actually write up an offer in the real estate agent's absence.

Chapter Summary

1. Listing properties is a vital part of a real estate agent's business. Listings can be found by farming, by making cold calls, by approaching expired listings and FSBOs, and through referrals.

2. Before making a listing presentation, the agent should research the property, visit the property, and prepare a competitive market analysis. At the listing presentation, the agent will present the competitive market analysis, tell the seller about the services the agent will provide, review the listing agreement, and discuss the net proceeds to the seller.

3. Once the listing is obtained, the agent must service the listing. This means advising the seller on preparing the property, advertising the property, holding an open house, and showing the home. If the listing does not sell, the listing agent and seller may agree to a listing modification or extension.

4. In addition to listing properties for sellers, agents need to find buyers for properties. Buyers can be found by advertising, by holding open houses, and by working floor duty. When a prospective buyer is found, the agent needs to determine the price range of affordable homes and to prioritize what the buyer wants in a home.

5. The agent must comply with certain license law restrictions on presenting offers and counteroffers. When making offers in a competitive market, it is important for a selling agent to paint a picture of the buyers and sell the buyers to the sellers; it is also important for buyers to be preapproved for financing.

6. An agent must be aware of a number of safety issues. Agents need to protect the physical safety of their clients and customers, protect the possessions of sellers, and protect themselves from danger.

7. An agent may need to hire a real estate assistant in order to make better use of her time. An assistant can help with a number of activities, such as maintaining files, updating listing information, communicating with clients, and setting up open houses. An agent must be careful that an unlicensed assistant does not perform any tasks that require a real estate license.

Key Terms

Farming: A sales technique that involves choosing a neighborhood where you wish to concentrate your activities, and then becoming a well-known name in that neighborhood by implementing various marketing activities.

Cold calls: A sales method that involves calling (in person or by phone) prospects, without any previous contact, to see if they are interested in your product or services.

For sale by owner (FSBO): A property that is being sold by the owner without the help of a real estate agent.

One-party listing: A listing agreement that is effective only for one particular buyer.

Curb appeal: The attractiveness of a property to a prospective buyer, based solely on its external appearance.

Truth in Lending Act: A federal law that requires lenders to make disclosures concerning loan costs (including the total finance charge and the annual percentage rate) to applicants for consumer loans (including any mortgage loan that will be used for personal, family, or household purposes), and that also requires certain disclosures in advertisements concerning consumer credit.

Trigger term: Under the Truth in Lending Act, a specific financing term that, when used in an advertisement, triggers the requirement that the annual percentage rate and other financing terms must also be disclosed in the ad.

Annual percentage rate (APR): All of the charges that a borrower will pay for the loan (including the interest, loan fee, discount points, and mortgage insurance costs), expressed as an annual percentage of the loan amount.

Preapproval: Formal loan approval given before the buyer has chosen a property to purchase, establishing the maximum loan amount that the lender is willing to provide.

Chapter Quiz

1. Agent Kalliwaki spends one hour every day randomly calling 20 homeowners to ask if they are interested in selling their homes. This practice is known as:
   a. farming
   b. cold calling
   c. FSBO-ing
   d. showing

2. Which of the following may be used in a competitive market analysis?
   a. Recently sold homes
   b. Current listings
   c. Recently expired listings
   d. All of the above

3. A homeowner wants to list his property for $245,900. The agent informs the homeowner that five similar homes have recently sold for around $235,000, there are five similar homes currently listed for around $239,000, and two similar, recently expired listings were priced at around $244,000. Which of the following statements is true?
   a. The upper ceiling of value is around $239,000
   b. The recently sold homes are the best indicators of value
   c. $245,900 is too high, because buyers refused to purchase similar homes for $244,000
   d. All of the above

4. A broker is advertising a client's property for sale, but neglects to include a licensee designation in the ad. The broker:
   a. is violating the real estate license law
   b. has created a blind ad
   c. doesn't need to include his designation unless he's selling his own property
   d. Both a) and b)

5. The following ad is placed in a local newspaper: "Fixer-upper going cheap. Two-bedroom, one-bathroom. Good foundation and plumbing, but needs a lot of TLC. Seller offers financing with small downpayment." This ad:
   a. violates the Truth in Lending Act
   b. must include the APR of the seller financing
   c. complies with the Truth in Lending Act
   d. must include the interest rate of the seller financing

6. Open houses:
   a. are often held to generate potential buyers for other listings
   b. should be conducted with the sellers present
   c. are held just before the listing is submitted to the MLS
   d. are a good way to determine what repairs need to be completed before the house will sell

7. Agent Brown receives two offers on the same house in the same hour. One offer is full price; the other is $25,000 below the listing price.
   a. Brown must submit both offers to the seller immediately
   b. Brown need submit only the most advantageous offer to the seller
   c. Brown has the authority to accept the best offer on behalf of the seller
   d. Brown must submit the best offer immediately, but can wait until the following day to submit the less advantageous offer

8. Now that the Knolls' last child has gone off to college, they are looking for a smaller house with easier upkeep. They can afford a significant downpayment using the equity from their current house. The Knolls would be considered:
   a. first-time buyers
   b. trade-up buyers
   c. empty-nesters
   d. retirees

9. Which of the following is not a safety precaution that agents should take?
   a. Warn sellers to remove valuable items from the home prior to showing
   b. Request that customers meet them at the property rather than at their office
   c. Work in pairs when showing properties or holding open houses, when possible
   d. Leave word with the office where they are going and when they will return

10. Which of the following activities should an unlicensed real estate assistant not perform?
    a. Maintain information in transaction folders
    b. Prepare flyers for mass mailings
    c. Coordinate appointments
    d. Advise buyers about obtaining financing

Answer Key

1. **b.** Cold calling is an unsolicited inquiry, usually by phone, made to a homeowner in order to obtain a listing.

2. **d.** Recently sold listings, current listings, and expired listings are all used in a CMA.

3. **d.** All of the options are true. Recent sales always provide the best indicators of value, and recently expired listings are likely to have been priced too high.

4. **d.** A broker advertising property other than his own must include a licensee designation; if the ad does not include this information, it will be considered a blind ad, which is a violation of the license law.

5. **c.** The ad complies with the Truth in Lending Act as no trigger terms are used.

6. **a.** People who walk into open houses rarely buy that particular home, but they are often interested in having the agent show them other homes.

7. **a.** Both offers must be submitted to the seller immediately. It is up to the seller to decide which offer to accept, not the agent.

8. **c.** The Knolls would be considered empty-nesters, since their children have moved out and they are looking for a smaller, easier-to-maintain property.

9. **b.** To be safe, agents should request that clients meet them at the broker's office first, rather than at an empty house.

10. **d.** An unlicensed real estate assistant should not answer questions about financing; this should be done only by licensees.

6

Preparing and Negotiating Offers

Making an Offer to Purchase

- Preparing an offer
- How offers are presented
- Multiple offers
- Backup offers
- Revoking an offer

Counteroffers and Negotiations

- Making a counteroffer
- Multiple counteroffers
- Negotiation process

Accepting an Offer

Contract Amendments

Contract Cancellation

Good Faith Deposits

- Size of the deposit
- Handling the deposit
- Refund or forfeiture

Fair Housing Considerations

Introduction

When a buyer finds a house he wants and decides to make an offer on it, what happens next? How and when are offers presented to a seller? What is your role as negotiator? What if you're representing the seller instead of the buyer?

In this chapter, we will discuss preparing and presenting an offer to purchase, negotiating terms, and the point at which an offer becomes a binding contract. We will also explain the procedures for handling the good faith deposit that customarily accompanies an offer.

Making an Offer to Purchase

You're helping your buyers—a married couple—look for a house that meets their needs: at least 1,800 square feet, three bedrooms, two baths, a large kitchen, and a double garage, in the $580,000 price range. After you've shown them several houses that fulfill these requirements, the buyers find one they are really interested in. You can tell, because they linger there a little longer, ask specific questions ("How old is the roof?" "How far is it to the elementary school?"), and mentally "move in" to the house, visualizing where their own furniture would go. They may make plans to come back and see the house again, perhaps bringing a third party—such as a parent or a more experienced friend—to examine the property with them.

After the buyers have had a chance to look at the property on their own and discuss it between themselves, you review the property's features and benefits and how well it meets their housing needs. You discuss a few concerns raised by the buyers, and ultimately they decide they're ready to make an offer to purchase the house. They ask you to write up their offer for them and present it to the seller.

Preparing an Offer

Under the statute of frauds, an offer to purchase real property must be in writing and signed by the offeror (the buyer). The statute of frauds is the law that requires certain types of contracts to be in writing.

An offer to purchase residential property is usually written up on a standard purchase agreement form (see Chapter 7). It must set forth all of the essential terms of the buyer's offer, including the purchase price, the buyer's good faith deposit, how he will pay the purchase price, and the proposed closing date. It's important to include all of the terms on which the buyer is willing to purchase the property, because once the document is signed by both the buyer and the seller, it becomes a binding contract—their **purchase agreement**. Since the purchase agreement traditionally also served as a receipt for the buyer's deposit, in California it is sometimes referred to as the **deposit receipt**.

What if a buyer wants to make an offer that is unrealistically low or contains too many conditions? Of course the buyer wants to get the property for the lowest price possible, but she needs to make an offer that the seller will take seriously. This is especially important if the seller receives multiple offers, as we'll discuss later in this chapter. It's part of your role to make sure the buyer understands this.

Although price is almost always the most important element of an offer, other factors can make an offer more or less attractive to the seller. The seller wants to get the best price for his home, but is also interested in a smooth, problem-free transaction. Anything the buyer can do to demonstrate greater commitment to the purchase will strengthen the offer. For example, making an earnest money deposit of at least 3% (the liquidated damages limit) shows the seller that the buyer is serious. An even larger deposit, exceeding that limit, may influence some sellers, even though the excess would have to be refunded in the event of default. (We'll explain the liquidated damages limit later in this chapter.)

Similarly, an offer with few or no contingencies means there's a greater chance of the sale closing smoothly. Submitting a "clean offer" with no conditions is ideal. Preapproval by a lender also makes an offer more attractive, since the buyer's ability to obtain financing is guaranteed (as long as the property meets the lender's standards). An all-cash offer is even better, since loan approval is completely unnecessary in that case.

It may be necessary to persuade your buyer to restructure her offer to make it more attractive. If the buyer wants to make a lowball offer, explain that the seller isn't likely to take the offer seriously and may in fact be offended. However, when discussing how to strengthen an offer, never encourage the buyer to eliminate an important contract condition or to make a higher offer than he can afford.

Who Can Prepare an Offer. Whose job is it to prepare the offer to purchase? A buyer could write her own offer; it is always legal (although generally not advisable) for the parties to a transaction to draw up their own contract. Or an attorney at law could draft the buyer's offer for her. What about you, the real estate agent? Can you prepare the buyer's offer?

When someone draws up a contract on behalf of others, he is considered to be practicing law. Only licensed attorneys may practice law, so as a general rule, contracts must be drafted by an attorney. However, there is an exception to this rule: real estate agents may prepare routine purchase agreements using standard forms that were originally written and approved by attorneys with expertise in real estate law. But even this exception is limited. A real estate agent may only fill out a purchase agreement form in connection with a transaction that she is handling. Also, an agent cannot charge a separate fee (in addition to her share of the brokerage commission) for completing the forms.

Note that when you fill out a contract form, you will be held to the same standard of care that is required of a lawyer. If, through negligence, you make a mistake when filling out a contract form, you may be liable for any harm suffered by the buyer or the seller as a result of the mistake.

Also, remember that you are only allowed to fill in the blanks on a standard form. Writing special clauses to insert into the pre-printed form or advising the parties on the legal effect of certain provisions may constitute the unauthorized practice of law, which is a criminal offense.

Reviewing the Offer. After filling out the purchase agreement form, check it over to see if it's complete and accurate. Then go over the form with the buyer, to make sure he understands and is satisfied with all of the terms. If the buyer has questions about the legal consequences of particular provisions, refer him to a real estate lawyer.

When you review the financial aspects of the offer, it is helpful to use a "Buyer's Estimated Net Cost" worksheet to calculate the buyer's closing costs and explain approximately how much cash will be needed to close the transaction if the seller accepts the offer. (See Figure 11.4 in Chapter 11.)

After going through the offer with the buyer, have him sign it, and then immediately give him a copy of the signed form. At this point, the buyer may give you a good faith deposit (discussed later in this chapter), which you will usually turn over to your broker.

Legal Requirements. In addition to being in writing and signed, a buyer's offer must meet certain other basic legal requirements to serve as the basis for a binding contract. To be valid, the offer must be definite and certain in its terms, not vague or incomplete. If you fill out the purchase agreement form properly, including the price, the closing date, and all of the other important terms, the buyer's offer will meet this requirement.

A valid offer must also clearly express a willingness to enter into a contract. Again, a standard purchase agreement fulfills this requirement.

When to Seek Advice. In filling out a purchase agreement form, problems most often occur in three areas:

- **Property description.** The property must be correctly described for the offer (and the subsequent purchase contract) to be enforceable. A full legal description is not required, but one should be used whenever possible.
- **Method of payment.** The offer must state how the buyer intends to pay the purchase price. Will the buyer obtain institutional financing, pay cash, or take advantage of seller financing?
- **Contingencies or special arrangements.** If the offer is contingent (on loan approval, on inspection results, or on the sale of the buyer's current residence, for example), the contingency provision must clearly state the circumstances under which the contingency will be considered fulfilled. Any special arrangements that the buyer wants to make, such as taking possession before the closing date, need to be spelled out in the offer.

These are areas you should pay extra attention to, but of course all of the terms of the offer are important. When you feel there may be a problem with one of the terms of the buyer's offer, or if you think you may have made a mistake, ask your broker for advice right away. Remember, you are preparing the offer as your broker's agent.

Occasionally, your broker will instruct you to get in touch with a real estate attorney. (Larger brokerages often have their own legal staff.) You should also consult an attorney in any of these situations:

- You have a question and your broker is not available.
- Because of special terms in the offer, you can't use a pre-printed purchase agreement or addendum. (Remember, you may not draft an agreement or even a complicated clause.)
- You need legal documents, such as an easement or a road maintenance agreement, to be prepared.

How Offers are Presented

It's usually the listing agent—the seller's own agent—who presents an offer to the seller. But the buyer's agent can also play an important role. We'll look at the presentation of a buyer's offer to a seller first from the buyer's agent's point of view and then from the listing agent's.

Buyer's Agent's Role. If you are the buyer's agent and the listing agent is going to present the offer to the seller, you should thoroughly explain it to the listing agent first. You may also want to go along when the listing agent meets with the seller, so that you can answer questions about the buyer or the offer.

> **Example:** The terms of your buyers' offer include paying cash for the seller's home—without any financing—and closing the transaction within 15 days. Because a cash sale is so unusual, you want to be there when the listing agent presents the offer to the seller. The seller might be suspicious of the buyers and want to know who they are, where they got their money, and why they want to close the transaction so quickly. You can relieve the seller's concerns by explaining the situation: the buyers recently received a large inheritance, and they want to move into a new house quickly because they are expecting their first baby soon. Making this explanation in person may be more effective than simply asking the listing agent to relay the information.

If the buyer is especially likable or in a situation that could evoke sympathy, it may be a good idea to ask the buyer to prepare a personal letter to give to the seller. Though financial considerations will be the primary basis for the seller's decision, he may view the offer more favorably if he thinks about the buyer as a real person rather than in the abstract. On the other hand, in a competitive market sellers receive a lot of these letters, and some agents dispute their value.

Note that if you go along when the offer is presented to the seller, you must disclose your agency status to the seller.

Naturally, you should give the seller the opportunity to discuss the offer privately with the listing agent. Whatever the seller decides to do about the offer, it is your job to convey that decision to the buyer.

Listing Agent's Role. If you are the listing agent and receive a written offer to purchase, you should arrange to meet with the seller to discuss the offer right away. Any and all offers to purchase that you receive must be presented to the seller as soon as possible.

When you meet with the seller, you should go over the terms of the offer and make sure the seller understands them. When there is more than one seller, it's a good idea to give each of them a copy of the offer. For instance, if the sellers are a married couple, make a photocopy of the offer so that each spouse can have a copy to look at as you discuss it. Then go through the offer line by line, answering the sellers' questions. It's especially important to discuss the following provisions:

- the proposed closing date and date of possession;
- the list of included items (any personal property that would be transferred to the buyers along with the real property);
- any contingencies (such as whether the buyers need to sell their own house first); and
- any obligations the sellers would have to fulfill before closing, such as completing repairs or cleanup.

If the sellers have legal questions, recommend that they consult an attorney. Do not try to answer legal questions yourself.

The sellers may ask questions about the buyers—who they are, whether they can afford the home, and how motivated they are to buy. When you describe the buyers, take care to avoid doing so in terms that might lead to a violation of the fair housing laws. Certain characteristics—race, national origin, religion, and so on—should not be mentioned.

When you review the financial aspects of the sale, it's helpful to use a "Seller's Estimated Net Proceeds" worksheet, which will make it easier to calculate the selling costs and the amount of cash the sellers can expect to receive at closing. (See Figure 11.5 in Chapter 11.)

Multiple Offers

Sometimes a seller has more than one offer to consider at the same time. Two or more offers may come in simultaneously, or an additional offer may come in while the seller is considering an earlier one. You must present every offer you receive to your seller, even if the seller has already decided to accept another offer.

Example: You presented an offer to the sellers two days ago. They've been considering it very seriously, and this morning they told you that they're almost sure they will accept it. They just want a little more time to think it over.

A few minutes ago, a buyer's agent faxed you another offer on the sellers' house. This offer is not nearly as attractive as the first one. Even so, you are required to present the new offer to the sellers right away. You can't wait around to see whether they accept or reject the first offer.

In a competitive real estate market, multiple offers are not uncommon. From a seller's point of view, multiple offer situations are desirable. Competing buyers may eliminate contingencies and increase offer amounts to make their offers more attractive, driving up the final sales price. For these same reasons, buyers try to avoid multiple offer situations.

Buyer's Agent's Role. If you represent a buyer in a multiple offer situation, your goal is to work with the buyer to make the offer as attractive as possible, without compromising too much. Depending on your client's financial situation, this may mean increasing the amount of the good faith deposit, or perhaps offering an unusually short closing period. As discussed in the previous chapter, a written statement or letter from the buyers may be helpful. Lender preapproval is almost a requirement; the seller is far less likely to consider an offer from an unapproved buyer if a similar offer has been submitted by an approved buyer. You may be able to find out from the seller's agent if the seller wants any special terms or concessions. For example, if the seller wants to sell quickly but remain in the home for an extra six months, you could add a sale-leaseback clause to your client's offer.

Make sure that any terms and concessions are really worth it to your client. It's easy for an anxious buyer to get caught up in a bidding war, and he may want to offer more than he can afford, or agree to unreasonable seller demands.

Listing Agent's Role. On the other hand, if you represent the seller in a multiple offer situation, your goal is to ensure that the seller accepts an offer that maximizes her profit but minimizes the chance that the sale will fall through.

One possible pitfall of a bidding war can occur if the price is driven up beyond what the home is truly worth. The seller may accept the highest offer but see the deal fall through when the buyer's lender appraises the house for less than the offered amount. Or the sale may fail for a different reason, and when the seller begins the negotiating process again, she may have inflated expectations of her home's value.

It is the listing agent's job to explain to the seller that simply accepting the highest offer isn't necessarily the wisest move. It may make more sense, for example, to choose a lower, all-cash offer over a higher offer requiring lender approval.

When faced with multiple offers, a seller has a number of options. The seller may decide to:

- reject all of the offers,
- accept one of the offers and reject the others,
- make a counteroffer on one offer and reject the others,
- make multiple counteroffers, or
- accept one offer and make a contingent counteroffer on another.

The last of these alternatives, the contingent counteroffer, brings us to the subject of backup offers.

Backup Offers

Some buyers are so interested in a particular house that they are willing to make a backup offer—an offer that's contingent on the failure of a previous sales contract.

Example: You showed Clark's house to Lenihan a week ago, and this morning Lenihan called to say he wants to make an offer on it. You contact the listing agent and learn that the seller has already signed a purchase agreement. Your client, Lenihan, is extremely disappointed. You explain that he can make a backup offer that is contingent on the failure of the first contract. He agrees to this, and you submit Lenihan's backup offer to the listing agent.

A listing agent is required to present additional offers received while the seller is already considering an offer; he must also present offers that come in after the seller has signed a contract, up until that sale actually closes. However, when an offer is submitted after the seller has signed a contract, the prospective buyer should make the offer contingent on the first sale's failure to close. You may use an addendum such as the one shown in Figure 6.1 to add a backup contingency clause to the second buyer's offer.

Contingent Counteroffer. Suppose you're representing a seller who has already signed a purchase agreement, and another buyer makes an offer. The seller is interested in accepting this as a backup offer, but it isn't contingent on the failure of the first contract. You should advise the seller to make a contingent counteroffer. The counteroffer will repeat the buyer's offer but add a contingency clause regarding the first contract.

Fig. 6.1 Back-up offer addendum

CALIFORNIA ASSOCIATION OF REALTORS®

BACK-UP OFFER ADDENDUM
(C.A.R. Form BUO, Revised 11/14)

This is an addendum to the ☐ California Residential Purchase Agreement, ☐ Counter Offer No._____, ☐ Other_____
_____, ("Agreement"), dated _____,
on property known as _____ ("Property"),
between _____ ("Buyer"),
and_____ ("Seller").

1. The Agreement is in back-up position number _____, and is contingent upon written cancellation of any prior contracts and related escrows ("Prior Contracts") between Seller and other buyers. Seller and other buyers may mutually agree to modify or amend the terms of Prior Contracts. Buyer may cancel the Agreement in writing at any time before Seller provides Buyer Copies of written cancellations of Prior Contracts Signed by all parties to those contracts. If Seller is unable to provide such written Signed cancellations to Buyer by _____ (date), then either Buyer or Seller may cancel the Agreement in writing.

2. **BUYER'S DEPOSIT** shall not be delivered to Escrow Holder until 3 business days After Copies of the written cancellations Signed by all parties to the Prior Contracts are provided to Buyer; OR (if checked) ☐ shall immediately be handled as provided in the Agreement.

3. **TIME PERIODS** in the Agreement for Investigations, contingencies, covenants and other obligations **(i)** shall begin on the Day After Seller provides Buyer Copies of Signed cancellations of Prior Contracts; OR **(ii)** (if checked) ☐ all time periods shall begin as provided in the Agreement. However, if the date for Close Of Escrow is a specific calendar date, that date shall NOT be extended, unless agreed to in writing by Buyer and Seller.

By signing below Buyer and Seller acknowledge that each has read, understands, has received a copy of and agrees to the terms of the Agreement and this Back-Up Offer Addendum.

Date _____   Date _____
Buyer _____   Seller _____
Buyer _____   Seller _____

Published and Distributed by:
REAL ESTATE BUSINESS SERVICES, INC.
a subsidiary of the California Association of REALTORS®
525 South Virgil Avenue, Los Angeles, California 90020

BUO REVISED 11/14 (PAGE 1 OF 1)

Reviewed by _____ Date _____

BACK-UP OFFER ADDENDUM (BUO PAGE 1 OF 1)

Reprinted with permission, California Association of Realtors®. Endorsement not implied.

Example: Your sellers have accepted an offer from the Browns. The Browns' offer is for the full listing price, but it's by no means certain that the Browns will qualify for the financing they need to complete the purchase. So when you present an offer from Finney, the sellers are very interested. Finney's offer is for $4,000 less than the Browns' offer, but Finney is already preapproved for the necessary loan.

The sellers want to accept Finney's offer as a backup offer. However, Finney's offer does not include a clause that makes it contingent on the failure of the first agreement. So you advise the sellers to make a counteroffer. They offer Finney the same terms set forth in his original offer, but they include a purchase agreement addendum making the sale to Finney contingent on the failure of the sale to the Browns. Finney accepts the sellers' counteroffer. Now if the Browns fail to qualify for financing, the sellers will have a binding contract with Finney.

Backup Offers and Breach of Contract. If a seller were to accept a second offer without a backup contingency clause, she would end up obligated to sell the house under two different contracts. Because one contract couldn't be fulfilled without breaching the other, the seller would be liable for breach of contract to the potential buyer who didn't get the property.

Example: Returning to the previous example, suppose your sellers accepted Finney's offer without adding the contingency provision. They would then be obligated to sell the property both to Finney and to the Browns. Obviously, the sellers can only transfer the property to one of the buyers. So if the sale to the Browns closed, Finney could sue the sellers for breach of his contract.

Never try to convince a seller to break an existing agreement in order to accept another offer, even if the second offer is much better. If you were to do that, you could be found guilty of a tort (a civil wrong) called "tortious interference with a contractual relationship." You could be held liable for damages caused by the breach of contract.

Example: Now suppose that Finney's offer is substantially better than the Browns' offer. Finney is offering $5,000 more than the listing price, will pay all of the closing costs, and is sure to qualify for the necessary financing. The sellers would be better off with this offer, and so would you (your commission would be larger because of the higher purchase price). But you should not suggest that the sellers breach their contract with the Browns in order to accept Finney's offer. If you did, the Browns could sue you for damages, and you could also lose your real estate license.

If your clients express an interest in breaching a contract in favor of another offer, you should strongly recommend that they talk to a real estate attorney before taking any action.

Notice to Backup Buyer. When a seller has accepted a backup offer and the first sale fails to close, the seller needs to notify the backup buyer that their contingent agreement is now a binding contract. Depending on how the backup offer was worded, the seller may also need to provide the backup buyer with a copy of the written cancellation of the first purchase agreement.

Revoking an Offer

A buyer can revoke an offer to purchase at any time until she is notified that the seller is accepting the offer. Once the acceptance is communicated, the offer becomes a binding contract, and the buyer can't back out without breaching it.

Even if an offer gives the seller a specific length of time to consider it, the buyer can revoke the offer sooner than that, as long as she acts before the seller sends his acceptance.

Example: Grant offers to buy Rush's house for $515,000. The offer states that it will terminate in 48 hours. If the 48 hours pass without an acceptance, Grant's offer will terminate automatically. But if Grant changes her mind about buying the house before that (for example, 30 hours after making the offer) and Rush has not yet accepted it, Grant is free to revoke the offer. Rush cannot force her to keep the offer open for the full 48 hours.

If a time limit is not stated in the offer, it will terminate after a reasonable amount of time.

Example: Now suppose that Grant's offer to Rush doesn't have a termination date. Rush doesn't respond to the offer for weeks. Finally, six weeks after receiving the offer, Rush notifies Grant that he's accepting it. It's too late, however. It's not reasonable to expect that an offer to purchase a house will be kept open for six weeks. If Grant has changed her mind about buying, she's no longer bound by her offer.

Counteroffers and Negotiations

Unless a buyer has made an offer that matches all of the seller's terms, the parties are likely to negotiate. In fact, negotiation is the norm rather than the exception. Sellers don't generally expect full-price offers, and buyers aren't surprised when the seller rejects their first offer and counters with another offer. The most common objections to initial offers concern:

- price,
- the size of the good faith deposit,
- the proposed closing date and date of possession,
- which furnishings or fixtures are included in the sale, and
- financing terms.

Making a Counteroffer

If the seller decides to counter the buyer's offer with another offer, you may be able to make the seller's changes on the original purchase agreement form.

Example: Gordon has offered Lamont $275,000 for her condo, with a closing date of June 16. He is making a good faith deposit of $2,500. Lamont is pleased with nearly all of the terms of Gordon's offer, but she wants a larger deposit—$5,000. Lamont's agent simply crosses out the $2,500 deposit figure on the form submitted by Gordon and writes in $5,000. Lamont initials the change, and her agent presents the counteroffer (the revised purchase agreement form) to Gordon.

For simple changes such as the one in the example, this might work just fine. But it's usually better to use a separate counteroffer form, such as the California Association of REALTORS® form shown in Figure 6.2, especially when the changes are numerous or complicated. Otherwise the purchase agreement may become confusing and, as a result, unenforceable.

On the seller's counteroffer form in Figure 6.2, you identify the original offer by filling in the date it was signed by the buyer, the property description, and the names of the buyer and seller. (The California Association of REALTORS® also publishes a similar but separate form for buyer's counteroffers.)

The counteroffer states that all of the terms of the original offer are accepted by the seller, except for the changes noted. There is space on the form for the seller's proposed changes, or an addendum may be attached, if necessary. There's a provision for setting a deadline, to indicate how long the buyer has to consider the counteroffer before it will terminate. The seller then signs the counteroffer and presents it to the buyer for approval or rejection.

Fig. 6.2 Seller counteroffer form

CALIFORNIA ASSOCIATION OF REALTORS®

SELLER COUNTER OFFER   No. _____
May not be used as a multiple counter offer.
(C.A.R. Form SCO, 11/14)

Date _____
This is a counter offer to the: ☐ California Residential Purchase Agreement, ☐ Buyer Counter Offer No.___, or ☐ Other_____ ("Offer"),
dated _____, on property known as _____ ("Property"),
between _____ ("Buyer") and _____ ("Seller").

1. **TERMS:** The terms and conditions of the above referenced document are accepted subject to the following:
    A. Paragraphs in the Offer that require initials by all parties, but are not initialed by all parties, are excluded from the final agreement unless specifically referenced for inclusion in paragraph 1C of this or another Counter Offer or an addendum.
    B. Unless otherwise agreed in writing, down payment and loan amount(s) will be adjusted in the same proportion as in the original Offer.
    C. **OTHER TERMS:** _____
    _____
    _____
    _____
    _____
    _____
    _____
    _____
    _____
    _____

    D. The following attached addenda are incorporated into this Seller Counter offer: ☐ Addendum No. _____
        ☐ _____   ☐ _____

2. **EXPIRATION:** This Seller Counter Offer shall be deemed revoked and the deposits, if any, shall be returned:
    A. Unless by 5:00pm on the third Day After the date it is signed in paragraph 3 (if more than one signature then, the last signature date)(or by _____ ☐ AM ☐ PM on _____ (date)) (i) it is signed in paragraph 4 by Buyer and (ii) a copy of the signed Seller Counter Offer is personally received by Seller or _____, who is authorized to receive it.
OR B. If Seller withdraws it in writing (CAR Form WOO) anytime prior to Acceptance.

3. **OFFER: SELLER MAKES THIS COUNTER OFFER ON THE TERMS ABOVE AND ACKNOWLEDGES RECEIPT OF A COPY.**
    Seller _____ Date _____
    Seller _____ Date _____

4. **ACCEPTANCE: I/WE** accept the above Seller Counter Offer **(If checked ☐ SUBJECT TO THE ATTACHED COUNTER OFFER)** and acknowledge receipt of a Copy.
    Buyer _____ Date _____ Time _____ AM/PM
    Buyer _____ Date _____ Time _____ AM/PM

CONFIRMATION OF ACCEPTANCE:

(_____/_____) (Initials) **Confirmation of Acceptance:** A Copy of Signed Acceptance was personally received by Seller, or Seller's authorized agent as specified in paragraph 2A on (date) _____ at _____ AM/PM. **A binding Agreement is created when a Copy of Signed Acceptance is personally received by Seller or Seller's authorized agent whether or not confirmed in this document.**

Published and Distributed by:
REAL ESTATE BUSINESS SERVICES, INC.
a subsidiary of the California Association of REALTORS®
525 South Virgil Avenue, Los Angeles, California 90020

Reviewed by _____ Date _____

SCO 11/14 (PAGE 1 OF 1)   Print Date

SELLER COUNTER OFFER (SCO PAGE 1 OF 1)

Reprinted with permission, California Association of Realtors®. No endorsement implied.

When your seller decides to make a counteroffer, be sure to explain that the counteroffer will terminate the original offer and all of the buyer's obligations under that offer.

Example: Returning to the previous example, suppose that Gordon rejects Lamont's counteroffer. He doesn't want to make a $5,000 good faith deposit. In that case, Gordon has no further obligation to Lamont. That's because Lamont's counteroffer had the same effect as a rejection of Gordon's original offer would have had: it terminated the offer. So when Gordon refuses to pay a larger deposit, Lamont can't simply change her mind and decide to accept Gordon's original offer. His offer has already been terminated by rejection. If Gordon still wants to buy the property, he can renew his offer to Lamont; but if he no longer wants to buy it (or buy it on the terms he originally offered), he is not obligated to do so.

If you are presenting a counteroffer to a buyer, review every term the seller has altered. You may want to prepare another "Buyer's Estimated Costs" worksheet if the counteroffer changes the buyer's costs.

If the buyer decides to accept the counteroffer, have her sign the counteroffer form and then notify the seller that the counteroffer has been accepted. Alternatively, the buyer may choose to respond with a counteroffer of her own. Each counteroffer may be made using a new copy of the appropriate counteroffer form.

Multiple Counteroffers

Sometimes a seller receives more than one attractive offer, but the seller still wants to negotiate some additional terms. One option is for the seller to make a counteroffer to the buyer who's made the most attractive offer and reject the other offers, but this limits the seller to negotiating with only one buyer. If the buyer rejected the counteroffer and no longer wanted to buy the property, the seller would no longer have the other offers to fall back on.

So in this situation, the seller might choose to make multiple counteroffers— in other words, counteroffers to more than one of the potential buyers. The seller must inform each buyer that she is making multiple counteroffers. The seller multiple counteroffer form in Figure 6.3, specifically created for this situation, allows the seller to do so.

To protect the seller from becoming obligated under more than one contract, both the counteroffer form and the multiple counteroffer form provide that the buyer's acceptance of the counteroffer won't automatically create a binding

Fig. 6.3 Seller multiple counteroffer form

CALIFORNIA ASSOCIATION OF REALTORS®

SELLER MULTIPLE COUNTER OFFER No. ________

(C.A.R. Form SMCO, 11/13)

Date ________________

This is a counter offer to the: ☐ California Residential Purchase Agreement, ☐ Other ________________ ("Offer"), dated ________________, on property known as ________________ ("Property"), between ________________ ("Buyer") and ________________ ("Seller").

1. **TERMS:** The terms and conditions of the above referenced document are accepted subject to the following:
   - **A.** Paragraphs in the Offer that require initials by all parties, but are not initialed by all parties, are excluded from the final agreement unless specifically referenced for inclusion in paragraph 1C of this or another Counter Offer.
   - **B.** Unless otherwise agreed in writing, down payment and loan amount(s) will be adjusted in the same proportion as in the original Offer.
   - **C.** OTHER TERMS: ________________
   - **D.** The following attached addenda are incorporated into this Multiple Counter Offer: ☐ Addendum No. ________ ☐ ________ ☐ ________
2. **EXPIRATION:** Seller is making Multiple Counter Offers to other prospective Buyers on terms that may or may not be the same as in this Multiple Counter Offer. This Multiple Counter Offer shall be deemed revoked and the deposits, if any, shall be returned:
   - **A.** Unless by 5:00PM on the third Day After the date Seller signs in paragraph 3 (if more than one Seller, then the last date) (or by ____ ☐ AM ☐ PM on ________ (Date)) all of the following occur:
     - (i) Buyer has signed this Counter Offer
     - AND (ii) A copy of the Counter Offer signed by Buyer is personally received by Seller or ________________, who is authorized to receive it.
     - AND (iii) After Buyer signs in paragraph 4, Seller signs in paragraph 5.
     - AND (iv) A copy of this Multiple Counter Offer with Seller's signed selection in paragraph 5 is personally received by Buyer or ________________ who is authorized to receive it. (Note: Prior to the completion of 2A(i,)(ii),(iii), and (iv) Buyer and Seller shall have no duties or obligations for the purchase or sale of the Property.)
   - **OR B.** If Seller withdraws this Multiple Counter Offer anytime prior to Acceptance (C.A.R. form WOO may be used).
3. **SELLER MAKES THIS MULTIPLE COUNTER OFFER ON THE TERMS ABOVE AND ACKNOWLEDGES RECEIPT OF A COPY.**

   ________________ Date ________

   ________________ Date ________
4. **ACCEPTANCE:** Buyer accepts the above Multiple Counter Offer (If checked ☐ SUBJECT TO THE ATTACHED COUNTER OFFER # ___) and acknowledges receipt of a Copy.

   ________________ Date ________ Time ________ AM/PM

   ________________ Date ________ Time ________ AM/PM
5. SELECTION OF ACCEPTED MULTIPLE COUNTER OFFER: By signing below, Seller accepts this Multiple Counter Offer. NOTE TO SELLER: Do NOT sign in this box until after Buyer signs in paragraph 4.

   ________________ Date ________ Time ______ AM/PM

   ________________ Date ________ Time ______ AM/PM

(_____/_____) (Initials) Confirmation of Acceptance: A Copy of the Signed Seller Selection was personally received by Buyer or Buyer's authorized agent on (date) ________________ at ________ AM/PM. A binding Agreement is created when a Copy of the Signed Seller Selection is personally received by Buyer or Buyer's authorized agent whether or not confirmed in this document.

Published and Distributed by:
REAL ESTATE BUSINESS SERVICES, INC.
a subsidiary of the California Association of REALTORS®
525 South Virgil Avenue, Los Angeles, California 90020

Reviewed by ______ Date ______

EQUAL HOUSING OPPORTUNITY

Reprinted with permission, California Association of Realtors®. No endorsement implied.

contract. Instead, the contract will be formed if the seller re-signs the counteroffer after the buyer has accepted it. That way, if more than one buyer accepts a counteroffer from the seller, the seller can choose which one to go with.

The Negotiation Process

In some cases, the parties will trade counteroffers back and forth a number of times. The negotiation process can be frustrating or even nerve-wracking. Remember to maintain your professionalism and do what you can to keep the parties from becoming hostile. Refrain from making negative comments about either party. It's your responsibility to serve the best interests of your client, and a transaction that satisfies both parties is in your client's best interests, whether you're representing the buyer or the seller.

Don't forget to give the parties copies of any documents they sign when they sign them. Each party who makes a counteroffer should get a copy of it immediately after signing it, and both parties should get a copy of the final agreement as soon as it is signed.

Like any offer, a counteroffer can be revoked at any time until the other party accepts it. You should notify the other party as quickly as possible that the offer is being withdrawn.

Accepting an Offer

When an offer (or a counteroffer) is accepted, a contract is formed and the parties are legally bound by it. There are three rules to keep in mind concerning the acceptance of an offer.

The acceptance:

1. must be communicated to the person who made the offer,
2. must be made in the specified manner, and
3. cannot change any of the terms of the offer.

Communicating Acceptance

To be effective and create a valid contract, the offeree's acceptance must be communicated to the offeror. (The offeree is the person to whom the offer was made, and the offeror is the person who made it.) A seller may have decided to accept a buyer's offer, but until the seller delivers an acceptance to the buyer, the buyer can still revoke it.

Example: White is selling his home. Hathaway makes an offer to buy it, and White's agent presents the offer to White.

In the meantime, Hathaway finds another house she likes better. She immediately notifies White that she's revoking her offer.

White protests, claiming that he had already signed Hathaway's offer before she revoked it. But since White hadn't given the signed contract to Hathaway yet, the acceptance was not communicated. As a result, Hathaway still had the right to revoke the offer.

Mailbox Rule. Acceptance of an offer may be communicated in a number of ways. When the seller's acceptance is delivered to the buyer in person, acceptance is deemed to take place at the time of delivery. But there are times when a seller may use the mail to notify the buyer of an acceptance. In this situation, the "mailbox rule" may apply: the acceptance creates a binding contract when the seller drops it in the mailbox, even though the buyer will not receive it right away.

The mailbox rule, however, may be trumped by a contrary provision in the agreement. For example, the California Association of REALTORS® purchase agreement states that delivery, regardless of the method used (mail, email, fax, etc.), is effective only upon personal receipt.

Communication to Agent. Acceptance is also considered to be communicated when the seller delivers it to the buyer's agent, even before the buyer's agent relays the acceptance to the buyer.

Manner of Acceptance

Because a contract to purchase real estate must be in writing, an offer to purchase real estate must be accepted in writing. A spoken acceptance does not create an enforceable contract.

Example: Adams submits a written offer to purchase Baker's property. Baker finds the offer very attractive, so she immediately calls Adams and accepts the offer over the phone. Two hours later, Baker receives an even better offer. Baker can still withdraw her acceptance of the offer because the acceptance wasn't in writing.

Sometimes an offer calls for a particular manner of acceptance. If so, the acceptance must be made in the specified manner to be binding.

Example: Wallace offers to buy Sanchez's property. But Wallace is leaving town shortly, so he adds this provision to the offer: "This offer shall become a binding contract when written acceptance is hand-delivered to my attorney at 437 First Avenue, Suite 312." Sanchez can only accept the offer by having the acceptance hand-delivered to Wallace's attorney at the specified address.

If the offer does not call for a particular manner of acceptance, it may be accepted by any reasonable medium of communication. A medium is considered reasonable if it is the same one that was used by the buyer, if it is one that is customarily used in similar transactions, or if it has been used by the parties in previous transactions. For instance, if the buyer sent the offer to the seller by email, it's reasonable for the seller to send the acceptance to the buyer by email. (Note that if you email offers and acceptances, it's a good idea to get signed originals from both parties.)

Acceptance Cannot Change Terms

To create a contract, the seller must accept the buyer's terms exactly as offered. The seller can't modify the terms of the offer or add any new terms. An acceptance with modifications is actually a counteroffer, not an acceptance.

Contract Amendments

Accepting an offer to purchase (or a counteroffer) creates a binding contract. After that, the terms of the agreement can't be changed without the consent of both parties.

If the buyer and seller agree to modify their contract, you should use a separate form instead of writing the changes on the original purchase agreement. For example, amendments to the California Association of REALTORS® purchase agreement form may be made using the addendum form shown in Chapter 7 (Figure 7.4).

The form used for an amendment should identify the original contract, provide space to write in the changes, and require the signatures of both parties. The signed amendment form should be attached to the original agreement. Each party should be given a copy of the amendment as soon as he or she signs it.

Fig. 6.4 Cancellation of contract form

CALIFORNIA ASSOCIATION OF REALTORS®

CANCELLATION OF CONTRACT, RELEASE OF DEPOSIT AND CANCELLATION OF ESCROW
(C.A.R. Form CC, Revised 11/14)

In accordance with the terms and conditions of the: ☐ California Residential Purchase Agreement; or ☐ Other _____ ("Agreement"), dated _____, including all amendments and related documents, on property known as _____ ("Property"), between _____ ("Buyer") and _____ ("Seller").

Paragraphs 1 and 2 below constitute escrow instructions to Escrow Holder. Release of funds (pursuant to paragraph 2) requires mutually Signed release instructions from Buyer and Seller, judicial decision or arbitration award. A party may be subject to a civil penalty of up to $1,000 for refusal to sign such instructions if no good faith dispute exists as to who is entitled to the deposited funds (Civil Code §1057.3).

1. **CANCELLATION OF CONTRACT:** ☐ Buyer ☐ Seller ☐ both Buyer and Seller cancel(s) the Agreement for the following reason:
   A. ☐ As permitted by the good faith exercise of paragraph(s) _____ of the Agreement.
   OR B. ☐ Buyer has failed to remove the applicable contingency after being given a Notice to Buyer to Perform (C.A.R. Form NBP).
   OR C. ☐ Buyer has failed to take the applicable contractual action after being given a Notice to Buyer to Perform (C.A.R. Form NBP).
   OR D. ☐ Seller has failed to take the applicable contractual action after being given a Notice to Seller to Perform (C.A.R. Form NSP).
   OR E. ☐ Seller has failed to remove the applicable contingency after being given a Notice to Seller to Perform (C.A.R. Form NSP).
   OR F. ☐ Per mutual agreement.
   OR G. ☐ Other _____.

   _____   _____
   Buyer's or Seller's Signature (party cancelling the contract)   Date

   _____   _____
   Buyer's or Seller's Signature (party cancelling the contract)   Date

2. **RELEASE OF DEPOSIT and CANCELLATION OF ESCROW**
   Buyer and Seller cancel escrow # _____ with _____ and
   A. ☐ Seller authorizes release of Buyer's deposit, less Buyer's fees and costs, to Buyer.

   OR B. ☐ Buyer authorizes release of Buyer's deposit, less Seller's fees and costs, to Seller. (☐ Pursuant to a properly executed liquidated damages clause, Buyer's authorization of release of deposit to Seller is limited to no more than 3% of the purchase price. Any additional deposit shall be returned to Buyer.)

   OR C. ☐ Both Buyer and Seller acknowledge mutual cancellation of the Agreement and authorize Escrow Holder to continue to hold the deposit until receiving subsequent mutual instructions, judicial decision or arbitration award.

   OR D. ☐ Other: _____

   Unless otherwise specified, Buyer and Seller (i) mutually release each other from all obligation to buy, sell or exchange the Property under the Agreement, and from all claims, actions and demands that each may have against the other(s) by reason of the Agreement; and (ii) intend that all rights and obligations arising out of the Agreement are null and void.
   Date _____   Date _____
   Buyer _____   Seller _____
   Buyer _____   Seller _____

Published and Distributed by:
REAL ESTATE BUSINESS SERVICES, INC.
a subsidiary of the California Association of REALTORS®
525 South Virgil Avenue, Los Angeles, California 90020

Reviewed by _____ Date _____

CC REVISED 11/14 (PAGE 1 OF 1) Print Date

CANCELLATION OF CONTRACT, RELEASE OF DEPOSIT AND CANCELLATION OF ESCROW (CC PAGE 1 OF 1)

Reprinted with permission, California Association of Realtors®. No endorsement implied.

When you're filling out a form to amend a contract, remember that writing a special provision for the parties would be considered the unauthorized practice of law. When a transaction requires a special provision, ask your broker. She is likely to have one or more standard clauses drafted by lawyers that are appropriate for your transaction.

Contract Cancellation

Sometimes both the buyer and the seller change their minds, and they agree to rescind or cancel their contract. The parties are always free to terminate their contract by mutual agreement. To do this, the buyer and the seller should sign a cancellation agreement, which officially terminates the purchase agreement. An example of a cancellation form is shown in Figure 6.4.

A cancellation agreement should describe how the good faith deposit will be handled. When a purchase agreement is canceled by mutual agreement, the buyer and the seller may agree to let the listing and selling brokers split the deposit in lieu of receiving the commission. Technically, the seller is still liable for the brokerage commission, but the brokers are usually willing to share the good faith deposit instead.

For the brokers' protection, a cancellation form may have a safety clause similar to the ones that appear in listing agreements. Under this provision, if the seller enters into a new purchase agreement with this same buyer within a specified period (such as six months) after canceling their original agreement, the seller must pay the brokers their full commission.

The parties may also use a cancellation agreement when a purchase agreement terminates because a contingency has not been fulfilled. This is discussed in Chapter 8.

Good Faith Deposits

An important part of helping a buyer make an offer to purchase a home is handling the deposit. As you know, it's traditional for the buyer to give the seller a good faith deposit (sometimes called earnest money) as evidence of the buyer's good faith intention to buy the property on the terms he has offered.

There's no law that requires a buyer to give the seller a good faith deposit, but nearly every seller expects one. A seller doesn't want to take her home off the market, possibly for several weeks, unless the buyer is actually going to follow through on his promise to buy the property. Since the buyer usually forfeits the deposit if he backs out, the deposit gives the seller some assurance that the buyer really is ready, willing, and able to buy the property.

The Size of the Deposit

There is no "standard" deposit amount or percentage. In fact, the size of the good faith deposit usually depends on the buyer's circumstances. A buyer who is planning to make a large cash downpayment generally won't have any trouble making a substantial deposit; the deposit is simply applied toward the downpayment when the sale closes. On the other hand, if the buyer plans to finance the purchase with a no-downpayment VA loan, for example, he may not have enough cash for a big deposit.

As a general rule, the deposit should be large enough to give the buyer an economic incentive to complete the transaction. It should also be large enough to compensate the seller for the time and expense involved in taking the house off the market if the buyer fails to complete the transaction.

Example: Bernhardt offers to buy Warren's property for $550,000. He makes a $1,300 deposit. Two weeks later, Bernhardt finds another property he likes more than Warren's for only $530,000. He decides to walk away from his contract with Warren, forfeit the $1,300 deposit, and purchase the other property. Even though Bernhardt is legally obligated to purchase Warren's home, Warren is unlikely to go to the trouble and expense of suing Bernhardt for breach of contract. Instead, like most sellers, Warren will just keep the deposit as payment for his time and trouble. But in this case, the deposit was too small to serve its purpose. The $1,300 deposit was not enough money to convince Bernhardt to honor his contract, nor was it enough to compensate Warren for taking his property off the market for three weeks.

Handling the Deposit

How a good faith deposit is handled depends on the terms of the purchase agreement. The agreement may provide that the buyer will give the deposit directly to the escrow agent; for example, the California Association of REALTORS® purchase agreement form states that (unless the parties provide otherwise) the buyer will deliver the good faith deposit to the escrow holder within three business days after the offer is accepted.

Alternatively, the agreement may provide that the buyer will give the good faith deposit to the selling agent. By law, when a real estate broker receives trust funds, she has three business days to deposit them:

1. with the principal,
2. into a neutral escrow account, or
3. into the broker's trust account.

When trust funds are given to a salesperson, instead of directly to the broker, the salesperson must turn the funds over to the broker immediately, or else (if directed to do so by the broker) deposit the funds as listed above.

However, there is an exception to these rules that allows a broker to hold a deposit check uncashed, provided that:

1. the check is not negotiable by the broker, or the buyer has given written instructions to hold the check uncashed until the offer is accepted; and
2. the seller is informed, before or when the offer is presented, that the check is being held uncashed.

Once the offer is accepted, the broker has three business days to deposit the check as listed above, unless the seller gives written authorization to continue to hold the check uncashed.

Some purchase agreements provide that the broker may hold the check for the good faith deposit uncashed until the seller accepts the offer. The broker is directed to deposit the check into his trust account within a specified number of days after the seller's acceptance. If the seller rejects the offer, the check is returned to the buyer. If the seller makes a counteroffer that the buyer rejects, the buyer may ask for his check back. If the buyer accepts the seller's counteroffer, the broker must then deposit the check into his trust account within the specified number of days. If the buyer rejects the counteroffer and makes another counter-offer, the broker should continue to hold the check until there is an acceptance or a final rejection.

Broker's Responsibilities. Legal responsibility for handling a good faith deposit properly generally falls on the broker who receives the deposit. That's typically the broker of the agent who's working with the buyer, rather than the listing broker.

Example: You work for Blue Hills Realty and you're helping the Snyders look for a home. They want to make an offer on a property listed with Green Valley

Homes. You prepare the offer and the Snyders give you a check for the deposit, with instructions to hold it until their offer is accepted or rejected. Your broker, Blue Hills Realty, is responsible for the check, not the listing broker.

Every brokerage firm should establish office procedures for handling good faith deposits. For example, agents should be instructed what to do if they receive a good faith deposit after business hours.

Bounced or Stopped Checks. After the broker deposits a good faith check into the appropriate trust account, problems can still arise. The check may fail to clear, or the buyer may stop payment for some reason.

> **Example:** On Tuesday, Green made an offer on Bowen's property. He gave you a $10,000 personal check for the deposit, and you immediately turned it over to your broker.
>
> Wednesday morning, your broker deposited the check into her trust account. Wednesday evening, Bowen rejected Green's offer, so Green asked for a refund of his deposit. Thursday morning, your broker wrote Green a $10,000 check from her trust account.
>
> On Friday morning, the bank calls your broker to inform her that Green's check failed to clear his bank due to insufficient funds. Now Green has your broker's $10,000, your broker's trust account is overdrawn, and your broker may face disciplinary action for the shortfall.

To prevent this type of problem, the purchase agreement may include a provision that requires the buyer to wait until his check clears before requesting a refund of the good faith deposit. Of course, if the agreement provides that the broker will hold the deposit until the seller accepts the offer, this problem is avoided altogether.

Form of the Deposit. Up to this point, we have discussed good faith deposits in the form of a check. But a buyer might offer a deposit in a different form, such as cash, a promissory note, or even personal property. If a real estate agent accepts a good faith deposit from a buyer, the agent must tell the seller—before the seller accepts the buyer's offer—the amount of the deposit and what form it takes. Is it cash, a money order, a personal check, a cashier's check, a postdated check, or a promissory note? You could face disciplinary action if you knowingly misrepresent the form or amount of the deposit to the seller.

> **Example:** You're the listing agent for Peterson's house. When Thompson makes an offer, he tells you that he'll give you a $5,000 good faith deposit

check. However, he explains that he can't write the deposit check until he has transferred funds into his checking account. He assures you that he'll bring you a check tomorrow. He asks you to present the offer to Peterson right away.

When you present the offer, you tell Peterson that Thompson is making a $5,000 deposit, but neglect to mention that he hasn't given you the check yet. You could be subject to disciplinary action for failing to disclose this information.

Peterson accepts Thompson's offer without asking to see the check. She assumes that you already have it and will give it to your broker in the usual way. The next day, Thompson puts you off for one more day. The day after that, he refuses to give you the check and tells you he's decided to back out of his contract with Peterson. Now, not only are you subject to disciplinary action, but Peterson could sue your broker for the money she should have received as compensation for Thompson's breach of contract.

Now let's consider the advantages and disadvantages of the various forms that a good faith deposit may take.

Personal checks. If a real estate agent accepts a deposit in the form of a personal check, she should make sure that the check is made payable to the brokerage (or the escrow agent) that will actually deposit the check if the buyer's offer is accepted.

Example: You work for Hadley Realty. Morris, an unrepresented buyer, is going to make an offer on one of your listings and give you a personal check for the deposit. The check should be made payable to Hadley Realty, not to you or the seller.

Some brokers require a cashier's check or a money order instead of a personal check. You should know your firm's policy regarding personal checks.

Sometimes a buyer wants to use a postdated check, which can't be deposited until the date on the check. Again, know your broker's policies; some brokers won't accept postdated checks. If you do accept a postdated check, you must tell the seller. It's wise to make this disclosure in writing.

As an alternative to a postdated check, the buyer can make a small good faith deposit with the offer and state in the offer that she will make an additional deposit within a certain period of time.

Example: Hassam wants to make an offer on a home. She has a certificate of deposit that will mature in ten days, and she's planning to use those funds for the downpayment. Right now, however, she only has enough cash available to make a $1,300 good faith deposit. She doesn't want to cash in her certificate of deposit before it matures, because she would have to pay a penalty for early withdrawal. Instead, she gives you a $1,300 check with her offer and agrees in writing to make an additional good faith deposit in the amount of $2,500 in ten days.

Cash. Sometimes a buyer will offer to make the good faith deposit in cash. But accepting a deposit in cash increases the chance of loss or improper handling.

Example: A buyer wants to make an offer for a property on Friday evening. He gives you a cash deposit of $1,200. You can't turn the cash over to your broker until Monday. What do you do with the cash over the weekend? You can't deposit it in your own account (that would be commingling trust funds with personal funds), but you will be responsible if the cash is lost or stolen.

Your broker may have a policy against accepting cash deposits. Once you explain some of the problems with a cash deposit, most buyers are willing to use a money order or a check instead of cash.

If you do take a cash deposit, you must turn it over to the broker in its original cash form. You may not deposit it into your account and then write a check against the deposit. Similarly, you can't purchase a money order or a cashier's check with the cash.

Promissory notes. Although it's risky to accept a promissory note as a good faith deposit, sometimes a seller is willing to do so. When you tell the seller that the deposit is in the form of a note, be sure he understands the risk. If the buyer refuses to pay the note when it comes due, a lawsuit would be the only way to collect the money owed.

Personal property. In unusual cases, a buyer may want to use an item of personal property as a good faith deposit. For instance, you might encounter a buyer who wants to use stock certificates, bonds, or a boat as part or all of the deposit. It is up to the seller to decide whether to accept such an item as a deposit. The parties and your broker would have to arrange an appropriate method of safekeeping for the item in question.

Refund or Forfeiture of Deposit

If the buyer and seller have signed a purchase agreement, but the sale fails to close, the deposit is either returned to the buyer or forfeited to the seller. The purchase agreement should make clear the circumstances under which it will be refunded or forfeited. This is the best way to prevent disputes over who is entitled to the deposit.

Typically, the buyer is entitled to a refund of the deposit if:

- the seller rejects the offer;
- the buyer withdraws the offer before it is accepted;
- the buyer rescinds the contract based on information in the transfer disclosure statement;
- the buyer discovers a material inaccuracy in the disclosures, or any material misrepresentations concerning the property; or
- the seller accepts the offer, but a contingency provision is not fulfilled, so the contract is terminated.

Example: Lindor and Jones have a purchase agreement that's contingent on Lindor obtaining a conventional loan to finance the purchase. Lindor applies to three lenders, but they all reject his loan application. The contingency hasn't been fulfilled, so the contract is terminated, and Lindor is entitled to a refund of the deposit.

On the other hand, the deposit will generally be forfeited to the seller if the buyer simply changes her mind and backs out of the sale. Most purchase agreements provide that the deposit will be treated as **liquidated damages** in the event of a breach of contract. If the buyer defaults, the seller will keep the deposit as liquidated damages rather than suing the buyer for actual damages.

Liquidated Damages. There are some statutory restrictions on using a buyer's good faith deposit as liquidated damages. If a real estate purchase agreement provides for liquidated damages in the event that the buyer defaults, that provision is enforceable only if the contract has a liquidated damages provision in either 10-point bold type or 8-point red type that is separately signed and initialed by both buyer and seller.

In addition, if it's residential property with up to four units and the buyer intended to live in one of the units, the total amount forfeited as liquidated damages generally may not exceed 3% of the purchase price. Any excess must be refunded to the buyer.

Disbursement. Before the good faith deposit is disbursed to either the seller or the buyer, the broker or the escrow agent holding the funds should ask the parties to agree to the disbursement in writing. If they disagree as to which of them is entitled to the deposit, the matter may have to go to arbitration or a court proceeding.

Remember, it is the broker or the escrow agent—not the salesperson—who is responsible for disbursing a good faith deposit. If a buyer or seller has questions about how the deposit will be handled, always refer him to your broker or the escrow agent. Never try to answer these questions yourself.

Some purchase agreements provide that any expenses already incurred that were to be paid by the seller at closing will be deducted from the good faith deposit before it's forfeited to the seller. Also, listing agreements typically provide that the seller will pay half of the remainder of the deposit to the listing broker in place of the commission. The listing broker may then share that amount with the buyer's broker.

Fair Housing Considerations

As you prepare offers and negotiate counteroffers, you must be sure to avoid discrimination based on race, color, religion, ancestry, national origin, sex, disability, medical condition, genetic information, age, sexual orientation, gender, gender identity, gender expression, familial status, or marital status. We discussed discriminatory listing and marketing practices in Chapter 3; in this section, we'll discuss discrimination in the context of working with buyers and negotiating contracts.

The potential for discrimination against a buyer begins with your first meeting. Even before you show the buyer a house, prepare an offer, or negotiate a sale, you could engage in discriminatory conduct.

It's important to remember that you do not have to intend to discriminate in order to violate state or federal law. Acting in a discriminatory manner, or with a discriminatory effect, is enough. (See Chapter 3.)

Federal and state fair housing laws make a wide array of discriminatory actions toward home buyers illegal. It is a violation of these laws to engage in any of the following actions based on race, religion, or one of the other protected characteristics:

- refusing to receive or failing to transmit a bona fide offer;
- refusing to negotiate for the sale of property, or otherwise making it unavailable;
- changing the terms of the sale for different potential buyers;
- discriminating in providing services or facilities in connection with a real estate transaction;

- representing that a property is not available for inspection or sale when it is in fact available;
- failing to advise a prospect about a property listing;
- using any application form or making any record or inquiry which indicates, directly or indirectly, an intent to discriminate; and
- discriminating in the negotiation or execution of any service or item (such as title insurance or mortgage insurance) in connection with a real estate transaction.

These actions involving discrimination against buyers can be categorized into three groups: refusing to show a property based on discriminatory considerations, steering, and treating certain types of buyers less favorably than others.

You should never refuse to show a buyer a particular house because of the buyer's race or another characteristic protected under the fair housing laws. Any buyer who asks to see a particular property should be shown the property.

Example: You have shown Hernandez, a Hispanic buyer, several houses. Hernandez looks over the entries in your multiple listing book and asks to be shown a particular house. He thinks it might be just the place he's looking for. From office rumors, you know that the seller will probably refuse to accept an offer from any minority buyer. You are anxious to avoid a confrontation, so you tell Hernandez that the seller has already accepted an offer and the house is no longer available. You have just discriminated against Hernandez by representing that the property is not available when in fact it is.

As explained in Chapter 3, steering refers to channeling prospective buyers or tenants toward or away from specific neighborhoods based on their race (or national origin, religion, or another protected class) in order to maintain or change the character of those neighborhoods.

Example: There are thirteen white agents and four African-American agents in your office. African-American buyers are directed to the African-American agents, who are "encouraged" to show them homes only in the one neighborhood in the city that's mainly African-American. This is done on the principle that these buyers would be more comfortable living there. Your real estate office is guilty of steering.

You must also be sure to treat all buyers the same in terms of client and customer services. It would obviously be discriminatory to ignore minority prospects when they enter your office, or to refuse to drive them to see the listed houses that interest them (if that's a service you ordinarily provide).

Because so many actions could be considered discriminatory, it's important to develop sales practices that will ensure your compliance with fair housing laws. Here are a few guidelines to follow when interviewing buyers, showing homes, and presenting and negotiating offers:

- Never imply that a person of a particular race, color, religion, national origin, etc., will have a harder time getting financing.
- Always offer to show your prospects all the listed properties in your market area that meet their objective criteria. Don't make assumptions about a buyer's housing needs or neighborhood preferences based on stereotypes.
- Be sure to treat all prospects equally when setting up showings, making keys available, setting appointments to present offers, or conducting negotiations.
- Report any suspected discriminatory act or statement on the part of a seller to your broker immediately. Check with your broker (or a lawyer, if necessary) on what you should do about a rejection that seemed to be based on discriminatory reasons.

Chapter Summary

1. As a real estate agent, you may fill out a standard purchase agreement form, but only for a transaction you are handling, and only if you do not charge a separate fee for the service. You can't draft special clauses or give advice about the legal effect of provisions in the form. If you have any questions or concerns when filling out a form, you should talk to your broker or a real estate attorney.

2. All offers to purchase, regardless of their merit, must be presented to the seller. You must even present offers received after the seller has already accepted another offer. (These backup offers should be made contingent on the failure of the first sales contract.) Offers are usually presented to the seller by the listing agent. You must disclose your agency status before presenting an offer to purchase.

3. When a seller "accepts" an offer with modifications, the seller is actually rejecting the offer and making a counteroffer. When a party wants to make a counteroffer, it is best to use a separate form. When you present a counteroffer, be sure to explain each term that has been changed and discuss the financial ramifications of the changes.

4. If an offer does not have a time limit, it will terminate after a reasonable period of time. An offer can be revoked at any time up until it is accepted. To be effective, the acceptance must be communicated to the person who made the offer. An offer to purchase real property must be in writing. The acceptance also must be in writing, and must comply with any other stipulations about the manner of acceptance.

5. When an offer (or counteroffer) is properly accepted, this creates a binding contract. It can't be modified without the written consent of both parties. The parties may mutually agree to terminate the contract, although the seller may still owe the broker the sales commission. If the contract is terminated, the parties should sign a cancellation agreement.

6. If a buyer gives a good faith deposit to a real estate agent, it generally must be delivered to the seller, deposited in the broker's trust account, or deposited into escrow within three business days of receipt. However, a deposit check may be held uncashed if: (1) the check is not negotiable by the broker, or the buyer has given written instructions not to cash the check until the buyer accepts the offer; and (2) the seller is informed that the check is being held.

7. An agent accepting a buyer's good faith deposit must disclose the amount and the form of the deposit to the seller and also disclose any problems with the deposit. Most deposits are personal checks, but they may also be in the form of cash, a money order, a cashier's check, a promissory note, or personal property.

8. If the sale closes, the good faith deposit is credited against the buyer's downpayment. If the sale fails to close, the deposit is either returned to the buyer or forfeited to the seller, depending on the circumstances.

9. In showing homes, preparing offers, and negotiating sales, be sure not to discriminate against the buyers you're working with. Discrimination does not have to be intentional to violate fair housing laws.

Key Terms

Purchase agreement: A contract in which a seller promises to convey title to real property to a buyer in exchange for the purchase price. Also called a deposit receipt, sales contract, or contract of sale.

Backup offer: An offer that's contingent on the failure of a previous sales contract.

Counteroffer: A response to a contract offer, changing some of the terms of the original offer. It operates as a rejection of the original offer (not as an acceptance).

Revoking an offer: When someone who made an offer withdraws the offer; as when a buyer withdraws his offer to purchase property.

Acceptance: Agreeing to the terms of an offer to enter into a contract, thereby creating a binding contract.

Mailbox rule: A common law rule under which an acceptance communicated by mail is effective when the message has been sent (put into the mailbox), even though the offeror won't receive it right away.

Cancellation: Termination of a contract without undoing acts that have already been performed under the contract.

Good faith deposit: A deposit that a prospective buyer gives the seller as evidence of her good faith intent to complete the transaction.

Liquidated damages: A sum that the parties to a contract agree in advance (at the time the contract is made) will serve as full compensation in the event of a breach.

Chapter Quiz

1. Which of the following statements about an offer to purchase real property is true?
   a. The offer needs to be in writing, but the acceptance does not
   b. Both the offer and the acceptance must be in writing
   c. Neither the offer nor the acceptance needs to be in writing, but the deed to transfer title must be in writing
   d. The offer does not have to be in writing, but the acceptance must include all of the terms of the offer

2. Which of the following statements about preparing an offer to purchase is true?
   a. The buyer cannot write her own offer without engaging in the unauthorized practice of law
   b. A real estate agent may write special clauses for the parties as long as they are inserted into a pre-printed form written and approved by attorneys
   c. A real estate agent may not prepare an offer if he is also representing one of the parties
   d. A real estate agent may be held liable for losses resulting from the agent's negligence in preparing an offer

3. A contingent counteroffer would be appropriate when:
   a. the seller has already signed a purchase agreement, and then receives an attractive offer from another buyer
   b. the seller wants to accept the buyer's offer, but modify some of the terms
   c. the buyer wants to accept the seller's counteroffer, but isn't sure if he'll qualify for financing
   d. the seller has received multiple offers and wants to withdraw her previous counteroffer to one buyer and accept another buyer's offer

4. The seller's acceptance would be effective (so that the buyer could no longer withdraw his offer) in all of the following situations, except:
   a. the seller accepts the buyer's offer over the phone
   b. the seller uses a fax machine to transmit her acceptance
   c. the seller sends her acceptance in the mail, with delivery confirmation
   d. the seller sends her acceptance in the mail, but without delivery confirmation

5. Once it has been signed by both the buyer and the seller, a purchase agreement can be modified only if:
   a. a contingency clause is not fulfilled
   b. the buyer accepts the seller's counteroffer in writing
   c. both parties agree to the modifications in writing
   d. the seller failed to disclose certain information he was legally required to disclose

6. Which of the following is least likely to be found in a cancellation agreement?
   a. A safety clause
   b. A notice to the backup buyer
   c. An agreement to allow the listing and selling brokers to share the good faith deposit in lieu of a commission
   d. The signatures of both parties

7. After accepting a good faith deposit from a buyer, you are required to tell the seller:
   a. what form the deposit is in
   b. if the deposit is a postdated check
   c. the amount of the deposit
   d. All of the above

8. If you accept cash as a good faith deposit, you:
   a. must turn the deposit over to the broker in its original cash form
   b. should use the cash to purchase a certified check, to prevent the funds from being lost or stolen
   c. should have the buyer's receipt notarized
   d. may face disciplinary action for violating the Real Estate Law

9. Many purchase agreement forms have a provision allowing the broker to hold a check for the good faith deposit for a specified period without depositing it in a trust account. One advantage of this is that:
   a. it gives the seller more time to consider the offer
   b. the broker can simply return the check to the buyer if the offer is rejected
   c. it ensures that the buyer has sufficient funds in her account
   d. the check can be postdated by a week or more

10. A buyer signs a purchase agreement for a duplex that she intends to occupy. If she forfeits the good faith deposit as liquidated damages for breach of the purchase agreement:
    a. the full amount of the deposit will be split between the selling broker and the listing broker in lieu of a commission
    b. any amount in excess of 3% of the purchase price must be refunded to the buyer
    c. any amount in excess of $10,000 must be refunded to the buyer
    d. the seller will be entitled to keep the entire amount, less any expenses incurred by the listing broker

Answer Key

1. b. The statute of frauds requires both an offer to purchase real property and the acceptance of the offer to be in writing.

2. d. If a real estate agent makes a mistake in filling out a contract form, the agent (or the agent's broker) may be held liable for losses resulting from the agent's negligence.

3. a. A contingent counteroffer allows a seller to accept a second offer, contingent on the failure of the first contract.

4. a. In order to form a contract to purchase real estate, the acceptance must be made in writing. Telephone communication is not a valid form of acceptance. The mailbox rule would apply to all of the other situations listed.

5. c. Once a contract has been formed, the terms of the contract can't be changed without the written consent of both parties. The parties may agree to amend the contract for any reason.

6. b. A contract cancellation agreement should be signed by both parties and describe how the good faith deposit will be handled. It may include a safety clause for the brokers' protection. If the seller has accepted a backup offer, the notice to the backup buyer will be handled separately.

7. d. A real estate agent who accepts a good faith deposit is required to disclose the amount and form of the deposit to the seller. The agent should follow office policies regarding the form and handling of the deposit, and also inform the seller of anything unusual about the deposit, such as the fact that the buyer's check is postdated.

8. a. If you accept a good faith deposit in cash, you must turn the cash over to your broker so that it can be placed in the trust account in cash. Although accepting a good faith deposit in cash increases the chance of loss or improper handling, it is not in itself grounds for disciplinary action.

9. b. Purchase agreements often allow the broker to hold the good faith deposit check without depositing it until the seller accepts the offer. This makes it easier to return the good faith deposit to the buyer if the offer is rejected.

10. b. If the buyer breaches the purchase agreement, no more than 3% of the purchase price can be retained as liquidated damages. After expenses incurred by the brokers have been deducted, the seller usually keeps half of the remainder and gives the listing broker the other half. The listing broker will usually split this portion with the selling broker.

7

Purchase Agreements

Requirements for a Valid Agreement

Typical Provisions in a Residential Purchase Agreement

- Identifying the parties
- Property description
- Agency disclosure
- Purchase price and method of payment
- Good faith deposit
- Allocation of costs
- Closing date
- Transfer of possession
- Closing agent
- Disclosure provisions
- Included and excluded items
- Buyer's investigation and repairs
- Conveyance and title
- Sale of buyer's property
- Default provisions
- Dispute resolution
- Time is of the essence
- Addenda
- Offer and acceptance
- Signatures

Introduction

There are a variety of techniques you can learn that will help you find potential buyers, show properties, and negotiate offers. Your broker will undoubtedly give you training in these matters. However, learning the functions of a purchase agreement and understanding its provisions may be just as important to your career. If you make a mistake in filling out a purchase agreement form, you could face the loss of your commission, a lawsuit by the buyer or the seller, and disciplinary action. This chapter describes the requirements for a valid purchase agreement, the provisions typically found in a residential purchase agreement form, and some of the addenda commonly used in residential transactions.

Requirements for a Valid Purchase Agreement

When the seller signs the buyer's written offer, agreeing to the buyer's terms, a contract is formed. The contract holds the buyer and seller to their agreement until the sale is ready to close. But the contract won't be enforceable unless it includes all of the terms that are legally required for a valid purchase agreement.

A valid purchase agreement must meet the basic legal requirements for any contract. The parties must be competent, and there must be mutual consent (offer and acceptance), a lawful objective, and consideration (the seller's promise to sell and the buyer's promise to buy).

In addition, a purchase agreement must:

1. be in writing;
2. identify the parties and describe the property;
3. state the price and method of payment;
4. list the liens or other encumbrances the buyer will assume or take title subject to;
5. specify the amount and terms of financing to be obtained by the buyer; and
6. describe any conditions of the sale.

While these are the minimum requirements for validity, most purchase agreement forms are quite detailed. It is important for the agreement between the parties to be stated fully; anything that isn't made clear at the outset can give rise to a dispute later on, and might prevent the transaction from closing.

Typical Provisions in a Residential Purchase Agreement

There is no standard purchase agreement form that all real estate agents must use. A variety of forms are available from multiple listing services, other professional organizations, and legal form publishers. As an example, Figure 7.1 shows the residential purchase agreement form that the California Association of REALTORS® (C.A.R.) uses. Of course, you need to become familiar with the terms of the purchase agreement form that is used in your office. Our discussion will be an overview of the provisions found in most purchase agreement forms.

To fill out a purchase agreement form, you need to be able to answer these questions:

1. What information needs to be filled in?
2. Which provisions are pertinent to this transaction?
3. Which provisions should be crossed out?
4. What other provisions need to be attached to the form as addenda?

Contract forms should always be filled in completely. If an entry doesn't apply to the transaction, write in "N/A" (for "not applicable") instead of leaving the space blank.

Also, a form must be used only for its intended purpose. For instance, the form in Figure 7.1 is intended for residential sales only. It shouldn't be used for any other type of transaction.

Identifying the Parties

We generally refer to the parties to a purchase agreement as the buyer and the seller. But in many transactions there's more than one buyer and/or more than one seller.

You must make sure that everyone who has an ownership interest in the property signs the contract. If any owner fails to sign it, the buyer may only be able to enforce the sale of a partial interest in the property, or the contract may not be enforceable at all.

Fig. 7.1 Residential purchase agreement

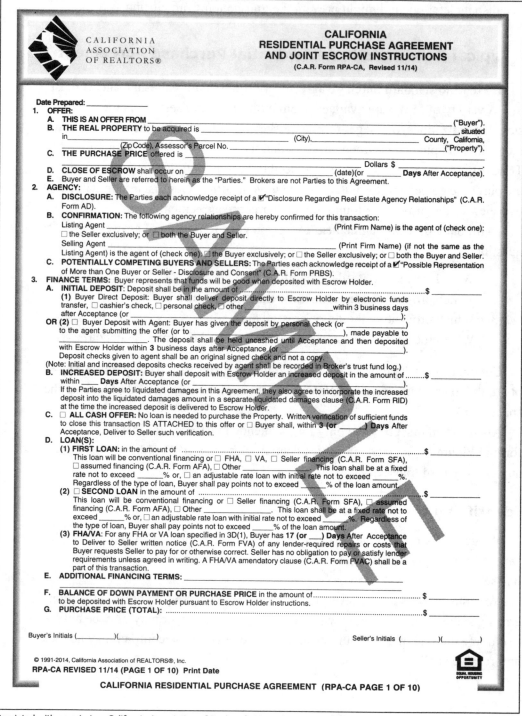

Reprinted with permission, California Association of Realtors®. No endorsement implied.

Property Address: _____   Date: _____

H.   VERIFICATION OF DOWN PAYMENT AND CLOSING COSTS: Buyer (or Buyer's lender or loan broker pursuant to paragraph 3J(1)) shall, within **3 (or ___) Days** After Acceptance, Deliver to Seller written verification of Buyer's down payment and closing costs. (☐ Verification attached.)

I.   APPRAISAL CONTINGENCY AND REMOVAL: This Agreement is (**or** ☐ is NOT) contingent upon a written appraisal of the Property by a licensed or certified appraiser at no less than the purchase price. Buyer shall, as specified in paragraph 14B(3), in writing, remove the appraisal contingency or cancel this Agreement within **17 (or ___) Days** After Acceptance.

J.   LOAN TERMS:

(1) LOAN APPLICATIONS: Within **3 (or ___) Days** After Acceptance, Buyer shall Deliver to Seller a letter from Buyer's lender or loan broker stating that, based on a review of Buyer's written application and credit report, Buyer is prequalified or preapproved for any NEW loan specified in paragraph 3D. If any loan specified in paragraph 3D is an adjustable rate loan, the prequalification or preapproval letter shall be based on the qualifying rate, not the initial loan rate. (☐ Letter attached.)

(2) LOAN CONTINGENCY: Buyer shall act diligently and in good faith to obtain the designated loan(s). Buyer's qualification for the loan(s) specified above **is a contingency** of this Agreement unless otherwise agreed in writing. If there is no appraisal contingency or the appraisal contingency has been waived or removed, then failure of the Property to appraise at the purchase price does not entitle Buyer to exercise the cancellation right pursuant to the loan contingency if Buyer is otherwise qualified for the specified loan. Buyer's contractual obligations regarding deposit, balance of down payment and closing costs **are not contingencies** of this Agreement.

(3) LOAN CONTINGENCY REMOVAL:
Within **21 (or ___) Days** After Acceptance, Buyer shall, as specified in paragraph 14, in writing, remove the loan contingency or cancel this Agreement. If there is an appraisal contingency, removal of the loan contingency shall not be deemed removal of the appraisal contingency.

(4) ☐ NO LOAN CONTINGENCY: Obtaining any loan specified above is NOT a contingency of this Agreement. If Buyer does not obtain the loan and as a result does not purchase the Property, Seller may be entitled to Buyer's deposit or other legal remedies.

(5) LENDER LIMITS ON BUYER CREDITS: Any credit to Buyer, from any source, for closing or other costs that is agreed to by the Parties ("Contractual Credit") shall be disclosed to Buyer's lender. If the total credit allowed by Buyer's lender ("Lender Allowable Credit") is less than the Contractual Credit, then (i) the Contractual Credit shall be reduced to the Lender Allowable Credit, and (ii) in the absence of a separate written agreement between the Parties, there shall be no automatic adjustment to the purchase price to make up for the difference between the Contractual Credit and the Lender Allowable Credit.

K.   BUYER STATED FINANCING: Seller is relying on Buyer's representation of the type of financing specified (including but not limited to, as applicable, all cash, amount of down payment, or contingent or non-contingent loan). Seller has agreed to a specific closing date, purchase price and to sell to Buyer in reliance on Buyer's covenant concerning financing. Buyer shall pursue the financing specified in this Agreement. Seller has no obligation to cooperate with Buyer's efforts to obtain any financing other than that specified in the Agreement and the availability of any such alternate financing does not excuse Buyer from the obligation to purchase the Property and close escrow as specified in this Agreement.

4.   SALE OF BUYER'S PROPERTY:

A. This Agreement and Buyer's ability to obtain financing are NOT contingent upon the sale of any property owned by Buyer.

OR B. ☐ This Agreement and Buyer's ability to obtain financing are contingent upon the sale of property owned by Buyer as specified in the attached addendum (C.A.R. Form COP).

5.   ADDENDA AND ADVISORIES:

A.   ADDENDA: ☐ Addendum # _____ (C.A.R. Form ADM)
☐ Back Up Offer Addendum (C.A.R. Form BUO)   ☐ Court Confirmation Addendum (C.A.R. Form CCA)
☐ Septic, Well and Property Monument Addendum (C.A.R. Form SWPI)
☐ Short Sale Addendum (C.A.R. Form SSA)   ☐ Other _____

B.   BUYER AND SELLER ADVISORIES: ☑ Buyer's Inspection Advisory (C.A.R. Form BIA)
☐ Probate Advisory (C.A.R. Form PAK)   ☐ Statewide Buyer and Seller Advisory (C.A.R. Form SBSA)
☐ Trust Advisory (C.A.R. Form TA)   ☐ REO Advisory (C.A.R. Form REO)
☐ Short Sale Information and Advisory (C.A.R. Form SSIA)   ☐ Other _____

6.   OTHER TERMS: _____
_____
_____
_____

7.   ALLOCATION OF COSTS

A.   INSPECTIONS, REPORTS AND CERTIFICATES: Unless otherwise agreed in writing, this paragraph only determines who is to pay for the inspection, test, certificate or service ("Report") mentioned; it **does not determine who is to pay for any work recommended or identified in the Report.**

(1) ☐ Buyer ☐ Seller shall pay for a natural hazard zone disclosure report, including tax ☐ environmental ☐ Other: _____ _____ prepared by _____ .
(2) ☐ Buyer ☐ Seller shall pay for the following Report _____ prepared by _____ .
(3) ☐ Buyer ☐ Seller shall pay for the following Report _____ prepared by _____ .

Buyer's Initials (_____)(_____)   Seller's Initials (_____)(_____)

RPA-CA REVISED 11/14 (PAGE 2 OF 10) Print Date

CALIFORNIA RESIDENTIAL PURCHASE AGREEMENT (RPA-CA PAGE 2 OF 10)

Property Address: _____ Date: _____

B. GOVERNMENT REQUIREMENTS AND RETROFIT:

(1) □ Buyer □ Seller shall pay for smoke alarm and carbon monoxide device installation and water heater bracing, if required by Law. Prior to Close Of Escrow ("COE"), Seller shall provide Buyer written statement(s) of compliance in accordance with state and local Law, unless Seller is exempt.

(2) (i) □ Buyer □ Seller shall pay the cost of compliance with any other minimum mandatory government inspections and reports if required as a condition of closing escrow under any Law.
(ii) □ Buyer □ Seller shall pay the cost of compliance with any other minimum mandatory government retrofit standards required as a condition of closing escrow under any Law, whether the work is required to be completed before or after COE.
(iii) Buyer shall be provided, within the time specified in paragraph 14A, a copy of any required government conducted or point-of-sale inspection report prepared pursuant to this Agreement or in anticipation of this sale of the Property.

C. ESCROW AND TITLE:

(1) (a) □ Buyer □ Seller shall pay escrow fee _____.
(b) Escrow Holder shall be _____.
(c) The Parties shall, within **5 (or ___) Days** After receipt, sign and return Escrow Holder's general provisions.

(2) (a) □ Buyer □ Seller shall pay for **owner's** title insurance policy specified in paragraph 13E _____.
(b) Owner's title policy to be issued by _____.
(Buyer shall pay for any title insurance policy insuring Buyer's **lender**, unless otherwise agreed in writing.)

D. OTHER COSTS:

(1) □ Buyer □ Seller shall pay County transfer tax or fee _____.
(2) □ Buyer □ Seller shall pay City transfer tax or fee _____.
(3) □ Buyer □ Seller shall pay Homeowners' Association ("HOA") transfer fee _____.
(4) Seller shall pay HOA fees for preparing documents required to be delivered by Civil Code §4525.
(5) □ Buyer □ Seller shall pay HOA fees for preparing all documents other than those required by Civil Code §4525.
(6) □ Buyer □ Seller shall pay for any private transfer fee _____.
(7) □ Buyer □ Seller shall pay for _____.
(8) □ Buyer □ Seller shall pay for _____.
(9) □ Buyer □ Seller shall pay for the cost, not to exceed $ _____, of a standard (or □ upgraded) one-year home warranty plan, issued by _____, with the following optional coverages: □ Air Conditioner □ Pool/Spa □ Other: _____.
Buyer is informed that home warranty plans have many optional coverages in addition to those listed above. Buyer is advised to investigate these coverages to determine those that may be suitable for Buyer.

OR □ Buyer waives the purchase of a home warranty plan. **Nothing in this paragraph precludes Buyer's purchasing a home warranty plan during the term of this Agreement.**

8. ITEMS INCLUDED IN AND EXCLUDED FROM SALE:

A. NOTE TO BUYER AND SELLER: Items listed as included or excluded in the MLS, flyers or marketing materials are **not** included in the purchase price or excluded from the sale unless specified in paragraph 8 B or C.

B. ITEMS INCLUDED IN SALE: Except as otherwise specified or disclosed,

(1) All EXISTING fixtures and fittings that are attached to the Property;

(2) EXISTING electrical, mechanical, lighting, plumbing and heating fixtures, ceiling fans, fireplace inserts, gas logs and grates, solar power systems, built-in appliances, window and door screens, awnings, shutters, window coverings, attached floor coverings, television antennas, satellite dishes, air coolers/conditioners, pool/spa equipment, garage door openers/remote controls, mailbox, in-ground landscaping, trees/shrubs, water features and fountains, water softeners, water purifiers, security systems/alarms and the following if checked: □ all stove(s), except _____; □ all refrigerator(s) except _____; □ all washer(s) and dryer(s), except _____.

(3) Existing integrated phone and home automation systems, including necessary components such as intranet and Internet-connected hardware or devices, control units (other than non-dedicated mobile devices, electronics and computers) and applicable software, permissions, passwords, codes and access information, are (□ are NOT) included in the sale.

(4) **LEASED OR LIENED ITEMS AND SYSTEMS:** Seller shall, within the time specified in paragraph 14A, (i) disclose to Buyer if any item or system specified in paragraph 8B or otherwise included in the sale is leased, or not owned by Seller, or specifically subject to a lien or other encumbrance, and (ii) Deliver to Buyer all written materials (such as lease, warranty, etc.) concerning any such item. Buyer's ability to assume any such lease, or willingness to accept the Property subject to any such lien or encumbrance, is a contingency of this Agreement as specified in paragraph 14B.

(5) The following additional items: _____

(6) Seller represents that all items included in the purchase price, unless otherwise specified, (i) are owned by Seller and shall be transferred free and clear of liens and encumbrances, except the items and systems identified pursuant to 8B(4) and _____ , and (ii) are transferred without Seller warranty regardless of value.

C. ITEMS EXCLUDED FROM SALE: Unless otherwise specified, the following items are excluded from sale: (i) audio and video components (such as flat screen TVs, speakers and other items) if any such item is not itself attached to the Property, even if a bracket or other mechanism attached to the component or item is attached to the Property; (ii) furniture and other items secured to the Property for earthquake purposes; and (iii) _____
_____. **Brackets attached to walls, floors or ceilings for any such component, furniture or item shall remain with the Property (or □ will be removed and holes or other damage shall be repaired, but not painted).**

Buyer's Initials (_____)(_____)   Seller's Initials (_____)(_____)

RPA-CA REVISED 11/14 (PAGE 3 OF 10) Print Date

CALIFORNIA RESIDENTIAL PURCHASE AGREEMENT (RPA-CA PAGE 3 OF 10)

Property Address: _____   Date: _____

9. CLOSING AND POSSESSION:

A. Buyer intends (or ☐ does not intend) to occupy the Property as Buyer's primary residence.

B. **Seller-occupied or vacant property:** Possession shall be delivered to Buyer: (i) at 6 PM or (_____ ☐ AM/☐ PM) on the date of Close Of Escrow; (ii) ☐ no later than ____ calendar days after Close Of Escrow; or (iii) ☐ at _____ ☐ AM/☐ PM on _____.

C. **Seller remaining in possession After Close Of Escrow:** If Seller has the right to remain in possession after Close Of Escrow, (i) the Parties are advised to sign a separate occupancy agreement such as ☐ C.A.R. Form SIP, for Seller continued occupancy of less than 30 days, ☐ C.A.R. Form RLAS for Seller continued occupancy of 30 days or more; and (ii) the Parties are advised to consult with their insurance and legal advisors for information about liability and damage or injury to persons and personal and real property; and (iii) Buyer is advised to consult with Buyer's lender about the impact of Seller's occupancy on Buyer's loan.

D. **Tenant-occupied property: Property shall be vacant** at least 5 (or ___) **Days** Prior to Close Of Escrow, unless otherwise agreed in writing. **Note to Seller: If you are unable to deliver Property vacant in accordance with rent control and other applicable Law, you may be in breach of this Agreement.**

   OR ☐ **Tenant to remain in possession** (C.A.R. Form TIP).

E. At Close Of Escrow: Seller assigns to Buyer any assignable warranty rights for items included in the sale; and Seller shall Deliver to Buyer available Copies of any such warranties. Brokers cannot and will not determine the assignability of any warranties.

F. At Close Of Escrow, unless otherwise agreed in writing, Seller shall provide keys, passwords, codes and/or means to operate all locks, mailboxes, security systems, alarms, home automation systems and intranet and Internet-connected devices included in the purchase price, and garage door openers. If the Property is a condominium or located in a common interest subdivision, Buyer may be required to pay a deposit to the Homeowners' Association ("HOA") to obtain keys to accessible HOA facilities.

10. STATUTORY AND OTHER DISCLOSURES (INCLUDING LEAD-BASED PAINT HAZARD DISCLOSURES) AND CANCELLATION RIGHTS:

A. **(1)** Seller shall, within the time specified in paragraph 14A, Deliver to Buyer: (i) if required by Law, a fully completed: Federal Lead-Based Paint Disclosures (C.A.R. Form FLD) and pamphlet ("Lead Disclosures"); and **(ii)** unless exempt, fully completed disclosures or notices required by sections 1102 et. seq. and 1103 et. seq. of the Civil Code ("Statutory Disclosures"). Statutory Disclosures include, but are not limited to, a Real Estate Transfer Disclosure Statement ("TDS"), Natural Hazard Disclosure Statement ("NHD"), notice or actual knowledge of release of illegal controlled substance, notice of special tax and/or assessments (or, if allowed, substantially equivalent notice regarding the Mello-Roos Community Facilities Act of 1982 and Improvement Bond Act of 1915) and, if Seller has actual knowledge, of industrial use and military ordnance location (C.A.R. Form SPQ or SSD).

   (2) Any Statutory Disclosure required by this paragraph is considered fully completed if Seller has answered all questions and completed and signed the Seller section(s) and the Listing Agent, if any, has completed and signed the Listing Broker section(s), or, if applicable, an Agent Visual Inspection Disclosure (C.A.R. Form AVID). Nothing stated herein relieves a Buyer's Broker, if any, from the obligation to (i) conduct a reasonably competent and diligent visual inspection of the accessible areas of the Property and disclose, on Section IV of the TDS, or an AVID, material facts affecting the value or desirability of the Property that were or should have been revealed by such an inspection or (ii) complete any sections on all disclosures required to be completed by Buyer's Broker.

   (3) Note to Buyer and Seller: Waiver of Statutory and Lead Disclosures is prohibited by Law.

   (4) Seller, unless exempt from the obligation to provide a TDS, shall, within the time specified in paragraph 14A, complete and provide Buyer with a Seller Property Questionnaire (C.A.R. Form SPQ) **OR** ☐ Supplemental Contractual and Statutory Disclosure (C.A.R. Form SSD).

   (5) Buyer shall, within the time specified in paragraph 14B(1), return Signed Copies of the Statutory, Lead and other disclosures to Seller.

   (6) In the event Seller or Listing Broker, prior to Close Of Escrow, becomes aware of adverse conditions materially affecting the Property, or any material inaccuracy in disclosures, information or representations previously provided to Buyer, Seller shall promptly provide a subsequent or amended disclosure or notice, in writing, covering those items. **However, a subsequent or amended disclosure shall not be required for conditions and material inaccuracies** of which Buyer is otherwise aware, or which are **disclosed in reports provided to or obtained by Buyer** or ordered and paid for by Buyer.

   (7) If any disclosure or notice specified in paragraph 10A(1), or subsequent or amended disclosure or notice is Delivered to Buyer after the offer is Signed, Buyer shall have the right to cancel this Agreement within **3 Days** After Delivery in person, or **5 Days** After Delivery by deposit in the mail, by giving written notice of cancellation to Seller or Seller's agent.

B. **NATURAL AND ENVIRONMENTAL HAZARD DISCLOSURES AND OTHER BOOKLETS:** Within the time specified in paragraph 14A, Seller shall, if required by Law: **(i)** Deliver to Buyer earthquake guide(s) (and questionnaire), environmental hazards booklet, and home energy rating pamphlet; **(ii)** disclose if the Property is located in a Special Flood Hazard Area; Potential Flooding (Inundation) Area; Very High Fire Hazard Zone; State Fire Responsibility Area; Earthquake Fault Zone; and Seismic Hazard Zone; and **(iii)** disclose any other zone as required by Law and provide any other information required for those zones.

C. **WITHHOLDING TAXES:** Within the time specified in paragraph 14A, to avoid required withholding, Seller shall Deliver to Buyer or qualified substitute, an affidavit sufficient to comply with federal (FIRPTA) and California withholding Law (C.A.R. Form AS or QS).

D. **MEGAN'S LAW DATABASE DISCLOSURE:** Notice: Pursuant to Section 290.46 of the Penal Code, information about specified registered sex offenders is made available to the public via an Internet Web site maintained by the Department of Justice at **www.meganslaw.ca.gov.** Depending on an offender's criminal history, this information will include either the address at which the offender resides or the community of residence and ZIP Code in which he or she resides. (Neither Seller nor Brokers are required to check this website. If Buyer wants further information, Broker recommends that Buyer obtain information from this website during Buyer's inspection contingency period. Brokers do not have expertise in this area.)

E. **NOTICE REGARDING GAS AND HAZARDOUS LIQUID TRANSMISSION PIPELINES:** This notice is being provided simply to inform you that information about the general location of gas and hazardous liquid transmission pipelines is available to the public via the National Pipeline Mapping System (NPMS) Internet Web site maintained by the United States Department of Transportation at **http://www.npms.phmsa.dot.gov/.** To seek further information about possible transmission pipelines near the Property, you may contact your local gas utility or other pipeline operators in the area. Contact information for pipeline operators is searchable by ZIP Code and county on the NPMS Internet Web site.

Buyer's Initials (_____)(_____)   Seller's Initials (_____)(_____)

Property Address: _____   Date: _____

F. CONDOMINIUM/PLANNED DEVELOPMENT DISCLOSURES:
(1) SELLER HAS: 7 (or ____) Days After Acceptance to disclose to Buyer if the Property is a condominium, or is located in a planned development or other common interest subdivision (C.A.R. Form SPQ or SSD).
(2) If the Property is a condominium or is located in a planned development or other common interest subdivision, Seller has **3 (or ____) Days** After Acceptance to request from the HOA (C.A.R. Form HOA1): **(i)** Copies of any documents required by Law; **(ii)** disclosure of any pending or anticipated claim or litigation by or against the HOA; **(iii)** a statement containing the location and number of designated parking and storage spaces; **(iv)** Copies of the most recent 12 months of HOA minutes for regular and special meetings; and **(v)** the names and contact information of all HOAs governing the Property (collectively, "CI Disclosures"). Seller shall itemize and Deliver to Buyer all CI Disclosures received from the HOA and any CI Disclosures in Seller's possession. Buyer's approval of CI Disclosures is a contingency of this Agreement as specified in paragraph 14B(3). The Party specified in paragraph 7, as directed by escrow, shall deposit funds into escrow or direct to HOA or management company to pay for any of the above.

11. CONDITION OF PROPERTY: Unless otherwise agreed in writing: **(i)** the Property is sold **(a)** "AS-IS" in its PRESENT physical condition as of the date of Acceptance and **(b)** subject to Buyer's Investigation rights; **(ii)** the Property, including pool, spa, landscaping and grounds, is to be maintained in substantially the same condition as on the date of Acceptance; and **(iii)** all debris and personal property not included in the sale shall be removed by Close Of Escrow.
A. Seller shall, within the time specified in paragraph 14A, DISCLOSE KNOWN MATERIAL FACTS AND DEFECTS affecting the Property, including known insurance claims within the past five years, and make any and all other disclosures required by law.
B. Buyer has the right to conduct Buyer Investigations of the Property and, as specified in paragraph 14B, based upon information discovered in those investigations: **(i)** cancel this Agreement; or **(ii)** request that Seller make Repairs or take other action.
C. **Buyer is strongly advised to conduct Investigations of the entire Property in order to determine its present condition. Seller may not be aware of all defects affecting the Property or other factors that Buyer considers important. Property improvements may not be built according to code, in compliance with current Law, or have had permits issued.**
12. BUYER'S INVESTIGATION OF PROPERTY AND MATTERS AFFECTING PROPERTY:
A. Buyer's acceptance of the condition of, and any other matter affecting the Property, is a contingency of this Agreement as specified in this paragraph and paragraph 14B. Within the time specified in paragraph 14B(1), Buyer shall have the right, at Buyer's expense unless otherwise agreed, to conduct inspections, investigations, tests, surveys and other studies ("Buyer Investigations"), including, but not limited to, the right to: **(i)** inspect for lead-based paint and other lead-based paint hazards; **(ii)** inspect for wood destroying pests and organisms. Any inspection for wood destroying pests and organisms shall be prepared by a registered Structural Pest Control company; shall cover the main building and attached structures; may cover detached structures; shall NOT include water tests of shower pans on upper level units unless the owners of property below the shower consent; shall NOT include roof coverings; and, if the Property is a unit in a condominium or other common interest subdivision, the inspection shall include only the separate interest and any exclusive-use areas being transferred, and shall NOT include common areas; and shall include a report ("Pest Control Report") showing the findings of the company which shall be separated into sections for evident infestation or infections (Section 1) and for conditions likely to lead to infestation or infection (Section 2); **(iii)** review the registered sex offender database; **(iv)** confirm the insurability of Buyer and the Property including the availability and cost of flood and fire insurance; **(v)** review and seek approval of leases that may need to be assumed by Buyer; and **(vi)** satisfy Buyer as to any matter specified in the attached Buyer's Inspection Advisory (C.A.R. Form BIA). Without Seller's prior written consent, Buyer shall neither make nor cause to be made: **(i)** invasive or destructive Buyer Investigations except to the extent required to prepare a Pest Control Report; or **(ii)** inspections by any governmental building or zoning inspector or government employee, unless required by Law.
B. Seller shall make the Property available for all Buyer Investigations. Buyer shall **(i)** as specified in paragraph 14B, complete Buyer Investigations and either remove the contingency or cancel this Agreement, and **(ii)** give Seller, at no cost, complete Copies of all such Investigation reports obtained by Buyer, which obligation shall survive the termination of this Agreement.
C. Seller shall have water, gas, electricity and all operable pilot lights on for Buyer's Investigations and through the date possession is made available to Buyer.
D. **Buyer indemnity and seller protection for entry upon property:** Buyer shall: **(i)** keep the Property free and clear of liens; **(ii)** repair all damage arising from Buyer Investigations; and **(iii)** indemnify and hold Seller harmless from all resulting liability, claims, demands, damages and costs. Buyer shall carry, or Buyer shall require anyone acting on Buyer's behalf to carry, policies of liability, workers' compensation and other applicable insurance, defending and protecting Seller from liability for any injuries to persons or property occurring during any Buyer Investigations or work done on the Property at Buyer's direction prior to Close Of Escrow. Seller is advised that certain protections may be afforded Seller by recording a "Notice of Non-Responsibility" (C.A.R. Form NNR) for Buyer Investigations and work done on the Property at Buyer's direction. Buyer's obligations under this paragraph shall survive the termination of this Agreement.
13. TITLE AND VESTING:
A. Within the time specified in paragraph 14, Buyer shall be provided a current preliminary title report ("Preliminary Report"). The Preliminary Report is only an offer by the title insurer to issue a policy of title insurance and may not contain every item affecting title. Buyer's review of the Preliminary Report and any other matters which may affect title are a contingency of this Agreement as specified in paragraph 14B. The company providing the Preliminary Report shall, prior to issuing a Preliminary Report, conduct a search of the General Index for all Sellers except banks or other institutional lenders selling properties they acquired through foreclosure (REOs), corporations, and government entities. Seller shall within 7 Days After Acceptance, give Escrow Holder a completed Statement of Information.
B. Title is taken in its present condition subject to all encumbrances, easements, covenants, conditions, restrictions, rights and other matters, whether of record or not, as of the date of Acceptance except for: **(i)** monetary liens of record (which Seller is obligated to pay off) unless Buyer is assuming those obligations or taking the Property subject to those obligations; and **(ii)** those matters which Seller has agreed to remove in writing.
C. Within the time specified in paragraph 14A, Seller has a duty to disclose to Buyer all matters known to Seller affecting title, whether of record or not.
D. At Close Of Escrow, Buyer shall receive a grant deed conveying title (or, for stock cooperative or long-term lease, an assignment of stock certificate or of Seller's leasehold interest), including oil, mineral and water rights if currently owned by Seller. Title shall vest as designated in Buyer's supplemental escrow instructions. THE MANNER OF TAKING TITLE MAY HAVE SIGNIFICANT LEGAL AND TAX CONSEQUENCES. CONSULT AN APPROPRIATE PROFESSIONAL.

Buyer's Initials (_____)(_____)   Seller's Initials (_____)(_____)

Property Address: _____ Date: _____

E. Buyer shall receive a CLTA/ALTA "Homeowner's Policy of Title Insurance", if applicable to the type of property and buyer. If not, Escrow Holder shall notify Buyer. A title company can provide information about the availability, coverage, and cost of other title policies and endorsements. If the Homeowner's Policy is not available, Buyer shall choose another policy, instruct Escrow Holder in writing and shall pay any increase in cost.

14. **TIME PERIODS; REMOVAL OF CONTINGENCIES; CANCELLATION RIGHTS: The following time periods may only be extended, altered, modified or changed by mutual written agreement. Any removal of contingencies or cancellation under this paragraph by either Buyer or Seller must be exercised in good faith and in writing (C.A.R. Form CR or CC).**

A. **SELLER HAS: 7 (or ___) Days** After Acceptance to Deliver to Buyer all Reports, disclosures and information for which Seller is responsible under paragraphs 5, 6, 7, 8B(4), 10A, B, C, and F, 11A and 13A. If, by the time specified, Seller has not delivered any such item, Buyer after first Delivering to Seller a Notice to Seller to Perform (C.A.R. Form NSP) may cancel this Agreement.

B. **(1) BUYER HAS: 17 (or ___) Days** After Acceptance, unless otherwise agreed in writing, to:
   (i) complete all Buyer Investigations; review all disclosures, reports, lease documents to be assumed by Buyer pursuant to paragraph 8B(4), and other applicable information, which Buyer receives from Seller; and approve all matters affecting the Property; and **(ii)** Deliver to Seller Signed Copies of Statutory and Lead Disclosures and other disclosures Delivered by Seller in accordance with paragraph 10A.
   (2) Within the time specified in paragraph 14B(1), Buyer may request that Seller make repairs or take any other action regarding the Property (C.A.R. Form RR). Seller has no obligation to agree to or respond to (C.A.R. Form RRRR) Buyer's requests.
   (3) By the end of the time specified in paragraph 14B(1) (or as otherwise specified in this Agreement), Buyer shall Deliver to Seller a removal of the applicable contingency or cancellation (C.A.R. Form CR or CC) of this Agreement. However, if any report, disclosure or information for which Seller is responsible is not Delivered within the time specified in paragraph 14A, then Buyer has **5 (or ___) Days** After Delivery of any such items, or the time specified in paragraph 14B(1), whichever is later, to Deliver to Seller a removal of the applicable contingency or cancellation of this Agreement.
   (4) Continuation of Contingency: Even after the end of the time specified in paragraph 14B(1) and before Seller cancels, if at all, pursuant to paragraph 14C, Buyer retains the right, in writing, to either (i) remove remaining contingencies, or (ii) cancel this Agreement based on a remaining contingency. Once Buyer's written removal of all contingencies is Delivered to Seller, Seller may not cancel this Agreement pursuant to paragraph 14C(1).

C. **SELLER RIGHT TO CANCEL:**
   (1) Seller right to Cancel; Buyer Contingencies: If, by the time specified in this Agreement, Buyer does not Deliver to Seller a removal of the applicable contingency or cancellation of this Agreement, then Seller, after first Delivering to Buyer a Notice to Buyer to Perform (C.A.R. Form NBP), may cancel this Agreement. In such event, Seller shall authorize the return of Buyer's deposit, except for fees incurred by Buyer.
   (2) Seller right to Cancel; Buyer Contract Obligations: Seller, after first delivering to Buyer a NBP, may cancel this Agreement if, by the time specified in this Agreement, Buyer does not take the following action(s): **(i)** Deposit funds as required by paragraph 3A, or 3B or if the funds deposited pursuant to paragraph 3A or 3B are not good when deposited; **(ii)** Deliver a notice of FHA or VA costs or terms as required by paragraph 3D(3) (C.A.R. Form FVA); **(iii)** Deliver a letter as required by paragraph 3J(1); **(iv)** Deliver verification, or a satisfactory verification if Seller reasonably disapproves of the verification already provided, as required by paragraph 3C or 3H; **(v)** Return Statutory and Lead Disclosures as required by paragraph 10A(5); or **(vi)** Sign or initial a separate liquidated damages form for an increased deposit as required by paragraphs 3B and 21B; or **(vii)** Provide evidence of authority to sign in a representative capacity as specified in paragraph 19. In such event, Seller shall authorize the return of Buyer's deposit, except for fees incurred by Buyer.

D. **NOTICE TO BUYER OR SELLER TO PERFORM:** The NBP or NSP shall: **(i)** be in writing; **(ii)** be signed by the applicable Buyer or Seller; and **(iii)** give the other Party at least **2 (or ___) Days** After Delivery (or until the time specified in the applicable paragraph, whichever occurs last) to take the applicable action. A NBP or NSP may not be Delivered any earlier than **2 Days** Prior to the expiration of the applicable time for the other Party to remove a contingency or cancel this Agreement or meet an obligation specified in paragraph 14.

E. **EFFECT OF BUYER'S REMOVAL OF CONTINGENCIES:** If Buyer removes, in writing, any contingency or cancellation rights, unless otherwise specified in writing, Buyer shall conclusively be deemed to have: **(i)** completed all Buyer Investigations, and review of reports and other applicable information and disclosures pertaining to that contingency or cancellation right; **(ii)** elected to proceed with the transaction; and **(iii)** assumed all liability, responsibility and expense for Repairs or corrections pertaining to that contingency or cancellation right, or for the inability to obtain financing.

F. **CLOSE OF ESCROW:** Before Buyer or Seller may cancel this Agreement for failure of the other Party to close escrow pursuant to this Agreement, Buyer or Seller must first Deliver to the other Party a demand to close escrow (C.A.R. Form DCE). The DCE shall: **(i)** be signed by the applicable Buyer or Seller; and **(ii)** give the other Party at least **3 (or ___) Days** After Delivery to close escrow. A DCE may not be Delivered any earlier than **3 Days** Prior to the scheduled close of escrow.

G. **EFFECT OF CANCELLATION ON DEPOSITS:** If Buyer or Seller gives written notice of cancellation pursuant to rights duly exercised under the terms of this Agreement, the Parties agree to Sign mutual instructions to cancel the sale and escrow and release deposits, if any, to the party entitled to the funds, less fees and costs incurred by that party. Fees and costs may be payable to service providers and vendors for services and products provided during escrow. Except as specified below, **release of funds will require mutual Signed release instructions from the Parties, judicial decision or arbitration award.** If either Party fails to execute mutual instructions to cancel, one Party may make a written demand to Escrow Holder for the deposit (C.A.R. Form BDRD or SDRD). Escrow Holder, upon receipt, shall promptly deliver notice of the demand to the other Party. If, within 10 Days After Escrow Holder's notice, the other Party does not object to the demand, Escrow Holder shall disburse the deposit to the Party making the demand. If Escrow Holder complies with the preceding process, each Party shall be deemed to have released Escrow Holder from any and all claims or liability related to the disbursal of the deposit. Escrow Holder, at its discretion, may nonetheless require mutual cancellation instructions. **A Party may be subject to a civil penalty of up to $1,000 for refusal to sign cancellation instructions if no good faith dispute exists as to who is entitled to the deposited funds (Civil Code §1057.3).**

15. **FINAL VERIFICATION OF CONDITION:** Buyer shall have the right to make a final verification of the Property within **5 (or ☐ ___) Days** Prior to Close Of Escrow, NOT AS A CONTINGENCY OF THE SALE, but solely to confirm: **(i)** the Property is maintained pursuant to paragraph 11; **(ii)** Repairs have been completed as agreed; and **(iii)** Seller has complied with Seller's other obligations under this Agreement (C.A.R. Form VP).

Buyer's Initials (_____)(_____)   Seller's Initials (_____)(_____)

RPA-CA REVISED 11/14 (PAGE 6 OF 10) Print Date
CALIFORNIA RESIDENTIAL PURCHASE AGREEMENT (RPA-CA PAGE 6 OF 10)

Property Address: _____ Date: _____

16. REPAIRS: Repairs shall be completed prior to final verification of condition unless otherwise agreed in writing. Repairs to be performed at Seller's expense may be performed by Seller or through others, provided that the work complies with applicable Law, including governmental permit, inspection and approval requirements. Repairs shall be performed in a good, skillful manner with materials of quality and appearance comparable to existing materials. It is understood that exact restoration of appearance or cosmetic items following all Repairs may not be possible. Seller shall: **(i)** obtain invoices and paid receipts for Repairs performed by others; **(ii)** prepare a written statement indicating the Repairs performed by Seller and the date of such Repairs; and **(iii)** provide Copies of invoices and paid receipts and statements to Buyer prior to final verification of condition.

17. PRORATIONS OF PROPERTY TAXES AND OTHER ITEMS: Unless otherwise agreed in writing, the following items shall be PAID CURRENT and prorated between Buyer and Seller as of Close Of Escrow: real property taxes and assessments, interest, rents, HOA regular, special, and emergency dues and assessments imposed prior to Close Of Escrow, premiums on insurance assumed by Buyer, payments on bonds and assessments assumed by Buyer, and payments on Mello-Roos and other Special Assessment District bonds and assessments that are now a lien. The following items shall be assumed by Buyer WITHOUT CREDIT toward the purchase price: prorated payments on Mello-Roos and other Special Assessment District bonds and assessments and HOA special assessments that are now a lien but not yet due. Property will be reassessed upon change of ownership. Any supplemental tax bills shall be paid as follows: **(i)** for periods after Close Of Escrow, by Buyer; and **(ii)** for periods prior to Close Of Escrow, by Seller (see C.A.R. Form SPT or SBSA for further information). TAX BILLS ISSUED AFTER CLOSE OF ESCROW SHALL BE HANDLED DIRECTLY BETWEEN BUYER AND SELLER. Prorations shall be made based on a 30-day month.

18. BROKERS:

    A. COMPENSATION: Seller or Buyer, or both, as applicable, agree to pay compensation to Broker as specified in a separate written agreement between Broker and that Seller or Buyer. Compensation is payable upon Close Of Escrow, or if escrow does not close, as otherwise specified in the agreement between Broker and that Seller or Buyer.

    B. SCOPE OF DUTY: Buyer and Seller acknowledge and agree that Broker: **(i)** Does not decide what price Buyer should pay or Seller should accept; **(ii)** Does not guarantee the condition of the Property; **(iii)** Does not guarantee the performance, adequacy or completeness of inspections, services, products or repairs provided or made by Seller or others; **(iv)** Does not have an obligation to conduct an inspection of common areas or areas off the site of the Property; **(v)** Shall not be responsible for identifying defects on the Property, in common areas, or offsite unless such defects are visually observable by an inspection of reasonably accessible areas of the Property or are known to Broker; **(vi)** Shall not be responsible for inspecting public records or permits concerning the title or use of Property; **(vii)** Shall not be responsible for identifying the location of boundary lines or other items affecting title; **(viii)** Shall not be responsible for verifying square footage, representations of others or information contained in Investigation reports, Multiple Listing Service, advertisements, flyers or other promotional material; **(ix)** Shall not be responsible for determining the fair market value of the Property or any personal property included in the sale; **(x)** Shall not be responsible for providing legal or tax advice regarding any aspect of a transaction entered into by Buyer or Seller; and **(xi)** Shall not be responsible for providing other advice or information that exceeds the knowledge, education and experience required to perform real estate licensed activity. Buyer and Seller agree to seek legal, tax, insurance, title and other desired assistance from appropriate professionals.

19. REPRESENTATIVE CAPACITY: If one or more Parties is signing this Agreement in a representative capacity and not for him/herself as an individual then that Party shall so indicate in paragraph 31 or 32 and attach a Representative Capacity Signature Disclosure (C.A.R. Form RCSD). Wherever the signature or initials of the representative identified in the RCSD appear on this Agreement or any related documents, it shall be deemed to be in a representative capacity for the entity described and not in an individual capacity, unless otherwise indicated. The Party acting in a representative capacity (i) represents that the entity for which that party is acting already exists and (ii) shall Deliver to the other Party and Escrow Holder, within 3 Days After Acceptance, evidence of authority to act in that capacity (such as but not limited to: applicable trust document, or portion thereof, letters testamentary, court order, power of attorney, resolution, or formation documents of the business entity).

20. JOINT ESCROW INSTRUCTIONS TO ESCROW HOLDER:

    A. The following paragraphs, or applicable portions thereof, of this Agreement constitute the joint escrow instructions of Buyer and Seller to Escrow Holder, which Escrow Holder is to use along with any related counter offers and addenda, and any additional mutual instructions to close the escrow: paragraphs 1, 3, 4B, 5A, 6, 7, 10C, 13, 14G, 17, 18A, 19, 20, 26, 29, 30, 31, 32 and paragraph D of the section titled Real Estate Brokers on page 10. If a Copy of the separate compensation agreement(s) provided for in paragraph 18A, or paragraph D of the section titled Real Estate Brokers on page 10 is deposited with Escrow Holder by Broker, Escrow Holder shall accept such agreement(s) and pay out from Buyer's or Seller's funds, or both, as applicable, the Broker's compensation provided for in such agreement(s). The terms and conditions of this Agreement not set forth in the specified paragraphs are additional matters for the information of Escrow Holder, but about which Escrow Holder need not be concerned. Buyer and Seller will receive Escrow Holder's general provisions, if any, directly from Escrow Holder and will execute such provisions within the time specified in paragraph 7C(1)(c). To the extent the general provisions are inconsistent or conflict with this Agreement, the general provisions will control as to the duties and obligations of Escrow Holder only. Buyer and Seller will execute additional instructions, documents and forms provided by Escrow Holder that are reasonably necessary to close the escrow and, as directed by Escrow Holder, within 3 (or ____) Days, shall pay to Escrow Holder or HOA or HOA management company or others any fee required by paragraphs 7, 10 or elsewhere in this Agreement.

    B. A Copy of this Agreement including any counter offer(s) and addenda shall be delivered to Escrow Holder within **3** Days After Acceptance (or _____). Buyer and Seller authorize Escrow Holder to accept and rely on Copies and Signatures as defined in this Agreement as originals, to open escrow and for other purposes of escrow. The validity of this Agreement as between Buyer and Seller is not affected by whether or when Escrow Holder Signs this Agreement. Escrow Holder shall provide Seller's Statement of Information to Title company when received from Seller. If Seller delivers an affidavit to Escrow Holder to satisfy Seller's FIRPTA obligation under paragraph 10C, Escrow Holder shall deliver to Buyer a Qualified Substitute statement that complies with federal Law.

    C. Brokers are a party to the escrow for the sole purpose of compensation pursuant to paragraph 18A and paragraph D of the section titled Real Estate Brokers on page 10. Buyer and Seller irrevocably assign to Brokers compensation specified in paragraph 18A, and irrevocably instruct Escrow Holder to disburse those funds to Brokers at Close Of Escrow or pursuant to any other mutually executed cancellation agreement. Compensation instructions can be amended or revoked only with the written consent of Brokers. Buyer and Seller shall release and hold harmless Escrow Holder from any liability resulting from Escrow Holder's payment to Broker(s) of compensation pursuant to this Agreement.

Buyer's Initials (_____)(_____)   Seller's Initials (_____)(_____)

RPA-CA REVISED 11/14 (PAGE 7 OF 10) Print Date

CALIFORNIA RESIDENTIAL PURCHASE AGREEMENT (RPA-CA PAGE 7 OF 10)

Property Address: _____ Date: _____

D. Upon receipt, Escrow Holder shall provide Seller and Seller's Broker verification of Buyer's deposit of funds pursuant to paragraph 3A and 3B. Once Escrow Holder becomes aware of any of the following, Escrow Holder shall immediately notify all Brokers: **(i)** if Buyer's initial or any additional deposit or down payment is not made pursuant to this Agreement, or is not good at time of deposit with Escrow Holder; or **(ii)** if Buyer and Seller instruct Escrow Holder to cancel escrow.

E. A Copy of any amendment that affects any paragraph of this Agreement for which Escrow Holder is responsible shall be delivered to Escrow Holder within **3 Days** after mutual execution of the amendment.

21. REMEDIES FOR BUYER'S BREACH OF CONTRACT:

A. Any clause added by the Parties specifying a remedy (such as release or forfeiture of deposit or making a deposit non-refundable) for failure of Buyer to complete the purchase in violation of this Agreement shall be deemed invalid unless the clause independently satisfies the statutory liquidated damages requirements set forth in the Civil Code.

B. LIQUIDATED DAMAGES: If Buyer fails to complete this purchase because of Buyer's default, Seller shall retain, as liquidated damages, the deposit actually paid. If the Property is a dwelling with no more than four units, one of which Buyer intends to occupy, then the amount retained shall be no more than 3% of the purchase price. Any excess shall be returned to Buyer. Except as provided in paragraph 14G, release of funds will require mutual, Signed release instructions from both Buyer and Seller, judicial decision or arbitration award. AT THE TIME OF ANY INCREASED DEPOSIT BUYER AND SELLER SHALL SIGN A SEPARATE LIQUIDATED DAMAGES PROVISION INCORPORATING THE INCREASED DEPOSIT AS LIQUIDATED DAMAGES (C.A.R. FORM RID).

Buyer's Initials _____/_____   Seller's Initials _____/_____

22. DISPUTE RESOLUTION:

A. MEDIATION: The Parties agree to mediate any dispute or claim arising between them out of this Agreement, or any resulting transaction, before resorting to arbitration or court action through the C.A.R. Real Estate Mediation Center for Consumers (**www.consumermediation.org**) or through any other mediation provider or service mutually agreed to by the Parties. The Parties also agree to mediate any disputes or claims with Broker(s), who, in writing, agree to such mediation prior to, or within a reasonable time after, the dispute or claim is presented to the Broker. Mediation fees, if any, shall be divided equally among the Parties involved. If, for any dispute or claim to which this paragraph applies, any Party (i) commences an action without first attempting to resolve the matter through mediation, or (ii) before commencement of an action, refuses to mediate after a request has been made, then that Party shall not be entitled to recover attorney fees, even if they would otherwise be available to that Party in any such action. THIS MEDIATION PROVISION APPLIES WHETHER OR NOT THE ARBITRATION PROVISION IS INITIALED. **Exclusions from this mediation agreement are specified in paragraph 22C.**

B. ARBITRATION OF DISPUTES:

The Parties agree that any dispute or claim in Law or equity arising between them out of this Agreement or any resulting transaction, which is not settled through mediation, shall be decided by neutral, binding arbitration. The Parties also agree to arbitrate any disputes or claims with Broker(s), who, in writing, agree to such arbitration prior to, or within a reasonable time after, the dispute or claim is presented to the Broker. The arbitrator shall be a retired judge or justice, or an attorney with at least 5 years of residential real estate Law experience, unless the parties mutually agree to a different arbitrator. The Parties shall have the right to discovery in accordance with Code of Civil Procedure §1283.05. In all other respects, the arbitration shall be conducted in accordance with Title 9 of Part 3 of the Code of Civil Procedure. Judgment upon the award of the arbitrator(s) may be entered into any court having jurisdiction. Enforcement of this agreement to arbitrate shall be governed by the Federal Arbitration Act. **Exclusions from this arbitration agreement are specified in paragraph 22C.**

"NOTICE: BY INITIALING IN THE SPACE BELOW YOU ARE AGREEING TO HAVE ANY DISPUTE ARISING OUT OF THE MATTERS INCLUDED IN THE 'ARBITRATION OF DISPUTES' PROVISION DECIDED BY NEUTRAL ARBITRATION AS PROVIDED BY CALIFORNIA LAW AND YOU ARE GIVING UP ANY RIGHTS YOU MIGHT POSSESS TO HAVE THE DISPUTE LITIGATED IN A COURT OR JURY TRIAL. BY INITIALING IN THE SPACE BELOW YOU ARE GIVING UP YOUR JUDICIAL RIGHTS TO DISCOVERY AND APPEAL, UNLESS THOSE RIGHTS ARE SPECIFICALLY INCLUDED IN THE 'ARBITRATION OF DISPUTES' PROVISION. IF YOU REFUSE TO SUBMIT TO ARBITRATION AFTER AGREEING TO THIS PROVISION, YOU MAY BE COMPELLED TO ARBITRATE UNDER THE AUTHORITY OF THE CALIFORNIA CODE OF CIVIL PROCEDURE. YOUR AGREEMENT TO THIS ARBITRATION PROVISION IS VOLUNTARY."

"WE HAVE READ AND UNDERSTAND THE FOREGOING AND AGREE TO SUBMIT DISPUTES ARISING OUT OF THE MATTERS INCLUDED IN THE 'ARBITRATION OF DISPUTES' PROVISION TO NEUTRAL ARBITRATION."

Buyer's Initials _____/_____   Seller's Initials _____/_____

C. ADDITIONAL MEDIATION AND ARBITRATION TERMS:

(1) EXCLUSIONS: The following matters are excluded from mediation and arbitration: **(i)** a judicial or non-judicial foreclosure or other action or proceeding to enforce a deed of trust, mortgage or installment land sale contract as defined in Civil Code §2985; **(ii)** an unlawful detainer action; and **(iii)** any matter that is within the jurisdiction of a probate, small claims or bankruptcy court.

(2) PRESERVATION OF ACTIONS: The following shall not constitute a waiver nor violation of the mediation and arbitration provisions: **(i)** The filing of a court action to enable the recording of a notice of pending action, for order of attachment, receivership, injunction, or other provisional remedies; or **(ii)** the filing of a mechanic's lien.

(3) BROKERS: Brokers shall not be obligated nor compelled to mediate or arbitrate unless they agree to do so in writing. Any Broker(s) participating in mediation or arbitration shall not be deemed a party to this Agreement.

Buyer's Initials (_____)(_____)   Seller's Initials (_____)(_____)

RPA-CA REVISED 11/14 (PAGE 8 of 10)   Print Date

CALIFORNIA RESIDENTIAL PURCHASE AGREEMENT (RPA-CA PAGE 8 OF 10)

Property Address: _____ Date: _____

23. **SELECTION OF SERVICE PROVIDERS:** Brokers do not guarantee the performance of any vendors, service or product providers ("Providers"), whether referred by Broker or selected by Buyer, Seller or other person. Buyer and Seller may select ANY Providers of their own choosing.

24. **MULTIPLE LISTING SERVICE ("MLS"):** Brokers are authorized to report to the MLS a pending sale and, upon Close Of Escrow, the sales price and other terms of this transaction shall be provided to the MLS to be published and disseminated to persons and entities authorized to use the information on terms approved by the MLS.

25. **ATTORNEY FEES:** In any action, proceeding, or arbitration between Buyer and Seller arising out of this Agreement, the prevailing Buyer or Seller shall be entitled to reasonable attorney fees and costs from the non-prevailing Buyer or Seller, except as provided in paragraph 22A.

26. **ASSIGNMENT:** Buyer shall not assign all or any part of Buyer's interest in this Agreement without first having obtained the separate written consent of Seller to a specified assignee. Such consent shall not be unreasonably withheld. Any total or partial assignment shall not relieve Buyer of Buyer's obligations pursuant to this Agreement unless otherwise agreed in writing by Seller (C.A.R. Form AOAA).

27. **EQUAL HOUSING OPPORTUNITY:** The Property is sold in compliance with federal, state and local anti-discrimination Laws.

28. **TERMS AND CONDITIONS OF OFFER:**
This is an offer to purchase the Property on the above terms and conditions. The liquidated damages paragraph or the arbitration of disputes paragraph is incorporated in this Agreement if initialed by all Parties or if incorporated by mutual agreement in a counter offer or addendum. If at least one but not all Parties initial, a counter offer is required until agreement is reached. Seller has the right to continue to offer the Property for sale and to accept any other offer at any time prior to notification of Acceptance. The Parties have read and acknowledge receipt of a Copy of the offer and agree to the confirmation of agency relationships. If this offer is accepted and Buyer subsequently defaults, Buyer may be responsible for payment of Brokers' compensation. This Agreement and any supplement, addendum or modification, including any Copy, may be Signed in two or more counterparts, all of which shall constitute one and the same writing.

29. **TIME OF ESSENCE; ENTIRE CONTRACT; CHANGES:** Time is of the essence. All understandings between the Parties are incorporated in this Agreement. Its terms are intended by the Parties as a final, complete and exclusive expression of their Agreement with respect to its subject matter, and may not be contradicted by evidence of any prior agreement or contemporaneous oral agreement. If any provision of this Agreement is held to be ineffective or invalid, the remaining provisions will nevertheless be given full force and effect. Except as otherwise specified, this Agreement shall be interpreted and disputes shall be resolved in accordance with the Laws of the State of California. **Neither this Agreement nor any provision in it may be extended, amended, modified, altered or changed, except in writing Signed by Buyer and Seller.**

30. **DEFINITIONS:** As used in this Agreement:
    A. **"Acceptance"** means the time the offer or final counter offer is accepted in writing by a Party and is delivered to and personally received by the other Party or that Party's authorized agent in accordance with the terms of this offer or a final counter offer.
    B. **"Agreement"** means this document and any incorporated addenda, counter offers and written terms Signed by all Parties collectively forming the binding agreement between the Parties. All terms and conditions of any addenda checked and Signed are incorporated into this Agreement.
    C. **"C.A.R. Form"** means the most current version of the specific form referenced or another comparable form agreed to by the parties.
    D. **"Close Of Escrow"**, including "COE", means the date the grant deed, or other evidence of transfer of title, is recorded.
    E. **"Copy"** means copy by any means including photocopy, NCR, facsimile and electronic.
    F. **"Days"** means calendar days. However, after Acceptance, the last **Day** for performance of any act required by this Agreement (including Close Of Escrow) shall not include any Saturday, Sunday, or legal holiday and shall instead be the next Day.
    G. **"Days After"** means the specified number of calendar days after the occurrence of the event specified, not counting the calendar date on which the specified event occurs, and ending at 11:59 PM on the final day.
    H. **"Days Prior"** means the specified number of calendar days before the occurrence of the event specified, not counting the calendar date on which the specified event is scheduled to occur.
    I. **"Deliver"**, **"Delivered"** or **"Delivery"**, unless otherwise specified in writing, means and shall be effective upon: personal receipt by Buyer or Seller or the individual Real Estate Licensee for that principal as specified in the section titled Real Estate Brokers on page 10, regardless of the method used (i.e., messenger, mail, email, fax, other).
    J. **"Electronic Copy"** or **"Electronic Signature"** means, as applicable, an electronic copy or signature complying with California Law. Buyer and Seller agree that electronic means will not be used by either Party to modify or alter the content or integrity of this Agreement without the knowledge and consent of the other Party.
    K. **"Law"** means any law, code, statute, ordinance, regulation, rule or order, which is adopted by a controlling city, county, state or federal legislative, judicial or executive body or agency.
    L. **"Repairs"** means any repairs (including pest control), alterations, replacements, modifications or retrofitting of the Property provided for under this Agreement.
    M. **"Signed"** means either a handwritten or electronic signature on an original document, Copy or any counterpart.

31. **EXPIRATION OF OFFER:** This offer shall be deemed revoked and the deposit, if any, shall be returned to Buyer unless the offer is Signed by Seller and a Copy of the Signed offer is personally received by Buyer, or by _____, who is authorized to receive it, by 5:00 PM on the third Day after this offer is signed by Buyer (or by ☐ _____ ☐AM/☐PM, on _____(date)).

☐ One or more Buyers is signing this Agreement in a representative capacity and not for him/herself as an individual. See attached Representative Capacity Signature Disclosure (C.A.R. Form RCSD) for additional terms.

Date _____ BUYER _____

(Print name) _____

Date _____ BUYER _____

(Print name) _____

☐ Additional Signature Addendum attached (C.A.R. Form ASA).

RPA-CA REVISED 11/14 (PAGE 9 of 10)   Print Date   Seller's Initials (_____)(_____)

CALIFORNIA RESIDENTIAL PURCHASE AGREEMENT (RPA-CA PAGE 9 OF 10)

Property Address: _____   Date: _____

32. ACCEPTANCE OF OFFER: Seller warrants that Seller is the owner of the Property, or has the authority to execute this Agreement. Seller accepts the above offer and agrees to sell the Property on the above terms and conditions. Seller has read and acknowledges receipt of a Copy of this Agreement, and authorizes Broker to Deliver a Signed Copy to Buyer.

☐ (If checked) SELLER'S ACCEPTANCE IS **SUBJECT TO ATTACHED COUNTER OFFER (C.A.R. Form SCO or SMCO) DATED:** _____.

☐ One or more Sellers is signing this Agreement in a representative capacity and not for him/herself as an individual. See attached Representative Capacity Signature Disclosure (C.A.R. Form RCSD) for additional terms.

Date _____ SELLER _____

(Print name) _____

Date _____ SELLER _____

(Print name) _____

☐ Additional Signature Addendum attached (C.A.R. Form ASA).

(____/____) **(Do not initial if making a counter offer.) CONFIRMATION OF ACCEPTANCE:** A Copy of Signed Acceptance was
(Initials) personally received by Buyer or Buyer's authorized agent on (date) _____ at _____
☐AM/☐PM. **A binding Agreement is created when a Copy of Signed Acceptance is personally received by Buyer or Buyer's authorized agent whether or not confirmed in this document. Completion of this confirmation is not legally required in order to create a binding Agreement; it is solely intended to evidence the date that Confirmation of Acceptance has occurred.**

REAL ESTATE BROKERS:
A. Real Estate Brokers are not parties to the Agreement between Buyer and Seller.
B. Agency relationships are confirmed as stated in paragraph 2.
C. If specified in paragraph 3A(2), Agent who submitted the offer for Buyer acknowledges receipt of deposit.
D. **COOPERATING BROKER COMPENSATION:** Listing Broker agrees to pay Cooperating Broker **(Selling Firm)** and Cooperating Broker agrees to accept, out of Listing Broker's proceeds in escrow, the amount specified in the MLS, provided Cooperating Broker is a Participant of the MLS in which the Property is offered for sale or a reciprocal MLS. If Listing Broker and Cooperating Broker are not both Participants of the MLS, or a reciprocal MLS, in which the Property is offered for sale, then compensation must be specified in a separate written agreement (C.A.R. Form CBC). Declaration of License and Tax (C.A.R. Form DLT) may be used to document that tax reporting will be required or that an exemption exists.

Real Estate Broker (Selling Firm) _____ CalBRE Lic. # _____
By _____ CalBRE Lic. # _____ Date _____
By _____ CalBRE Lic. # _____ Date _____
Address _____ City _____ State _____ Zip _____
Telephone _____ Fax _____ E-mail _____

Real Estate Broker (Listing Firm) _____ CalBRE Lic. # _____
By _____ CalBRE Lic. # _____ Date _____
By _____ CalBRE Lic. # _____ Date _____
Address _____ City _____ State _____ Zip _____
Telephone _____ Fax _____ E-mail _____

ESCROW HOLDER ACKNOWLEDGMENT:
Escrow Holder acknowledges receipt of a Copy of this Agreement, (if checked, ☐ a deposit in the amount of $ _____),
counter offer numbers _____ ☐ Seller's Statement of Information and _____
_____, and agrees to act as Escrow Holder subject to paragraph 20 of this Agreement, any supplemental escrow instructions and the terms of Escrow Holder's general provisions.

Escrow Holder is advised that the date of Confirmation of Acceptance of the Agreement as between Buyer and Seller is _____

Escrow Holder _____ Escrow # _____
By _____ Date_____
Address _____
Phone/Fax/E-mail_____
Escrow Holder has the following license number # _____
☐ Department of Business Oversight, ☐ Department of Insurance, ☐ Bureau of Real Estate.

PRESENTATION OF OFFER: (_____) Listing Broker presented this offer to Seller on _____ (date).
                          Broker or Designee Initials

REJECTION OF OFFER: (_____)(_____) No counter offer is being made. This offer was rejected by Seller on_____ (date).
                        Seller's Initials

Published and Distributed by:
REAL ESTATE BUSINESS SERVICES, INC.
a subsidiary of the CALIFORNIA ASSOCIATION OF REALTORS®
525 South Virgil Avenue, Los Angeles, California 90020

Reviewed by _____
Broker or Designee _____

RPA-CA REVISED 11/14 (PAGE 10 of 10)   Print Date

Buyer's Initials (_____)(_____)

CALIFORNIA RESIDENTIAL PURCHASE AGREEMENT (RPA-CA PAGE 10 OF 10)

Example: A property is owned by three cousins who inherited it from their grandfather. One of the cousins has lived in South America for several years, and the other two cousins have managed the property. When they ask you to handle the sale of the property, you must be sure that the third cousin will be available to sign the sales contract, either in person or through a representative (such as an attorney in fact). Otherwise, a buyer would only be able to purchase a partial interest in the property. (Note that the absent cousin must also sign the listing agreement.)

You should also consider whether everyone who is signing the contract has contractual capacity. If one of the parties is a minor (younger than 18) or mentally incompetent, the contract should be signed by that party's legal guardian. Otherwise, the purchase agreement will be void.

Marital Property. Find out whether or not each buyer or seller who is going to sign the purchase agreement is married, and make sure each married party's spouse is going to sign the agreement too. In California, when community real property is bought or sold, both spouses must join in the contract.

Example: Henry and Deborah's house is community property. They've been talking about selling it for some time. While Deborah's out of town, Henry decides to surprise her. He signs a purchase agreement with the Bentleys, agreeing to sell their house for $625,000. When Deborah comes home and hears the news, she's aghast. She believes their house is worth much more than $625,000, and she isn't ready to move so soon. Deborah can call off the sale, because the house is community property and she didn't sign the contract.

Although a married person can sell his or her separate property without the spouse's consent, it's often difficult to know when real property owned by a married person is community property or separate property. It's not your job to determine the status of the property, so it's always best to get both spouses to sign all documents related to the transaction. If they have questions about the separate or community status of their property, they should consult an attorney.

When filling in the names of a married couple, state each name separately; for example, "Edward K. Hardy and Joanna T. Hardy, a married couple."

Other Forms of Co-ownership. When property is owned as a tenancy in common or in joint tenancy, all of the owners must sign the purchase agreement in order to convey full ownership to the buyer. However, an individual tenant in common or joint tenant can convey her own interest without the consent of the other owner(s).

Business Entities as Parties. When one of the parties to the contract is a partnership, the names of all of the general partners (and their spouses) and the name of the partnership itself should appear in the contract. For partnerships, corporations, and limited liability companies, the company's address and the state in which it is organized or incorporated should also be shown.

Legal authority to enter into the transaction must be established. Before closing, the escrow agent needs documentation proving that the person signing the contract has authority to do so on behalf of the entity. The documentation could be in the form of a power of attorney (see below) or a resolution of the board of directors. If there's any doubt about who needs to sign the documents, consult a lawyer.

Estates and Trusts. When property that is part of an estate is sold, the personal representative or executor of the estate must sign the purchase agreement and other documents. To sell property that is part of a trust, the trustee must sign the documents.

Attorneys in Fact. If a party to a contract is unavailable or unable to sign the contract documents, a personal representative may be authorized to sign on his behalf. Authorization to sign for someone else is granted by a written document called a **power of attorney**. The authorized person is referred to as an **attorney in fact**. The power of attorney is valid only while the person who granted it is still alive and mentally competent. A power of attorney pertaining to real property should be recorded in the county where the property is located.

When an attorney in fact signs for another person, she usually signs that person's name and then writes her own name beneath it:

Michelle H. Plunkett
by Sarah R. Johnson, her Attorney in Fact

If an attorney in fact is going to sign any of the documents in a sale you're involved in, ask to see a copy of the power of attorney and verify its validity by checking with the person who granted the power.

Property Description

To be enforceable, a purchase agreement must contain an unambiguous description of the property. You should always use a complete legal description. Don't rely on the street address or the property tax identification number. Tax numbers are subject to change, and the description in the tax statement might be incomplete.

When there isn't enough room for the property's legal description on the form, you should attach an addendum containing the description. Put a reference to the addendum in the space provided for the property description (for example, "See Addendum A"). If the legal description is complicated, photocopy it from the seller's deed or get a photocopy from a title company (or copy and paste it from a digital version). That way, you'll avoid the transcription mistakes that commonly occur when a complicated description is retyped.

Agency Disclosure

As we discussed in Chapter 1, the real estate agents involved in a transaction must inform both the buyer and the seller which party (or parties) they represent. An agency disclosure must be made to the buyer before the buyer signs the offer to purchase, and to the seller before the seller signs the offer. The disclosures must be confirmed in writing, either in the purchase agreement or in a separate agency confirmation form.

Purchase Price and Method of Payment

The full purchase price, including any mortgages or other liens that the buyer is going to assume, should be stated in the agreement. For example, if the buyer is going to assume the seller's mortgage, which has a remaining principal balance of $397,000, and also give the seller $55,000 in cash at closing, then you should fill in $452,000 as the purchase price on the purchase agreement form.

Most residential purchase agreements are contingent on financing; in other words, the agreement will not be binding unless the buyer obtains a loan. This contingency is set forth in an addendum or as a provision in the agreement itself. The financing contingency specifies the downpayment the buyer will make, the loan amount, and any key loan terms important to the buyer. Financing contingencies are discussed in Chapter 8.

Some transactions are financed completely or partially by the seller. The seller may accept a cash downpayment with a real estate contract or a deed of trust for all or part of the remainder of the purchase price. In that case, the interest rate, payment amount, and other terms for the seller financing must be included in the purchase agreement. The parties can use a form such as the seller financing addendum shown in Figure 7.2 to include the additional financing terms. (For more information about seller financing, see Chapter 10. Seller financing disclosure requirements are discussed in Chapter 9.)

Good Faith Deposit

The purchase agreement should state the amount of the buyer's good faith deposit and how the deposit will be handled. As we explained in Chapter 6, the agreement should also state the form of the deposit, such as cash or a personal check.

The purchase agreement may direct the buyer to deliver the deposit directly to the escrow agent. Alternatively, the buyer may give the selling agent a personal check for the deposit, and the purchase agreement provides that the selling broker will hold the check undeposited until the seller has accepted the buyer's offer. That makes it easy to return the deposit to the buyer if the seller rejects the offer.

Allocation of Costs

A residential real estate transaction may involve a wide variety of closing costs (see Chapter 11). Whether the buyer or the seller pays a particular closing cost usually depends on what's customary in the local area, but the parties can allocate most costs however they wish in their contract. Provisions concerning inspection fees, the cost of compliance with certain regulations, and the escrow fee are commonly included in the purchase agreement.

Inspections. In California, residential lenders typically require a structural pest control inspection, performed by a licensed pest control inspector. Usually a seller will order an inspection at the time the house is listed. In the purchase agreement, you can indicate the inspection company used and which party is responsible for the inspection cost.

A buyer may want to order inspections of other aspects of the property. (See the discussion of inspection contingencies in Chapter 8.) The purchase agreement will state what inspections are required and the party who will pay for each inspection. The agreement may also specify who will pay for any necessary repairs.

Fig. 7.2 Seller financing addendum

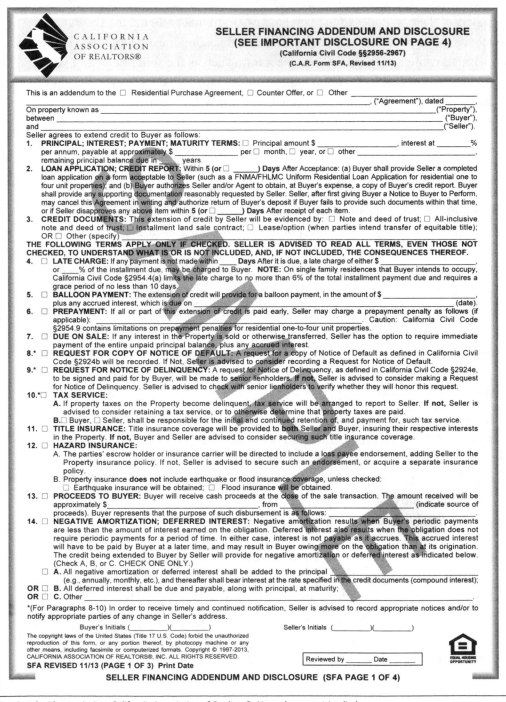

Reprinted with permission, California Association of Realtors®. No endorsement implied.

Property Address: _____ Date: _____

15. ☐ **ALL-INCLUSIVE DEED OF TRUST; INSTALLMENT LAND SALE CONTRACT:** This transaction involves the use of an all-inclusive (or wraparound) deed of trust or an installment land sale contract. That deed of trust or contract shall provide as follows:

   A. In the event of an acceleration of any senior encumbrance, the party responsibile for payment, or for legal defense is: ☐ Buyer ☐ Seller ; OR ☐ **Is not** specified in the credit or security documents.

   B. In the event of the prepayment of a senior encumbrance, the responsibilities and rights of Buyer and Seller regarding refinancing, prepayment penalties, and any prepayment discounts are: _____;
   OR ☐ **Are not** specified in the documents evidencing credit.

   C. Buyer will make periodic payments to _____ (Seller, collection agent, or any neutral third party), who will be responsible for disbursing payments to the payee(s) on the senior encumbrance(s) and to Seller. NOTE: The Parties are advised to designate a neutral third party for these purposes.

16. ☐ **TAX IDENTIFICATION NUMBERS:** Buyer and Seller shall each provide to each other their Social Security Numbers or Taxpayer Identification Numbers.

17. ☐ **OTHER CREDIT TERMS** _____

18. ☐ **RECORDING:** The documents evidencing credit (paragraph 3) will be recorded with the county recorder where the Property is located. If not, Buyer and Seller are advised that their respective interests in the Property may be jeopardized by intervening liens, judgments, encumbrances, or subsequent transfers.

19. ☐ **JUNIOR FINANCING:** There will be additional financing, secured by the Property, junior to this Seller financing. Explain: _____

20. SENIOR LOANS AND ENCUMBRANCES: The following information is provided on loans and/or encumbrances that will be senior to Seller financing. NOTE: The following are estimates, unless otherwise marked with an asterisk (*). If checked: ☐ A separate sheet with information on additional senior loans/encumbrances is attached

		1st	2nd
A.	Original Balance	$ _____	$ _____
B.	Current Balance	$ _____	$ _____
C.	Periodic Payment (e.g. $100/month):	$ _____	$ _____ /
	Including Impounds of:	$ _____	$ _____ /
D.	Interest Rate (per annum)	_____ %	_____ %
E.	Fixed or Variable Rate:	_____	_____
	If Variable Rate: Lifetime Cap (Ceiling)	_____	_____
	Indicator (Underlying Index)	_____	_____
	Margins	_____	_____
F.	Maturity Date	_____	_____
G.	Amount of Balloon Payment	$ _____	$ _____
H.	Date Balloon Payment Due	_____	_____
I.	Potential for Negative Amortization? (Yes, No, or Unknown)	_____	_____
J.	Due on Sale? (Yes, No, or Unknown)	_____	_____
K.	Pre-payment penalty? (Yes, No, or Unknown)	_____	_____
L.	Are payments current? (Yes, No, or Unknown)	_____	_____

21. BUYER'S CREDITWORTHINESS: (CHECK EITHER A OR B. Do not check both.) In addition to the loan application, credit report and other information requested under paragraph 2:

   A. ☐ No other disclosure concerning Buyer's creditworthiness has been made to Seller;

OR **B.** ☐ The following representations concerning Buyer's creditworthiness are made by Buyer(s) to Seller:

Borrower	**Co-Borrower**
1. Occupation _____	1. Occupation _____
2. Employer _____	2. Employer _____
3. Length of Employment _____	3. Length of Employment _____
4. Monthly Gross Income _____	4. Monthly Gross Income _____
5. Other _____	5. Other _____

22. ADDED, DELETED OR SUBSTITUTED BUYERS: The addition, deletion or substitution of any person or entity under this Agreement or to title prior to close of escrow shall require Seller's written consent. Seller may grant or withhold consent in Seller's sole discretion. Any additional or substituted person or entity shall, if requested by Seller, submit to Seller the same documentation as required for the original named Buyer. Seller and/or Brokers may obtain a credit report, at Buyer's expense, on any such person or entity.

Buyer's Initials (_____)(_____)   Seller's Initials (_____)(_____)

SFA REVISED 11/13 (PAGE 2 OF 4)   Reviewed by _____ Date _____

SELLER FINANCING ADDENDUM AND DISCLOSURE (SFA PAGE 2 OF 4)

Property Address: _____ Date: _____

23. CAUTION:

    A. If the Seller financing requires a balloon payment, Seller shall give Buyer written notice, according to the terms of Civil Code §2966, at least 90 and not more than 150 days before the balloon payment is due if the transaction is for the purchase of a dwelling for not more than four families.

    B. If **any** obligation secured by the Property calls for a balloon payment, Seller and Buyer are aware that refinancing of the balloon payment at maturity may be difficult or impossible, depending on conditions in the conventional mortgage marketplace at that time. There are no assurances that new financing or a loan extension will be available when the balloon prepayment, or any prepayment, is due.

    C. If **any** of the existing or proposed loans or extensions of credit would require refinancing as a result of a lack of full amortization, such refinancing might be difficult or impossible in the conventional mortgage marketplace.

    D. In the event of default by Buyer: (1) Seller may have to reinstate and/or make monthly payments on any and all senior encumbrances (including real property taxes) in order to protect Seller's secured interest; (2) Seller's rights are generally limited to foreclosure on the Property, pursuant to California Code of Civil Procedure §580b; and (3) the Property may lack sufficient equity to protect Seller's interests if the Property decreases in value.

If this three-page Addendum and Disclosure is used in a transaction for the purchase of a dwelling for not more than four families, it shall be prepared by an Arranger of Credit as defined in California Civil Code §2957(a). (The Arranger of Credit is usually the agent who obtained the offer.)

_____

Arranger of Credit - (Print Firm Name) _____ By _____ Date _____

Address _____ City _____ State _____ Zip _____

Phone _____ Fax _____

> BUYER AND SELLER ACKNOWLEDGE AND AGREE THAT BROKERS: (A) WILL NOT PROVIDE LEGAL OR TAX ADVICE; (B) WILL NOT PROVIDE OTHER ADVICE OR INFORMATION THAT EXCEEDS THE KNOWLEDGE, EDUCATION AND EXPERIENCE REQUIRED TO OBTAIN A REAL ESTATE LICENSE; OR (C) HAVE NOT AND WILL NOT VERIFY ANY INFORMATION PROVIDED BY EITHER BUYER OR SELLER. BUYER AND SELLER AGREE THAT THEY WILL SEEK LEGAL, TAX AND OTHER DESIRED ASSISTANCE FROM APPROPRIATE PROFESSIONALS. BUYER AND SELLER ACKNOWLEDGE THAT THE INFORMATION EACH HAS PROVIDED TO THE ARRANGER OF CREDIT FOR INCLUSION IN THIS DISCLOSURE FORM IS ACCURATE. BUYER AND SELLER FURTHER ACKNOWLEDGE THAT EACH HAS RECEIVED A COMPLETED COPY OF THIS DISCLOSURE FORM.

Buyer _____ Date _____
         (signature)
Address _____ City _____ State _____ Zip _____
Phone _____ Fax _____ E-mail _____

Buyer _____ Date _____
         (signature)
Address _____ City _____ State _____ Zip _____
Phone _____ Fax _____ E-mail _____

Seller _____ Date _____
         (signature)
Address _____ City _____ State _____ Zip _____
Phone _____ Fax _____ E-mail _____

Seller _____ Date _____
         (signature)
Address _____ City _____ State _____ Zip _____
Phone _____ Fax _____ E-mail _____

Published and Distributed by:
REAL ESTATE BUSINESS SERVICES, INC.
a subsidiary of the California Association of REALTORS®
525 South Virgil Avenue, Los Angeles, California 90020

Reviewed by _____ Date _____

SFA REVISED 11/13 (PAGE 3 OF 4)

SELLER FINANCING ADDENDUM AND DISCLOSURE (SFA PAGE 3 OF 4)

Property Address: _____ Date: _____

IMPORTANT SELLER FINANCING DISCLOSURE - PLEASE READ CAREFULLY

The Dodd-Frank Wall Street Reform and Consumer Protection Act (Dodd-Frank) has made significant and important changes affecting seller financing on residential properties. Effective January 10, 2014, sellers who finance the purchase of residential property containing 1-4 units may be considered "loan originators" required to comply with certain Truth In Lending Act ("TILA") requirements. Even under Dodd-Frank however, the following two exemptions exist:

1. The seller finances only **ONE** property in any 12 month period and:
   a. The seller is a natural person, a trust or an estate, and
   b. The seller did not construct the property, and
   c. The financing has a fixed rate or does not adjust for the first 5 years, and
   d. The financing does not result in negative amortization.

   OR

2. The seller finances no more than **THREE** properties in any 12 month period and:
   a. The seller is a natural person or organization (corporation, LLC, partnership, trust, estate, association, etc.), and
   b. The seller did not construct the property, and
   c. The loan is fully amortized, i.e., no balloon payment, and
   d. The financing has a fixed rate or does not adjust for the first 5 years, and
   e. The borrow has the reasonable ability to repay the loan.

Sellers who finance the purchase of residential property containing 1-4 units meeting either of the two exemptions are not subject to the TILA requirements above may continue to, and are required by California Law to, use the Seller Financing Addendum.

Sellers who finance the purchase of residential property containing 1-4 units who do not meet either of the two tests above should still complete the Seller Finance Addendum and speak to a lawyer about other TILA disclosures that may be required.

Sellers who finance the purchase of residential property containing 5 or more units, vacant land, or commercial properties are not subject to the TILA disclosures nor are they required to use the Seller Financing Addendum.

A seller who originates a single extension of credit through a mortgage broker and additionally meets the definition of a "high-cost" mortgage under Dodd-Frank may be subject to the Truth in Lending Act's requirement to verify the borrower's ability to repay.

Buyer's Initials (_____)(_____)   Seller's Initials (_____)(_____)

SFA REVISED 11/13 (PAGE 4 OF 4)

Reviewed by _____ Date _____

SELLER FINANCING ADDENDUM AND DISCLOSURE (SFA PAGE 4 OF 4)

Meeting Government Requirements. The law requires residential properties to have smoke detectors and properly braced water heaters. Depending on the property, carbon monoxide detectors may also be required. In addition, some communities require certain retrofit repairs, such as the installation of low-flow toilets. The parties can designate who will pay the costs of compliance in the purchase agreement.

Escrow Fee and Prorated Expenses. The purchase agreement should state who will pay the escrow agent's fee; it is typically split between the parties. In addition, the agreement should set forth how property expenses such as property taxes and homeowners association dues will be shared. These are ordinarily prorated as of the closing date, unless otherwise agreed. We'll discuss closing costs and explain how to do prorations in Chapter 11.

Closing Date

The closing date is the date when the proceeds of the sale are disbursed to the seller, the deed is delivered to the buyer, and all the appropriate documents are recorded. The purchase agreement usually sets the date for closing.

In choosing a closing date, it's important to consider how long it will take to meet any conditions that the purchase agreement is contingent on (see Chapter 8) and any obligations it imposes. For example, even if the buyer has been preapproved, the property still has to be appraised, a title report prepared, and the transaction evaluated before the lender will give final approval and make the loan funds available for closing. (The lender can probably give you some idea of how long this will take.) And after an inspection is performed, repairs may be necessary, followed by reinspection. The chosen closing date must allow enough time for the parties to fulfill these conditions and obligations.

If the closing date is approaching and repairs have not been completed, a final loan approval has not been obtained, or some other contingency has not yet been satisfied, the parties may want to change the closing date by executing a written extension agreement. The purchase agreement will terminate on the date set for closing, so try to get an extension agreement signed as soon as possible. Failure to extend the closing date may result in an unenforceable agreement. A special form may be used for an extension agreement, or you may use a general amendment addendum form and state that the parties agree to defer the closing to a later date.

On the other hand, if all conditions and obligations have been fulfilled well before the date set for closing, the buyer and seller may agree to move the closing date up. This amendment should also be in writing and signed by both parties.

Transfer of Possession

Most purchase agreement forms have a space for including the date of possession, when the seller will relinquish possession of the property to the buyer. The seller usually agrees that the property will be maintained in its present condition until the buyer takes possession.

Possession is normally transferred to the buyer at closing. Sometimes the buyer wants to take possession a few days or even a few weeks earlier, or the seller wants a few extra days to vacate the property.

Example: Jenkins is buying Hahn's home. The sale will close on October 17. However, the sale of Jenkins's current home will close on October 10. Jenkins wants to move into Hahn's home on October 7 to avoid the nuisance of moving twice. Hahn agrees to move out by October 6.

If possession is transferred before (or after) the closing date, the parties should execute a separate rental agreement. An example of a rental agreement that can be used for occupancy before closing is shown in Figure 7.3. This agreement sets forth the dates of occupancy, the rental rate, and other terms that will govern possession during the rental period.

Both buyers and sellers should consult their lawyers and insurance companies before entering into a leasing arrangement, because there are potential problems. For example, a buyer/tenant who moves in early might refuse to move out if the sale falls through.

Closing Agent

The buyer should designate an escrow agent or other closing agent on the purchase agreement form. In many cases, the escrow department of the buyer's lender serves as the closing agent.

Closing agents may perform a wide variety of tasks, such as ordering title insurance, arranging for liens to be paid off and released, and preparing documents on behalf of both the buyer and the seller. They also hold funds and documents in escrow for the parties, distributing them only when specified conditions have been fulfilled. All of these conditions are set forth in the escrow instructions for the transaction. While the escrow instructions may be a separate document, the C.A.R. purchase agreement form incorporates the escrow instructions into the purchase agreement. (See paragraph 20 in Figure 7.1. Escrow instructions and the closing process are discussed in Chapter 11.)

Fig. 7.3 Interim occupancy agreement

CALIFORNIA
ASSOCIATION
OF REALTORS®

INTERIM OCCUPANCY AGREEMENT
Buyer in Possession Prior to Close of Escrow
(C.A.R. Form IOA, Revised 1/06)

_____ ("Seller/Landlord")
and _____ ("Buyer/Tenant")
have entered into a purchase agreement for the real property described below. Close of escrow for the purchase agreement is scheduled
to occur on _____ (date). Seller, as Landlord, and Buyer, as Tenant, agree as follows:

1. **PROPERTY:**
   A. Landlord rents to Tenant and Tenant rents from Landlord, the real property and improvements described as: _____
      _____ ("Premises").
   B. The Premises are for the sole use as a personal residence by the following named persons **only:** _____
      _____
   C. The personal property listed in the purchase agreement, maintained pursuant to paragraph 11, is included.

2. **TERM:** The term begins on (date) _____ ("Commencement Date") and shall terminate
   at _____ ☐AM/☐PM on the earliest of: **(a)** the date scheduled for close of escrow of the purchase agreement as specified above,
   or as modified in writing; or **(b)** mutual cancellation of the purchase agreement. Tenant shall vacate the Premises upon termination
   of this Agreement, unless: **(i)** Landlord and Tenant have signed a new agreement, **(ii)** mandated by local rent control law, or **(iii)**
   Landlord accepts Rent from Tenant (other than past due Rent), in which case a month-to-month tenancy shall be created which
   either party may terminate pursuant to California Civil Code § 1946.1. Rent shall be at a rate agreed to by Landlord and Tenant, or
   as allowed by law. All other terms and conditions of this Agreement shall remain in full force and effect.

3. **RENT:** "Rent" shall mean all monetary obligations of Tenant to Landlord under the terms of this Agreement, except security deposit.
   A. Tenant agrees to pay $ _____ per month for the term of this Agreement.
   B. Rent is payable in advance on the **1st (or ☐** _____ **) day** of each calendar week, and is delinquent on the next day; or ☐ in full
      at close of escrow; or ☐ _____.
   C. PAYMENT: The Rent shall be paid by ☐ personal check, ☐ money order, ☐ cashier's check, ☐ through escrow (per escrow
      instructions), or ☐ other _____ to (name) _____
      (phone) _____ at (address) _____,
      (or at any other location subsequently specified by Landlord in writing to Tenant) between the hours of _____ and _____
      on the following days: _____. If any payment is returned
      for non-sufficient funds ("NSF") or because tenant stops payment, then, after that: (i) Landlord may, in writing, require Tenant
      to pay Rent in cash for three months and (ii) all future Rent shall be paid by ☐ money order, or ☐ cashier's check.

4. **SECURITY DEPOSIT:**
   A. Tenant agrees to pay $ _____ as a security deposit. Security deposit will be
      ☐ transferred to and held by Seller; ☐ held in Seller's Broker's trust account; or ☐ held in escrow (per escrow instructions).
   B. (1) If the tenancy is terminated due to the close of escrow by Buyer under the purchase agreement, the full amount of the
          security deposit, less any deductions below, shall be credited to Buyer's down payment on the purchase (or, if checked ☐
          returned to Buyer from Seller's proceeds in escrow). If required by lender for closing, Seller shall place the security deposit
          into escrow prior to the signing of loan documents by Buyer.
      (2) All or any portion of the security deposit may be used, as reasonably necessary, to: **(i)** cure Tenant's default in payment of Rent
          (which includes Late Charges, NSF fees or other sums due); **(ii)** repair damage, excluding ordinary wear and tear, caused by
          Tenant or by a guest or licensee of Tenant; **(iii)** clean Premises, if necessary, upon termination of the tenancy; and **(iv)** replace or
          return personal property or appurtenances. **SECURITY DEPOSIT SHALL NOT BE USED BY TENANT IN LIEU OF
          PAYMENT OF LAST MONTH'S RENT.** If all or any portion of the security deposit is used during the tenancy, Tenant agrees
          to reinstate the total security deposit within 5 Days after written notice is delivered to Tenant.
      (3) Within 21 days after Tenant vacates the Premises, Landlord shall: **(i)** furnish Tenant an itemized statement indicating the
          amount of any security deposit received and the basis for its disposition; and **(ii)** return any remaining portion of the security
          deposit to Tenant.
   C. **Except when escrow closes, security deposit will not be returned until all Tenants have vacated the Premises. Any security
      deposit returned by check shall be made out to all Tenants named on this Agreement, or as subsequently modified.**
   D. No interest will be paid on security deposit unless required by local Law.
   E. If the security deposit is held by Seller, Tenant agrees not to hold Broker responsible for its return. If the security deposit is held in
      Seller's Broker's trust account, **and** Broker's authority is terminated before expiration of this Agreement, **and** security deposit is
      released to someone other than Tenant, **then** Broker shall notify Tenant, in writing, where and to whom security deposit has been
      released. Once Tenant has been provided such notice, Tenant agrees not to hold Broker responsible for the security deposit.

5. **MOVE-IN COSTS RECEIVED/DUE:** Move-in funds made payable to _____ shall
   be paid by ☐ personal check, ☐ money order, ☐ cashier's check, or ☐ through escrow (per escrow instructions).

Category	Total Due	Payment Received	Balance Due	Date Due
Rent from _____ to _____ (date)				
*Security Deposit				
Other _____				
Other _____				
Total				

*The maximum amount Landlord may receive as security deposit, however designated, cannot exceed two months' Rent for unfurnished premises, or
three months' Rent for furnished premises.

Tenant's Initials (_____)(_____)
Landlord's Initials (_____)(_____)

IOA REVISED 1/06 (PAGE 1 OF 6) Print Date

Reviewed by _____ Date _____

EQUAL HOUSING
OPPORTUNITY

INTERIM OCCUPANCY AGREEMENT (IOA PAGE 1 OF 6)

Premises: _____ Date: _____

6. LATE CHARGE; RETURNED CHECKS:

   A. Tenant acknowledges either late payment of Rent or issuance of a returned check may cause Landlord to incur costs and expenses, the exact amounts of which are extremely difficult and impractical to determine. These costs may include, but are not limited to, processing, enforcement and accounting expenses, and late charges imposed on Landlord. If any installment of Rent due from Tenant is not received by Landlord within **5 (or ☐ _____) calendar days** after the date due, or if a check is returned, Tenant shall pay to Landlord, respectively, an additional sum of $_____ or _____% of the Rent due as a Late Charge and $25.00 as a NSF fee for the first returned check and $35.00 as a NSF fee for each additional returned check, either or both of which shall be deemed additional Rent.

   B. Landlord and Tenant agree these charges represent a fair and reasonable estimate of the costs Landlord may incur by reason of Tenant's late or NSF payment. Any Late Charge or NSF fee due shall be paid with the current installment of Rent. Landlord's acceptance of any Late Charge or NSF fee shall not constitute a waiver as to any default of Tenant. Landlord's right to collect a Late Charge or NSF fee shall not be deemed an extension of the date Rent is due under paragraph 3 or prevent Landlord from exercising any other rights and remedies under this Agreement and as provided by law.

7. PARKING: (Check A or B)

   ☐ **A.** Parking is permitted as follows: _____

   The right to parking ☐ is ☐ is not included in the Rent charged pursuant to paragraph 3. If not included in the Rent, the parking rental fee shall be an additional $ _____ per month. Parking space(s) are to be used for parking properly licensed and operable motor vehicles, except for trailers, boats, campers, buses or trucks (other than pick-up trucks). Tenant shall park in assigned space(s) only. Parking space(s) are to be kept clean. Vehicles leaking oil, gas or other motor vehicle fluids shall not be parked on the Premises. Mechanical work or storage of inoperable vehicles is not permitted in parking space(s) or elsewhere on the Premises.

   OR ☐ B. Parking is not permitted on the Premises.

8. STORAGE: (Check A or B)

   ☐ **A.** Storage is permitted as follows: _____

   The right to storage space ☐ is ☐ is not included in the Rent charged pursuant to paragraph 3. If not included in the Rent, storage space fee shall be an additional $ _____ per month. Tenant shall store only personal property Tenant owns, and shall not store property claimed by another or in which another has any right, title or interest. Tenant shall not store any improperly packaged food or perishable goods, flammable materials, explosives, hazardous waste or other inherently dangerous material, or illegal substances.

   OR ☐ B. Storage is not permitted on the Premises.

9. UTILITIES: Tenant agrees to pay for all utilities and services, and the following charges: _____ except _____, which shall be paid for by Landlord. If any utilities are not separately metered, Tenant shall pay Tenant's proportional share, as reasonably determined and directed by Landlord. If utilities are separately metered, Tenant shall place utilities in Tenant's name as of the Commencement Date. Landlord is only responsible for installing and maintaining one usable telephone jack and one telephone line to the Premises. Tenant shall pay any cost for conversion from existing utilities service provider.

10. CONDITION OF PREMISES: Tenant has examined Premises, all furniture, furnishings, appliances, landscaping, if any, and fixtures, including smoke detector(s).

   (Check all that apply:)

   ☐ **A.** Tenant acknowledges these items are clean and in operable condition, with the following exceptions: _____
   _____.

   ☐ **B.** Tenant's acknowledgment of the condition of these items is contained in an attached statement of condition (C.A.R. Form MIMO).

   ☐ **C.** Tenant will provide Landlord a list of items that are damaged or not in operable condition within **3 (or ☐ _____) Days** after Commencement Date, not as a contingency of the Agreement but rather as an acknowledgment of the condition of the Premises.

   ☐ **D.** Other: _____.

11. MAINTENANCE:

   A. Tenant shall properly use, operate and safeguard Premises, including if applicable, any landscaping, furniture, furnishings and appliances, and all mechanical, electrical, gas and plumbing fixtures, and keep them and the Premises clean, sanitary and well ventilated. Tenant shall be responsible for checking and maintaining all smoke detectors and any additional phone lines beyond the one line and jack that Landlord shall provide and maintain. Tenant shall immediately notify Landlord, in writing, of any problem, malfunction or damage. Tenant shall be charged for all repairs or replacements caused by Tenant, pets, guests or licensees of Tenant, excluding ordinary wear and tear. Tenant shall be charged for all damage to Premises as a result of failure to report a problem in a timely manner. Tenant shall be charged for repair of drain blockages or stoppages, unless caused by defective plumbing parts or tree roots invading sewer lines.

   B. ☐ Landlord ☐ Tenant shall water the garden, landscaping, trees and shrubs, except: _____
   _____.

   C. ☐ Landlord ☐ Tenant shall maintain the garden, landscaping, trees and shrubs, except: _____
   _____.

   D. ☐ Landlord ☐ Tenant shall maintain _____.

IOA REVISED 1/06 (PAGE 2 OF 6)

Tenant's Initials (_____)(_____)
Landlord's Initials (_____)(_____)

Reviewed by _____ Date _____

INTERIM OCCUPANCY AGREEMENT (IOA PAGE 2 OF 6)

Premises: _____ Date: _____

E. Tenant's failure to maintain any item for which Tenant is responsible shall give Landlord the right to hire someone to perform such maintenance and charge Tenant to cover the cost of such maintenance.

F. The following items of personal property are included in the Premises without warranty and Landlord will not maintain, repair or replace them: _____.

12. NEIGHBORHOOD CONDITIONS: Tenant is advised to satisfy him or herself as to neighborhood or area conditions, including schools, proximity and adequacy of law enforcement, crime statistics, proximity of registered felons or offenders, fire protection, other governmental services, availability, adequacy and cost of any speed-wired, wireless internet connections or other telecommunications or other technology services and installations, proximity to commercial, industrial or agricultural activities, existing and proposed transportation, construction and development that may affect noise, view, or traffic, airport noise, noise or odor from any source, wild and domestic animals, other nuisances, hazards, or circumstances, cemeteries, facilities and condition of common areas, conditions and influences of significance to certain cultures and/or religions, and personal needs, requirements and preferences of Tenant.

13. PETS: Unless otherwise provided in California Civil Code § 54.2, no animal or pet shall be kept on or about the Premises without Landlord's prior written consent, except: _____

14. RULES;REGULATIONS:

A. Tenant agrees to comply with all Landlord rules and regulations that are at any time posted on the Premises or delivered to Tenant. Tenant shall not, and shall ensure that guests and licensees of Tenant shall not, disturb, annoy, endanger or interfere with other tenants of the building or neighbors, or use the Premises for any unlawful purposes, including, but not limited to, using, manufacturing, selling, storing, or transporting illicit drugs or other contraband, or violate any law or ordinance, or commit a waste or nuisance on or about the Premises.

B. (If applicable, check one:)
☐ **(1)** Landlord shall provide Tenant with a copy of the rules and regulations within _____ Days or _____.
OR ☐ **(2)** Tenant has been provided with, and acknowledges receipt of, a copy of the rules and regulations.

15. ☐ **(If checked) CONDOMINIUM;PLANNED UNIT DEVELOPMENT:**

A. The Premises is a unit in a condominium, planned unit, development or other common interest subdivision governed by a homeowners' association ("HOA"). The name of the HOA is_____
Tenant agrees to comply with all HOA covenants, conditions and restrictions, bylaws, rules and regulations and decisions. Tenant shall reimburse Landlord for any fines or charges imposed by HOA or other authorities, due to any violation by Tenant, or the guests or licensees of Tenant.

B. (Check one:)
☐ **(1)** Landlord shall provide Tenant with a copy of the HOA rules and regulations within _____ Days or _____.
OR ☐ **(2)** Tenant has been provided with, and acknowledges receipt of, a copy of the HOA rules and regulations.

16. ALTERATIONS; REPAIRS: Unless otherwise specified by law or paragraph 27C or pursuant to the purchase agreement, without Landlord's prior written consent: **(i)** Tenant shall not make any repairs, alterations or improvements in or about the Premises including: painting, wallpapering, adding or changing locks, installing antenna or satellite dish(es), placing signs, displays or exhibits, or using screws, fastening devices, large nails or adhesive materials; **(ii)** Landlord shall not be responsible for the costs of repairs, alterations or improvements made by Tenant; **(iii)** Tenant shall not deduct from Rent the costs of any repairs, alterations or improvements; and **(iv)** any deduction made by Tenant shall be considered unpaid Rent. Tenant shall immediately notify Landlord if Tenant, individually or by or through others, commences any work on the Premises. Tenant shall be charged for any costs Landlord incurs to post and record a Notice of Non-Responsibility for any such work. Upon completion of any such work, Tenant shall notify Landlord. Tenant shall be charged for any costs Landlord incurs to post and record a Notice of Completion relating to any such work. Tenant agrees to indemnify, defend and hold harmless Landlord for any mechanic's lien attaching to the Premises or other claim resulting from any work ordered by Tenant.

17. KEYS; LOCKS:

A. Tenant acknowledges receipt of (or Tenant will receive ☐ prior to the Commencement Date, or ☐ _____):
☐ _____ key(s) to Premises,   ☐ _____ remote control device(s) for garage door/gate opener(s),
☐ _____ key(s) to mailbox,   ☐ _____.
☐ _____ key(s) to common area(s),   ☐ _____
B. Tenant acknowledges that locks to the Premises ☐ have, ☐ have not, been re-keyed.
C. If Tenant re-keys existing locks or opening devices, Tenant shall immediately deliver copies of all keys to Landlord. Tenant shall pay all costs and charges related to loss of any keys or opening devices. Tenant may not remove locks, even if installed by Tenant.

18. ENTRY:

A. Tenant shall make Premises available to Landlord or Landlord's representative for the purpose of entering to make necessary or agreed repairs, decorations, alterations, or improvements, or to supply necessary or agreed services, or to show Premises to prospective or actual purchasers, tenants, mortgagees, lenders, appraisers, or contractors.

B. Landlord and Tenant agree that 24-hour written notice shall be reasonable and sufficient notice, except as follows. 48-hour written notice is required to conduct an inspection of the Premises prior to the Tenant moving out, unless the Tenant waives the right to such notice. Notice may be given orally to show the Premises to actual or prospective purchasers provided Tenant has been notified in writing within 120 Days preceding the oral notice that the Premises are for sale and that oral notice may be given to show the Premises. No notice is required to **(i)** enter in case of an emergency; **(ii)** if the Tenant is present and consents at the time of entry or **(iii)** the Tenant has abandoned or surrendered the Premises. No written notice is required if Landlord and Tenant orally agree to an entry for agreed services or repairs if the date and time of entry are within one week of the oral agreement.

Tenant's Initials (_____)(_____)
Landlord's Initials (_____)(_____)
Reviewed by _____ Date _____

INTERIM OCCUPANCY AGREEMENT (IOA PAGE 3 OF 6)

Premises: _____ Date: _____

C. ☐ (If checked) Tenant authorizes the use of a keysafe/lockbox to allow entry into the Premises and agrees to sign a keysafe/lockbox addendum (C.A.R. Form KLA).

19. SIGNS: Tenant authorizes Landlord to place FOR SALE/LEASE signs on the Premises.

20. ASSIGNMENT; SUBLETTING: Tenant shall not sublet all or any part of Premises, or assign or transfer this Agreement or any interest herein, without Landlord's prior written consent. Unless such consent is obtained, any assignment, transfer or subletting of Premises or this Agreement or tenancy, by voluntary act of Tenant, operation of law or otherwise, shall at the option of Landlord, terminate the Agreement. Any proposed assignee, transferee or sublessee shall submit to Landlord an application and credit information for Landlord's approval and, if approved, sign a separate written agreement with Landlord and Tenant. Landlord's consent to any one assignment, transfer or sublease shall not be construed as consent to any subsequent assignment, transfer or sublease and does not release Tenant of Tenant's obligations under this Agreement.

21. JOINT AND INDIVIDUAL OBLIGATIONS: If there is more than one Tenant, each one shall be individually and completely responsible for the performance of all obligations of Tenant under this Agreement, jointly with every other Tenant, and individually, whether or not in possession.

22. ☐ **LEAD-BASED PAINT (If checked):** Premises was constructed prior to 1978. In accordance with federal law, Landlord gives and Tenant acknowledges receipt of the disclosures on the attached form (C.A.R. Form FLD) and a federally approved lead pamphlet.

23. ☐ **MILITARY ORDNANCE DISCLOSURE:** (If applicable and known to Landlord) Premises is located within one mile of an area once used for military training, and may contain potentially explosive munitions.

24. ☐ **PERIODIC PEST CONTROL:** Landlord has entered into a contract for periodic pest control treatment of the Premises and shall give Tenant a copy of the notice originally given to Landlord by the pest control company.

25. ☐ **METHAMPHETAMINE CONTAMINATION:** Prior to signing this Agreement, Landlord has given Tenant a notice that a health official has issued an order prohibiting occupancy of the property because of methamphetamine contamination. A copy of the notice and order are attached.

26. DATABASE DISCLOSURE: Notice: Pursuant to Section 290.46 of the Penal Code, information about specified registered sex offenders is made available to the public via an Internet Web site maintained by the Department of Justice at www.meganslaw.ca.gov. Depending on an offender's criminal history, this information will include either the address at which the offender resides or the community of residence and ZIP Code in which he or she resides. (Neither Landlord nor Brokers, if any, are required to check this website. If Tenant wants further information, Tenant should obtain information directly from this website.)

27. POSSESSION:

A. Tenant is not in possession of the premises. If Landlord is unable to deliver possession of Premises on Commencement Date, such Date shall be extended to the date on which possession is made available to Tenant. If Landlord is unable to deliver possession within 5 (or ☐ _____) calendar days after agreed Commencement Date, Tenant may terminate this Agreement by giving written notice to Landlord, and shall be refunded all Rent and security deposit paid. Possession is deemed terminated when Tenant has returned all keys to the Premises to Landlord.

B. ☐ Tenant is already in possession of the Premises.

28. TENANT'S OBLIGATIONS UPON VACATING PREMISES: If the tenancy is terminated due to any reason other than close of escrow by Buyer under the purchase agreement, upon termination of this Agreement:

A. Tenant shall: **(i)** give Landlord all copies of all keys or opening devices to Premises, including any common areas; **(ii)** vacate and surrender Premises to Landlord, empty of all persons; **(iii)** vacate any/all parking and/or storage space; **(iv)** clean and deliver Premises, as specified in paragraph C below, to Landlord in the same condition as referenced in paragraph 10; **(v)** remove all debris; **(vi)** give written notice to Landlord of Tenant's forwarding address; and **(vii)** _____.

B. All alterations/improvements made by or caused to be made by Tenant, with or without Landlord's consent, become the property of Landlord upon termination. Landlord may charge Tenant for restoration of the Premises to the condition it was in prior to any alterations/improvements.

C. **Right to Pre-Move-Out Inspection and Repairs as follows: (i)** After giving or receiving notice of termination of a tenancy (C.A.R. Form NTT), or before the end of a lease, Tenant has the right to request that an inspection of the Premises take place prior to termination of the lease or rental (C.A.R. Form NRI). If Tenant requests such an inspection, Tenant shall be given an opportunity to remedy identified deficiencies prior to termination, consistent with the terms of this Agreement. **(ii)** Any repairs or alterations made to the Premises as a result of this inspection (collectively, "Repairs") shall be made at Tenant's expense. Repairs may be performed by Tenant or through others, who have adequate insurance and licenses and are approved by Landlord. The work shall comply with applicable law, including governmental permit, inspection and approval requirements. Repairs shall be performed in a good, skillful manner with materials of quality and appearance comparable to existing materials. It is understood that exact restoration of appearance or cosmetic items following all Repairs may not be possible. **(iii)** Tenant shall: **(a)** obtain receipts for Repairs performed by others; **(b)** prepare a written statement indicating the Repairs performed by Tenant and the date of such Repairs; and **(c)** provide copies of receipts and statements to Landlord prior to termination.

29. BREACH OF CONTRACT; EARLY TERMINATION: In addition to any obligations established by paragraph 27, in event of termination by Tenant prior to completion of the original term of the Agreement, Tenant shall also be responsible for lost Rent, rental commissions, advertising expenses and painting costs necessary to ready Premises for re-rental. Landlord may withhold any such amounts from Tenant's security deposit.

IOA REVISED 1/06 (PAGE 4 OF 6)

Tenant's Initials (_____)(_____)
Landlord's Initials (_____)(_____)

| Reviewed by _____ Date _____ |

INTERIM OCCUPANCY AGREEMENT (IOA PAGE 4 OF 6)

Premises: _____ Date: _____

30. TEMPORARY RELOCATION: Subject to local law, Tenant agrees, upon demand of Landlord, to temporarily vacate Premises for a reasonable period, to allow for fumigation (or other methods) to control wood destroying pests or organisms, or other repairs to Premises. Tenant agrees to comply with all instructions and requirements necessary to prepare Premises to accommodate pest control, fumigation or other work, including bagging or storage of food and medicine, and removal of perishables and valuables. Tenant shall only be entitled to a credit of Rent equal to the per diem Rent for the period of time Tenant is required to vacate Premises.

31. DAMAGE TO PREMISES: If, by no fault of Tenant, Premises are totally or partially damaged or destroyed by fire, earthquake, accident or other casualty that render Premises totally or partially uninhabitable, either Landlord or Tenant may terminate this Agreement by giving the other written notice. Rent shall be abated as of the date Premises become totally or partially uninhabitable. The abated amount shall be the current monthly Rent prorated on a 30-day period. If this Agreement is not terminated, Landlord shall promptly repair the damage, and Rent shall be reduced based on the extent to which the damage interferes with Tenant's reasonable use of Premises. If damage occurs as a result of an act of Tenant or Tenant's guests, only Landlord shall have the right of termination, and no reduction in Rent shall be made.

32. INSURANCE: Tenant's or guest's personal property and vehicles are not insured by Landlord, manager or, if applicable, HOA, against loss or damage due to fire, theft, vandalism, rain, water, criminal or negligent acts of others, or any other cause. **Tenant is advised to carry Tenant's own insurance (renter's insurance) to protect Tenant from any such loss or damage.** Tenant shall comply with any requirement imposed on Tenant by Landlord's insurer to avoid: **(i)** an increase in Landlord's insurance premium (or Tenant shall pay for the increase in premium); or **(ii)** loss of insurance.

33. WATERBEDS: Tenant shall not use or have waterbeds on the Premises unless: **(i)** Tenant obtains a valid waterbed insurance policy; **(ii)** Tenant increases the security deposit in an amount equal to one-half of one month's Rent; and **(iii)** the bed conforms to the floor load capacity of Premises.

34. WAIVER: The waiver of any breach shall not be construed as a continuing waiver of the same or any subsequent breach.

35. NOTICE: Notices may be served at the following address, or at any other location subsequently designated:
Landlord: _____ Tenant: _____
_____

36. TENANT ESTOPPEL CERTIFICATE: Tenant shall execute and return a tenant estoppel certificate delivered to Tenant by Landlord or Landlord's agent within 3 Days after its receipt. Failure to comply with this requirement shall be deemed Tenant's acknowledgment that the tenant estoppel certificate is true and correct, and may be relied upon by a lender or purchaser.

37. TENANT REPRESENTATIONS; CREDIT: Tenant warrants that all statements in Tenant's rental application are accurate. Tenant authorizes Landlord and Broker(s) to obtain Tenant's credit report periodically during the tenancy in connection with modification or enforcement of this Agreement. Landlord may cancel this Agreement: **(i)** before occupancy begins; **(ii)** upon disapproval of the credit report(s); or **(iii)** at any time, upon discovering that information in Tenant's application is false. A negative credit report reflecting on Tenant's record may be submitted to a credit reporting agency if Tenant fails to fulfill the terms of payment and other obligations under this Agreement.

38. MEDIATION:
A. Consistent with paragraphs B and C below, Landlord and Tenant agree to mediate any dispute or claim arising between them out of this Agreement, or any resulting transaction, before resorting to court action. Mediation fees, if any, shall be divided equally among the parties involved. If, for any dispute or claim to which this paragraph applies, any party commences an action without first attempting to resolve the matter through mediation, or refuses to mediate after a request has been made, then that party shall not be entitled to recover attorney fees, even if they would otherwise be available to that party in any such action.
B. The following matters are excluded from mediation: **(i)** an unlawful detainer action; **(ii)** the filing or enforcement of a mechanic's lien; and **(iii)** any matter within the jurisdiction of a probate, small claims or bankruptcy court. The filing of a court action to enable the recording of a notice of pending action, for order of attachment, receivership, injunction, or other provisional remedies, shall not constitute a waiver of the mediation provision.
C. Landlord and Tenant agree to mediate disputes or claims involving Listing Agent, Leasing Agent or property manager ("Broker"), provided Broker shall have agreed to such mediation prior to, or within a reasonable time after, the dispute or claim is presented to such Broker. Any election by Broker to participate in mediation shall not result in Broker being deemed a party to this Agreement.

39. ATTORNEY FEES: In any action or proceeding arising out of the Agreement, the prevailing party between Landlord and Tenant shall be entitled to reasonable attorney fees and costs, except as provided in paragraph 37A.

40. C.A.R. FORM: C.A.R. Form means the specific form referenced or another comparable from agreed to by the parties.

41. OTHER TERMS AND CONDITIONS; SUPPLEMENTS: ☐ Interpreter/Translator Agreement (C.A.R. Form ITA); ☐ Keysafe/Lockbox Addendum (C.A.R. Form KLA); ☐ Lead-Based Paint and Lead-Based Paint Hazards Disclosure (C.A.R. Form FLD)
The following ATTACHED supplements are incorporated into this Agreement: _____
_____

42. TIME OF ESSENCE; ENTIRE AGREEMENT: Time is of the essence. All understandings between the parties are incorporated in this Agreement. Its terms are intended by the parties as a final, complete and exclusive expression of their Agreement with respect to its subject matter, and may not be contradicted by evidence of any prior agreement or contemporaneous oral agreement. If any provision of this Agreement is held to be ineffective or invalid, the remaining provisions will nevertheless be given full force and effect. Neither this Agreement nor any provision in it may be extended, amended, modified, altered or changed except in writing. This Agreement is subject to California landlord-tenant law and shall incorporate all changes required by amendment or successors to such law. The Agreement and any supplement, addendum or modification, including any copy, may be signed in two or more counterparts, all of which shall constitute one and the same writing.

Tenant's Initials (_____)(_____)
Landlord's Initials (_____)(_____)

IOA REVISED 1/06 (PAGE 5 OF 6)

Reviewed by _____ Date _____

INTERIM OCCUPANCY AGREEMENT (IOA PAGE 5 OF 6)

Premises: _____ Date: _____

43. AGENCY:

A. CONFIRMATION: The following agency relationship(s) are hereby confirmed for this transaction:
Listing Agent: (Agent representing the Seller in the purchase agreement)
(Print firm name) _____ is
the agent of (check one): ☐ the Landlord exclusively; or ☐ both the Landlord and Tenant.
Selling Agent: (Agent representing the Buyer in the purchase agreement)
(Print firm name) _____ (if
not same as Listing Agent) is the agent of (check one): ☐ the Tenant exclusively; or ☐ the Landlord exclusively; or ☐
both the Tenant and Landlord.

B. DISCLOSURE: ☐ (If checked): The term of this lease exceeds one year. A disclosure regarding real estate agency
relationships (C.A.R. Form AD) has been provided to Landlord and Tenant, who each acknowledge its receipt.

44. ☐ INTERPRETER/TRANSLATOR: The terms of this Agreement have been interpreted for Tenant into the following language:
_____. Landlord and Tenant acknowledge receipt of
the attached interpretator/translator agreement, (C.A.R. Form ITA).

45. FOREIGN LANGUAGE NEGOTIATION: If this Agreement has been negotiated by Landlord and Tenant primarily in
Spanish, Chinese, Tagalog, Korean, Vietnamese or pursuant to the California Civil Code, Tenant shall be provided a
translation of this Agreement in the language used for the negotiation.

45. RECEIPT: If specified in paragraph 5, Landlord or Broker, acknowledges receipt of move-in funds.

Landlord and Tenant acknowledge and agree Brokers: **(a)** do not guarantee the condition of the Premises; **(b)**
cannot verify representations made by others; **(c)** cannot provide legal or tax advice; **(d)** will not provide other advice
or information that exceeds the knowledge, education or experience required to obtain a real estate license.
Furthermore, Brokers: **(e)** do not decide what rental rate a Tenant should pay or Landlord should accept; and **(f)** do not
decide upon the length or other terms of tenancy. Landlord and Tenant agree they will seek legal, tax, insurance and
other desired assistance from appropriate professionals.

Tenant/Buyer _____ Date _____
Address _____ City _____ State _____ Zip _____
Telephone _____ Fax _____ E-mail _____
Tenant/Buyer _____ Date _____
Address _____ City _____ State _____ Zip _____
Telephone _____ Fax _____ E-mail _____
Landlord /Seller _____ Date _____
Landlord /Seller _____ Date _____
Landlord Address _____ City _____ State _____ Zip _____
Telephone _____ Fax _____ E-mail _____

REAL ESTATE BROKERS:
A. Brokers are not a party to the Agreement between Landlord and Tenant.
B. Agency relationships are confirmed as above.

Real Estate Broker _____ License # _____
(Agent representing the Buyer in the purchase agreement)
By (Agent) _____ License # _____ Date _____
Address _____ City _____ State _____ Zip _____
Telephone _____ Fax _____ E-mail _____

Real Estate Broker _____ License # _____
(Agent representing the Seller in the purchase agreement)
By (Agent) _____ License # _____ Date _____
Address _____ City _____ State _____ Zip _____
Telephone _____ Fax _____ E-mail _____

SURE TRAC
The System for Success®

Reviewed by _____ Date _____

EQUAL HOUSING
OPPORTUNITY

IOA REVISED 1/06 (PAGE 6 OF 6)

INTERIM OCCUPANCY AGREEMENT (IOA PAGE 6 OF 6)

Disclosure Provisions

In transactions that involve housing built before 1978, the seller must disclose information about lead-based paint on the property to potential buyers. (See Chapter 2.) Specific warnings must be included in the purchase agreement, along with signed statements from the parties acknowledging that the requirements of the law have been fulfilled. The signed acknowledgments must be kept for at least three years as proof of compliance.

Other disclosures that sellers in residential transactions are required to make may be included or referenced in the purchase agreement. For example, the form must include a provision that explains how to access the "Megan's Law" database on the Internet. The database lists areas where registered sex offenders are residing.

Included and Excluded Items

An included and excluded items paragraph often begins by listing items that are included in the sale unless otherwise noted in the purchase agreement. The list usually includes carpeting, built-in appliances, window coverings, air conditioning equipment, shrubs, and so forth. Even without this provision in the contract, many of the items listed as included would be considered fixtures or attachments and included in the sale. However, the provision helps prevent disputes over these items.

Similarly, the paragraph usually contains a list of items that are excluded from the sale unless otherwise noted.

Of course, the parties can alter the lists of included and excluded items. Some purchase agreement forms have blank lines in the paragraph for this purpose; otherwise, you can use an addendum.

Buyer's Investigation and Repairs

It's always best for a buyer to inspect a property thoroughly before purchasing it. And most buyers don't want to be obligated to go through with the transaction if an inspection reveals serious flaws. For this reason, the purchase agreement form typically gives the buyer the right to investigate the property, and makes the buyer's offer contingent on her approval of the property's condition. The buyer has a set period of time to complete her inspections and then either remove the contingency or cancel the agreement.

If the inspections reveal any problems, the buyer must decide whether she wants those problems corrected before she purchases the property. If the buyer does want corrective work completed before the sale, the parties must negotiate who will complete and pay for the repair work. (Inspection contingencies are also discussed in Chapter 8.)

Conveyance and Title

A purchase agreement form includes provisions pertaining to the conveyance of the property and the condition of title. The type of deed that the seller will execute in favor of the buyer (ordinarily a grant deed) is specified. Typically, the seller agrees to provide the buyer with a preliminary title report listing liens and other encumbrances. The buyer usually agrees to take title subject to existing non-financial encumbrances (easements and restrictive covenants), with a home-owner's coverage title insurance policy. The seller agrees to pay off any liens at closing (if not before), unless the buyer is assuming or taking title subject to an existing lien.

The seller is required to disclose to the buyer any information he has about matters affecting the title, whether or not these issues appear in the title report. If the seller is a party to a legal action—such as a bankruptcy, a divorce, or a foreclosure action—the seller may not be able to convey clear title. This is a material fact and should be disclosed to the buyer. If the buyer has questions about the legal ramifications of the seller's court proceedings, the buyer should consult an attorney.

Sale of Buyer's Property

Often a buyer needs to sell her current home in order to have the money to purchase a new home. The buyer does not want to be obligated to go through with the purchase if she can't sell her current home. This problem can be solved by making the purchase agreement contingent on the sale of the buyer's current home. The contingency should be listed in the purchase agreement, with the appropriate contingency addendum form filled out and attached to the contract. We'll discuss this type of contingency in more detail in the next chapter.

Default Provisions

A purchase agreement usually states the remedies available to the buyer or the seller if the other party defaults, and explains how the good faith deposit will be handled in case of default.

Seller's Remedies. In California, most residential purchase agreements have a liquidated damages provision similar to Paragraph 21 in the C.A.R. form shown in Figure 7.1. If both parties to the contract initial and date this provision, the good faith deposit will be treated as liquidated damages. If they choose this option, the parties agree that liquidated damages will be the seller's only remedy in the event that the buyer defaults. The seller will keep the good faith deposit as compensation for the buyer's breach of contract, but the seller can't seek any additional compensation.

Under California law, if a purchase agreement provides for liquidated damages, the provision must be in bold or red type and separately initialed by both the buyer and the seller to show that each of them consented to it. Otherwise the provision is unenforceable, which means that the seller will be allowed to choose what legal remedy to pursue if the buyer defaults. (Typically, the seller would file a lawsuit against the buyer in this situation.)

There's an additional rule that applies to transactions involving residential property with up to four units, if the buyer intends to reside in one of the units. In these transactions, no more than 3% of the purchase price can be treated as liquidated damages. So if the buyer's good faith deposit was more than 3% of the price, the seller must return the excess if the buyer forfeits the deposit. (The law concerning liquidated damages is also covered in Chapter 6.)

Dispute Resolution

Unfortunately, disputes arising out of a real estate transaction are sometimes unavoidable. The purchase agreement form should establish the procedures for resolving disputes between the buyer and the seller. Most agreements provide for mediation and arbitration as alternatives to a lawsuit.

Mediation. As we explained in Chapter 2, in mediation a neutral third party (the mediator) helps the parties involved in a dispute reach a mutually satisfactory solution. The C.A.R. purchase agreement form contains a mediation clause. In this provision, the buyer and seller agree that they will try to mediate any disputes before turning to arbitration or filing a lawsuit. If one of them resorts to arbitration or a lawsuit without attempting mediation first, he will not be entitled to have his attorney's fees paid by the other party if he wins. (Attorney's fees are discussed below.) The buyer and seller also agree to split the cost of the mediation.

Arbitration. The C.A.R. purchase agreement form also contains an arbitration clause. This provision, unlike the mediation clause, applies only if it's initialed by both the buyer and the seller. By initialing the arbitration clause, the parties agree in advance to arbitrate any disputes that haven't been resolved through mediation. They give up the right to file a lawsuit and the right to appeal the arbitrator's decision to a court. It's important that both parties understand these consequences before deciding to initial the arbitration clause.

Arbitration proceedings are conducted according to California state law. Both parties are entitled to discovery, which means they may request documents and interview witnesses. The arbitrator will be a retired judge or an experienced real estate attorney, unless the buyer and seller agree to a different arbitrator. The arbitrator's decision may be filed with the court and made into an enforceable court order. By contrast, a mediator's decision is not legally binding on the parties.

Attorney's Fees. A purchase agreement typically includes an attorney's fees provision. Under this type of provision, if a dispute ends up in arbitration or in court, the attorney's fees of the winning party must be paid by the losing party. Remember that the C.A.R. purchase agreement form provides that if a party takes legal action without attempting to mediate the dispute first, that party will not be entitled to attorney's fees even if she prevails in the legal proceeding.

Time is of the Essence

Purchase agreements usually state that "time is of the essence." This phrase doesn't simply mean that the parties hope the sale progresses as quickly as possible; it means they are legally required to meet all deadlines set in the agreement. Performance on or before the specified dates (not just within a reasonable time thereafter) is an essential term of the agreement. Failure to meet any of the deadlines breaches the contract.

Addenda

A purchase agreement often has a number of addenda attached to it that become part of the contract between the buyer and the seller. We've already mentioned various addendum forms, such as the seller financing addendum and the sale of buyer's property contingency addendum. To incorporate the addenda into the agreement, they should be listed in the space provided on the purchase agreement form and then attached to the main document. The parties must sign or initial and date each page of the attachments.

In some cases the buyer and seller may want to add other contract terms that are not covered in a specific addendum form. If the additional terms are simple, you can use a general addendum form, such as the one shown in Figure 7.4, for this purpose. But if the additional terms are at all complicated or unusual, an attorney must draft them. As we've discussed, real estate agents can't write complicated clauses to include in a purchase agreement.

Offer and Acceptance

A purchase agreement form typically has space for the buyer to set a deadline for acceptance of the offer. The manner in which the seller is to communicate acceptance may also be specified. The C.A.R. form, for example, provides that the seller's acceptance isn't effective until a copy of the agreement signed by the seller is received by the buyer or the buyer's agent. An offer that is not accepted in this manner expires when the deadline passes, and the good faith deposit will be refunded to the buyer.

A purchase agreement may also set a deadline for the buyer's acceptance of a counteroffer. Remember that a counteroffer isn't an acceptance, so the buyer isn't contractually bound unless he accepts the seller's counteroffer.

Signatures

Of course, a purchase agreement provides space for each party's signature. The buyer's signature makes the form an offer to purchase, and the seller's signature turns it into a binding contract. On many forms, the listing and selling agents are also supposed to sign and fill in the names of their brokerages. Note that the purchase agreement must include the license identification number of any licensee acting as an agent in the transaction.

Fig. 7.4 Addendum

CALIFORNIA ASSOCIATION OF REALTORS®

ADDENDUM
(C.A.R. Form ADM, Revised 4/12)

No. _____

The following terms and conditions are hereby incorporated in and made a part of the: ☐ Residential Purchase Agreement, ☐ Manufactured Home Purchase Agreement, ☐ Business Purchase Agreement, ☐ Residential Lease or Month-to-Month Rental Agreement, ☐ Vacant Land Purchase Agreement, ☐ Residential Income Property Purchase Agreement, ☐ Commercial Property Purchase Agreement, ☐ Other _____,

dated _____, on property known as _____,

in which _____ is referred to as ("Buyer/Tenant")

and _____ is referred to as ("Seller/Landlord").

_____
_____
_____
_____

The foregoing terms and conditions are hereby agreed to, and the undersigned acknowledge receipt of a copy of this document.

Date _____   Date _____

Buyer/Tenant _____   Seller/Landlord _____

Buyer/Tenant _____   Seller/Landlord _____

Published and Distributed by:
REAL ESTATE BUSINESS SERVICES, INC.
a subsidiary of the California Association of REALTORS®
525 South Virgil Avenue, Los Angeles, California 90020

Reviewed by _____ Date _____

EQUAL HOUSING OPPORTUNITY

ADM REVISED 4/12 (PAGE 1 OF 1)   Print Date

ADDENDUM (ADM PAGE 1 OF 1)

Reprinted with permission, California Association of Realtors®. No endorsement implied.

Chapter Summary

1. A properly executed purchase agreement is a binding contract that holds the parties to the terms of their agreement until all conditions have been fulfilled and the transaction closes.

2. The parties to a purchase agreement are the buyer(s) and the seller(s). All parties must have contractual capacity. Everyone with an interest in the property must sign the agreement. The spouse of any married seller or buyer should also sign, even if that spouse has no ownership interest.

3. In California, a purchase agreement should include an agency disclosure paragraph, stating that the real estate agents involved in the transaction made the required disclosures concerning which party or parties they were representing.

4. Every purchase agreement must have an adequate description of the property, specify the total purchase price and the method of payment, list the liens and encumbrances the buyer will assume, specify the amount and terms of the buyer's financing, and describe the conditions of sale.

5. Purchase agreements almost always contain a "time is of the essence" clause, which makes the dates agreed to a material term of the contract. Closing must take place on or before the date stated in the agreement, unless the parties agree in writing to an extension.

6. In most residential transactions, the buyer gives the seller a good faith deposit. The purchase agreement may provide that the buyer will deliver the deposit directly to the escrow agent, or that the broker will hold the deposit until the seller has accepted or rejected the buyer's offer.

Key Terms

Community property: Property owned jointly by a married couple in California and other community property states, as distinguished from each spouse's separate property; generally, any property acquired through the labor or skill of either spouse during marriage.

Power of attorney: An instrument authorizing one person (the attorney in fact) to act as another's agent, to the extent stated in the instrument.

Closing date: The date on which all the terms of a purchase agreement must be met, or the contract is terminated.

Closing agent: A neutral third party who holds funds, documents, or other valuables on behalf of the parties to a transaction, releasing these items to the parties only when certain conditions in the escrow instructions have been fulfilled.

Mediation: A negotiation to resolve a dispute that is led by an impartial third party.

Arbitration: Submitting a disputed matter to a private party (rather than to the judicial system) for resolution.

Time is of the essence: A clause in a contract that means performance on or before the exact dates specified is an essential element of the contract. Failure to perform on time is a material breach.

Chapter Quiz

1. If the seller is a minor, the purchase agreement should be signed by:
   a. the seller's husband or wife
   b. the seller's nearest living relative
   c. the seller's legal guardian
   d. both the seller and the seller's attorney in fact

2. The purchase price stated in the purchase agreement should include any:
   a. mortgages or other liens being assumed by the buyer
   b. seller financing
   c. new loan to be obtained by the buyer
   d. All of the above

3. The buyer usually gives the good faith deposit to either the escrow agent or the:
   a. selling agent
   b. seller
   c. listing broker
   d. listing agent

4. The included and excluded items paragraph is used to:
   a. disclose the encumbrances on the property
   b. list the documents that are being attached to the agreement
   c. determine how closing costs will be allocated
   d. specify fixtures and personal property that will be part of the sale

5. In setting a closing date, you should take into account all of the following except:
   a. when the next installment of the property taxes will be due
   b. how long the seller needs to make any necessary repairs
   c. whether the buyer needs to sell her current home
   d. the time needed for all of the inspections that will be required

6. The parties are required to initial the liquidated damages clause in a purchase agreement:
   a. if the buyer's deposit exceeds 3% of the sales price
   b. to show that they were aware of the provision and consented to it
   c. to provide that the selling broker can hold the good faith deposit check uncashed until the seller accepts the offer
   d. to allow the seller to choose what remedy to pursue in the event that the buyer defaults

7. Because a purchase agreement has a "time is of the essence" clause:
   a. a check for the good faith deposit can be held for no more than three days
   b. the seller must accept the buyer's offer within five days, or the offer will terminate
   c. failure to meet a deadline set in the agreement is a breach of contract
   d. the closing must take place within 45 days after the agreement is signed

8. To be enforceable, an arbitration clause in a purchase agreement must be:
   a. in a separate addendum
   b. initialed by the buyer and seller
   c. initialed by the selling agent and the listing agent
   d. All of the above

9. Which document should be prepared if the buyer plans to take possession before the closing date?
   a. Backup offer
   b. Sale of buyer's home contingency
   c. Bump notice
   d. Rental agreement

10. If a buyer defaults on a purchase agreement, the good faith deposit is typically:
    a. returned to the buyer
    b. split between the buyer and seller
    c. forfeited to the listing broker
    d. forfeited to the seller

Answer Key

1. c.   If one of the parties to a contract is a minor (under 18 years of age), the contract should be signed by that party's legal guardian.

2. d.   The purchase price stated in the agreement should be the full price being paid for the property, including the downpayment, any mortgages or liens the buyer is assuming, and any financing, whether the financing is provided by the seller or by a lender.

3. a.   In most cases, the buyer will give the good faith deposit either directly to the escrow agent or to the selling agent (and the deposit will be held in trust or delivered to an escrow agent by the selling broker).

4. d.   The included and excluded items paragraph lists items that are included in or excluded from the sale unless otherwise noted. (Many of the items listed as included would be considered fixtures or attachments to the real property and included in the sale even without this provision.)

5. a.   In setting a closing date, it's important to consider how long it will take the parties to fulfill their obligations and satisfy any contingencies in the purchase agreement. The due date for the property taxes is irrelevant, since the taxes will be prorated.

6. b.   The liquidated damages clause must be initialed by the buyer and the seller to show that they were aware of the provision and specifically consented to it. (If the clause is initialed, liquidated damages are the seller's only remedy for breach of contract.)

7. c.   The purpose of a "time is of the essence" clause is to make the dates and deadlines specified in the agreement material terms of the contract. As a result, one party's failure to meet a deadline may be treated as a breach of contract by the other party.

8. b.   An arbitration clause in a purchase agreement is enforceable only if it has been initialed by both the buyer and the seller.

9. d.   If the parties plan to transfer possession of the property either before or after the closing date, they should sign a rental agreement.

10. d. When a buyer defaults on a purchase agreement, her good faith deposit is forfeited to the seller. In many cases, the seller will split the deposit with the listing broker, who will then split his share with the selling broker.

8

Contingent Transactions

How Contingencies Work

- Termination or removal
- Good faith effort required
- Basic elements of a contingency clause

Types of Contingencies

- Financing contingencies
- Inspection contingencies
- Sale of buyer's home contingencies
- Purchase of replacement property contingencies
- Other types of contingencies

Unfulfilled Contingencies

- Notices to perform
- Canceling the purchase agreement

Introduction

In many cases a buyer wants to make an offer on a house, but does not want to become bound by a contract with the seller unless a particular event occurs first. For instance, the buyer may need to get a purchase loan approved, or she may want to have the house inspected by an expert. However, the buyer doesn't want to wait until that event occurs before making an offer on the house—by that time, the seller might have sold the property to someone else. In this situation, the buyer needs to make her offer conditional or contingent on the occurrence of the event in question.

To help a buyer prepare a contingent offer, you need to know how contingency clauses work, the essential elements of a contingency, the common types of contingencies, and the various pre-printed forms you can use to establish a contingency.

How Contingencies Work

Many purchase agreements are enforceable only if a certain event occurs. The event is called a **contingency**, or a **condition** of the sale. If the specified event occurs, then both the buyer and the seller are bound to carry out the terms of their contract. If the specified event does not occur, the agreement may be terminated and, in most cases, the buyer is entitled to a refund of the good faith deposit.

Termination or Removal

A contingency provision is typically included in a contract for the benefit of one of the parties rather than both of them. If the contingency is not fulfilled—if the specified event does not happen—the benefiting party has two choices. He may:

1. terminate the contract without penalty, or
2. remove the condition and proceed with the contract.

Only the benefiting party has the right to choose between terminating the contract or removing the condition. By removing the condition, the party waives the option to terminate the contract and gives up the rights associated with the contingency. If the benefiting party is willing to remove the condition, the other party cannot refuse to go through with the sale because the condition has not been met.

Example: Suppose a purchase agreement is contingent on the buyer obtaining a fixed-rate conventional loan with a $20,000 downpayment within 30 days of the seller's acceptance of the offer. This contingency benefits the buyer. It protects the buyer from being forced to complete the purchase if he can't get the financing he needs.

If the buyer gets the loan within the 30-day period, he must buy the seller's property. If the buyer got the loan but refused to purchase the property anyway, the seller could keep the buyer's good faith deposit as liquidated damages or (depending on the terms of their agreement) sue the buyer.

On the other hand, if he doesn't get the loan, the buyer can take one of two courses of action. He can give the seller notice that the condition has not been met, terminate the agreement, and get the deposit back. Alternatively, he can remove the financing contingency and go ahead with the transaction. This would mean that he has to come up with the purchase price from some other source by the closing date, or else forfeit his deposit.

If the buyer decides to go ahead with the purchase, the seller cannot then refuse to complete the transaction because the condition was not met. Since the condition was included in the purchase agreement for the benefit of the buyer, only the buyer can choose whether to remove the condition or terminate the sale.

In the unusual case when a contingency clause benefits both parties to a contract, the condition can only be removed with the consent of both parties. In other words, if the condition were not met, either party would have the option of terminating the contract, even if the other party wanted to proceed with it.

For the Buyer's Benefit. Contingency provisions in a purchase agreement are usually for the benefit of the buyer. They protect the buyer from becoming obligated to go through with the purchase if something doesn't work out in her own situation, or if it turns out that the property is unsuitable in some way—for instance, because it can't be subdivided, or it's infested with termites, or the well water is contaminated. Common contingency provisions in real estate transactions concern the buyer's financing (as in the example above); the sale of property the buyer currently owns; a satisfactory pest, soil, septic, well, or structural inspection; obtaining approval for a rezone, variance, or subdivision from the local planning commission; or the issuance of some sort of license needed to operate an establishment (such as a liquor license).

Good Faith Effort Required

Whenever a contract contains a contingency clause, the benefited party has an implied legal obligation to make a reasonable, good faith effort to fulfill the contingency.

Example: Hanson's agreement to purchase Moore's house is contingent on Hanson getting a 90% fixed-rate loan at 6% interest. Three days after signing the agreement, Hanson decides she doesn't want to buy Moore's property after all. So she doesn't even bother to apply for a loan. Hanson then tells Moore that she's terminating the contract because the contingency hasn't been fulfilled, and she demands the return of her good faith deposit.

However, Hanson had a legal obligation to make a reasonable effort to get a loan. Because she didn't fulfill that obligation, she has breached the purchase agreement and is not entitled to a refund of her deposit.

If the responsible party does not make a good faith effort to satisfy the contingency, then it is dropped from the contract. That party is bound by the contract even though the condition has not been met. Under these circumstances, as in the example above, the seller could keep the deposit if the buyer failed to go through with the purchase.

Although the obligation to make a good faith effort to fulfill a condition is always implied in the contract, the contingency clause should spell out that obligation. For example, the financing contingency contained in the California Association of REALTORS® purchase agreement form (see Figure 8.1) includes the following language:

Buyer shall act diligently and in good faith to obtain the designated loan(s).

Basic Elements of a Contingency Clause

Any contingency provision, whether it concerns financing, inspections, or something else, should contain the following elements:

1. What the condition is and what has to be done to fulfill it.
2. The procedure for notifying the other party of either satisfaction or removal of the condition.
3. A deadline by which the condition must be met or removed.
4. The rights of the parties if the condition is not met or removed by the specified date.

While it's important to know the elements a contingency clause should have, you shouldn't try to draft one yourself. When necessary, you can use a pre-printed, attorney-approved contingency form that can be attached as an addendum to the purchase agreement. In the case of the C.A.R. purchase agreement form, a number of contingency clauses, including a financing contingency and an inspection contingency, are already included in the form itself. If you were to write your own provision instead of using a pre-printed contingency clause or form, that could be considered the unauthorized practice of law.

Types of Contingencies

In purchase agreements for residential transactions, three types of contingency clauses are very common: financing contingencies, inspection contingencies, and contingencies concerning the sale of the buyer's home.

Financing Contingencies

Most residential purchase agreements are contingent on financing. If the buyer can't obtain the loan she needs in order to pay the seller the agreed price, then the contract will terminate unless the buyer chooses to proceed with the transaction anyway (and has an alternative source of funds). Standard purchase agreement forms may include a financing contingency clause in the form itself; otherwise, the parties would use an addendum.

A financing contingency usually states the type of financing the buyer will apply for, sets deadlines for the loan application and fulfillment or removal of the contingency, specifies the notice periods, and describes how lender-required inspections and repairs will be handled.

Financing Terms. The financing terms set forth in the contingency clause may be general or specific. In this regard, the parties have conflicting interests. The buyer may want the contract to be contingent on a specific and very favorable financing arrangement, one that is as affordable as possible. On the other hand, the seller—who wants to hold the buyer to the agreement, or to keep the deposit if the buyer backs out—would prefer a financing contingency that simply calls for a typical institutional loan in the current marketplace. The seller probably won't agree to a financing contingency that specifies a below-market interest rate or unusually low loan fees, because it's much less likely that the buyer will be able to obtain that type of financing.

Figure 8.1 shows the financing contingency provisions on the first two pages of the C.A.R. purchase agreement form. Unless otherwise noted, this purchase agreement is automatically contingent on financing. If the buyer doesn't want her offer to include a financing contingency, she must specify this by checking Paragraph 3J(4).

This financing contingency allows you to set forth quite specific financing terms. You're given space to state the amount of the buyer's loan, the type of loan, the interest rate, and whether the rate is fixed or adjustable. You'll need to fill in additional information if the buyer plans to seek FHA or VA financing. Again, a very specific financing contingency is ordinarily to the buyer's advantage and the seller's disadvantage.

Deadlines. A financing contingency usually states that the buyer must apply for the loan within a certain number of days. In addition, the provision will set a deadline for fulfilling the contingency or notifying the seller that the contingency is removed. If the buyer has not notified the seller that the contingency has been fulfilled or removed by that deadline, the seller can terminate their agreement.

The seller must first notify the buyer that she intends to terminate the agreement, by sending the buyer a notice to perform (discussed at the end of this chapter). The buyer gets a final chance to remove the contingency after receiving this notice. The contingency provision gives the required notice period, and also states the seller's obligation to return the good faith deposit to the buyer if the purchase agreement terminates.

Appraisal Provisions. Because the buyer's loan amount depends in part on the appraised value of the property, the financing contingency may include an appraisal contingency. This makes the agreement contingent on whether the property appraises at the agreed sales price (or a higher value). If the appraisal indicates that the property isn't worth at least as much as the buyer agreed to pay, the buyer may cancel the agreement without forfeiting the good faith deposit.

If the appraisal is low, it may be possible to get a reappraisal. See Chapter 4 for a more general discussion of the low appraisal problem.

Lender-required Inspections. Before approving a loan application, many lenders require the property to be inspected. If the inspection report says that repairs are needed, the lender may require the repairs to be completed, at the seller's cost, as a condition of loan approval. If the seller opts not to make or pay for these repairs, the buyer can cancel the agreement without losing the good faith deposit.

Fig. 8.1 Financing contingency in residential purchase agreement

Reprinted with permission, California Association of Realtors®. No endorsement implied.

Property Address: _____ Date: _____

H. **VERIFICATION OF DOWN PAYMENT AND CLOSING COSTS:** Buyer (or Buyer's lender or loan broker pursuant to paragraph 3J(1)) shall, within **3 (or ____) Days** After Acceptance, Deliver to Seller written verification of Buyer's down payment and closing costs. (☐ Verification attached.)

I. **APPRAISAL CONTINGENCY AND REMOVAL:** This Agreement is (or ☐ is NOT) contingent upon a written appraisal of the Property by a licensed or certified appraiser at no less than the purchase price. Buyer shall, as specified in paragraph 14B(3), in writing, remove the appraisal contingency or cancel this Agreement within **17 (or ____) Days** After Acceptance.

J. **LOAN TERMS:**

(1) LOAN APPLICATIONS: Within **3 (or ____) Days** After Acceptance, Buyer shall Deliver to Seller a letter from Buyer's lender or loan broker stating that, based on a review of Buyer's written application and credit report, Buyer is prequalified or preapproved for any NEW loan specified in paragraph 3D. If any loan specified in paragraph 3D is an adjustable rate loan, the prequalification or preapproval letter shall be based on the qualifying rate, not the initial loan rate. (☐ Letter attached.)

(2) LOAN CONTINGENCY: Buyer shall act diligently and in good faith to obtain the designated loan(s). Buyer's qualification for the loan(s) specified above **is a contingency** of this Agreement unless otherwise agreed in writing. If there is no appraisal contingency or the appraisal contingency has been waived or removed, then failure of the Property to appraise at the purchase price does not entitle Buyer to exercise the cancellation right pursuant to the loan contingency if Buyer is otherwise qualified for the specified loan. Buyer's contractual obligations regarding deposit, balance of down payment and closing costs **are not contingencies** of this Agreement.

(3) LOAN CONTINGENCY REMOVAL:

Within **21 (or ____) Days** After Acceptance, Buyer shall, as specified in paragraph 14, in writing, remove the loan contingency or cancel this Agreement. If there is an appraisal contingency, removal of the loan contingency shall not be deemed removal of the appraisal contingency.

(4) ☐ NO LOAN CONTINGENCY: Obtaining any loan specified above is NOT a contingency of this Agreement. If Buyer does not obtain the loan and as a result does not purchase the Property, Seller may be entitled to Buyer's deposit or other legal remedies.

(5) LENDER LIMITS ON BUYER CREDITS: Any credit to Buyer, from any source, for closing or other costs that is agreed to by the Parties ("Contractual Credit") shall be disclosed to Buyer's lender. If the total credit allowed by Buyer's lender ("Lender Allowable Credit") is less than the Contractual Credit, then (i) the Contractual Credit shall be reduced to the Lender Allowable Credit, and (ii) in the absence of a separate written agreement between the Parties, there shall be no automatic adjustment to the purchase price to make up for the difference between the Contractual Credit and the Lender Allowable Credit.

K. **BUYER STATED FINANCING:** Seller is relying on Buyer's representation of the type of financing specified (including but not limited to, as applicable, all cash, amount of down payment, or contingent or non-contingent loan). Seller has agreed to a specific closing date, purchase price and to sell to Buyer in reliance on Buyer's covenant concerning financing. Buyer shall pursue the financing specified in this Agreement. Seller has no obligation to cooperate with Buyer's efforts to obtain any financing other than that specified in the Agreement and the availability of any such alternate financing does not excuse Buyer from the obligation to purchase the Property and close escrow as specified in this Agreement.

4. **SALE OF BUYER'S PROPERTY:**

A. This Agreement and Buyer's ability to obtain financing are NOT contingent upon the sale of any property owned by Buyer.

OR B. ☐ This Agreement and Buyer's ability to obtain financing are contingent upon the sale of property owned by Buyer as specified in the attached addendum (C.A.R. Form COP).

5. **ADDENDA AND ADVISORIES:**

A. ADDENDA:

	☐ Addendum # _____ (C.A.R. Form ADM)
☐ Back Up Offer Addendum (C.A.R. Form BUO)	☐ Court Confirmation Addendum (C.A.R. Form CCA)
☐ Septic, Well and Property Monument Addendum (C.A.R. Form SWPI)	
☐ Short Sale Addendum (C.A.R. Form SSA)	☐ Other _____

B. BUYER AND SELLER ADVISORIES:

☑ Buyer's Inspection Advisory (C.A.R. Form BIA)	
☐ Probate Advisory (C.A.R. Form PAK)	☐ Statewide Buyer and Seller Advisory (C.A.R. Form SBSA)
☐ Trust Advisory (C.A.R. Form TA)	☐ REO Advisory (C.A.R. Form REO)
☐ Short Sale Information and Advisory (C.A.R. Form SSIA)	☐ Other _____

6. **OTHER TERMS:** _____

_____

_____

_____

7. **ALLOCATION OF COSTS**

A. **INSPECTIONS, REPORTS AND CERTIFICATES:** Unless otherwise agreed in writing, this paragraph only determines who is to pay for the inspection, test, certificate or service ("Report") mentioned; it **does not determine who is to pay for any work recommended or identified in the Report.**

(1) ☐ Buyer ☐ Seller shall pay for a natural hazard zone disclosure report, including tax ☐ environmental ☐ Other: _____
_____ prepared by _____.

(2) ☐ Buyer ☐ Seller shall pay for the following Report _____
prepared by_____

(3) ☐ Buyer ☐ Seller shall pay for the following Report _____
prepared by _____.

Buyer's Initials (_____)(_____)   Seller's Initials (_____)(_____)

RPA-CA REVISED 11/14 (PAGE 2 OF 10) Print Date

CALIFORNIA RESIDENTIAL PURCHASE AGREEMENT (RPA-CA PAGE 2 OF 10)

Inspection Contingencies

Another very common type of contingency in residential purchase agreements is an inspection contingency. The contract may be made contingent on one or more expert inspections of the property: for example, a general home inspection, a geological inspection, a hazardous substances inspection, and/or a structural pest control inspection.

An inspection contingency should establish:

- which party is responsible for ordering and paying for the inspection;
- a deadline for the buyer to review inspection results and either remove the contingency or cancel the agreement; and
- an opportunity for reinspection by the buyer if the seller needs to make repairs.

Buyer's Inspections. Most inspection contingencies provide a deadline for the buyer to complete inspections and either remove the contingency or cancel the purchase agreement. The inspections must be ordered and completed, and the buyer must decide whether she approves or disapproves of the inspection report, before the contingency deadline. The seller is required to make the property available for the inspections.

Unless the property is brand-new, the inspections will almost certainly reveal at least a few issues with the property. Depending on the number and seriousness of the issues, the buyer may:

- ask the seller to make repairs to the property,
- negotiate a lower purchase price,
- remove the inspection contingency, or
- cancel the purchase agreement.

Request for Repair. If the buyer wants the seller to make repairs, she can give the seller a request for repair form, such as the one shown in Figure 8.2. Each problem the buyer wants corrected should be listed on the form. It's a good idea to attach copies of any inspection reports or other documents describing the problems to help clarify the requested repair work.

If the seller is willing to make the repairs, the repairs are generally subject to reinspection and approval. If the seller refuses to make the requested repairs, the buyer then must decide whether to remove the condition and proceed with the transaction, or else terminate the purchase agreement.

Sometimes a seller responds to the buyer by offering to make only some of the requested repairs, or by offering to modify their contract in some way (for example, by lowering the purchase price). It is then up to the buyer to accept or reject the seller's offer. The parties may go back and forth in this way several times before a compromise is reached or the buyer decides to give up and terminate the contract.

Example: A purchase agreement with an inspection contingency is signed on January 1. The purchase agreement gives the buyer, Ellen, 15 days to have her inspections completed and notify the seller, Ralph, whether she will remove the contingency or cancel the agreement.

Ellen has the house inspected on January 4. On January 6, Ellen gives Ralph her request for repairs. She objects to the condition of the roof, attaches the portion of the written inspection report that describes the roof's condition, and asks Ralph to have the roof repaired. Ralph now must decide whether or not he wants to correct the roof's condition. Ellen and Ralph discuss lowering the sales price as an alternative to making repairs, but they can't agree on the amount of the price reduction and no written agreement is ever signed. On January 11, Ralph gives Ellen his response to the request for repairs, stating that he rejects the request to repair the roof.

Ellen now has five days to decide whether to remove the contingency or cancel the agreement. Ellen decides she does not want to purchase a house with roof problems, and she gives notice of cancellation on the 15th. The purchase agreement is now canceled, and the good faith deposit must be returned to Ellen.

By requesting and agreeing to make repairs, the parties are changing the terms of their contract. That means repair negotiations should always be handled in writing. Both the buyer's request for repairs and the seller's response should be in writing, preferably on forms intended specifically for those purposes.

Code Violations. Sellers should be aware that if an inspection reveals violations of the building code or other laws, public authorities could order them to correct the violations, whether or not the sale to the buyer proceeds.

Sale of Buyer's Home Contingencies

Unless you're helping them buy their first home, your buyers will often have to sell their current home before buying a new one. For one thing, they probably

Fig. 8.2 Request for repair

CALIFORNIA ASSOCIATION OF REALTORS®

REQUEST FOR REPAIR No. _____
(Or other Corrective Action)
(C.A.R. Form RR, Revised 11/14)

In accordance with the terms and conditions of the: ☐ California Residential Purchase Agreement or ☐ Other _____ ("Agreement"), dated _____, on property known as _____ ("Property"), between _____ ("Buyer"), and _____ ("Seller").

BUYER REQUEST:

1. **(a)** ☐ Buyer requests that Seller, prior to final verification of condition, repair or take the other specified action for each item listed below or ☐ on the attached list dated _____:

    _____
    _____
    _____
    _____
    _____
    _____
    _____
    _____
    _____
    _____
    _____
    _____
    _____

    (b) (i) ☐ **SECTION 1:** Buyer requests Seller pay to have Section 1 work completed as specified in the attached Pest Control Report dated _____ and prepared by _____

    (ii) ☐ **SECTION 2:** Buyer requests Seller pay to have Section 2 work completed as specified in the attached Pest Control Report dated _____ and prepared by _____

    (iii) If Buyer requests either Section 1 or Section 2 work above, the request includes the following. Seller shall, no later than 5 (or ___)Days Prior to Close of Escrow, Deliver to Buyer a written pest control certification showing the corrective work has been completed.

    (c) ☐ Buyer requests that Seller credit Buyer $ _____ at Close of Escrow.

    (d) ☐ Buyer requests that Seller reduce the purchase price to $ _____

2. A copy of the following inspection or other report is attached.
    ☐ _____   ☐ _____
    ☐ _____   ☐ _____

Buyer _____ Date _____
Buyer _____ Date _____

RR REVISED 11/14 (PAGE 1 OF 1)

Reviewed by _____ Date _____

REQUEST FOR REPAIR (RR PAGE 1 OF 1)

Reprinted with permission, California Association of Realtors®. No endorsement implied.

need to sell their current home to generate the cash for the downpayment on the new home. Also, not many buyers can afford the mortgage payments on two houses at the same time. For both of these reasons, it's very common to make the sale of the buyer's current home a condition of the contract for the purchase of the new home.

Depending on the terms of the purchase agreement, this condition may actually be a "hidden contingency." In other words, the agreement may be contingent on the sale of the buyer's home even though that contingency is not expressly stated in the agreement.

> **Example:** Wilder has agreed to purchase Greenbaum's home. The sale is contingent on financing: unless Wilder obtains a purchase loan from an institutional lender, the contract will not be binding.
>
> When Wilder applies for a loan, she doesn't have enough cash for the downpayment she'll be required to make. She plans to sell her current home to get the necessary cash. The lender processes the application and approves the loan on the condition that Wilder obtain the necessary cash before closing. If Wilder can't sell her home before the closing date set in her contract with Greenbaum, she won't have the cash for the downpayment and the lender will refuse to fund the loan. Thus, the sale of Greenbaum's home is actually contingent on the sale of Wilder's home, even though this contingency was not stated in their purchase agreement.

Naturally, it's better to state the terms of any contingency clearly rather than leave it unstated or hidden behind another contingency. The seller needs to know all the contingencies of the sale to make an informed decision about whether to accept the buyer's offer. This is particularly important when the buyer must sell her own property before completing the purchase. If this contingency is not made clear to the seller, the seller may believe that the buyer has a much better chance of getting a loan than she actually does. If the transaction doesn't close because the buyer can't sell her home (and thus get the loan), the seller could claim that by failing to disclose the hidden contingency, you misrepresented the buyer's financial ability to complete the purchase.

In the C.A.R. purchase agreement form, paragraph 4A states that this sale and the buyer's ability to obtain financing are not contingent on the sale of the buyer's home (or other property). However, paragraph 4B contains a checkbox allowing the parties to make the transaction contingent on such a sale if they want. If the box in 4B is checked, then you must fill out and attach the Contingency for Sale of Buyer's Property addendum form shown in Figure 8.3.

Fig. 8.3 Sale of buyer's property contingency addendum

CALIFORNIA
ASSOCIATION
OF REALTORS ®

**CONTINGENCY FOR SALE
OF BUYER'S PROPERTY**
(C.A.R. Form COP, Revised 11/14)

This is an addendum to the ☐ California Residential Purchase Agreement, ☐ Counter Offer, ☐ Other _____
_____ ("Agreement"), dated _____,
on property known as _____ ("Seller's Property"),
between _____ ("Buyer")
and _____ ("Seller").

SALE OF BUYER'S PROPERTY:
1. **LENGTH OF CONTINGENCY:**
   A. The Agreement is contingent on the close of escrow of Buyer's property, described as: _____
      _____ ("Buyer's Property").
   B. If Buyer's Property does not close escrow by the earliest of: **(i)** the scheduled close of escrow of Seller's Property; **(ii)** the date
      specified in paragraph 3B; or **(iii)** Other ☐ _____, then either Seller, after first giving Buyer a
      Notice to Buyer to Perform (C.A.R. Form NBP), or Buyer may cancel the Agreement in writing.
2. ☐ **BUYER'S PROPERTY NOT IN ESCROW:** (If checked) Buyer's Property is not now in escrow and (check boxes as applicable):
   A. ☐ is not yet listed for sale.
   B. ☐ is listed for sale with _____ company and is offered for
      sale in the _____ MLS, # _____.
   C. Buyer has 17 (or ☐ ____) Days to enter into escrow fo the sale of Buyer's Property.
   D. Buyer shall, within the time specified in 2C, provide Seller with Copies of the contract, escrow instructions and all
      related documents ("Escrow Evidence") for the sale of Buyer's Property showing that Buyer's Property has entered escrow.
3. ☐ **BUYER'S PROPERTY IN ESCROW:** (If checked) Buyer's Property is in escrow.
   A. Escrow holder is _____, (escrow # _____)
   B. Escrow is scheduled to close escrow on _____ (date).
   C. Buyer shall, within **5 Days** After Acceptance, deliver to Seller Escrow Evidence that Buyer's Property is in escrow.
4. **INTENT TO CANCEL ESCROW FOR BUYER'S PROPERTY:** If Buyer's Property is in or enters escrow, Buyer shall give Seller written
   notice if either party to that escrow gives notice to the other of intent to cancel.
5. **SELLER ADDITIONAL RIGHT TO CANCEL:** Seller, after first giving Buyer a Notice to Buyer to Perform, may cancel the Agreement
   in writing,
   A. If Buyer fails to provide Seller Escrow Evidence within the time specified in paragraph 2(D) or 3(C), or
   B. If, pursuant to paragraph 4, Buyer gives notice to Seller of either party's intent to cancel the escrow for Buyer's Property.
6. **BUYER ADDITIONAL RIGHT TO CANCEL:** Buyer may cancel the Agreement in writing if, **prior** to Buyer's removal of the contingency
   for sale of Buyer's Property, the buyer for Buyer's Property gives notice of intent to cancel the escrow for Buyer's Property.
7. **BACK UP OFFERS AND SELLER RIGHT TO HAVE BUYER REMOVE CONTINGENCIES OR CANCEL:** After Acceptance, Seller
   shall have the right to continue to offer Seller's Property for sale for Back-up Offers. If Seller accepts a written back-up offer:
   A. **Immediate Right to Notify Buyer to Remove Sale of Property Contingency:** Seller shall have the right to immediately give
      written notice to Buyer to, in writing: **(i)** remove this contingency; **(ii)** remove the loan contingency, if any; **(iii)** provide verification
      of sufficient funds to close escrow without the sale of Buyer's Property; and **(iv)** comply with the following additional requirement(s):
      _____. If Buyer fails to complete these actions within
      3 (or ☐ ___) Days after receipt of such notice, Seller may then immediately cancel the Agreement in writing.
   OR B. ☐ (If checked) **Delayed Right to Notify Buyer:** Seller shall not invoke the notice provisions in paragraph 7A: **(i)** within the
      first **17 (or ☐ ___) Days** After Acceptance; or **(ii)** (if checked) ☐ during the term of the Agreement.

By signing below, Buyer and Seller each acknowledge that they have read, understand, accept and have received a copy of this
Addendum.

Date _____   Date _____

Buyer _____   Seller _____

Buyer _____   Seller _____

Reviewed by _____ Date _____

COP Revised 11/14 (PAGE 1 OF 1)

CONTINGENCY FOR SALE OF BUYER'S PROPERTY (COP PAGE 1 OF 1)

Reprinted with permission, California Association of Realtors®. No endorsement implied.

Acceptance or Closing. What constitutes a "sale" in a sale of buyer's home contingency? There are basically two choices. The agreement can state that the sale occurs: 1) when the buyer accepts an offer to purchase his current home, or 2) when the sale of the buyer's current home actually closes. The first choice means the seller doesn't have to wait until the buyer's sale closes to know whether she and the buyer have a binding contract. However, the C.A.R. contingency addendum in Figure 8.3 goes with the second choice. It requires the sale to actually close, which is generally a more practical approach; unless that sale closes, the buyer probably can't afford to pay the purchase price for the seller's property.

> **Example:** Whitfield is offering to buy Mayer's home for $329,000, with a $33,000 downpayment. The purchase agreement will be contingent on the sale of Whitfield's current home.
>
> Whitfield wants the contingency clause to be written so that the condition will be fulfilled only if the sale of his home actually closes within 90 days and he nets enough cash to make his $33,000 downpayment. He's afraid of what would happen if the condition were fulfilled when he accepted an offer for his home, but that sale failed to close for some reason. He wouldn't be able to go through with his purchase of Mayer's home (because he wouldn't have the money for the downpayment). As a result, Whitfield would be in default on the purchase agreement, and he would forfeit his good faith deposit to Mayer.
>
> On the other hand, Mayer wants the contingency clause to be written so that the condition will be fulfilled if Whitfield accepts an offer on his current home within 30 days of signing the purchase agreement with Mayer. Mayer doesn't want to wait up to 90 days to see whether Whitfield's sale is actually going to close. He wants to know that they have an enforceable contract much sooner than that. Otherwise, he would rather wait for another offer.

Sometimes a seller won't agree to a sale of buyer's home contingency, or perhaps the buyer doesn't want to complicate her offer by including such a contingency. An alternative for the buyer whose purchase funds are tied up in her current home is to apply for a **swing loan** (also called a bridge loan or gap loan). This loan provides the buyer with the funds to close the purchase of the new house secured by the equity in the buyer's old house. It creates a lien against the old house, and the buyer will pay it off out of the proceeds when the sale of the old house eventually closes.

Deadlines. The buyer generally wants as much time as possible to fulfill this type of contingency, so that she can get the highest possible price for her property. The seller, on the other hand, usually wants the present transaction to close as soon as possible, so that he'll have the money from the sale more quickly. So the parties must agree on a compromise that gives the buyer a reasonable length of time to market her house without delaying the resolution of the present transaction (either a successful closing or the failure of the condition) for too long.

It's extremely important to make sure that the dates in the contingency clause agree with the other dates in the purchase agreement. For example, the contingency should not give the buyer 120 days to sell her home if the current sale is supposed to close within 90 days.

Release Clauses. When a purchase agreement is contingent on the sale of the buyer's home, it's common to include a provision that gives the seller the right to keep the house on the market and accept another offer. This provision, known as a "release clause" or a "72-hour clause," may be used with any type of contingency, but it's most commonly used with a sale of the buyer's home contingency. That's because this contingency tends to involve greater uncertainty and a longer wait than other types. While you can usually predict whether a buyer can get a loan or a satisfactory pest inspection, it's harder to predict whether a buyer will be able to sell his home by a certain date on terms that will generate a certain amount of cash.

A release clause helps reconcile the buyer's need for time to sell his current home with the seller's need for a timely resolution of her contingent contract with the buyer. Essentially, a release clause allows the seller to accept an uncertain offer without having to take her property off the market.

The contingency addendum in Figure 8.3 includes a release clause. It allows the seller to continue to market her property until the buyer notifies her that the contingency has been satisfied or removed. If the seller receives and accepts a second offer during this period, the seller notifies the buyer of this acceptance. Once that happens, the buyer has a short period of time—the default period is 72 hours—to notify the seller that the sale of buyer's home contingency and the financing contingency have both been either satisfied or removed. Otherwise, the seller may cancel the transaction and the deposit will be returned to the buyer.

Purchase of Replacement Property Contingencies

Just like buyers who are selling their current home to buy a new one, sellers often want to buy another home when they sell their current property. Occasionally a seller will want to make the purchase agreement contingent on whether she's able to find a new home to buy. This is known as a contingency for the purchase of replacement property.

This type of contingency is much less common than a sale of buyer's home contingency. While a purchase agreement may fall apart if the buyer can't sell his current home, a delay in finding a new home usually won't prevent the seller from going through with the sale.

The contingency form in Figure 8.3 is used to make a sale contingent on the sale of the buyer's current home. A similar form is used to make the sale contingent on the seller's purchase of a replacement property.

Other Types of Contingencies

The financing contingency, inspection contingency, and sale of buyer's home contingency are the types of contingencies you will encounter most often. But the parties can agree to make their contract contingent on almost anything that might affect whether one or both of them want to go through with the transaction. If the buyer or seller wants to make the purchase agreement contingent on a specific event, check with your broker about what forms to use.

Unfulfilled Contingencies

As we discussed at the beginning of this chapter, the party that benefits from a contingency provision must make a good faith effort to fulfill it. Naturally, your job as a real estate agent is to help the parties satisfy any contingencies so that they can successfully complete the transaction. But sometimes, despite your best efforts, a contingency can't be fulfilled, and the benefiting party will decide to cancel the purchase agreement.

Notices to Perform

A contingency provision should always set a deadline for the benefiting party (usually the buyer) to fulfill or remove the condition. If the buyer doesn't meet this deadline, the seller may terminate the purchase agreement. Before allowing this, however, the contingency clause usually requires the seller to give the buyer a notice to perform. This lets the buyer know that the deadline has passed and gives her one last chance to decide if she wants to remove the contingency and proceed with the transaction.

Fig. 8.4 Notice to buyer to perform

CALIFORNIA ASSOCIATION OF REALTORS®

NOTICE TO BUYER TO PERFORM
No. _____
(C.A.R. Form NBP, Revised 11/14)

In accordance with the terms and conditions of the ☐ California Residential Purchase Agreement (C.A.R. Form RPA) or ☐ Residential Income Property Purchase Agreement (C.A.R. Form RIPA), or ☐ Commercial Property Purchase Agreement (C.A.R. Form CPA), or ☐ Vacant Land Purchase Agreement (C.A.R. Form VLPA),or ☐ Other _____ ("Agreement"),
dated _____, on property known as _____ ("Property"),
between _____ ("Buyer"),
and _____ ("Seller").

SELLER hereby gives Buyer notice to remove the following contingencies or take the specified contractual action:

I. Contingency

☐ **ALL CONTINGENCIES**

A. ☐ Loan (Paragraph 3J(3))
B. ☐ Appraisal (Paragraph 3I)
C. ☐ Disclosures/Reports (Paragraphs 7, 10 and 11)
D. ☐ Condominium/Planned Development Disclosures (HOA or OA) (Paragraph 10F)
E. ☐ Buyer Investigation, including insurability(Paragraph 12)
F. ☐ Title: Preliminary Report (Paragraph 13)
G. ☐ Sale of Buyer's Property (Paragraph 4)
H. ☐ _____
I. ☐ _____
J. ☐ _____
K.

II. Contractual Action

L. ☐ Initial Deposit (Paragraph 3A)
M. ☐ Increased Deposit (Paragraph 3B)
N. ☐ Form FVA (Paragraph 3D)
O. ☐ Loan Application Letter (Paragraph 3J(1))
P. ☐ Down Payment Verification (Paragraph 3H)
Q. ☐ All Cash Verification (Paragraph 3C)
R. ☐ Return of Statutory Disclosures (Paragraph 10A(5))
S. ☐ Return of Lead Disclosures (Paragraph 10A(5))
T. ☐ Receipt for Increased Deposit (Paragraph 21B)
U. ☐ Escrow Evidence, Sale of Buyer's Property (C.A.R. Form COP, Paragraph 2(C) or 3(B))
V. ☐ Delivery of a Representative Capacity Signature Addendum and evidence of authority to act (Paragraphs 19 and 31)
W. ☐ _____

NOTE: Paragraph numbers refer to the California Residential Purchase Agreement (C.A.R. Form RPA-CA). Applicable paragraph numbers for each contingency or contractual action in other C.A.R. contracts are found in Contract Paragraph Matrix (C.A.R. Form CPM).

BUYER: If you do not remove the contingency(ies) (C.A.R. Forms CR or RR) or take the contractual actions specified above within 2 (or ☐ _____) Days After Delivery (but no less than the time specified in the Agreement) of this Notice to Buyer to Perform, Seller may cancel the Agreement.

_____
Seller   Date

_____
Seller   Date

(_____/_____) (Initials) **CONFIRMATION OF RECEIPT:** A Copy of this Signed Notice to Buyer to Perform was personally received by Buyer or authorized agent on _____ (date), at _____ ☐ AM ☐ PM.

Reviewed by _____ Date _____

NBP REVISED 11/14 (PAGE 1 OF 1) Print Date

NOTICE TO BUYER TO PERFORM (NBP PAGE 1 OF 1)

Reprinted with permission, California Association of Realtors®. No endorsement implied.

The C.A.R. Notice to Buyer to Perform is shown in Figure 8.4. It can be used if the buyer misses the deadline to remove a contingency, or if the buyer is late in meeting an obligation set forth in the purchase agreement. Similarly, the buyer can give the seller a notice to perform if the seller has not satisfied some of his obligations under the purchase agreement.

If the buyer decides to remove the contingency and proceed with the transaction, he should give the seller written notice that he is doing so. If the seller has sent a Notice to Buyer to Perform, the buyer can use a contingency removal form to respond. In that case, the contingency no longer applies and the parties can close the sale. (A buyer who removes a financing contingency or a sale of buyer's home contingency must have another source of funds ready.)

Canceling the Purchase Agreement

When a purchase agreement terminates because a contingency was neither satisfied nor removed, the seller usually still wants to sell the property. In some cases, the seller has already entered into a backup agreement conditioned on the failure of the first agreement. But uncertainties about the rights and obligations of the buyer and seller under the first agreement may cause problems for a subsequent sale. Thus, a second sale should not proceed until the first agreement has been officially terminated and it is clearly established that the first buyer has no right to enforce that earlier agreement. This is done by having the first buyer and the seller sign a cancellation agreement.

As explained in Chapter 6, a cancellation agreement formally terminates a purchase agreement. It should authorize the party who holds the good faith deposit—either the broker or the escrow agent—to disburse it to the appropriate party. Remember, if the parties disagree about how the deposit should be handled, the broker should not disburse the funds to either of them. Instead, mediation, arbitration, or a court proceeding is necessary to determine who receives the funds. An example of a cancellation agreement is shown in Chapter 6 (Figure 6.4).

Chapter Summary

1. Most purchase agreements are contingent on the occurrence of a specified event (or events). Unless the event occurs, the party benefiting from the contingency (usually the buyer) can terminate the transaction without penalty. However, the party benefiting from the contingency has an obligation to make a good faith effort to fulfill it.

2. A contingency provision should state what the condition is and what has to occur to fulfill it, the time limit for fulfilling or removing the condition, and what happens if the condition is not fulfilled or removed.

3. The three most common types of contingencies in residential purchase agreements are financing contingencies, inspection contingencies, and sale of the buyer's home contingencies.

4. A financing contingency gives the buyer the right to be released from the agreement without forfeiting her deposit if she can't get the financing she needs. The financing contingency may be specific or general about the terms of the loan the buyer will apply for.

5. An inspection contingency conditions the sale on a satisfactory structural, pest, soil, geological, or hazardous substances inspection. The inspection contingency should state who is responsible for ordering and paying for the inspection and set a deadline for reviewing results and either removing the contingency or canceling the agreement.

6. An offer may be conditioned on the sale of the buyer's current home. The contingency provision should state whether the condition will be fulfilled by the acceptance of an offer, or not until the sale of the buyer's home closes; the deadline for fulfillment or removal of the contingency; and what happens if the seller gets another offer during the contingency period.

7. A release clause allows the seller to continue actively marketing her property during the contingency period. If the seller accepts another offer, the seller notifies the first buyer and gives the first buyer a short time to either meet or remove the contingency. If the buyer does neither, the first contract will terminate.

8. If a contingent transaction fails, the buyer and seller should sign a cancellation agreement. A cancellation agreement formally terminates the purchase agreement and authorizes the disbursement of the good faith deposit. Once a cancellation agreement has been signed by the first buyer and the seller, the seller can safely enter into a purchase agreement with another buyer.

Key Terms

Contingency: A provision in a contract that makes the parties' rights and obligations dependent on the occurrence (or nonoccurrence) of a particular event.

Good faith effort: A reasonable effort, such as when attempting to fulfill a contingency.

Financing contingency: A contingency that makes the sale dependent on the buyer's ability to obtain the financing needed to complete the sale.

Inspection contingency: A contingency that makes the sale dependent on the satisfactory results of an inspection (such as a general home inspection, a geological inspection, a hazardous substances inspection, or a structural pest control inspection).

Sale of buyer's home contingency: A contingency that makes the sale dependent on the sale of the buyer's existing home, because the buyer needs the proceeds from that sale to close this transaction.

Notice to perform: A notice from one party to the other that lets the second party know that a deadline for meeting a contingency has passed, and that the second party must meet or waive the contingency or the transaction will terminate.

Chapter Quiz

1. If a contingency clause benefits both parties to a contract, it:
   a. can only be removed with the consent of both parties
   b. cannot be removed by either party
   c. can be removed by either party
   d. can be removed by the buyer, but not by the seller

2. All of the following are typically found in contingency provisions except:
   a. a procedure for notifying the other party that the condition has been waived or satisfied
   b. a deadline for waiving or satisfying the condition
   c. statutorily required language advising the parties to seek legal advice
   d. the rights of the parties if a condition isn't waived or satisfied

3. Which of the following is least likely to be included in a financing contingency provision?
   a. The parties' options in case of a low appraisal
   b. The amount of the buyer's downpayment
   c. The terms of the seller financing arrangement
   d. A deadline for applying for the loan

4. If an inspection reveals building code violations, which of the following is true?
   a. The buyer's lender may require the seller to correct the violations as a condition of loan approval
   b. The buyer may require the seller to correct the violations before proceeding with the contract
   c. Public authorities may order the seller to correct the violations whether or not the transaction closes
   d. All of the above

5. An inspection contingency provision will often contain a:
   a. hidden contingency
   b. clause providing for a reinspection of the property after any repairs are made
   c. schedule of adjustments in the purchase price for different problems that may be found during the inspection
   d. release clause allowing the seller to keep the property on the market and accept other offers

6. After an inspection, the buyer requests that the seller make certain repairs. Which of the following is not one of the ways in which the seller can respond?
   a. Removing the inspection contingency
   b. Refusing to make the requested repairs
   c. Offering to modify the contract
   d. Offering to make only some of the requested repairs

7. A sale of buyer's home contingency will usually state:
   a. a price at which the buyer will be required to accept an offer on his current home
   b. that the seller may continue to market her property until the contingency is removed or fulfilled
   c. that all contingencies must be waived on any offer on the buyer's current home
   d. a deadline for applying for a swing loan

8. With a sale of buyer's home contingency, the common approaches to resolving the conflicting needs of the buyer and seller do not include:
   a. having the buyer get the funds to close the purchase of the seller's home with a swing loan
   b. allowing the seller to keep his property on the market and accept other offers
   c. a release clause
   d. a cancellation agreement

9. Which of the following is true of most contingencies?
   a. The seller wants the contingency resolved quickly so that he knows whether the transaction will go through
   b. The benefiting party is not required to make any effort to fulfill the contingency
   c. Before the buyer removes the contingency, she must give the seller a notice to perform
   d. The seller is usually the party that benefits from the contingency

10. Which of the following ways of including a contingency in a purchase agreement would *not* be advisable?
    a. Using a pre-printed contingency addendum form
    b. Checking a contingency clause in the purchase agreement form itself
    c. Having an attorney draft a special contingency clause
    d. Writing a special contingency clause yourself on an addendum form

Answer Key

1. a. When a contingency clause benefits both parties to a contract, the condition can only be removed with the consent of both parties. If the condition isn't satisfied, either party can terminate the contract.

2. c. Generally, contingency provisions don't require language advising the parties to seek counsel, although obtaining legal advice is often a good idea.

3. c. If the seller is going to provide financing for the buyer, the terms should be set forth in another addendum, and the financing forms that will be used must be attached. (Seller financing is not ordinarily treated as a contingency.)

4. d. Either the buyer or the buyer's lender may require repairs based on an inspection report. And if an inspection reveals violations of the building code or other laws, public authorities could order the seller to correct the violations, regardless of whether the sale moves forward.

5. b. If the seller makes repairs to address problems revealed by an inspection, the seller typically must allow the property to be reinspected once the repairs have been completed.

6. a. The inspection contingency is for the benefit of the buyer, so only the buyer has the ability to remove it.

7. b. A typical sale of buyer's home contingency will include a release clause, which allows the seller to keep her property on the market and consider other offers.

8. d. A cancellation agreement terminates a purchase agreement, so it would only be used if the contingency was not fulfilled.

9. a. Most contingencies benefit the buyer, and the seller wants the contingency to be resolved as soon as possible. The seller doesn't want to take the property off the market for long if the transaction is not certain to go through.

10. d. You should never try to draft a contingency clause yourself, since that might be considered the unauthorized practice of law.

9

Loan Qualifying

Preapproval

- Preapproval process
- Advantages of preapproval

The Underwriting Process

- Income analysis
- Net worth
- Credit reputation
- Low-documentation loans
- Subprime lending

Choosing a Loan

- Truth in Lending Act
- Other finance disclosure laws
- Locking in the interest rate
- Other considerations

Predatory Lending

Introduction

Some buyers, especially first-time buyers, have only a vague idea of what they can afford to pay for a home. Other buyers think they know how much they can afford to pay for housing, but don't realize that a lender would find the percentage of income they're prepared to spend on a mortgage payment unacceptably high.

While financing the sale is the buyer's responsibility, and judging the creditworthiness of the buyer is the lender's responsibility, it's still important for you to understand the loan approval process so that you can discuss financing options with buyers. This chapter explains preapproval and describes the underwriting process lenders use to evaluate the creditworthiness of residential mortgage loan applicants. It also discusses how a buyer can compare different loans.

Preapproval

At one time, buyers used to do their house-hunting before they'd been approved for a mortgage loan. Often a real estate agent would "prequalify" a buyer by asking her questions about her income, assets, debts, and credit history and use that information to estimate how large a loan she was likely to qualify for. Based on that estimate, the agent would suggest an affordable price range for the buyer and then start showing her homes.

Now it's common practice for buyers to apply for a loan and get preapproved before they start house-hunting in earnest. In a preapproval, the lender carefully evaluates the buyer's financial situation, then decides on a maximum loan amount—how much the lender is willing to loan this buyer for a home purchase. Armed with this information, the buyer can shop for houses with a very clear idea of what price range he can afford.

Preapproval is especially important in an active market, when sellers rarely even consider offers from buyers who aren't preapproved. Even in a slower market, an offer may not get serious consideration unless the buyer has been preapproved. Buyer's agents typically urge their clients to get preapproved no matter what the market is like; few agents want to spend time showing clients properties they can't afford.

The Preapproval Process

To get preapproved, buyers must complete a loan application and provide the required supporting documentation, just as if they were applying for a loan after finding a house. Much of this can be accomplished online.

The lender evaluates an application for preapproval in the same way as an ordinary loan application, except that there's no property appraisal or title report at this point, since the buyers have not yet chosen a home to buy. If the buyers are creditworthy, the lender uses their income and net worth information to set a maximum loan amount. The lender gives the buyers a **preapproval letter**, agreeing to loan them up to the specified amount when they find the home they want to buy, as long as the property meets the lender's standards. The preapproval letter will expire at the end of a specified period—for example, after one or two months. If the buyers haven't found the house they want by then, the lender may agree to an extension.

Advantages of Preapproval

A preapproval letter can be an extremely useful tool in negotiating with a seller. It gives the seller confidence that if he accepts the buyers' offer, the financing contingency won't be a problem; the buyers are ready, willing, and able to buy. In an active market, a listing agent might advise her sellers to consider offers only from preapproved buyers. Certainly, a seller weighing two or more offers should always take into account whether each buyer has been preapproved or not.

In negotiations with sellers, there's one potential disadvantage to a preapproval letter from a lender. The lender's letter will ordinarily state the *maximum* amount that the buyer is preapproved for. This is fine if the buyer is looking for a home near the upper limit of her price range, but it can be a drawback if she is making an offer on a home that's well within the limit.

Example: The buyer has a preapproval letter that says she's financially qualified to purchase property worth up to $485,000. But the buyer is interested in a home that's listed for only $452,000, and she wants to make a starting offer of $440,000. The seller will be able to tell from the buyer's preapproval letter that the buyer could easily afford to pay the full listing price for his home. That's likely to make the seller much less inclined to accept a lower offer than he might otherwise be.

There is a way around this problem. To make an offer on this property, the buyer could ask her lender for a special version of the preapproval letter indicating that the buyer is preapproved to purchase a $455,000 home. This would assure the seller that the buyer is financially qualified to buy his home, without revealing the buyer's full purchasing power.

In addition to its value in negotiations, preapproval helps streamline the closing process. The lender has already fully evaluated the buyers, and only the appraisal and title report remain to be done before the lender can make the final decision to approve (or reject) the transaction.

The Underwriting Process

Before you can discuss financing options with your buyers, you need to understand the criteria that a lender uses to qualify a buyer for a loan. These criteria are referred to as **qualifying standards** or **loan underwriting standards**.

Loan underwriting is the process a lender goes through to evaluate the buyer and the property to determine whether the proposed loan would be a good risk. The lender has employees called loan underwriters (or credit underwriters) who carry out the underwriting process and decide whether to accept or reject the loan application.

Every loan carries some degree of risk. In fact, every time a lender makes a loan, the lender assumes two risks:

1. the risk that the borrower will not pay off the loan as agreed; and
2. the risk that, if the borrower does default, the property will be worth less than the amount that the borrower still owes the lender.

If a loan underwriter feels that these events are likely to occur, the loan is considered too risky, and the application will be rejected.

To evaluate the lender's risk, the underwriter tries to answer two questions during the underwriting process:

1. Can the borrower be expected to make the monthly loan payments on time, based on his overall financial situation?
2. If the borrower defaults, will the security property generate enough money in a foreclosure sale to pay off the loan balance?

To help answer these two questions, the underwriter applies underwriting standards to both the prospective borrower (the buyer) and the property. The underwriter's evaluation of the property is based on an appraisal. The appraisal process is similar to the process used to price property (discussed in Chapter 4), but it is more rigorous. In this chapter, we will focus on the standards that are applied to the borrower.

Although lenders may establish their own qualifying standards, the standards set by the major secondary market entities (Fannie Mae and Freddie Mac) are very influential. Lenders want to be able to sell their loans on the secondary market, and conventional loans that don't meet the standards set by Fannie Mae and Freddie Mac (referred to as **nonconforming** loans) are more difficult to sell. Also, lenders who want to make loans through a particular loan program must comply with the program's qualifying standards. For example, a loan will only be eligible for FHA insurance or a VA guaranty if it meets FHA or VA standards.

While qualifying standards vary, the underwriting process is basically the same no matter what type of loan the buyer has applied for. This section focuses on the basic underwriting process. The specific qualifying standards for the major loan programs are discussed in the next chapter.

Lenders now handle most aspects of the underwriting process by computer. This is known as **automated underwriting**. Fannie Mae and Freddie Mac each have an automated underwriting system (AUS) that lenders can use for loans they're planning to sell on the secondary market, and some large lenders have their own systems. An AUS can analyze a borrower's loan application and credit report and provide a recommendation for or against approval.

However, while computer programs speed up the underwriting process, the analysis of a loan application can't be entirely automated. As a general rule, the ultimate decision—whether or not to approve the loan—is still made by human beings, not by a computer.

When qualifying a buyer, a lender examines the information included in the loan application, plus additional information acquired from a credit report and verification forms. The lender uses all this information to evaluate the buyer's complete financial situation. This information can be broken down into three basic categories:

1. income,
2. net worth, and
3. credit reputation.

Income Analysis

An underwriter analyzes a loan applicant's income to see if the applicant can really afford the monthly mortgage payment for the requested loan. This analysis is a two-step process. First, the underwriter decides how much of the applicant's income is acceptable income, generally referred to as **stable monthly income**. Next, the underwriter decides whether the loan applicant has enough stable monthly income to reliably make the monthly mortgage payments.

Characteristics of Stable Monthly Income. To be considered stable monthly income, a loan applicant's income must be of a high quality, and it must also be durable.

Quality. To evaluate the quality of an applicant's income, the underwriter looks at the source. High-quality income comes from a dependable source. For example, if the income is salary income, the more established the employer, the higher the quality of the income.

Example: Your buyer, Hathaway, has applied for a loan. She works for the U.S. Postal Service. Because the Postal Service is a government agency, it is considered a very dependable source of income. Therefore, Hathaway's salary will be considered high-quality income.

The less dependable the source of the income, the lower the quality of that income.

Example: Suppose instead that Hathaway works for a new construction company that is struggling to make ends meet. The underwriter might decide that the company is not a very dependable source of income, and therefore consider Hathaway's salary low-quality income.

Durability. Income is considered durable if it can be expected to continue for a long period of time. Durable income typically includes wages from permanent employment, disability benefits, and interest on established investments. An example of income that isn't considered durable is income from unemployment benefits. Unemployment benefits, by their very nature, are not expected to continue for a long period of time.

Acceptable Types of Income. Lenders have rules of thumb that they follow when determining what is or is not stable monthly income. Let's take a look at some of those rules.

Permanent employment. Lenders accept a loan applicant's income from permanent employment as stable monthly income only if he has a history of continuous, stable employment. Generally speaking, a loan applicant should have been continuously employed in the same field for at least two years. However, even without a two-year work history, there may be extenuating circumstances that would warrant loan approval, such as having recently finished college or left the armed services. Special training or education can make up for minor weaknesses in job history. If you're working with a buyer who has an inadequate employment history, recommend that the buyer write a brief explanation of any extenuating circumstances and include it in her loan application.

Another point to keep in mind: if your buyer has changed jobs recently to advance her career, this is a good sign. But if she has changed jobs repeatedly without any advancement, the lender will probably see this as a problem.

Self-employment. Self-employment income is considered less durable and dependable than other types of employment income, so in some cases lenders won't count it as stable monthly income.

A buyer who has been self-employed for less than two years may have a hard time qualifying for a loan; it will be even more difficult if he has been in business for less than one year. A lender only counts the self-employment income of a buyer who's been in business for a short time if the buyer has a history of employment in the same field and can document a reasonable chance for success based on market feasibility studies and pro forma financial statements.

Other employment income. In addition to a salary or wages from a full-time job, a buyer can use other types of employment income to qualify for a loan. Bonuses, commissions, and part-time earnings can be considered stable monthly income if they've been a regular part of a loan applicant's overall earnings pattern for at least one, but preferably two, years. Lenders prefer not to treat overtime as stable income, but they will if it's clearly a regular part of the applicant's earnings.

Example: Schwinn's salary is $3,500 a month. Over the last three months, she worked many hours of overtime. She averaged an additional $1,000 a month in overtime during those three months. A lender will not count that additional $1,000 a month as stable income, because Schwinn only earned it for three months.

If, however, Schwinn could show that she earned an average of $1,000 a month in overtime over the previous 14 months, the lender would probably consider that part of her stable monthly income. Or if Schwinn could show that she earned an average of $3,000 a year in seasonal overtime from September to November every year for the past three years, and that this pattern is likely to continue, the lender would probably be willing to count the overtime as stable income.

Secondary income sources. There are other acceptable income sources besides employment income. For example, **pension and social security payments** are also considered part of a loan applicant's stable monthly income.

Alimony or spousal support payments are only considered stable monthly income if the payments are reliable. So the underwriter will look to see whether the payments are required by a court decree, how long the loan applicant has been receiving the payments, the financial status of the ex-spouse, and the applicant's ability to compel payment.

Child support payments are accepted as stable monthly income under the same conditions: if they are required by a court decree and there is proof of regular payment. If payments are missed, or regularly late, the underwriter may decide to exclude the child support from the loan applicant's stable monthly income. Also, child support payments typically stop when the child turns 18. So the closer the child is to age 18, the less durable the child support income is. If the child is over 15, the underwriter probably won't count the support payments as part of the loan applicant's stable monthly income.

Example: Martinez gets court-ordered child support for her daughter, who is 16, and for her son, who is 13. Martinez has received the child support regularly for three years. The lender will probably consider only the child support for the son as part of Martinez's stable monthly income. The child support for the daughter will only last another two years, so it isn't durable.

Income from **public assistance programs** may also be acceptable income. The Equal Credit Opportunity Act prohibits lenders from discriminating against loan applicants on the basis that all or part of their income is from a public assistance program, such as welfare or food stamps. Public assistance payments count as stable monthly income if they are durable—that is, if they are expected to continue for a sufficiently long time (at least the first few years of the loan term). If the loan applicant's eligibility for the program will terminate shortly, then the lender is unlikely to treat the payments as part of the applicant's stable monthly income.

Example: A loan applicant receives monthly income from a public assistance program. Although the lender generally treats public assistance payments as stable monthly income, the loan applicant's eligibility for this particular program will run out in just about a year. These payments are not durable enough to be counted when calculating the applicant's stable monthly income.

Dividends or **interest** from an investment is also part of stable monthly income, unless the loan applicant needs to cash in the investment to have enough funds for a downpayment or to pay for closing costs.

Net income from rental property can count as stable monthly income. This may be property the loan applicant already owns or the property being purchased. When possible, the lender uses detailed information about the property's income and expenses to determine a monthly net income figure. In other cases, the lender might use a certain percentage (for example, 75%) of the gross rent as a rough estimate of the net income.

Example: Your buyer is purchasing a duplex. She'll occupy one unit; the other is currently leased for $2,000 per month. To allow for maintenance expenses and possible vacancies or rent collection losses, the lender will count only 75% of the gross rent, or $1,500, as stable monthly income.

Sometimes it's very clear that a buyer won't have enough income to support the loan application. In that case, a **co-mortgagor** can be used. A co-mortgagor is simply a co-borrower—someone who (along with the primary borrower) signs the mortgage and note and is obligated to pay off the loan. For instance, parents may use their income history and financial status to help their children qualify for a loan.

Like the primary borrower, a co-mortgagor must have an income, net worth, and credit reputation that are acceptable to the lender. The co-mortgagor's resources must be sufficient to cover both his own housing expense and also whatever amount the primary borrower wouldn't qualify for on her own.

Unacceptable Types of Income. Some types of income are not considered to be stable monthly income. As mentioned earlier, **unemployment benefits** last only for a limited period of time, so they are virtually never considered stable monthly income.

Also, lenders are generally not interested in the **earnings of family members** other than the loan applicants themselves. For instance, if a married couple is applying for a loan, the lender will take into account the income of both spouses.

However, income that the couple's teenage children earn will not be considered, because the children won't necessarily be sharing their parents' home for much longer.

Income from full- or part-time **temporary work** is not considered stable monthly income because it does not pass the test of durability. Note that a job doesn't have to have a termination date for the lender to consider it temporary. Other factors can be taken into account, such as the nature of the work itself.

> **Example:** A recent flood has damaged a large portion of an industrial complex. The property manager has hired several full-time workers to help clean up the mess left by the flood and repair the damage. These jobs have no termination date, but are by their nature temporary. The income generated by these jobs wouldn't be considered stable monthly income.

However, income from temporary work may be accepted if the loan applicant has supported herself through a particular type of temporary work for years. The income from temporary work is then considered self-employment income.

> **Example:** Ingraham works in the computer industry as a temporary employee. She goes from job to job, helping to set up databases. Each job is temporary. However, Ingraham has supported herself for four years with this kind of temporary work. At this point, a lender might regard these temporary jobs as a form of self-employment and consider Ingraham's earnings to be stable monthly income.

Verifying Income. Lenders need to verify the income information given to them by loan applicants. A lender may send an income verification form (containing a release signed by the applicant) directly to the applicant's employer. The employer fills out the form and sends it directly back to the lender.

In some cases a lender uses an alternative income verification method. The loan applicant gives the lender W-2 forms for the previous two years, and payroll stubs or vouchers for the previous 30-day period. The lender then confirms the employment and income information with a phone call to the employer.

In addition to verifying the applicant's regular wages or salary, the lender also needs to verify any other types of income included in the applicant's stable month income. For example, if the applicant is relying on commission income, the lender will require copies of the applicant's federal income tax returns for the previous two years.

A self-employed loan applicant is usually required to give the lender audited financial statements and federal income tax returns for the two years prior to the loan application.

For alimony or child support income, the lender will require a copy of the court decree and proof that the payments are received. A bank statement showing that the checks have been deposited into the applicant's account may be good enough, or the lender might require copies of the deposited checks.

To verify rental income, the loan applicant usually has to submit copies of recent income tax returns. Additional documentation (such as copies of current leases) may also be required.

In some cases a lender may approve a loan application with less documentation than is usually required. Low-documentation loans are discussed later in this chapter.

Calculating Monthly Income. The lender wants to know the amount of the loan applicant's income in monthly terms. If a buyer works full-time (40 hours per week) for an hourly wage, you can calculate monthly income by multiplying the hourly wage by 173.33.

> **Example:** The buyer makes $17.50 an hour. To calculate her monthly earnings, multiply $17.50 by 173.33. $17.50 × 173.33 = $3,033.28. She earns $3,033 a month.

If a buyer gets paid twice a month, simply multiply the amount of the paycheck by two.

> **Example:** The buyer gets paid $2,700 twice a month. $2,700 × 2 = $5,400. His monthly income is $5,400.

It's a little more complicated if the buyer gets paid every two weeks. First, you must multiply the payment by 26 to get the annual income figure, and then you must divide that figure by 12 to get the monthly income figure.

> **Example:** The buyer gets paid $2,700 every two weeks. $2,700 × 26 = $70,200. Her annual income is $70,200. Now divide $70,200 by 12. $70,200 ÷ 12 = $5,850. Her monthly income is $5,850.

Using Income Ratios. Now the lender has a rough idea of how much stable monthly income the buyer has. Next comes the second part of the income analysis—determining if that income is enough.

The lender usually uses two numbers, called **income ratios** or **qualifying ratios**, to measure the buyer's income. The rationale behind income ratios is that if a loan applicant's regular monthly expenses exceed a certain percentage of his monthly income, the applicant may have a difficult time making loan payments. The lender wants some assurance that the applicant can make the mortgage payment and still have enough income left over for other expenses, such as food, clothing, doctor bills, car payments, and other necessities.

There are two types of income ratios:

1. a debt to income ratio, and
2. a housing expense to income ratio.

A debt to income ratio measures the monthly mortgage payment plus any other regular debt payments against the monthly income. A housing expense to income ratio measures only the monthly mortgage payment against the monthly income. For the purposes of income ratios, the monthly mortgage payment includes principal, interest, property taxes, and hazard insurance, plus mortgage insurance and homeowners association dues, if any. This is sometimes referred to as the **PITI payment**, which stands for principal, interest, taxes, and insurance. (If homeowners association dues are included, it may be called the PITIA payment.)

Each ratio is expressed as a percentage. For instance, a loan applicant's housing expense to income ratio would be 29% if her proposed mortgage payment represented 29% of her monthly income.

Each loan program has its own income ratio requirements. For example, the maximum acceptable debt to income ratio might be 36% or 41%, depending on the loan program. We will discuss the income ratio limits used for various loan programs in the next chapter. For now, just to show you how income ratios work, we'll use the general rule that the monthly mortgage payment should not exceed 28% of the loan applicant's income.

Example: Robinson's annual salary is $62,000. During the last four months, she made an extra $300 per month in overtime. For the past three years she has received an annual bonus of $2,600. She recently inherited a rental house that rents for $2,100 a month.

First decide which portions of Robinson's employment income a lender is likely to count. Her salary is stable monthly income, but you should exclude the overtime, because it hasn't been a regular part of her earnings history. You can include her annual bonus, because she's received a bonus for at least two years in a row. So add $2,600 to her annual salary of $62,000.

$$\$62,000 + \$2,600 = \$64,600$$

To calculate Robinson's stable monthly income from employment, divide this annual figure by 12 to arrive at a monthly figure.

$$\$64,600 \div 12 = \$5,383$$

Now take 75% of her regular rental income (to allow for maintenance expenses and vacancies or rent collection losses) and add that to her monthly employment income.

$$\$2,100 \times .75 = 1,575$$
$$\$1,575 + \$5,383 = \$6,958$$

Robinson's stable monthly income totals about $6,958. To get a rough idea of the maximum loan payment she would qualify for, multiply her stable monthly income by 28%.

$$\$6,958 \times .28 = \$1,948$$

Robinson could probably qualify for a monthly housing payment of $1,948. About 15% of that ($292) would go to taxes and insurance; the rest ($1,656) is her maximum principal and interest payment.

Net Worth

Along with income, a lender will also analyze the buyer's net worth. Net worth is the buyer's "bottom line"—the value of his total financial holdings, in dollars and cents. To calculate his net worth, you simply subtract his liabilities (debts) from his assets.

Example: Brown owns a house, a car, and some furniture, and he has $2,900 in savings. The total value of these assets is $277,000. Brown owes $5,000 on the car and $243,000 on the house; he owns the furniture free and clear.

To determine Brown's net worth, subtract the money he owes (his liabilities) from the value of his assets. $277,000 – $248,000 = $29,000. Brown's net worth is $29,000.

Net worth is important to lenders for a number of reasons. First, lenders feel that if a loan applicant has accumulated a significant amount of net worth, that's a sign that she will be a good credit risk. A healthy net worth is especially important if the loan application is weak in another area. For instance, if a loan applicant's income is marginal, an above-average net worth can mean the difference between loan approval and rejection.

Example: Carter has been out of college for four years. She makes $3,800 a month. She paid cash for her car, which is worth about $10,000. She has $9,600 in an IRA, $4,200 in mutual funds, and $6,500 in a savings account set aside for the downpayment and closing expenses. Her monthly bills consist of a revolving charge card payment of $45 and a college loan payment of $55. She's applied for a loan that would require monthly payments of $1,178.

Using the lender's income ratios, the highest payment Carter can qualify for is $1,064. However, because Carter has managed to accumulate a significant amount of assets in a short period of time, the lender may approve the loan anyway. Carter's accumulation of assets shows that she's an able money manager and a good credit risk.

Significant net worth—particularly cash—also tells the lender that the loan applicant will have sufficient funds to complete the purchase. The applicant needs enough cash to cover the downpayment, the closing costs, and any other expenses involved in buying the property.

Also, lenders often require a loan applicant to have **reserves** left over after making the downpayment and paying the closing costs. Typically, the reserves must be enough to cover two or three months' worth of mortgage payments. Reserves give the lender confidence that the applicant could handle a temporary financial emergency without defaulting on the loan.

Thus, a significant net worth tells the lender that the loan applicant:

1. knows how to manage money,
2. has enough cash to close the transaction, and
3. can weather a financial emergency without missing a loan payment.

Types of Assets. A buyer should list all of his assets on the loan application. An asset is anything of value, including real estate, cars, furniture, jewelry, stocks, bonds, or the cash value in a life insurance policy.

Liquid assets. Liquid assets are generally more important to an underwriter than non-liquid assets. Liquid assets include cash and any other assets that can be quickly converted to cash. For example, stocks (which can easily be sold) are preferred over real estate. And cash in the bank is best of all.

Verifying account information. A loan applicant must give the lender information about her bank accounts and sign a release so that the lender can verify the applicant's cash deposits.

The lender may use a "Request for Verification of Deposit" form to verify that the loan applicant actually has the money in his bank accounts that he claims to have. This form is sent directly to the bank and returned directly to the lender. In many cases lenders are willing to accept a faster, alternative method of verification: the loan applicant is asked to submit original bank statements for the previous three months.

The lender looks for four things when it verifies deposits:

1. Does the verified information agree with the amounts claimed in the loan application?
2. Does the loan applicant have enough money in the bank to meet the expenses of purchasing the property?
3. Has the bank account been opened only recently (within the last couple of months)?
4. Is the present balance significantly higher than the average balance?

If the account was opened recently or has a higher balance than normal, the lender may become suspicious. These are strong indications that the loan applicant borrowed the funds for the downpayment and closing costs, which generally is not allowed. However, if the funds are a gift, the lender may find this acceptable. (See the discussion of gift funds, below.)

Real estate. When a buyer is selling one home in order to buy another (usually more expensive) home, she can use her **net equity** in the home she's selling as a liquid asset. Net equity is the market value of the property minus the sum of the liens against the property and the selling expenses. In other words, net equity is the money the buyer expects to receive from the sale of her current home.

To estimate the amount of equity the buyer can apply toward the new purchase, take the appraised value of the current home (or the sales price, if a sale is already pending), subtract any outstanding mortgages or other liens, and then subtract the estimated selling costs (which are commonly between 10% and 13% of the sales price).

Example: The buyer's current home is valued at $350,000. There's a mortgage with a $294,000 balance to be paid off when the home is sold. To calculate the buyer's gross equity, subtract the mortgage balance from the market value.

$$\$350,000 - \$294,000 = \$56,000$$

The gross equity is $56,000. From the gross equity, deduct the estimated selling expenses, which come to $38,500.

$$\$56,000 - \$38,500 = \$17,500$$

Your buyer will have approximately $17,500 in net equity to apply to the purchase of a new home.

Sometimes equity in other property is the primary source of the cash that the buyer will use to purchase the new property. In this situation, the lender will require proof that the property has been sold and that the buyer has received the sale proceeds before it will make the new loan.

If it looks as though the buyer won't be able to sell his other property quickly enough, then he may be able to arrange a swing loan, as we explained in Chapter 8. The swing loan provides the cash to close the buyer's purchase transaction, and when the other property eventually sells, the buyer will pay the swing loan off out of the sale proceeds.

A buyer may also own real estate that she is not planning to sell. The property may be a rental house, a small apartment building, or vacant land. In any case, the property must be included in the loan application. Again, it is the equity in this other real estate that is important, not just the appraised value. If the buyer has little or no equity in the property, the lender will view it as a liability rather than an asset.

Liabilities. As we explained earlier, to determine net worth, the lender subtracts liabilities from assets. So after listing all his assets on the loan application, a buyer must then list all his liabilities.

Liabilities include balances owing on credit cards, charge accounts, student loans, car loans, and other installment debts. Other types of debts, such as income taxes that are currently payable, are also liabilities.

Gift Funds. Sometimes a buyer has enough income to qualify for a loan, but lacks the liquid assets necessary to close the loan. (In other words, she doesn't have enough cash for the downpayment and other expenses.) In some cases the buyer's family is willing to make up the deficit. Most lenders allow that, as long as the money supplied by the family is a gift and not a loan.

A gift of money from a relative must be confirmed with a **gift letter**. The letter should clearly state that the money is a gift to the buyer and does not have to be repaid, and it must be signed by the donor. Lenders often have their own form for gift letters and may require the donor to use their form.

The lender will have to verify the gift funds, so the donor should give them to the buyer as soon as possible.

Many loan programs have limits on the amount of gift funds that can be used in a transaction. These limits are intended to ensure that the buyer invests at least a small amount of his own money in the property he's buying.

Credit Reputation

The third part of the qualifying process is analyzing the loan applicant's credit reputation. The lender does this by obtaining a credit report from a credit reporting agency. The applicant (the buyer) normally pays the fee for the credit report.

A personal credit report includes information about an individual's debts and repayment history for the preceding seven years. A credit report primarily covers credit cards and loans. Other bills, such as utility bills, usually aren't listed unless they were turned over to a collection agency.

Derogatory Credit Information. If a loan applicant's credit report shows a history of slow payment or other credit problems, the loan application could be declined. Derogatory credit information includes all of the following.

- **Slow payments.** If the loan applicant is chronically late in paying bills, this will show up on the credit report. Slow payments may be a sign that the applicant is unable to pay on time, perhaps because she is already financially overextended. They may also be a sign that she does not take debt repayment seriously.

- **Debt consolidation and refinancing.** A pattern of continually increasing liabilities and periodic "bailouts" through refinancing and debt consolidation is a red flag to a lender. It suggests that the loan applicant has a tendency to live beyond a prudent level.

- **Collections.** After several attempts to get a debtor to pay a bill, a frustrated creditor may turn the bill over to a collection agency. Collections show up on the debtor's credit report for seven years.

- **Repossessions.** If someone purchases personal property on credit and fails to make the payments, the creditor may be able to repossess the item. Repossessions stay on the debtor's credit report for seven years.

- **Foreclosure.** A real estate foreclosure stays on the debtor's credit report for seven years. (Some alternatives to foreclosure, such as a short sale, will also appear on a credit report.)
- **Judgments.** If someone successfully sued the loan applicant, that, too, will show up on the credit report. A judgment is listed on a credit report for seven years after it is entered in the public record.
- **Bankruptcy.** Not surprisingly, lenders look at bankruptcy with disfavor. A bankruptcy stays on the debtor's credit report longer than other credit problems—for ten years instead of seven.

Credit Scores. Underwriters use **credit scores** to help evaluate a loan applicant's credit history. A credit reporting agency calculates an individual's credit score using the information that appears in his credit report and a quantitative model developed by a national credit scoring company. Credit scoring models, which are based on statistical analysis of large numbers of mortgages, are designed to predict the likelihood of successful repayment of or default on a mortgage. In general, someone with a poor credit score is much more likely to default than someone with a good credit score.

There are a variety of credit scoring models in use. The most widely used credit scores are FICO® scores. FICO® scores range from 300 to 850. A relatively high FICO® score (for example, over 700) is a positive sign.

How credit scores are used. In some cases, underwriters use credit scores to decide what level of review to apply to a loan applicant's credit history. For example, if an applicant has a very good credit score, the underwriter might perform a basic review, simply confirming that the information in the credit report is complete and accurate without investigating further. Aside from a foreclosure or a bankruptcy, the underwriter probably won't question the applicant about derogatory information in the report, because it's already been taken into account in calculating the credit score. On the other hand, if the applicant has a mediocre or poor credit score, the underwriter will perform a more complete review, looking into the circumstances that led to credit problems.

A loan applicant's credit score may also be a factor in determining the interest rate that will apply if the loan is approved. If the credit score is mediocre, instead of rejecting the application altogether, the lender might approve the loan but charge a higher interest rate or additional loan fees (called loan-level price adjustments) to make up for the increased risk of default.

Maintaining a good credit score. Any information that appears on a person's credit report may affect his credit score, but credit activity within the last two years has the greatest impact.

While most people would expect chronically late payments and collection problems to hurt someone's credit rating, they might be surprised at some of the other factors that can also lower a credit rating. For example, with a revolving credit card, maintaining a balance near the credit limit ("maxing out" the card) will have a negative impact on the cardholder's credit score, even if the borrower always makes the minimum monthly payment on time.

Applying for too much credit can also have a negative effect. Each time a person applies for credit (a store charge card, a car loan, a home equity loan, and so on), the creditor makes a "credit inquiry" that becomes part of the applicant's credit history. Occasional inquiries are fine, but more than a few inquiries within the past year can detract from the applicant's credit score. From a lender's point of view, too many credit inquiries may be an indication that the applicant is becoming overextended.

An exception applies when a number of credit inquiries are made within a short period. This could happen, for example, if someone were applying for a car loan or mortgage loan from various lenders, intending to compare loan offers and accept the best one. To allow for that type of situation, all of the credit inquiries within a certain period (ranging from 14 to 45 days) are treated as a single inquiry when the applicant's credit score is calculated.

Obtaining Credit Information. It's a good idea for prospective home buyers to obtain their credit reports and find out their credit scores well before they apply for a mortgage. (Obtaining a copy of your own credit report does not count as a credit inquiry.) A credit report may contain incorrect information, and the Fair Credit Reporting Act, a federal law, requires credit reporting agencies to investigate complaints and make corrections. This process can take a month or more.

There are three major credit reporting agencies: Equifax, Experian, and TransUnion. A buyer should obtain a credit report from each of the three agencies. Credit scores should also be requested; they are not automatically part of the credit report.

Explaining Credit Problems. A negative credit report or a poor credit score won't necessarily prevent a buyer from getting a loan at a reasonable interest rate. Credit problems can often be explained. If the lender is convinced that the past problems don't reflect the buyer's overall attitude toward credit and that the circumstances leading to the problems were temporary and are unlikely to recur, the loan application may well be approved. By obtaining her credit report before applying for a mortgage loan, the buyer can be prepared to discuss any problems with the lender.

Most people try to meet their credit obligations on time; when they don't, there's usually a reason. Loss of a job, divorce, hospitalization, prolonged illness, or a death in the family can create extraordinary financial pressures and adversely affect bill-paying habits. If a buyer has a poor credit score, it may be possible to show that the credit problems occurred during a specific period for an understandable reason, and that the buyer has handled credit well both before and since that period. The buyer should put this explanation in writing and be prepared to provide supporting documentation (such as hospital records) from a third party.

Fig. 9.1 Mortgage loan underwriting

Income Analysis
- Stable monthly income: quality and durability
- Income verification
- Income ratios measure adequacy of stable monthly income

Net Worth
- Assets minus liabilities
- Reserves required after closing
- Liquid vs. non-liquid assets
- Asset verification
- Gift fund limits

Credit Reputation
- Credit report (covers seven years)
- Credit scores
- Mitigating circumstances for past problems

When a buyer explains a credit problem to a lender, it's a mistake to blame the problem on the creditor. Lenders hear too many excuses from loan applicants who refuse to accept responsibility for their own actions. The lender's reaction is predictable: skepticism and rejection of the loan application. The lender will reason that someone who won't take responsibility for previous credit problems won't take responsibility for future ones, either.

Even serious credit problems can be resolved with time. When buyers tell you they have had credit problems in the past, don't simply assume that they can't qualify for a good loan. Refer them to a lender and get an expert's opinion.

Low-Documentation Loans

At times, some lenders have been willing to make low-documentation ("low-doc") loans to certain buyers. For example, if a buyer with a high credit score could make a large downpayment, a lender might waive some of the requirements for proof of income and assets in exchange for a higher interest rate. This was convenient for self-employed buyers and others with complicated financial situations.

However, the practice got out of hand during the subprime boom (see below). Some lenders made low-doc and even "no-doc" loans to less creditworthy buyers, including some who claimed income and assets they didn't actually have. Many of them eventually defaulted. Low-doc loans are much less common now, and no-doc loans have virtually disappeared.

Subprime Lending

Buyers who won't qualify for a loan under standard underwriting requirements may be able to obtain a subprime mortgage. Subprime lenders apply more flexible underwriting standards in order to take on riskier borrowers and riskier loans. To offset the increased risk, subprime lenders charge significantly higher interest rates and fees. In addition, subprime loans are more likely to involve prepayment penalties, balloon payments, and negative amortization.

Many subprime borrowers are buyers with poor or limited credit histories. However, subprime financing has also been used by buyers who:

- can't (or would rather not have to) meet the income and asset documentation requirements of prime lenders;
- have good credit but carry more debt than prime lenders allow; or
- want to purchase nonstandard properties that prime lenders don't regard as acceptable collateral.

Beginning in the late 1990s, the mortgage industry experienced a boom in subprime lending, enabling many subprime borrowers to buy homes. However, by 2008 a significant number of these borrowers were defaulting on their loans. The resulting wave of foreclosures hurt housing prices generally and the economy as a whole. It is now much more difficult to get subprime financing.

Choosing a Loan

In many cases, a buyer will be offered a choice of different loans, either by a single lender or by competing lenders. Comparing the loans and choosing between them can be a challenge. The buyer must compare the cost of the loans and also consider how the structure of each loan (the downpayment, repayment period, and other features) would affect his circumstances in both the short term and the long term. Financing disclosure laws, including the Truth in Lending Act, the Mortgage Loan Broker Law, and the Seller Financing Disclosure Law, are designed to ensure that buyers will have the information they need to choose the best loan for their situation.

Truth in Lending Act

To tell which of two or more possible loans is the least expensive, it isn't enough to compare the quoted interest rates. Loan fees and other financing charges also need to be taken into account.

The federal Truth in Lending Act (TILA) requires lenders to disclose information about loan costs in consumer credit transactions. The disclosures help loan applicants compare credit costs and shop around for the best terms.

TILA is implemented by **Regulation Z** and enforced by the Consumer Financial Protection Bureau. The law does not set limits on interest rates or other finance charges, but it does regulate the disclosure of these charges.

The most important disclosure required under TILA is the loan's **annual percentage rate** (APR). The APR expresses the relationship between the total finance charge and the total amount financed as an annualized percentage. The **total finance charge** that's used to calculate the APR includes interest, the loan origination fee, any discount points that will be paid by the borrower, and mortgage insurance premiums (see Chapter 10).

Because it takes into account these other charges as well as the interest, the APR for a real estate loan is virtually always higher than the quoted interest rate.

For example, a loan that bears an annual interest rate of 4% might have a 4.25% APR because of the origination fee and mortgage insurance. By comparing only the interest rates quoted by different lenders, a buyer could easily be misled. For instance, if a lender quotes a very low interest rate, but charges a large origination fee or several discount points, the total cost of the loan may actually exceed the total cost of a loan from a competitor with a higher interest rate. The APRs of the two loans will reveal this difference in cost.

To help prospective borrowers evaluate and compare loans, TILA and the Real Estate Settlement Procedures Act (discussed in Chapter 11) require lenders in most residential transactions to give the loan applicant a disclosure form. Beginning in October 2015, to comply with both laws, lenders must use the loan estimate form that's shown in Figure 9.2. The form discloses key information about the loan, including the APR, monthly payment amount, finance charges, and other closing costs, along with a list of services the borrower can shop around for (such as title insurance).

The lender has three business days after receiving the loan application to mail or deliver the loan estimate form. Most lenders give the estimate to the applicant at the time of application. If any of the estimated figures change over the course of the transaction, the lender has three days to give the borrower an updated estimate. Generally the lender must do this at least seven days before consummation of the loan transaction (the point at which the buyer becomes contractually obligated to the lender).

While a buyer won't get the loan estimate form until after applying for a loan, it's possible to find out the estimated APR and other loan details with a phone call to the lender or by checking the lender's website.

Other Finance Disclosure Laws

Whether or not a real estate finance transaction is subject to the federal Truth in Lending Act, other disclosures may be required by state law. California's finance disclosure laws include the Mortgage Loan Broker Law and the Seller Financing Disclosure Law. Like the Truth in Lending Act, they help buyers decide whether a particular loan meets their needs. In some cases, it's the real estate agent who has to make the disclosures required by these laws. In addition, the Real Estate Commissioner's regulations impose a number of disclosure requirements on a real estate licensee advertising financing options.

Fig. 9.2 Sample loan estimate form

FICUS BANK
4321 Random Boulevard · Somecity, ST 12340

Save this Loan Estimate to compare with your Closing Disclosure.

Loan Estimate

DATE ISSUED 2/15/20XX
APPLICANTS Michael Jones and Mary Stone
123 Anywhere Street
Anytown, ST 12345
PROPERTY 456 Somewhere Avenue
Anytown, ST 12345
SALE PRICE $240,000

LOAN TERM 30 years
PURPOSE Purchase
PRODUCT 5 Year Interest Only, 5/3 Adjustable Rate
LOAN TYPE ☒ Conventional ☐ FHA ☐ VA ☐ _____
LOAN ID # 123456789
RATE LOCK ☐ NO ☒ YES, until 4/16/20XX at 5:00 p.m. EDT

Before closing, your interest rate, points, and lender credits can change unless you lock the interest rate. All other estimated closing costs expire on 3/4/20XX at 5:00 p.m. EDT

Loan Terms

		Can this amount increase after closing?
Loan Amount	$211,000	**NO**
Interest Rate	4%	**YES** • Adjusts **every 3 years** starting in year 6 • Can go **as high as 12%** in year 15 • See **AIR Table on page 2** for details
Monthly Principal & Interest *See Projected Payments below for your Estimated Total Monthly Payment*	$703.33	**YES** • Adjusts **every 3 years** starting in year 6 • Can go **as high as $2,068** in year 15 • Includes **only interest** and **no principal** until year 6 • See **AP Table on page 2** for details
		Does the loan have these features?
Prepayment Penalty		**NO**
Balloon Payment		**NO**

Projected Payments

Payment Calculation	Years 1-5	Years 6-8	Years 9-11	Years 12-30
Principal & Interest	$703.33 *only interest*	$1,028 min $1,359 max	$1,028 min $1,604 max	$1,028 min $2,068 max
Mortgage Insurance	+ 109	+ 109	+ 109	+ —
Estimated Escrow *Amount can increase over time*	+ 0	+ 0	+ 0	+ 0
Estimated Total Monthly Payment	$812	$1,137–$1,468	$1,137–$1,713	$1,028–$2,068

Estimated Taxes, Insurance & Assessments *Amount can increase over time*	$533 a month	**This estimate includes** ☒ Property Taxes ☒ Homeowner's Insurance ☐ Other: *See Section G on page 2 for escrowed property costs. You must pay for other property costs separately.*	**In escrow?** NO NO

Costs at Closing

Estimated Closing Costs	$8,791	Includes $5,851 in Loan Costs + $2,940 in Other Costs – $0 in Lender Credits. *See page 2 for details.*
Estimated Cash to Close	$27,791	Includes Closing Costs. *See Calculating Cash to Close on page 2 for details.*

Visit **www.consumerfinance.gov/mortgage-estimate** for general information and tools.

LOAN ESTIMATE

PAGE 1 OF 3 · LOAN ID # 123456789

Source: Consumer Financial Protection Bureau.

Closing Cost Details

Loan Costs

A. Origination Charges	$3,110
1 % of Loan Amount (Points)	$2,110
Application Fee	$500
Processing Fee	$500

B. Services You Cannot Shop For	$820
Appraisal Fee	$305
Credit Report Fee	$30
Flood Determination Fee	$35
Lender's Attorney Fee	$400
Tax Status Research Fee	$50

C. Services You Can Shop For	$1,921
Pest Inspection Fee	$125
Survey Fee	$150
Title – Courier Fee	$32
Title – Lender's Title Policy	$665
Title – Settlement Agent Fee	$325
Title – Title Search	$624

D. TOTAL LOAN COSTS (A + B + C)	$5,851

Other Costs

E. Taxes and Other Government Fees	$152
Recording Fees and Other Taxes	$152
Transfer Taxes	

F. Prepaids	$1,352
Homeowner's Insurance Premium (12 months)	$1,000
Mortgage Insurance Premium (months)	
Prepaid Interest ($23.44 per day for 15 days @ 4.00%)	$352
Property Taxes (months)	

G. Initial Escrow Payment at Closing			
Homeowner's Insurance	per month for	mo.	
Mortgage Insurance	per month for	mo.	
Property Taxes	per month for	mo.	

H. Other	$1,436
Title – Owner's Title Policy (optional)	$1,436

I. TOTAL OTHER COSTS (E + F + G + H)	$2,940

J. TOTAL CLOSING COSTS	$8,791
D + I	$8,791
Lender Credits	

Calculating Cash to Close

Total Closing Costs (J)	$8,791
Closing Costs Financed (Paid from your Loan Amount)	$0
Down Payment/Funds from Borrower	$29,000
Deposit	– $10,000
Funds for Borrower	$0
Seller Credits	$0
Adjustments and Other Credits	$0
Estimated Cash to Close	$27,791

Adjustable Payment (AP) Table

Interest Only Payments?	YES for your first 60 payments
Optional Payments?	NO
Step Payments?	NO
Seasonal Payments?	NO

Monthly Principal and Interest Payments

First Change/Amount	$1,028 – $1,359 at 61st payment
Subsequent Changes	Every three years
Maximum Payment	$2,068 starting at 169th payment

Adjustable Interest Rate (AIR) Table

Index + Margin	MTA + 4%
Initial Interest Rate	4%
Minimum/Maximum Interest Rate	3.25%/12%

Change Frequency

First Change	Beginning of 61st month
Subsequent Changes	Every 36th month after first change

Limits on Interest Rate Changes

First Change	2%
Subsequent Changes	2%

Additional Information About This Loan

LENDER	Ficus Bank	**MORTGAGE BROKER**	
NMLS/__ LICENSE ID		**NMLS/__ LICENSE ID**	
LOAN OFFICER	Joe Smith	**LOAN OFFICER**	
NMLS/__ LICENSE ID	12345	**NMLS/__ LICENSE ID**	
EMAIL	joesmith@ficusbank.com	**EMAIL**	
PHONE	123-456-7890	**PHONE**	

Comparisons		Use these measures to compare this loan with other loans.
In 5 Years	$54,944	Total you will have paid in principal, interest, mortgage insurance, and loan costs.
	$0	Principal you will have paid off.
Annual Percentage Rate (APR)	4.617%	Your costs over the loan term expressed as a rate. This is not your interest rate.
Total Interest Percentage (TIP)	81.18%	The total amount of interest that you will pay over the loan term as a percentage of your loan amount.

Other Considerations

Appraisal	We may order an appraisal to determine the property's value and charge you for this appraisal. We will promptly give you a copy of any appraisal, even if your loan does not close. You can pay for an additional appraisal for your own use at your own cost.
Assumption	If you sell or transfer this property to another person, we ☐ will allow, under certain conditions, this person to assume this loan on the original terms. ☒ will not allow assumption of this loan on the original terms.
Homeowner's Insurance	This loan requires homeowner's insurance on the property, which you may obtain from a company of your choice that we find acceptable.
Late Payment	If your payment is more than *15* days late, we will charge a late fee of *5% of the monthly principal and interest payment.*
Refinance	Refinancing this loan will depend on your future financial situation, the property value, and market conditions. You may not be able to refinance this loan.
Servicing	We intend ☐ to service your loan. If so, you will make your payments to us. ☒ to transfer servicing of your loan.

Confirm Receipt

By signing, you are only confirming that you have received this form. You do not have to accept this loan because you have signed or received this form.

_____   _____   _____   _____

Applicant Signature   Date   Co-Applicant Signature   Date

Mortgage Loan Broker Law. In order to close a sale, a real estate agent sometimes must take an active role in arranging financing. For instance, if the buyer can't qualify for a large enough primary loan to purchase the property, the agent might arrange secondary financing with another lender. California law permits real estate agents to negotiate mortgage loans and also to be compensated for helping buyers in this way. Note, however, that anyone acting in this role must comply with the federal SAFE Act, which requires mortgage loan originators to have an endorsement from the Nationwide Mortgage Licensing System and Registry.

When a real estate agent arranges a loan, she must comply with California's Mortgage Loan Broker Law (also known as the Real Property Loan Law). This law requires an agent negotiating a loan to disclose to the borrower the loan fees, the interest rate, any liens against the property, and other similar information. The agent must use a state-mandated form to make these disclosures. The law also limits the commission and costs that the agent may charge for arranging a loan for less than $30,000.

Seller Financing Disclosure Law. A real estate agent who arranges seller financing in a transaction may need to make disclosures to the buyer and the seller regarding the terms of the financing. California's Seller Financing Disclosure Law applies to the purchase of a one- to four-unit residential property when the seller extends credit to the buyer in any arrangement that involves a finance charge or more than four payments in addition to the downpayment.

The seller financing disclosure statement must disclose:

- the financing terms;
- existing liens against the property;
- the buyer's credit and employment history;
- whether title insurance has been or will be obtained;
- whether a tax service has been arranged to ensure that property taxes are paid;
- whether the deed of trust will be recorded; and
- the amount, source, and purpose of any funds the buyer is to receive from the transaction.

The form must also include a warning about the hazards of refinancing and an explanation of the possible effects of negative amortization.

The buyer and the seller must sign the disclosure statement. The real estate agent also has to sign the form as an "arranger of credit" if she helped to negotiate the financing or prepare the loan documents. The statement must be delivered to the parties before a promissory note is executed. The arranger of credit must keep a signed copy of the disclosure statement on file for three years.

Note that a seller financing disclosure statement is not required if the transaction is already covered under another disclosure law, such as the Truth in Lending Act or the Mortgage Loan Broker Law. An example of a seller financing addendum and disclosure statement can be found in Chapter 7 (Figure 7.2).

Advertising Regulations. When a real estate agent advertises financing options, she must comply with the disclosure requirements in the Real Estate Commissioner's regulations. These regulations prohibit the agent from making false, misleading, or deceptive statements or representations. More specific requirements apply when advertising certain types of financing. For example, if an agent advertises a low-documentation loan (discussed earlier in this chapter), the ad must include a statement that the loan may have a higher interest rate, more points, and more fees than other types of loans.

Locking in the Interest Rate

If a buyer chooses a lender because of a low interest rate, she should consider asking the lender to **lock in** the rate for a certain period. If the rate is not locked in, the lender may change it at any time before closing. So even if the rate is 4.25% when the loan application is submitted, by the time the loan closes, the rate could be 4.5%. The buyer might end up with a much higher monthly loan payment than originally anticipated—even an unaffordable payment.

A buyer who wants to lock in the interest rate typically pays a lock-in fee or a slightly higher rate of interest. If the closing date gets postponed, the buyer may have to pay an extension fee to maintain the rate lock.

A rate lock can be expensive. If the buyer thinks market interest rates may drop in the next few weeks, it probably doesn't make sense to lock in the rate. The lender may charge the buyer the locked-in rate even if market rates went down in the period before closing.

Fig. 9.3 Buyer's considerations in choosing a loan

- Interest rate and loan fees

- Short-term cost of financing vs. overall long-term cost

- Savings remaining after home purchase

- Spending money remaining after monthly mortgage payment

- How long does the buyer intend to own this home?

- How rapidly will equity build?

- How soon will the mortgage be paid off?

- How much house will this financing enable the buyer to purchase?

- What alternative investment opportunities are available?

Other Considerations in Choosing a Loan

The interest rate and the overall cost of a loan are important considerations for any buyer, but they are by no means the only ones. In comparing different financing options, buyers should think about a variety of other issues: How much money will they have left in savings after the loan closes? How much spending money will they have left over each month after paying their mortgage payment? How long do they plan to stay in the home they're buying? With income ratios and other qualifying standards, a lender takes certain aspects of the buyers' situation into account before agreeing to make a loan. But only the buyers themselves can decide which financing alternative is most comfortable for them and fits in best with their own financial plans.

Some buyers are only planning to live in the house they're purchasing for a few years. These buyers generally want to minimize the short-term cost of the property, and they're less concerned with the long-term, overall cost. For example, a buyer who plans to sell the property in less than five years might be a candidate for an adjustable-rate mortgage with a five-year fixed-rate period at the outset. He can take advantage of the lower starting interest rate without worrying about how high the market rates may rise in the future.

Buyers who hope to retire early or reduce their workload may be most concerned with building equity and paying off their mortgage as soon as possible. They might prefer a loan with a 15-year or 20-year term, rather than the standard 30-year term, even though it means they will qualify for a smaller loan amount and have to buy a less expensive home than they otherwise would.

Some first-time buyers with limited buying power want to purchase the largest home they can afford. They may be interested in financing arrangements that can boost their price range: an adjustable interest rate, a high loan-to-value ratio, a 40-year loan term, discount points, or secondary financing.

On the other hand, some buyers don't want to borrow as much money for a house as lenders would allow. They may want to invest their money differently, or they may simply prefer to avoid the financial stress that the maximum monthly mortgage payment would represent for them.

In short, buyers must evaluate every potential loan in light of their own goals and preferences. The downpayment and other cash requirements, a fixed or adjustable interest rate, the monthly payment amount, and the loan term are all variables to consider in choosing a loan. We'll be discussing these and other loan features in the next chapter.

Predatory Lending

We can't end our discussion of loan qualifying without mentioning predatory lending. The term predatory lending is used to describe an array of mortgage practices used to take advantage of unsophisticated borrowers. Predatory lenders tend to target elderly or minority borrowers, especially those with limited income or limited English skills.

Examples of predatory lending practices include:

- **Predatory steering:** Steering a buyer toward a more expensive loan when the buyer could qualify for a less expensive one.
- **Fee packing:** Charging interest rates, points, or processing fees that far exceed the norm and aren't justified by the cost of the services provided.
- **Loan flipping:** Encouraging repeated refinancing even though there is no benefit to the borrower. (The predatory lender benefits from the loan fees.)

- **Disregarding borrower's ability to pay:** Making a loan based on the property's value, without using appropriate qualifying standards to determine the borrower's ability to afford the loan payments.
- **Balloon payment abuses:** Making a partially amortized or interest-only loan with low monthly payments, without disclosing to the borrower that a large balloon payment will be required after a short period.
- **Fraud:** Misrepresenting or concealing unfavorable loan terms or excessive fees, falsifying documents, or using other fraudulent means to induce a prospective borrower to enter into a loan agreement.

Predatory lending is often associated with subprime mortgages, and is considered to have contributed to the subprime mortgage crisis. Many states, including California, have enacted statutes intended to help prevent predatory lending.

California's **Predatory Lending Law** applies to purchase loans as well as home equity loans. The loan must be secured by residential property with no more than four dwelling units, and it must be the applicant's principal residence.

The law applies only to loans defined as "high cost." For instance, it applies to a loan if the total points and fees exceed 6% of the loan amount. In addition, the law applies only if the loan amount is less than the conforming loan limit (a limit that is set by the Federal Housing Finance Agency and adjusted annually; see Chapter 10).

Here are some of the prohibitions and requirements that apply to loans covered by this law:

- Loan applicants may not be steered toward a subprime loan if they could qualify for a standard loan, or toward a loan with a higher interest rate and fees if they could actually qualify for a less expensive loan.
- Loan applicants must be given a disclosure statement entitled *Consumer Caution and Home Ownership Counseling Notice*.
- The loan agreement can't include an acceleration clause that allows the lender to accelerate the loan at its discretion (even if the borrower hasn't defaulted).
- A prepayment penalty can't be charged if the loan is accelerated due to default.
- Refinancing isn't allowed if it doesn't result in an identifiable benefit to the consumer.

Anyone who willfully and knowingly violates this state law faces a possible civil penalty of up to $25,000 per violation, and may also owe damages to the consumer. Additionally, a real estate agent who participates in a predatory lending scheme could lose his license or suffer other license law penalties.

Chapter Summary

1. Home buyers usually get preapproved for a loan before beginning their house hunt. Preapproval requires submission of a loan application and all supporting documentation, just like applying for a loan after finding the property.

2. When a mortgage loan application is submitted to a lender, the lender's underwriters evaluate it to determine whether the applicant is a good credit risk and can afford the proposed loan. The underwriter analyzes the applicant's income, net worth, and credit reputation.

3. Stable monthly income is income that meets the lender's standards of quality (how dependable the source is) and durability (how long the income is likely to continue). Verified income from employment, pensions, social security, spousal maintenance, child support, public assistance, dividends, interest, and rental property may be counted as stable monthly income.

4. Income ratios are used to measure the adequacy of a loan applicant's income. In many cases the underwriter will apply both a debt to income ratio and a housing expense to income ratio. A debt to income ratio states the applicant's monthly mortgage payment (PITI), plus any other monthly obligations, as a percentage of her stable monthly income. A housing expense to income ratio states the PITI payment alone as a percentage of stable monthly income.

5. Net worth is calculated by subtracting liabilities from assets. A loan applicant's net worth indicates to a lender whether the applicant knows how to manage money, has the cash required for closing, and has adequate reserves in case of a financial emergency. Liquid assets are generally more helpful to a loan application than non-liquid assets. If the loan applicant owns real estate, the lender will be concerned with the applicant's net equity. Lenders place limits on the amount of gift funds a buyer can use to close the transaction.

6. A credit report lists credit problems that have occurred within the past seven years (ten years for a bankruptcy). A loan applicant's credit score provides an overall measure of creditworthiness and may be used to determine the level of review applied to the application. It may also be a factor in setting the loan's interest rate.

7. Subprime lending involves making riskier loans, usually in exchange for higher interest rates and fees. Many subprime borrowers have poor or limited credit histories; others simply want to purchase nonstandard properties that prime lenders don't regard as acceptable collateral.

8. The Truth in Lending Act and the Real Estate Settlement Procedures Act require residential lenders to provide loan applicants with a loan estimate form within three days after receiving an application. The form must disclose the annual percentage rate (APR) of the proposed loan and provide estimates of finance charges and the monthly payment amount.

9. A real estate agent who helps a buyer obtain institutional financing or negotiates seller financing may be required to provide a disclosure statement to comply with the Mortgage Loan Broker Law or the Seller Financing Disclosure Law.

10. Remember that it is not always a good idea for buyers to borrow the maximum loan amount and buy the most expensive home they can. Buyers need to consider their entire financial situation, short-term and long-term, when choosing a home to buy and a loan to finance the purchase.

11. Predatory lenders take advantage of unsophisticated borrowers, often targeting elderly or minority borrowers. Predatory lending practices include predatory steering, fee packing, loan flipping, disregarding a borrower's ability to pay, balloon payment abuses, and fraud.

Key Terms

Preapproval: Formal loan approval given before the buyer has chosen property to purchase, establishing the maximum loan amount that the lender is willing to provide.

Preapproval letter: A letter from a lender in which the lender agrees to loan the borrower up to a specified amount when she finds a home she wants to buy, provided the property meets the lender's standards.

Qualifying (or underwriting) standards: The standards a lender requires a loan applicant to meet before a loan will be approved.

Nonconforming loan: A loan that does not meet the underwriting standards of Fannie Mae and Freddie Mac.

Automated underwriting system: A computerized system used to analyze a borrower's loan application and credit report, and provide a recommendation for or against approval.

Stable monthly income: A loan applicant's gross monthly income that meets the lender's tests of quality and durability.

Income ratios: A standard used in qualifying a buyer for a loan, to determine whether he has sufficient income. The buyer's debts and proposed housing expense should not exceed a specified percentage of his income.

Net worth: An individual's personal financial assets, minus her personal liabilities.

Liquid assets: Cash and other assets that can be readily turned into cash (liquidated), such as stock.

Liabilities: Financial debts or obligations.

Credit reputation: An individual's record of bill payment and debt repayment, as revealed in a credit report compiled by a credit rating bureau.

Credit score: A figure used in underwriting that encapsulates the likelihood that a loan applicant will default, calculated using a credit scoring model and the information from the applicant's credit report.

Low-documentation loan: A loan where the lender waives some of the requirements for proof of income and assets in the underwriting process, in exchange for a higher interest rate.

Subprime lending: When lenders apply more flexible underwriting standards in order to take on riskier borrowers and riskier loans, in return for higher loan fees and interest rates.

Truth in Lending Act (TILA): A federal law that requires lenders to make disclosures concerning loan costs to applicants for consumer loans (including any mortgage loan that will be used for personal, family, or household purposes). It also requires certain disclosures in advertisements concerning consumer credit.

Annual percentage rate (APR): All of the charges that a borrower will pay for the loan (including the interest, loan fee, discount points, and mortgage insurance costs), expressed as an annualized percentage of the total amount financed.

Mortgage Loan Broker Law: A California law that requires loan brokers to give their customers a disclosure statement, and also limits the size of the commissions and other costs they can charge for smaller loans.

Predatory lending: Lending practices used to take advantage of unsophisticated borrowers.

Chapter Quiz

1. When a potential buyer approaches a lender prior to looking for a house, in order to obtain a promise of a loan up to a certain amount, this is known as:
   a. prequalification
   b. predetermination
   c. preapproval
   d. prepayment

2. A buyer may find it useful to have a preapproval letter because it:
   a. does not commit the lender to making a loan
   b. gives the seller confidence that the financing contingency won't be a problem
   c. tells the seller the maximum amount the buyer can afford
   d. allows the buyer to extend the closing process

3. If a loan applicant's primary source of income is self-employment, the lender will consider this stable monthly income if the loan applicant:
   a. does not have any other source of income
   b. also has secondary sources of income
   c. has been self-employed for at least five years
   d. has a history of employment in the same field and can document a reasonable chance for success

4. Which of the following would a lender consider an acceptable secondary income source?
   a. Rental income, with a percentage deducted to allow for vacancies or uncollected rent
   b. Interest on investments that the loan applicant will cash in to pay for closing costs
   c. Child support payments for the loan applicant's 17-year-old daughter
   d. Regular monthly income from a public assistance program, if the loan applicant's eligibility will expire at the end of the year

5. In contrast to a debt to income ratio, a housing expense to income ratio:
   a. takes into account principal and interest on the mortgage, but not taxes and insurance
   b. is based on the monthly mortgage payment alone, not on all of the loan applicant's debt payments
   c. uses the applicant's current housing expense instead of the proposed mortgage payment
   d. takes into account the loan applicant's net worth as well as monthly income

6. Which of the following is true about how a lender evaluates net worth?
   a. When verifying bank accounts, the lender wants the present balance to be significantly higher than the average balance in the past
   b. The lender prefers non-liquid assets to liquid assets
   c. The lender is primarily concerned with the appraised value of the real estate that the loan applicant owns
   d. If the loan applicant's income is marginal, the lender may approve the loan anyway if the applicant has significant net worth

7. How would a lender calculate the net equity in real estate the loan applicant owns?
   a. Take the market value of the property and deduct the sum of the liens against the property, plus the selling expenses
   b. Subtract the balance of the existing mortgage from the assessed value of the property
   c. Take the market value of the property and subtract between 10% and 13% for the estimated selling costs
   d. Add the buyer's downpayment to the market value of the property, then subtract the sum of the liens against the property

8. Which of the following would be most likely to have a negative effect on an individual's credit rating?
   a. Obtaining a copy of his own credit report
   b. Unemployment
   c. Debt consolidation
   d. A high FICO® score

9. The APR for a real estate loan:
   a. must be disclosed before a loan application is submitted
   b. expresses the relationship of the total finance charge to the total amount financed
   c. includes interest, points, lock-in fees, closing costs, and the downpayment
   d. is usually lower than the quoted interest rate

10. Fee packing, loan flipping, and balloon payment abuses are all examples of:
    a. preapproval techniques
    b. derogatory credit information
    c. rate lock-ins
    d. predatory lending practices

Answer Key

1. **c.** A buyer who would like to be preapproved will go directly to a lender and submit a loan application. Prequalification, by contrast, can be performed by a real estate agent and is merely a determination of an appropriate price range.

2. **b.** Preapproval makes a buyer's offer more attractive because the seller can be confident that the buyer will qualify for financing.

3. **d.** A lender will count the income of a self-employed loan applicant who has been in business for a short time, but only if the loan applicant has a history of employment in the same field and can document a reasonable chance for success with pro forma financial statements and market feasibility studies.

4. **a.** Income from sources besides employment must still be reliable and durable. Rental income is acceptable if the loan applicant can prove that rental payments are made regularly, but the lender will usually consider only a certain percentage because vacancies and rent collection problems are unpredictable.

5. **b.** A housing expense to income ratio measures the adequacy of the loan applicant's income using only the monthly mortgage payment (principal, interest, taxes, and insurance). A debt to income ratio also takes payments on other debts into account.

6. **d.** Above-average net worth can mean the difference between approval and rejection if the loan applicant's income is marginal.

7. **a.** Net equity is the amount of money the loan applicant can expect to receive from the sale of the property. This is often the primary source of cash that will be used to buy the new property.

8. **c.** A pattern of increasing liabilities followed by debt consolidation suggests that the individual tends to live beyond his means.

9. **b.** The annual percentage rate (APR) helps loan applicants compare the overall cost of different loans. A loan's APR expresses the relationship between the total finance charge and the total amount financed.

10. **d.** These are all examples of predatory lending practices.

10

Financing Programs

Basic Loan Features

- Repayment period
- Amortization
- Loan-to-value ratio
- Secondary financing
- Loan fees
- Fixed and adjustable interest rates

Conventional Loans

- Conventional loans and the secondary market
- Characteristics of conventional loans
- Underwriting conventional loans
- Making conventional loans more affordable

Government-sponsored Loan Programs

- FHA-insured loans
- VA-guaranteed loans
- Cal-Vet loans
- Rural Housing Service loans

Seller Financing

- How seller financing works
- Types of seller financing
- Other ways sellers can help

Introduction

As discussed in the previous chapter, the size of loan a particular buyer can get depends on the buyer's income, net worth, and credit history. But it also depends on the features of the loan and the way it's structured. How long is the repayment period? How much of a downpayment does the lender require? Is the interest rate fixed or adjustable? Changes in the loan features offered by residential lenders reflect the changing conditions in the mortgage finance market. Lenders want to make loans that will enable buyers to purchase homes, but they have to structure the loans to control the risk of default and protect their investments. The mortgage loans that make business sense to a lender vary with the state of the market: Are interest rates high or low, and are they headed up or down? Is this a buyer's market or a seller's market?

As a real estate agent, you can help your buyers get the financing they need by keeping abreast of currently available options. Lenders will frequently send you information about their latest loan programs, and you should keep an eye out for new developments. First-time buyers are especially likely to benefit from special programs. This chapter will provide you with the background information needed to understand the various types of loans lenders offer. In the first part of the chapter, we'll review the basic features of a mortgage loan; it is differences in these features that distinguish the various loan programs. In the second part of the chapter, we'll look at the main categories of mortgage loan programs: conventional loans and government-sponsored loans. We'll also discuss seller financing.

Basic Loan Features

The basic features of a mortgage loan include the repayment period; amortization; the loan-to-value ratio; a secondary financing arrangement (in some cases); loan fees; and a fixed or adjustable interest rate.

Repayment Period

The repayment period of a loan is the number of years the borrower has to repay the loan. The repayment period may also be referred to as the loan term.

Thirty years is generally considered the standard repayment period for a residential mortgage, but many lenders also offer 15-year and 20-year loans. In some programs a term as short as 10 years or as long as 40 years is allowed.

The length of the repayment period affects two important aspects of a mortgage loan:

1. the amount of the monthly payment, and
2. the total amount of interest paid over the life of the loan.

To see the impact that the repayment period has on the monthly payment and the total interest paid, let's compare a 30-year loan with a 15-year loan.

Monthly Payment Amount. The main reason 30 years became the standard term for a residential mortgage is that a longer repayment period reduces the amount of the monthly payment. Thus, a 30-year loan is more affordable than a 15-year loan.

> **Example:** The monthly payment on a $100,000 30-year loan at 7% interest is $665.30. The monthly payment on the same loan amortized over a 15-year period is $898.83.

The higher monthly payment required for a 15-year loan means that the borrower will build equity in the home much faster. But the higher payment also makes it much more difficult to qualify for a 15-year loan than for the same size loan with a 30-year term. A buyer who wants a 15-year loan and has sufficient funds might decide to make a larger downpayment and borrow less money in order to make the monthly payment amount more affordable. Or the buyer might choose instead to buy a much less expensive home than what he could afford with a 30-year loan.

Total Interest. Probably the biggest advantage of a shorter repayment period is that it substantially decreases the amount of interest paid over the life of the loan. With a 15-year mortgage, a borrower will end up paying less than half as much interest over the life of the loan as a 30-year mortgage would require.

> **Example:** Let's look at our $100,000 loan at 7% interest again. By the end of a 30-year loan term, the borrower will pay a total of $239,509. But by the end of a 15-year term, the borrower will pay only $161,789. After deducting the original $100,000 principal amount, you can see that the 30-year loan will require $139,509 in interest, while the 15-year loan will require only $61,789 in interest.

So the 30-year mortgage has more affordable payments, but requires the borrower to pay a lot more interest over the life of the loan. On the other hand, the

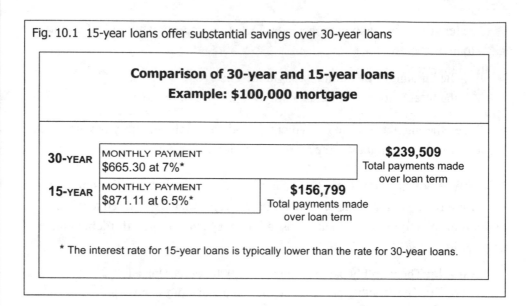

Fig. 10.1 15-year loans offer substantial savings over 30-year loans

Comparison of 30-year and 15-year loans
Example: $100,000 mortgage

30-YEAR
MONTHLY PAYMENT
$665.30 at 7%*

$239,509
Total payments made
over loan term

15-YEAR
MONTHLY PAYMENT
$871.11 at 6.5%*

$156,799
Total payments made
over loan term

* The interest rate for 15-year loans is typically lower than the rate for 30-year loans.

15-year loan has much higher monthly payments, but allows the borrower to pay far less interest over the life of the loan.

Interest Rates for 15-Year Loans. To simplify our comparison of a 15-year loan and a 30-year loan, we applied the same interest rate—7%—to both loans. In fact, however, a lender is likely to charge a significantly lower interest rate on a 15-year loan than it charges for a comparable 30-year loan. That's because a 15-year loan represents less of a risk for the lender.

The interest rate on a 15-year loan might be half a percentage point lower than the rate on a 30-year loan. If the interest rate on the 15-year loan in our example were only 6.5% instead of 7%, the monthly payment would be $871.11. The total interest paid over the life of the loan would be $56,799.

Amortization

Amortization refers to how the principal and interest are paid over a loan's repayment period. Most loans made by institutional lenders like banks and savings and loans are **fully amortized**. A fully amortized loan is completely paid off by the end of the repayment period by means of regular monthly payments. The amount of the monthly payment remains the same throughout the repayment period. Each monthly payment includes both a principal portion and an interest portion. As each payment is made, the principal amount of the debt is reduced.

With each succeeding payment, a slightly smaller portion of the payment is applied to interest and a slightly larger portion is applied to the principal, until at last the final payment pays off the loan completely.

In the early years of a fully amortized loan, the principal portion of the payment is quite small, so it takes several years for the borrower's equity to increase significantly through debt reduction. But toward the end of the loan period, the borrower's equity increases more rapidly.

Example: A fully amortized, 30-year $100,000 loan at 6% interest calls for monthly payments of $599.55. Only $99.55 of the first payment is applied to the principal. But by the twentieth year of the loan term, $327.89 of the $599.55 payment is applied to the principal.

The alternatives to fully amortized loans include partially amortized loans and interest-only loans. Like a fully amortized loan, a **partially amortized** loan requires monthly payments of both principal and interest. However, the monthly payments are not enough to completely pay off the debt by the end of the repayment period. At the end of the repayment period, some principal remains unpaid. It must then be paid off in one lump sum called a **balloon payment**.

Example: A partially amortized $400,000 loan might have a $171,000 balance at the end of the loan term. The borrower will have to make a balloon payment of $171,000 to pay off the loan.

Fig. 10.2 Payments for a fully-amortized loan

EXAMPLE: **$100,000** LOAN @ **6%**, **30**-YEAR TERM, MONTHLY PAYMENTS					
PAYMENT NUMBER	BEGINNING BALANCE	TOTAL PAYMENT	INTEREST PORTION	PRINCIPAL PORTION	ENDING BALANCE
1	$100,000.00	$599.55	$500.00	$99.55	$99,900.45
2	$99,900.45	$599.55	$499.50	$100.05	$99,800.40
3	$99,800.40	$599.55	$499.00	$100.55	$99,699.85
4	$99,699.85	$599.55	$498.50	$101.05	$99,598.80
5	$99,598.80	$599.55	$497.99	$101.56	$99,497.24

In most cases, the borrower comes up with the funds for the balloon payment by refinancing. (Refinancing means using the funds from a new mortgage loan to pay off an existing mortgage.)

The term **interest-only loan** may be used in two different ways. In the first of these, an interest-only loan is one that calls for payments during the loan term that cover only the interest accruing on the loan, without paying off any of the principal. The entire principal amount—the amount originally borrowed—is due at the end of the term. For example, in this sense, someone who borrows $600,000 on an interest-only basis will make monthly interest payments to the lender during the loan term; at the end of the term, the borrower will be required to repay the lender the entire $600,000 principal amount as a lump sum.

In the alternative usage (the more common one now), an interest-only loan is one that allows the borrower to make interest-only payments for a specified period at the beginning of the loan term. At the end of this period, the borrower must begin making amortized payments that will pay off all of the principal, along with the additional interest that accrues, by the end of the term. Though popular for a few years, this type of loan is no longer widely available, as we'll discuss shortly.

Loan-to-Value Ratio

A **loan-to-value ratio** (LTV) expresses the relationship between the loan amount and the value of the home being purchased. If a buyer is purchasing a $100,000 home with an $80,000 loan and a $20,000 downpayment, the loan-to-value ratio is 80%. If the loan amount were $90,000 and the downpayment were $10,000, the LTV would be 90%. The higher the LTV, the larger the loan amount and the smaller the downpayment.

A loan with a low LTV is generally less risky than one with a high LTV. The borrower's investment in her home is greater, so she'll try harder to avoid defaulting on the loan and losing the home. And if the borrower does default, the outstanding loan balance is less, so it's more likely that the lender will be able to recoup the entire amount in a foreclosure sale.

Lenders use LTVs to set maximum loan amounts. For example, under the terms of a particular loan program, the maximum loan amount might be 95% of the sales price or appraised value of the property, whichever is less. The borrower would be required to make a downpayment of at least 5%.

Secondary Financing

Sometimes a buyer may want to get two loans at the same time. One of the loans is a **primary loan** for most of the purchase price, and the other is generally used to pay part of the downpayment or closing costs required for the first loan. The second loan is referred to as **secondary financing**.

Secondary financing can come from a variety of sources. It may come from the same lender who is making the primary loan, a second institutional lender, the seller, or a private third party.

A lender making a primary loan will usually place restrictions on the type of secondary financing arrangement the borrower may enter into. The borrower generally must be able to qualify for the combined payment on the primary and secondary loans. And in most cases the borrower must make at least a minimum downpayment out of his own funds.

Loan Fees

Of course, lenders don't loan money free of charge. For mortgage loans, lenders not only charge borrowers interest on the principal, they also charge points. The term "point" is short for "percentage point." A point is one percentage point (1%) of the loan amount. For example, on a $100,000 loan, one point would be $1,000; six points would be $6,000. Any lender charges that are a percentage of the loan amount may be referred to as points; the chief examples are loan origination fees and discount points.

Origination Fees. A loan origination fee covers administrative costs the lender incurs in processing a loan; it is sometimes called a service fee, an administrative charge, or simply a loan fee. An origination fee is charged in almost every residential mortgage loan transaction, with the exception of "no-fee loans," which usually carry a slightly higher interest rate over the entire loan term instead.

Discount Points. The second type of point is a discount point. Discount points are used to increase the lender's upfront yield, or profit, on the loan. By charging discount points, the lender not only gets interest throughout the loan term, it collects an additional sum of money up front, when the loan is funded. As a result, the lender is willing to "discount" the loan—that is, make the loan at a lower interest rate than it would have without the discount points. In effect, the borrower pays the lender a lump sum to avoid paying more interest later. A lower interest rate also translates into a lower monthly payment.

Discount points are not charged in all residential loan transactions, but they are quite common. The number of discount points charged usually depends on how the loan's interest rate compares to market interest rates. Typically, a lender that offers an especially low rate charges more points to make up for it.

Fixed and Adjustable Interest Rates

A loan's interest rate can be either fixed or adjustable. With a fixed-rate loan, the interest rate charged on the loan remains constant throughout the entire loan term. If a borrower obtains a 30-year home loan with a 7% fixed interest rate, the interest rate remains 7% for the whole 30-year period, no matter what happens to market interest rates during that time. If market rates increase to 9%, or if they drop to 5%, the interest rate charged on the loan will still be 7%.

Until the early 1980s, virtually all mortgage loans had a fixed interest rate. During the 1980s, however, market interest rates rose dramatically and fluctuated constantly. Suddenly, many borrowers could no longer afford to take out a home loan. And many lenders (who were unable to predict future interest rates) became uncomfortable lending money for 30 years at a fixed interest rate. The **adjustable-rate mortgage** (ARM) was introduced as the solution to both of these problems.

An ARM allows the lender to periodically adjust the loan's interest rate to reflect changes in market interest rates. The lender's ability to change the loan's interest rate during the loan term passes much of the risk of interest rate increases on to the borrower. Because of this shift in risk, lenders are often willing to

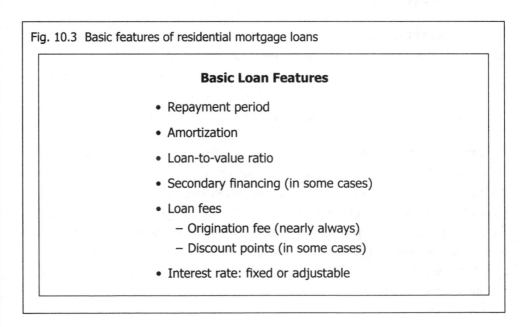

Fig. 10.3 Basic features of residential mortgage loans

Basic Loan Features

- Repayment period
- Amortization
- Loan-to-value ratio
- Secondary financing (in some cases)
- Loan fees
    - Origination fee (nearly always)
    - Discount points (in some cases)
- Interest rate: fixed or adjustable

charge a lower rate on ARMs. For example, if a borrower could get a fixed interest rate loan at 6%, he might be able to get an adjustable-rate loan at an initial rate between 5% and 5½%.

Of course, while the initial interest rate of an adjustable-rate loan appears attractive, the borrower is assuming a greater risk. With an ARM, it is the borrower who pays the price of an increase in market interest rates. When market rates go up, the borrower's interest rate and mortgage payments also go up. On the other hand, if market rates decrease, the borrower's interest rate and mortgage payments also decrease.

ARM Features. The features of an adjustable-rate loan include the note rate, the index, the margin, a rate adjustment period, a payment adjustment period, rate caps, payment caps, a negative amortization cap, and a conversion option.

Note rate. The note rate is the ARM's initial interest rate. It's commonly referred to as the note rate because it's the rate stated in the promissory note.

Index. An index is a widely published statistical report that is considered a reliable indicator of changes in the cost of money. Examples include the one-year Treasury securities index, the Eleventh District cost of funds index, and the LIBOR index.

Margin. An ARM's margin is the difference between the index rate and the interest rate the lender charges the borrower. The margin is how the lender earns a profit on the loan. A typical margin is between two and three percentage points.

Example: Suppose the current index rate is 2.5% and the lender's margin is 2%. 2.5% + 2% = 4.5%. The lender charges the borrower 4.5% interest on the loan. The 2% margin is the lender's income from the loan.

Rate adjustment period. An ARM's rate adjustment period determines how often the lender will adjust the loan's interest rate, if an increase or decrease is indicated. The most common rate adjustment period is one year, but it could be every six months, every three years, or some other time period. At the end of each period, the lender checks the index. If the index rate has increased, the lender can increase the borrower's interest rate. If the index rate has decreased, the lender must decrease the borrower's interest rate.

Some ARMs have a two-tiered rate adjustment structure. They provide for a longer initial period before the first rate adjustment, with more frequent rate adjustments after that. These are sometimes called **hybrid ARMs**, because they're a cross between adjustable-rate and fixed-rate mortgages.

Example: The borrowers are financing their home with a 30-year ARM that has an initial rate adjustment period of three years, with annual rate adjustments from then on. The interest rate charged on their loan won't change during the first three years of the repayment period, but it will change each year after that.

The hybrid loan in the example would be called a 3/1 ARM. There are also 5/1 ARMs, 7/1 ARMs, and 10/1 ARMs. In each case, the first number is the number of years in the initial rate adjustment period, and the second number means that subsequent rate adjustments will occur once a year. Some borrowers who choose hybrid ARMs intend to sell or refinance their home before the end of the initial adjustment period. As a general rule, the longer the initial adjustment period, the higher the initial interest rate. But the initial rate will still be lower than the rate for a comparable fixed-rate loan.

Mortgage payment adjustment period. An ARM's mortgage payment adjustment period determines when the lender changes the amount of the borrower's monthly payment to reflect a change in the interest rate charged on the loan. For most ARMs, the payment adjustment period coincides with the interest rate adjustment period. In that case, when the lender increases the interest rate on the loan, the payment amount immediately goes up as well. And when the lender decreases the loan's interest rate, the payment amount immediately goes down.

Rate caps. ARM borrowers may run the risk of "payment shock." Payment shock occurs when a borrower's monthly payment amount increases so much that she can no longer afford the payments. This could happen to an ARM borrower if there is a sharp jump in market interest rates, or if market rates keep rising steadily over an extended period.

To help borrowers avoid payment shock, lenders generally include interest rate caps in their ARMs. A rate cap limits how much the interest rate on the loan can go up, regardless of what its index does. Limiting interest rate increases prevents the monthly payment from increasing too much.

Many ARMs have two kinds of rate caps. One limits the amount that the interest rate can increase in any one adjustment period. The other limits the amount that the interest rate can increase over the entire life of the loan. Common rate caps are 2% per year and 6% over the life of the loan.

Payment cap. A mortgage payment cap serves the same purpose as a rate cap: limiting how much the borrower's monthly mortgage payment can increase. A payment cap directly limits how much the lender can raise the monthly mort-

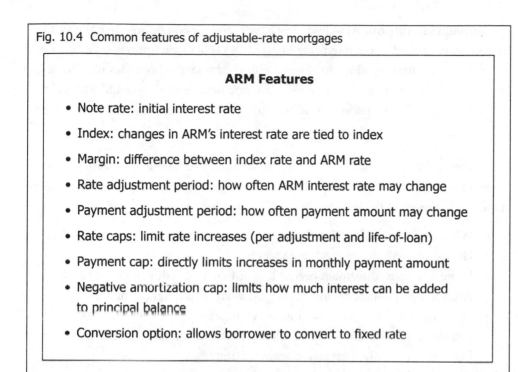

Fig. 10.4 Common features of adjustable-rate mortgages

ARM Features

- Note rate: initial interest rate
- Index: changes in ARM's interest rate are tied to index
- Margin: difference between index rate and ARM rate
- Rate adjustment period: how often ARM interest rate may change
- Payment adjustment period: how often payment amount may change
- Rate caps: limit rate increases (per adjustment and life-of-loan)
- Payment cap: directly limits increases in monthly payment amount
- Negative amortization cap: limits how much interest can be added to principal balance
- Conversion option: allows borrower to convert to fixed rate

gage payment, regardless of what is happening to the mortgage interest rate. For example, a payment cap might limit payment increases to 7.5% annually. However, a payment cap unaccompanied by a rate cap can lead to negative amortization. We'll discuss that issue next.

Negative amortization cap. If an ARM has a payment cap but no rate cap, payment increases don't always keep up with increases in the loan's interest rate. The same thing can happen if the payment adjustment period differs from the rate adjustment period. As a result, the monthly payments don't cover the full amount of the interest that has accrued. So the lender adds the unpaid interest to the loan's principal balance. This is called **negative amortization**. A loan's principal balance ordinarily declines steadily over the loan term, but negative amortization makes the balance go up instead of down. The borrower can end up owing the lender more money than the original loan amount.

A negative amortization cap limits the amount of unpaid interest that can be added to the principal balance. A typical negative amortization cap limits the total amount a borrower can owe to 110% of the original loan amount (although caps can be as high as 125%). Most ARMs today are structured to prevent negative amortization in the first place.

Conversion option. An ARM may have a conversion option that allows the borrower to convert it to a fixed-rate loan. Most conversion options give the borrower a limited time in which to convert. For example, the borrower may be able to convert the ARM to a fixed-rate loan anytime between the first and fifth year of the loan term. Conversion is usually considerably less expensive than refinancing the loan.

ARM Checklist. Adjustable-rate loans are complicated. A buyer considering an ARM needs to know the answers to the following questions. If she doesn't understand some aspect of the loan, she should ask the lender for clarification.

- What will my initial interest rate be?
- How often will my interest rate change?
- Is the first rate adjustment period longer than later adjustment periods?
- Are there any limits on how much my interest rate can be increased?
- How often will my payment amount change?
- Are there any limits on how much my payment can be increased?
- Does my ARM allow negative amortization?
- Can my ARM be converted to a fixed-rate loan?

Conventional Loans

Now let's turn our attention to loan programs. Loans made by institutional lenders (such as banks, savings and loans, or mortgage companies) can be divided into two main categories: conventional loans and government-sponsored loans. A **conventional loan** is any institutional loan that is not insured or guaranteed by a government agency. For example, a loan made by a commercial bank and insured by a private mortgage insurance company is a conventional loan. A loan that is insured by the FHA (Federal Housing Administration) or guaranteed by the VA (Department of Veterans Affairs) is not a conventional loan. We'll discuss conventional loan programs first, and then we'll look at government loan programs.

Conventional Loans and the Secondary Market

Lenders sometimes make conventional "portfolio" loans. A portfolio loan is one that the lender plans on keeping in its own portfolio of investments, as opposed to selling it on the secondary market. With some limitations, portfolio loans can be made according to the lender's own underwriting standards.

However, lenders generally want to have the option of selling their loans on the secondary market instead of keeping them in portfolio. Conventional loans are much easier to sell if the lender makes them in accordance with the underwriting standards and other rules set by the major secondary market entities, Fannie Mae (the Federal National Mortgage Association) and Freddie Mac (the Federal Home Loan Mortgage Corporation). Loans that conform to the rules of Fannie Mae and/or Freddie Mac are called **conforming loans**; by contrast, loans that don't meet Fannie Mae or Freddie Mac's standards are **nonconforming loans**. Because the standards of the secondary market entities have been very influential, our discussion of conventional loan programs is primarily based on rules set by Fannie Mae and Freddie Mac.

Characteristics of Conventional Loans

A conventional loan's characteristics are determined by rules concerning loan amounts, loan-to-value ratios, private mortgage insurance, risk-based loan fees, secondary financing, prepayment penalties, and assumption.

Conventional Loan Amounts. In order for a loan to be eligible for purchase by Fannie Mae or Freddie Mac, the loan amount must not exceed the applicable **conforming loan limit**. Conforming loan limits for dwellings with one, two, three, or four units are set by the Federal Housing Finance Agency (the agency that oversees the secondary market entities) based on median housing prices nationwide. The limits may be adjusted annually to reflect changes in median housing prices.

For 2015, the conforming loan limit for single-family homes and other one-unit dwellings in most parts of the country is $417,000. In high-cost areas—areas where housing is more expensive—there are higher limits based on area median housing prices, up to a maximum of $625,500. (Special limits apply in Alaska, Hawaii, Guam, and the Virgin Islands, where housing is exceptionally expensive. The 2015 maximum for high-cost loans in these places is $938,250.)

Although they're generally ineligible for sale to the major secondary market entities, conventional loans that exceed the conforming loan limits are also available in many areas. For these larger loans, sometimes called **jumbo loans**, lenders are likely to charge higher interest rates and fees and apply stricter underwriting standards.

Conventional LTVs. A mortgage loan for 80% of the property's sales price or appraised value is generally regarded as a very safe investment for the lender. The 20% downpayment gives the borrower a substantial incentive to avoid default, and if foreclosure becomes necessary, the lender is likely to recover the full amount owed.

At one time, 80% was the standard loan-to-value ratio for a conventional loan. That started changing in the 1980s. More and more lenders became comfortable making conventional loans with higher LTVs. By the late 1990s, high-LTV loans had become more common than 80% loans. Lenders routinely made conventional loans with LTVs up to 95%, requiring only a 5% downpayment.

By the 2000s, some lenders were even making 100% conventional loans, allowing the borrowers to put no money down. In 2007 and 2008, when home values began dropping around the country, many high-LTV borrowers who had started out with little or no equity suddenly had "negative equity." In other words, they owed their lenders more than their homes were worth. If borrowers in that situation could no longer afford to pay their mortgages, they often lost their homes to foreclosure, and their lenders often incurred serious losses. As we discussed in the previous chapter, a nationwide foreclosure crisis developed. Because of the crisis, conventional loans with LTVs over 95% are no longer common, although some lenders still offer them through special programs. (See the discussion of low-downpayment programs later in this chapter.)

Conventional loans with loan-to-value ratios up to 95% are still available, however. Applicants for conventional loans with LTVs over 90% typically must meet stricter qualifying standards than they'd have to for a lower-LTV loan, and they can expect to pay a higher interest rate and higher loan fees. Some lenders also require these loans to have a fixed interest rate, because the unpredictability of changes in the interest rate and monthly payment amount of an adjustable-rate mortgage makes default more likely with an ARM than with a fixed-rate loan.

Private Mortgage Insurance. With a conventional loan, if the downpayment is less than 20% of the property's value, the lender requires the borrower to purchase private mortgage insurance (PMI). The mortgage insurance protects the lender against the additional risk that a higher loan-to-value ratio represents. Fannie Mae and Freddie Mac both require PMI on all conventional loans they purchase that have loan-to-value ratios greater than 80%.

With PMI, the mortgage insurance company insures the lender against losses that might result if the borrower defaults on the loan. The mortgage insurance covers only the upper portion of the loan amount—for example, it might cover the upper 25%. In this way, the insurance company assumes only part of the risk of loss rather than the entire risk.

Example: Wilson is buying a $400,000 home. She's financing the purchase with a $360,000 loan, so the loan-to-value ratio is 90%. Because the LTV is over 80%, the lender requires Wilson to purchase PMI. In exchange for the PMI premiums, the mortgage insurance company insures the top 25% of the loan amount, or $90,000. The insurance company is assuming the risk that the lender may lose up to $90,000 on a foreclosure sale in the event that Wilson defaults.

If the borrower defaults on a loan covered by PMI, the lender has two options. The lender can foreclose on the property, and if the foreclosure sale results in a loss, file a claim with the insurance company to cover the loss, up to the policy amount. Or the lender can simply relinquish the property to the insurer and make a claim for actual losses up to the policy amount. Most lenders choose the first option.

Premiums. The premiums for private mortgage insurance can be paid by the lender or another party, but they are usually paid by the borrower. (As in the example above, the lender requires the borrower to purchase the insurance as a condition of making the loan.) Mortgage insurers offer various payment plans, such as:

- a flat monthly premium amount added to the monthly mortgage payment;
- an initial premium paid at closing, plus annual renewal premiums; or
- a one-time premium paid at closing or financed along with the loan amount.

Cancellation of PMI. If all goes well, the borrower will gradually pay off the principal. And unless the property depreciates in value, the loan-to-value ratio will decrease as the principal balance goes down. Eventually the mortgage insurance should no longer be necessary.

A federal law called the Homeowners Protection Act requires lenders to cancel a conventional loan's PMI and refund any unearned premium to the borrower once certain conditions are met.

Here are the basic rules for standard loans covered by PMI (different rules apply to loans classified as high-risk and outside standard guidelines):

- The lender must automatically cancel the PMI when the loan's principal balance is scheduled to reach 78% of the home's original value, unless the borrower is delinquent on the payments.
- The borrower may send the lender a written request to cancel the PMI earlier, when the principal balance is scheduled to reach 80% of the original value. The request must be granted if the borrower's payment history is good, the value of the home has not decreased, and the borrower has not taken out any other loans on the home.

The Homeowners Protection Act requires lenders to send all borrowers with private mortgage insurance an annual notice concerning their PMI cancellation rights.

Risk-based Loan Fees. Conventional borrowers are nearly always expected to pay an origination fee, and they may also agree to pay discount points. In addition, if their loan is going to be sold to Fannie Mae or Freddie Mac, they will probably be charged one or more **loan-level price adjustments** (LLPAs), which the lender will pass on to the borrower. Loan-level price adjustments shift some of the risk (that is, the cost) of mortgage default to the borrower. As a general rule, the riskier the loan, the more the borrower is required to pay in LLPAs.

Nearly all loans sold to the secondary market entities are subject to an LLPA. The amount of the LLPA varies depending on the borrower's credit score and the loan-to-value ratio; the riskier the loan, the larger the LLPA. For instance, a borrower with a credit score of 650 and an 80% loan-to-value ratio might be required to pay an LLPA of 2.50% of the loan amount at closing, while a borrower with a credit score of 710 and a 90% loan might be charged only 1.00%.

There are also LLPAs for certain types of transactions that involve more risk, such as investor loans and loans with secondary financing. One or more of these other LLPAs may be charged in addition to the one that's based on the credit score and loan-to-value ratio.

Secondary Financing and Conventional Loans. Secondary financing can be used in conjunction with a conventional loan, but most lenders require a series of rules to be met. These rules are designed to keep the borrower from overextending himself, thus reducing the risk that he will default on the primary loan. For example, a second loan generally isn't allowed to have a repayment period of less than five years. This prevents the second lender from requiring the borrower to make a balloon payment during the first five years after closing, when the risk of default on the primary loan is the greatest. If your buyer is interested in secondary financing, he should check with the lender to find out what types of secondary financing arrangements are acceptable.

Prepayment Penalties. Some mortgage loan agreements allow the lender to charge the borrower a prepayment penalty if the borrower pays off all of the principal, or a substantial portion of it, before it is due. A prepayment penalty is not considered a standard provision in a conventional loan. However, some lenders offer reduced loan fees or a lower interest rate in exchange for including a prepayment penalty provision in the loan agreement. While this can be a reasonable arrangement, the borrower should carefully consider the consequences before agreeing to a prepayment penalty.

California law places some restrictions on prepayment penalties for loans secured by owner-occupied residential property with up to four units. For these loans, the lender may charge prepayment penalties only during the first five years of the loan term. There is also a limit on the amount of the prepayment penalties that may be charged during those first five years. When the loan is made, the lender must give the borrower a written disclosure calling attention to the prepayment penalty provision and explaining the conditions under which the penalty will be charged.

The federal Dodd-Frank Act of 2010 also imposed restrictions on prepayment penalties. These restrictions apply to loans secured by a dwelling with up to four units. A prepayment penalty is prohibited if the loan has an adjustable interest rate or if it meets the definition of a "higher-priced" loan (if the fees charged exceed average loan costs by a certain amount). For other loans secured by a dwelling, a prepayment penalty can be charged only during the first three years of the loan term, and the amount of the penalty is also limited.

Assumption. A conventional loan usually includes a due-on-sale clause (alienation clause), which means the loan can be assumed only with the lender's permission. The lender will evaluate the new buyers to make sure they are creditworthy. The buyers will be expected to pay an assumption fee, and the lender may also raise the interest rate on the loan.

Underwriting Conventional Loans

Now let's look at the underwriting guidelines Fannie Mae and Freddie Mac require lenders to follow in qualifying a buyer for a conforming conventional loan.

Fannie Mae treats the applicant's credit reputation, as reflected in his credit score, as one of two primary risk factors. The other is the cash investment the applicant will be making, measured by the loan-to-value ratio. Based on the credit score and the LTV, a proposed loan is ranked as having a low, moderate, or high primary risk, and that ranking determines the level of review applied to the rest of the loan application. Fannie Mae treats the other aspects of the application, such as the applicant's debt to income ratio and cash reserves, as contributory risk factors that may increase or decrease the risk of default.

Freddie Mac's approach involves a separate evaluation of each of the main components of creditworthiness—credit reputation, capacity to repay (income and net worth), and collateral (the value of the property)—and an evaluation of the "overall layering of risk." This means that strength in one component of the application may compensate for weakness in another. But even if each of the main components seems acceptable on its own, the combined risk factors in the application as a whole may amount to excessive layering of risk. In that case, the loan should be denied.

The differences between Freddie Mac's approach and Fannie Mae's aren't as great as they may sound; there's a lot of common ground. In both, each aspect of the application is to be considered as part of the overall picture, and negative factors may be offset by positive ones.

Credit Scores. Both Fannie Mae and Freddie Mac expect lenders to use applicants' credit scores as a key tool in evaluating creditworthiness. In addition, as explained earlier, credit scores are used in determining the risk-based loan fees (loan-level price adjustments) that borrowers will be charged. Fannie Mae will not purchase loans made to borrowers with credit scores below 620. Freddie Mac will consider scores below 620, though some programs may require higher scores. Borrowers with lower scores are charged higher fees.

Income Ratios. As with any type of residential mortgage loan, the first step in the income analysis for a conventional loan is calculating the applicant's stable monthly income. (See Chapter 9.) The next step is measuring the adequacy of the stable monthly income using income ratios. Both Fannie Mae and Freddie Mac require lenders to use the first ratio we'll talk about: the debt to income ratio.

The debt to income ratio measures the relationship between the loan applicant's monthly income and his total monthly debt. The total monthly debt is made up of the proposed housing expense (which includes PITI: principal, interest, property taxes, hazard insurance, and any mortgage insurance or homeowners association dues), plus any other recurring liabilities. These other recurring liabilities fall into three categories:

- installment debts (which have a definite beginning and ending date and fixed monthly payments);
- revolving debts (such as credit card payments); and
- other obligations (such as child support or spousal support).

Note that an installment debt usually counts as part of the applicant's total monthly debt only if there are more than ten payments remaining.

Example: George has applied for a conventional loan. Among other debts, he has a student loan that requires payments of $108 per month. However, he only has to make ten more payments to pay off the loan. As a result, the $108 payment won't be included in George's total monthly debt.

That rule also applies to child support or spousal support (alimony): if the required payments will end in ten months or less, they don't count as part of the loan applicant's total monthly debt.

There is an exception to the ten-payment rule, however. Even if there are no more than ten payments remaining on a debt, if the payment amount is large enough to potentially interfere with the borrower's ability to pay the mortgage, then the debt should be counted in calculating the debt to income ratio.

The standard or benchmark debt to income ratio for conventional loans is 36%. In other words, a loan applicant's income is generally considered adequate for a conventional loan if the total monthly debt does not exceed 36% of the applicant's stable monthly income.

Example: The Browns' stable monthly income is $4,800. Their monthly debts include a $40 minimum payment on a credit card, a $250 car loan payment, and a $150 personal loan payment.

To estimate how large a mortgage payment the Browns might qualify for if they apply for a conventional loan, first multiply $4,800 by 36%. $4,800 × .36 = $1,728. The benchmark 36% debt to income ratio would allow them to have up to $1,728 in total monthly debt, including their housing expense.

Now subtract the Browns' monthly payments on their debts from that figure: $1,728 − $40 charge card payment − $250 car loan payment − $150 personal loan payment = $1,288. So $1,288 is the maximum monthly housing expense that the Browns could qualify for under the 36% debt to income ratio guideline.

Freddie Mac guidelines also call for lenders to consider the loan applicant's housing expense to income ratio. The proposed housing expense generally should not exceed 28% of the applicant's stable monthly income.

Example: Let's go back to the Browns' situation. Their stable monthly income is $4,800. To apply the housing expense to income ratio, multiply $4,800 by 28%, or .28. $4,800 × .28 = $1,344. So $1,344 is the maximum housing expense the Browns could qualify for under the 28% housing expense to income ratio guideline.

The maximum housing expense figure arrived at with the debt to income ratio is compared to the one arrived at with the housing expense to income ratio, and the smaller of the two figures is treated as the maximum allowable housing expense. In our example, the Browns' maximum housing expense would be $1,288 (the figure indicated by the debt to income ratio) rather than $1,344.

It's important to understand that both Fannie Mae and Freddie Mac consider their income ratios as benchmarks or guidelines rather than rigid limits. They may be willing to purchase a loan even though the borrower's debt to income ratio exceeds 36%, as long as there are compensating factors that justify making the loan in spite of the higher income ratio. For example, one or more of the following factors (especially the first one) might offset the extra risk:

- a large downpayment;
- substantial net worth;
- demonstrated ability to incur few debts and accumulate savings;
- demonstrated ability to devote extra income to housing expenses;
- education, job training, or employment history that indicates strong potential for increased earnings; or
- significant energy-efficient features in the home being purchased.

On the other hand, when a proposed loan would involve other factors that represent increased rather than decreased risk, then a debt to income ratio in excess of 36% is generally unacceptable. For example, many lenders would be unwilling to accept a high debt to income ratio for a loan with a loan-to-value ratio over 90% or for an adjustable-rate loan.

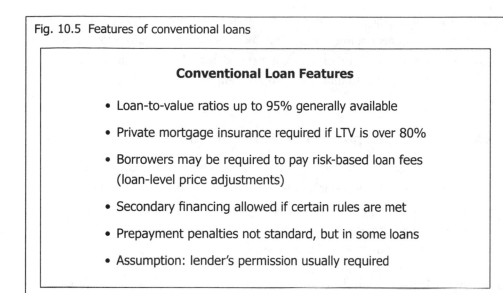

Fig. 10.5 Features of conventional loans

Conventional Loan Features

- Loan-to-value ratios up to 95% generally available

- Private mortgage insurance required if LTV is over 80%

- Borrowers may be required to pay risk-based loan fees (loan-level price adjustments)

- Secondary financing allowed if certain rules are met

- Prepayment penalties not standard, but in some loans

- Assumption: lender's permission usually required

When compensating factors make it acceptable to have a debt to income ratio over 36%, how much higher than the benchmark can the ratio be? If the loan application is manually underwritten, neither Fannie Mae nor Freddie Mac will accept a debt to income ratio over 45%, no matter how many compensating factors are present. If the application is submitted to an automated underwriting system, there's no set maximum; the AUS will analyze whether the high ratio is acceptable in the context of the overall default risk that the application presents.

Reserves. Conventional loan applicants generally should have the equivalent of at least two months of mortgage payments in reserve after making the down-payment and paying all closing costs. That's not necessarily treated as a strict requirement, but less than that in reserve will weaken an application, and more will strengthen it. Some lenders do require at least two months of reserves, and some require even more for riskier loans. For example, a lender might require three months of reserves for a 95% loan. The reserves must be cash or liquid assets that could easily be converted to cash if necessary (for example, the cash value of a life insurance policy, or the vested portion of a retirement account).

Gift Funds. Lenders also apply a number of rules regarding the use of gift funds to close a transaction financed with a conventional loan. The donor usually must be someone who has a particular connection with the borrower—for example, a family member, fiancé, or employer. A nonprofit organization or a municipality may also be an acceptable donor. The donor is usually required to sign a gift letter to confirm that the funds are a gift and not a loan. And in some cases the borrower is required to make a downpayment of at least 5% out of her own funds.

Making Conventional Loans More Affordable

Sometimes a buyer can't qualify for a standard fixed-rate loan and wouldn't be comfortable with an adjustable-rate loan. There are quite a few other options that can make a conventional loan more affordable. These include buydowns, low-downpayment programs, programs targeted at low-income borrowers or low-income neighborhoods, and loans with lower initial payments.

Buydown Plans. One of the easiest ways to make a loan less expensive is with a buydown. A buydown lowers the borrower's monthly payment and can make it easier to qualify for the loan. When the loan is made, the seller or a third party pays the lender a lump sum that is used to reduce the borrower's payments either early in the loan term or throughout the loan term.

A buydown has the same effect as discount points (mentioned earlier in the chapter). The lump sum payment at closing increases the lender's upfront yield on the loan, and in return the lender charges a lower interest rate, which lowers the amount of the borrower's monthly mortgage payment. But a buydown is typically proposed to the lender by the parties; unlike ordinary discount points, it's not a component of the lender's initial rate quote.

Note that when a seller agrees to pay for a buydown, he doesn't have to come up with cash to do so. The amount of the buydown is simply deducted from the seller's net proceeds at closing and transferred to the lender. As you might expect, buydowns are especially popular when market interest rates are high.

A buydown can be permanent or temporary. With a permanent buydown, the borrower pays the lower interest rate (and a lower monthly payment) for the entire loan term. With a temporary buydown, the interest rate and the monthly payment are reduced only during the first years of the loan term.

Permanent buydowns. If a borrower's interest rate is bought down permanently, the buydown reduces the note rate, which is the interest rate stated in the promissory note. The cost of a permanent buydown depends on how much the interest rate is reduced; the greater the rate reduction, the higher the cost.

Example: Bowen needs to borrow $150,000 to buy Sanderson's property. The lender quoted a 10% interest rate, and Bowen can't quite qualify for the loan at that rate. Sanderson offers to buy down Bowen's interest rate by 1% to help her qualify for the loan.

Based on market conditions, the lender estimates it will take about six points to increase the yield on a 30-year loan by 1%. So the lender agrees to make the buydown for six points, or 6% of the loan amount. To determine how much the buydown will cost Sanderson, multiply the loan amount by 6%. $150,000 × .06 = $9,000. At closing, the lender will withhold $9,000 from the loan funds, reducing Sanderson's proceeds from the sale.

The 1% buydown will reduce Bowen's mortgage payment by more than $100 per month, enabling her to qualify for the loan. The lender will charge Bowen 9% interest instead of 10% throughout the 30-year loan term, which will save Bowen nearly $39,400 over the life of the loan. In that way, the buydown is of much greater value to Bowen than simply reducing the purchase price by $9,000 (although a lower purchase price might have meant a somewhat smaller downpayment).

As the example indicates, the cost of a buydown is affected by market conditions, including market interest rates and the average time loans are outstanding before they are paid off. The amount that the lender will actually charge should be confirmed before the parties sign an agreement.

Temporary buydowns. A temporary buydown reduces the buyer's monthly payment in the early years of the loan. Temporary buydowns appeal to buyers who believe they can grow into a larger payment, but need time to get established. They also cost sellers less than permanent buydowns.

There are two types of temporary buydown plans: level payment and graduated payment. A level payment plan calls for an interest reduction that stays the same throughout the buydown period. For example, a seller might buy a buyer's interest rate down by 2% for two years. The buyer would pay the lower interest rate during the first two years, and then the lender would begin charging the note rate at the start of the third year.

With a graduated payment plan, the interest rate reduction changes at set points during the buydown period. For example, one graduated payment plan is the 3-2-1 buydown. It calls for a 3% reduction in the interest rate during the first year, 2% during the second year, and 1% during the third year. The lender begins charging the note rate in the fourth year. This gives the buyer a chance to get used to higher payments gradually.

With a temporary buydown, because the buyer will eventually have to afford a larger payment based on the full note rate, the lender will not be willing to qualify the buyer at the buydown rate. Instead, the lender will usually qualify the buyer based on the note rate. Special rules apply for adjustable-rate loans.

Limits on buydowns and other contributions. Fannie Mae and Freddie Mac limit the financial contributions a buyer may accept from the seller or another interested party, such as the builder or a real estate agent involved in the transaction. The contributions can't exceed a certain percentage of the property's sales price or appraised value, whichever is less. These limits apply to buydowns, to payment of closing costs customarily paid by the buyer, and to similar contributions.

Low-Downpayment Programs. For many potential home buyers, especially first-time buyers, coming up with enough cash is the biggest challenge in buying a home. They have a steady, reliable income, but they don't have the savings to cover the downpayment, closing costs, and reserves required for a standard conventional loan. Even the 5% downpayment required for a 95% loan may be beyond their means. Buyers in this situation may want to consider special programs that have reduced cash requirements and allow them to draw on alternative sources for the cash they need.

The details of these programs vary. But here are examples of the types of loans that buyers can look for:

- A loan with a 95% LTV that requires a 3% downpayment from the borrower's own funds, with 2% from alternative sources.
- A loan with a 97% LTV that requires a 3% downpayment from the borrower's own funds, plus a 3% contribution to closing costs that may come from alternative sources.

Depending on the program, the allowable alternative sources of funds may include gifts, grants, or unsecured loans. The funds may come from a relative, an employer, a public agency, a nonprofit organization, or a private foundation. More than one source may be tapped to get the necessary funds together.

Some of these programs don't require the borrower to have any reserves after closing. Others require only one month's mortgage payment in reserve.

Targeted programs. Although some conventional low-downpayment programs are open to any prospective home buyer, many are targeted at low- and moderate-income buyers. As a general rule, a buyer can qualify for one of these targeted programs if his stable monthly income does not exceed the median income in the metropolitan area in question. (An increased income limit applies in a high-cost area such as San Francisco.) To make it even easier for low- and moderate-income buyers to get a mortgage, these programs may allow a debt to income ratio of 38% or even 40% without compensating factors, and may have no maximum housing expense to income ratio.

To encourage neighborhood revitalization, the targeted programs often waive their income limits for buyers who are purchasing homes in low-income or run-down neighborhoods. Thus, a buyer whose income is well above the area median could still qualify for a targeted low-downpayment program if she's buying a home in a neighborhood that meets the program's standards.

Other conventional low-downpayment programs are offered to specific groups such as teachers, police officers, and firefighters. These programs are intended to enable the borrowers to purchase homes in the urban communities they serve, instead of being priced out into the suburbs.

Loans with Lower Initial Payments. Some borrowers have adequate funds for a downpayment, but don't have enough income to qualify for a loan with high monthly payments. If these borrowers expect their income to increase steadily (for example, perhaps they're young adults just starting out on their careers), so that they'll be able to grow into larger payments later on, they might be able to afford a more expensive home by getting a loan with lower initial payments.

We've already discussed some types of loans that fall into this category. One is the hybrid ARM, an adjustable-rate mortgage with a two-tiered rate adjustment schedule, such as a 5/1 ARM: the interest rate and payment amount start out lower than the rate and payment for a fixed-rate loan, and they don't change during the first five years; the lender makes annual adjustments after that.

Another option (also discussed earlier) is the type of interest-only loan where the borrower pays only interest on the principal during the early years of the term, and later must start making amortized payments that will pay off the balance by the end of the term. This switch will cause the monthly payment amount to rise considerably.

Over the years lenders have offered a variety of other types of loans with lower initial payments. For example, a **graduated payment mortgage** (GPM) is set up so that the payments are low to begin with, increase by a certain amount each year for the first three or five years of the loan term, and then stay level after that. Another example is the **two-step mortgage**: the interest rate adjusts to the market rate at one point (usually at the five- or seven-year mark), but there are no further adjustments; the payments stay level for the rest of the term.

Fig. 10.6 Making conventional loans more affordable

Conventional Affordability Plans and Programs

- Buydowns: permanent or temporary
- Low-downpayment programs
  - typically allow LTVs up to 97%
  - borrower may use some funds from alternative sources
  - targeted programs: low- or moderate-income
    buyers, or neighborhoods that need revitalization
- Low initial payment programs

Most of these options aren't widely used today, however. In the wake of the foreclosure crisis, lenders tend to be leery of loans where the payment amount may increase sharply and create the risk of payment shock; interest-only loans fell into particular disfavor as a result of the crisis. Hybrid ARMs, such as the 5/1, satisfy most of the demand today for loans with low initial payments.

Government-Sponsored Loan Programs

Now let's turn to government-sponsored mortgage loan programs. The two major programs established by the federal government are the FHA-insured loan program and the VA-guaranteed loan program. In California, the state government also sponsors the Cal-Vet program. We'll look at each of these in turn, and also discuss Rural Housing Service loans.

FHA-Insured Loans

The federal government created the Federal Housing Administration (FHA) in 1934, during the Great Depression, to help people with low and moderate incomes buy homes. For much of the twentieth century, the FHA-insured loan program was the main source of low-downpayment mortgage loans for U.S. home buyers. FHA loans continue to play an important role in residential lending.

The FHA is an agency within the U.S. Department of Housing and Urban Development. The FHA does not make loans; it insures loans made by banks and other institutional lenders. In effect, the FHA is a giant mortgage insurance agency. Its insurance program, the Mutual Mortgage Insurance Plan, is funded with premiums paid by FHA borrowers. If a lender that makes an FHA-insured loan suffers a loss because the borrower defaults, the FHA will compensate the lender for its loss.

In exchange for insuring a loan, the FHA regulates most of the loan's terms and conditions. The FHA has various programs for specific types of mortgage loans, such as home rehabilitation loans and energy efficiency loans. But the central program for single-family home purchase loans is the 203(b) program. The rules we'll be discussing here apply to loans made through the 203(b) program.

Characteristics of FHA Loans. Here are some of the key characteristics of FHA loans:

- Although FHA programs are intended to help home buyers with low or moderate incomes, there are no maximum income limits. (Instead, the maximum loan amount rules ensure that FHA loans can generally only be used to purchase relatively modest homes.)
- An FHA loan requires a comparatively small downpayment, and the loan fees and other charges may be lower than they would be for a typical conventional loan. Overall, an FHA borrower may need significantly less cash for closing.
- FHA loan amounts can't exceed specified maximums that are based on median housing prices. In some areas, the FHA maximum loan amounts are considerably lower than the maximums for conforming conventional loans.
- The qualifying standards for an FHA loan are not as strict as those for a standard conventional loan.
- The property purchased with an FHA loan may have up to four dwelling units. The borrowers must intend to occupy one of the units as their primary residence. The FHA does not insure loans made to investors, as opposed to owner-occupants.
- If there are any other mortgage liens against the property, the FHA loan must have first lien position.
- The interest rate on an FHA loan may be fixed or adjustable.
- Most FHA loans have 30-year terms, although 15-year loans are also available. (However, if the interest rate is adjustable, the term must be 30 years.)
- In addition to an origination fee, an FHA borrower may be charged discount points, which can be paid by either the borrower or the property seller.

- Mortgage insurance is required on all FHA loans.
- FHA loans never call for a prepayment penalty. They can be paid off at any time with no penalty.

FHA Loan Amounts. The loan amount for a transaction financed with an FHA loan can't exceed the local limit that applies in the area where the property is located. Local limits are based on median housing prices and tied to the conforming loan limits for conventional loans. They may be adjusted annually.

For 2015, the FHA maximum loan amount for single-family homes and other one-unit dwellings is generally $271,050, but it can be as much as $625,500 in high-cost areas. (There are special limits for Alaska, Hawaii, Guam, and the Virgin Islands.)

Loan-to-value ratios. The loan amount for a particular transaction is determined not just by the FHA loan ceiling for the local area, but also by the FHA's rules concerning loan-to-value ratios. The maximum LTV for an FHA loan depends on the borrower's credit score. If the borrower's credit score is 580 or above, the maximum LTV is 96.5%. If his score is 500 to 579, the maximum LTV is 90%. Someone with a score below 500 isn't eligible for an FHA loan.

Minimum Cash Investment. The difference between the maximum loan amount and the appraised value or sales price (whichever is less) is called the borrower's **minimum cash investment**. In effect, this is the required downpayment for an FHA loan. In a transaction with maximum financing (a 96.5% LTV), the borrower must make a minimum cash investment of 3.5%. Closing costs, discount points, and prepaid expenses (interim interest on the loan and impounds for taxes and insurance) don't count toward the minimum cash investment.

FHA Insurance Premiums. The mortgage insurance premiums for FHA loans are called the MIP. Usually, an FHA borrower pays both a one-time premium and annual premiums.

Upfront premium. The one-time premium is called the **upfront MIP**. Either the borrower or the seller can pay the upfront premium in cash at closing. The borrower also has the option of financing the upfront premium over the loan term. When the upfront premium is financed, it's simply added to the base loan amount (the amount determined by the maximum loan amount and minimum cash investment rules). The monthly payments are then set to pay off the total amount financed by the end of the loan term. When the upfront premium is financed in this way, the total loan amount (the base loan amount plus the upfront premium) can't exceed 100% of the property's appraised value. The current upfront insurance premium is 1.75% of the loan amount.

Annual premium. In addition to the upfront MIP, an annual premium is also required for most FHA loans. The annual premium ranges from .45% to 1.05% of the loan balance, depending on the base loan amount, loan term, and LTV. For loans with an original LTV of over 90%, the borrower must pay the annual MIP for the entire loan term. For loans with an original LTV of 90% or less, the annual MIP will be canceled after 11 years. Even if the annual premium is canceled, the mortgage insurance policy will remain in force for the full term of the loan.

Seller Contributions. As you've seen, to make the home more affordable, sometimes a seller agrees to buy down the buyer's interest rate. Or the seller might help pay all or part of the buyer's closing costs or discount points. When the sale is financed with an FHA loan, contributions from the seller—or from another interested party, such as a real estate broker—may not exceed 6% of the sales price or the appraised value, whichever is less. Any amount over that limit must be subtracted from the sales price before calculating the loan-to-value ratio and minimum cash investment.

Secondary Financing. An FHA borrower is allowed to use secondary financing. In fact, the amount of the first and second mortgages added together can exceed the FHA's local loan ceiling, so in some cases secondary financing makes it possible to buy a more expensive house. As a general rule, however, the combined loan-to-value ratio can't exceed the FHA's maximum allowable LTV. That means secondary financing ordinarily can't be used for the minimum cash investment. (There are exceptions to this rule when the secondary financing is provided by a family member, a nonprofit, or a governmental agency, or when the borrower is 60 or older.)

A number of other restrictions apply to secondary financing supplementing an FHA loan. For example, the second loan can't require a balloon payment within a certain number of years after closing, and it can't have a prepayment penalty.

Underwriting FHA Loans. Qualifying a buyer for an FHA loan involves essentially the same steps as conventional underwriting: the lender analyzes the applicant's income, net worth, and credit reputation. But the FHA's underwriting standards are not as strict as the standards used for conventional loans. The less stringent FHA standards make it easier for low- and moderate-income buyers to qualify for a mortgage.

Income ratios. The FHA's term for stable monthly income is **effective income**. An FHA loan applicant's effective income is his monthly gross income from all sources that can be expected to continue for the first three years of the loan term.

Two ratios are applied to evaluate the adequacy of the applicant's effective income. These are the fixed payment to income ratio (which is essentially another term for the debt to income ratio) and the housing expense to income ratio. As a general rule, an FHA loan applicant's fixed payment to income ratio may not exceed 43%. In addition, the applicant's housing expense to income ratio generally may not exceed 31%. The applicant must qualify under both ratios.

The fixed payment to income ratio takes into account the proposed monthly housing expense plus all recurring monthly charges. The housing expense includes principal and interest (based on the total amount financed), property taxes, hazard insurance, one-twelfth of the annual premium for the FHA mortgage insurance, and any dues owed to a homeowners association. Recurring monthly charges include the monthly payments on any debt with ten or more payments remaining. Alimony and child support payments, installment debt payments, and payments on revolving credit accounts are all counted.

Example: Miriam is applying for an FHA loan. She has a reliable monthly salary of $2,750. She also receives $740 a month in Social Security payments for her young children, which began when their father died three years ago. Miriam's effective income totals $3,490 a month. She pays the following monthly recurring charges: a $235 car payment, a $50 minimum MasterCard payment, and a $125 personal loan payment.

To get a general idea of how large a house payment Miriam can qualify for with FHA financing, use the FHA's two income ratios. First multiply her effective income by 43% to see how much she can spend per month on her total monthly obligations. $3,490 × .43 = $1,501. Then subtract her recurring monthly charges from her maximum total monthly obligations. $1,501 − $235 car payment − $50 MasterCard payment − $125 personal loan payment = $1,091. Miriam could qualify for a $1,091 monthly housing expense under the debt to income ratio.

Next, apply the housing expense to income ratio by multiplying Miriam's effective income by 31%. $3,490 × .31 = $1,082. So $1,082 is the maximum monthly housing expense Miriam could qualify for under this ratio. Since Miriam must qualify under both ratios, $1,082 is her maximum monthly housing expense for an FHA loan.

If a loan applicant's income ratios exceed the 43% and 31% limits, he might not qualify for an FHA loan. However, the loan can be approved if there are compensating factors that will reduce the risk of default. For example, if the applicant has a conservative attitude toward credit and has at least three months' mortgage payments in reserve after closing, the underwriter could approve the loan in spite of a debt to income ratio over 43%. If a loan applicant's debt to income ratio exceeds 43% and the applicant's credit score is below 620, the FHA requires the application to be manually underwritten. The underwriter will document the compensating factors taken into account in the underwriting process.

A temporary buydown can be used with an FHA loan, as long as the loan has a fixed interest rate. However, the underwriter will use the note rate to qualify the borrower. So even if the interest rate on the loan were bought down from 4% to 3% for the first two years of the loan term, the buyer would still be required to qualify for the loan at 4%, the note rate.

Fig. 10.7 Features of FHA-insured loans

FHA Loan Features

- For residential properties with one to four units
- Borrower must occupy property as primary residence
- FHA mortgage insurance (MIP) on all loans
- Maximum loan amount based on local median housing prices
- Borrower's minimum cash investment: 3.5% of price or value
- Secondary financing allowed
- Income ratio guidelines:
    - 43% debt to income ratio
    - 31% housing expense to income ratio
- Assumption: lender's approval required

Funds for closing. At closing, an FHA borrower must have enough cash to cover the minimum cash investment, discount points, prepaid expenses, and other out-of-pocket expenses. Ordinarily, no reserves are required. The borrower may use gift funds to help close the transaction. The donor of the gift funds must be the borrower's employer or labor union, a close relative, a close friend with a clearly defined interest in the borrower, a charitable organization, or a government agency.

An FHA borrower also has other options for coming up with the necessary funds. As we discussed earlier, a close family member may provide secondary financing to cover the minimum cash investment and other funds needed for closing. Alternatively, a close family member may simply loan the funds to the borrower without requiring a second mortgage or any form of security in return.

Also, the borrower may be permitted to borrow the cash needed for closing from someone other than a family member, as long as the loan is secured by collateral other than the property being purchased with the FHA mortgage. For example, if the applicant can borrow money against his car or vacation property, the loan funds may be used to close the sale. Note that this loan must be from an independent third party, not from the seller or a real estate agent involved in the transaction. It must be clear that the loan is a bona fide business transaction and that the collateral is truly worth the loan proceeds.

Assumption. FHA loans contain due-on-sale clauses, and various limitations on assumption apply. With some exceptions, the buyer must intend to occupy the property as his primary residence. The lender will review the creditworthiness of the buyer before agreeing to the assumption.

VA-Guaranteed Loans

The VA home loan program allows veterans to finance the purchase of their homes with low-cost loans that offer a number of advantages over conventional and FHA loans. A VA loan, like an FHA loan, is made by an institutional lender, not a government agency. However, the loan is guaranteed by the Department of Veterans Affairs (VA), and that significantly reduces the lender's risk. If the borrower defaults, the VA will reimburse the lender for its losses, up to the guaranty amount.

A VA loan can be used to finance the purchase or construction of an owner-occupied single-family residence, or a multi-family residence with up to four units, as long as the veteran will occupy one of the units.

Characteristics of VA Loans. One of the biggest advantages of VA financing is that, unlike most loans, a typical VA loan does not require a downpayment. Within certain limitations, a VA loan can equal the sales price or appraised value of the home, whichever is less. This allows many veterans who would otherwise be unable to buy homes to do so.

Equally important to many veterans, the underwriting standards for VA loans are more relaxed than the standards for conventional loans. So not only will a veteran need less cash to buy a home with a VA loan, he will also find it easier to qualify for the loan.

There are no income limits on VA borrowers, nor are there official restrictions on the size of a VA loan. This means that VA loans aren't limited to low- or moderate-income buyers.

VA loans are fully amortized and typically have 30-year terms. The lender may not impose any prepayment penalties.

The VA doesn't set a maximum interest rate for VA loans; the interest rate is negotiable between the lender and borrower. The lender may charge the borrower a flat fee of no more than 1% of the loan amount to cover administrative costs (the equivalent of an origination fee). The lender may also charge reasonable discount points, which can be paid by the borrower, the seller, or a third party.

VA loans do not require mortgage insurance. The borrower doesn't have to pay for the private mortgage insurance required for many conventional loans, or the MIP required for all FHA-insured loans. However, a VA borrower usually has to pay a **funding fee**, which the lender will remit to the VA. (Veterans with service-connected disabilities are exempt.) For a member of the regular military obtaining a no-downpayment loan, the funding fee is 2.15% of the loan amount; it's 2.4% for a member of the National Guard or Reserves. If the borrower makes a downpayment of 5% or more, the fee is reduced. The funding fee can be paid at closing or financed along with the loan amount.

Another important feature of VA loans is the leniency extended to VA borrowers who are experiencing temporary financial difficulties, such as illness, injury, unemployment, or the death of a spouse. A VA loan officer can help a borrower whose loan becomes delinquent to negotiate a repayment plan.

Eligibility. To obtain a VA loan, a veteran must have a Certificate of Eligibility issued by the VA. To be eligible, the veteran must have served a certain minimum amount of time on active duty service. The minimum amount varies depending on when the veteran served, and it ranges from 90 days to two years of active duty. Buyers who want to determine whether they're eligible for a VA loan can do so online or check with the local VA office.

VA Guaranty. Like private mortgage insurance, the VA guaranty covers only a portion of the loan amount. The guaranty amount available for a particular transaction depends on the loan amount. For larger loans, it also depends on median home prices in the county where the property being purchased is located.

For example, for a VA loan used to purchase a one-unit property, if the loan amount is between $144,000 and $417,000, the guaranty amount is 25% of the loan amount. (So that's a $104,250 guaranty for a $417,000 loan.) For loan amounts over $417,000, the guaranty is 25% of the loan amount, up to the maximum specified for the county.

For 2015, in most parts of the country, a county's maximum guaranty is $104,250; however, the maximum is higher in high-cost areas. In California, the 2015 maximum guaranty amount ranges from $104,250 in the least expensive counties, such as Plumas and Tulare counties, up to $156,375 in the most expensive counties, such as San Francisco and San Mateo counties.

Loan Amount. The amount of a VA loan can't exceed the appraised value of the home or the sales price. The VA puts no other restrictions on the loan amount. However, most lenders do have rules about VA loan amounts. The most common rule is that for a no-downpayment VA loan, most lenders require the guaranty amount to equal at least 25% of the value or sales price of the property, whichever is less. For example, with a guaranty amount of $104,250 (the 2015 maximum in most places that don't have high housing prices), this restriction means that most lenders won't make a no-downpayment VA loan for more than $417,000 ($104,250 ÷ 25% = $417,000).

Lenders who follow that rule will still approve a larger loan if the borrower can make a downpayment. They typically want the total of the guaranty amount and the veteran's downpayment to equal 25% of the value or the sales price, whichever is less. This 25% rule means that the downpayment a veteran may have to make is still likely to be fairly modest.

Example: Sharon Vincent is eligible for a VA loan. She wants to buy a home for $430,000. The maximum guaranty amount in her county is $104,250, so her lender won't make a no-downpayment VA loan larger than $417,000. That means Sharon will have to make a downpayment in order to purchase the home.

However, because of the lender's 25% rule, Sharon doesn't have to pay the difference between the $430,000 sales price and $417,000 to get the loan. Her downpayment only has to equal 25% of the difference. The combination of the guaranty and the downpayment must equal 25% of the sales price. 25% of $430,000 is $107,500. $107,500 – $104,250 guaranty amount = $3,250. Sharon only has to make a $3,250 downpayment in order to purchase the home.

The other situation in which a VA borrower has to make a downpayment is when the property's sales price exceeds its appraised value. The borrower must make up the difference out of his own funds.

Secondary Financing. If he doesn't have enough cash, a VA borrower can obtain secondary financing to cover a downpayment required by the lender. The total financing (the VA loan plus the secondary financing) can't exceed the appraised value of the property, the borrower must be able to qualify for the payments on both loans, and the second loan cannot have more stringent conditions than the VA loan.

Secondary financing that meets these standards can be used for the borrower's closing costs, as well as for a downpayment required by the lender. But secondary financing cannot be used when the downpayment is required because the sales price exceeds the property's appraised value.

Assumption and Release of Liability. A VA loan can be assumed by any buyer, either a veteran or a non-veteran, as long as the buyer is creditworthy. The parties must obtain the VA's prior approval for the assumption. The interest rate on a VA loan is not changed on assumption. The VA charges a 0.5% funding fee, and the lender may charge limited processing and underwriting fees.

An assumption will be granted, and the original borrower will be released from further liability in connection with the loan, if the following conditions are met:

1. the loan payments are current;
2. the new buyer is an acceptable credit risk; and
3. the new buyer contractually assumes the veteran's obligations on the loan.

Restoration of Entitlement. The guaranty amount available to a particular veteran is sometimes called the veteran's "entitlement." After using his entitlement, a veteran can obtain another VA loan only if the entitlement is restored.

Fig. 10.8 Features of VA-guaranteed loans

VA Loan Features

- For residential properties with one to four units
- Borrower must occupy property as primary residence
- 100% financing allowed – no downpayment required
- 1% origination fee (discount points also allowed)
- Funding fee required, but no mortgage insurance
- No maximum loan amount
- Maximum guaranty amount is tied to county median home price and varies with loan amount
- Lender may require downpayment if guaranty is less than 25% of loan amount
- Secondary financing allowed for downpayment
- Loan can be assumed by creditworthy veteran or non-veteran
- Income ratio guideline: 41% debt to income ratio
- Residual income requirements

Example: Joe McDowell used a VA loan to buy a home in 2002. This year Joe decided to sell the property. He paid off his VA loan out of the sale proceeds. When he repaid the loan, Joe's guaranty entitlement was restored. If Joe decides to buy another home, he can use his entitlement to get another VA loan.

It's possible for a veteran to have his entitlement restored even if the loan is assumed instead of paid off when the home is sold. For this to work, the new buyer must also be a veteran who agrees to substitute her entitlement for the seller's entitlement. The loan payments must be current, and the buyer must also be an acceptable credit risk. If all of these conditions are met, the veteran can formally request a substitution of entitlement from the VA.

Qualifying for a VA Loan. To qualify for a VA loan, a veteran must meet the underwriting standards set by the Department of Veterans Affairs. A VA loan applicant's income is analyzed with two different methods, an income ratio method and a residual income method. The veteran must qualify under both methods.

The income ratio method for analyzing a veteran's income is similar to the method used for conventional and FHA loans. However, only one ratio—the debt to income ratio—is used, instead of two ratios. As a general rule, the loan applicant's debt to income ratio should not be more than 41%.

Example: Robert Garcia is eligible for a VA loan. He makes $2,800 a month, and his total monthly obligations add up to $375 a month. To estimate how large a house payment he can qualify for, multiply $2,800 by 41%. $2,800 × .41 = $1,148. Now subtract his monthly obligations of $375 from $1,148. $1,148 – $375 = $773. So the VA's 41% maximum debt to income ratio would allow Robert to qualify for a $773 monthly housing expense.

The second method used to qualify a VA loan applicant is the **residual income method**, also called cash flow analysis. The proposed housing expense (the PITI payment), estimated property maintenance and utility costs, all other recurring obligations, and certain taxes (including federal income tax, any state or local income tax, Social Security tax, Medicare tax, and any other taxes deducted from the veteran's paychecks) are subtracted from the veteran's gross monthly income to determine his residual income. The monthly maintenance and utility cost estimate is calculated by multiplying the number of square feet of living area in the house by 14 cents. (The VA refers to the borrower's PITI payment plus the maintenance and utility cost estimate as the monthly shelter expense.)

The loan applicant's residual income should be at least one dollar more than the VA's minimum requirement. The minimum requirement varies, depending on where the veteran lives, his family size, and the size of the proposed loan (see Figure 10.9). For example, the residual income required for a family of three living in California when the loan amount is less than $80,000 is $859. The residual income required for a family of four living in California when the loan amount is $80,000 or more is $1,117.

Example: Robert lives in California; he's divorced and has one child. He wants to buy a 1,500 square-foot home that costs $107,000. The VA requires him to have at least $823 in residual income to qualify for a loan.

To calculate Robert's residual income, start with his monthly gross income, $2,800. Subtract his federal income tax, which is $300, and subtract another $50 for state income tax. His Social Security and Medicare taxes also have to

Fig. 10.9 VA residual income requirements

Table of Residual Incomes by Region For loan amounts of $79,999 and below				
Family Size	Northeast	Midwest	South	West
1	$390	$382	$382	$425
2	$654	$641	$641	$713
3	$788	$772	$772	$859
4	$888	$868	$868	$967
5	$921	$902	$902	$1,004
Over 5: Add $75 for each additional member up to a family of 7.				

Table of Residual Incomes by Region For loan amounts of $80,000 and above				
Family Size	Northeast	Midwest	South	West
1	$450	$441	$441	$491
2	$755	$738	$738	$823
3	$909	$889	$889	$990
4	$1,025	$1,003	$1,003	$1,117
5	$1,062	$1,039	$1,039	$1,158
Over 5: Add $80 for each additional member up to a family of 7.				

be subtracted; they total $214. Next, subtract his recurring monthly obligations, which are $375. Calculate the monthly maintenance and utility costs ($0.14 × 1,500 square feet = $210) and subtract that figure. Then subtract Robert's proposed housing expense (PITI), which is, at most, $773 (the figure obtained from applying the 41% debt to income ratio).

$$\$2,800 - \$300 - \$50 - \$214 - \$375 - \$210 - \$773 = \$878$$

Robert's residual income is above his required minimum ($823) so he should have no problem qualifying for the loan.

The VA emphasizes that its minimum residual income figures are only guidelines. If the veteran fails to meet the guidelines, it should not mean an automatic rejection of the loan application. The lender should take other factors into consideration, such as the applicant's ability to accumulate a significant net worth, and the number and ages of any dependents.

The VA's 41% income ratio is also flexible. A lender can approve a VA loan even though the applicant's income ratio is above 41% if the application presents other favorable factors, such as an excellent credit history, a substantial amount of reserves, a substantial downpayment, or significantly more residual income than the minimum amount required by the VA. Extra residual income is an especially important compensating factor. If the applicant's residual income is at least 20% over the required minimum, the lender can approve the loan even though the income ratio is well over 41% and there are no other compensating factors.

Cal-Vet Loans

Veterans who live in California may also be eligible for a loan to purchase a single-family residential or farm property through the California Veterans Farm and Home Purchase Program, better known as the Cal-Vet program. The California Department of Veterans Affairs processes, originates, and services loans made through the program.

The Cal-Vet program works very differently from the federal programs, which directly insure or guarantee loans made by lenders. Instead, when a veteran purchases property using a Cal-Vet loan, the state of California actually purchases the property and takes title to it, and then sells the property to the veteran using a land contract. The buyer holds only an equitable interest in the property until the land contract is fully paid, at which point he receives a grant deed.

Eligibility. To be eligible for a Cal-Vet loan, a veteran generally must have served at least 90 days of active duty and been honorably discharged. (At one time, wartime service was required, but that's no longer true.) Veterans discharged before 90 days because of a service-connected disability are also eligible, as are veterans who were called to active duty from the Reserves or National Guard by Presidential Order.

In addition, current service members are eligible for a Cal-Vet loan after 90 days of active duty. Members of the California National Guard or the U.S. Reserves are eligible if they've served at least one year of a six-year obligation and are first-time home buyers (or are purchasing homes in certain economically distressed areas).

A veteran's surviving unremarried spouse may apply for a Cal-Vet loan if the veteran died of injuries suffered in the line of duty, is designated as missing or a prisoner of war, or died after applying for a Cal-Vet loan.

Restrictions. Some Cal-Vet loans are subject to the following restrictions:

- the purchase price of the property can't exceed a specified limit that's based on average prices in the area; and
- the borrower's family income can't exceed a specified limit that varies depending on family size and the county where the property is located.

Keep in mind that these restrictions don't apply to all applicants. Someone interested in a Cal-Vet loan should check with the California Department of Veterans Affairs to determine whether they apply in her case.

Characteristics. A Cal-Vet loan is fully amortized and typically has a 30-year loan term. The state sets a below-market interest rate for the loan. The rate may vary over the loan's term, but there is a cap on rate increases.

Even though the state is selling the property to the veteran through a land contract, the state obtains either a federal VA guaranty or private mortgage insurance to protect its interest, unless there's a downpayment of 20% or more. To pay for the guaranty or insurance, the veteran is usually charged a funding fee of between 1.25% and 3.3% of the loan amount, depending on the size of the downpayment and the veteran's military status.

If the Cal-Vet loan has a VA guaranty, no downpayment is required. Otherwise, a downpayment of at least 3% is usually required, so that the maximum loan-to-value ratio is 97%. Secondary financing is allowed, but the total amount borrowed can't exceed the appraised value of the property.

Cal-Vet loans are subject to a maximum loan amount that varies from county to county. The highest loan amount available anywhere in the state in 2015 is $521,250.

An application for a Cal-Vet loan may be submitted to an authorized mortgage broker or directly to the California Department of Veterans Affairs. The veteran must pay a 1% origination fee, but does not pay any discount points. The only other fees are an application fee, an appraisal fee, and a credit report fee. Cal-Vet loans do not have a prepayment penalty.

The borrower or his immediate family must occupy the home within 60 days after the Cal-Vet loan is funded. The property may not be transferred, encumbered, or leased without the permission of the California Department of Veterans Affairs. Cal-Vet loans cannot be assumed.

A Cal-Vet borrower under age 62 has the option of purchasing life insurance through the Cal-Vet program. If the borrower dies during the loan term, part or

Fig. 10.10 Cal-Vet loan characteristics

Cal-Vet Loan Characteristics

- State sells property to veteran through land contract
- Below-market variable interest rate with cap on rate increases
- High loan-to-value ratio
- Loan amount varies among counties
- Available only for owner-occupied single-family residence, condo unit, or mobile home

all of the loan balance will be paid out of the insurance proceeds. In addition, the Cal-Vet borrower purchases low-cost homeowner's insurance through the program, which includes flood and earthquake protection.

Rural Housing Service Loans

The Rural Housing Service (RHS) is a federal agency within the U.S. Department of Agriculture that makes and guarantees loans used to purchase, build, or rehabilitate homes in rural areas. These are often referred to as rural development (or RD) loans.

A rural area is generally defined as open country or a town with a rural character and a population of 10,000 or less. However, an area with a population of up to 20,000 may be considered rural if it is outside a metropolitan area and suffers from a serious lack of mortgage credit. (Even an area with a population up to 25,000 may qualify as a rural area under certain circumstances.)

To be eligible for an RHS program, a borrower must currently be without adequate housing. The borrower must also be able to afford the proposed mortgage payments and have a reasonable credit history. A home purchased, built, or improved with a rural development loan must be modest in both size and design.

Direct Loans. Low-income borrowers (whose income is no more than 80% of the area median income) may obtain financing from the RHS for 100% of the purchase price. The loan term may be as long as 38 years, depending on the borrower's income level. The RHS sets the interest rate and will service the loan.

Guaranteed Loans. The Rural Housing Service also guarantees loans made by approved lenders to borrowers whose income is no more than 115% of the area median income. Approved lenders include any state housing agency, FHA- and VA-approved lenders, and lenders participating in RHS-guaranteed loan programs. The loan amount may be 100% of the purchase price. The loan term is 30 years, and the interest rate is set by the lender.

Seller Financing

Institutional lenders such as banks, savings and loans, and mortgage companies are not the only sources of residential financing. In some cases, the home seller may also be a source. When a seller helps a buyer finance the purchase of a home, it's called **seller financing**. Seller financing can take a variety of forms, ranging from the simple to the complex.

How Seller Financing Works

As you know, institutional lenders require both a promissory note and a security instrument (a mortgage or a deed of trust) when they make a loan. The promissory note is evidence of the debt, and the security instrument makes the property collateral for the loan. In many cases, these same documents are used in seller financing. The buyer signs a promissory note, promising to pay the seller the amount of the debt, and then signs a mortgage or deed of trust that gives the seller a security interest in the home being purchased. This kind of seller financing arrangement is often called a **purchase money loan** or a **carryback loan**.

Purchase money loans are quite different from institutional loans. With an institutional loan, the lender gives the borrower cash, which is then given to the seller in return for the deed to the property. With a purchase money loan, the seller simply extends credit to the buyer. Essentially, the buyer is allowed to pay off the purchase price in installments over time, instead of having to pay the total purchase price in cash at closing.

In some instances, the seller may choose to use a land contract instead of the promissory note and mortgage or deed of trust. With a land contract, the buyer takes immediate possession of the land, but does not acquire legal title until the entire purchase price is paid off. A land contract is another way a seller can offer credit to the buyer.

In a seller-financed transaction, the seller usually decides which type of financing documents to use. If your seller is unsure about which type to use, you

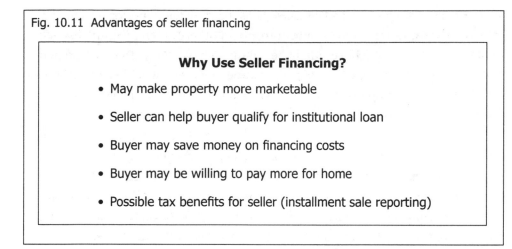

Fig. 10.11 Advantages of seller financing

Why Use Seller Financing?

- May make property more marketable

- Seller can help buyer qualify for institutional loan

- Buyer may save money on financing costs

- Buyer may be willing to pay more for home

- Possible tax benefits for seller (installment sale reporting)

should recommend that she speak to an attorney. Never advise a seller about the legal consequences of using the various types of documents. And always recommend that an attorney prepare any documents used in a seller-financed transaction. If your seller wishes to prepare the documents herself, strongly recommend that an attorney review them before they are signed by the parties.

Why Use Seller Financing? Setting up a seller-financed transaction can be complicated. The seller has to decide what kinds of documents to use and, typically, one or more attorneys get involved somewhere along the way. But there are several good reasons to use seller financing. One important reason is to make the property more marketable. This is especially true when market interest rates are high or loans are difficult to obtain. When interest rates are high, mortgage payments are also high. Potential buyers may have a difficult time qualifying for a loan with high mortgage payments, or they may be simply unwilling to take on a long-term loan at such high interest rates. By offering seller financing at a lower-than-market interest rate, a seller can make his home more attractive to potential buyers.

Seller financing can also help a buyer who could not qualify for institutional financing to complete the purchase of a home. With seller financing, the buyer avoids some of the costs of borrowing money from a lender, such as the loan origination fee and any discount points. Also, the seller may agree to a smaller downpayment than an institutional lender would require. Both of these factors mean a buyer can close a seller-financed sale with much less cash than an institutional loan would demand.

Because of the potential advantages that seller financing has for buyers, the seller may be able to get more for her property. For example, if the seller was asking $350,000 cash, a buyer might be willing to pay $360,000 for the property and attractive seller financing terms. In essence, the buyer would pay an additional $10,000 for the property to get the advantages of a low downpayment, fewer closing costs, a favorable interest rate, and lower monthly payments.

Seller financing can also provide tax benefits for the seller. Because the buyer will be paying the purchase price for the property in installments, over a period of years, the seller can spread out any taxable gain from the sale over that same period. In other words, the seller does not have to report the full taxable profit from the sale on her tax return in the year of sale. Only the amount of profit actually received in a given year is taxed in that year. The seller can spread the tax payments out over a longer period, and may be able to take advantage of a lower tax rate as a result.

Always advise a seller to consult an accountant or attorney about the tax implications of seller financing. There may be some tax disadvantages to a particular transaction that the seller may not be aware of.

Concerns of the Parties. When structuring a seller financing arrangement, it's important to pay close attention to the particular needs of the buyer and the seller. The buyer will be concerned with the cost of the financing, especially the interest rate and the amount of the downpayment. If the seller requires a balloon payment in a few years, the buyer should have some idea where he is going to get the money to make that payment. Will the buyer have the cash to make the balloon payment, or will he have to refinance the transaction? Financing that involves a balloon payment always presents a risk for the buyer. This kind of arrangement often works out fine, but the buyer should make plans about the balloon payment sooner rather than later.

Seller financing raises different concerns for the seller. Obviously, the seller doesn't want to extend financing to a buyer who can't afford the monthly payments. The seller should also be concerned about whether the buyer will be able to make any required balloon payment. But there are other equally important issues for the seller to consider.

First of all, the seller needs to decide whether she can really afford to offer seller financing, or whether she needs to be cashed out. For example, if the seller is purchasing a new home, she may need all of her equity from the old home in cash at closing. And even if the seller does not need all of the equity right away,

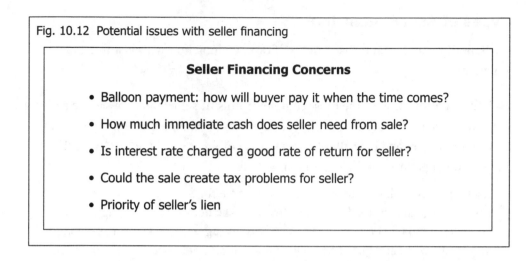

Fig. 10.12 Potential issues with seller financing

Seller Financing Concerns

- Balloon payment: how will buyer pay it when the time comes?

- How much immediate cash does seller need from sale?

- Is interest rate charged a good rate of return for seller?

- Could the sale create tax problems for seller?

- Priority of seller's lien

will the buyer's anticipated downpayment be enough cash to meet the seller's needs?

Most sellers who offer seller financing do so because they don't need the cash right away and a steady monthly income is attractive. Is the mortgage payment the buyer is going to pay on the seller financing enough to meet the seller's monthly needs? Is the interest rate charged on the seller financing a good rate of return? If the seller would charge 5% interest on the second mortgage, but could get a 7% return from investing in a mutual fund, the seller may want to rethink the transaction. Also, depending on the rate of interest charged, the seller could be faced with tax penalties based on the "imputed interest" rule. Under the imputed interest rule, if a seller charges an interest rate that is below a specified minimum, the IRS will treat some of the principal received in each installment payment as interest, and thus taxable. If the seller runs afoul of the imputed interest rule, many of the benefits the seller thought he was getting by offering seller financing could be eliminated. Again, it is imperative to advise your sellers to seek competent tax advice before they enter into a seller-financed transaction.

Finally, lien priority is an important consideration in any seller financing arrangement. It is almost certain that any new or existing institutional loan will have a higher priority than the seller's loan. In the event of default, the higher priority loan will be repaid first. If there is nothing left after the institutional loan has been repaid, the seller will get nothing. Thus, like an institutional lender, the seller must consider the relationship between the liens and the property's value. Would the property sell for enough at a foreclosure sale to pay off the seller financing as well as the liens with higher priority?

Types of Seller Financing

Seller financing can be used by itself or in conjunction with institutional financing.

Seller Seconds. One of the most common forms of seller financing is the seller second. With a seller second, the buyer pays most of the purchase price with an institutional loan, and the seller finances some of what would normally be the buyer's downpayment with a second mortgage.

> **Example:** Schmidt is buying Earnshaw's home for $200,000. She is getting an institutional loan for $170,000. However, she doesn't have enough cash to make a $30,000 downpayment, so Earnshaw agrees to take back a second mortgage in the amount of $15,000. Now Schmidt only has to come up with $15,000 for the downpayment.

There are several advantages to a seller second. As in this example, a seller second allows the buyer to make a smaller downpayment than she might otherwise have to make. A seller second can also help a marginal buyer qualify for an institutional loan. Institutional lenders have certain rules that must be followed when the buyer is going to use secondary financing. The lender should always be consulted to make sure the seller second is acceptable.

As long as the parties stay within the institutional lender's guidelines, they can come up with virtually unlimited ways to structure their financing package.

Primary Seller Financing. Seller financing may also be used as the main or only source of financing. This is called primary seller financing. Seller financing is at its most flexible when it is the only financing. Lender guidelines for secondary loans no longer have to be followed, and qualifying standards can be virtually ignored if the parties choose to do so.

Unencumbered property. Seller financing can be used when the property is either encumbered by a previous mortgage or unencumbered. Property is unencumbered when the seller owns it free and clear of any liens. When the property is unencumbered, seller financing is usually very straightforward. All the buyer and seller have to do is negotiate the sales price and the terms of the financing, and then have the appropriate finance documents prepared.

If the seller financing is the only financing, the seller will have first lien position as long as she records the loan documents promptly. However, the seller still has to be prepared to protect her security interest. A first mortgage does not have priority over all other liens. For example, real property tax liens and special assessment liens take priority over mortgages, no matter what the recording date. If the buyer fails to pay the property taxes, the property could be foreclosed on and the seller could take a loss at the foreclosure sale.

Destruction of the premises is another danger. Suppose the buyer fails to keep the property insured and the house burns down. The buyer then defaults on the loan, and the seller has to foreclose. Since the property is now probably worth much less than the amount of the remaining debt, the seller is likely to lose a great deal of money in the foreclosure sale.

The seller can protect her interest in the property by setting up an impound account for taxes and insurance, just as many institutional lenders do. Along with the loan payment, the buyer would make monthly tax and insurance payments, which would be deposited into the impound account. The funds in the impound account would then be used to pay the property taxes and insurance premiums when they become due. Many banks, savings and loans, and mortgage companies are willing to provide and service impound accounts for private parties.

Encumbered property. It's relatively uncommon for a seller to own his property free and clear of any other mortgage liens. Typically, the seller financed the purchase of the property and still owes money on that loan when he decides to sell. When the property is encumbered with a mortgage loan, it's a rare seller who can pay off the first loan with savings or the buyer's downpayment alone.

For instance, suppose Brown is selling his home for $200,000. He'd prefer to finance the sale and receive payments on an installment basis. However, there's a first mortgage on the property in the amount of $125,000. Brown doesn't have enough cash to pay off a $125,000 loan at closing, and a buyer is unlikely to have that much cash to invest in the home as a downpayment. It's possible that the buyer could assume Brown's existing mortgage, and Brown could finance the rest of the purchase price with a seller second. But there is another alternative that may be more attractive: wraparound financing.

With a **wraparound loan** (also called an all-inclusive trust deed), the buyer does not assume the seller's mortgage. Nor does the seller try to pay off this mortgage at closing. Instead, the buyer takes the property "subject to" the existing mortgage. This means the seller remains primarily responsible for making the payments on this mortgage. The seller finances the complete purchase price for the buyer, less the downpayment. The seller then uses part of the monthly payment received from the buyer to make the monthly payment on the existing mortgage (referred to as the **underlying mortgage**), and keeps the balance.

Example: Brown owes $125,000 on his house. The mortgage payment is $1,200. Brown sells his house to Morgan for $300,000. Morgan gives him a $35,000 downpayment, and Brown finances the remaining $265,000 purchase price at 7% interest. Morgan's monthly payment is $1,900. Brown uses part of the $1,900 to make the $1,200 payment on the underlying mortgage, then keeps the remaining $700 for himself.

Wraparound financing is only possible if the underlying loan does not have a due-on-sale clause. If there's a due-on-sale clause, the lender may call the underlying note, and it will become immediately due and payable.

When there is a due-on-sale clause in the underlying mortgage, it is dangerous to try to get away with a wraparound loan by keeping the lender in the dark about the sale. This is called a "silent" wrap, and it could easily backfire. Real estate agents should never get involved in silent wraps.

With wraparound financing, the buyer typically needs a little extra protection. If the seller fails to make the payments on the underlying loan, the institutional lender could foreclose, and the buyer could lose the property as well as all the monthly payments she has already made.

The best way to protect the buyer is to set up an escrow account for the loan payments. An independent third party in charge of the escrow account uses part of the buyer's payment to make the underlying loan payments and sends the remainder to the seller. Thus, the buyer is assured that the underlying loan payments will always be made in a timely manner. The seller can require the buyer to deposit tax and hazard insurance payments into the same account, thus protecting the seller's security interest in the property as well.

Other Ways Sellers Can Help

In many cases a seller can't afford to offer seller financing to a buyer, usually because the seller can't wait several years to be cashed out. However, there are a number of other ways in which a seller can help a buyer close the transaction. We've already mentioned buydowns and seller contributions to closing costs. A seller may also help out by agreeing to an equity exchange.

In an **equity exchange**, the seller accepts another asset—such as recreational property, a car, or a boat—as all or part of the required downpayment, instead of cash. This enables the buyer to close the sale with significantly less cash.

The other form of seller assistance we'll mention here is the **lease/option**. Sometimes a prospective buyer may simply not be ready to purchase a home. She may need time to save up for a downpayment, pay off debts, or improve her credit rating. Or perhaps the buyer needs more time to sell a property she already owns. In situations like these, a lease/option arrangement may help the buyer purchase the seller's home. A lease/option combines a lease with an option to purchase. The seller leases the property to the prospective buyer for a specific period of time. At the same time, the seller gives the buyer an option to purchase the property at a certain price during the lease period.

Whenever you're handling a sale that involves seller financing, make sure that both parties understand all the ramifications of the transaction. While you can't give them legal advice, it is appropriate to raise the concerns we've discussed here, such as the seller's lien priority and the importance of an impound account. As a real estate agent, you should not prepare the documents used in a seller-financed transaction, and you should strongly recommend that both the buyer and the seller get advice from their attorneys or accountants, or both.

Chapter Summary

1. The basic features of a residential mortgage loan are the repayment period, amortization, the loan-to-value ratio, secondary financing (in some cases), loan fees, and a fixed or adjustable interest rate.

2. Conventional loans with loan-to-value ratios of up to 95% are generally available. Private mortgage insurance is required for conventional loans with LTVs over 80%. As a general rule, the maximum debt to income ratio for a conventional loan applicant is 36%, unless there are compensating factors. The maximum housing expense to income ratio is ordinarily 28%, although lenders don't always apply that limit.

3. FHA loans are characterized by less stringent qualifying standards, low downpayment requirements, and FHA mortgage insurance (with both a one-time premium and annual premiums). Unless there are compensating factors, an FHA loan applicant's fixed payment to income ratio shouldn't exceed 43%, and the housing expense to income ratio shouldn't exceed 31%.

4. VA loans generally require no downpayment and no mortgage insurance. The maximum guaranty for VA loans is adjusted annually. Although the VA does not set a maximum loan amount, most lenders require the guaranty to cover at least 25% of the loan amount. Compared to conventional standards, VA qualifying standards are lenient. A VA loan applicant's debt to income ratio should not exceed 41% without compensating factors, and the applicant must also have residual income that meets VA standards.

5. In a Cal-Vet loan transaction, the California Department of Veterans Affairs purchases the property and sells it back to the veteran through a land contract. The maximum loan amount varies from county to county, and the state sets a below-market interest rate.

6. Rural development (RD) loans are made or guaranteed by the Rural Housing Service. They're available to low-income borrowers in rural areas.

7. When a seller helps the buyer finance the transaction, it's called seller financing. The most common form of seller financing is the seller second: the buyer pays most of the purchase price with an institutional loan, and the seller finances some of the buyer's downpayment. Seller financing may also be the buyer's only source of financing.

Key Terms

Fully amortized loan: A loan that requires regular installment payments of both principal and interest, with the installment payments paying off the full amount of the principal and all of the interest by the end of the repayment period.

Partially amortized loan: A loan where the installment payments will cover only part of the principal, so that a balloon payment of the remaining principal balance is required at the end of the repayment period.

Interest-only loan: A loan that allows the borrower to pay only the interest accruing during the initial years of the loan term; at the end of the interest-only period, the borrower begins making amortized principal and interest payments that will pay off the loan by the end of its term. Also, a loan that requires interest payments but no repayment of principal during its term.

Loan-to-value ratio (LTV): The relationship between the loan amount and either the sales price or the appraised value of the property (whichever is less), expressed as a percentage.

Secondary financing: Money borrowed to pay part of the required downpayment or closing costs for a first loan, when the second loan is secured by the same property that secures the first loan.

Origination fee: A fee a lender charges a borrower upon making a new loan, intended to cover the administrative costs of making the loan.

Discount points: A percentage of the principal amount of a loan, collected by the lender at the time a loan is originated, to give the lender an additional yield.

Adjustable-rate mortgage: A loan in which the interest rate is periodically increased or decreased to reflect changes in the cost of money.

Note rate: The interest rate stated in a promissory note.

Index: A published statistical report that indicates changes in the cost of money; used as the basis for interest rate adjustments in an ARM.

Margin: In an adjustable-rate mortgage, the difference between the index rate and the interest rate charged to the borrower.

Negative amortization: The addition of unpaid interest to the principal balance of a loan, thereby increasing the amount owed.

Conversion option: A provision in many adjustable-rate mortgages that gives the borrower the option of converting to a fixed interest rate at certain times during the first years of the loan term; if the borrower chooses to do this, the loan will remain at that fixed rate for the remainder of the term.

Conventional loan: An institutional loan that is not insured or guaranteed by a government agency.

Private mortgage insurance: Insurance provided by private companies to conventional lenders for loans with loan-to-value ratios over 80%.

Reserves: Cash or other liquid assets that a borrower will have left over after closing (after making the downpayment and paying the closing costs) and could use to pay the mortgage in the event of a financial emergency.

Gift funds: Money that a relative (or other third party) gives to a buyer who otherwise would not have enough cash to close the transaction.

Buydown: The payment of discount points to a lender to reduce (buy down) the interest rate charged to the borrower; especially when a seller pays discount points to help the buyer/borrower qualify for financing.

FHA-insured loan: A loan made by an institutional lender and insured by the Federal Housing Administration, so that the FHA will reimburse the lender for losses that result if the borrower defaults.

Mortgage insurance premium (MIP): Most often used to refer to the fee charged for FHA insurance coverage. The initial FHA premium is referred to as the UFMIP (upfront MIP).

VA-guaranteed loan: A home loan made by an institutional lender to an eligible veteran, where the Department of Veterans Affairs will reimburse the lender for losses if the veteran borrower defaults.

VA guaranty amount: The portion of a VA loan guaranteed by the Department of Veterans Affairs; the maximum amount that the VA will pay the lender for a loss resulting from the borrower's default.

Cal-Vet loan: A loan made through the California Veterans Farm and Home Purchase Program.

Rural development (RD) loan: A loan made or guaranteed by the federal Rural Housing Service, available to low-income borrowers in rural areas.

Seller financing: When a seller extends credit to a buyer to finance the purchase of the property, as opposed to having the buyer obtain a loan from a third party, such as an institutional lender.

Purchase money loan: When a seller extends credit to a buyer to finance the purchase of the property, accepting a deed of trust or mortgage instead of cash.

Wraparound loan: A purchase money loan arrangement in which the seller uses part of the buyer's payments to make the payments on an existing loan (called the underlying loan). The buyer takes title subject to the underlying loan, but does not assume it.

Chapter Quiz

1. A loan requires monthly payments of both principal and interest, but leaves some of the principal to be paid off in a balloon payment at the end of the loan term. This loan is:
   a. fully amortized
   b. negatively amortized
   c. non-amortized
   d. partially amortized

2. A lender will usually charge a higher interest rate in which of the following situations?
   a. The borrower wants an ARM instead of a fixed-rate mortgage
   b. The seller is offering a buydown
   c. The borrower wants a 5/1 ARM instead of an ARM with a one-year initial rate adjustment period
   d. The borrower wants a 15-year loan instead of a 30-year loan

3. A portfolio loan is a loan that:
   a. the lender plans to keep as an investment
   b. conforms to the rules of Fannie Mae and Freddie Mac
   c. is insured or guaranteed by a government agency
   d. is sold on the secondary market

4. To compensate for the extra risk, a lender making a conventional loan with a high loan-to-value ratio:
   a. might apply stricter qualifying standards
   b. might charge higher loan fees
   c. will require private mortgage insurance
   d. All of the above

5. The Homeowners Protection Act requires:
   a. borrowers to send a written request to their lender in order to cancel private mortgage insurance
   b. all loans to be covered by private mortgage insurance
   c. lenders to send all borrowers with private mortgage insurance an annual notice concerning their PMI cancellation rights
   d. lenders to automatically cancel the PMI when a loan's principal balance reaches 78% of the home's current appraised value

6. All of the following factors might justify making a conventional loan when the borrower's income ratios exceed the standard benchmarks, except:

   a. substantial net worth
   b. significant energy-efficient features in the home being purchased
   c. a high loan-to-value ratio
   d. education that indicates strong potential for increased earnings

7. With a graduated payment buydown plan for a fixed-rate loan, what rate will a lender probably use to qualify the buyer for the loan?

   a. A rate somewhere between the initial rate the borrower will pay and the full note rate
   b. The note rate
   c. A rate 1% or 2% above the note rate
   d. The buydown rate

8. Which of the following can the borrower count as part of the minimum cash investment required for an FHA loan?

   a. Discount points
   b. Closing costs
   c. Prepaid expenses
   d. None of the above

9. Jack, a veteran who wants to buy a house with a VA loan, has full guaranty entitlement. Which of the following is true?

   a. The VA guaranty will cover only a portion of the loan amount
   b. The VA guaranty will cover the entire loan amount
   c. Jack cannot be required to make a downpayment, regardless of the loan amount
   d. Jack is guaranteed a VA loan, so the VA's usual qualifying standards will be waived

10. If a seller wants to help a prospective buyer qualify for an institutional loan, which of the following options may reduce the interest rate used to qualify the buyer?

    a. Buydown
    b. Lease/option
    c. Silent wrap
    d. Equity exchange

Answer Key

1. d. With a partially amortized loan, not all of the principal is paid off through the monthly payments, and the borrower must make a balloon payment at the end of the loan term.

2. c. With adjustable-rate loans, as a general rule, the longer the initial rate adjustment period, the higher the interest rate. The interest rate on a 5/1 ARM is not adjusted during the first five years, but may be adjusted annually after that.

3. a. If a lender plans to keep a loan as an investment instead of selling it on the secondary market, the lender is keeping the loan "in portfolio."

4. d. For a high-LTV conventional loan, many lenders apply stricter qualifying standards and charge a higher interest rate and loan fees. Private mortgage insurance is generally required on any conventional loan with an LTV over 80%.

5. c. The Homeowners Protection Act requires lenders to send an annual notice to borrowers with PMI, regardless of whether their loans are subject to the other provisions of the act. (PMI must be canceled automatically when the principal balance reaches 78% of the home's original value, not 78% of the current appraised value.)

6. c. If the borrower exceeds the income ratio guidelines, the lender may consider other factors that indicate the borrower will be able to make the monthly payments. A high loan-to-value ratio, however, means the borrower has less invested in the property and is more likely to default.

7. b. Because a buyer with a graduated payment buydown will eventually have to pay interest at the full note rate, the lender wants to make sure the buyer will be able to handle the increased monthly payments. As a result, the lender will usually qualify the borrower using the note rate.

8. d. Discount points paid by the borrower do not count towards the required minimum cash investment, nor do the closing costs or prepaid expenses.

9. a. The VA guaranty covers only a portion of the loan amount. Even veterans who have full guaranty entitlement must meet the VA's qualifying standards in order to obtain a VA-guaranteed loan.

10. a. With a permanent buydown, the seller lowers the interest rate on the buyer's loan, which may allow the buyer to get a loan he would not otherwise qualify for. (A temporary buydown also lowers the buyer's interest rate for a certain period, but the buyer is likely to be qualified using the note rate instead of the bought-down rate.)

11

Closing the Transaction

The Closing Process

- Escrow
- Steps in closing a transaction
- Real estate agent's role

Closing Costs

- Costs and credits
- Estimating the buyer's net cost
- Estimating the seller's net proceeds

Laws that Affect Closing

- Income tax requirements
- Real Estate Settlement Procedures Act

Introduction

You helped your buyers find an affordable house that suits their needs. They made an offer on the house, and the sellers accepted it. The buyers must now order inspections, apply for or finalize their financing, and obtain a preliminary title report. The sellers must pay off the liens against the property, arrange for required repairs, and execute the deed. In other words, the buyers and the sellers must go through the closing process.

As a real estate agent, you will be shepherding your buyers and sellers through closing. Many of your clients will be unfamiliar with the process; you'll need to calm their anxieties and answer their questions. How long will it take to close the sale? What responsibilities does each party have? How much cash will the buyer need to close the sale? How much cash will the seller receive at closing?

In this chapter, we will discuss the closing process, closing costs and which party usually pays them, and how to estimate the buyer's net cost and the seller's net proceeds. We'll also cover some laws that affect closing, including the Real Estate Settlement Procedures Act.

The Closing Process

The phrase "closing a sale" actually has two meanings in the real estate field. Sometimes it refers to getting a buyer to make an offer, or getting a seller to accept one. For instance, a seller's agent can "close a sale" by overcoming the buyer's objections and convincing the buyer that it's the right time to make an offer on the house. Here, however, we'll be using "closing the sale" in its other sense, to mean completing all the tasks that have to be taken care of before title can be transferred to the buyer and the purchase price can be disbursed to the seller.

For every sale you handle as a real estate agent, it's part of your job to make sure that all of the closing requirements are met on time. You probably won't be completing all, or even most, of the necessary tasks yourself, but you have to know what needs to be done, who's responsible for doing it, and whether it's being done in a timely manner. If the closing process doesn't go smoothly, it can cause considerable delay and inconvenience, and in some cases the transaction will fall apart altogether.

To help keep track of the steps in the closing process and make sure that everything's getting done, you might want to use a closing checklist, such as the

Fig. 11.1 Checklist for closing

Closing Checklist

Property: _____

Buyer: _____

Seller: _____

Other party's agent: _____

Financing		**Inspection 1**	
Lender: _____		Company: _____	
Loan application submitted	_____	Inspection ordered	_____
Appraisal ordered	_____	Inspection report issued	_____
Appraisal completed	_____	Approval or disapproval	_____
Loan package submitted	_____	Seller's response	_____
Loan approved	_____	Repairs completed	_____
Loan documents signed	_____	Repairs reinspected	_____
Loan funds disbursed	_____	Reinspection approved	_____

Closing Requirements		**Inspection 2**	
Good faith deposit	_____	Company: _____	
Escrow opened	_____	Inspection ordered	_____
Escrow instructions	_____	Inspection report issued	_____
Seller's information	_____	Approval or disapproval	_____
Title search ordered	_____	Seller's response	_____
Preliminary title report	_____	Repairs completed	_____
Demand for payoff	_____	Repairs reinspected	_____
All conditions fulfilled	_____	Reinspection approved	_____
All documents signed	_____		
Buyer deposits funds	_____	**Moving**	
Hazard insurance policy	_____	Seller's belongings out	_____
Documents recorded	_____	Yard cleanup	_____
Title policies issued	_____	Interior cleaning	_____
Settlement statements	_____	Keys for buyer	_____

one shown in Figure 11.1. Review the purchase agreement to remind yourself of the basic terms and any unusual provisions; add any special requirements to the checklist. As the days go by, refer to your list on a regular basis, check off what has been accomplished and fill in the date of completion, and note what still needs to be done.

Escrow

Most transactions in California are closed through the escrow process. An **escrow agent** or **closing agent** handles the closing. This agent, who owes fiduciary duties to both the buyer and the seller, holds money and documents on their behalf in accordance with their written **escrow instructions**. The agent releases the money and documents to the appropriate parties only when all of the conditions in the escrow instructions have been fulfilled.

Benefits of Escrow. There are two major benefits to closing a transaction through escrow. First, escrow helps ensure that both parties will go through with the transaction as agreed. For example, once a signed deed has been placed in escrow, it's much more difficult for the seller to change his mind at the last moment and refuse to transfer title to the buyer. The escrow agent has legally binding instructions to deliver the deed to the buyer when the buyer pays the purchase price. The seller can't just demand the deed back from the escrow agent. So if the seller changes his mind, a lawsuit may be required to resolve the matter.

The second benefit of escrow is convenience. It isn't necessary for everyone involved in the transaction to be present at the same time for the sale to close.

Escrow Agents. In addition to holding items on behalf of the parties and disbursing them at the proper time, the escrow agent or closing agent is also responsible for seeing that legal documents are prepared and recorded, prorating the settlement costs, preparing the settlement statements, and various other tasks.

Licensing and exemptions. In California, escrow agents (independent escrow companies) must be licensed with the Department of Corporations. Only a corporation—not a partnership or an individual—can be licensed as an escrow agent.

However, attorneys, title companies, banks, savings and loans, and insurance companies may provide escrow services without an escrow license. Real estate brokers who provide escrow services for transactions they are handling are also exempt from the escrow licensing requirement, and they may charge a fee for their escrow services.

Example: Yamamoto is buying Farley's house, and you're the broker representing Farley. You may act as the closing agent for the transaction, even if your firm isn't licensed as an escrow agent. You may provide the closing services free of charge, or you may charge Yamamoto and Farley an escrow fee in addition to your regular commission.

Terminology. Sometimes the term "escrow agent" is reserved for a licensed independent escrow company, while "closing agent" is used as a general term that refers to any person or entity providing escrow services in a real estate transaction (whether that's a lawyer, a bank, a real estate broker, or a licensed escrow agent). In other cases, the two terms are used interchangeably to mean any person or entity that is providing escrow services in a real estate transaction. Thus, when a lawyer or a real estate broker is performing the same tasks as an escrow company, you may hear the lawyer or the broker referred to either as the closing agent or as the escrow agent for the transaction.

The escrow process is handled differently in different parts of the state. In northern California, closing services are usually provided by title insurance companies. In southern California, many transactions are closed by independent escrow companies. Also, statewide, many lenders have in-house escrow departments to handle transactions that they are financing.

Steps in Closing a Transaction

Certain steps must be completed during the closing process in almost every residential transaction. We'll give you an overview of these steps, and then consider some of them in more detail.

Overview. Our overview will include a brief look at inspections, financing, appraisal, and other key parts of the closing process.

Ordering inspections. If the sale is contingent on one or more inspections—for example, a home inspection and a soil test—the inspections should be ordered as soon as possible after the purchase agreement is signed. This is usually done by the buyer or the buyer's real estate agent.

The inspector sends the inspection report to her client (the buyer or the lender) and also to any other recipients the client has indicated (such as the seller, for example). If the report shows that repairs are needed, the buyer and the seller often negotiate about who will pay for the repairs (see Chapter 8).

Buyer's loan. The buyer should arrange for financing as soon as possible. The buyer must either apply for a loan or, if he has been preapproved for a loan, fulfill any additional requirements set by the lender. In any case, the lender will order a property appraisal before issuing a final loan commitment.

Opening escrow. The buyer's lender may open escrow by delivering a copy of the purchase agreement to its escrow department. Alternatively, a real estate agent may open escrow by delivering a copy of the agreement to the escrow agent specified by the parties.

Either way, the escrow agent sets up the escrow and conducts the closing based on escrow instructions signed by the buyer and seller. The C.A.R. purchase agreement form (see Figure 7.1 in Chapter 7) includes the escrow instructions for the transaction. If the purchase agreement lacks escrow instructions, the escrow agent must prepare a separate document for the parties to sign, based on the purchase agreement. (The conditions and deadlines in the escrow instructions must match the terms of the purchase agreement.)

Appraisal. The appraiser sends the appraisal report to the buyer's lender, because the lender is the appraiser's client. The lender generally sends a copy of the report to the buyer (and is required to do so in connection with certain loans).

Title report. The escrow agent orders a preliminary title report, if the lender has not already done so. The title insurance company sends the report, which describes the condition of the seller's title to the property, to the lender and the buyer for approval. Any unexpected title problems revealed in the report must be addressed.

Seller's loan payoff. In most transactions, the seller has a mortgage or deed of trust on the property that will be paid off at closing. Whoever is preparing the closing disclosure (the buyer's lender or the escrow agent) requests a final payoff figure from the seller's lender. A form called a "Demand for Payoff" or a "Request for Beneficiary's Statement" is used to make this request. The disclosure preparer also needs to obtain exact payoff figures for any other liens that must be removed.

Buyer's loan approval. When the buyer's loan is approved, the lender informs the buyer of the exact terms on which it was approved and the date on which the loan commitment will expire. The lender also gives the buyer an updated estimate of her closing costs. The lender sends all of the loan documents—the promissory note and the mortgage or deed of trust—to the escrow agent, who arranges for the buyer to review and sign them. Once the loan documents have been signed, they are returned to the lender, who then coordinates loan funding with the escrow agent.

Buyer's funds. When all of the contingencies listed in the purchase agreement (such as the inspections, the financing arrangements, or the sale of the buyer's home) have been satisfied, the buyer deposits the downpayment and the closing costs into escrow. Some lenders disburse the loan funds to the escrow

Fig. 11.2 Steps in the closing process

Closing a Residential Transaction

- Inspections ordered by buyer or real estate agent
- Financing applied for or finalized by buyer
- Appraisal ordered by lender
- Escrow opened by lender or real estate agent
- Escrow instructions signed by the parties
- Preliminary title report ordered by closing agent
- Loan payoff amount requested from seller's lender by closing agent
- Loan documents signed by buyer
- Downpayment and closing costs deposited by buyer
- Loan funds deposited by lender
- Settlement statements prepared by closing agent
- Funds disbursed by closing agent
- Title policy Issued by title company
- Documents filed for recording
- Hazard insurance policy issued to buyer

---

agent at this point, but many lenders wait until the title has been transferred and the buyer's deed and mortgage or deed of trust have been recorded. The title company will file the documents with the county clerk for recording.

Closing date. On the closing date, the escrow agent disburses the funds held in escrow to the seller, the real estate broker, and other individuals or entities that are entitled to payment. The title insurance policies are issued, as is the buyer's hazard or homeowner's insurance policy. The deed and the other documents are filed with the county clerk for recording. Once this has all been done, the sale has officially closed.

Next, let's look at certain aspects of the closing process in more detail. We'll discuss property inspections, financing and the appraisal, hazard insurance, and title insurance.

Inspections. For each inspection required by the parties' agreement or by the lender, an initial inspection must be ordered; then the inspection report must be approved or rejected by the buyer or the lender, repairs must be completed and reinspected, and the parties must be notified about the results of the reinspection. (For more information about the addenda and notice forms that can be used for inspection contingencies, see Chapter 8.) It's very important for inspections to be ordered early in the closing process; if repairs are required, they need to be completed early enough so that they don't delay the closing.

Types of inspections. There are many different types of real estate inspections. Here are brief descriptions of the inspections most commonly performed in residential transactions. The first three on the list are usually carried out by a single expert called a **home inspector**.

- **Structural inspection.** The inspector identifies the materials used in the construction, the type of construction, and the accessibility of the various areas that are to be inspected. In addition, the inspector checks for major and minor problems in the structural systems of the building, including the foundation and the floor, wall, and roof framing.
- **Electrical and plumbing inspection.** The inspector checks the electrical and plumbing systems for capacity, safety, and life expectancy. Plumbing systems are also checked for unsanitary conditions. Upgrades and repairs may be recommended. If the property's water source is a private well, it may also be inspected for water quality and quantity.
- **Interior inspection.** The inspector checks the walls, floors, and ceilings for signs of water damage, settling, fire hazards, or other problems. Ventilation and energy conservation issues are noted. Appliances may also be examined for operational problems.
- **Pest inspection.** A pest inspector checks for damage caused by wood-eating insects such as termites, wood-boring beetles, and carpenter ants.
- **Soil inspection.** A soil inspector or geologist examines the soil conditions to see if there are existing or potential settling or drainage problems.
- **Environmental inspection.** An environmental inspection addresses concerns such as radon, urea formaldehyde, asbestos, lead-based paint, underground storage tanks, or contaminated water. (These problems are discussed in Chapter 3.)

Choosing an inspector. For a particular inspection, your buyer may have an inspector in mind, or he may ask you to recommend someone reputable. Some real estate firms require their agents to give the buyer at least three names to choose from. (Ask your broker or the other agents in your office for suggestions, if necessary.) If you refer someone to an inspector with whom you have (or had) any type of personal or business relationship, you should disclose that relationship in writing.

To help a buyer choose a home inspector, you might suggest that he ask the inspector the following questions:

1. How long has the inspection firm (or individual inspector) been in business? (A minimum of five years' experience is recommended.)
2. Does the firm belong to the American Society of Home Inspectors? (Membership requires actual experience, passing a written examination, inspection reviews, and continuing education.)
3. Has the firm changed its name recently? If so, why?
4. What type of report does the firm prepare? How long does it take to complete the report and get it back to the client?
5. How many inspectors does the firm have? Are they full-time or part-time?
6. Does the firm engage in other businesses in addition to inspections? (In other words, is home inspection only a sideline?)
7. Does the firm also offer to make any of the repairs recommended by the inspection? (Inspection companies that also make repairs may not give unbiased reports.)
8. Does the firm provide references? If the buyer requests them, an inspector should be willing to give several references.

It's also a good idea to check with the Better Business Bureau to see if any complaints have been lodged against the inspection firm.

Inspection reports. After an inspection is completed, the inspector prepares an inspection report. The report summarizes the major points of concern and states which problems need to be repaired or otherwise addressed promptly.

A home inspection report should include information about substandard workmanship and also about deterioration, such as rotting wood or corroded piping. The report should put the property into perspective by comparing it to similar properties. A 15-year-old house can't be expected to be in the same condition as a brand new one.

In addition, the report should project a five-year budget for anticipated repair work and identify potential remodeling problems. For instance, if the buyer were to add rooms onto the house, the entire electrical system might need to be upgraded. Or the septic system might only be adequate for a three-bedroom house, and if another bedroom were added, a new septic tank would be required.

Repairs. After an inspection report has been issued, the party who requested it (the buyer or the lender) must either approve or disapprove the report. Depending on the terms of the inspection contingency provision, the seller may have to complete the repairs before the transaction can close. If the buyer's lender required the inspection, the repairs may be a condition of loan approval, as we'll discuss in a moment.

Ideally, the parties have already agreed who will pay for any required repairs, but that isn't always the case. The purchase agreement may commit the seller to paying up to a specified amount, but no more than that. If the repair costs significantly exceed that amount, it may be necessary for the seller to negotiate a price adjustment or some other concession to persuade the buyer to go forward.

In many cases, the repairs have to be completed and reinspected—and the buyer or lender has to approve the reinspection report—before the sale can close or the loan can be funded. In some circumstances, however, the closing can take place even though the repairs won't be completed by the closing date.

Structural pest control inspections. Structural pest control inspections can be particularly important, and most lenders in California require one. In addition, the FHA and the VA require this type of inspection in certain parts of the state. Pest control inspectors must file the addresses of properties they inspect with the state Structural Pest Control Board. If a home was inspected within the previous two years, anyone can obtain a copy of the report by submitting a request to the board.

Typically, a seller will order a structural pest control inspection when the house is first listed so that any problems found can be corrected as soon as possible. The seller must give a copy of the pest inspector's report to the buyer. In most cases, the seller will pay for corrective repairs, but the buyer is responsible for any preventive measures.

Financing. A home sale can't close unless the buyers have enough money to pay the purchase price. The buyers usually borrow the money they need from a bank or other lender. As explained in Chapter 9, it's now common for buyers to get preapproved for financing. Before choosing a house to buy, the buyers submit a fully completed loan application and the supporting documentation. The lender performs a credit analysis and qualifies the buyers for a certain loan amount at a specified interest rate. If the buyers find a house that can be purchased with that loan, and if the property meets the lender's standards, the lender will issue a final loan commitment.

Employees of the buyer's lender are actively involved in closing the transaction. The lender's team orders and evaluates the appraisal, reviews the preliminary title report, and may also order inspections and require repairs. They prepare the financing documents for the buyer to sign, and they are responsible for funding the loan—that is, depositing the loan amount into escrow so that it can be disbursed at closing. As we indicated earlier, in some cases the entire closing is handled by the lender's escrow department.

Because of their role, the loan officer and other employees of the lender can have a big impact on the closing. If they're reputable and competent, they'll make sure that the loan process is completed smoothly and quickly, with a minimum of errors. Find out which lenders have good or bad reputations by asking experienced real estate agents; if your buyers haven't chosen a lender yet, pass that information along to them before they make their choice.

Appraisal. The buyer's lender orders the appraisal as part of the loan underwriting process. The property as well as the buyer must be qualified for the requested loan. Regardless of the buyer's financial situation, it's the property that serves as the security for the debt. If the loan is not repaid as agreed, the lender will foreclose on the property to recover the money owed. Before approving the loan, the lender wants assurance that it is lending based on fair market value, so that if the borrower defaults, any loss on the foreclosure sale will be as small as possible. Also, borrowers with little or no equity in their property are much more likely to default, so lenders want borrowers to start out with at least some equity. To ensure that they will have some, the maximum loan amount for a transaction is tied to the property's appraised value (see Chapter 10).

The residential appraisal process has a lot in common with the competitive market analysis that real estate agents use to help price a home (see Chapter 4). In fact, the CMA method is based on the sales comparison approach to appraisal, which is the most important approach for residential appraisals.

You should understand the appraisal process well enough to give a brief explanation to the buyer and seller. They are often anxious about the appraisal, since their transaction depends on the appraiser's opinion.

Hazard Insurance. Virtually all lenders require the escrow agent to make sure the borrower's property is insured up to its replacement cost before the loan funds are disbursed. In most cases, the minimum insurance policy is the HO-3 policy. This type of policy provides coverage against most perils, but it excludes floods and earthquakes, as well as war, nuclear hazard, and certain other things.

A buyer who is concerned about floods or earthquakes should consider buying supplemental coverage. But this type of coverage can be expensive, and it isn't available in all areas or for all properties. For instance, a house may need seismic retrofitting before the buyer can obtain earthquake coverage.

Applying for hazard insurance used to be a part of the closing process that was taken for granted. Buyers rarely had trouble obtaining ordinary coverage. However, because of stricter insurance underwriting standards, it's no longer so unusual for a buyer to be turned down. As a result, some purchase agreement forms now have a hazard insurance contingency provision, which makes the sale contingent on whether the buyer can obtain adequate coverage. The hazard insurance contingency may be regarded as part of the financing contingency. (See Chapter 8.)

Title Insurance. Title insurance insures the buyer or the buyer's lender against financial losses that could result from problems with the seller's title that haven't been discovered yet. As we said earlier, the escrow agent or the lender orders a preliminary title report on the property.

The title report should be ordered early in the closing process to allow time for problems to be resolved. For example, if the title report indicates that there is a judgment lien against the property, the seller has to clear away the lien so that marketable title can be transferred to the buyer at closing. Depending on the circumstances, the seller may simply arrange to pay the lienholder at closing, out of the sale proceeds. Or the seller may need to prove to the title company's satisfaction that there is no lien against the property. (Perhaps the title searcher overlooked a recorded release; or the lien might be against a completely different property owned by someone who has the same name as the seller.)

Types of title policies. As a condition of the buyer's loan, the lender requires the buyer to purchase a **lender's title insurance policy** for the lender. The lender's policy (sometimes referred to as a mortgagee's policy) protects the lender's security interest.

Example: After closing, it comes to light that there's a lien against the property that has higher priority than the lender's deed of trust. That other lien was not discovered by the title searcher and listed in the title report. As a result, the lien was not paid off before closing; but it also wasn't listed as an exception to coverage in the title policy. If the lender suffers a financial loss because it doesn't have first lien position, the title company will have to reimburse the lender, up to the face amount of the policy.

An **owner's title insurance policy** is for the protection of the buyer, the new owner of the property. It protects the buyer's ownership interest against undiscovered title problems such as a forged deed or a gap in the chain of title. If someone makes a claim against the title that is covered by the policy, the title insurance company will pay the cost of defending the title against the claim. If the claim is successful in spite of this defense, the company will compensate the policy holder (the buyer) for the financial loss, up to the face amount of the policy.

It's never wise for a buyer to purchase a home without an owner's title insurance policy. (Keep in mind that the lender's policy offers no protection to the buyer.) This type of policy isn't particularly expensive, and although title problems are unlikely to surface, they could be very costly if they did. As we'll discuss later, which party pays for the owner's policy depends on local custom, unless otherwise agreed.

Extent of coverage. Title insurance policies are also categorized according to the type or extent of the coverage they provide. There is standard coverage, extended coverage, and homeowner's coverage.

Standard coverage title insurance protects the policy holder against title problems that concern matters of record—that is, deeds and liens and other interests that appear in the public record.

Extended coverage protects against all of the same problems that standard coverage does, plus problems that should be discovered in an actual inspection of the property. These include encroachments, adverse possession, construction that may result in a lien that hasn't been recorded yet, and other problems that do not show up in the public record. The title company sends an inspector to the property to look for indications that there may be one of these problems. Lenders require lender's policies to be extended coverage policies.

A third type of coverage, **homeowner's coverage**, is available for transactions involving residential property with up to four units. This covers most of the same matters as extended coverage, as well as some additional issues such as violations of restrictive covenants. This is the type of coverage selected for the owner's policy (the policy protecting the buyer) in most residential transactions in California.

The Real Estate Agent's Role in the Closing Process

As your sale progresses toward closing, it's important to keep track of the details. Don't assume that everything's going smoothly while you turn your attention to other listings and other buyers.

Communication. Throughout the closing process, keep your client up to date on what's happening. Let her know when the appraisal is completed, when the loan is approved, and so on. This will ease her anxieties and reassure her that someone—you—is looking after her interests. Communication is especially important when problems crop up. If there's a delay in getting a preliminary title report or the pest inspection looks bad, tell your client immediately. Explain the problem, suggest what can be done about it, and then work with the client to find a solution.

Communication with the other party's agent is also very important. You need to promote your client's interests, but you should always do your best to get along with the other agent and the other party. Although their interests will sometimes conflict with those of your client, in most cases all of you ultimately want the sale to close. Don't agree to unreasonable demands, but work with the other agent to complete the transaction successfully.

Preventing Problems. Here is a list of questions and suggestions that will help you prevent problems and make the closing process smoother. Of course, what you do in a particular transaction will depend in part on whether you're representing the buyer or the seller.

Preparing the purchase agreement. Have the forms used for the buyer's offer and any counteroffers been filled out carefully? Do the parties understand the terms of their agreement? Is the legal description of the property correct? Consider whether the deadlines in the agreement make sense under all of the current conditions. How long will it take to fulfill the contingencies in this market? The contingencies may include inspections, financing, and even the sale of the buyer's current home. When does the buyer need to move? Is it realistic to expect that the seller can be completely moved out by that date?

Opening escrow. Does the escrow agent have a copy of every addendum and amendment as well as a copy of the purchase agreement itself? If the escrow instructions are separate from the purchase agreement form, do they accurately reflect all the terms of the purchase agreement? The parties can sign amended instructions if necessary.

Inspections. Are you responsible for ordering any inspections? If so, do it right away. And if someone else has that responsibility, make sure they take care of it as soon as possible. Later, check to see whether the inspection report has been delivered to the appropriate parties. Does the report seem thorough and accurate? If the report recommends repairs, do the recommendations seem reasonable? If the transaction is contingent on the results of this inspection, help your client prepare or respond to the inspection notice (see Chapter 8). If repairs are agreed to, they should be ordered and completed as soon as possible. Have arrangements for a timely reinspection been made?

Financing. If the buyer hasn't been preapproved for a loan, has she gathered all of the personal information that she'll need for the loan application? Has she chosen a competent lender? Check with the lender periodically to find out how the loan process is going.

Appraisal. If the appraisal comes in low, does a request for reconsideration of value seem appropriate? (See Chapter 4.)

Special provisions. Are there any special provisions in the purchase agreement that require your attention? Are both parties clear on which personal property items and fixtures are included in the sale, and which the seller is going to take with him?

Title insurance. Has a preliminary title report been ordered? When the report becomes available, find out whether there are any title problems that need to be cleared up.

Hazard insurance. Has the buyer applied for and obtained a new homeowner's insurance policy? Has a copy of the policy been delivered to the escrow agent or the lender?

Moving out. Is the seller packing his belongings and preparing to move out on time? Will he leave the house reasonably clean and the yard in reasonably good shape? Many sellers gladly pay to have junk hauled away, or to have a team of house cleaners go over the house once it's empty. You should be able to recommend junk hauling services and house cleaning services. Ask the other agents in your office which companies they recommend.

Moving in. If the buyer will move in before closing, or the seller can't move out until after closing, has an interim rental agreement been prepared and signed? (See Chapter 7.) Whenever the buyer moves in, will the seller have all of the house keys ready to turn over to the buyer? If the buyer finds personal property that may have been left behind accidentally or if there's mail that should be forwarded to the seller, it's usually more appropriate to contact the seller's agent rather than the seller himself.

Last-Minute Problems. In the closing process, the risk that the transaction will fall apart is usually greatest before the contingencies have been fulfilled, but something can go wrong at any point, right up through the last few days before closing.

> **Example:** The sale of your client's house to the Friedmans has been going well. The seller and the buyers have been taking care of their responsibilities on time, and the financing contingency and inspection contingencies have been satisfied.
>
> But just a week before the date set for closing, you get a call from the seller. He says that there's a problem with the house that he never told you about. There's some rot in the crawl spaces. He should have listed this in the transfer disclosure statement, but he decided not to. The home inspector apparently missed the problem. Now the seller's conscience (and fear of liability) has prompted him to let you know about it. He wants to know what he should do.

How you handle this situation may mean the difference between closing the sale on time and not closing it at all. The problem must be disclosed to the buyers, and they could use it as grounds for canceling the contract. You should do whatever you can to prevent that. For instance, you might go to the house and investigate the extent of the problem, consult with your broker and a home inspector, help the seller decide on an appropriate price concession to offer the buyers, and then call the buyers' agent. By dealing with this problem in a straightforward and professional manner, you can make it much more likely that the sale will go through.

To summarize, always stay on top of the closing process. Keep in touch with your client, with the other party's agent, and with the escrow agent. Handle any problems that come up as promptly as you can. Your role in getting the transaction to close can be just as important as your role in negotiating the sale in the first place.

Closing Costs

One of your tasks as a real estate agent is explaining the various costs involved in closing a real estate transaction to your clients. Some examples of closing costs are inspection fees, title insurance fees, recording fees, escrow fees, and loan fees. Some of these are paid by the buyer, some are paid by the seller, and some are split between the two parties.

As a real estate agent, you need to be able to give the buyers and sellers you work with a reasonable estimate of how much their closing costs will be. Sellers want to know how much money they'll get from a sale, and buyers want to know how much they'll actually end up paying at closing. They will often ask you about this before they make or accept an offer or counteroffer.

To estimate a seller's **net proceeds** (the amount of cash the seller will walk away with) or a buyer's **net cost** (the amount of cash the buyer must bring to closing), you have to know how the various closing costs are typically allocated on a settlement statement.

A **settlement statement** (also called a closing statement) sets out all of the financial details of a real estate transaction, including the closing costs each party must pay. In residential transactions, the settlement statement is part of the required closing disclosure form, which we'll discuss later in the chapter. In preparing a settlement statement or closing disclosure form, the lender or closing agent allocates each closing cost to the buyer or the seller (or both) as indicated in the purchase agreement; if the agreement doesn't specify which party is responsible for a particular cost, it is allocated according to local custom. For your estimates, you'll allocate the parties' closing costs in the same way.

Many agents use worksheets to help them calculate—and explain—net costs and net proceeds for their buyers and sellers. A buyer's estimated net cost worksheet is shown later in the chapter, in Figure 11.4. A seller's estimated net proceeds worksheet is shown in Figure 11.5. Your broker may have similar worksheets available for you to use.

You'll need to do some math to calculate the amount of certain closing costs. And some expenses will have to be **prorated** between the buyer and the seller. To prorate an expense is to divide and allocate it proportionately between two or more parties, according to time, interest, or benefit. Figure 11.3 shows the steps involved in proration.

Costs and Credits

On a settlement statement, the costs that a party must pay at closing are referred to as that party's **debits** (the opposite of credits). The buyer's debits increase the amount of money the buyer will have to bring to closing. The seller's debits decrease the seller's net proceeds.

In addition to their debits, each party will usually have some credits that also must be taken into account (and in some cases prorated). Credits are payments that will be made to the buyer or the seller at closing. The buyer's credits decrease the buyer's net cost. The seller's credits increase the seller's net proceeds.

Note that some closing costs are charges that one party owes the other party. At closing, each of these will be treated as a debit for the party that must pay it and as a credit for the other party. For example, the buyer may be required to pay the seller a prorated share of the annual property taxes, because the seller paid the taxes in advance. The prorated amount is a debit for the buyer and a credit for the seller on the settlement statement. On your worksheets, add it to the buyer's net cost, and also add it to the seller's net proceeds.

Other closing costs are charges that one party must pay to a third party. For example, the seller will have to pay the broker the sales commission. This is a debit for the seller (subtracted from the net proceeds), but it does not affect the buyer.

Also, some of the credits a party receives at closing come from a third party. For example, the seller's lender must refund any unused tax and insurance reserves to the seller at closing. This is a credit for the seller (added to the net proceeds), and it does not affect the buyer.

Residential transactions involve many standard closing costs. As we said, some are allocated according to the terms of the purchase agreement and some are allocated according to custom; a few are allocated according to law. We'll first go through the process of estimating a buyer's net cost. After that, we'll turn to the seller's net proceeds.

Estimating the Buyer's Net Cost

Certain costs are the buyer's responsibility in every transaction, or almost every transaction. Responsibility for other costs—whether they'll be paid by the buyer or by the seller, or shared between them—may vary. To estimate a buyer's net cost, add up all of the charges the buyer will have to pay to close the sale and offset them with the credits owed to the buyer.

Purchase Price. Of course, the purchase price is the major cost for the buyer in every transaction. Use this as the starting point on your buyer's net cost worksheet (see Figure 11.4). The price is offset by the buyer's good faith deposit and the financing.

Good faith deposit. In most transactions, the buyer gives the seller a good faith deposit, and the deposit is applied to the purchase price if the sale closes. Since the buyer has already paid the good faith deposit, it is treated as a credit for the buyer on the settlement statement. On the net cost worksheet, subtract the amount of the deposit from the purchase price.

Financing. Many buyers pay a large part of the purchase price with borrowed money. Any financing arrangement—a new loan, the assumption of the seller's loan, or seller financing—is treated as a credit for the buyer. On the buyer's worksheet, subtract the loan amount and/or the amount of other financing from the purchase price.

Loan Costs. Borrowing money isn't free; in addition to the interest paid over the life of the loan, the borrower must pay a number of charges to obtain the loan. Unless the seller has agreed to pay some of them, the buyer will pay all of the closing costs associated with the loan. That means you should add these closing costs to the purchase price on your buyer's net cost worksheet.

Appraisal. The buyer's lender requires the appraisal, so the buyer pays the appraisal fee.

Credit report. The buyer's lender charges the buyer for the credit investigation, so this is also a cost for the buyer.

Origination fee. This is the lender's one-time charge to the borrower for setting up the loan (see Chapter 10). It's almost always paid by the buyer. If the buyer is assuming the seller's loan, an assumption fee will be charged instead of an origination fee.

Discount points. As we discussed in Chapter 10, by paying the lender discount points at closing, a borrower can get the loan at a lower interest rate than the lender would otherwise have charged. Like other loan fees, discount points are ordinarily paid by the buyer. When a seller agrees to pay discount points on the buyer's behalf, it's called a buydown (see Chapter 10); in that case, the discount points would be a cost for the seller instead.

Prepaid interest. As a general rule, the first payment date of a new loan is not the first day of the month immediately following closing, but rather the first day of the next month after that. For instance, if a sale closes on April 14, the first payment on the new loan is due on June 1 instead of May 1. This gives the buyer a chance to recover a little from the financial strain of closing.

Even though the first loan payment isn't due for an extra month, interest begins accruing on the loan on the closing date. Interest on a real estate loan is almost always paid in arrears. In other words, the interest that accrues during a given month is paid at the end of that month. For instance, a loan payment that is due on September 1 includes the interest that accrued during August. So if the transaction closes on April 14, the first payment will be due on June 1, and that payment will cover the interest accrued in May. However, it won't cover the interest accrued between April 14 and April 30. Instead, the lender will require the buyer to pay the interest for those 17 days in April at closing. This is called **prepaid interest** or **interim interest**. It is almost always paid by the buyer.

Fig. 11.3 Prorating an expense

Step 1
Divide the expense by the number of days it covers to find the per diem (daily) rate.
- Divide annual expenses by 365.
- Divide monthly expenses by the number of days in the month in question.

Step 2
Determine the number of days for which one party is responsible for the expense.

Step 3
Multiply the number of days by the per diem rate to find that party's share of the expense.

Expense paid in arrears (overdue):
- Seller's share is a debit for the seller.

Expense paid in advance:
- Seller's share is a credit for the seller.

Expense continues after closing:
- Buyer's share is a credit for the buyer if paid in arrears.
- Buyer's share is a debit for the buyer if paid in advance.

Example: The buyer is borrowing $335,000 at 6.5% interest to finance the purchase. The annual interest on the loan during the first year will be $21,775 ($335,000 × .065 = $21,775). Divide that annual figure by 365 to get the per diem interest rate.

$$\$21,775 \div 365 = \$59.66 \text{ per diem}$$

There are 17 days between the closing date (April 14) and the first day of the following month, so the lender will expect the buyer to prepay 17 days' worth of interest at closing.

$$\$59.66 \times 17 \text{ days} = \$1,014.22 \text{ prepaid interest}$$

The escrow agent will enter $1,014.22 as a debit to the buyer on the settlement statement. When you are preparing your estimated net cost worksheet for the buyer, you can go through the same process to come up with a figure for the prepaid interest. Add it to the buyer's net cost.

The buyer and the seller both owe interest for the closing date (unless the buyer is assuming the seller's loan or the buyer is paying all cash). That's because there are two different loans at issue—one that ends on the closing date and the other that begins on that date. If the buyer is assuming the seller's loan, the parties must agree on who pays the interest for the closing date.

Lender's title insurance premium. As explained earlier, the lender requires the buyer to provide a policy to protect the lender's lien priority. The premium for the lender's policy is paid by the buyer, unless otherwise agreed. In northern California, the buyer also typically pays for the owner's title insurance policy.

Inspection Fees. The cost of an inspection is allocated by agreement between the parties. Customarily, the buyer pays for the inspection fees.

Hazard Insurance. The lender generally requires the buyer to pay for one year of hazard insurance coverage in advance, at closing.

Attorney's Fees. A buyer who is represented by an attorney in the transaction pays her own attorney's fees. (The same is true for the seller.) In many transactions, the attorney's fees are not handled through escrow. Instead, each lawyer simply bills his client directly.

Recording Fees. The fees for recording the various documents involved in the transaction are usually charged to the party who benefits from the recording. Thus, the buyer pays the fees for recording the deed and the new mortgage or deed of trust.

Escrow Fee. Also called a settlement fee or closing fee, this is the escrow agent's charge for her services. The buyer and the seller commonly agree to split the escrow fee, so that each of them pays half.

Property Taxes. The seller is responsible for the property taxes up to the day of closing; the buyer is typically responsible for them on the day of closing and thereafter. If the seller has already paid some or all of the property taxes in advance, he receives a prorated refund from the buyer at closing. The amount of the refund is a debit for the buyer and a credit for the seller.

Fig. 11.4 Buyer's estimated net cost worksheet

Buyer's Estimated Net Cost	
Purchase Price	**$370,000.00**
Good faith deposit (credit)	− 10,000.00
Financing (credit)	− 335,000.00
Remainder (price less offsets)	**$25,000.00**
Buyer's Closing Costs	
Appraisal fee	+ 275.00
Credit report	+ 40.00
Origination fee	+ 3,350.00
Discount points	+ 10,050.00
Prepaid interest	+ 1,028.33
Lender's title insurance	+ 600.00
Inspection fees	+ 400.00
Hazard insurance	+ 375.00
Attorney's fees	+ 350.00
Recording fees	+ 50.00
Escrow fee	+ 250.00
Property taxes	+ 641.37
Estimated Net Cost	**$42,409.70**

Example: The sale is closing on April 14. This year the property taxes on the house are $2,996.65. Calculate the per diem rate by dividing that figure by 365.

$$\$2,996.65 \div 365 = \$8.21 \text{ per diem}$$

The seller is responsible for the property taxes from January 1 through April 13—in other words, for the first 103 days of the year. The buyer is responsible for them from April 14 to the end of the tax year, which in California is June

30. Annual property taxes in California are paid in two equal installments, so each installment for this property would be $1,498.33 ($2,996.65 ÷ 2 = $1,498.33).

The seller has already paid taxes through the end of June, so at closing he receives a credit for the share that is the buyer's responsibility. Multiply the number of days for which the seller is responsible by the per diem rate to determine the seller's share of the taxes. Then subtract the seller's share from the semi-annual figure to find the buyer's share.

$$103 \text{ days} \times \$8.21 = \$845.63 \text{ (Seller's share)}$$
$$\$1,498.33 - \$845.63 = \$652.70 \text{ (Buyer's share)}$$

This $652.70 will be a debit (a cost) for the buyer and a credit for the seller at closing. For your net cost estimate, add $652.70 to the buyer's net cost. (For a net proceeds estimate, you'd also add a credit of $652.70 to the seller's net proceeds.)

Estimated Total Cost. When all of the appropriate items on your net cost worksheet have been filled in, you're ready to calculate the buyer's estimated net cost. Subtract the buyer's credits from the purchase price, and then add all of the buyer's costs. The result is the net cost, the amount of money that the buyer will have to give to the escrow agent in order to close the sale.

Be sure your buyer knows what kind of check the escrow agent will accept. A certified check or cashier's check, rather than a personal check, is usually required.

Estimating the Seller's Net Proceeds

Now let's look at the costs and credits involved in estimating a seller's net proceeds.

Sales Price. The largest credit for the seller is, naturally, the sales price. It should be the starting point in your net proceeds calculation (see Figure 11.5). You'll add any other credits that the seller will receive at closing to the price, then subtract the costs that the seller must pay.

Refunds. The seller may be entitled to certain refunds at closing. As you've already seen, if the seller has paid the property taxes in advance, the buyer will have to refund the share for which she's responsible to the seller. That will increase the seller's net proceeds. (On the other hand, if the seller hasn't paid the taxes yet, he will have to pay a prorated share of them at closing, which will decrease the net proceeds.)

Another possible credit for the seller is a refund of funds remaining in the reserve account (or impound account) for the seller's loan. A seller often has reserves on deposit with his lender to cover future property taxes and hazard insurance premiums. When the seller's loan is paid off, the unused balance in the reserve account is refunded to the seller by the lender. If your seller will receive this type of refund, add it to the seller's net proceeds. The seller's lender can help you determine how much the refund of reserves will be.

Any other refunds that the seller will receive at closing should be treated in the same way.

Total Proceeds. On your net proceeds worksheet, add all of the seller's credits to the sales price to determine the seller's total proceeds. You'll be subtracting the seller's costs from this figure.

Seller Financing or Loan Assumption. We explained earlier that any type of financing is a credit for the buyer. Thus, just like a new loan, seller financing or an assumed loan is subtracted from the buyer's net cost. But unlike a new loan, seller financing or an assumed loan is also subtracted from the seller's net proceeds. That's because either of these financing arrangements will reduce the amount of cash the seller will receive at closing. (Note, however, that if the buyer obtains a new loan from a bank or other third-party lender, the loan amount has no effect on the seller's net proceeds.)

Payoff of Seller's Loan. If, like most sellers, your seller will have to pay off his existing mortgage loan, his net will be reduced by the payoff amount. This is the unpaid principal balance, plus any unpaid interest, as of the closing date. Even if you don't have a specific closing date yet, you can get a good idea of the payoff amount by asking the seller's lender what the current principal balance is.

The actual payoff amount will probably be somewhat less than the current balance (since it's likely that the seller will have to make at least one more mortgage payment before closing). But you don't need to be too concerned about the difference. Your estimate of the seller's net proceeds won't match the actual net proceeds exactly, and it's better if the estimate turns out to be somewhat lower than the actual figure, rather than somewhat higher. That way, the seller will be pleased rather than disappointed at closing. (For the same reason, it's better if the buyer's estimated net cost is a little higher than the actual figure.)

Interest on Seller's Loan. Because interest on a real estate loan is paid in arrears, when a transaction closes in the middle of the payment period the seller owes his lender some interest after paying off the principal balance.

> **Example:** The closing date is April 14. Although the seller made a mortgage payment on his loan on April 1, that payment did not include any of the interest that is accruing during April. The seller owes the lender interest for the period from April 1 through April 14. The escrow agent prorates the interest, charging the seller only for those days, rather than for the whole month.
>
> Suppose the remaining principal balance is $156,000 and the annual interest rate is 7%. First find the per diem amount.

$$156,000 \times .07 = \$10,920 \text{ annual interest}$$
$$\$10,920 \div 365 = \$29.92 \text{ per diem interest}$$
$$\$29.92 \times 14 \text{ days} = \$418.88$$

The seller owes the lender $418.88 in interest. Subtract this from the seller's net proceeds.

Suppose the seller in this example had arranged for the buyer to assume his loan. In that case, the buyer's first payment to the lender would be due May 1, and it would pay all of the interest for April. The seller would be debited for the interest owed up to April 14, and the buyer would be credited for the same amount.

Prepayment Penalty. This is a charge the seller's lender may impose on the seller for paying the loan off before the end of its term. If the seller must pay a prepayment penalty, contact the lender to determine approximately how much the penalty will be. Subtract the estimated penalty from the seller's net proceeds. Prepayment penalties are prohibited or limited in many types of loans (see Chapter 10).

Sales Commission. The real estate broker's commission is almost always paid by the seller. The amount of the commission is usually determined by multiplying the sales price by the commission rate.

> **Example:** Your listing agreement says that the seller will pay a brokerage commission of 7% of the sales price. The house sells for $370,000. $370,000 × .07 = $25,900. The amount of the brokerage commission is $25,900.

Fig. 11.5 Seller's estimated net proceeds worksheet

Seller's Estimated Net Proceeds	
Sales Price	**$370,000.00**
Prorated property taxes (credit)	+ 641.37
Reserve account (credit)	+ 1,000.64
Total Proceeds to Seller	**$371,642.01**
Seller's Closing Costs	
Loan payoff	– 156,000.00
Interest due on loan	– 424.62
Prepayment penalty	– 0.00
Other liens and assessments	– 0.00
Brokerage commission	– 25,900.00
Owner's title insurance	– 725.00
Seller-paid discount points	– 0.00
Documentary transfer tax	– 407.00
Repairs	– 500.00
Attorney's fees	– 0.00
Recording fees	– 24.00
Escrow fee	– 250.00
Estimated Net Proceeds	**$187,411.39**

Since the commission is one of the seller's costs, you should subtract it from the sales price when you're calculating the seller's net proceeds.

Owner's Title Insurance Premium. The premium for the owner's title insurance policy (which protects the buyer) is customarily paid by the seller in southern California. In northern California, the premium for the owner's policy is usually paid by the buyer, although in some counties the parties split the fee.

Discount Points. If the seller has agreed to pay discount points or other costs involved in the buyer's loan, these will be a debit for the seller on the settlement statement. Subtract them from the seller's net proceeds.

Documentary Transfer Tax. A documentary transfer tax is imposed on most sales of real property in California. As a general rule, the amount of the tax is 55 cents per every $500 of the selling price, or fraction thereof. (In certain cities, the rate is higher.) The documentary transfer tax is customarily paid by the seller.

> **Example:** A property's selling price is $370,000. The seller would owe $407 in documentary transfer tax. The tax would be calculated this way:

$$\$370,000 \div \$500 = 740$$
$$740 \times \$0.55 = \$407.00$$

If the buyer is assuming the seller's mortgage, the loan balance is subtracted from the selling price before the documentary transfer tax is calculated.

Repair Costs. The cost of repairs that the seller agreed to pay for will be deducted from the seller's proceeds at closing, unless the seller has already paid for them.

Attorney's Fees. The seller pays his own attorney's fees if he is represented by a lawyer. As we said, lawyers often bill their clients directly, rather than getting paid through the closing process.

Recording Fees. The seller pays the recording fees for the documents that are recorded for his benefit. For instance, the seller customarily pays the fee for recording a deed of reconveyance to release the property from the lien of the deed of trust he has paid off.

Escrow Fee. As we mentioned earlier, the seller customarily pays half of the escrow fee.

Estimated Net Proceeds. When you subtract the seller's loan payoff and all of the seller's closing costs from the seller's total proceeds, you arrive at the seller's estimated net proceeds, the amount he can expect to take away from closing. The escrow agent may offer the seller different options for receiving these funds, such as a cashier's check or direct deposit.

Laws that Affect Closing

To end the chapter, we'll discuss some laws that must be complied with when a real estate transaction closes. These include some laws related to income taxes, and also the Real Estate Settlement Procedures Act.

Income Tax Requirements

There are tax-related reporting and withholding requirements connected with closing that you should be aware of. The escrow agent (or other closing agent) is primarily responsible for ensuring that these requirements are met.

Form 1099 Reporting. A closing agent is generally required to report a real estate sale to the Internal Revenue Service. IRS Form 1099-S is used to report the seller's name and social security number and the gross proceeds from the sale. In most cases, the gross proceeds figure is the same as the property's sales price.

There are several exemptions from this reporting requirement. Most significantly, the form isn't required in the sale of a principal residence if: 1) the seller certifies in writing that none of the gain is taxable; and 2) the sale is for $250,000 or less ($500,000 or less if the seller is married).

Note that the closing agent is not permitted to charge an extra fee for filling out the 1099-S form.

Form 8300 Reporting. To help prevent money laundering and tax evasion, transactions involving large sums of cash must be reported to the federal government. A closing agent who receives more than $10,000 in cash must report the cash payment on IRS Form 8300. That's true even if the cash isn't received all at one time.

> **Example:** ABC Escrow is handling the closing for a real estate sale. To finalize the transaction, the buyer must deposit $12,000 into escrow. He wants to give the escrow agent the money in cash instead of writing a check, and he also wants to split it into two separate payments. He gives ABC Escrow $8,000 in cash on Thursday and another $4,000 in cash on Friday. Although each payment was less than $10,000, ABC Escrow will need to submit Form 8300 to the IRS because the two payments relate to the same transaction.

The closing agent must file Form 8300 within 15 days of receiving the cash, and a copy of the form should be kept on file for five years.

FIRPTA. The Foreign Investment in Real Property Tax Act (FIRPTA) helps prevent foreign investors from evading tax liability on income generated from the sale of real estate in the United States. To comply with FIRPTA, the buyer must determine whether the seller is a "foreign person" (someone who is not a U.S. citizen or a resident alien). If the seller is a foreign person, then the buyer must withhold 10% of the amount realized from the sale and forward that amount to the Internal Revenue Service. (The amount realized is usually the sales price.) This must occur within 20 days after the transfer date. In most cases, the closing agent handles these requirements on behalf of the buyer.

Many purchase agreement forms have a provision concerning FIRPTA compliance. The seller and the buyer agree to sign any documents necessary to comply with FIRPTA (or with the state withholding law discussed below).

Unless the transaction is exempt from FIRPTA, the closing agent will usually prepare a certification for the seller to sign, stating that the seller is not a "foreign person" under the terms of this law. But if the seller is a foreign person, the closing agent will withhold the required amount instead.

Various types of transactions are exempt from FIRPTA's requirements. For example, a residential transaction is exempt if the buyer is purchasing the property for use as her home and the purchase price is $300,000 or less.

California Withholding Law. In some transactions, the closing agent must withhold 3.33% of the sales price from the seller as a prepayment of any state income tax due on the gain. (Alternatively, the seller can opt for a withholding amount based on his estimated gain from the sale.) The funds withheld must be transmitted to the Franchise Tax Board.

This law also has a number of exemptions. For example, a real estate transaction is exempt if the sales price is $100,000 or less, or if the property was the seller's principal residence.

Real Estate Settlement Procedures Act

The Real Estate Settlement Procedures Act (RESPA) affects how closing is handled in most residential transactions financed with institutional loans. The law has two main goals:

- to provide borrowers with information about their closing costs; and
- to eliminate kickbacks and referral fees that unnecessarily increase closing costs.

Transactions Covered by RESPA. RESPA applies to "federally related" loan transactions. A loan is federally related if:

1. it will be secured by a mortgage or deed of trust against:
   * property on which there is (or on which the loan proceeds will be used to build) a dwelling with four or fewer units;
   * a condominium unit or a cooperative apartment; or
   * a lot with (or on which the loan proceeds will be used to place) a mobile home; and
2. the lender is federally regulated, has federally insured accounts, is assisted by the federal government, makes loans in connection with a federal program, sells loans to Fannie Mae, Ginnie Mae, or Freddie Mac, or makes real estate loans that total more than $1,000,000 per year.

In short, the act applies to almost all institutional lenders and to most residential loans.

Exemptions. RESPA does not apply to the following loan transactions:

* a loan used to purchase 25 acres or more;
* a loan primarily for a business, commercial, or agricultural purpose;
* a loan used to purchase vacant land, unless there will be a one- to four-unit dwelling built on it or a mobile home placed on it;
* temporary financing, such as a construction loan; or
* an assumption for which the lender's approval is neither required nor obtained.

Note that RESPA also does not apply to seller-financed transactions, since they are not federally regulated.

RESPA Requirements. RESPA has the following requirements for federally related loan transactions:

1. Within three business days of receiving a loan application, the lender must mail or deliver to every applicant:
   * a copy of a booklet (meeting government standards) that explains RESPA and closing costs;
   * a loan estimate form* providing estimates of the closing costs that the borrower will pay; and

---

* This is the same form required by the Truth in Lending Act (see Chapter 9). To comply with RESPA and TILA, in October 2015 lenders must start using the loan estimate form and the closing disclosure form described on the following pages and shown in Figure 11.6.

- a mortgage servicing disclosure statement, to inform the borrower whether the lender plans to have a different entity service the loan (collect the payments owed).

2. If a lender or other settlement service provider requires the borrower to use a particular attorney, credit reporting agency, or appraiser, that requirement must be disclosed to the borrower at the time of the loan application or service agreement.

3. If any settlement service provider is in a position to refer a borrower to an "affiliated" provider, that joint business relationship must be fully disclosed at the time of referral, along with fee estimates and language that the referral is optional.

4. No later than three business days before closing, the lender must give the borrower a closing disclosure form (discussed below) showing the actual closing costs the borrower will pay, along with other information.

5. If the borrower will be required to make deposits into an impound account to cover taxes, insurance, and other recurring costs, the lender cannot require excessive deposits (more than necessary to cover the expenses when they come due, plus a two-month cushion).

6. A lender or other settlement service provider (such as a title company or a real estate agent) may not:
   - pay or accept kickbacks or referral fees (a payment from one settlement service provider to another provider for referring customers);
   - pay or accept unearned fees (a charge that one settlement service provider shares with another provider who hasn't actually performed any services in exchange for the payment); or
   - charge a fee for the preparation of the loan estimate form, the closing disclosure form, or an impound account statement.

7. The seller may not require the buyer to use a particular title company.

RESPA's prohibition on referral fees and unearned fees (number 6 above) is intended to prevent practices that were once widespread and that generally benefited lenders, real estate agents, and other settlement service providers at the expense of home buyers. Note that this prohibition doesn't apply to referral fees that one real estate licensee or firm pays to another for referring potential brokerage customers or clients, or to commission sharing arrangements between real estate licensees.

Closing Disclosure Form. RESPA and the Truth in Lending Act require lenders to disclose the parties' actual closing costs on a closing disclosure form. (See Figure 11.6.)

The closing disclosure form generally tracks the contents of the loan estimate form, but it also includes the seller's closing costs and credits and any amounts paid by third parties. To present this information clearly, the second and third pages are laid out in a detailed grid that takes the place of a settlement statement.

As noted earlier, the buyer and the seller must receive the closing disclosure form no later than three business days before closing. They should check it closely.

The law limits how much certain categories of loan costs can increase between the time the buyer receives the loan estimate form and the closing date. These limits on increases, referred to as "tolerances," help prevent bait and switch tactics: giving a buyer low estimates when the loan application is submitted, but charging much more than the estimated amounts after the buyer has committed to the lender. If the buyer doesn't have the option of shopping for a particular service (because the lender requires the use of a certain settlement service provider), then a "zero tolerance" rule applies; in other words, the buyer can't be charged any more than the estimate that was given for that service.

A key section of the closing disclosure form is the table at the top of the second page. It directly compares the estimated closing costs that appeared on the buyer's loan estimate form to the actual charges that the buyer is paying at closing.

Lenders can avoid penalties for excessive increases in their initial cost estimates by providing the buyer with an amended loan estimate form. If a buyer pays an excessive charge, the lender must refund the excess within 60 days after closing.

Fig. 11.6 Sample closing disclosure form

Closing Disclosure

This form is a statement of final loan terms and closing costs. Compare this document with your Loan Estimate.

Closing Information

Date Issued	4/15/20XX
Closing Date	4/15/20XX
Disbursement Date	4/15/20XX
Settlement Agent	Epsilon Title Co.
File #	12-3456
Property	456 Somewhere Ave
	Anytown, ST 12345
Sale Price	$180,000

Transaction Information

Borrower	Michael Jones and Mary Stone
	123 Anywhere Street
	Anytown, ST 12345
Seller	Steve Cole and Amy Doe
	321 Somewhere Drive
	Anytown, ST 12345
Lender	Ficus Bank

Loan Information

Loan Term	30 years
Purpose	Purchase
Product	Fixed Rate
Loan Type	☒ Conventional ☐ FHA
	☐ VA ☐ _____
Loan ID #	123456789
MIC #	000654321

Loan Terms

		Can this amount increase after closing?
Loan Amount	$162,000	**NO**
Interest Rate	3.875%	**NO**
Monthly Principal & Interest *See Projected Payments below for your Estimated Total Monthly Payment*	$761.78	**NO**
		Does the loan have these features?
Prepayment Penalty		**YES** • **As high as $3,240** if you pay off the loan during the first 2 years
Balloon Payment		**NO**

Projected Payments

Payment Calculation	Years 1-7	Years 8-30
Principal & Interest	$761.78	$761.78
Mortgage Insurance	+ 82.35	+ —
Estimated Escrow *Amount can increase over time*	+ 206.13	+ 206.13
Estimated Total Monthly Payment	**$1,050.26**	**$967.91**

Estimated Taxes, Insurance & Assessments *Amount can increase over time* *See page 4 for details*	$356.13 a month	**This estimate includes** ☒ Property Taxes ☒ Homeowner's Insurance ☒ Other: Homeowner's Association Dues *See Escrow Account on page 4 for details. You must pay for other property costs separately.*	**In escrow?** YES YES NO

Costs at Closing

Closing Costs	$9,712.10	Includes $4,694.05 in Loan Costs + $5,018.05 in Other Costs – $0 in Lender Credits. *See page 2 for details.*
Cash to Close	$14,147.26	Includes Closing Costs. *See Calculating Cash to Close on page 3 for details.*

CLOSING DISCLOSURE

PAGE 1 OF 5 • LOAN ID # 123456789

Source: Consumer Financial Protection Bureau.

Closing Cost Details

Loan Costs		Borrower-Paid		Seller-Paid		Paid by Others
		At Closing	Before Closing	At Closing	Before Closing	
A. Origination Charges		**$1,802.00**				
01 0.25 % of Loan Amount (Points)		$405.00				
02 Application Fee		$300.00				
03 Underwriting Fee		$1,097.00				
04						
05						
06						
07						
08						
B. Services Borrower Did Not Shop For		**$236.55**				
01 Appraisal Fee	to John Smith Appraisers Inc.					$405.00
02 Credit Report Fee	to Information Inc.		$29.80			
03 Flood Determination Fee	to Info Co.	$20.00				
04 Flood Monitoring Fee	to Info Co.	$31.75				
05 Tax Monitoring Fee	to Info Co.	$75.00				
06 Tax Status Research Fee	to Info Co.	$80.00				
07						
08						
09						
10						
C. Services Borrower Did Shop For		**$2,655.50**				
01 Pest Inspection Fee	to Pests Co.	$120.50				
02 Survey Fee	to Surveys Co.	$85.00				
03 Title – Insurance Binder	to Epsilon Title Co.	$650.00				
04 Title – Lender's Title Insurance	to Epsilon Title Co.	$500.00				
05 Title – Settlement Agent Fee	to Epsilon Title Co.	$500.00				
06 Title – Title Search	to Epsilon Title Co.	$800.00				
07						
08						
D. TOTAL LOAN COSTS (Borrower-Paid)		**$4,694.05**				
Loan Costs Subtotals (A + B + C)		$4,664.25	$29.80			

Other Costs						
E. Taxes and Other Government Fees		**$85.00**				
01 Recording Fees	Deed: $40.00 Mortgage: $45.00	$85.00				
02 Transfer Tax	to Any State			$950.00		
F. Prepaids		**$2,120.80**				
01 Homeowner's Insurance Premium (12 mo.) to Insurance Co.		$1,209.96				
02 Mortgage Insurance Premium (mo.)						
03 Prepaid Interest ($17.44 per day from 4/15/13 to 5/1/13)		$279.04				
04 Property Taxes (6 mo.) to Any County USA		$631.80				
05						
G. Initial Escrow Payment at Closing		**$412.25**				
01 Homeowner's Insurance $100.83 per month for 2 mo.		$201.66				
02 Mortgage Insurance per month for mo.						
03 Property Taxes $105.30 per month for 2 mo.		$210.60				
04						
05						
06						
07						
08 Aggregate Adjustment		– 0.01				
H. Other		**$2,400.00**				
01 HOA Capital Contribution	to HOA Acre Inc.	$500.00				
02 HOA Processing Fee	to HOA Acre Inc.	$150.00				
03 Home Inspection Fee	to Engineers Inc.	$750.00			$750.00	
04 Home Warranty Fee	to XYZ Warranty Inc.			$450.00		
05 Real Estate Commission	to Alpha Real Estate Broker			$5,700.00		
06 Real Estate Commission	to Omega Real Estate Broker			$5,700.00		
07 Title – Owner's Title Insurance (optional) to Epsilon Title Co.		$1,000.00				
08						
I. TOTAL OTHER COSTS (Borrower-Paid)		**$5,018.05**				
Other Costs Subtotals (E + F + G + H)		$5,018.05				
J. TOTAL CLOSING COSTS (Borrower-Paid)		**$9,712.10**				
Closing Costs Subtotals (D + I)		$9,682.30	$29.80	$12,800.00	$750.00	$405.00
Lender Credits						

CLOSING DISCLOSURE

Calculating Cash to Close

Use this table to see what has changed from your Loan Estimate.

	Loan Estimate	Final	Did this change?
Total Closing Costs (J)	$8,054.00	$9,712.10	YES · See **Total Loan Costs (D)** and **Total Other Costs (I)**
Closing Costs Paid Before Closing	$0	– $29.80	YES · You paid these Closing Costs **before closing**
Closing Costs Financed (Paid from your Loan Amount)	$0	$0	NO
Down Payment/Funds from Borrower	$18,000.00	$18,000.00	NO
Deposit	– $10,000.00	– $10,000.00	NO
Funds for Borrower	$0	$0	NO
Seller Credits	$0	– $2,500.00	YES · See Seller Credits in **Section L**
Adjustments and Other Credits	$0	– $1,035.04	YES · See details in **Sections K and L**
Cash to Close	$16,054.00	$14,147.26	

Summaries of Transactions

Use this table to see a summary of your transaction.

BORROWER'S TRANSACTION

K. Due from Borrower at Closing	$189,762.30
01 Sale Price of Property	$180,000.00
02 Sale Price of Any Personal Property Included in Sale	
03 Closing Costs Paid at Closing (J)	$9,682.30
04	
Adjustments	
05	
06	
07	

Adjustments for Items Paid by Seller in Advance

08 City/Town Taxes to	
09 County Taxes to	
10 Assessments to	
11 HOA Dues 4/15/13 to 4/30/13	$80.00
12	
13	
14	
15	

L. Paid Already by or on Behalf of Borrower at Closing	$175,615.04
01 Deposit	$10,000.00
02 Loan Amount	$162,000.00
03 Existing Loan(s) Assumed or Taken Subject to	
04	
05 Seller Credit	$2,500.00
Other Credits	
06 Rebate from Epsilon Title Co.	$750.00
07	
Adjustments	
08	
09	
10	
11	

Adjustments for Items Unpaid by Seller

12 City/Town Taxes 1/1/13 to 4/14/13	$365.04
13 County Taxes to	
14 Assessments to	
15	
16	
17	

CALCULATION

Total Due from Borrower at Closing (K)	$189,762.30
Total Paid Already by or on Behalf of Borrower at Closing (L)	– $175,615.04
Cash to Close ☒ From ☐ To Borrower	**$14,147.26**

SELLER'S TRANSACTION

M. Due to Seller at Closing	$180,080.00
01 Sale Price of Property	$180,000.00
02 Sale Price of Any Personal Property Included in Sale	
03	
04	
05	
06	
07	
08	

Adjustments for Items Paid by Seller in Advance

09 City/Town Taxes to	
10 County Taxes to	
11 Assessments to	
12 HOA Dues 4/15/13 to 4/30/13	$80.00
13	
14	
15	
16	

N. Due from Seller at Closing	$115,665.04
01 Excess Deposit	
02 Closing Costs Paid at Closing (J)	$12,800.00
03 Existing Loan(s) Assumed or Taken Subject to	
04 Payoff of First Mortgage Loan	$100,000.00
05 Payoff of Second Mortgage Loan	
06	
07	
08 Seller Credit	$2,500.00
09	
10	
11	
12	
13	

Adjustments for Items Unpaid by Seller

14 City/Town Taxes 1/1/13 to 4/14/13	$365.04
15 County Taxes to	
16 Assessments to	
17	
18	
19	

CALCULATION

Total Due to Seller at Closing (M)	$180,080.00
Total Due from Seller at Closing (N)	– $115,665.04
Cash ☐ From ☒ To Seller	**$64,414.96**

CLOSING DISCLOSURE

PAGE 3 OF 5 · LOAN ID # 123456789

Additional Information About This Loan

Loan Disclosures

Assumption

If you sell or transfer this property to another person, your lender

☐ will allow, under certain conditions, this person to assume this loan on the original terms.

☒ will not allow assumption of this loan on the original terms.

Demand Feature

Your loan

☐ has a demand feature, which permits your lender to require early repayment of the loan. You should review your note for details.

☒ does not have a demand feature.

Late Payment

If your payment is more than *15* days late, your lender will charge a late fee of *5% of the monthly principal and interest payment.*

Negative Amortization (Increase in Loan Amount)

Under your loan terms, you

☐ are scheduled to make monthly payments that do not pay all of the interest due that month. As a result, your loan amount will increase (negatively amortize), and your loan amount will likely become larger than your original loan amount. Increases in your loan amount lower the equity you have in this property.

☐ may have monthly payments that do not pay all of the interest due that month. If you do, your loan amount will increase (negatively amortize), and, as a result, your loan amount may become larger than your original loan amount. Increases in your loan amount lower the equity you have in this property.

☒ do not have a negative amortization feature.

Partial Payments

Your lender

☒ may accept payments that are less than the full amount due (partial payments) and apply them to your loan.

☐ may hold them in a separate account until you pay the rest of the payment, and then apply the full payment to your loan.

☐ does not accept any partial payments.

If this loan is sold, your new lender may have a different policy.

Security Interest

You are granting a security interest in

456 Somewhere Ave., Anytown, ST 12345

You may lose this property if you do not make your payments or satisfy other obligations for this loan.

Escrow Account

For now, your loan

☒ will have an escrow account (also called an "impound" or "trust" account) to pay the property costs listed below. Without an escrow account, you would pay them directly, possibly in one or two large payments a year. Your lender may be liable for penalties and interest for failing to make a payment.

Escrow		
Escrowed Property Costs over Year 1	$2,473.56	Estimated total amount over year 1 for your escrowed property costs: *Homeowner's Insurance Property Taxes*
Non-Escrowed Property Costs over Year 1	$1,800.00	Estimated total amount over year 1 for your non-escrowed property costs: *Homeowner's Association Dues* You may have other property costs.
Initial Escrow Payment	$412.25	A cushion for the escrow account you pay at closing. See Section G on page 2.
Monthly Escrow Payment	$206.13	The amount included in your total monthly payment.

☐ will not have an escrow account because ☐ you declined it ☐ your lender does not offer one. You must directly pay your property costs, such as taxes and homeowner's insurance. Contact your lender to ask if your loan can have an escrow account.

No Escrow	
Estimated Property Costs over Year 1	Estimated total amount over year 1. You must pay these costs directly, possibly in one or two large payments a year.
Escrow Waiver Fee	

In the future,

Your property costs may change and, as a result, your escrow payment may change. You may be able to cancel your escrow account, but if you do, you must pay your property costs directly. If you fail to pay your property taxes, your state or local government may (1) impose fines and penalties or (2) place a tax lien on this property. If you fail to pay any of your property costs, your lender may (1) add the amounts to your loan balance, (2) add an escrow account to your loan, or (3) require you to pay for property insurance that the lender buys on your behalf, which likely would cost more and provide fewer benefits than what you could buy on your own.

Loan Calculations

Total of Payments. Total you will have paid after you make all payments of principal, interest, mortgage insurance, and loan costs, as scheduled.	$285,803.36
Finance Charge. The dollar amount the loan will cost you.	$118,830.27
Amount Financed. The loan amount available after paying your upfront finance charge.	$162,000.00
Annual Percentage Rate (APR). Your costs over the loan term expressed as a rate. This is not your interest rate.	4.174%
Total Interest Percentage (TIP). The total amount of interest that you will pay over the loan term as a percentage of your loan amount.	69.46%

Questions? If you have questions about the loan terms or costs on this form, use the contract information below. To get more information or make a complaint, contact the Consumer Financial Protection Bureau at **www.consumerfinance.gov/mortgage-closing**

Other Disclosures

Appraisal
If the property was appraised for your loan, your lender is required to give you a copy at no additional cost at least 3 days before closing. If you have not yet received it, please contact your lender at the information listed below.

Contract Details
See your note and security instrument for information about
• what happens if you fail to make your payments,
• what is a default on the loan,
• situations in which your lender can require early repayment of the loan, and
• the rules for making payments before they are due.

Liability after Foreclosure
If your lender forecloses on this property and the foreclosure does not cover the amount of unpaid balance on this loan,
☒ state law may protect you from liability for the unpaid balance. If you refinance or take on any additional debt on this property, you may lose this protection and have to pay any debt remaining even after foreclosure. You may want to consult a lawyer for more information.
☐ state law does not protect you from liability for the unpaid balance.

Refinance
Refinancing this loan will depend on your future financial situation, the property value, and market conditions. You may not be able to refinance this loan.

Tax Deductions
If you borrow more than this property is worth, the interest on the loan amount above this property's fair market value is not deductible from your federal income taxes. You should consult a tax advisor for more information.

Contact Information

	Lender	Mortgage Broker	Real Estate Broker (B)	Real Estate Broker (S)	Settlement Agent
Name	Ficus Bank		Omega Real Estate Broker Inc.	Alpha Real Estate Broker Co.	Epsilon Title Co.
Address	4321 Random Blvd. Somecity, ST 12340		789 Local Lane Sometown, ST 12345	987 Suburb Ct. Someplace, ST 12340	123 Commerce Pl. Somecity, ST 12344
NMLS ID					
ST License ID			Z765416	Z61456	Z61616
Contact	Joe Smith		Samuel Green	Joseph Cain	Sarah Arnold
Contact NMLS ID	12345				
Contact ST License ID			P16415	P51461	PT1234
Email	joesmith@ ficusbank.com		sam@omegare.biz	joe@alphare.biz	sarah@ epsilontitle.com
Phone	123-456-7890		123-555-1717	321-555-7171	987-555-4321

Confirm Receipt

By signing, you are only confirming that you have received this form. You do not have to accept this loan because you have signed or received this form.

_____   _____   _____   _____
Applicant Signature   Date   Co-Applicant Signature   Date

CLOSING DISCLOSURE   PAGE 5 OF 5 • LOAN ID # 123456789

Chapter Summary

1. Most real estate transactions in California are closed through the escrow process. The buyer and seller deposit money and documents with the escrow agent (or other closing agent), who holds those deposits until they can be disbursed or delivered to the proper parties. The escrow agent may also handle a variety of other tasks, such as preparing documents for the parties to sign, ordering the preliminary title report, and calculating and prorating closing costs.

2. Some of the most important aspects of the closing process are inspections and repairs, approval of the buyer's loan, the appraisal, and the purchase of hazard insurance and title insurance. As a real estate agent, you should have a checklist of what needs to be done and make sure everything is getting done in time for the closing date. It's part of your job to keep the sale on track.

3. You should be able to provide good estimates of the buyer's net cost and the seller's net proceeds. To do this, you need to be familiar with the standard closing costs and who typically pays them. You must also be able to prorate certain expenses, such as property taxes and hazard insurance.

4. The income tax requirements that apply to real estate closings include the Form 1099 and Form 8300 reporting rules, the Foreign Investment in Real Property Tax Act, and the California withholding law. In some transactions, a portion of the seller's proceeds must be withheld and sent to the IRS or the Franchise Tax Board.

5. The Real Estate Settlement Procedures Act helps home buyers and sellers understand their closing costs. RESPA applies to most residential real estate transactions financed with institutional loans. Key requirements include the loan estimate and closing disclosure forms. The prohibition on kickbacks and referral fees for settlement service providers is another important aspect of RESPA.

Key Terms

Escrow: An arrangement in which something of value (such as money or a deed) is held on behalf of the parties to a transaction by an escrow agent until specified conditions have been fulfilled.

Escrow agent: An agent who holds things of value on behalf of the parties to a transaction in an escrow arrangement.

Hazard insurance: Insurance against damage to real property caused by fire, theft, vandalism, and other covered perils.

Settlement statement: A document that presents a final, detailed accounting for a real estate transaction, listing each party's debits and credits and the amount each will receive or pay at closing.

Debits and credits: A debit is a charge or debt owed by a party, and a credit is a payment owed to a party.

Prepaid (interim) interest: Interest on a new loan that must be paid at the time of closing; covers the interest due for the first month of the loan term.

FIRPTA: The Foreign Investment in Real Property Tax Act, which requires that an escrow agent must withhold funds from the sale of real property by a seller who is not a U.S. citizen, in order to prevent tax evasion.

RESPA: A federal law that governs residential real estate closings, requiring disclosure of closing costs and prohibiting payment of kickbacks to settlement service providers.

Closing disclosure form: A form required by RESPA and TILA in most residential transactions; it discloses each party's closing costs and also shows how the actual loan charges compare to the estimates in the buyer's loan estimate form.

Chapter Quiz

1. Although the terms are often used interchangeably, the technical difference between an escrow agent and a closing agent is that:
   a. an escrow agent is a licensed escrow company, while a closing agent is anyone providing escrow services
   b. a closing agent represents the interests of only one party to a transaction, while an escrow agent acts on behalf of both parties
   c. the term "closing agent" refers specifically to a real estate broker who is providing escrow services
   d. None of the above; there is no difference

2. Which of the following is not one of the steps in the inspection process?
   a. Ordering the inspection
   b. Approval or disapproval of the inspection report
   c. Appraisal of the property
   d. Reinspection of any required repairs

3. When choosing a home inspector, a buyer should look for a firm that:
   a. has recently changed its name
   b. will offer to make the repairs recommended by the inspection
   c. belongs to the American Society of Home Inspectors
   d. does other business in addition to inspections

4. An HO-3 hazard insurance policy would cover damages resulting from:
   a. floods
   b. fires
   c. earthquakes
   d. encroachments

5. If a home buyer is concerned about title problems that do not show up in the public record, he should:
   a. make sure there are no problems listed in the preliminary title report
   b. require the seller to purchase a standard coverage title insurance policy
   c. rely on the lender's title insurance policy
   d. get a homeowner's coverage title insurance policy

6. On a settlement statement, the debits represent:
   a. the amount of financing in the transaction
   b. amounts that are owed to a party at closing
   c. costs that a party must pay at closing
   d. costs that the buyer must pay to the seller

7. The good faith deposit is:
   a. retained by the broker at closing as her commission
   b. applied toward the purchase price at closing
   c. a credit for the buyer on the settlement statement
   d. Both b and c

8. Prepaid interest refers to:
   a. the charge that the buyer must pay at closing to cover interest that will accrue on his loan during the last part of the month in which closing occurs
   b. the refund to the seller of reserves on deposit in an impound account with her lender
   c. the interest owed by the seller at closing after paying off the principal balance of her loan
   d. the fact that mortgage interest is usually paid in advance

9. The seller customarily pays the fee for recording the:
   a. deed of reconveyance
   b. deed from the seller to the buyer
   c. new mortgage or deed of trust
   d. None of the above

10. A loan secured by a deed of trust on the home the buyer is purchasing will be considered a "federally related" loan if the:
    a. person responsible for closing must report the sale to the IRS
    b. lender sells loans to Fannie Mae
    c. closing agent is required to withhold part of the proceeds under FIRPTA
    d. loan is used to purchase more than 25 acres

Answer Key

1. a.   The two terms are often used interchangeably, but technically the term "escrow agent" refers to a licensed escrow company. "Closing agent" refers to anyone providing escrow services—a lawyer, an escrow company, a broker, a lender, etc.

2. c.   During the closing process, the initial inspection needs to be ordered, and then the inspection report must be approved or rejected by the buyer and/or the lender. If the seller makes repairs, a reinspection will be necessary. (The appraisal is a separate matter, not part of the inspection process.)

3. c.   Membership in the American Society of Home Inspectors requires actual experience, passing a written examination, inspection reviews, and continuing education.

4. b.   Floods and earthquakes are not covered by a typical hazard insurance policy, although supplemental coverage may be available. (Protection against encroachments would be provided by extended coverage title insurance, not by hazard insurance.)

5. d.   A homeowner's coverage title insurance policy will protect the buyer against problems that do not appear in the public record, such as an encroachment or adverse possession.

6. c.   Debits are costs that a party must pay at closing, either to the other party or to a third party. The buyer's debits increase the amount of money the buyer will need to pay at closing. The seller's debits decrease the seller's net proceeds.

7. d.   The good faith deposit is applied toward the purchase price at closing; it's part of the buyer's downpayment. Because the buyer has already paid the good faith deposit, it is treated as a credit for the buyer on his settlement statement.

8. a.   The buyer's first payment on a new loan is not due the first day of the month immediately after closing, but the first day of the month after that. To cover the interest that accrues during the remainder of the month in which closing occurs, the buyer must pay prepaid or interim interest at closing.

9. a. The seller would pay the fee for recording a deed of reconveyance to release the property from the lien of a deed of trust. The recording fee for a document is generally paid by the party who benefits most from having that document recorded.

10. b. For RESPA purposes, a loan is federally related if the lender is federally regulated, has federally insured accounts, is assisted by the federal government, makes loans in connection with a federal program, sells loans to Fannie Mae, Ginnie Mae, or Freddie Mac, or makes real estate loans that total more than $1,000,000 per year.

12

Property Management

Investing in Real Estate

- Investment characteristics
- Advantages of investing in real estate

Types of Managed Properties

- Residential rental property
- Other types of property

The Property Management Agreement

The Management Plan

- Preliminary study
- Management proposal

Management Functions

- Leasing and tenant relations
- Recordkeeping and manager/owner relations
- Maintenance

Introduction

You successfully helped the Herreras complete the purchase of a new home. Now, perhaps a few years later, they are doing well financially and are looking to buy an investment property. They liked working with you and ask you to represent them again this time. Not only do they want your help with the purchase, they also want to know if you can manage the property for them.

Many brokerage offices engage in property management to some degree, so all real estate agents should have an understanding of property management principles. We'll begin by covering the basics of investing in real estate and the differences between types of managed properties. Then, focusing on income-producing residential property, we'll discuss how the management of real estate is organized, examining the property management agreement, the management plan, and the various functions of a property manager.

Investing in Real Estate

Real property has value for two basic reasons: it has value because it can be used, and it also has investment value. For property owners who do not live on or otherwise make use of their property, the investment aspect is the most important. Someone who owns property as an investment may not have time to devote a lot of attention to it, but still wants the investment to perform well. To ensure this, the owner usually hires someone else to manage the property. A person other than the owner who supervises the operation of income-producing property in exchange for a fee is called a **property manager**.

A property manager's job begins after someone has decided to invest in income-producing property, such as an apartment building, office building, or shopping center. The manager's primary function is to help the property owner achieve her investment goals. So before discussing the nuts and bolts of property management, let's take a brief look at general investment principles and at real estate as an investment. (A word of caution: real estate agents should not act as investment counselors; they should always refer clients to an accountant, attorney, or investment specialist for investment advice.)

Investment Characteristics

An investment is an asset that is expected to generate a **return** (a profit). A return on an investment can take various forms, including interest, dividends, or appreciation in value. An asset appreciates in value because of inflation, and may also appreciate because of a rising demand for the asset. For example, a parcel of prime vacant land appreciates in value as developable land becomes increasingly scarce.

An investor considers any investment in terms of liquidity, safety, and total return on the investment (sometimes called **yield**). These three characteristics are interrelated. For example, liquidity and safety generally go together. On the other hand, in exchange for a high return an investor often sacrifices safety or liquidity, or both.

A **liquid asset** is one that can be converted into cash quickly. Money in a bank account is extremely liquid: to convert it into cash, the investor need only present the bank with a withdrawal slip or check. Mutual funds, stocks, and bonds are less liquid—they take a little longer (perhaps a week or so) to convert into cash. Other items, such as jewelry or coin collections, are not liquid at all, because an investor might have to wait months to exchange those assets for cash. Real estate is not a liquid asset.

Liquid investments do not offer very high returns. In general, the more liquid the asset, the lower the return. For example, the money in your wallet is the most liquid asset you can have, but it earns no return (interest) at all. Money in a savings account is a little less liquid—you have to go to the bank to withdraw it—but it offers a modest return in the form of a low rate of interest. By contrast, real estate can offer a very high rate of return, but it is not at all liquid.

The most liquid investments are generally considered the safest. With liquid assets, there is little risk of losing the asset itself. Money in the bank is both liquid and safe. Since your deposit is insured by the federal government (up to $250,000), there is little chance of losing your investment. Other, less liquid types of investments, such as gold or real estate, are not as safe. For example, if a property owner must sell when real estate values are low, the owner may lose a good portion of his original investment in the property.

Investments that are both safe and liquid offer the lowest returns. In a sense, investors "pay" for safety and liquidity with a low return. Savings accounts and certificates of deposit, both safe investments, offer relatively low returns. Mutual funds, gold, and real estate can generate high returns, but at a considerable risk to the investor. For some types of assets, such as real estate, the safety of the investment will increase if the investor can afford to keep the investment for a long period of time. For example, if an investor does not need to cash out her investment in real estate for ten or fifteen years, chances are good that she will reap a high return. This is true because the investor will have more control over when to sell the asset, and so will be able to take full advantage of healthy market conditions.

> **Example:** Jeanne and Harold both invest $20,000 in rental homes in the same year. One year later, Jeanne desperately needs some cash and is forced to sell her rental home at a loss. She ends up with only $17,000 out of her original $20,000 investment.
>
> Harold, on the other hand, keeps his rental home for 12 years. He's in no hurry to sell his property, so he can wait for optimal market conditions. He sells at the peak of a real estate cycle, when property values are high. Because Harold could choose when to sell his property, he walks away from the transaction with $45,000, a healthy return on his original $20,000 investment.

Advantages of Investing in Real Estate

People invest in real estate for many reasons. The advantages of investing in real estate can be broken down into three general categories:

- appreciation,
- leverage, and
- cash flow.

Appreciation. Appreciation refers to an increase in a property's value due to changes in the economy or other outside factors. As we have seen in recent years, real estate values fluctuate; they can go down as well as up. However, it's generally safe to assume that over an extended period of time real estate will increase in value at a rate equal to or higher than the rate of inflation. Thus, real estate may be considered an effective hedge against inflation. When buildable property becomes scarce, the value of properties in prime locations increases even more rapidly.

Appreciation causes a property owner's equity to increase. **Equity** is the difference between the value of the property and the liens against it, so an increase in the property's value increases the owner's equity in the property. Also, each monthly mortgage payment typically increases the owner's equity, in proportion to the reduction of the principal amount of the loan. Equity adds to the investor's net worth and can also be used to secure an equity loan (a mortgage against the owner's equity in the property). So even though real estate is not considered a liquid asset, equity in real estate can be used to generate cash funds.

Leverage. Real estate investors can take advantage of **leverage**, which is defined as using borrowed money to invest in an asset. If the asset appreciates, then the investor earns money on the money borrowed, as well as on the money he invested.

> **Example:** Martin purchases a rental home for $315,000. He makes a $63,000 downpayment and borrows the rest of the purchase price. The rent generated by the property covers all the expenses of operating the property, plus the mortgage payment and income taxes. The property appreciates at 3% per year for five years. At the end of the five years, Martin sells the property for $365,000. He's made a $50,000 profit over five years on his $63,000 investment. This represents a 79% return over the five-year period. The property appreciated at 3% per year, but because he only invested 20% of the purchase price, Martin was able to generate a 79% return on his investment.

Cash Flow. Many real estate investments not only appreciate in value, but also generate a positive cash flow. **Cash flow** is the difference between the income generated by the property and the expenses associated with it, including operating costs, mortgage payments, and the owner's income taxes.

Cash flow may be either positive or negative, depending on whether or not the income from the investment exceeds the expenses. Some real estate investors are mainly interested in generating a return through appreciation and may be willing to accept a negative cash flow; but most hope for a positive cash flow as well as appreciation. When a real estate investment generates a positive cash flow, the investor's monthly income increases. Thus, a real estate investment can increase both the investor's net worth (through appreciation of the property) and her income (through positive cash flow). Investors sometimes use the term "cash on cash," which refers to a property's annual cash flow divided by the initial investment. This figure gives a quick sense of the immediate return the investor is earning.

Another way in which a piece of real estate can generate cash is through a **sale-leaseback** arrangement. In a sale-leaseback, someone who owns a building that he uses for his business sells the building to an investor, but then leases it back from the investor and continues to use it. The money generated by the sale can be used for expansion, acquiring inventory, or investment elsewhere. The seller obtains more cash through the sale than would ordinarily be possible by mortgaging the property, since lenders will not often lend 100% of the value. At the same time, the seller can deduct the rent paid to lease the property from his income taxes as a business expense.

Types of Managed Properties

Now let's consider the different types of properties that a property manager may be called upon to manage. There are four basic types of income-producing properties:

1. residential rental property,
2. office buildings,
3. retail property, and
4. industrial property.

Each type of property has its own unique characteristics and management needs. Because each type of property demands a different kind of expertise, property managers often specialize in one particular type. In the following paragraphs, we'll discuss some of the differences between property types.

Residential Rental Property

A property owner may need the services of a property manager to operate anything from a single-family rental home to a large apartment complex. The homeowners associations that run condominiums and co-ops also frequently rely on outside property managers.

Apartment buildings are the most common type of managed residential property. They typically offer six-month or one-year leases and have a relatively high turnover rate. As a result, residential property managers tend to spend a lot of time marketing and leasing out space.

The owner and property manager of a residential rental property must fulfill certain legal requirements that do not apply to other types of property. The operation of a residential rental property must comply with the landlord-tenant laws, which are designed to protect the rights of residential tenants. In addition, a number of cities in California have rent control ordinances. If the property is located in an area that has rent controls, the property manager must determine whether the property falls under the ordinance.

Other Types of Property

Obviously, properties used for commercial purposes are very different from residential properties. Nevertheless, while our discussion focuses primarily on managing residential properties, most of the principles and practices we describe apply to the management of any type of property. Let's look briefly at the special characteristics of different types of nonresidential property.

Office Buildings. Office buildings have very different maintenance requirements than residential buildings. For example, they have facilities that get continuous use, such as elevators and public restrooms, and thus need frequent cleaning and maintenance. Also, management is often responsible for cleaning the tenants' spaces as well as the common areas of the building.

Lease negotiations are also very different for office space than for residential units. Office leases are for longer periods of time, and rent payments are set up differently. Rent is typically based on a price per square foot (rather than per unit), and the lease often includes an escalation clause that provides for automatic increases in rent. Landlords commonly offer major concessions to attract office tenants, such as extensive remodeling to suit the tenant's needs, or free rent for a limited period.

Retail Property. Leasing space to an appropriate tenant is a concern with any type of property, but it's especially important when managing a shopping center. The success of each tenant in a shopping center depends in part on the customers that each of the other tenants attracts, so it is vital to lease to strong tenants. Also, a portion of the rent is often based on the store's income, so the property owner has a strong interest in the financial success of each tenant. The tenant mix must appeal to the widest variety of potential shoppers, while avoiding too much direct competition within the shopping center itself.

Industrial Property. Many industrial properties are specialized and expensive to build. As a result, the lease for an industrial property is usually for a much longer term than for other properties. An industrial lease runs 20 years or longer.

Because of the long lease term, it's essential to find the right tenant for an industrial property. Many property managers rely on leasing agents to find industrial tenants. The leasing agent will study the physical aspects of the property, the nearby transportation services, and the supply of and demand for the prospective tenant's products, to find a suitable tenant.

Warehouse and storage space is one type of industrial property where long-term leases are not generally used. This is because the property is not specialized to a particular tenant's needs. Many different tenants can use the space, and tenants tend to come and go more frequently. So for the manager of a warehouse property, finding new tenants is an important part of the job, much as it is with a residential rental property.

The Property Management Agreement

The first step in the management process is entering into a property management agreement. The property management agreement establishes the working relationship between the property manager and the property owner. In the same way that a listing agreement creates an agency relationship between a seller and a firm providing brokerage services, a management agreement creates an agency relationship between an owner and a firm providing management services. However, for purposes of this discussion we use the term "property manager" to refer to the individual licensee who performs duties for the property owner on behalf of the real estate firm.

Since the property management agreement is an agency agreement, it must meet the requirements imposed on other types of real estate agency agreements (such as listing agreements). The agreement must be in writing and signed by both the manager and the owner. It must also state:

- the term of the agreement;
- the scope of the manager's authority;
- the manager's compensation; and
- the property description (as always, it's best to use a legal description).

In describing the manager's authority, the agreement should make clear what decisions the manager can make, and what issues must be referred to the owner. For example, suppose several units in an apartment building need new carpets. Could the manager replace the carpets without consulting the owner, or is this a decision the owner wants to make? Other areas where questions might arise include the manager's authority to sign leases, hire and fire employees, make major repairs, choose an insurance company and policy for the property, or embark on a major advertising campaign.

The property manager's compensation may be a percentage of gross income, a commission on new rentals, a fixed fee, or some combination of these. Sometimes different forms of compensation apply to different duties, such as renting units, handling evictions, preparing units for rental or sale, or managing units during periods of vacancy. The property management agreement should state exactly how the compensation will be determined.

A typical property management agreement goes into considerable detail, as you can see from the C.A.R. property management agreement form shown in Figure 12.1. In most cases, a management agreement authorizes the property manager to collect rents and to hold and refund tenants' security deposits. It also usually authorizes her to pay expenses related to the management of the property, so that she can purchase supplies and compensate contractors for routine maintenance and repairs. The agreement should specify what reports the manager must make to the owner. In addition, if the manager is expected to cover some property expenses out of her fee, those need to be specified.

The property manager must bear in mind that after the management agreement is signed, an agency relationship exists between the manager and the owner. As a result, the manager must fulfill all the duties of an agent (see Chapter 1).

The Management Plan

Once a property manager has entered into a management agreement, the actual business of managing begins. The first step in managing a property is drawing up a management plan. The management plan outlines the manager's strategy for the financial management and physical upkeep of the property in light of the owner's goals.

It's important to realize that different property owners have different reasons for investing in real property and different management goals. For instance, one property owner may simply want a steady, reliable stream of income. Another owner may want a tax shelter. Another may want to increase the property's value in order to reap a bigger profit in later years.

An owner's goals can change over time. The property manager should review the management plan periodically with the owner. If circumstances have changed, the management plan may need to be updated accordingly.

Example: When he's in his early forties, Greg decides to purchase a small apartment building. He has other sources of income, so he's most interested in the long-term investment and tax shelter aspects of real estate ownership. However, as the years pass, Greg's needs change. After he retires, he is suddenly more interested in receiving a steady cash flow from his property. The management plan for the property needs to be revised to reflect Greg's new goals.

Fig. 12.1 Property management agreement

PROPERTY MANAGEMENT AGREEMENT

CALIFORNIA ASSOCIATION OF REALTORS®

(C.A.R. Form PMA, Revised 11/13)

_____ ("Owner"), and
_____ ("Broker"), agree as follows:

1. **APPOINTMENT OF BROKER:** Owner hereby appoints and grants Broker the exclusive right to rent, lease, operate and manage the property(ies) known as _____,
_____ and any additional property that may later be added to this Agreement ("Property"), upon the terms below, for the period beginning (date) _____ and ending (date) _____, at 11:59 PM.
(If checked:) ☐ Either party may terminate this Property Management Agreement ("Agreement") on at least 30 days written notice _____ months after the original commencement date of this Agreement. After the exclusive term expires, this Agreement shall continue as a non-exclusive agreement that either party may terminate by giving at least 30 days written notice to the other.

2. **BROKER ACCEPTANCE:** Broker accepts the appointment and grant, and agrees to:
   A. Use due diligence in the performance of this Agreement.
   B. Furnish the services of its firm for the rental, leasing, operation and management of the Property.

3. **AUTHORITY AND POWERS:** Owner grants Broker the authority and power, at Owner's expense, to:
   A. **ADVERTISING:** Display FOR RENT/LEASE and similar signs on the Property and advertise the availability of the Property, or any part thereof, for rental or lease.
   B. **RENTAL; LEASING:** Initiate, sign, renew, modify or cancel rental agreements and leases for the Property, or any part thereof; collect and give receipts for rents, other fees, charges and security deposits. Any lease or rental agreement executed by Broker for Owner shall not exceed _____ year(s) or ☐ shall be month-to-month. Unless Owner authorizes a lower amount, rent shall be: ☐ at market rate; OR ☐ a minimum of $ _____ per _____; OR ☐ see attachment.
   C. **TENANCY TERMINATION:** Sign and serve in Owner's name notices that are required or appropriate; commence and prosecute actions to evict tenants; recover possession of the Property in Owner's name; recover rents and other sums due; and, when expedient, settle, compromise and release claims, actions and suits and/or reinstate tenancies.
   D. **REPAIR; MAINTENANCE:** Make, cause to be made, and/or supervise repairs, improvements, alterations and decorations to the Property; purchase, and pay bills for, services and supplies. Broker shall obtain prior approval of Owner for all expenditures over $ _____ for any one item. Prior approval shall not be required for monthly or recurring operating charges or, if in Broker's opinion, emergency expenditures over the maximum are needed to protect the Property or other property(ies) from damage, prevent injury to persons, avoid suspension of necessary services, avoid penalties or fines, or suspension of services to tenants required by a lease or rental agreement or by law, including, but not limited to, maintaining the Property in a condition fit for human habitation as required by Civil Code §§ 1941 and 1941.1 and Health and Safety Code §§ 17920.3 and 17920.10.
   E. **REPORTS, NOTICES AND SIGNS:** Comply with federal, state or local law requiring delivery of reports or notices and/or posting of signs or notices.
   F. **CONTRACTS; SERVICES:** Contract, hire, supervise and/or discharge firms and persons, including utilities, required for the operation and maintenance of the Property. Broker may perform any of Broker's duties through attorneys, agents, employees, or independent contractors and, except for persons working in Broker's firm, shall not be responsible for their acts, omissions, defaults, negligence and/or costs of same.
   G. **EXPENSE PAYMENTS:** Pay expenses and costs for the Property from Owner's funds held by Broker, unless otherwise directed by Owner. Expenses and costs may include, but are not limited to, property management compensation, fees and charges, expenses for goods and services, property taxes and other taxes, Owner's Association dues, assessments, loan payments and insurance premiums.
   H. **SECURITY DEPOSITS:** Receive security deposits from tenants, which deposits shall be n given to Owner, or n placed in Broker's trust account and, if held in Broker's trust account, pay from Owner's funds all interest on tenants' security deposits if required by local law or ordinance. Owner shall be responsible to tenants for return of security deposits and all interest due on security deposits held by Owner.
   I. **TRUST FUNDS:** Deposit all receipts collected for Owner, less any sums properly deducted or disbursed, in a financial institution whose deposits are insured by an agency of the United States government. The funds shall be held in a trust account separate from Broker's personal accounts. Broker shall not be liable in event of bankruptcy or failure of a financial institution.
   J. **RESERVES:** Maintain a reserve in Broker's trust account of $ _____
   K. **DISBURSEMENTS:** Disburse Owner's funds held in Broker's trust account in the following order:
      (1) Compensation due Broker under paragraph 6.
      (2) All other operating expenses, costs and disbursements payable from Owner's funds held by Broker.
      (3) Reserves and security deposits held by Broker.
      (4) Balance to Owner.
   L. **OWNER DISTRIBUTION:** Remit funds, if any are available, monthly (or ☐ _____), to Owner.
   M. **OWNER STATEMENTS:** Render monthly (or ☐ Quarterly or ☐ _____), and year-end statements of receipts, expenses and charges for each Property.
   N. **BROKER FUNDS:** Broker shall not advance Broker's own funds in connection with the Property or this Agreement.

Owner's Initials (_____)(_____)   Broker's Initials (_____)(_____)

PMA REVISED 11/13 (PAGE 1 OF 4)

Reviewed by _____ Date _____

PROPERTY MANAGEMENT AGREEMENT (PMA PAGE 1 OF 4)

Reprinted with permission, California Association of Realtors®. No endorsement implied.

Owner Name: _____ Date: _____

O. **KEYSAFE/LOCKBOX:** ☐ (If checked) Owner authorizes the use of a keysafe/lockbox to allow entry into the Property and agrees to sign a keysafe/ lockbox addendum (C.A.R., Form KLA).

4. **OWNER RESPONSIBILITIES:** Owner shall:
   A. Provide all documentation, records and disclosures as required by law or required by Broker to manage and operate the Property, and immediately notify Broker if Owner becomes aware of any change in such documentation, records or disclosures, or any matter affecting the habitability of the Property.
   B. Indemnify, defend and hold harmless Broker, and all persons in Broker's firm, regardless of responsibility, from all costs, expenses, suits, liabilities, damages, attorney fees and claims of every type, including but not limited to those arising out of injury or death of any person, or damage to any real or personal property of any person, including Owner, for: **(i)** any repairs performed by Owner or by others hired directly by Owner; or **(ii)** those relating to the management, leasing, rental, security deposits, or operation of the Property by Broker, or any person in Broker's firm, or the performance or exercise of any of the duties, powers or authorities granted to Broker.
   C. Maintain the Property in a condition fit for human habitation as required by Civil Code §§ 1941 and 1941.1 and Health and Safety Code §§ 17920.3 and 17920.10 and other applicable law.
   D. Pay all interest on tenants' security deposits if required by local law or ordinance.
   E. Carry and pay for: **(i)** public and premises liability insurance in an amount of no less than $1,000,000; and **(ii)** property damage and worker's compensation insurance adequate to protect the interests of Owner and Broker. Broker shall be, and Owner authorizes Broker to be, named as an additional insured party on Owner's policies.
   F. Pay any late charges, penalties and/or interest imposed by lenders or other parties for failure to make payment to those parties, if the failure is due to insufficient funds in Broker's trust account available for such payment.
   G. Immediately replace any funds required if there are insufficient funds in Broker's trust account to cover Owner's responsibilities.

5. **OWNER REPRESENTATIONS:** Owner represents that, unless otherwise specified in writing, Owner is unaware of: **(i)** any recorded Notice of Default affecting the Property; **(ii)** any delinquent amounts due under any loan secured by, or other obligation affecting, the Property; **(iii)** any bankruptcy, insolvency or similar proceeding affecting the Property; **(iv)** any litigation, arbitration, administrative action, government investigation, or other pending or threatened action that does or may affect the Property or Owner's ability to transfer it; and **(v)** any current, pending or proposed special assessments affecting the Property. Owner shall promptly notify Broker in writing if Owner becomes aware of any of these items during the term of this Agreement.

6. **TAX WITHHOLDING:**
   A. If owner is not a California Resident or a corporation or LLC qualified to conduct business in California, owner authorizes Broker to withhold and transmit to California Franchise Tax Board ("FTB") 7% of the GROSS payments to owner that exceed $1,500 received by Broker, unless owner completes and transmits to Broker FTB form 600, nonresident reduced withholding request, FTB form 589, nonresident withholding waiver, or FTB form 590, withholding exemption certificate.
   B. If Owner is a nonresident alien individual, a foreign entity, or other non-U.S. person (Foreign Investor) Owner authorizes Broker to withhold and transmit to the Internal Revenue Service (IRS) 30% of the GROSS rental receipts unless Owner elects to treat rental income as "effectively connected income" by submitting to Broker a fully completed IRS form W-8ECI, Certificate of Foreign Person's Claim for Exemption From Withholding on Income Effectively Connected With the Conduct of a Trade of Business in the United States. A Foreign Investor Owner will need to obtain a U.S. tax payer identification number and file a declaration with the IRS regarding effectively connected income in order to complete the form given to Broker. Further, the Foreign Investor Owner will be responsible for making any necessary estimated tax payments.

7. **DISCLOSURE:**
   A. **LEAD-BASED PAINT**
      (1) ☐ The Property was constructed on or after January 1, 1978.
      OR **(2)** ☐ The Property was constructed prior to 1978.
         (i) Owner has no knowledge of lead-based paint or lead-based paint hazards in the housing except: _____
         (ii) Owner has no reports or records pertaining to lead-based paint or lead-based paint hazards in the housing, except the following, which Owner shall provide to Broker: _____
   B. **POOL/SPA DRAIN**
      Any pool or spa on the property does (or, ☐ does not) have an approved anti-entrapment drain cover, device or system.

8. **COMPENSATION:**
   A. Owner agrees to pay Broker fees in the amounts indicated below for:
      (1) Management: _____
      (2) Renting or Leasing: _____
      (3) Evictions: _____
      (4) Preparing Property for rental or lease: _____
      (5) Managing Property during extended periods of vacancy: _____
      (6) An overhead and service fee added to the cost of all work performed by, or at the direction of, Broker: _____
      (7) Other: _____
   B. This Agreement does not include providing on-site management services, property sales, refinancing, preparing Property for sale or refinancing, modernization, fire or major damage restoration, rehabilitation, obtaining income tax, accounting or legal advice, representation before public agencies, advising on proposed new construction, debt collection, counseling, attending Owner's Association meetings or _____

   If Owner requests Broker to perform services not included in this Agreement, a fee shall be agreed upon before these services are performed.

Owner's Initials (_____)(_____)   Broker's Initials (_____)(_____)

Reviewed by _____ Date _____

Owner Name: _____ Date: _____

    C. Broker may divide compensation, fees and charges due under this Agreement in any manner acceptable to Broker.

    D. Owner further agrees that:

        (1) Broker may receive and keep fees and charges from tenants for: **(i)** requesting an assignment of lease or sublease of the Property; **(ii)** processing credit applications; **(iii)** any returned checks and/or (☐ if checked) late payments; and **(iv)** any other services that are not in conflict with this Agreement.

        (2) Broker may perform any of Broker's duties, and obtain necessary products and services, through affiliated companies or organizations in which Broker may own an interest. Broker may receive fees, commissions and/or profits from these affiliated companies or organizations. Broker has an ownership interest in the following affiliated companies or organizations: _____

        Broker shall disclose to Owner any other such relationships as they occur. Broker shall not receive any fees, commissions or profits from unaffiliated companies or organizations in the performance of this Agreement, without prior disclosure to Owner.

        (3) Other: _____

9. **AGENCY RELATIONSHIPS:** Broker may act, and Owner hereby consents to Broker acting, as dual agent for Owner and tenant(s) in any resulting transaction. If the Property includes residential property with one-to-four dwelling units and this Agreement permits a tenancy in excess of one year, Owner acknowledges receipt of the "Disclosure Regarding Agency Relationships" (C.A.R. Form AD). Owner understands that Broker may have or obtain property management agreements on other property, and that potential tenants may consider, make offers on, or lease through Broker, property the same as or similar to Owner's Property. Owner consents to Broker's representation of other owners' properties before, during and after the expiration of this Agreement.

10. **NOTICES:** Any written notice to Owner or Broker required under this Agreement shall be served by sending such notice by first class mail or other agreed-to delivery method to that party at the address below, or at any different address the parties may later designate for this purpose. Notice shall be deemed received three (3) calendar days after deposit into the United States mail OR ☐ _____

11. **DISPUTE RESOLUTION:**

    A. **MEDIATION:** Owner and Broker agree to mediate any dispute or claim arising between them out of this Agreement, or any resulting transaction, before resorting to arbitration or court action. Mediation fees, if any, shall be divided equally among the parties involved. If, for any dispute or claim to which this paragraph applies, any party (i) commences an action without first attempting to resolve the matter through mediation, or (ii) before commencement of an action, refuses to mediate after a request has been made, then that party shall not be entitled to recover attorney fees, even if they would otherwise be available to that party in any such action. THIS MEDIATION PROVISION APPLIES WHETHER OR NOT THE ARBITRATION PROVISION IS INITIALED. **Exclusions from this mediation agreement are specified in paragraph 11C.**

    B. **ARBITRATION OF DISPUTES:**

        Owner and Broker agree that any dispute or claim in Law or equity arising between them out of this Agreement or any resulting transaction, which is not settled through mediation, shall be decided by neutral, binding arbitration. The arbitrator shall be a retired judge or justice, or an attorney with at least 5 years of residential real estate Law experience, unless the parties mutually agree to a different arbitrator. The parties shall have the right to discovery in accordance with Code of Civil Procedure §1283.05. In all other respects, the arbitration shall be conducted in accordance with Title 9 of Part 3 of the Code of Civil Procedure. Judgment upon the award of the arbitrator(s) may be entered into any court having jurisdiction. Enforcement of this agreement to arbitrate shall be governed by the Federal Arbitration Act. Exclusions from this arbitration agreement are specified in paragraph 11C.

        "NOTICE: BY INITIALING IN THE SPACE BELOW YOU ARE AGREEING TO HAVE ANY DISPUTE ARISING OUT OF THE MATTERS INCLUDED IN THE 'ARBITRATION OF DISPUTES' PROVISION DECIDED BY NEUTRAL ARBITRATION AS PROVIDED BY CALIFORNIA LAW AND YOU ARE GIVING UP ANY RIGHTS YOU MIGHT POSSESS TO HAVE THE DISPUTE LITIGATED IN A COURT OR JURY TRIAL. BY INITIALING IN THE SPACE BELOW YOU ARE GIVING UP YOUR JUDICIAL RIGHTS TO DISCOVERY AND APPEAL, UNLESS THOSE RIGHTS ARE SPECIFICALLY INCLUDED IN THE 'ARBITRATION OF DISPUTES' PROVISION. IF YOU REFUSE TO SUBMIT TO ARBITRATION AFTER AGREEING TO THIS PROVISION, YOU MAY BE COMPELLED TO ARBITRATE UNDER THE AUTHORITY OF THE CALIFORNIA CODE OF CIVIL PROCEDURE. YOUR AGREEMENT TO THIS ARBITRATION PROVISION IS VOLUNTARY."

        "WE HAVE READ AND UNDERSTAND THE FOREGOING AND AGREE TO SUBMIT DISPUTES ARISING OUT OF THE MATTERS INCLUDED IN THE 'ARBITRATION OF DISPUTES' PROVISION TO NEUTRAL ARBITRATION."

Owner's Initials	/	Broker's Initials	/

    C. **ADDITIONAL MEDIATION AND ARBITRATION TERMS: The following matters shall be excluded from mediation and arbitration: (i) a judicial or non-judicial foreclosure or other action or proceeding to enforce a deed of trust, mortgage or installment land sale contract as defined in Civil Code §2985; (ii) an unlawful detainer action; (iii) the filing or enforcement of a mechanic's lien; and (iv) any matter that is within the jurisdiction of a probate, small claims or bankruptcy court. The filing of a court action to enable the recording of a notice of pending action, for order of attachment, receivership, injunction, or other provisional remedies, shall not constitute a waiver or violation of the mediation and arbitration provisions.**

Owner's Initials (_____)(_____)   Broker's Initials (_____)(_____)

PMA REVISED 11/13 (PAGE 3 OF 4)

Reviewed by _____ Date _____

PROPERTY MANAGEMENT AGREEMENT (PMA PAGE 3 OF 4)

Owner Name: _____ Date:_____

12. **EQUAL HOUSING OPPORTUNITY:** The Property is offered in compliance with federal, state and local anti-discrimination laws.

13. **ATTORNEY FEES:** In any action, proceeding or arbitration between Owner and Broker regarding the obligation to pay compensation under this Agreement, the prevailing Owner or Broker shall be entitled to reasonable attorney fees and costs from the non-prevailing Owner or Broker, except as provided in paragraph 11A.

14. **ADDITIONAL TERMS:** ☐ Keysafe/Lockbox Addendum (C.A.R. Form KLA); ☐ Lead-Based Paint and Lead-Based Paint Hazards Disclosure (C.A.R. Form FLD) _____
_____
_____

15. **TIME OF ESSENCE; ENTIRE CONTRACT; CHANGES:** Time is of the essence. All understandings between the parties are incorporated in this Agreement. Its terms are intended by the parties as a final, complete and exclusive expression of their Agreement with respect to its subject matter, and may not be contradicted by evidence of any prior agreement or contemporaneous oral agreement. If any provision of this Agreement is held to be ineffective or invalid, the remaining provisions will nevertheless be given full force and effect. Neither this Agreement nor any provision in it may be extended, amended, modified, altered or changed except in writing. This Agreement and any supplement, addendum or modification, including any copy, may be signed in two or more counterparts, all of which shall constitute one and the same writing.

Owner warrants that Owner is the owner of the Property or has the authority to execute this Agreement. Owner acknowledges Owner has read, understands, accepts and has received a copy of the Agreement.

Owner _____ Date _____
Owner _____
     Print Name   Social Security/Tax ID # (for tax reporting purposes)
Address _____ City _____ State _____ Zip _____
Telephone _____ Fax _____ Email _____

Owner _____ Date _____
Owner _____
     Print Name   Social Security/Tax ID # (for tax reporting purposes)
Address _____ City _____ State _____ Zip _____
Telephone _____ Fax _____ Email _____

Real Estate Broker (Firm) _____ CalBRE Lic. #: _____
By (Agent) _____ CalBRE Lic. #: _____ Date _____
Address _____ City _____ State _____ Zip _____
Telephone _____ Fax _____ Email _____

PMA REVISED 11/13 (PAGE 4 OF 4)

Reviewed by _____ Date _____

PROPERTY MANAGEMENT AGREEMENT (PMA PAGE 4 OF 4)

The Preliminary Study

A management plan can be created only after a comprehensive study of all aspects of the property, including its location, physical characteristics, financial status, and policies of operation. This preliminary study includes a regional analysis, neighborhood analysis, property analysis, and market analysis.

Regional Analysis. Preparing a management plan begins with a study of the region (the city or metropolitan area) in which the property is located. The manager analyzes the general economic conditions, physical attributes, and population growth and distribution. Among the most significant considerations are trends in occupancy rates, market rental rates, employment levels, and (for residential property) family size and lifestyle.

Occupancy rates. According to the law of supply and demand, when the demand for an item is greater than the supply, the price or value of the item increases. And when the supply exceeds the demand, the price or value of the item decreases. This basic rule applies to rental properties just as it applies to other commodities.

From a property manager's point of view, the supply of rental units is the total number of units available for occupancy in the area where the managed property is located. The demand for rental units is the total number of potential tenants in that area who can afford to rent those units. When demand exceeds supply, rental rates go up; when supply exceeds demand, rental rates go down.

There is a **technical oversupply** of property when there are more units than potential tenants. There is an **economic oversupply** when there are enough potential tenants, but they are unable to pay the current rent. Likewise, there may be a **technical shortage** (when there are more potential tenants than units) or an **economic shortage** (when there are more able-to-pay tenants than units).

To set rental rates for a managed property, a property manager must determine the occupancy trend for the area. If the trend is toward higher occupancy levels, the value of the units will increase as space becomes scarce. It is during these times that managers raise rents and reduce services. On the other hand, if there is a trend toward higher vacancy rates, a unit's value will decrease. In periods of high vacancy, tenants are likely to resist rent increases or make more demands for services or repairs when leases are renewed.

Occupancy levels fluctuate constantly. The direction and speed of those changes will affect the property manager's operating and marketing policies.

Market rental rates. In addition to evaluating occupancy trends, a property manager should keep track of market rental rates—the rates charged for comparable rental units. The manager should set rental rates for the managed units at a level that makes them competitive.

Various published reports provide information about rental rates, such as the Department of Labor's statistics on rents paid for residential units. A property manager may also collect data on local rental rates from rental advertising and online resources like Zillow. This research can give the manager a basic picture of market trends.

Labor force. A property manager should follow local employment trends, since employment levels affect how many potential tenants can afford to rent. A manager should also know whether earnings are increasing or decreasing. Falling wages put downward pressure on rents.

Family size and lifestyle. Family size has a great deal to do with the value of particular residential units. If the average family size is three (two parents and one child), five-bedroom units have little appeal and two-bedroom units are very attractive. Thus, two-bedroom units will command a higher price per square foot than five-bedroom units. A property manager needs to be aware of the national trend toward smaller and even single-person households, and also any local trends in family size and lifestyle.

Neighborhood Analysis. After the regional analysis, the next step in the preliminary study is to analyze the neighborhood where the property is located. The definition of a neighborhood varies considerably from one place to another. In rural areas, a neighborhood may consist of many square miles. In an urban area, a neighborhood may be only a few blocks.

The qualities of the neighborhood have a significant bearing on the property's value and use. Important neighborhood characteristics include:

- the character of the buildings and amenities of the neighborhood;
- the level of maintenance (whether the buildings are well cared for, or in poor condition);
- a growth or decline in population; and
- the economic status of the residents.

A property manager should discover the reasons behind any neighborhood trends. Is the population density increasing because of new multifamily developments or because single-family homes are changing into rooming houses? The building of new apartments is a sign of economic prosperity; rooming house tenancies are not.

A neighborhood analysis helps a property manager factor location into the management plan. No matter how effectively a property is operated, location has a big impact on profitability. Realistic management goals must take location into account.

Property Analysis. Of course, to develop a management plan the manager must become very familiar with the physical characteristics of the property itself. She will inspect the property, noting its architectural design, physical condition, facilities, and general layout.

The following characteristics are particularly important:

- number and size of the living units, or number of rentable square feet;
- appearance of the property and the rental spaces (age, architectural style, layout, view, fixtures);
- physical condition of the building (roof, elevators, windows);
- physical condition of the rental spaces (floor coverings, stairways, shades or blinds, walls, entryways);
- amenities provided (laundry room, recreational facilities);
- services provided (janitorial services, repair services, or security);
- relationship of the land to the building (Is the land used efficiently? Is there adequate parking?);
- occupancy rate and tenant composition; and
- size and efficiency of the staff.

Market Analysis. The last step in the preliminary study for a management plan is the market analysis, which provides information on competing properties. To do a market analysis, the manager must first define the pertinent market. The major divisions of the real estate market are residential, office, retail, and industrial. Each of these can be broken down into subcategories. For instance, the residential market can be divided into single-family rental homes, duplexes, townhouses, walk-up apartments, small multi-story apartments, and large apartment complexes.

Once the manager has identified the managed property's market, he must determine the:

- number of units available in the market;
- average age and character of the buildings in which the units are located;
- quality of the average unit in the market (size, condition, layout, facilities);
- number of potential tenants in the market;
- price for the average unit; and
- occupancy rate for the average unit.

The property manager compares the managed property to competing properties in order to understand the property's relative advantages and disadvantages. Armed with this information, she can establish an effective management strategy.

The Management Proposal

After completing the preliminary study, the property manager develops a management proposal and submits it to the property owner for approval. The manager's proposal will include a rental schedule, income and expense projections, a schedule of day-to-day operations, and perhaps suggestions for physical changes to the property itself.

Rental Schedule. A property's rental schedule lists the types of units and their rental rates. For example, an apartment building may consist of studio apartments, one-bedroom apartments, and two-bedroom apartments. Some apartments may have views, others may not. Rental rates vary accordingly.

Rental schedules are based on all the data collected during the regional, neighborhood, property, and market analyses. This information helps the manager determine the maximum rent that can be charged while maintaining the desired occupancy level. To set the rate for a particular type of unit, the manager can adjust the market rental rate for the average comparable unit up or down to reflect the differences between the comparable and the type of unit in question. In other words, the manager can apply competitive market analysis to rental rates (see Chapter 4). Because this method of setting rates depends on market conditions, the rental schedule should be reexamined periodically to see if it's current. Either an unusually high vacancy rate or an unusually low vacancy rate indicates that the property's rental rates may be out of line with the market. If the vacancy rate

---

Fig. 12.2 Property management documents

Management Agreement

- Contract between property manager and owner
- Creates an agency relationship
- Establishes scope of manager's authority

Management Proposal

- Based on a comprehensive study of the property and market conditions
- When approved by owner, proposal becomes management plan

Management Plan

- Includes rental schedule and plans for day-to-day operations
- Budget projects future income and expenses
- Implements owner's goals

---

is too high, the rent may be too expensive; if the vacancy rate is unusually low, the rent may be below the norm.

Budgets. The property manager also sets up a budget of income and operating expenses. The manager lists the total value of all rentable space at the scheduled rental rates, then subtracts a figure for projected delinquent rental payments and vacancies (sometimes called a **vacancy factor**). Any other income sources, such as laundry facilities, vending machines, or parking, should also be listed.

Next, the manager lists the estimated operating expenses, both fixed expenses and variable expenses. **Fixed expenses** occur at regular intervals and generally don't vary in response to changes in the property's occupancy rate. They include such items as insurance premiums, property taxes, and employee salaries. **Variable expenses** include items such as utilities, maintenance, repairs, and management fees. After calculating the projected operating expenses, the manager deducts those expenses from projected revenues to arrive at a net income figure.

Day-to-Day Operations. In addition to long-range financial planning, the management proposal includes the manager's plans for the property's day-to-day operations. The manager has to decide how much (if any) staffing is required and settle on employment policies and procedures. The manager should also address the type and amount of marketing and maintenance that will be needed.

Physical Alterations. In some cases, the property manager's proposal includes recommendations for remodeling, rehabilitation, or other physical alterations to the property. For instance, after a thorough examination of the property, the customer base, and the market, a manager might decide that the property would be worth much more if the building were altered to match current family size and lifestyle trends.

> **Example:** An older building is made up of three- and four-bedroom units in a neighborhood predominantly made up of one- and two-person households. If the apartments are converted to smaller units, the owner's profits should increase significantly.

Owner's Approval. Once completed, the management proposal is presented to the property owner. If the owner has suggestions or concerns, the management proposal may need to be adjusted. When the proposal is approved, it becomes the management plan: the blueprint for managing the property.

Management Functions

Property managers must possess the skills necessary to perform a variety of management functions. They must be able to market the property, negotiate leases, and handle tenant relations. They must be able to keep and understand detailed financial records and report to the property owner on a regular basis. They must also be able to arrange for the maintenance and repairs that will preserve the value of the property.

Leasing and Tenant Relations

The property manager's tasks involved in leasing and tenant relations include marketing the rental spaces, negotiating leases, addressing tenants' complaints, and collecting rents.

Marketing. As a general rule, the more people who view a rental space, the more likely it is that the manager will lease it to a good tenant. However, different types of properties require different types and amounts of advertising. For some properties, advertising is necessary only when there is a vacancy to fill. Or if the property is in a prominent location and attractive to potential tenants, advertising may not be necessary at all. On the other hand, if the property is in an isolated location, continuous advertising may be required to generate enough interest to fill vacancies when they occur. (Such advertising should be general; a licensee may not advertise specific vacancies that don't exist.)

Successful advertising brings in a good number of potential tenants in the least amount of time for the lowest cost. Property managers often evaluate the effectiveness of their advertising in terms of the number of potential tenants for the advertising dollars spent. For example, based on experience, a property manager might have a general rule of thumb that the cost of advertising should not exceed $25 to $35 per prospect. Thus, newspaper advertising that costs $300 should bring in nine to twelve prospective tenants to view the property.

To reach the greatest number of potential tenants for the lowest possible cost, a property manager must be familiar with the various types of advertising and know which will be most effective for the property in question. A manager may consider using signs, print advertising, online advertising and websites, direct mail, or some combination of these media.

Signs. Small, tasteful signs are often used, whether there is a vacancy or not, to inform passersby of the name of the manager and how to acquire rental information. The use of signs is most successful for large apartment complexes, office buildings, and shopping centers.

Newspaper advertising. Newspaper advertising includes classified ads and display ads. Classified ads (relatively inexpensive line-type advertising that appears in the newspaper's classified ads section) were once the most popular way to advertise residential rental space, but in most cases newspaper advertising has given way to Internet advertising, as discussed below. Display ads are larger and more expensive than classified ads. A display ad often includes a photograph of the property, and it may appear in any section of the newspaper. Display advertising might be used to advertise space in a new office building, industrial park, or shopping center.

Internet advertising. Classified ads can also be placed online, through advertising websites such as craigslist. Online classifieds have a number of advantages over newspaper classifieds; for example, they can include photographs of the property, and many websites allow listings to be posted free of charge.

Depending on the scope of her business, a property manager may want to maintain her own website to advertise all of the properties she's managing. And it often makes sense to have a website dedicated to a particular apartment complex, office building, or other property.

Direct mail. To be effective, direct mail advertising must be received by potential tenants, not just the general public. So a property manager who wants to use direct mail must compile or purchase a mailing list. With a good mailing list and a brochure designed to appeal to prospective tenants, direct mail can be an effective means of advertising. Also, the same brochure can be handed out to those who visit the property.

Leasing. A prospect sees an advertisement and comes to look at the available rental space. Now it is the property manager's job to convince the prospect that the rental space is desirable. They will usually tour the property together, and during the tour the manager will emphasize all of the property's positive qualities and amenities. He'll point out the advantages of the neighborhood, such as nearby freeway access and excellent public transportation, and might also provide some information about the other tenants. If it's commercial property, the manager and the prospect may discuss how the space could be altered to suit the prospect's requirements, and how additional space could be incorporated if the business needs to expand.

After the tour, if the prospect is still interested in the property, it's the property manager's responsibility to make sure that the prospect is qualified to lease it. Naturally, financial stability is a key consideration, but the manager must also look at other factors. The manager should consider whether the prospect is likely to be a responsible and cooperative tenant. For certain types of property, the tenant must be appropriate for the property. In the case of a shopping center, for example, the manager must make sure that the prospect's business complements the other stores.

Ultimately, whether to accept a particular tenant is a matter of judgment—the property manager's judgment and/or the owner's, if she retains or shares this authority under the management agreement. However, the decision maker(s) must be very careful to avoid violating antidiscrimination laws (see Chapter 3). If the decision is in favor of the prospect, the next step is to sign a rental agreement or lease.

Signing a lease. A lease is a contract between the landlord (the property owner) and the tenant, allowing the tenant to occupy and use the property. In exchange, the tenant pays rent to the landlord. For the protection of both parties, a lease should always be put into writing and signed by the landlord and the tenant. A lease for a fixed term must be in writing to be enforceable. The property manager may sign the lease as the landlord's agent, if the manager has been authorized to execute leases.

The lease should include the names of the parties, a description of the property, the amount of the rent, and the duration of the tenancy. A residential lease must include the name, address, and telephone number of the manager, and also an address where legal notices can be sent to the owner or the owner's agent. The lease should also clearly spell out the responsibilities of the parties and any restrictions imposed on the tenant. These additional terms could cover issues such as utilities or maintenance that are the tenant's responsibility, restrictions on alterations to the property, and whether the tenant can sublease the property or assign the lease to another party.

Security deposits. Both commercial and residential tenants are typically required to provide a security deposit at the beginning of the lease term. The security deposit gives the property owner some protection if the tenant damages the property or defaults on rent payments.

The lease agreement should include the amount of the security deposit and clearly state the conditions under which the deposit will be returned to the tenant. California law limits the amount of residential security deposits to no more than two months' rent for an unfurnished property, and no more than three months' rent for a furnished property. When a tenant moves out, the landlord must provide the tenant with an itemized list of deposit deductions within three weeks, and refund any balance of the deposit that remains.

Use of premises. Unless limitations are stated in the lease, a tenant may use the property for any legal purpose. However, most leases do place restrictions on the tenant's use of the property. For instance, a lease for retail space in a shopping center would typically restrict the tenant to a specific kind of business, to maintain the desired mix of stores and prevent harm to the business of other tenants.

Lease renewal. Unless the tenant has caused problems, in most cases a property manager would much rather renew an existing lease than find a new tenant. Renewal avoids a vacancy between the time one tenant moves out and another moves in. A building has greater stability with long-term tenants, and it is usually easier and less expensive to satisfy the requirements of an existing tenant than to improve the space for a new tenant.

A property manager should be aware of which tenants are nearing the end of their lease terms and notify them that their leases are about to expire. Then the manager should follow up on the notices, by phone or in person, to inquire whether the tenant wants to renew. If so, the terms of the new lease must be negotiated.

Some leases contain an **automatic renewal clause**. Under this provision, the lease will be automatically renewed on the same terms unless one party notifies the other of his or her intent to terminate the lease.

Note that even if the parties don't renew the lease, a residential tenancy often continues on a month-to-month basis.

Tenant Complaints. Of course, keeping tenants happy is an important part of the property manager's job. Making sure that the property is kept clean and in good repair is essential, and so is responding promptly and professionally to requests and complaints.

Rent Collection. Rental property cannot be profitable unless the rents are collected when due. Careful selection of tenants in the first place is one of the most effective ways of avoiding delinquent rents. A high occupancy rate doesn't benefit the property owner unless the tenants meet their financial obligations.

The manager of a residential property should check every rental applicant's references and employment information, and contact the applicant's previous landlord. Credit checks are also helpful in determining whether a prospective tenant is likely to meet financial obligations in a timely manner. For a commercial lease, the prospective tenant is usually required to provide extensive financial information.

The lease should clearly state the amount of the rent, the time and place for rent payment, and any penalties imposed for late payment. The manager needs to follow a collection plan that includes adequate recordkeeping, immediate notification of late payments, and consistent enforcement. When all collection attempts fail, the manager must be prepared to take legal action to evict the tenant. The legal eviction process is called an **unlawful detainer action**.

Recordkeeping and Manager/Owner Relations

A property manager must account to the owner for all money received and disbursed. It's up to the owner to decide how frequent and detailed operating reports should be. This depends on how involved the owner wants to be in the management of the property. For example, an owner with extensive property holdings who is also engaged in another full-time occupation may not want to be bothered with detailed, time-consuming reports. But a retired person with only one or two income-producing properties might want to be very involved in their management and may ask the manager for lots of information.

Statement of Operations. In many cases, the property manager's report to the owner takes the form of a monthly statement of operations. A statement of operations typically includes the following sections: a summary of operations, the rent roll, a statement of disbursements, and a narrative report of operations.

The **summary of operations** briefly describes the property's income and expenses, making it easier for the owner to evaluate the property's monthly financial performance. The information in the rest of the statement of operations supports the summary.

The **rent roll** is a report on rent collection. Both occupied and vacant units are listed in the rent roll, as well as the total of rental income earned, both collected and uncollected. The rent roll breaks down rental figures into the previous balance, current rent, total amount received, and balance due.

The information in the rent roll is obtained from the individual ledger sheets kept on each tenant and rental space. A ledger sheet typically shows the tenant's name, unit, phone number, regular rent, other recurring charges, security deposit information, move-in date, lease term, payments made, and balances owed.

The **statement of disbursements** lists all of the expenses paid during the pertinent time period. A written order should be prepared for every purchase and payment so that an accurate account can be made of all expenditures, including the purpose of each one. Disbursements are usually classified according to type, to make analysis easier. For example, maintenance expenses, tax and insurance expenses, and administrative expenses are grouped separately.

In addition to the numerical accounts given to the owner, it is often helpful to include a **narrative report of operations** in the statement of operations. This is simply a letter explaining the information set forth in the other sections of the statement. The narrative report adds a personal touch, and it is especially important if the income was lower or the expenses were higher than expected. If there is a deviation from the normal cash flow, the owner will want a clear explanation. If the reason for a drop in cash flow is not explained, the owner may doubt the competence or integrity of the property manager.

Keeping in Touch. In addition to sending the owner reports and statements, the manager should contact the owner in person from time to time. A telephone call or an appointment to explain a particular proposal or problem or to ask a question is much more effective than a letter. A formal meeting is a good idea if the monthly report is especially unusual.

Maintenance

In addition to leasing, tenant relations, recordkeeping, and reporting to the owner, a property manager is also responsible for the supervision of property maintenance. There are four basic categories of maintenance activities:

1. **Preventive maintenance:** Work done to preserve the physical condition of the premises and prevent deterioration. (Cleaning the gutters is an example of preventive maintenance.) Good preventive maintenance reduces corrective maintenance costs.
2. **Corrective maintenance:** Actual repairs that keep equipment, utilities, and amenities functioning in a proper manner. (Fixing a leaking faucet is an example of corrective maintenance.)
3. **Housekeeping:** Cleaning the common areas and grounds on a regular basis to keep the property attractive (for example, vacuuming hallways and cleaning elevators).
4. **New construction:** This includes alterations made for the benefit of a tenant, as well as cosmetic changes designed to make the building more attractive (for example, redecorating the lobby).

Most maintenance activities are handled by building maintenance employees or by outside maintenance services. The property manager must be able to recognize the maintenance needs of the property and see that they are fulfilled.

The manager should direct the activities of the maintenance staff or independent contractors by giving them a schedule of inspection and maintenance. First the manager should inventory the building's equipment and physical elements (such as the plumbing, heating system, elevators, floors, and walls). Then the manager should set a schedule of regular inspections, cleaning, and repairs. For instance, the schedule might call for an annual inspection of the roof.

It's also important for the property manager to keep accurate and up-to-date records on when the various elements were inspected, serviced, replaced, or repaired. These routine inspections and maintenance activities will help preserve the value of the building and prevent major repair expenses.

When managing commercial or industrial property, a property manager is often required to alter the interior of the building to meet the needs of a new tenant. These alterations can range from simply repainting to completely redesigning or rebuilding the space. (If the property is new construction, the interior is often left incomplete so that it can be built to fit the needs of the individual tenants.) Commercial property managers dealing with remodeling or new construction must be aware of the Americans with Disabilities Act, the federal law that requires public accommodations to be accessible to the disabled (see Chapter 3).

Chapter Summary

1. An investment is an asset that is expected to generate a return for the investor. Three basic characteristics of an investment are safety, liquidity, and yield. The advantages of real estate investment include appreciation, leverage, and cash flow.

2. There are four main types of income-producing properties: residential, office, retail, and industrial. Each type has unique characteristics and management needs. Property managers often specialize in one type of property.

3. A property manager must have a written management agreement with the property owner. The agreement should contain all of the terms of the management arrangement, including the manager's compensation, the manager's duties and authority, and the allocation of costs. It should also provide that the manager will submit reports to the owner on a regular basis.

4. Before preparing a management plan, the manager should conduct a regional analysis, a neighborhood analysis, a property analysis, and a market analysis. The information gathered during this preliminary study will help the manager set a rental schedule, prepare a budget, and plan the day-to-day operations.

5. The functions of a property manager include marketing the property, leasing, handling tenant complaints, rent collection, recordkeeping, preparing reports for the owner, and arranging for the maintenance of the property.

Key Terms

Return: A profit from an investment.

Yield: The amount of profit on an investment, stated as a percentage of the amount invested.

Appreciation: An increase in value; the opposite of depreciation.

Equity: An owner's unencumbered interest in his or her property; the difference between the value of the property and the liens against it.

Leverage: The effective use of borrowed money to finance an investment such as real estate.

Cash flow: A property's residual income after deducting operating expenses, mortgage payments, and income taxes from gross income.

Sale-leaseback: A form of real estate financing in which the owner of industrial or commercial property sells the property and leases it back from the buyer.

Market rental rate: The rental rates currently being charged for comparable rental units.

Rental schedule: A list of all the rental rates assigned to the different types of units in a building. For example, a rental schedule for an apartment building might list the rates of its studio apartments, one-bedroom apartments, and two-bedroom apartments.

Vacancy factor: A percentage deducted from a property's potential gross income to determine the effective gross income, estimating the income that will probably be lost because of vacancies and tenants who don't pay.

Fixed expenses: Recurring property expenses, such as general real estate taxes and hazard insurance.

Variable expenses: Expenses incurred in connection with property that do not occur on a set schedule, such as the cost of repairing a roof damaged in a storm.

Security deposit: Money a tenant gives a landlord at the beginning of the tenancy to protect the landlord in case the tenant fails to comply with the terms of the lease. The landlord may retain all or part of the deposit to cover unpaid rent or repair costs at the end of the tenancy.

Summary of operations: A brief description of the property's income and expenses; this report makes it easier for the owner to evaluate the property's monthly financial performance.

Rent roll: A monthly report on rent collection, listing both occupied and vacant units and the total rental income earned, both collected and uncollected.

Statement of disbursements: A report that lists all of the expenses paid during the pertinent time period.

Preventive maintenance: A program of regular inspection and servicing for a property and its fixtures and equipment, to prevent potential problems.

Corrective maintenance: Repairs that keep equipment, utilities, and amenities functioning in a proper manner (such as fixing a leaking faucet).

Unlawful detainer—A lawsuit filed by a landlord to evict a defaulting tenant.

Chapter Quiz

1. The main disadvantage of investing in real estate is:
   a. the use of leverage to increase returns
   b. lack of liquidity
   c. uniformly low returns
   d. a constantly increasing supply, which decreases values

2. The contract between a property manager and the owner of the property is the:
   a. property management agreement
   b. management plan
   c. lease-back agreement
   d. management proposal

3. The property manager's main purpose must be to fulfill:
   a. his or her career goals
   b. the owner's objectives
   c. the government's affordable housing goals
   d. his or her office's cash flow goals

4. If a regional analysis shows that the typical family size is four, with two parents and two children, which of the following apartment units is most marketable?
   a. Studio
   b. Five-bedroom
   c. Three-bedroom
   d. It is unlikely that one type of unit would be preferred over any other

5. The type of property that ordinarily demands the most marketing is:
   a. residential
   b. office
   c. retail
   d. industrial

6. By completing a market analysis, a property manager discovers that the average rental rate for comparable residential units is $1,650. For the subject property, the property manager should set a rental rate of approximately:
   a. $1,550 per unit, to undercut the competition
   b. $1,725 per unit, because tenants are not very well informed and will probably pay a higher-than-average price
   c. $1,650 per unit, to remain competitive
   d. None of the above; a fixed rental rate should not be set

7. What document states the frequency and level of detail required in management reports?
   a. Management agreement
   b. Management plan
   c. Statement of operations
   d. Preliminary analysis

8. Insurance premiums would be categorized as a:
   a. variable expense
   b. daily expense
   c. fixed expense
   d. pro rata expense

9. To see which tenants are behind in their rent, a property owner would check the:
   a. rental schedule
   b. statement of disbursements
   c. narrative report of operations
   d. rent roll

10. The most effective way to reduce expensive repair bills is to:
    a. emphasize preventive maintenance
    b. put off repairs for as long as possible
    c. institute a policy of tenant-paid repairs
    d. find cheap repair companies

Answer Key

1. b.   Because it takes some time to convert real property into cash, the lack of liquidity is the main disadvantage of investing in real estate.

2. a.   The contract is called the property management agreement. It creates an agency relationship between the manager and the owner. Entering into a property management agreement is the first step in the management process.

3. b.   A property manager's primary responsibility is to work to achieve the property owner's objectives. The property manager should design a management plan that focuses on achieving the owner's goals as effectively as possible.

4. c.   In this situation, a family of typical size would be more likely to rent a three-bedroom unit than either a studio or a five-bedroom apartment.

5. a.   Because residential lease terms are relatively short, managing residential property tends to involve more marketing than managing other types of property.

6. c.   Rental rates should not be much lower or much higher than the rates for competitive properties. The rental schedule should be reexamined periodically to make sure it is current.

7. a.   The management agreement lists the manager's duties, including how frequent and how detailed reports to the owner must be.

8. c.   Fixed expenses remain the same, regardless of rental income. Insurance premiums are a fixed expense.

9. d.   The rent roll is a report on rent collection. It lists all units individually and breaks down rental figures in detail, including uncollected amounts.

10. a.   Preventive maintenance preserves the physical integrity of the property and reduces the need for corrective maintenance.

Glossary

The definitions given here explain how the listed terms are used in the real estate field. Some of the terms have additional meanings, which can be found in a standard dictionary.

Abstract of Title—See: Title, Abstract of.

Acceleration Clause—A provision in a promissory note or security instrument allowing the lender to declare the entire debt due immediately if the borrower breaches one or more provisions of the loan agreement. Also referred to as a call provision.

Acceptance—1. Agreeing to the terms of an offer to enter into a contract, thereby creating a binding contract. 2. Taking delivery of a deed from the grantor.

Acceptance, Qualified—See: Counteroffer.

Acquisition Cost—The amount of money a buyer was required to expend in order to acquire title to a piece of property; in addition to the purchase price, this might include closing costs, legal fees, and other expenses.

Acre—A measure of area for land; one acre is 43,560 square feet.

Adjustable-Rate Mortgage—See: Mortgage, Adjustable-Rate.

Ad Valorem—A Latin phrase that means "according to value," used to refer to taxes that are assessed on the value of property.

Agency—A relationship of trust created when one person (the principal) grants another (the agent) authority to represent the principal in dealings with third parties.

Agency Disclosure—Real estate agents involved in a transaction must disclose in writing which party or parties they are representing (usually, this is done in the purchase and sale agreement).

Agency, Apparent—When third parties are given the impression that someone who has not been authorized to represent another is that person's agent, or else given the impression that an agent has been authorized to perform acts which are in fact beyond the scope of her authority. Also called ostensible agency.

Agency, Dual—When an agent represents both parties to a transaction, as when a broker represents both the buyer and the seller.

Agency, Exclusive—See: Listing, Exclusive.

Agency, Ostensible—See: Agency, Apparent.

Agency Coupled with an Interest—When an agent has a claim against the property that is the subject of the agency, so that the principal cannot revoke the agent's authority.

Agent—A person authorized to represent another (the principal) in dealings with third parties.

Agent, Dual—See: Agency, Dual.

Agent, General—An agent authorized to handle all of the principal's affairs in one area or in specified areas.

Agent, Special—An agent with limited authority to do a specific thing or conduct a specific transaction.

Agent, Universal—An agent authorized to do everything that can be lawfully delegated to a representative.

Agreement—See: Contract.

Alienation—The transfer of ownership or an interest in property from one person to another, by any means.

Alienation, Involuntary—Transfer of an interest in property against the will of the owner, or without action by the owner, occurring through operation of law, natural processes, or adverse possession.

Alienation, Voluntary—When an owner voluntarily transfers an interest to someone else.

Alienation Clause—A provision in a security instrument that gives the lender the right to declare the entire loan balance due immediately if the borrower sells or otherwise transfers the security property. Also called a due-on-sale clause.

All-Inclusive Trust Deed—See: Mortgage, Wraparound.

ALTA—American Land Title Association, a nationwide organization of title insurance companies. An extended coverage title policy is sometimes referred to as an ALTA policy.

Amendment—A change to a contract, such as a purchase and sale agreement, after the contract is signed. All parties must agree to the change; generally a separate form is used when amending purchase and sale agreements.

Amenities—Features of a property that contribute to the pleasure or convenience of owning it, such as a fireplace, a beautiful view, or its proximity to a good school.

Americans with Disabilities Act—A federal law requiring facilities that are open to the public to ensure accessibility to disabled persons, even if that accessibility requires making architectural modifications. The ADA also requires employers to make reasonable accommodations for disabled employees.

Amortization, Negative—When unpaid interest on a loan is added to the principal balance, increasing the amount owed.

Amortize—To gradually pay off a debt with installment payments that include both principal and interest. See also: Loan, Amortized.

Annual Percentage Rate (APR)—All of the charges that the borrower will pay for the loan (including the interest, loan fee, discount points, and mortgage insurance costs), expressed as an annual percentage of the loan amount.

Anticipation, Principle of—An appraisal principle which holds that value is created by the expectation of benefits to be received in the future.

Appraisal—An estimate or opinion of the value of a piece of property as of a particular date. Also called valuation.

Appraiser—One who estimates the value of property, especially an expert qualified to do so by training and experience.

Appreciation—An increase in value; the opposite of depreciation.

Appurtenances—Rights that go along with ownership of a particular piece of property, such as air rights or mineral rights; they are ordinarily transferred with the property, but may, in some cases, be sold separately.

APR—See: Annual Percentage Rate.

Area—The size of a surface, usually in square units of measure, such as square feet or square miles. The area of a piece of land may also be stated in acres.

Arbitration—Submitting a disputed matter to a private party (rather than to the judicial system) for resolution.

ARM—See: Mortgage, Adjustable-Rate.

Arm's Length Transaction—A transaction in which there is no pre-existing family or business relationship between the parties.

Asbestos—A carcinogenic substance that was used in insulation for many years and that should be enclosed or removed if found.

Assessment—The valuation of property for purposes of taxation.

Assessor—An official who determines the value of property for taxation.

Asset—Anything of value that a person owns.

Assets, Liquid—Cash and other assets that can be readily liquidated (turned into cash), such as stock.

Assign—To transfer rights (especially contract rights) or interests to another.

Assignee—One to whom rights or interests have been assigned.

Assignment—1. A transfer of contract rights from one person to another. 2. In the case of a lease, when the original tenant transfers his entire leasehold estate to another. Compare: Sublease.

Assignor—One who has assigned her rights or interest to another.

Assumption—When a buyer takes on personal liability for paying off the seller's existing mortgage or deed of trust.

Assumption Fee—A fee paid to the lender, usually by the buyer, when a mortgage or deed of trust is assumed.

Attorney in Fact—Any person authorized to represent another by a power of attorney; not necessarily a lawyer (an attorney at law).

Automated Underwriting—See: Underwriting, Automated.

Authority, Actual—Authority actually given to an agent by the principal, either expressly or by implication.

Authority, Apparent—Authority to represent another that someone appears to have and that the principal is estopped from denying, although no actual authority has been granted.

Authority, Implied—An agent's authority to do everything reasonably necessary to carry out the principal's express orders.

Backup Offer—An offer that's contingent on the failure of a previous sales contract.

Balloon Payment—A payment on a loan (usually the final payment) that is significantly larger than the regular installment payments.

Bankruptcy—1. When the liabilities of an individual, corporation, or firm exceed the assets. 2. When a court declares an individual, corporation, or firm to be insolvent, so that the assets and debts will be administered under bankruptcy laws.

Beneficiary—1. One for whom a trust is created and on whose behalf the trustee administers the trust. 2. The lender in a deed of trust transaction. 3. One entitled to receive real or personal property under a will; a legatee or devisee.

Bill of Sale—A document used to transfer title to personal property from one person to another.

Binder—1. An instrument providing immediate insurance coverage until the regular policy is issued. 2. Any payment or preliminary written statement intended to make an agreement legally binding until a formal contract has been drawn up.

Blind Ad—An advertisement placed by a real estate licensee that does not include the broker's name.

Blockbusting—Attempting to induce owners to list or sell their homes by predicting that members of another racial, ethnic, or religious group, or people with a disability, will be moving into the neighborhood; this violates antidiscrimination laws. Also called panic selling.

Board of Directors—The body responsible for governing a corporation on behalf of the shareholders, which oversees the corporate management.

Bona Fide—In good faith; genuine; not fraudulent.

Breach—Violation of an obligation, duty, or law; especially an unexcused failure to perform a contractual obligation.

Broker—One who is licensed to represent members of the public in real estate transactions for compensation; may be an individual, a corporation, or a partnership.

Broker, Associate—A person who has qualified as a broker, but is affiliated with another broker.

Broker, Designated—A corporate officer or general partner who is authorized to act as the broker for a licensed corporation or partnership.

Brokerage—A real estate broker's business.

Brokerage Fee—The commission or other compensation charged for a real estate broker's services.

Bureau of Real Estate (CalBRE)—The state agency in charge of administering the Real Estate Law in California. Formerly called the Department of Real Estate.

Business Opportunity—A business that is for sale.

Buydown—When discount points are paid to a lender to reduce (buy down) the interest rate charged to the borrower; especially when a seller pays discount points to help the buyer/borrower qualify for financing.

Buyer Representation Agreement—A representation agreement between a prospective property buyer and a real estate broker. The buyer hires the broker to locate a suitable property for the buyer to purchase.

California Environmental Quality Act—A California state law similar to NEPA, requiring an environmental impact report for public or private projects that may have a significant effect on the environment.

Call Provision—See: Acceleration Clause.

Cancellation—Termination of a contract without undoing acts that have been already performed under the contract. Compare: Rescission.

Capacity—The legal ability or competency to perform some act, such as enter into a contract or execute a deed or will.

Capital—Money (or other forms of wealth) available for use in the production of more money.

Capitalization—A method of appraising real property by converting the anticipated net income from the property into the present value. Also called the income approach to value.

Capitalize—1. To provide with cash, or another form of capital. 2. To determine the present value of an asset using capitalization.

CAR—The California Association of Realtors®.

Carryback Loan—See: Loan, Purchase Money.

Cash Equivalent Financing—Financing terms that do not affect the market value of the financed property.

Cash Flow—The residual income after deducting all operating expenses and debt service from gross income. Also called spendable income.

CERCLA—See: Comprehensive Environmental Response, Compensation, and Liability Act.

CEQA— See: California Environmental Quality Act.

Certificate of Eligibility—A document issued by the Department of Veterans Affairs as evidence of a veteran's eligibility for a VA-guaranteed loan.

Certificate of Sale—The document given to the purchaser at a mortgage foreclosure sale, instead of a deed; replaced with a sheriff's deed only after the redemption period expires.

Chain of Title—See: Title, Chain of.

Change, Principle of—An appraisal principle which holds that property values are in a state of flux, increasing and decreasing in response to social, economic, and governmental forces.

Civil Law—The body of law concerned with the rights and liabilities of one individual in relation to another; includes contract law, tort law, and property law. Compare: Criminal Law.

Civil Rights—Fundamental rights guaranteed to individuals by the law. The term is primarily used in reference to constitutional and statutory protections against discrimination or government interference.

Civil Suit—A lawsuit in which one private party sues another private party (as opposed to a criminal suit, in which an individual is sued—prosecuted—by the government).

Client—One who employs a broker, lawyer, appraiser, or other professional. A real estate broker's client can be a seller, a buyer, a landlord, or a tenant.

Closing—The final stage in a real estate transaction, when the seller receives the purchase money, the buyer receives the deed, and title is transferred. Also called settlement.

Closing Disclosure Form—A settlement statement form created by the Consumer Financial Protection Bureau showing closing costs and credits. Both RESPA and TILA require use of the form in residential loan transactions.

Closing Costs—Expenses incurred in the transfer of real estate in addition to the purchase price; for example, the appraisal fee, title insurance premium, broker's commission, and excise tax.

Closing Date—The date on which all the terms of a purchase agreement must be met, or the contract is terminated.

Closing Statement—See: Settlement Statement.

Cloud on Title—A claim, encumbrance, or apparent defect that makes the title to a property unmarketable. See: Title, Marketable.

Code of Ethics—A body of rules setting forth accepted standards of conduct, reflecting principles of fairness and morality; especially one that the members of an organization are expected to follow.

Cold Calling—A marketing technique involving calling homeowners on the telephone and asking if they are interested in selling.

Collateral—Anything of value used as security for a debt or obligation.

Color of Title—See: Title, Color of.

Commingling—Illegally mixing trust funds held on behalf of a client with personal funds.

Commission—1. The compensation paid to a broker for services in connection with a real estate transaction (usually a percentage of the sales price). 2. A group of people organized for a particular purpose or function; usually a governmental body, such as the Real Estate Advisory Commission.

Commitment—In real estate finance, a lender's promise to make a loan. A loan commitment may be "firm" or "conditional"; a conditional commitment is contingent on something, such as a satisfactory credit report on the borrower.

Community Property—In California and other community property states, property owned jointly by a married couple, as distinguished from each spouse's separate property; generally, any property acquired through the labor or skill of either spouse during marriage.

Co-Mortgagor—Someone (usually a family member) who accepts responsibility for the repayment of a mortgage loan along with the primary borrower, to help the borrower qualify for the loan.

Comparable—A recently sold property similar to a subject property, used as a basis for estimating value in the sales comparison approach to appraisal or a competitive market analysis.

Competent—1. Of sound mind, for the purposes of entering into a contract or executing an instrument. 2. Both of sound mind and having reached the age of majority.

Competition, Principle of—An appraisal principle which holds that profits tend to encourage competition, and excess profits tend to result in ruinous competition.

Competitive Market Analysis—A comparison of homes that are similar in location, style, and amenities to the subject property, in order to set a realistic listing price. Similar to the sales comparison approach to value.

Compliance Inspection—A building inspection to determine, for the benefit of a lender, whether building codes, specifications, or conditions established after a prior inspection have been met before a loan is made.

Comprehensive Environmental Response, Compensation, and Liability Act—A federal law allocating liability for the costs of cleanup of toxic waste.

Condition—1. A provision in a contract that makes the parties' rights and obligations depend on the occurrence (or non-occurrence) of a particular event. Also called a contingency clause. 2. A provision in a deed that makes title depend on compliance with a particular restriction.

Conditional Commitment—See: Commitment.

Conforming Loan—See: Loan, Conforming.

Conformity, Principle of—An appraisal principle which holds that the maximum value of property is realized when there is a reasonable degree of social and economic homogeneity in the neighborhood.

Consideration—Anything of value (such as money, goods, services, or a promise) given to induce another to enter into a contract. Sometimes called valuable consideration.

Conspiracy—An agreement or plan between two or more persons to perform an unlawful act.

Construction Lien—See: Lien, Mechanic's.

Consumer Financial Protection Bureau—A federal agency that enforces a number of consumer protection laws that affect the real estate business, such as the Truth in Lending Act.

Contingency Clause—See: Condition.

Contract—An agreement between two or more persons to do or not do a certain thing, for consideration.

Contract, Bilateral—A contract in which each party has made a binding promise to perform (as distinguished from a unilateral contract).

Contract, Broker and Salesperson—An employment contract between a broker and an affiliated salesperson, outlining their mutual obligations.

Contract, Conditional Sales—See: Contract, Land.

Contract, Executed—A contract in which both parties have completely performed their contractual obligations.

Contract, Executory—A contract in which one or both parties have not yet completed performance of their obligations.

Contract, Express—A contract that has been put into words, either spoken or written.

Contract, Implied—A contract that has not been put into words, but is implied by the actions of the parties.

Contract, Installment Sales—See: Contract, Land.

Contract, Land—A contract for the sale of real property in which the buyer (the vendee) pays in installments; the buyer takes possession of the property immediately, but the seller (the vendor) retains legal title until the full price has been paid. Also called a conditional sales contract, installment sales contract, real estate contract, or contract for deed.

Contract, Oral—A spoken agreement that has not been written down.

Contract, Real Estate—1. Any contract pertaining to real estate. 2. A land contract.

Contract, Sales—See: Purchase Agreement.

Contract, Unenforceable—An agreement that a court would refuse to enforce; for example, because its contents can't be proven or the statute of limitations has run out.

Contract, Unilateral—A contract that is accepted by performance; the offeror has promised to perform her side of the bargain if the other party performs, but the other party has not promised to perform. Compare: Contract, Bilateral.

Contract, Valid—A binding, legally enforceable contract.

Contract, Void—An agreement that is not a valid contract, because it lacks a required element (such as consideration) or is defective in some other respect.

Contract, Voidable—A contract that one of the parties can disaffirm without liability, because of lack of capacity or a negative factor such as fraud or duress.

Contract for Deed—See: Contract, Land.

Contract of Sale—See: Purchase Agreement.

Contribution, Principle of—An appraisal principle which holds that the value of real property is greatest when the improvements produce the highest return commensurate with their cost (the investment).

Conventional Financing—See: Loan, Conventional.

Conversion—Misappropriating property or funds belonging to another; for example, converting trust funds to one's own use.

Conveyance—The transfer of title to real property from one person to another by means of a written document, especially a deed.

Cooperative Sale—A sale in which the buyer and the seller are brought together by salespersons working for different brokers.

Corporation—An association organized according to certain laws, in which individuals may purchase ownership shares; treated by the law as an artificial person, separate from the individual shareholders. Compare: Partnership.

Cost—The amount paid for anything in money, goods, or services.

Cost, Replacement—In appraisal, the current cost of constructing a building with the same utility as the subject property using modern materials and construction methods.

Cost, Reproduction—In appraisal, the cost of constructing a replica (an exact duplicate) of the subject property, using the same materials and construction methods that were originally used, but at current prices.

Cost Approach to Value—One of the three main methods of appraisal, in which an estimate of the subject property's value is arrived at by estimating the cost of replacing (or reproducing) the improvements, then deducting the estimated accrued depreciation and adding the estimated market value of the land.

Counteroffer—A response to a contract offer, changing some of the terms of the original offer; it operates as a rejection of the original offer (not as an acceptance). Also called qualified acceptance.

Covenant—1. A contract. 2. A promise. 3. A guarantee (express or implied) in a document such as a deed or lease. 4. A restrictive covenant.

Covenant, Restrictive—A promise to do or not do an act relating to real property, especially a promise that runs with the land; usually an owner's promise not to use the property in a specified manner.

Credit—A payment receivable (owed to a party), as opposed to a debit, which is a payment due (owed by a party).

Credit Score—A figure used in underwriting that encapsulates the likelihood that a loan applicant will default, calculated using a credit scoring model and the information from the applicant's credit report.

Creditor—One who is owed a debt.

Creditor, Secured—A creditor with a security interest in or a lien against specific property; if the debt is not repaid, the creditor can repossess the property or (in the case of real estate) foreclose on the property and collect the debt from the sale proceeds.

Criminal Law—The body of law under which the government can prosecute an individual for crimes, wrongs against society. Compare: Civil Law.

Customer—A party to a sale whom the broker does not represent. For a listing agent, the customer is usually the buyer; for the buyer's agent, the customer is usually the seller.

Damages—In a civil lawsuit, an amount of money the defendant is ordered to pay the plaintiff.

Damages, Compensatory—Damages awarded to a plaintiff as compensation for injuries (personal injuries, property damage, or financial losses) caused by the defendant's act or failure to act.

Damages, Liquidated—A sum that the parties to a contract agree in advance (at the time the contract is made) will serve as full compensation in the event of a breach.

Damages, Punitive—In a civil lawsuit, an award added to compensatory damages, to punish the defendant for outrageous or malicious conduct and discourage others from similar conduct.

Debit—A charge payable by a party; in a real estate transaction, the purchase price is a debit to the buyer, for example, and the sales commission is a debit to the seller.

Debtor—One who owes money to another.

Debt Service—The amount of money required to make the periodic payments of principal and interest on an amortized debt, such as a mortgage.

Debt to Income Ratio—The debt to income ratio measures the relationship between the loan applicant's monthly income and his total monthly debt.

Deed—An instrument which, when properly executed and delivered, conveys title to real property from the grantor to the grantee.

Deed, Grant—A deed that uses the word "grant" in its words of conveyance and carries two implied warranties: (1) the grantor has not previously conveyed title to anyone else, and (2) the grantor has not caused any encumbrances to attach to the property other than those already disclosed to the grantee.

Deed, Quitclaim—A deed that conveys any interest in a property that the grantor has at the time the deed is executed, without warranties.

Deed, Special Warranty—A deed in which the grantor warrants title only against defects that may have arisen during his period of ownership; rarely used in California.

Deed, Tax—A deed given to a purchaser of property at a tax foreclosure sale.

Deed, Trust—See: Deed of Trust.

Deed, Warranty—1. A deed in which the grantor warrants the title against defects that might have arisen before or during her period of ownership; rarely used in California. 2. Any type of deed that carries warranties.

Deed in Lieu of Foreclosure—A deed given by a borrower to the lender, relinquishing ownership of the security property, to satisfy the debt and avoid foreclosure.

Deed of Reconveyance—The instrument used to release the security property from the lien created by a deed of trust when the debt has been repaid.

Deed of Trust—An instrument that creates a voluntary lien on real property to secure the repayment of a debt, and which includes power of sale clause permitting nonjudicial foreclosure; the parties are the grantor or trustor (borrower), the beneficiary (the lender), and the trustee (a neutral third party).

Deed Release Provision—See: Release Clause.

Deed Restrictions—Provisions in a deed that restrict use of the property, and which may be either covenants or conditions.

Default—Failure to fulfill an obligation, duty, or promise, as when a borrower fails to make payments, or a tenant fails to pay rent.

Defendant—1. The person being sued in a civil lawsuit. 2. The accused person in a criminal lawsuit.

Deferred Maintenance—Maintenance or repairs that were postponed, causing physical deterioration of the building.

Delivery—The legal transfer of a deed from the grantor to the grantee, which results in the transfer of title.

Deposit—Money offered as an indication of commitment or as a protection, and which may be refunded under certain circumstances, such as a buyer's good faith deposit or a tenant's security deposit.

Deposit Receipt—See: Purchase Agreement.

Depreciation—1. A loss in value (caused by deferred maintenance, functional obsolescence, or external obsolescence). 2. For the purpose of income tax deductions, apportioning the cost of an asset over a period of time.

Disbursements—Money paid out or expended.

Disclaimer—A denial of legal responsibility.

Discount—1. (verb) To sell a promissory note at less than its face value. 2. (noun) An amount withheld from the loan amount by the lender when the loan is originated; discount points.

Discount Points—A percentage of the principal amount of a loan, collected by the lender at the time a loan is originated, to give the lender an additional yield.

Discrimination—Treating people unequally because of their race, religion, sex, national origin, age, or some other characteristic.

Do Not Call Registry—A list, administered by the Federal Trade Commission, of persons who may not be cold called.

Downpayment—The part of the purchase price of property that the buyer is paying in cash; the difference between the purchase price and the financing.

Drainage—A system to draw water off land, either artificially (e.g., with pipes) or naturally (e.g., with a slope).

Dual Agency—See: Agency, Dual.

Due-on-Sale Clause—See: Alienation Clause.

Duress—Unlawful force or constraint used to compel someone to do something (such as sign a contract) against his will.

Earnest Money—See: Good Faith Deposit.

Easement—An irrevocable right to use some part of another person's real property for a particular purpose.

Elements of Comparison—In the sales comparison approach to appraisal, considerations taken into account in selecting comparables and comparing comparables to the subject property; they include date of sale, location, physical characteristics, and terms of sale.

Employee—Someone who works under the direction and control of another. Compare: Independent Contractor.

Encumber—To place a lien or other encumbrance against the title to a property.

Encumbrance—A nonpossessory interest in real property; a right or interest held by someone other than the property owner, which may be a lien, an easement, a profit, or a restrictive covenant.

Endangered Species Act—A federal law that limits development in habitats of endangered or threatened species.

Encumbrance, Financial—A lien.

Encumbrance, Nonfinancial—An easement, a profit, or a restrictive covenant.

Equity—1. An owner's unencumbered interest in his or her property; the difference between the value of the property and the liens against it. 2. A judge's power to soften or set aside strict legal rules, to bring about a fair and just result in a particular case.

Escrow—An arrangement in which something of value (such as money or a deed) is held on behalf of the parties to a transaction by a third party (an escrow agent) who is acting as an agent for both parties until specified conditions have been fulfilled.

Estate—1. An interest in real property that is or may become possessory; either a freehold or a leasehold. 2. The property left by someone who has died.

Estoppel—A legal doctrine that prevents a person from asserting rights or facts that are inconsistent with her earlier actions or statements.

Estoppel Certificate—A document that prevents a person who signs it from later asserting facts different from those stated in the document. Also called an estoppel letter.

Ethics—A system of accepted principles or standards of moral conduct. See: Code of Ethics.

Exclusive Listing—See: Listing, Exclusive.

Execute—1. To sign an instrument and take any other steps (such as acknowledgment) that may be necessary to its validity. 2. To perform or complete. See: Contract, Executed.

Exemption—A provision holding that a law or rule does not apply to a particular person or group; for example, a person entitled to a tax exemption is not required to pay the tax.

Express—Stated in words, whether spoken or written. Compare: Implied.

Extender Clause—See: Safety Clause.

External Obsolescence—See: Obsolescence, External.

Failure of Purpose—When the intended purpose of an agreement or arrangement can no longer be achieved; in most cases, this releases the parties from their obligations.

Fair Employment and Housing Act—A California state law making it illegal to discriminate in the selling or leasing of housing. Also known as the Rumford Act.

Fair Housing Act—A federal law prohibiting discrimination based on race, color, religion, sex, national origin, disability, or familial status, in the sale or lease of residential property. Part of the Civil Rights Act of 1968.

Fannie Mae—Popular name for the Federal National Mortgage Association (FNMA).

Fed—The Federal Reserve.

Fee—See: Fee Simple.

Fee, Qualified—A fee simple estate that is subject to termination if a certain condition is not met or if a specified event occurs. It may be a fee simple determinable or a fee simple subject to condition subsequent. Also called a conditional fee or defeasible fee.

Fee Simple—The highest and most complete form of ownership, which is of potentially infinite duration. Also called a fee or a fee simple absolute.

FEHA—See: Fair Employment and Housing Act.

FHA—Federal Housing Administration. See also: Loan, FHA.

Fiduciary Relationship—A relationship of trust and confidence, where one party owes the other (or both parties owe each other) loyalty and a higher standard of good faith than is owed to third parties. For example, an agent is a fiduciary in relation to the principal; husband and wife are fiduciaries in relation to one another.

Finance Charge—Any charge a borrower is assessed, directly or indirectly, in connection with a loan. See also: Total Finance Charge.

Financing Contingency—A contingency that makes the sale dependent on the buyer's ability to obtain the financing needed to complete the sale.

Financial Statement—A summary of facts showing the financial condition of an individual or a business, including a detailed list of assets and liabilities. Also called a balance sheet.

Financing Statement—A brief instrument that is recorded to perfect and give constructive notice of a creditor's security interest in an article of personal property.

Finder—Someone who introduces a real estate buyer and seller, but does not help them negotiate their contract. A finder is not the agent of either party and does not have to be licensed. Also called a middleman.

Firm Commitment—See: Commitment.

First Lien Position—The position held by a mortgage or deed of trust that has higher lien priority than any other mortgage or deed of trust against the property.

Fixed-Rate Loan—See: Loan, Fixed-Rate.

Fixed Term—A period of time that has a definite beginning and ending.

Foreclosure—When a lienholder causes property to be sold against the owner's wishes, so that the unpaid lien can be satisfied from the sale proceeds.

Foreclosure Consultant—Anyone who offers (in exchange for compensation) to help a homeowner stop or slow a foreclosure, repair credit, or provide certain other related services to a homeowner.

Foreclosure, Judicial—1. The sale of property pursuant to court order to satisfy a lien. 2. A lawsuit filed by a lender to foreclose on the security property when the borrower has defaulted.

Foreclosure, Nonjudicial—Foreclosure by a trustee under the power of sale clause in a deed of trust.

Forfeiture—Loss of a right or something else of value as a result of failure to perform an obligation or fulfill a condition.

For Sale by Owner—A property that is being sold by the owner without the help of a real estate agent. Also called a FSBO (often pronounced "fizz-bo").

Fraud—An intentional or negligent misrepresentation or concealment of a material fact, which is relied upon by another, who is induced to enter a transaction and harmed as a result.

Fraud, Actual—Deceit or misrepresentation with the intention of cheating or defrauding another.

Fraud, Constructive—A breach of duty that misleads the person to whom the duty was owed, without an intention to deceive; for example, if a seller gives a buyer inaccurate information about the property without realizing that it is false, that may be constructive fraud.

Freddie Mac—Popular name for the Federal Home Loan Mortgage Corporation (FHLMC).

Free and Clear—Ownership of real property completely free of any liens.

Freehold—A possessory interest in real property that has an indeterminable duration; it can be either a fee simple or an estate for life. Someone who has a freehold estate has title to the property (as opposed to someone with a leasehold estate, who is only a tenant).

Frontage—The distance a property extends along a street or a body of water; the distance between the two side boundaries at the front of the lot.

Front Foot—A measurement of property for sale or valuation, with each foot of frontage presumed to extend the entire depth of the lot.

Functional Obsolescence—See: Obsolescence, Functional.

Gift Funds—Money that a relative (or other third party) gives to a buyer who otherwise would not have enough cash to close the transaction.

Ginnie Mae—Popular name for the Government National Mortgage Association (GNMA).

Good Faith Deposit—A deposit that a prospective buyer gives the seller (usually when the buyer's offer is presented) as evidence of his or her good faith intent to complete the transaction. The deposit is applied to the purchase price if the sale closes.

Grant—To transfer or convey an interest in real property by means of a written instrument.

Grant Deed—See: Deed, Grant.

Grantee—One who receives a grant of real property.

Granting Clause—Words in a deed that indicate the grantor's intent to transfer an interest in property.

Grantor—One who grants an interest in real property to another.

Group Boycott—An agreement between two or more real estate brokers to exclude other brokers from equal participation in real estate activities.

Guardian—A person appointed by a court to administer the affairs of a minor or an incompetent person.

Heir—Someone entitled to inherit another's property under the laws of intestate succession.

Highest and Best Use—The use which, at the time of appraisal, is most likely to produce the greatest net return from the property over a given period of time.

Housing Financial Discrimination Act—A California state law requiring lenders to make lending decisions based on the merits of the borrower and the security property, not racial characteristics of the property's neighborhood. Also known as the Holden Act.

HUD—The U.S. Department of Housing and Urban Development.

Hypothecate—To make property security for an obligation without giving up possession of it. Compare: Pledge.

Implied—Not expressed in words, but understood from actions or circumstances. Compare: Express.

Impound Account—A bank account maintained by a lender for payment of property taxes and insurance premiums on the security property; the lender requires the borrower to make regular deposits, and then pays the expenses out of the account when they are due. Also called a reserve account or escrow account.

Improvements—Manmade additions to real property.

Improvements, Misplaced—Improvements that do not fit the most profitable use of the site; they can be overimprovements or underimprovements.

Imputed Knowledge—A legal doctrine stating that a principal is considered to have notice of information that the agent has, even if the agent never told the principal.

Included Items—Items that are included in the sale of real estate, unless otherwise noted in the purchase agreement (such as carpeting, built-in appliances, window coverings, etc.).

Income, Disposable—Income remaining after income taxes have been paid.

Income, Effective Gross—A measure of a rental property's capacity to generate income; calculated by subtracting a vacancy factor from the economic rent (potential gross income).

Income, Gross—A property's total income before making any deductions (for bad debts, vacancies, operating expenses, etc.).

Income, Net—The income left over after subtracting the property's operating expenses (fixed expenses, maintenance expenses, and reserves for replacement) from the effective gross income. In the income approach to value, it is capitalized to estimate the subject property's value.

Income, Potential Gross—A property's economic rent; the income it could earn if it were available for lease in the current market.

Income, Residual—The amount of income that an applicant for a VA loan has left over after taxes, recurring obligations, and the proposed housing expense have been deducted from her gross monthly income.

Income, Spendable—The income that remains after deducting operating expenses, debt service, and income taxes from a property's gross income. Also called net spendable income or cash flow.

Income Approach to Value—One of the three main methods of appraisal, in which an estimate of the subject property's value is based on the net income it produces; also called the capitalization method or investor's method of appraisal.

Income Property—Property that generates rent or other income for the owner, such as an apartment building. In the federal income tax code, it is referred to as property held for the production of income.

Income Ratio—A standard used in qualifying a buyer for a loan, to determine whether he has sufficient income; the buyer's debts and proposed housing expense should not exceed a specified percentage of his income.

Incompetent—Not legally competent; not of sound mind.

Independent Contractor—A person who contracts to do a job for another, but retains control over how she will carry out the task, rather than following detailed instructions. Compare: Employee.

Index—A published statistical report that indicates changes in the cost of money; used as the basis for interest rate adjustments in an ARM.

In-House Transaction—A sale in which the buyer and the seller are brought together by salespersons working for the same broker.

Injunction—A court order prohibiting someone from performing an act, or commanding performance of an act.

Inspection Contingency—A contingency that makes the sale dependent on the satisfactory results of an inspection (such as a general home inspection, a geological inspection, a hazardous substances inspection, and a structural pest control inspection).

Installment Sale—Under the federal income tax code, a sale in which less than 100% of the sales price is received in the year the sale takes place.

Instrument—A legal document, usually one that transfers title (such as a deed), creates a lien (such as a mortgage), or establishes a right to payment (such as a promissory note or contract).

Insurance, Hazard—Insurance against damage to real property caused by fire, flood, theft, or other mishap. Also called casualty insurance.

Insurance, Homeowner's—Insurance against damage to a homeowner's real property and personal property; a form of hazard insurance.

Insurance, Mortgage—Insurance that protects a lender against losses resulting from the borrower's default.

Insurance, Mutual Mortgage—The mortgage insurance provided by the FHA to lenders who make loans through FHA programs.

Insurance, Private Mortgage (PMI)—Insurance provided by private companies to conventional lenders for loans with loan-to-value ratios over 80%.

Insurance, Title—Insurance that protects against losses resulting from undiscovered title defects. An owner's policy protects the buyer, while a lender's policy protects the lien position of the buyer's lender.

Insurance, Title, Extended Coverage—Title insurance that covers problems that should be discovered by an inspection of the property (such as encroachments and adverse possession), in addition to the problems covered by standard coverage policies. An extended coverage policy is sometimes referred to as an ALTA (American Land Title Association) policy.

Insurance, Title, Homeowner's Coverage—Title insurance that is available only in residential one- to four-unit transactions; covers the same issues as an extended coverage policy, plus some additional issues.

Insurance, Title, Standard Coverage—Title insurance that protects against latent title defects (such as forged deeds) and undiscovered recorded encumbrances, but does not protect against problems that would only be discovered by an inspection of the property. A standard coverage policy is sometimes referred to as a CLTA (California Land Title Association) policy.

Interest—1. A right or share in something (such as a piece of real estate). 2. A charge a borrower pays to a lender for the use of the lender's money.

Interest, Compound—Interest computed on both the principal and the interest that has already accrued. Compare: Interest, Simple.

Interest, Interim—See: Interest, Prepaid.

Interest, Prepaid—Interest on a new loan that must be paid at the time of closing; covers the interest due for the first month of the loan term. Also called interim interest.

Interest, Simple—Interest that is computed on the principal amount of the loan only, which is the type of interest charged in connection with real estate loans. Compare: Interest, Compound.

Invalid—Not legally binding or legally effective; not valid.

Joint Tenancy—A form of co-ownership in which the co-owners have unity of time, title, interest, and possession and the right of survivorship. Compare: Tenancy in Common.

Judgment—1. A court's binding determination of the rights and duties of the parties in a lawsuit. 2. A court order requiring one party to pay the other damages.

Judgment, Deficiency—A personal judgment entered against a borrower in favor of the lender if the proceeds from a foreclosure sale of the security property are not enough to pay off the debt.

Judgment Creditor—A person who is owed money as a result of a judgment in a lawsuit.

Judgment Debtor—A person who owes money as a result of a judgment in a lawsuit.

Judgment Lien—See: Lien, Judgment.

Judicial Foreclosure—See: Foreclosure, Judicial.

Kickback—A fee paid for a referral (for example, to an appraiser or inspector). The Real Estate Settlement Procedures Act prohibits kickbacks in most residential mortgage loan transactions.

Land Contract—See: Contract, Land.

Landlord—A landowner who has leased her property to another (a tenant). Also called a lessor.

Latent Defect—A defect that is not visible or apparent. Compare: Patent Defect.

Lawful Object—An objective or purpose of a contract that does not violate the law or a judicial determination of public policy.

Lease—A conveyance of a leasehold estate from the fee owner to a tenant; a contract in which one party pays the other rent in exchange for the possession of real estate. Also called a rental agreement.

Leaseback—See: Sale-Leaseback.

Legal Description—A precise description of a parcel of real property that would enable a surveyor to locate its exact boundaries. It may be a lot and block description, a metes and bounds description, or a government survey description.

Lender, Institutional—A bank, savings and loan, or similar organization that invests other people's funds in loans; as opposed to an individual or private lender, which invests its own funds.

Lessor—A landlord.

Lessee—A tenant.

Leverage—The effective use of borrowed money to finance an investment such as real estate.

Levy—To impose a tax.

Liability—1. A debt or obligation. 2. Legal responsibility.

Liability, Joint and Several—A form of liability in which two or more persons are responsible for a debt both individually and as a group.

Liability, Limited—When a business investor is not personally liable for the debts of the business, as in the case of a limited partner or a corporate shareholder.

Liability, Vicarious—A legal doctrine holding that a principal can be held liable for harm to third parties resulting from an agent's actions.

Liable—Legally responsible.

License—1. Official permission to do a particular thing that the law does not allow everyone to do. 2. Revocable, non-assignable permission to use another person's land for a particular purpose. Compare: Easement.

Lien—A nonpossessory interest in real property, giving the lienholder the right to foreclose if the owner doesn't pay a debt owed to the lienholder; a financial encumbrance on the owner's title.

Lien, Attachment—A lien intended to prevent transfer of the property pending the outcome of litigation.

Lien, Construction—A lien on property in favor of someone who provided labor or materials to improve the property. The term encompasses mechanic's liens and materialman's liens.

Lien, General—A lien against all the property of a debtor, rather than a particular piece of her property. Compare: Lien, Specific.

Lien, Involuntary—A lien that arises by operation of law, without the consent of the property owner.

Lien, Judgment—A general lien against a judgment debtor's property. The lien is created automatically in the county where the judgment was rendered and may be created in other counties by recording an abstract of judgment.

Lien, Materialman's—A construction lien in favor of someone who supplied materials for a project (as opposed to labor).

Lien, Mechanic's—A lien on property in favor of someone who provided labor or materials to improve it.

Lien, Property Tax—A specific lien on property to secure payment of property taxes.

Lien, Specific—A lien that attaches only to a particular piece of property. Compare: Lien, General.

Lien, Tax—A lien on property to secure the payment of taxes.

Lien, Voluntary—A lien placed against property with the consent of the owner; a deed of trust or a mortgage.

Lienholder, Junior—A secured creditor whose lien is lower in priority than another's lien.

Lien Priority—The order in which liens are paid off out of the proceeds of a foreclosure sale.

Limited Liability—See: Liability, Limited.

Liquidated Damages—See: Damages, Liquidated.

Liquidity—The degree of ease with which a non-cash asset can be converted into cash.

Listing—A written agency contract between a seller and a real estate broker, stipulating that the broker will be paid a commission for finding (or attempting to find) a buyer for the seller's property. Also called a listing agreement.

Listing Broker—The broker who takes a listing, and thus represents the seller.

Listing, Exclusive—Either an exclusive agency listing or an exclusive right to sell listing.

Listing, Exclusive Agency—A listing agreement that entitles the broker to a commission if anyone other than the seller finds a buyer for the property during the listing term.

Listing, Exclusive Right to Sell—A listing agreement that entitles the broker to a commission if anyone—including the seller—finds a buyer for the property during the listing term.

Listing, Multiple—A listing (usually an exclusive right to sell listing) that includes a provision allowing the broker to submit the listing to her multiple listing service for dissemination to cooperating brokers.

Listing, Net—A listing agreement in which the seller sets a net amount he is willing to accept for the property; if the actual selling price exceeds that amount, the broker is entitled to keep the excess as her commission.

Listing, Open—A nonexclusive listing, given by a seller to as many brokers as he chooses. If the property is sold, a broker is only entitled to a commission if she was the procuring cause of the sale.

Loan, Amortized—A loan that requires regular installment payments of both principal and interest (as opposed to an interest-only loan). It is fully amortized if the installment payments will pay off the full amount of the principal and all of the interest by the end of the repayment period. It is partially amortized if the installment payments will cover only part of the principal, so that a balloon payment of the remaining principal balance is required at the end of the repayment period.

Loan, Cal-Vet—A loan made through the California Veterans Farm and Home Purchase Program.

Loan, Called—A loan that has been accelerated by the lender. See: Acceleration Clause.

Loan, Carryback—See: Loan, Purchase Money.

Loan, Conforming—A loan made in accordance with the standardized underwriting criteria of the major secondary market agencies, Fannie Mae and Freddie Mac, and which therefore can be sold to those agencies.

Loan, Construction—A loan to finance the cost of constructing a building, usually providing that the loan funds will be advanced in installments as the work progresses. Also called an interim loan.

Loan, Conventional—An institutional loan that is not insured or guaranteed by a government agency.

Loan, FHA—A loan made by an institutional lender and insured by the Federal Housing Administration, so that the FHA will reimburse the lender for losses that result if the borrower defaults.

Loan, Fixed-Rate—A loan on which the interest rate will remain the same throughout the entire loan term. Compare: Mortgage, Adjustable-rate.

Loan, Guaranteed—A loan in which a third party has agreed to reimburse the lender for losses that result if the borrower defaults.

Loan, Home Equity—A loan secured by the borrower's equity in the home she already owns. Compare: Loan, Purchase Money.

Loan, Interest-Only—A loan that requires the borrower to pay only the interest during the loan term, with the principal due at the end of the term.

Loan, Interim—See: Loan, Construction.

Loan, Permanent—See: Loan, Take-out.

Loan, Purchase Money—1. When a seller extends credit to a buyer to finance the purchase of the property, accepting a deed of trust or mortgage instead of cash. Sometimes called a carryback loan. 2. In a more general sense, any loan the borrower uses to buy the security property (as opposed to a loan secured by property the borrower already owns).

Loan, Swing—A loan used by a borrower who intends to purchase a new house, funded by the equity in his old house, before selling his old house.

Loan, Take-Out—Long-term financing used to replace a construction loan (an interim loan) when construction has been completed. Also called a permanent loan.

Loan, VA-Guaranteed—A home loan made by an institutional lender to an eligible veteran and guaranteed by the Department of Veterans Affairs. The VA reimburses the lender for losses if the borrower defaults.

Loan Correspondent—An intermediary who arranges loans of an investor's money to borrowers, and then services the loans.

Loan Estimate—Lenders and mortgage brokers must provide a loan applicant with an estimate of closing costs on a form developed by the Consumer Financial Protection Bureau.

Loan Fee—A loan origination fee, an assumption fee, or discount points.

Loan-to-Value Ratio (LTV)—The relationship between the loan amount and either the sales price or the appraised value of the property (whichever is less), expressed as a percentage.

Loan Level Price Adjustment (LLPA)—A risk-based loan fee that varies depending on the borrower's credit score and the loan-to-value ratio (or certain other factors that affect risk), charged on many conventional conforming loans.

LTV—See: Loan-to-Value Ratio.

Mailbox Rule—A common law rule under which an acceptance communicated by mail is effective when the message has been sent (put into the mailbox), even though the offeror won't receive it right away. (This rule isn't used in the CAR purchase agreement form.)

Majority, Age of—The age at which a person becomes legally competent; in California, 18 years old. See: Minor.

Maker—The person who signs a promissory note, promising to repay a debt. Compare: Payee.

Margin—In an adjustable-rate mortgage, the difference between the index rate and the interest rate charged to the borrower.

Marketable Title—See: Title, Marketable.

Market Allocation—When competing brokers agree not to sell: 1) certain products or services in certain specified areas; 2) in specified areas; or 3) to certain customers in specified areas.

Market Data Approach—See: Sales Comparison Approach.

Market Price—1. The current price generally being charged for something in the marketplace. 2. The price actually paid for a property. Compare: Value, Market.

Material Fact—An important fact; one that is likely to influence a decision.

Maturity Date—The date by which a loan is supposed to be paid off in full.

Mediation—A negotiation to resolve a dispute that is conducted by an impartial third party.

Meeting of Minds—See: Mutual Consent.

Mello-Roos Lien—A special assessment that provides for community improvements within a special taxing district; the presence of such a lien must be disclosed to the buyer.

Middleman—See: Finder.

Minor—A person who has not yet reached the age of majority; in California, a person under 18.

MIP—Mortgage insurance premium; especially a premium charged in connection with an FHA-insured loan.

Misrepresentation—A false or misleading statement. See: Fraud.

MLS—See: Multiple Listing Service.

Monopoly—When a single entity or group has exclusive control over the production or sale of a product or service.

Mortgage—1. An instrument that creates a voluntary lien on real property to secure repayment of a debt, and which (unlike a deed of trust) ordinarily does not include a power of sale, so it can only be foreclosed judicially; the parties are the mortgagor (borrower) and mortgagee (lender). 2. The term is often used more generally, to refer to either a mortgage or a deed of trust—i.e., to any loan secured by real property. Note: If you do not find the specific term you are looking for here under "Mortgage," check the entries under "Loan."

Mortgage, Adjustable-Rate (ARM)—A loan in which the interest rate is periodically increased or decreased to reflect changes in the cost of money. Compare: Loan, Fixed-Rate.

Mortgage, Balloon—A partially amortized mortgage loan that requires a large balloon payment at the end of the loan term.

Mortgage, Blanket—A mortgage that is a lien against more than one parcel of property.

Mortgage, Budget—A loan in which the monthly payments include a share of the property taxes and insurance, in addition to principal and interest; the lender places the money for taxes and insurance in an impound account.

Mortgage, First—The mortgage on a property that has first lien position; the one with higher lien priority than any other mortgage against the property.

Mortgage, Hard Money—A mortgage given to a lender in exchange for cash, as opposed to one given in exchange for credit.

Mortgage, Junior—A mortgage that has lower lien priority than another mortgage against the same property. Sometimes called a secondary mortgage.

Mortgage, Level Payment—An amortized loan with payments that are the same amount each month, although the portion of the payment that is applied to principal steadily increases and the portion of the payment applied to interest steadily decreases. See: Loan, Amortized.

Mortgage, Package—A mortgage that is secured by certain items of personal property (such as appliances) in addition to the real property.

Mortgage, Satisfaction of—The document a mortgagee gives the mortgagor when the mortgage debt has been paid in full, acknowledging that the debt has been paid and the mortgage is no longer a lien against the property.

Mortgage, Secondary—See: Mortgage, Junior.

Mortgage, Senior—A mortgage that has higher lien priority than another mortgage against the same property; the opposite of a junior mortgage.

Mortgage, Wraparound—A purchase money loan arrangement in which the seller uses part of the buyer's payments to make the payments on an existing loan (called the underlying loan); the buyer takes title subject to the underlying loan, but does not assume it. When the security instrument used for wraparound financing is a deed of trust instead of a mortgage, it may be referred to as an all-inclusive trust deed.

Mortgage Banker—See Mortgage Company.

Mortgage Broker—An intermediary who brings real estate lenders and borrowers together and negotiates loan agreements between them.

Mortgage Company—A type of real estate lender that originates residential mortgage loans on behalf of large investors or for sale on the secondary market, and may also service the loans; not a depository institution. Also called a mortgage banking company or a mortgage banker.

Mortgage Foreclosure Consultant Law—A California state law protecting distressed homeowners from being victimized by foreclosure rescue scams.

Mortgage Loan—Any loan secured by real property, whether the actual security instrument used is a mortgage or a deed of trust.

Mortgagee—A lender who accepts a mortgage as security for repayment of the loan.

Mortgaging Clause—A clause in a mortgage that describes the security interest given to the mortgagee.

Mortgagor—A property owner (usually a borrower) who gives a mortgage to another (usually a lender) as security for payment of an obligation.

Multiple Listing Service (MLS)—An organization of brokers who share their exclusive listings.

Mutual Consent—When all parties freely agree to the terms of a contract, without fraud, undue influence, duress, menace, or mistake. Mutual consent is achieved through offer and acceptance; it is sometimes referred to as a "meeting of the minds."

NAR—National Association of Realtors®.

Narrative Report—A thorough appraisal report in which the appraiser summarizes the data and the appraisal methods used, to convince the reader of the soundness of the estimate; a more comprehensive presentation than a form report.

National Environmental Policy Act—A federal law requiring federal agencies to provide an environmental impact statement for agency actions having a significant effect on the environment.

Negligence—Conduct that falls below the standard of care that a reasonable person would exercise under the circumstances; carelessness or recklessness.

Negotiable Instrument—An instrument containing an unconditional promise to pay a certain sum of money, to order or to bearer, on demand or at a particular time. It can be a check, promissory note, bond, draft, or stock.

Net Income—See: Income, Net.

Net Listing—See: Listing, Net.

Net Worth—A person's financial assets minus liabilities.

Nominal Interest Rate—The interest rate stated in a promissory note. Also called the note rate or coupon rate. Compare: Annual Percentage Rate.

Nonconforming Loan—See: Loan, Conforming.

Notarize—To have a document certified by a notary public.

Notary Public—Someone who is officially authorized to witness and certify the acknowledgment made by someone signing a legal document.

Note—See: Note, Promissory.

Note, Demand—A promissory note that is due whenever the holder of the note demands payment.

Note, Installment—A promissory note that calls for regular payments of principal and interest until the debt is fully paid.

Note, Joint—A promissory note signed by two or more persons with equal liability for payment.

Note, Promissory—A written promise to repay a debt; it may or may not be a negotiable instrument.

Note, Straight—A promissory note that calls for regular payments of interest only, so that the entire principal amount is due in one lump sum at the end of the loan term.

Notice, Actual—Actual knowledge of a fact, as opposed to knowledge imputed by law (constructive notice).

Notice, Constructive—Knowledge of a fact imputed to a person by law. A person is held to have constructive notice of something when he should have known it (because he could have learned it through reasonable diligence or an inspection of the public record), even if he did not actually know it.

Notice of Default—A notice sent by a secured creditor to the debtor, informing the debtor that he has breached the loan agreement.

Notice of Sale—A notice stating that foreclosure proceedings have been commenced against a property.

Novation—1. When one party to a contract withdraws and a new party is substituted, relieving the withdrawing party of liability. 2. The substitution of a new obligation for an old one.

Obsolescence—Any loss in value (depreciation) due to reduced desirability and usefulness.

Obsolescence, External—Loss in value resulting from factors outside the property itself, such as proximity to an airport. Also called economic obsolescence or external inadequacy.

Obsolescence, Functional—Loss in value due to inadequate or outmoded equipment, or as a result of poor or outmoded design.

Offer—When one person (the offeror) proposes a contract to another (the offeree); if the offeree accepts the offer, a binding contract is formed.

Offer, Tender—See: Tender.

Offeree—One to whom a contract offer is made.

Offeror—One who makes a contract offer.

Officer—In a corporation, an executive authorized by the board of directors to manage the business of the corporation.

Off-Site Improvements—Improvements that add to the usefulness of a site but are not located directly on it, such as curbs, street lights, and sidewalks.

One-Party Listing—A listing agreement that is only effective in regard to one particular buyer.

Open House—Showing a listed home to the public for a certain number of hours.

Option—A contract giving one party the right to do something, without obligating her to do it.

Optionee—The person who receives (buys) an option.

Optionor—The person who gives (sells) an option.

Option to Purchase—An option giving the optionee the right to buy property owned by the optionor at an agreed price during a specified period.

Ordinance—A law passed by a local legislative body, such as a city or county council. Compare: Statute.

Orientation—The placement of a house on its lot, with regard to its exposure to the sun and wind, privacy from the street, and protection from outside noise.

Origination Fee—A fee a lender charges a borrower upon making a new loan, intended to cover the administrative costs of making the loan. Also called a loan fee or points.

"Or More"—A provision in a promissory note that allows the borrower to prepay the debt.

Ownership—Title to property, dominion over property; the rights of possession and control.

Ownership, Concurrent—When two or more individuals share ownership of one piece of property, each owning an undivided interest in the property (as in a tenancy in common or joint tenancy, or with community property). Also called co-ownership or co-tenancy.

Ownership in Severalty—Ownership by a single individual.

Panic Selling—See: Blockbusting.

Parcel—A lot or piece of real estate, especially a specified part of a larger tract.

Partial Reconveyance—The instrument given to the borrower when part of the security property is released from a blanket deed of trust under a partial release clause.

Partial Release Clause—See: Release Clause.

Partial Satisfaction—The instrument given to the borrower when part of the security property is released from a blanket mortgage under a partial release clause.

Partner, General—A partner who has the authority to manage and contract for a general or limited partnership, and who is personally liable for the partnership's debts.

Partner, Limited—A partner in a limited partnership who typically is merely an investor and does not participate in the management of the business. A limited partner isn't personally liable for the partnership's debts.

Partnership—An association of two or more persons to carry on a business for profit. The law regards a partnership as a group of individuals, not as an entity separate from its owners. Compare: Corporation.

Partnership, General—A partnership in which each member has an equal right to manage the business and share in the profits, as well as equal responsibility for the partnership's debts.

Partnership, Limited—A partnership made up of one or more general partners and one or more limited partners.

Patent Defect—A problem that is readily observable in an ordinary inspection of the property. Compare: Latent Defect.

Payee—In a promissory note, the party who is entitled to be paid; the lender. Compare: Maker.

Percolation Test—A test to determine the ability of the ground to absorb or drain water; used to determine whether a site is suitable for construction, particularly for installation of a septic tank system.

Personal Property—Any property that is not real property; movable property not affixed to land. Also called chattels or personalty.

Personalty—Personal property.

Physical Deterioration—Loss in value (depreciation) resulting from wear and tear or deferred maintenance.

Plaintiff—The party who brings or starts a civil lawsuit; the one who sues.

Pledge—When a debtor transfers possession of property to the creditor as security for repayment of the debt. Compare: Hypothecate.

PMI—See: Insurance, Private Mortgage.

Point—One percent of the principal amount of a loan.

Points—See: Discount Points; Origination Fee.

Portfolio—The mix of investments owned by an individual or company.

Possession—1. The holding and enjoyment of property. 2. Actual physical occupation of real property.

Power of Attorney—An instrument authorizing one person (the attorney in fact) to act as another's agent, to the extent stated in the instrument.

Power of Sale Clause—A clause in a deed of trust giving the trustee the right to foreclose nonjudicially (sell the debtor's property without a court action) if the borrower defaults.

Preapproval—Lender approval given before the buyer has chosen a property to purchase, establishing the maximum loan amount that the lender is willing to provide.

Predatory Lending—Lending practices used to take advantage of unsophisticated borrowers.

Prepayment—Paying off part or all of a loan before payment is due.

Prepayment Penalty—A penalty charged to a borrower who prepays.

Preventive Maintenance—A program of regular inspection and care of a property and its fixtures, allowing the prevention of potential problems or their immediate repair.

Price Fixing—The cooperative setting of prices by competing firms. Price fixing is an automatic violation of antitrust laws.

Primary Mortgage Market—The market in which mortgage loans are originated, where lenders make loans to borrowers. Compare: Secondary Mortgage Market.

Prime Rate—The interest rate a bank charges its largest and most desirable customers.

Principal—1. One who grants another person (an agent) authority to represent him in dealings with third parties. 2. One of the parties to a transaction (such as a buyer or seller), as opposed to those who are involved as agents or employees (such as a broker or escrow agent). 3. In regard to a loan, the amount originally borrowed, as opposed to the interest.

Procuring Cause—The real estate agent who is primarily responsible for bringing about a sale; for example, by negotiating the agreement between the buyer and seller.

Profit—A nonpossessory interest; the right to enter another person's land and take something (such as timber or minerals) away from it.

Progression, Principle of—An appraisal principle which holds that a property of lesser value tends to be worth more when it is located in an area with properties of greater value than it would be if located elsewhere. The opposite of the principle of regression.

Promisee—Someone who has been promised something; someone who is supposed to receive the benefit of a contractual promise.

Promisor—Someone who has made a contractual promise to another.

Promissory Note—See: Note, Promissory.

Property—1. The rights of ownership in a thing, such as the right to use, possess, transfer, or encumber it. 2. Something that is owned.

Property Tax—See: Tax, Property.

Proprietorship, Individual or Sole—A business owned and operated by one person.

Proration—The process of dividing or allocating something (especially a sum of money or an expense) proportionately, according to time, interest, or benefit.

Protection Clause—See: Safety Clause.

Public Accommodation—Any facility operated by a private entity and open to the public, where the operation of the facility affects commerce, such as a hotel, restaurant, theater, retail store, or service professional's office.

Public Record—The official collection of legal documents that persons have filed with the county recorder in order to make public the information contained in the documents.

Puffing—Statements of exaggerated praise for a property that should not be considered assertions of fact.

Purchase Agreement—A contract in which a seller promises to convey title to real property to a buyer in exchange for the purchase price. Also called a deposit receipt in California. Elsewhere, also called a purchase and sale agreement, earnest money agreement, sales contract, or contract of sale.

Qualifying Standards—The standards a lender requires a loan applicant to meet before a loan will be approved. Also called underwriting standards.

Quitclaim Deed—See: Deed, Quitclaim.

Radon—A naturally occurring carcinogenic gas formed in the earth's crust that can enter buildings through cracks in a foundation.

Ratify—To confirm or approve after the fact an act that was not authorized when it was performed.

Ready, Willing, and Able—A buyer is ready, willing, and able if he makes an offer that meets the seller's stated terms, and has the contractual capacity and financial resources to complete the transaction.

Real Estate—See: Real Property.

Real Estate Brokerage—1. A real estate broker's business. 2. As a licensed real estate agent, bringing a buyer and a seller together and negotiating a sales contract between the two parties.

Real Estate Contract—1. A purchase agreement. 2. A land contract. 3. Any contract having to do with real property.

Real Estate Investment Trust (REIT)—A real estate investment business with at least 100 investors, organized as a trust and entitled to special tax treatment under IRS rules.

Real Estate Settlement Procedures Act—See: RESPA.

Real Estate Transfer Disclosure Statement—A statement containing information about the property that a seller of residential property is required to give to the buyer.

Real Property—Land and everything attached to or appurtenant to it. Also called realty or real estate. Compare: Personal Property.

Realtor®—A real estate agent who is an active member of a state or local real estate board that is affiliated with the National Association of Realtors®.

Realty—See: Real Property.

Reconciliation—The final step in an appraisal, when the appraiser assembles and interprets the data in order to arrive at a final value estimate. Also called correlation.

Reconveyance—Releasing the security property from the lien created by a deed of trust, by recording a deed of reconveyance.

Recording—Filing a document at the county recorder's office, so that it will be placed in the public record.

Redemption—1. When a defaulting borrower prevents foreclosure by paying the full amount of the debt, plus costs. 2. When a mortgagor regains the property after foreclosure by paying whatever the foreclosure sale purchaser paid for it, plus interest and expenses.

Redlining—When a lender refuses to make loans secured by property in a certain neighborhood because of the racial or ethnic composition of the neighborhood.

Refinancing—When a homeowner takes out a new loan—usually to take advantage of lower interest rates—and uses that loan's proceeds to pay off the existing loan.

Regression, Principle of—An appraisal principle which holds that a valuable property surrounded by properties of lesser value will tend to be worth less than it would be in a different location; the opposite of the principle of progression.

Regulation Z—The federal regulation that implements the Truth in Lending Act.

Reinstate—To prevent foreclosure by curing the default.

Release—1. To give up a legal right. 2. A document in which a legal right is given up.

Release Clause—1. A provision in a purchase agreement that allows the seller to keep the property on the market while waiting for a contingency to be fulfilled; if the seller receives another good offer, he can require the buyer to either waive the contingency clause or terminate the contract. 2. A clause in a blanket mortgage or deed of trust which allows the borrower to get part of the security property released from the lien when a certain portion of the debt has been paid or other conditions are fulfilled. Also called a partial release clause.

Rent—Compensation paid by a tenant to the landlord in exchange for the possession and use of the property.

Rent Roll—A monthly report on rent collection, listing both occupied and vacant units and the total rental income earned, both collected and uncollected.

Rental Schedule—A list of all the rental rates assigned to the different types of units in a building. For example, a rental schedule for an apartment building might list the rates of its studio apartments, one-bedroom apartments, and two-bedroom apartments.

Replacement Cost—See: Cost, Replacement.

Reproduction Cost—See: Cost, Reproduction.

Request for Reconsideration of Value—A request to a lender to reconsider the appraised value of a property, when the appraisal comes in lower than expected. The request is supported by data on comparable sales that would support a higher market value for the subject property.

Rescission—When a contract is terminated and each party gives anything acquired under the contract back to the other party. (The verb form is rescind.) Compare: Cancellation.

Reserve Account—See: Impound Account.

Reserve Requirements—The percentage of deposits commercial banks must keep on reserve with the Federal Reserve Bank.

Reserves for Replacement—Regular allowances set aside by an investment property owner, a business, or a homeowners association to pay for the replacement of structures and equipment that are expected to wear out.

RESPA—Real Estate Settlement Procedures Act; a federal law that requires lenders to disclose certain information about closing costs to loan applicants.

Restitution—Restoring something (especially money) that a person was unjustly deprived of.

Restriction—A limitation on the use of real property.

Restriction, Deed—A restrictive covenant in a deed.

Restriction, Private—A restriction imposed on property by a previous owner, a neighbor, or the subdivision developer; a restrictive covenant or a condition in a deed.

Restriction, Public—A law or regulation limiting or regulating the use of real property.

Restrictive Covenant—See: Covenant, Restrictive.

Return—A profit from an investment, such as interest on a bank account.

Risk Analysis—See: Underwriting.

Safety Clause—A clause in a listing agreement providing that for a specified period after the listing expires, the broker will still be entitled to a commission if the property is sold to someone the broker dealt with during the listing term. Also called a protection clause or extender clause.

Sale-Leaseback—A transaction to raise capital in which the owner of real property used in his business sells the property and leases it back from the buyer. In addition to certain tax advantages, the seller/lessee obtains more cash through the sale than would normally be possible by borrowing and mortgaging the property, since lenders will not often lend 100% of the property's value.

Sales Comparison Approach to Value—One of the three main methods of appraisal, in which the sales prices of comparable properties are used to estimate the value of the subject property. Also called the market data approach.

Satisfaction of Mortgage—See: Mortgage, Satisfaction of.

Secondary Financing—Money borrowed to pay part of the required downpayment or closing costs for a first loan, when the second loan is secured by the same property that secures the first loan.

Secondary Mortgage Market—The market in which investors (including Fannie Mae, Freddie Mac, and Ginnie Mae) purchase real estate loans from lenders.

Secret Profit—A financial benefit that an agent takes from a transaction without informing the principal.

Security Instrument—A document that creates a voluntary lien, to secure repayment of a loan; for debts secured by real property, it is either a mortgage or a deed of trust.

Security Interest—The interest a creditor may acquire in the debtor's property to ensure that the debt will be paid.

Security Property—The property that a borrower gives a lender a voluntary lien against, so that the lender can foreclose if the borrower defaults.

Seller Financing—When a seller extends credit to a buyer to finance the purchase of the property; as opposed to having the buyer obtain a loan from a third party, such as an institutional lender.

Selling Broker—The broker responsible for procuring a buyer for real estate; may represent either the seller or the buyer.

Separate Property—Property owned by a married person that is not community property; includes property acquired before marriage or by gift or inheritance after marriage.

Settlement—1. An agreement between the parties to a civil lawsuit, in which the plaintiff agrees to drop the suit in exchange for money or the defendant's promise to do or refrain from doing something. 2. Closing.

Settlement Statement—A document that presents a final, detailed accounting for a real estate transaction, listing each party's debits and credits and the amount each will receive or be required to pay at closing. Also called a closing statement.

Severalty—See: Ownership in Severalty.

Shareholder—An individual who holds ownership shares (shares of stock) in a corporation, and has limited liability in regard to the corporation's debts. Also called a stockholder.

Sheriff's Sale—A foreclosure sale held after a judicial foreclosure. Sometimes called an execution sale.

Special Assessment—A tax levied only against the properties that have benefited from a public improvement (such as a sewer or a street light), to cover the cost of the improvement; creates a special assessment lien. Also called an improvement tax.

Special Warranty Deed—See: Deed, Special Warranty.

Specific Performance—A legal remedy in which a court orders someone who has breached to actually perform the contract as agreed, rather than simply paying money damages.

Stable Monthly Income—A loan applicant's gross monthly income that meets the lender's tests of quality and durability.

Statute—A law enacted by a state legislature or the U.S. Congress. Compare: Ordinance.

Statute of Frauds—A law that requires certain types of contracts to be in writing and signed in order to be enforceable.

Statute of Limitations—A law requiring a particular type of lawsuit to be filed within a specified time after the event giving rise to the suit occurred.

Steering—Channeling prospective buyers or tenants to or away from particular neighborhoods based on their race, religion, national origin, or ancestry.

Stockholder—See: Shareholder.

Subagent—A person that an agent has delegated authority to, so that the subagent can assist in carrying out the principal's orders; the agent of an agent.

Subcontractor—A contractor who, at the request of the general contractor, provides a specific service, such as plumbing or drywalling, in connection with the overall construction project.

Subject to—When a purchaser takes property subject to a trust deed or mortgage, he is not personally liable for paying off the loan; in case of default, however, the property can still be foreclosed on.

Sublease—When a tenant grants someone else the right to possession of the leased property for part of the remainder of the lease term; as opposed to a lease assignment, where the tenant gives up possession for the entire reminder of the lease term. Also called a sandwich lease.

Subordination Clause—A provision in a mortgage or deed of trust that permits a later mortgage or deed of trust to have higher lien priority than the one containing the clause.

Subprime Lending—When lenders apply more flexible underwriting standards in order to take on riskier borrowers and riskier loans, in return for higher loan fees and interest rates.

Substitution, Principle of—A principle of appraisal holding that the maximum value of a property is limited by the cost of obtaining another equally desirable property, assuming that there would not be a long delay or significant incidental expenses involved in obtaining the substitute property.

Survey—The process of precisely measuring the boundaries and determining the area of a parcel of land.

Syndicate—An association formed to operate an investment business. A syndicate is not a recognized legal entity; it can be organized as a corporation, LLC, partnership, or trust.

Tax, Ad Valorem—A tax assessed on the value of property.

Tax, Documentary Transfer—A state tax levied on most real estate sales, to be paid by the seller.

Tax, General Real Estate—An annual ad valorem tax levied on real property.

Tax, Improvement—See: Special Assessment.

Tax, Property—1. The general real estate tax. 2. Any ad valorem tax levied on real or personal property.

Tax Deed—See: Deed, Tax.

Tax Sale—Sale of property after foreclosure of a tax lien.

Tenancy in Common—A form of concurrent ownership in which two or more persons each have an undivided interest in the entire property, but no right of survivorship. Compare: Joint Tenancy.

Tenant—Someone in lawful possession of real property; especially, someone who has leased the property from the owner (also called a lessee).

Tender—An unconditional offer by one of the parties to a contract to perform her part of the agreement; made when the offeror believes the other party is breaching, it establishes the offeror's right to sue if the other party doesn't accept it. Also called a tender offer.

Term—A prescribed period of time; especially, the length of time a borrower has to pay off a loan, or the duration of a lease.

Third Party—1. A person seeking to deal with a principal through an agent. 2. In a transaction, someone who is not one of the principals.

Tie-In Arrangement—An agreement to sell one product, only on the condition that the buyer also purchases a different product.

Tight Money Market—When loan funds are scarce, leading lenders to charge high interest rates and discount points.

TILA—Truth in Lending Act. A federal law protecting loan applicants and borrowers by requiring disclosures about loan costs.

Time is of the Essence—A clause in a contract that means performance on the exact dates specified is an essential element of the contract; failure to perform on time is a material breach.

Title—Lawful ownership of real property. Also, the deed or other document that is evidence of that ownership.

Title, Abstract of—A brief, chronological summary of the recorded documents affecting title to a particular piece of real property.

Title, After-Acquired—A rule applicable to warranty deeds; if the title is defective at the time of transfer, but the grantor later acquires more perfect title, the additional interest passes to the grantee automatically.

Title, Chain of—1. The chain of deeds (and other documents) transferring title to a piece of property from one owner to the next, as disclosed in the public record. 2. A listing of all recorded documents affecting title to a particular property; more complete than an abstract.

Title, Clear—A good title to property, free from encumbrances or defects; marketable title.

Title, Color of—Title that appears to be good title, but which in fact is not; commonly based on a defective instrument, such as an invalid deed.

Title, Equitable—The vendee's interest in property under a land contract. Also called an equitable interest.

Title, Legal—The vendor's interest in property under a land contract.

Title, Marketable—Title free and clear of objectionable liens, encumbrances, or defects, so that a reasonably prudent person with full knowledge of the facts would not hesitate to purchase the property.

Title Company—A title insurance company.

Title Insurance—See: Insurance, Title.

Title Report—A report issued by a title company, disclosing the condition of the title to a specific piece of property, before the actual title insurance policy is issued. Sometimes called a preliminary title report.

Title Search—An inspection of the public record to determine the rights and encumbrances affecting title to a piece of property.

Topography—The contours of the surface of the land (level, hilly, steep, etc.).

Total Finance Charge—Under the Truth in Lending Act, the total finance charge on a loan includes interest, any discount points paid by the borrower, the loan origination fee, and mortgage insurance costs.

Tract—1. A piece of land of undefined size. 2. In the rectangular survey system, an area made up of 16 townships; 24 miles on each side.

Trigger Term—A specific finance term (such as monthly payment amount) that, when used in an advertisement, triggers the requirement of full disclosure of all the important financing terms, as required by the Truth in Lending Act (TILA).

Trust—A legal arrangement in which title to property (or funds) is vested in one or more trustees, who manage the property on behalf of the trust's beneficiaries, in accordance with instructions set forth in the document establishing the trust.

Trust Account—A bank account, separate from a real estate broker's personal and business accounts, used to segregate trust funds from the broker's own funds.

Trust Funds—Money or things of value received by an agent, not belonging to the agent but being held for the benefit of others.

Trustee—1. A person appointed to manage a trust on behalf of the beneficiaries. 2. A neutral third party appointed in a deed of trust to handle the nonjudicial foreclosure process in case of default.

Trustee in Bankruptcy—An individual appointed by the court to handle the assets of a person in bankruptcy.

Trustee's Deed—See: Deed, Trustee's.

Trustee's Sale—A nonjudicial foreclosure sale under a deed of trust.

Trustor—The borrower in a deed of trust. Also called the grantor.

Truth in Lending Act—See: TILA.

Underwriting—In real estate lending, the process of evaluating a loan application to determine the probability that the applicant would repay the loan, and matching the risk to an appropriate rate of return. Sometimes called risk analysis.

Underwriting, Automated—Underwriting using software that performs a preliminary analysis of a loan application and makes a recommendation for approval or additional scrutiny.

Undue Influence—Exerting excessive pressure on someone so as to overpower the person's free will and prevent him or her from making a rational or prudent decision; often involves abusing a relationship of trust.

Unenforceable—See: Contract, Unenforceable.

Unilateral Contract—See: Contract, Unilateral.

Unruh Civil Rights Act—A California state law prohibiting discrimination based on a number of protected classes, in all business establishments.

Urea Formaldehyde—A toxic substance found in adhesives used in pressed wood building products.

VA—The U.S. Department of Veterans Affairs (formerly the Veterans Administration).

Vacancy Factor—A percentage deducted from a property's potential gross income to determine the effective gross income, estimating the income that will probably be lost because of vacancies and tenants who don't pay.

Valid—The legal classification of a contract that is binding and enforceable in a court of law.

Valuable Consideration—See: Consideration.

Valuation—See: Appraisal.

Value—The present worth of the future benefits of owning a piece of real or personal property.

Value, Assessed—The value placed on property by the taxing authority (the county assessor, for example) for the purposes of taxation.

Value, Face—The value of an instrument, such as a promissory note or a security, that is indicated on the face of the instrument itself.

Value, Market—The most probable price which a property should bring in a competitive and open market under all conditions requisite to a fair sale, the buyer and seller each acting prudently and knowledgeably, and assuming the price is not affected by undue stimulus. (This is the definition from the Uniform Standards of Professional Appraisal Practice.) Market value is also called fair market value, value in exchange, or objective value. Compare: Market Price.

Value, Subjective—The value of a property in the eyes of a particular person, as opposed to its market value (objective value).

Value, Utility—The value of a property to its owner or to a user. (A form of subjective value.) Also called value in use.

Value in Exchange—See: Value, Market.

Value in Use—See: Value, Utility.

Vendee—A buyer or purchaser; particularly, someone buying property under a land contract.

Vendor—A seller; particularly, someone selling property by means of a land contract.

Void—Having no legal force or effect.

Voidable—See: Contract, Voidable.

Waiver—The voluntary relinquishment or surrender of a right.

Warranty, Implied—In a sale or lease of property, a guarantee created by operation of law, whether or not the seller or landlord intended to offer it.

Warranty Deed—See: Deed, Warranty.

Waste—Destruction, damage, or material alteration of property by someone in possession who holds less than a fee estate (such as a life tenant or lessee), or by a co-owner.

Wraparound Financing—See: Mortgage, Wraparound.

Yield—The return of profit to an investor on an investment, stated as a percentage of the amount invested.

Zoning—Government regulation of the uses of property within specified areas (zones such as retail, industrial, residential).

Index

A